WELCOME TO
EXPLORING STRATEG

Strategy is an exciting subject, essential to all organisations, from multinationals to entrepreneurs, through charities to government agencies, and many more. Strategy concerns organisations – how they grow, how they innovate and how they change. As a manager of tomorrow, you will be involved in shaping, informing or communicating these strategies.

Our aim in writing *Exploring Strategy* is to give you a comprehensive understanding of the issues and techniques of strategy, and to help you get a great time studying your course. Here's how you might make the most of the text:

- **Explore** hot topics in cutting-edge issues, such as competitive strategy, corporate governance, internationalisation, innovation and entrepreneurship, strategic change and acquisitions and alliances.

- **Consider** the key debates and the different strategy lenses to get new perspectives and set you on your way to better practice in your assignments and examinations.

- **Follow up** on the recommended readings at the end of each chapter. These are specially selected as accessible and valuable sources that will enhance your learning and give you an extra source for your coursework.

After you've registered with the access code included in the back of *Exploring Strategy* at **www.pearsoned.co.uk/mystrategylab** to find essential student learning material, including:

- **The Strategy Experience** simulation, which gives you a hands-on experience of strategic decision making at various companies. As a Director of the board, you must deal with opportunities as they arise – and your decisions will affect the organisation's performance. Choose wisely!

- **A personalised** study plan that gives you feedback on your strengths and weaknesses, then recommends a tailored set of resources that will help to develop your understanding of strategy.

- **Audio** and **video resources**, including case studies on IKEA, Land Rover and the Eden Project, that put a spotlight on strategy in practice.

We want *Exploring Strategy* to give you what you need: a comprehensive view of the subject, an ambition to put that into practice, and – of course – success in your studies. We hope that you'll be as excited by the key issues of strategy as we are!

So, read on and good luck!

Gerry Johnson
Richard Whittington
Kevan Scholes

Gerry Johnson, BA, PhD is Emeritus Professor of Strategic Management at Lancaster University School of Management and a Senior Fellow of the UK Advanced Institute of Management Research (AIM). He has also taught at Strathclyde Business School, Cranfield School of Management, Manchester Business School and Aston University. He is the author of numerous books and his research has been published in many of the foremost management research journals in the world. He also serves on the editorial boards of the *Academy of Management Journal*, the *Strategic Management Journal* and the *Journal of Management Studies*. He is a partner in the consultancy partnership Strategy Explorers (see www.strategyexplorers.com) where he works with senior management teams on issues of strategy development and strategic change.

Richard Whittington MA, MBA, PhD is Professor of Strategic Management at the Saïd Business School and Millman Fellow at New College, University of Oxford. He is author or co-author of nine books and has published many journal articles. He serves on the editorial boards of *Organization Science, Organization Studies*, the *Strategic Management Journal* and *Long Range Planning*, amongst others. He has had full or visiting positions at the Harvard Business School, HEC Paris, Imperial College London, the University of Toulouse and the University of Warwick. He is a partner in Strategy Explorers and active in executive education and consulting, working with organisations from across Europe, the USA and Asia (see www.strategyexplorers.com). His current research is focused on strategy practice and international management.

Kevan Scholes MA, PhD, DMS, CIMgt, FRSA is Principal Partner of Scholes Associates – specialising in strategic management. He is also Visiting Professor of Strategic Management and formerly Director of the Sheffield Business School, UK. He has extensive experience of teaching strategy to both undergraduate and postgraduate students at several universities. In addition, his corporate management development work includes organisations in manufacturing, many service sectors and a wide range of public service organisations. He has had regular commitments outside the UK – including Ireland, Australia and New Zealand. He has also been an advisor on management development to a number of national bodies and is a Companion of The Chartered Management Institute.

EXPLORING STRATEGY

NINTH EDITION

GERRY JOHNSON
Lancaster University Management School

RICHARD WHITTINGTON
Saïd Business School, University of Oxford

KEVAN SCHOLES
Sheffield Business School

Financial Times
Prentice Hall
is an imprint of

Harlow, England • London • New York • Boston • San Francisco • Toronto
Sydney • Tokyo • Singapore • Hong Kong • Seoul • Taipei • New Delhi
Cape Town • Madrid • Mexico City • Amsterdam • Munich • Paris • Milan

Pearson Education Limited
Edinburgh Gate
Harlow
Essex CM20 2JE
England

and Associated Companies throughout the world

Visit us on the World Wide Web at:
www.pearsoned.co.uk

First edition published under the Prentice Hall imprint 1984
Fifth edition published under the Prentice Hall imprint 1998
Sixth edition published under the Financial Times Prentice Hall imprint 2002
Seventh edition 2005
Eighth edition 2008
Ninth edition 2011

ISBN: 978-0-273-73549-6 (text only)
ISBN: 978-0-273-73202-0 (text and cases)

British Library Cataloguing-in-Publication Data
A catalogue record for this book is available from the British Library

Library of Congress Cataloging-in-Publication Data
A catalog record for this book is available from the Library of Congress

10 9 8 7 6 5 4 3 2 1
14 13 12 11

Typeset in 9.5/13.5pt Photina by 35
Printed and bound by Rotolito Lombarda, Italy

BRIEF CONTENTS

EXPLORING STRATEGY ONLINE

A wide range of supporting resources are available at:

PEARSON mystrategylab

Register to create your own personal account using the access code supplied with your copy of the book,* and access the following teaching and learning resources:

Resources for students

- **A dynamic eText** of the book that you can search, bookmark, annotate and highlight as you please
- **Self-assessment questions** that identify your strengths before recommending a personalised study plan that points you to the resources which can help you achieve a better grade
- **Key concept audio summaries** that you can download or listen to online
- **Video cases** that show managers talking about strategic issues in their own organisations
- **Revision flashcards** to help you prepare for your exams
- **A multi-lingual online glossary** to help explain key concepts
- Guidance on **how to analyse a case study**
- **Links** to relevant sites on the web so you can explore more about the organisations featured in the case studies
- **Classic cases** – over 30 case studies from previous editions of the book
- The **Strategy Experience simulation** gives you hands-on experience of strategic analysis and putting strategy into action

Resources for instructors

- **Instructor's manual**, including extensive teaching notes for cases and suggested teaching plans
- **PowerPoint slides**, containing key information and figures from the book
- **Secure testbank**, containing over 600 questions
- Support for the **Strategy Experience simulation** with guidance on the aims and objectives of the simulation, and instructions on how to set up simulation groups that enable you to monitor your student's performance

Also, the following instructor resources are available off-line:

- Instructor's manual in hard copy, with CD containing PowerPoint slides and classic cases
- Video resources on DVD

For more information, please contact your local Pearson Education sales representative or visit **www.pearsoned.co.uk/mystrategylab**

*If you don't have an access code, you can still access the resources.
Visit **www.pearsoned.co.uk/mystrategylab** for details.

CONTENTS

5 CULTURE AND STRATEGY

PART II
STRATEGIC CHOICES

LIST OF ILLUSTRATIONS
AND KEY DEBATES

ILLUSTRATIONS

KEY DEBATES BY CHAPTER

LIST OF FIGURES

LIST OF TABLES

PREFACE

We are delighted to offer this ninth edition of *Exploring Strategy*. With sales of previous editions above 900,000, we believe we have a well-tried product. Yet the strategy field is constantly changing. For this edition, therefore, we have thoroughly refreshed each chapter, with new concepts, new cases and new examples throughout. Here we would like to highlight four substantial changes, while recalling some of the classic features of the book.

The ninth edition's principal innovations are:

- **Our new title, *Exploring Strategy*:** we have dropped the reference to 'Corporate' in the title in order to reflect the wide scope the book has always had. To some, 'corporate' implied a focus on large, multi-business commercial organisations. *Exploring Strategy* is for all organisations, including small entrepreneurial businesses, not-for-profits and public sector organisations too.

- **A new chapter on Mergers, Acquisitions and Alliances:** mergers and acquisitions are an important method for many strategies, particularly diversification and internationalisation, and they often grab the headlines. Alliances too are a crucial feature of contemporary business. We have recognised the importance of these methods by granting them a new chapter of their own.

- **A separate chapter on Strategy Evaluation:** in the end, strategies have to be evaluated, not just described. This chapter introduces key evaluation techniques, financial and non-financial, encouraging students to apply them and assess their usefulness on real cases.

- **A new web-based strategy simulation, the Strategy Experience:** our simulation of an international advertising company gives students the chance to apply strategy frameworks in action, either individually or in teams. The simulation also provides teachers with an effective method of assessment and feedback. You can find this simulation at **www.MyStrategyLab.com**.

At the same time, *Exploring Strategy* retains its longstanding commitment to a comprehensive and real-world view of strategy. In particular, this entails a deep concern for:

- **Process:** we believe that the human processes of strategy, not only the economics of particular strategies, are central to achieving long-term organisational success. Throughout the book, we underline the importance of human processes, but in particular we devote Part III to processes of strategy formation, implementation and change.

- **Practice:** we conclude the book with a chapter on the Practice of Strategy (Chapter 15), focused on the practicalities of managing strategy. Throughout the book, we introduce concepts and techniques through practical illustrations and applications, rather than abstract descriptions.

Many people have helped us with the development of this new edition. Steve Pyle has taken leadership in coordinating the case collection. We have consulted carefully with our Advisory Board, made up of experienced adopters of the book. Many other adopters of the book provide more informal advice and suggestions – many of whom we have had the pleasure of meeting at our annual teachers' workshops. This kind of feedback is invaluable. Also, our students and clients at Sheffield, Lancaster and Oxford and the many other places where we teach are a constant source of ideas and stimulus. We also gain from our links across the world, particularly in Ireland, The Netherlands, Denmark, Sweden, France, Canada, Australia, New Zealand, Hong Kong, Singapore and the USA. Many contribute directly by providing case studies and illustrations and these are acknowledged in the text. But for other kinds of contributions we particularly thank Julia Balogun, Phyl Johnson, John Kind, Donald MacLean, Sam McPherson, Lance Moir, David Pettifer, Rob Pieters and Basak Yakis-Douglas.

Finally, we thank those organisations that have been generous enough to be written up as case studies. We hope that those using the book will respect the wishes of the case study organisations and *not* contact them directly for further information.

Gerry Johnson (gerry.johnson@lancaster.ac.uk)
Richard Whittington (richard.whittington@sbs.ox.ac.uk)
Kevan Scholes (KScholes@scholes.u-net.com)
May 2010

ADVISORY BOARD

Special thanks are due to the following members of the Advisory Board for their valued comments:

Clive Choo	Nanyang Technological University
David Oliver	HEC Montréal
Emiel Wubben	Wageningen University
Eric Cassells	Oxford Brookes University
Erik Wilberg	BI Oslo
Heather Farley	University of Ulster
Kenneth Wiltshire	University of Queensland
Laure Cabantous	Nottingham University
Lisa Barton	Cardiff University
Ludovic Cailluet	IAE Toulouse
Marian Crowley-Henry	Dublin Institute of Technology
Martin Lindell	Hanken School of Economics
Matthew Hinton	The Open University
Michael Mayer	University of Bath
Michael O'Keefe	King's College London
Moira Fischbacher-Smith	University of Glasgow
Shigefumi Makino	The Chinese University of Hong Kong

EXPLORING STRATEGY

This ninth edition of *Exploring Strategy* builds on the established strengths of this best-selling textbook. A range of in-text features and supplementary features have been developed to enable you and your students to gain maximum added value from the teaching and learning of strategy.

- **Outstanding pedagogical features**. Each chapter has clear learning outcomes, practical questions associated with real-life illustrations and examples which students can easily apply to what they have learnt.

- **Flexibility of use**. You can choose to use either the Text and Cases version of the book, or – if you don't use longer cases (or have your own) – the Text-only version. The provision of Key Debates, Commentaries and Strategy 'Lenses' allow you to dig deeper into the tensions and complexity of strategy.

The two versions are complemented by a concise version of the text, *Fundamentals of Strategy*, and instructors also have the option of further customising the text. Visit **www.pearsoned.co.uk/CustomPublishing** for more details.

- **Up-to-date materials**. As well as a new chapter on mergers, acquisitions and alliances, we have fully revised the other chapters, incorporating new research and updating references so that you can easily access the latest research.

- **Encouraging critical thinking**. As well as the Strategy Lenses, we encourage critical thinking by ending each chapter with a 'key debate', introducing students to research evidence and theory on key issues of the chapter and encouraging them to take a view.

Our 'three circles' model – depicting the overlapping issues of strategic position, strategic choices and strategy-in-action – also challenges a simple linear, sequential view of the strategy process.

- **Case and examples**. A wide range of Illustrations, Case Examples and (in the Text and Cases version) longer Case Studies are fresh and engage with student interests and day-to-day experience. The majority of these are entirely new to this edition; we have extensively revised the remainder. Finally, we draw these examples from all over the world and use examples from the public and voluntary sectors as well as the private.

- **Teaching and learning support**. You and your students can access a wealth of resources at **www.pearsoned.co.uk/mystrategylab**, including the following:

  For students

  - **The Strategy Experience** simulation, which puts the student in the driving seat and allows them to experience the real world of strategic decision-making.

  - A personalised study plan that helps students focus their attention and efforts on the areas where they're needed the most.

  - Flashcards, a multilingual glossary, and weblinks for revision and research.

For instructors

- An Instructor's Manual which provides a comprehensive set of teaching support, including guidance on the use of case studies and assignments, and advice on how to plan a programme using the text.

- PowerPoint slides.

- A test-bank of assessment questions.

- Classic Cases from previous editions of the book.

In addition to the website, a printed copy of the Instructor's Manual is also available.

- **Video resources on DVD**. A DVD has been specially created for in-class use and contains briefings on selected topics from the authors, and material to support some of the case studies in the book:

  1 'With the Experts' (the authors explain key concepts)
  Strategy in Different Contexts
  Porter's five forces
  Core Competencies
  Strategic Drift and the Cultural Web

  2 Case Study organisations
  SABMiller – international development
  eBay – success and sustainability
  Amazon.com – business-level strategy
  Manchester United – football club or business?
  easyJet – competitive strategy
  Marks & Spencer – two CEOs on managing turnaround

  You can order and find out more about these resources from your local Pearson Education representative (**www.pearsoned.co.uk/replocator**).

- **Teachers' workshop**. We run an annual workshop to facilitate discussion of key challenges and solutions in the teaching of strategic management. Details of forthcoming workshops can be found at **www.pearsoned.co.uk/ecsworkshop**.

GUIDED TOUR

→ Setting the scene

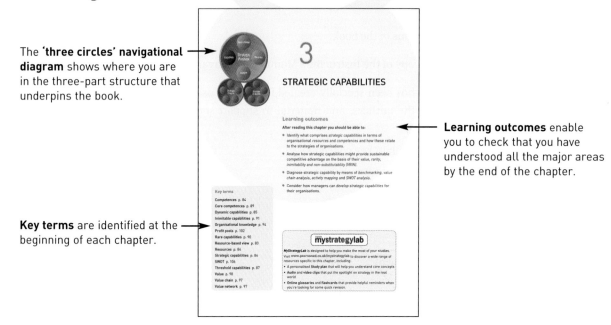

The **'three circles' navigational diagram** shows where you are in the three-part structure that underpins the book.

Learning outcomes enable you to check that you have understood all the major areas by the end of the chapter.

Key terms are identified at the beginning of each chapter.

→ Strategy in the real world

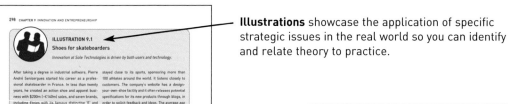

Illustrations showcase the application of specific strategic issues in the real world so you can identify and relate theory to practice.

Video cases enable you to engage with and learn from the experience of senior manangers responsible for determining and implementing strategy.

The **Case example** at the end of each chapter allows exploration of topics covered in the chapter.

→ Critical thinking and further study

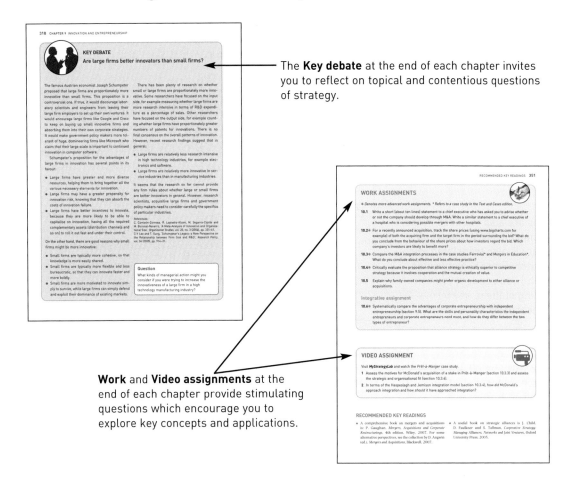

The **Key debate** at the end of each chapter invites you to reflect on topical and contentious questions of strategy.

Work and **Video assignments** at the end of each chapter provide stimulating questions which encourage you to explore key concepts and applications.

Commentaries at the end of each part of the book present a view of strategy through four 'lenses' to help you see strategic issues in different ways.

→ Check your understanding with mystrategylab*

Thus the long-term
long-term direction of
amines the practical
nt levels of strategy;
statement'.

Key concept icons in the text direct
you to audio and other resources in
MyStrategyLab where you can check
and reinforce your understanding of
key concepts.

These terms are also included in the
Glossary, found in **MyStrategyLab**.
(The Glossary is also translated into
Chinese, Dutch, French, Norwegian
and Swedish.) You can test your
understanding of these key terms
using **Flashcards** on the website.

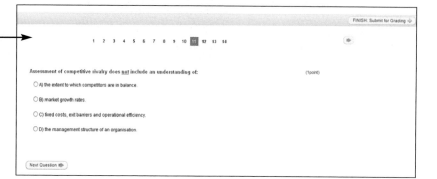

Need a little extra help?
Self-assessment tests will
help you to identify the areas
where you need to improve . . .

... and the **Personalised study plan**
will direct you to the specific resources
that can help you achieve a better grade.

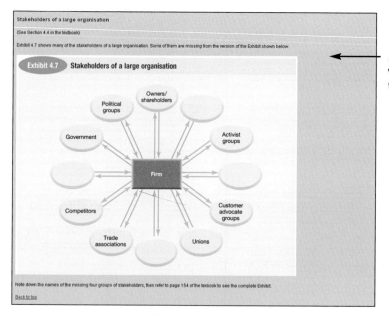

***Don't forget to register using your
access code at:**
www.pearsoned.co.uk/mystrategylab

The **Strategy Experience simulation** included in **MyStrategyLab**, puts you in the position of a strategic decision maker. You are the Director of the Board at WRSX Group, a global advertising and marketing communications business.

Multimedia resources and briefing documents help you to build an understanding of the WRSX Group's strategic position, as well as the choices that are available to the organisation.

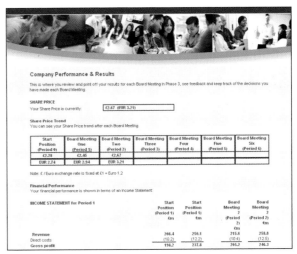

You apply your knowledge in the boardroom, where you are faced with a number of scenarios. Here you must make tough decisions that will shape the company's future.

Success will depend on how well you understand and can apply the concepts that are covered in *Exploring Strategy*. Choose wisely!

EXPLORING STRATEGY

1

INTRODUCING STRATEGY

Learning outcomes

After reading this chapter you should be able to:

- Summarise the strategy of an organisation in a *'strategy statement'*.

- Identify key issues for an organisation's strategy according to the *Exploring Strategy* model.

- Distinguish between *corporate*, *business* and *operational* strategies.

- Understand how different people contribute to strategy *at work*.

- Appreciate the contributions of different academic disciplines and *theoretical lenses* to practical strategy analysis.

Key terms

Business-level strategy p. 7

Corporate-level strategy p. 7

Exploring Strategy Model p. 14

Managing strategy in action p. 18

Operational strategies p. 7

Strategic choices p. 17

Strategic position p. 16

Strategy p. 3

Strategy lenses p. 20

Strategy statements p. 8

Three horizons framework p. 4

PEARSON
mystrategylab

MyStrategyLab is designed to help you make the most of your studies.

Visit **www.pearsoned.co.uk/mystrategylab** to discover a wide range of resources specific to this chapter, including:

- A personalised **Study plan** that will help you understand core concepts
- **Audio** and **video clips** that put the spotlight on strategy in the real world
- **Online glossaries** and **flashcards** that provide helpful reminders when you're looking for some quick revision.

(1.1) INTRODUCTION

Strategy is about key issues for the future of organisations. For example, how should Google – originally a search company – manage its entry into the market for mobile phones? Should universities concentrate their resources on research excellence or teaching quality or try to combine both? How should a small video games producer relate to dominant console providers such as Nintendo and Sony? What should a rock band do to secure revenues in the face of declining CD sales?

All these are strategy questions. Naturally they concern entrepreneurs and senior managers at the top of their organisations. But these questions matter more widely. Middle managers also have to understand the strategic direction of their organisations, both to know how to get top management support for their initiatives and to explain their organisation's strategy to the people they are responsible for. Anybody looking for a management-track job needs to be ready to discuss strategy with their potential employer. Indeed, anybody taking a job should first be confident that their new employer's strategy is actually viable. There are even specialist career opportunities in strategy, for example as a strategy consultant or as an in-house strategic planner, often key roles for fast-track young managers.

This book takes a broad approach to strategy, looking at both the economics of strategy and the people side of managing strategy in practice. It is a book about 'Exploring', because the real world of strategy rarely offers obvious answers. In strategy, it is typically important to explore several options, probing each one carefully before making choices. The book is also relevant to any kind of organisation responsible for its own direction into the future. Thus the book refers to large private-sector multinationals and small entrepreneurial start-ups; to public-sector organisations such as schools and hospitals; and to not-for-profits such as charities or sports clubs. Strategy matters to almost all organisations, and to everybody working in them.

(1.2) WHAT IS STRATEGY?[1]

In this book, **strategy is the long-term direction of an organisation**. Thus the long-term direction of Nokia is from mobile phones to mobile computing. The long-term direction of Disney is from cartoons to diversified entertainment. This section examines the practical implication of this definition of strategy; distinguishes between different levels of strategy; and explains how to summarise an organisation's strategy in a 'strategy statement'.

KEY CONCEPT

Strategy

1.2.1 Defining strategy

Defining strategy as the long-term direction of an organisation implies a more comprehensive view than some influential definitions. Figure 1.1 (over page) shows the strategy definitions of three leading strategy theorists: Alfred Chandler and Michael Porter, both from the Harvard Business School, and Henry Mintzberg, from McGill University, Canada. Each points to important but distinct elements of strategy. Chandler emphasises a logical flow from the determination of goals and objectives to the allocation of resources. Porter focuses on deliberate choices, difference and competition. On the other hand, Mintzberg uses the word 'pattern' to allow for the fact that strategies do not always follow a deliberately chosen and logical plan, but can

Figure 1.1 Definitions of strategy

'the determination of the long-run goals and objectives of an enterprise and the adoption of courses of action and the allocation of resource necessary for carrying out these goals'

Alfred D. Chandler

'Competitive strategy is about being different. It means deliberately choosing a different set of activities to deliver a unique mix of value'

Michael Porter

'a pattern in a stream of decisions'

Henry Mintzberg

'the long-term direction of an organisation'

Exploring Strategy

Sources: A.D. Chandler, *Strategy and Structure: Chapters in the History of American Enterprise*, MIT Press, 1963, p. 13; M.E. Porter, 'What is strategy?', *Harvard Business Review*, 1996, November–December, p. 60; H. Mintzberg, *Tracking Strategy: Toward a General Theory*, Oxford University Press, 2007, p. 3.

emerge in more ad hoc ways. Sometimes strategies reflect a series of incremental decisions that only cohere into a recognisable pattern – or 'strategy' – after some time.

All of these strategy definitions incorporate important elements of strategy. However, this book's definition of strategy as 'the long-term direction of an organisation' has two advantages. First, the long-term direction of an organisation can include both deliberate, logical strategy and more incremental, emergent patterns of strategy. Second, long-term direction can include both strategies that emphasise difference and competition, and strategies that recognise the roles of cooperation and even imitation.

The three elements of this strategy definition – the long term, direction and organisation – can each be explored further. The strategy of News Corporation, owner of social networking company MySpace, illustrates important points (see Illustration 1.1):

● *The long term.* Strategies are typically measured over years, for some organisations a decade or more. The importance of a long-term perspective on strategy is emphasised by the 'three horizons' framework in Figure 1.2 (over page). **The three horizons framework suggests that every organisation should think of itself as comprising three types of business or activity, defined by their 'horizons' in terms of years.** *Horizon 1* businesses are basically the current core activities. In the case of News Corporation, Horizon 1 businesses include the original print newspapers. Horizon 1 businesses need defending and extending but the expectation is that in the long term they will likely be flat or declining in terms of profits (or whatever else the organisation values). *Horizon 2* businesses are emerging activities that should provide new sources of profit. In News Corporation, those include the various internet initiatives, principally MySpace. Finally, there are *Horizon 3* possibilities, for which nothing is sure.

ILLUSTRATION 1.1

MySpace becomes part of a bigger network

Social networking site MySpace presents opportunities and challenges for the global media conglomerate News Corporation.

The social networking site MySpace was founded in California in 2003 by MBA graduate Chris DeWolfe and rock musician Tom Anderson. From the first, the networking site was strong on music, and helped launch the careers of the Arctic Monkeys and Lily Allen. By 2005, it had 22 million members, with more page views than Google. That was the point when the multinational media conglomerate News Corporation bought it for $580m (€406m).

News Corporation started in Australia in the newspaper business, acquiring the *Times* newspaper group in the United Kingdom and the *Wall Street Journal* in the United States. It also diversified into television (for example Fox News and BSkyB) and film, including 20th Century Fox, responsible for the hit film *Avatar*. Its chairman is Rupert Murdoch, whose family owns a controlling interest: Rupert Murdoch's son James is expected to succeed him at the top.

In 2005, with media audiences increasingly moving to the internet, Rupert Murdoch declared his ambition to create 'a leading and profitable internet presence'. The acquisition of MySpace seemed a good fit. Chris DeWolfe and Tom Anderson were retained at the head of MySpace, but within a new division providing oversight for all News Corporation's internet interests. Ross Levinsohn, long-time News Corporation insider and head of the new division, told the *Financial Times*: 'The MySpace guys were really freaked out that we were going to come in and turn it into Fox News. One of the things we said was: "We're going to leave it alone" '.

Some adjustments had to be made. Tom Anderson told *Fortune* magazine: 'Before, I could do whatever I wanted. Now it takes more time to get people to agree on things. All the budget reviews and processes. That can be a pain. But it's not stopping us.' News Corporation was able to fund a more robust technology platform to cope with the thousands of new users MySpace was getting each day. In 2006, MySpace signed a three year advertising contract with Google worth $900m, which paid for the original acquisition with money left over. Executives summed up MySpace's distinctive positioning by saying: 'Your mom uses Facebook'.

But business then got tougher. Facebook overtook MySpace in terms of unique visitors in 2008. News Corporation executives complained about the excessive new initiatives at MySpace and the failure to prioritise: DeWolfe and Anderson were even considering launching their own film studio. Then Rupert Murdoch announced a target of $1bn in advertising revenues for 2008, without consulting DeWolfe. MySpace missed the target by about 10 per cent. The push from News Corporation to increase advertisements on MySpace, and a reluctance to remove pages with advertising from the site, began to make MySpace increasingly less attractive for users.

During 2009, MySpace's share of the social networking market fell to 30 per cent, from a peak of 66 per cent. The company missed the online traffic targets set by the Google contract. Losses were expected to be around $100m. In March, Chris DeWolfe was removed as Chief Executive of MySpace. The new Chief Executive was Alan Van Natta, from Facebook. Van Natta told the *Financial Times* that MySpace was no longer competing with Facebook: 'we're very focused on a different space . . . MySpace can foster discovery [of music, films and TV] in a way that others can't'.

Sources: M. Garnham, 'The rise and fall of MySpace', *Financial Times*, 4 December 2009; P. Sellers, 'MySpace Cowboys', *Fortune*, 29 August 2006; S. Rosenbusch, 'News Corp's Place in MySpace', *Business Week*, 19 July 2005.

Questions

1 How valuable is MySpace's distinctive position in the social networking market?

2 How should News Corporation have managed MySpace?

Figure 1.2 Three horizons for strategy

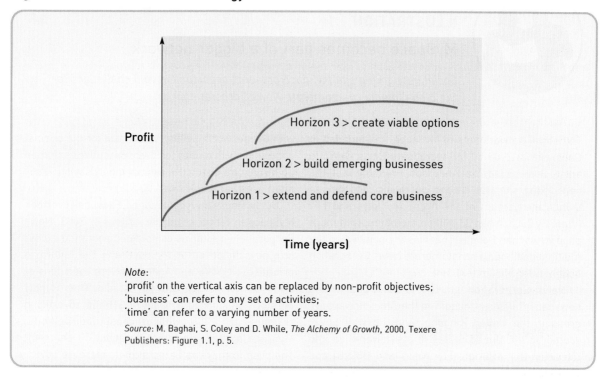

Note:
'profit' on the vertical axis can be replaced by non-profit objectives;
'business' can refer to any set of activities;
'time' can refer to a varying number of years.

Source: M. Baghai, S. Coley and D. While, *The Alchemy of Growth*, 2000, Texere
Publishers: Figure 1.1, p. 5.

These are typically risky Research & Development projects, start-up ventures, test-market pilots or similar, some of which may fuel growth in the future even if most are likely to fail. For a fast-moving internet organisation like MySpace, *Horizon 3* might only be a couple of years from the present time. In a pharmaceutical company, where the R&D and regulatory processes for a new drug take many years, *Horizon 3* might be a decade ahead. While timescales might differ, the basic point about the 'three horizons' framework is that managers need to avoid focusing on the short-term issues of their existing activities. Strategy involves pushing out Horizon 1 as far as possible, at the same time as looking to Horizons 2 and 3. Strategy for Horizons 2 and 3 will involve a good deal of *uncertainty*.

● *Strategic direction*. Over the years, strategies follow some kind of long-term direction or trajectory. The strategic direction of News Corporation is from print to internet media, as represented by MySpace. Sometimes a strategic direction only emerges as a coherent pattern over time. Typically, however, managers and entrepreneurs try to set the direction of their strategy according to long-term *objectives*. In private-sector businesses, the objective guiding strategic direction is usually maximising profits for shareholders. Thus Rupert Murdoch's acquisition of MySpace was driven by the objective to create a leading and profitable presence on the internet. However, profits do not always set strategic direction. First, public-sector and charity organisations may set their strategic direction according to other objectives: for example, a sports club's objective may be to move up from one league to a higher one. Second, even in the private sector profit is not always the sole criterion for strategy. Thus controlling families (such as perhaps News Corporation's Murdoch family) may sometimes sacrifice the maximisation of profits for family objectives, for example passing down the management of the business to the next generation. The objectives behind strategic direction always need close scrutiny.

- *Organisation.* In this book, organisations are not treated as discrete, unified entities. Organisations involve complex relationships, both internally and externally. This is because organisations typically have many internal and external *stakeholders*, in other words people and groups that depend on the organisation and upon which the organisation itself depends. Internally, organisations are filled with people, typically with diverse, competing and more or less reasonable views of what should be done. At MySpace, the News Corporation executives clashed over strategic direction with MySpace founder Chris DeWolfe. In strategy, therefore, it is always important to look *inside* organisations and to consider the people involved and their different interests and views. Externally, organisations are surrounded by important relationships, for example with suppliers, customers, alliance partners, regulators and shareholders. For MySpace, the relationship with Google was critical. Strategy therefore is also crucially concerned with an organisation's external *boundaries*: in other words, questions about what to include within the organisation and how to manage important relationships with what is kept outside.

Because strategy typically involves managing people, relationships and resources, the subject is sometimes called 'strategic management'. This book takes the view that managing is always important in strategy. Good strategy is about managing as well as strategising.

1.2.2 Levels of strategy

Inside an organisation, strategies can exist at three main levels. Again they can be illustrated by reference to MySpace and News Corporation (Illustration 1.1):

- **Corporate-level strategy is concerned with the overall scope of an organisation and how value is added to the constituent businesses of the organisational whole.** Corporate-level strategy issues include geographical scope, diversity of products or services, acquisitions of new businesses, and how resources are allocated between the different elements of the organisation. For News Corporation, diversifying from print journalism into television and social networking are corporate-level strategies. Being clear about corporate-level strategy is important: determining the range of businesses to include is the *basis* of other strategic decisions.

- **Business-level strategy is about how the individual businesses should compete in their particular markets** (for this reason, business-level strategy is often called 'competitive strategy'). These individual businesses might be stand-alone businesses, for instance entrepreneurial start-ups, or 'business units' within a larger corporation (as MySpace and Fox are inside News Corporation). Business-level strategy typically concerns issues such as innovation, appropriate scale and response to competitors' moves. In the public sector, the equivalent of business-level strategy is decisions about how units (such as individual hospitals or schools) should provide best-value services. Where the businesses are units within a larger organisation, business-level strategies should clearly fit with corporate-level strategy.

- **Operational strategies are concerned with how the components of an organisation deliver effectively the corporate- and business-level strategies in terms of resources, processes and people.** For example, MySpace engineers had to keep developing enough processing capacity to cope with the strategy of rapid growth. In most businesses, successful business strategies depend to a large extent on decisions that are taken, or activities that occur, at the operational level. Operational decisions need therefore to be closely linked to business-level strategy. They are vital to successful strategy implementation.

This need to link the corporate, business and operational levels underlines the importance of *integration* in strategy. Each level needs to be aligned with the others. The demands of integrating levels define an important characteristic of strategy. Strategy is typically *complex*, requiring careful and sensitive management. Strategy is rarely simple.

1.2.3 Strategy statements

David Collis and Michael Rukstad[2] at the Harvard Business School argue that all entrepreneurs and managers should be able to summarise their organisation's strategy with a 'strategy statement'. **Strategy statements should have three main themes: the fundamental *goals* that the organisation seeks, which typically draw on the organisation's stated mission, vision and objectives; the *scope* or domain of the organisation's activities; and the particular *advantages* or capabilities it has to deliver all of these.** These various contributing elements of a strategy statement are explained as follows, with examples in Illustration 1.2:

- *Mission*. This relates to goals, and refers to the overriding purpose of the organisation. It is sometimes described in terms of the apparently simple but challenging question: '*what business are we in?*'. The mission statement helps keep managers focused on what is central to their strategy.

- *Vision*. This too relates to goals, and refers to the desired future state of the organisation. It is an aspiration which can help mobilise the energy and passion of organisational members. The vision statement, therefore, should answer the question: '*what do we want to achieve?*'.

- *Objectives*. These are more precise and ideally quantifiable statements of the organisation's goals over some period of time. Objectives might refer to profitability or market share targets for a private company, or to examination results in a school. Objectives introduce discipline to strategy. The question here is: '*what do we have to achieve in the coming period?*'.

- *Scope*. An organisation's scope or domain refers to three dimensions: customers or clients; geographical location; and extent of internal activities ('vertical integration'). For a university, scope questions are twofold: first, which academic departments to have (a business school, an engineering department and so on); second, which activities to do internally themselves (vertically integrate) and which to externalise to subcontractors (for example, whether to manage campus restaurants in-house or to subcontract them).

- *Advantage*. This part of a strategy statement describes how the organisation will achieve the objectives it has set for itself in its chosen domain. In competitive environments, this refers to the *competitive* advantage: for example, how a particular company or sports club will achieve goals in the face of competition from other companies or clubs. In order to achieve a particular goal, the organisation needs to be better than others seeking the same goal. In the public sector, advantage might refer simply to the organisation's capability in general. But even public-sector organisations frequently need to show that their capabilities are not only adequate, but superior to other rival departments or perhaps to private-sector contractors.

Collis and Rukstad suggest that strategy statements covering goals, scope and advantage should be no more than 35 words long. Shortness keeps such statements focused on the essentials and makes them easy to remember and communicate. Thus for News Corporation, a strategy statement might be: 'to build a leading and profitable presence in both old and new media, drawing on competitive advantages in terms of the scale, diversity and international

ILLUSTRATION 1.2

Strategy statements

Both Nokia, the Finnish telecommunications giant, and University College Cork, based in the West of Ireland, publish a good deal about their strategies.

Nokia Vision and Strategy

Our vision is a world where everyone can be connected. Our promise is to help people feel close to what is important to them.

The businesses of Nokia
- Compelling consumer solutions with devices and services
- Strong infrastructure business with Siemens Networks

Our competitive advantage is based on scale, brand and services
- Scale-based assets and capabilities
- Leading brand
- Build further competitive advantage by differentiating our offering through services

Our business strategy
- Maximize Nokia's lifetime value to consumer
- Best mobile devices everywhere
  - Take share and drive value across price brands and geographies
  - Enhance and capture market growth in emerging markets
- Context-enriched services
  - Take share of the internet services market by delivering winning solutions
  - Take share of business mobility market

University College Cork (UCC), Strategic Plan 2009–2012

University College Cork (UCC) . . . is sited in Ireland's second city . . . UCC's motto *'Where Finbarr taught let Munster learn'* binds us to the sixth-century monastery and place of learning established by St. Finbarr . . . UCC was established in 1845 as one of three Queen's Colleges . . . The campus today is home to over 18,000 students including 2,000 international students from 93 countries. . . . A third of our staff are from overseas. Our strategic alliances with world-ranking universities in Asia, Europe and North America ensure that we learn from and contribute to the best standards of teaching, learning and research.

Vision
To be a world-class university that links the region to the globe.

Mission
In an environment which gives parity of esteem to teaching, learning and research and where students are our highest priority, the University's central roles are to create, preserve and communicate knowledge and to enhance intellectual, cultural, social and economic life locally, regionally and globally.

Targets by 2012 (selected from 'Teaching, Learning and the Student Experience')
- Achieve a first year retention rate of 93% or greater
- Increase the proportion of students at postgraduate level from 19% to 30%
- Increase flexible/part-time provision to 15% of undergraduate entrants

Sources: www.nokia.com; www.ucc.ie.

Questions

1 Construct short strategy statements covering the goals, scope and advantage of Nokia and University College Cork. How much do the different contexts matter?

2 Construct a strategy statement for your own organisation (university or employer). What implications might this statement have for your particular course or department?

range of our businesses'. The strategy statement of American financial advisory firm Edward Jones is more specific: 'to grow to 17,000 financial advisers by 2012 by offering trusted and convenient face-to-face financial advice to conservative individual investors through a national network of one-financial adviser offices'. Of course, such strategy statements are not always fulfilled. Circumstances may change in unexpected ways. In the meantime, however, they can provide a useful guide both to managers in their decision-making and to employees and others who need to understand the direction in which the organisation is going. The ability to give a clear strategy statement is a good test of managerial competence in an organisation.

As such, strategy statements are relevant to a wide range of organisations. For example, a small entrepreneurial start-up will need a strategy statement to persuade investors and lenders of its viability. Public-sector organisations need strategy statements not only for themselves, but to reassure external clients, funders and regulators that their priorities are the right ones. Voluntary organisations need to communicate persuasive strategy statements in order to inspire volunteers and donors. Thus organisations of all kinds frequently publish materials relevant to such strategy statements on their websites or annual reports. Illustration 1.2 provides published materials on the strategies of two very different organisations: the technology giant Nokia from the private sector and the medium-sized University College Cork from the public sector.

 ## 1.3 WORKING WITH STRATEGY

A theme so far is that almost all managers are concerned with strategy to some extent or another. Strategy is certainly a key issue for top management, but it is not just their preserve. Middle and lower-level managers have to meet the objectives set by their organisation's strategy and observe the constraints imposed by it. Managers have to communicate strategy to their teams, and will achieve greater performance from them the more convincing they are in doing so. Indeed, as responsibility is increasingly decentralised in many organisations, middle and lower-level managers play a growing part in shaping strategy themselves. Because they are closer to the daily realities of the business, lower-level managers can be a crucial source of ideas and feedback for senior management teams. Being able to participate in an organisation's 'strategic conversation' – engaging with senior managers on the big issues facing them – is therefore often part of what it takes to win promotion.[3]

Strategy, then, is part of many managers' work. However, there are specialist strategists as well, in both private and public sectors. Many large organisations have in-house strategic planning or analyst roles.[4] Typically requiring a formal business education of some sort, strategic planning is a potential career route for many readers of this book, especially after some operational experience. Strategy consulting has been a growth industry in the last decades, with the original leading firms such as McKinsey & Co., the Boston Consulting Group and Bain joined now by more generalist consultants such as Accenture, IBM Consulting and PwC, each with its own strategy consulting arm.[5] Again, business graduates are in demand for strategy consulting roles.[6]

The interviews in Illustration 1.3 (see over page) give some insights into the different kinds of strategy work that managers and strategy specialists can do. Galina, the manager of an international subsidiary, Masoud, working in a governmental strategy unit, and Chantal, a strategy consultant, all have different experiences of strategy, but there are some common themes also. All find strategy work stimulating and rewarding. The two specialists, Masoud and Chantal, talk more than Galina of analytical tools such as scenario analysis, sensitivity analysis and hypothesis testing. Galina discovered directly the practical challenges of real-world strategic planning, having to adapt the plan during the first few years in the United Kingdom. She emphasises the importance of flexibility in strategy and the value of getting her managers to see the 'whole picture' through involving them in strategy-making. But Masoud and Chantal too are concerned with much more than just analysis. Chantal emphasises the importance of gaining 'traction' with clients, building consensus in order to ensure implementation. Masoud likewise does not take implementation for granted, continuing to work with departments after the delivery of recommendations. He sees strategy and delivery as intimately connected, with people involved in delivery needing an understanding of strategy to be effective, and strategists needing to understand delivery. For him, strategy is a valuable stepping-stone in a career, something that will underpin his possible next move into a more operational role.

Strategy, therefore, is not just about abstract organisations: it is a kind of work that real people do. An important aim of this book is to equip readers to do this work better.

1.4 STUDYING STRATEGY

This book is both comprehensive and serious about strategy. To understand the full range of strategy issues, it is important to be open to the perspectives and insights of many academic disciplines, particularly economics, sociology and psychology. To be serious about strategy means to draw as far as possible on rigorous research about these issues. This book aims for an evidence-based approach to strategy, hence the articles and books referenced at the end of each chapter.[7]

This book therefore covers equally the three main branches of strategy as a subject: strategy *context*, strategy *content* and strategy *process*. Each of these is important to effective strategy-making, and each is underpinned by research streams whose characteristic analytical approaches can be applied to practical strategy issues as well. Figure 1.3 shows the three branches and the respective research streams: these are listed in the approximate historical order of their emergence as strong research streams, the arrows representing the continuously

Figure 1.3 Strategy's three branches

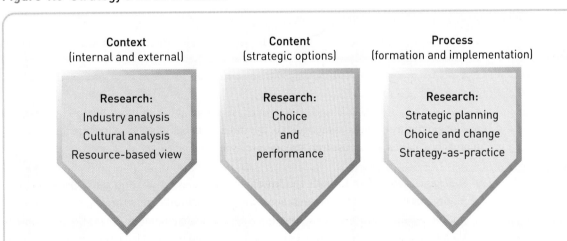

ILLUSTRATION 1.3

Strategists

For Galina, Masoud and Chantal, strategy is a large part of their jobs.

Galina

After a start in marketing, Galina became managing director of the British subsidiary of a Russian information-technology company at the age of 33. As well as developing the strategy for her local business, she has to interact regularly with the Moscow headquarters:

'Moscow is interested in the big picture, not just the details. They are interested in the future of the business.'

The original strategic plans for the subsidiary had had to be adapted heavily:

'When we first came here, we had some ideas about strategy, but soon found the reality was very different to the plans. The strategy was not completely wrong, but in the second stage we had to change it a lot: we had to change techniques and adapt to the market. Now we are in the third stage, where we have the basics and need to focus on trends, to get ahead and be in the right place at the right time.'

Galina works closely with her management team on strategy, taking them on an annual 'strategy away-day' (see Chapter 15):

'Getting people together helps them see the whole picture, rather than just the bits they are responsible for. It is good to put all their separate realities together.'

Galina is enthusiastic about working on strategy:

'I like strategy work, definitely. The most exciting thing is to think about where we have come from and where we might be going. We started in a pub five years ago and we have somehow implemented what we were hoping for then. Strategy gives you a measure of success. It tells you how well you have done.'

Her advice is:

'Always have a strategy – have an ultimate idea in mind. But take feedback from the market and from your colleagues. Be ready to adjust the strategy: the adjustment is the most important.'

Masoud

Aged 27, Masoud is a policy advisor in a central government strategy unit in the United Kingdom. He provides analysis and advice for ministers, often on a cross-departmental basis. He typically works on projects for several months at a time, continuing to work with responsible service departments after the delivery of recommendations. Projects involve talking to experts inside and outside government, statistical analysis, scenario analyses (see Chapter 2), sensitivity analyses (see Chapter 11), hypothesis testing (see Chapter 15) and writing reports and making presentations. As he has progressed, Masoud has become increasingly involved in the management of strategy projects, rather than the basic analysis itself.

Masoud explains what he likes most about strategy work in government:

---

developing nature of each. In more detail, the three branches and the characteristic analytical approaches of their main research streams are as follows:

- *Strategy context* refers to both the internal and the external contexts of organisations. All organisations need to take into account the opportunities and threats of their external environments. *Industry analysis* took off as a research tradition in the early 1980s, when Michael Porter showed how the tools of economics could be applied to understanding what makes industries attractive (or unattractive) to operate in.[8] From the 1980s too, *cultural*

'I like most the challenge. It's working on issues that really matter, and often it's what you are reading about in the newspapers. They are really tough issues; these are problems facing the whole of society.'

He thinks people should get involved in strategy:

'I would encourage people to do strategy, because it gets to the heart of problems. In all organisations, having some experience of working on strategy is very valuable, even if it is not what you want to major on your whole career.'

Masoud is considering moving into service delivery as the next step of his career, because he sees knowledge of strategy and knowledge of operations as so interconnected:

'Part of doing strategy is you have to understand what can be delivered; and part of doing delivery is you have to understand the strategy.'

Chantal

Chantal is in her early thirties and has worked in Paris for one of the top three international strategy consultancies since graduating in business. Consulting was attractive to her originally because she liked the idea of helping organisations improve. She chose her particular consultancy because

'I had fun in the interview rounds and the people were inspiring. I pictured myself working with these kinds of topics and with these kinds of people.'

Chantal enjoys strategy consulting:

'What I like is solving problems. It's a bit like working on a mystery case: you have a problem and then you have to find a solution to fit the company, and help it grow and to be better.'

The work is intellectually challenging:

'Time horizons are short. You have to solve your case in two to three months. There's lots of pressure. It pushes you and helps you to learn yourself. There are just three to four in a team, so you will make a significant contribution to the project even as a junior. You have a lot of autonomy and you're making a contribution right from the start, and at quite a high level.'

Consulting work can involve financial and market modelling (see Chapters 2 and 11), interviewing clients and customers, and working closely with the client's own teams. Chantal explains:

'As a consultant, you spend a lot of time in building solid fact-based arguments that will help clients make business decisions. But as well as the facts, you have to have the ability to get traction. People have to agree, so you have to build consensus, to make sure that recommendations are supported and acted on.'

Chantal summarises the appeal of strategy consulting:

'I enjoy the learning, at a very high speed. There's the opportunity to increase your skills. One year in consulting is like two years in a normal business.'

Source: interviews (interviewees anonymised).

Questions

1 Which of these strategy roles appeals to you most – manager of a business unit in a multinational, in-house strategy specialist or strategy consultant? Why?

2 What would you have to do to get such a role?

---

analysts have used sociological insights into human behaviour to point to the importance of shared cultural understandings about appropriate ways of acting. In the internal context, cultural analysts show that strategies are often influenced by the organisation's specific culture. In the external context, they show how strategies often have to fit with the surrounding industry or national cultures. *Resource-based view* researchers focus on internal context, looking for the unique characteristics of each organisation.[9] According to the resource-based view, the economic analysis of market imperfections, the psychological analysis of perceptual or emotional biases, and the sociological analysis of organisational cultures should reveal the particular characteristics (resources) that contribute to an organisation's specific competitive advantages and disadvantages.

● *Strategy content* concerns the content (or nature) of different strategies and their probability of success. Here the focus is on the merits of different strategic options. *Strategy and Performance* researchers started by using economic analysis to understand the success of different types of diversification strategies. This research continues as the enduring central core of the strategy discipline, with an ever-growing list of issues addressed. For example, contemporary Strategy and Performance researchers examine various new innovation strategies, different kinds of internationalisation and all the complex kinds of alliance and networking strategies organisations adopt today. These researchers typically bring a tough economic scrutiny to strategy options. Their aim is to establish which types of strategies pay best and under what conditions. They refuse to take for granted broad generalisations about what makes a good strategy.

● *Strategy process*, broadly conceived, examines how strategies are formed and implemented. Research here provides a range of insights to help managers in the practical processes of managing strategy.[10] From the 1960s, researchers in the *Strategic Planning* tradition have drawn from economics and management science in order to design rational and analytical systems for the planning and implementing of strategy. However, strategy involves people: since the 1980s, *Choice and Change* researchers have been pointing to how the psychology of human perception and emotions, and the sociology of group politics and interests, tend to undermine rational analysis. The advice of these researchers is to accept the irrational, messy realities of organisations, and to work with them, rather than to try to impose textbook rationality. Finally, *Strategy-as-Practice* researchers have recently been using micro-sociological approaches to closely examine the human realities of formal and informal strategy processes.[11] This tradition focuses attention on how people do strategy work, and the importance of having the right tools and skills.

From the above, it should be clear that studying strategy involves perspectives and insights from a range of academic disciplines. Issues need to be 'explored' from different points of view. A strategy chosen purely on economic grounds can easily be undermined by psychological and sociological factors. On the other hand, a strategy that is chosen on the psychological grounds of emotional enthusiasm, or for sociological reasons of cultural acceptability, is liable to fail if not supported by favourable economics. As underlined by the four strategy lenses to be introduced later, one perspective is rarely enough for good strategy. A complete analysis will typically need the insights of economics, psychology and sociology.

THE *EXPLORING STRATEGY* MODEL

This book is structured around a three-part model that encompasses issues of context, content and process equally. **The *Exploring Strategy* Model includes understanding *the strategic position* of an organisation (context); assessing *strategic choices* for the future (content); and managing *strategy in action* (process).** Figure 1.4 shows these elements and defines the broad coverage of this book. Together, the three elements provide a practical template for studying strategic situations. The following sections of this chapter will introduce the strategic issues that arise under each of these elements of the Exploring Strategy Model. But first it is important to understand why the model is drawn in this particular way.

Figure 1.4 **The *Exploring Strategy* Model**

Figure 1.4 could have shown the model's three elements in a linear sequence – first understanding the strategic position, then making strategic choices and finally turning strategy into action. Indeed, this logical sequence is implicit in the definition of strategy given by Alfred Chandler (Figure 1.1) and many other textbooks on strategy. However, as Henry Mintzberg recognises, in practice the elements of strategy do not always follow this linear sequence. Choices often have to be made before the position is fully understood. Sometimes too a proper understanding of the strategic position can only be built from the experience of trying a strategy out in action. The real-world feedback which comes from launching a new product is often far better at uncovering the true strategic position than remote analysis carried out in a strategic planning department at head office.

The interconnected circles of Figure 1.4 are designed to emphasise this potentially non-linear nature of strategy. Position, choices and action should be seen as closely related, and in practice none has priority over another. It is only for structural convenience that this book divides its subject matter into three sections; the book's sequence is not meant to suggest that the process of strategy must follow a logical path of distinct steps. The three circles are overlapping and non-linear. The evidence provided in later chapters will suggest that strategy rarely occurs in tidy ways and that it is better not to expect it to do so.

However, the Exploring Strategy Model does provide a comprehensive and integrated framework for analysing an organisation's position, considering the choices it has and putting strategies into action. Each of the chapters can be seen as asking fundamental strategy questions and providing the essential concepts and techniques to help answer them. Working systematically through questions and answers provides the basis for persuasive strategy recommendations.

1.5.1 Strategic position

Strategic position

The strategic position is concerned with the impact on strategy of the external environment, the organisation's strategic capability (resources and competences), the organisation's goals and the organisation's culture. Understanding these four factors is central for evaluating future strategy. These issues, and the fundamental questions associated with them, are covered in the four chapters of Part I of this book:

- *Environment.* Organisations operate in a complex political, economic, social and technological world. These environments vary widely in terms of their dynamism and attractiveness. The fundamental question here relates to the *opportunities* and *threats* available to the organisation in this complex and changing environment. Chapter 2 provides key frameworks to help in focusing on priority issues in the face of environmental complexity and dynamism.

- *Strategic capability.* Each organisation has its own strategic capabilities, made up of its *resources* (e.g. machines and buildings) and *competences* (e.g. technical and managerial skills). The fundamental question on capability regards the organisation's *strengths* and *weaknesses* (for example, where is it at a competitive advantage or disadvantage?). Are the organisation's capabilities adequate to the challenges of its environment and the demands of its goals? Chapter 3 provides tools and concepts for analysing such capabilities.

- *Strategic purpose.* Although sometimes unclear or contested, most organisations claim for themselves a particular purpose, as encapsulated in their *vision, mission* and *objectives*. The strategic purpose is a key criterion against which strategies must be evaluated. The third fundamental question therefore is: what is the organisation's strategic purpose; what does it seek to achieve? Here the issue of *corporate governance* is important: which stakeholders does the organisation primarily serve and how should managers be held accountable for this? Questions of purpose and accountability raise issues of *corporate social responsibility* and *ethics*: is the purpose an appropriate one and are managers achieving it? Chapter 4 provides concepts for addressing these issues of purpose.

- *Culture.* Organisational cultures can also influence strategy. So can the cultures of a particular industry or particular country. The impact of these influences can be *strategic drift*, a failure to create necessary change. The fundamental question here, therefore, is: how does culture shape strategy? Answering this typically requires an understanding of the organisation's *history*. Chapter 5 demonstrates how managers can analyse, challenge and sometimes turn to their advantage the various cultural influences on strategy.

Applying the Exploring Strategy Model to the positioning of News Corporation (Illustration 1.1) raises the following issues. News Corporation was threatened by an environmental shift from print to the internet. It also lacked the capabilities to develop a social networking business on its own. The company was determined to grow its internet business fast, setting demanding goals that MySpace struggled to meet. Finally, there appeared to be culture clashes between the traditional family-owned conglomerate and the young entrepreneurial start-up.

1.5.2 Strategic choices

Strategic choices involve the options for strategy in terms of both the *directions* in which strategy might move and the *methods* by which strategy might be pursued. For instance, an organisation might have a range of strategic directions open to it: the organisation could diversify into new products; it could enter new international markets; or it could transform its existing products and markets through radical innovation. These various directions could be pursued by different methods: the organisation could acquire a business already active in the product or market area; it could form alliances with relevant organisations that might help its new strategy; or it could try to pursue its strategies on its own. Typical strategic choices, and the related fundamental questions, are covered in the five chapters that make up Part II of this book, as follows:

- *Business strategy*. There are strategic choices in terms of how the organisation seeks to compete at the individual *business level*. Typically these choices involve strategies based on *cost* (for example, economies of scale) or *differentiation* (for example, superior quality). Crucial is deciding how to win against competitors (for this reason, business strategy is sometimes called 'competitive strategy'). The fundamental question here, then, is how should the business unit compete? Key dilemmas for business-level strategy, and ways of resolving them, are discussed in Chapter 6.

- *Corporate strategy and diversification*. The highest level of an organisation is typically concerned with corporate-level strategy, focused on questions of portfolio scope. The fundamental question in corporate-level strategy is therefore which businesses to include in the portfolio. This relates to the appropriate degree of *diversification*, in other words the spread of products and markets. Corporate-level strategy is also concerned both with the relationship between the various businesses that make up the corporate portfolio of the business and with how the corporate 'parent' (owner) adds value to the individual businesses. Chapter 7 provides tools for assessing diversification strategies and the appropriate relationships within the corporate portfolio.

- *International strategy*. Internationalisation is a form of diversification, but into new geographical markets. It is often at least as challenging as product or service diversification. Here the fundamental question is: where internationally should the organisation compete? Chapter 8 examines how to prioritise various international options and identifies key methods for pursuing them: export, licensing, direct investment and acquisition.

- *Innovation and entrepreneurship*. Most existing organisations have to innovate constantly simply to survive. Entrepreneurship, the creation of a new enterprise, is an act of innovation too. A fundamental question, therefore, is whether the organisation is innovating appropriately. Chapter 9 considers key choices about innovation and entrepreneurship, and helps in selecting between them.

- *Acquisitions and alliances*. Organisations have to make choices about methods for pursuing their strategies. Many organisations prefer to grow 'organically', in other words by building new businesses with their own resources. Other organisations might develop through mergers and acquisitions or strategic alliances with other organisations. The fundamental question here, then, is whether to buy another company, ally or to go it alone. How to choose between these alternative methods is discussed in Chapter 10.

Again, issues of strategic choice are live in the case of News Corporation and MySpace (Illustration 1.1). The Exploring Strategy Model asks the following kinds of questions here. Should MySpace compete against Facebook by emphasising its music strengths? Should a newspaper company try to enter the new social networking market and, if it does, is an acquisition the best method? How should News Corporation add value to its entrepreneurial new business? And should MySpace be allowed to continue to innovate in its old loosely disciplined style?

1.5.3 Strategy in action

Managing strategy in action is about how strategies are formed and how they are implemented. The emphasis is on the practicalities of managing. These issues are covered in the five chapters of Part III, and include the following, each with their own fundamental questions:

- *Strategy evaluation*. Once a set of strategic options has been established, it is time to evaluate their relative merits. The fundamental evaluation questions are as follows: are the options *suitable* in terms of matching opportunities and threats; are they *acceptable* in the eyes of significant stakeholders; and are they *feasible* in terms of the *capabilities* the organisation has available? Chapter 11 introduces a range of financial and non-financial techniques for evaluating suitability, acceptability and feasibility.

- *Strategy development processes*. Strategies are often developed through formal *planning* processes. However, while formal planning is important, in practice the strategies an organisation actually pursues are often *emergent* – in other words, accumulated patterns of ad hoc decisions, bottom-up initiatives and rapid responses to the unanticipated. Given the scope for emergence, the fundamental question is: what kind of strategy process should an organisation have? Should it try to plan strategy in detail or should it leave plenty of opportunities for emergence? Chapter 12 considers how strategic planning processes should be designed and the degree to which organisations should allow for other processes of strategy development.

- *Organising*. Once a strategy is developed, the organisation needs to organise for successful implementation. Each strategy requires its own specific configuration of *structures* and *systems*. The fundamental question, therefore, is: what kinds of structures and systems are required for the chosen strategy? Chapter 13 introduces a range of structures and systems and provides frameworks for deciding between them.

- *Leadership and strategic change*. In a dynamic world, strategy inevitably involves change. Managing change involves *leadership*, both at the top of the organisation and lower down. There is not just one way of leading change, however: there are different *styles* and different *levers* for change. So the fundamental question is: how should the organisation manage necessary changes entailed by the strategy? Chapter 14 therefore examines options for leading and managing change, and considers how to choose between them.

- *Strategy practice*. Inside the broad processes of strategy development and change is a lot of hard, detailed work. The fundamental question in managing this work is: who should do what in the strategy process? Chapter 15 thus provides guidance on which *people* should be included in the process; what *activities* they have to do; and which *methodologies* can help them do it. These kinds of practicalities are a fitting end to the book and essential equipment for those who will have to go out and participate in strategy work themselves.

Table 1.1 The strategy checklist

Fourteen fundamental questions in strategy		
Strategic position	**Strategic choices**	**Strategy in action**
• What are the environmental opportunities and threats? • What are the organisation's strengths and weaknesses? • What is the basic purpose of the organisation? • How does culture shape strategy?	• How should business units compete? • Which businesses to include in a portfolio? • Where should the organisation compete internationally? • Is the organisation innovating appropriately? • Should the organisation buy other companies, ally or go it alone?	• Which strategies are suitable, acceptable *and* feasible? • What kind of strategy-making process is needed? • What are the required organisation structures and systems? • How should the organisation manage necessary changes? • Who should do what in the strategy process?

With regard to strategy-in-action, the Exploring Strategy Model raises the following kinds of questions for News Corporation and MySpace. Should MySpace move towards a more disciplined strategy development process? Was it wise to organise MySpace under the authority of a divisional head responsible for all the existing internet businesses of News Corporation? Was this divisional head, Ross Levinson, the right person to provide leadership to the entrepreneurial MySpace? Which change levers were available to the new Chief Executive from Facebook, Alan Van Natta?

Thus the Exploring Strategy Model offers a comprehensive framework for analysing an organisation's position, considering alternative choices, and selecting and implementing strategies. In this sense, the fundamental questions in each chapter provide a comprehensive checklist for strategy. These fundamental questions are summed up in Table 1.1. Any assessment of an organisation's strategy will benefit from asking these questions systematically. The frameworks for answering these and related questions can be found in the respective chapters.

The logic of the Exploring Strategy Model can be applied to our personal lives as much as to organisations. We all have to make decisions with long-run consequences for our futures and the issues involved are very similar. For example, in pursuing a career strategy, a job-seeker needs to understand the job market, evaluate their strengths and weaknesses, establish the range of job opportunities and decide what their career goals really are (positioning issues). The job-seeker then chooses particular jobs and makes some applications (choice issues). Finally, the job-seeker takes a job and starts to work for their next promotion or job move (strategy-in-action). Just as in the non-linear, overlapping Exploring Strategy Model, work experience will frequently amend the original strategic goals. Putting a career strategy into action produces better understanding of strengths and weaknesses and frequently leads to the setting of new ambitions.

1.5.4 Exploring strategy in different contexts

The Exploring Strategy Model can be applied in many contexts, though in each context the typical balance of strategic issues may differ. For example, just within News Corporation

(Illustration 1.1), fast-growing challenger MySpace is likely to have quite different issues from static traditional newspapers such as *The Times*, even though both businesses are dealing with the internet. In applying the Exploring Strategy Model, it is therefore useful to ask what kinds of issues are likely to be particularly significant in the specific context being considered. To illustrate this general point, this section shows how issues arising from the Exploring Strategy Model can vary in three important contexts.

- *Small businesses.* With regard to positioning, small businesses will certainly need to attend closely to the environment, because they are so vulnerable to change. But, especially in small entrepreneurial and family businesses, the most important positioning issue will often be strategic purpose: this will not necessarily just be profit, but might include objectives such as independence, family control, handing over to the next generation and maybe even a pleasant lifestyle. The range of strategic choices is likely to be narrower: it is rare for a small business to make an acquisition itself, though small businesses may have to decide whether to allow themselves to be acquired by another business (as MySpace was). Some issues of strategy-in-action will be different, for example strategic change processes will not involve exactly the same challenges as for large, complex organisations.

- *Multinational corporations.* In this context, positioning in a complex global marketplace will be very important. Each significant geographical market may call for a separate analysis of the business environment. Likewise, operating in many different countries will raise positioning issues of culture: variations in national culture imply different demands in the marketplace and different managerial styles internally. Strategic choices are likely to be dominated by international strategy questions about which geographies to serve. The scale and geographical reach of most multinationals point to significant issues for strategy-in-action, particularly those of organisational structure and strategic change.

- *Public sector and not-for-profits.* Positioning issues of competitive advantage will be important even in these contexts. Charitable not-for-profits typically compete for funds from donors; public-sector organisations, such as schools and hospitals, often compete on measures such as quality or service. The positioning issue of purpose is likely to be very important too. In the absence of a clear, focused objective such as profit, purpose in the public sector and not-for-profits can be ambiguous and contentious. Strategic choice issues may be narrower than in the private sector: for example, there may be constraints on diversification. Strategy-in-action issues often need close attention, leadership and strategic change typically being very challenging in large public-sector organisations.

In short, while drawing on the same basic principles, strategy analysis is likely to vary in focus across different contexts. As the next section will indicate, it is often helpful therefore to apply different lenses to strategy problems.

(1.6) THE STRATEGY LENSES

Exploring means looking for new and different things. Exploring strategy involves searching for new angles on strategic problems. A comprehensive assessment of an organisation's strategy needs more than one perspective. **The strategy lenses are ways of looking at strategy issues differently in order to generate many insights.** Looking at problems in different ways will raise new issues and new solutions. Thus, although the lenses are drawn from academic research on strategy, they should also be highly practical in the job of doing strategy.

The four lenses are introduced more fully immediately after this chapter and will provide the framework for separate *commentaries* on each of the three parts of this book. This section introduces them briefly as follows:

- *Strategy as design.* This takes the view that strategy development can be 'designed' in the abstract, as an architect might design a building using pens, rulers and paper. The architect designs, and then hands over the plans for the builders actually to build. This design lens on strategy encourages a large investment in planning and analysis before making final decisions. It tends to exclude improvisation in strategy development and underplay the unpredictable, conservative or political aspects of human organisations. Taking a design lens to a strategic problem means being systematic, analytical and logical.

- *Strategy as experience.* The experience lens recognises that the future strategy of an organisation is often heavily influenced by its experience and that of its managers. Here strategies are seen as driven not so much by clear-cut analysis as by the taken-for-granted assumptions and ways of doing things embedded in people's personal experience and the organisational culture. Strategy is likely to build on and continue what has gone on before. Insofar as different views and expectations within the organisation exist, they will be resolved not through rational optimisation, as in the design lens, but through messy compromises and ad hoc deals. The experience lens suggests that the personal experience and interests of key decision-makers need to be understood. It sets low expectations of radical change.

- *Strategy as variety.*[12] Neither of the above lenses is likely to uncover radical new ideas in strategy. Design approaches risk being too rigid and top-down; experience builds too much on the past. How then are radical new ideas discovered? The variety lens sees strategy not so much as planned from the top as emergent from within and around organisations as people respond to an uncertain and changing environment with a variety of initiatives. New ideas bubble up through unpredictable and competitive processes. The variety lens therefore emphasises the importance of promoting diversity in and around organisations, in order to allow the seeding of as many genuinely new ideas as possible. Somebody with a variety lens would look for future strategies at the bottom and the periphery of organisations. They should be ready for surprises.

- *Strategy as discourse.* Managers spend most of their time talking, persuading and negotiating. They are always using language, or what is here called 'discourse'. The discourse lens points to how command of strategy discourse becomes a resource for managers by which to shape 'objective' strategic analyses to their personal views and to gain influence, power and legitimacy. Treating strategy as a discourse focuses attention on the ways managers use language to frame strategic problems, make strategy proposals, debate issues and then finally communicate strategic decisions. For believers in the discourse lens, strategy 'talk' matters. The discourse lens tries to look under the surface of strategy to uncover the personal interests and politicking in organisations. Taking a discourse lens thus encourages a somewhat sceptical view.

None of these lenses is likely to offer a complete view of a strategic situation. The point of the lenses is to encourage the exploration of different perspectives: to look at the situation first from one point of view (perhaps design) and then from another. These lenses help in recognising how otherwise logical strategic initiatives might be held back by cultural experience; in checking for unexpected ideas from the bottom or the periphery of the organisation; and in seeing through the formal strategy discourse to ask whose interests are really being served.

SUMMARY

- Strategy is the long-term direction of an organisation. A 'strategy statement' should cover the *goals* of an organisation, the *scope* of the organisation's activities and the *advantages* or *capabilities* the organisation brings to these goals and activities.

- *Corporate-level strategy* is concerned with an organisation's overall scope; *business-level strategy* is concerned with how to compete; and *operational strategy* is concerned with how resources, processes and people deliver corporate- and business-level strategies.

- Strategy work is done by *managers* throughout an organisation, as well as specialist *strategic planners* and *strategy consultants*.

- Research on strategy *context*, *content* and *process* shows how the analytical perspectives of economics, sociology and psychology can all provide practical insights for approaching strategy issues

- The Exploring Strategy Model has three major elements: understanding the *strategic position*, making *strategic choices* for the future and managing *strategy-in-action*.

- Strategic issues are best seen from a variety of perspectives, as exemplified by the four *strategy lenses* of *design*, *experience*, *variety* and *discourse*.

WORK ASSIGNMENTS

✳ *Denotes more advanced work assignments.* * *Refers to a case study in the Text and Cases edition.*

1.1 Drawing on Figure 1.2 as a guide, write a strategy statement for an organisation of your choice (for example, your university), drawing on strategy materials in the organisation's annual report or website.

1.2 Using the *Exploring Strategy* Model of Figure 1.4, map key issues relating to strategic position, strategic choices and strategy into action for either the Lego case* or an organisation with which you are familiar (for example, your university).

1.3 Go to the website of one of the major strategy consultants such as Bain, the Boston Consulting Group or McKinsey & Co. (see reference 5 below). What does the website tell you about the nature of strategy consulting work? Would you enjoy that work?

1.4✳ Using Figure 1.3 as a guide, show how the elements of strategic management differ in:

    (a) a small business (e.g. Ekomate*, Leax* or Web Reservations*)

    (b) a large multinational business (e.g. Marks & Spencer*, SABMiller*, Sony*)

    (c) a non-profit organisation (e.g. NHS Direct* or Queensland Rail*).

RECOMMENDED KEY READINGS

It is always useful to read around a topic. As well as the specific references below, we particularly highlight:

- For general overviews of the strategy discipline, R. Whittington, *What Is Strategy – and Does it Matter?*, 2nd edition, International Thompson, 2000; and H. Mintzberg, B. Ahlstrand and J. Lampel, *Strategy Safari: a Guided Tour through the Wilds of Strategic Management*, Simon & Schuster, 2000.

- Two accessible articles on what strategy is, and might not be, are M. Porter, 'What is strategy?', *Harvard Business Review*, November–December 1996, pp. 61–78; and F. Fréry, 'The fundamental dimensions of strategy', *MIT Sloan Management Review*, vol. 48, no. 1 (2006), pp. 71–75.

- For contemporary developments in strategy practice, business newspapers such as the *Financial Times*, *Les Echos* and the *Wall Street Journal* and business magazines such as *Business Week*, *The Economist*, *L'Expansion* and *Manager-Magazin*. See also the websites of the leading strategy consulting firms: www.mckinsey.com; www.bcg.com; www.bain.com.

REFERENCES

1. The question 'What is strategy?' is discussed in R. Whittington, *What Is Strategy – and Does it Matter?*, International Thomson, 1993/2000 and M.E. Porter, 'What is strategy?', *Harvard Business Review*, November–December 1996, pp. 61–78.

2. D. Collis and M. Rukstad, 'Can you say what your strategy is?', *Harvard Business Review*, April 2008, pp. 63–73.

3. F. Westley, 'Middle managers and strategy: microdynamics of inclusion', *Strategic Management Journal*, vol. 11, no. 5 (1990), 337–51.

4. For insights about in-house strategy roles, see D. Angwin, S. Paroutis and S. Mitson, 'Connecting up strategy: are strategy directors a missing link?', *California Management Review*, vol. 51, no. 3 (2009).

5. The major strategy consulting firms have a wealth of information on strategy careers and strategy in general: see www.mckinsey.com; www.bcg.com; www.bain.com.

6. University careers advisers can usually provide good advice on strategy consulting and strategic planning opportunities. See also www.vault.com.

7. For reviews of the contemporary state of strategy as a discipline, see H. Volberda, 'Crisis in strategy: fragmentation, integration or synthesis', *European Management Review*, vol. 1, no. 1 (2004), pp. 35–42; and J. Mahoney and A. McGahan, 'The field of strategic management within the evolving science of strategic organization', *Strategic Organization*, vol. 5, no. 1 (2007), 79–99.

8. See M.E. Porter, 'The Five Competitive Forces that shape strategy', *Harvard Business Review*, January 2008, pp. 57–91.

9. The classic statement of the resource-based view is J. Barney, 'Firm resources and sustained competitive advantage', *Journal of Management*, vol. 17, no. 1 (1991), pp. 91–120.

10. Two recent collections in the strategy process tradition are G. Szulanski, J. Porac and Y. Doz (eds), *Strategy Process: Advances in Strategic Management*, JAI Press, 2005; and S. Floyd, J. Roos, C. Jacobs and F. Kellermans (eds), *Innovating Strategy Process*, Blackwell, 2005.

11. For recent samples of Strategy-as-Practice research, see the special issues edited by P. Jarzabkowski, J. Balogun and D. Seidl, 'Strategizing: the challenge of a practice perspective', *Human Relations*, vol. 60, no. 1 (2007) and R. Whittington and L. Cailluet, 'The crafts of strategy', *Long Range Planning*, vol. 41, no. 3 (2008).

12. In earlier editions, this lens was called the 'ideas lens'.

Glastonbury – from hippy weekend to international festival

Steve Henderson, Leeds Metropolitan University

Glastonbury Festival has become a worldwide attraction for music fans and artists alike. In 2009, Bruce Springsteen was added to the long list of acts (from Paul McCartney to Oasis) that have appeared at the festival. It started in 1970 when 1,500 hippy revellers gathered on a farm near Glastonbury Tor to be plied with free milk and entertainment from a makeshift stage. Now, Glastonbury is a major international festival that attracts over 150,000 attenders. Without any knowledge of the line-up, the tickets for the 2010 Festival sold out in days.

In those early days, the Festival was developed by local farmer, Michael Eavis, whose passion for music and social principles led to a weekend of music as a means of raising funds for good causes. It was a social mission rooted in the hippy counter-culture of the 1960s and events such as Woodstock. Today, the Glastonbury Festival attender finds that those early days of hippy idealism are a long way off. The scale of the organisation demands strong management to support the achievement of the festival's social aims.

At first, the statutory requirements for an event held on private land were minimal. Jovial policemen looked over hedges whilst recreational drugs were sold from tables near the festival entrance as if this was just a slightly unusual village fête. Needless to say, the festival began to attract the attention of a number of different groups, especially as legislation around the running of events tightened. Eavis struggled with local residents who hated the invasion of their privacy; with hippy activist groups who felt that their contribution in helping at the festival gave them a sense of ownership; with drug dealers carrying on their activities on the fringes of the festival; and fans climbing over the fences to get free access.

The festival's continued expansion has resulted in a festival with over ten stages covering jazz, dance, classical, world music and other genres. Added to this, there is comedy, poetry, circus, theatre and children's entertainment alongside more esoteric street theatre performances. Much of this is organised into specific grassy field areas where, for example, the Dance Village uses a number of tents dedicated to different types of dance music. Indeed, such is the range of entertainment

Source: Getty Images.

on offer that some attenders spend the whole weekend at the festival without seeing a single live music act. Though the Eavis family remain involved with the main programme, much of the other entertainment is now managed by others. Reflecting this shift towards more diverse entertainment, the name of the festival was changed from Glastonbury Fayre (reflecting the ancient cultural heritage of the area) to the Glastonbury Festival for Contemporary Performing Arts.

In some years, the festival is forced to take a year off to allow the farmland to recover from the trampling of thousands of pairs of feet. Not only is this wise on an agricultural front but also gives the local residents a rest from the annual invasion of festival goers. Despite this, the festival has met with a number of controversies such as when a large number of gatecrashers spoilt the fun in 2000. This caused the festival to be fined due to exceeding the licensed attendance and excessive noise after the event. Furthermore, health and safety laws now require the event management to have a 'duty of care' to everyone on the festival site. To address these health and safety concerns, support was sought from Melvin Benn who ran festivals for the Mean Fiddler organisation. With a steel fence erected around the perimeter, Melvin Benn helped re-establish the festival in 2002 after a year off.

Ownership of the festival remained with the Eavis family but Melvin Benn was appointed Managing Director. However, concerns arose in 2006 when his employer, Mean Fiddler, was taken over by major music promoters, Live Nation and MCD Productions. In a worrying move, Live Nation announced that they would entice a number of major artists to appear on the weekend normally used by Glastonbury at a new UK festival called Wireless. Based in London, this seemed set to offer a city-based alternative to Glastonbury. At much the same time, Live Nation announced that they would launch their own online ticket agency to support the sales of their music events. This shift in power between the major music promoters indicated not only their interest in the ownership of key events but their desire to control income streams.

Elsewhere in the world of live entertainment, the success of Glastonbury had not gone unnoticed and the festival market showed considerable growth. Some of the other festivals tried to capitalise on features that Glastonbury could not offer. For example, Glastonbury was famous for its wet weather with pictures of damp revellers and collapsed tents being commonplace. Live Nation's city-based Wireless festival offered the opportunity to sleep under a roof at home or hotel, as opposed to risking the weather outdoors. Alternatively, Benicassim in southern Spain offered a festival with an excellent chance of sunshine and top acts for the price of a low cost airline ticket. Other festivals noted that Glastonbury attenders enjoyed the wider entertainment at the event. In doing this, they realised that many festival goers were attracted by the whole social experience. So, sidestepping major acts and their related high fees, smaller festivals were created for just a few thousand attenders. These offered entertainment in various formats, often in a family-friendly atmosphere. Sometimes described as boutique festivals, Freddie Fellowes, organiser of the Secret Garden Party, describes this type of festival as a chance 'to be playful, to break down barriers between people and create an environment where you have perfect freedom and perfect nourishment, intellectually and visually'. Festival Republic, the rebranded Mean Fiddler, created a boutique festival on a larger scale with their Latitude festival. Similarly, Rob da Bank, a BBC DJ, put together Bestival on the Isle of Wight where the attenders are encouraged to join in the fun by appearing in fancy dress. Quite clearly, audiences are now being presented with a wide range of festivals to consider for their leisure time entertainment.

Many of these festivals attract sponsors with some becoming prominent by acquiring naming rights on the festival. Others have low profile arrangements involving so-called 'contra' deals as opposed to sponsorship payments. For example, Glastonbury has official cider suppliers who typically boost their brand by giving the festival a preferential deal on their products in exchange for publicity. Though these commercial relationships are sometimes spurned by the smaller festivals that see the branding as an intrusion on their fun environment, larger festivals often need such relationships to survive. In order to attract sponsors, large festivals are turning to radio and television broadcasters as a means to expand the audience and offer wider exposure for the sponsor. Indeed, in 2009, the BBC sent over 400 staff members down to Glastonbury for broadcasting aimed at satisfying the interest of the armchair viewer/listener.

With such huge demand for their talents, artists can have a lucrative summer moving between festivals. Similarly, audiences can make lengthy treks to their favourite festivals. For some, this has caused environmental concerns with Glastonbury's rural location, poor transport links and large audience being cited as a specific problem. On the other hand, artists are not only finding that the festivals offer a good source of income but that private parties and corporate entertainment have emerged as alternative, often greater, income opportunities. One newspaper claimed that George Michael pocketed more than £1.5m (~€1.65m; ~$2.25m) to entertain revellers at the British billionaire retailer Sir Philip Green's 55th birthday party in the Maldives. Hence, for many artists, the summer has become a case of 'cherry picking' their favourite festivals or seeking out the most lucrative opportunities.

Over time, the shift from small, homespun event to corporate-controlled festival has provided awkward situations for Michael Eavis – from the difficulties with establishment figures who felt the event was out of control to the demands of counter-cultural groups such as the travelling hippies. However, along the way, the festival has maintained its aim of supporting charities like CND and, later, Greenpeace, Oxfam and a number of local charities. In the mind of the audience, this helps position the festival as a fun event with a social conscience. The continued expansion and shift in management of the festival has freed Michael Eavis to be the figurehead for the event and to pursue the original social mission of the festival.

Given this growing and increasingly competitive market, there is much to consider for the festivals involved. In recent years, Glastonbury has sold all its tickets and made donations to its favoured causes, confirming the financial viability of its current business model. Indeed, the festival's iconic status has traditionally meant that it is a rite of passage for many young music fans. Yet, in 2008, Eavis publicly registered concern over the age of the Glastonbury audience suggesting that selling tickets by phone would help attract a younger audience. Maybe Eavis was concerned by comments such as those in *The Times* newspaper that cruelly declared Glastonbury as suited to the 'the hip-op generation' and questioned whether young people thought it was 'cool' to go to the same music events as their parents. On the other hand, their parents belong to the 'baby boomer' generation that grew up with popular music and festivals like Glastonbury. So, there is no real surprise that they would enjoy this eclectic event. Whatever disturbed Eavis, he announced that Jay-Z, an American rap artist, was to headline in order to help attract a younger audience. With sales slower compared with previous sell-out years, he later stated 'We're not trying to get rid of anybody. The older people are fantastic, but we do need young people coming in as well.' Then, reflecting on the 2008 festival in 2009, Michael Eavis displayed concerns over the future of the festival saying 'Last year I thought that maybe we'd got to the end and we'd have to bite the bullet and fold it all up. A lot of the bands were saying Glastonbury had become too big, too muddy and too horrible.'

With such an established festival as Glastonbury, one would expect the management might be looking to leverage its brand with, for example, further events. Yet, the comments of Michael Eavis suggest not only a lack of clarity about the target audience but also concern over whether it can persist. Furthermore, Eavis seems nervous about the festival's appeal to artists who have lots of opportunities to make appearances over the summer. Audiences and artists are the two key factors that underpin financial success at these events, as successful festival promoters are well aware.

Sources: The history of Glastonbury is charted on its website (http://www.glastonburyfestivals.co.uk/history) whilst ownership and finances are available through Companies House.

Most of the background to the festival and related market has been drawn from online news resources such as the BBC, Times Online and the *Guardian*, or industry magazines such as *Music Week*.

More information on UK Festivals is available from Mintel.

Questions

1 Sticking to the 35 word limit suggested by Collis and Rukstad in section 1.2.3, what strategy statement would you propose for the Glastonbury Festival?

2 Carry out a 'three horizons' analysis (section 1.2.1) of the Glastonbury Festival, in terms of both existing activities and possible future ones. How might this analysis affect their future strategic direction?

3 Using the headings of environment, strategic capability, strategic purpose and culture seen in section 1.5.1, identify key positioning issues for the Glastonbury Festival and consider their relative importance.

4 Following on from the previous question and making use of section 1.5.2, what alternative strategies do you see for the Glastonbury Festival?

5 Converting good strategic thinking into action can be a challenge: examine how the Glastonbury Festival has achieved this by considering the elements seen in section 1.5.3.

COMMENTARY
THE STRATEGY LENSES

Chapter 1 showed that there are different academic disciplines underpinning the way strategy is understood. Exploring the subject in terms of different perspectives is helpful because it provides *different insights* on issues relating to strategy and the management of strategy. Think of everyday discussions you have. It is not unusual for people to say: 'But if you look at it this way . . .'. Taking one view can lead to a partial and perhaps biased understanding. A fuller picture, giving different insights, can be gained from multiple perspectives. In turn these different insights can prompt thinking about different *options or solutions* to strategic problems. There is, therefore, both conceptual and practical value in taking a multi-perspective approach to strategy.

This commentary builds on different perspectives on strategy to develop four *lenses* through which strategy in organisations can be viewed. They are:

- **Strategy as design views strategy development as a logical process of analysis and evaluation** to establish a clear picture of an organisation's strategic position as a basis for deciding future strategy and planning its implementation. So strategy viewed through the design lens emphasises the use of tools and concepts that encourage such objective analysis for making strategy. It is also the most commonly held view about how strategy is developed and what managing strategy is about.

- **Strategy as experience views strategy development as the outcome of people's (not least managers'), taken-for-granted assumptions and ways of doing things.** Strategy through the experience lens therefore puts people and their experience centre stage in strategy development.

- **Strategy as variety* is the view that strategy bubbles up from new ideas arising from the variety of people in and around organisations.** The variety lens therefore helps explain why some organisations may be more innovative than others. It also suggests that, if innovation is specially important, managing strategy is about creating the organisational context to benefit from such variety, foster the emergence of ideas and develop them as they emerge. Whereas the design lens suggests strategy develops in terms of planned direction from the top, the emphasis here is more on bottom-up strategy development. From this point of view it is important to look to the periphery and bottom of the organisation to discover the organisation's future strategy.

- **Strategy as discourse is the view that the language is important as a means by which managers communicate and explain and change strategy, but by which they also gain influence and power and establish their legitimacy and identity.** The discourse lens suggests it is important to unpick the language managers use to justify their strategy in order to uncover hidden assumptions and political interests: the view that language is a resource.

---

* In earlier editions the variety lens was called the 'ideas lens'. The authors believe, however, that the word 'variety' more accurately encapsulates the concepts explained in this section.

The rest of this commentary explains the lenses in more detail. In so doing, the discussion suggests how the lenses relate to and shed light on three key dimensions of managing strategy:

- *Rationality.* The extent to which the development of strategy is a rationally managed act. Of course the design lens assumes this is the case, but the other lenses raise questions about it.

- *Innovation and change.* The extent to which the management of strategy is likely to develop innovatory, change-oriented organisations; or conversely, consolidate strategies rooted in past experience, established ways of doing things and existing power structures.

- *Legitimacy.* How strategy and the involvement in the management of strategy provide a basis of power, authority and influence in their organisations.

The lenses are then used in commentaries at the end of each part of the book to identify implications that arise through viewing the content of the chapters in these different ways and to encourage readers to reflect on the issues that have been raised.

Strategy as design

The design lens builds on two main premises. The first is that managers are, or should be, rational decision-makers. The second is that they should be taking decisions about how to optimise economic performance of their organisations. The principles of economics and the guidelines provided by the decision sciences support and feed the notion that this is what strategic management is all about. Moreover most managers would probably agree that is what they are there to do.

Rational choice implies that managers can and should be able to weigh the benefits and disbenefits of different strategic options on the basis of evidence that informs them of likely outcomes of decisions they make.[1] This is the way strategic management is often explained in textbooks, by tutors and indeed by managers. Stated more fully, the assumptions typically underpinning a *design* view of strategy are as follows. First, in terms of *how strategic decisions are made*:

- *Systematic analysis.* Although there are many influences on an organisation's performance, careful analysis can identify those most likely to influence the organisation significantly. It may be possible to forecast, predict or build scenarios about future impacts so that managers can think through the conditions in which their organisation is likely to operate.

- *Strategic positioning.* This analysis provides a basis for the matching of organisational strengths and resources with changes in the environment so as to take advantage of opportunities and overcome or circumvent threats.

- *Analytic thinking precedes and governs action.* Strategy-making is often seen as a *linear process.* Decisions about what the strategy should be in terms of its content come first and are managed down through the organisation. Decisions about what the strategy should be are therefore separate from and precede its implementation.

- *Objectives* should be clear and explicit and the basis upon which *options are evaluated.* Given a thorough analysis of the factors internal and external to the organisation to inform management about the strategic position of the organisation, a range of options for future strategic direction are then considered and evaluated in terms of the objectives and that analysis. A strategic decision is then made on the basis of what is considered to be optimal, given all these considerations.

Second, the design lens makes assumptions about the *form and nature of organisations*:

- *Organisations are hierarchies*. It is the responsibility of top management to plan the destiny of the organisation. They make important decisions, and lower levels of management, and eventually the rest of the organisation, carry out these decisions and implement the strategy decided at the top.

- *Organisations are rational systems*. Since the complexity organisations face can be understood analytically such that logical conclusions are reached, the associated assumption is that people in the organisation will adopt and accept such logic. The system can be controlled rationally too. *Control systems* (for example, budgets, targets, appraisals) provide the means by which top management can measure whether or not others in the organisation are meeting expected objectives and behaving in line with the strategy.

- *Organisations are mechanisms* by which strategy can be put into effect. They are analogous to engineered systems or, perhaps, machines. So how an organisation is structured and controlled (see Chapter 13) needs to be suited to the strategy. Mechanisms to ensure that strategy is, indeed, being considered rationally and dispassionately are also needed.

Implications for management

Managers often talk as if strategy comes about – or *should* come about – much as the design lens suggests: it is seen as valuable by managers. Arguably there are five main reasons for this:

- *Dealing with complexity and uncertainty*. Strategy as design provides a means of coping with and talking about complex and uncertain issues in a rational, logical and structured way. Indeed there are many *concepts*, *tools* and *techniques* to help managers with this.

- *Management power and legitimacy*. Managers, particularly CEOs, face complex and often challenging situations. The assumptions, tools and techniques of design provide them with ways in which they can feel in control and exercise control in such circumstances.

- Rationality is *deeply rooted* in our way of thinking and in our systems of education. We also live in a world in which science and reasoned solutions to the problems we face seem to surround us and provide many benefits. In this sense the design lens is embedded in our human psyche. So, for example, even when managers admit that strategy is not actually developed in ways the design lens suggests, they often think it should be.

- *Stakeholder expectations*. Important stakeholders such as banks, financial analysts, investors and employees may expect and value such an approach. So it is an important means of gaining their support and confidence.

- *The language of strategy*. In many respects the design lens, especially in its emphasis on analysis and control, is the orthodox approach to strategy development most commonly written about in books, taught at business schools and verbalised by management when they discuss the strategy of their organisations. So it is a useful language to know (see the discourse lens below).

In summary, the design lens is a useful way of viewing the management of strategy on the basis of *analysis and planning*. The associated assumption is that change and innovation can, or at least should be able to, be achieved through such rational and mechanistic approaches. However, the emphasis on analysis and control may well result in conformity rather than innovation. Indeed insights from the experience and ideas lenses that follow help explain why this is so. As Figure C.i also shows, since a rational/analytic approach is typically seen as being

Figure C.i Design lens

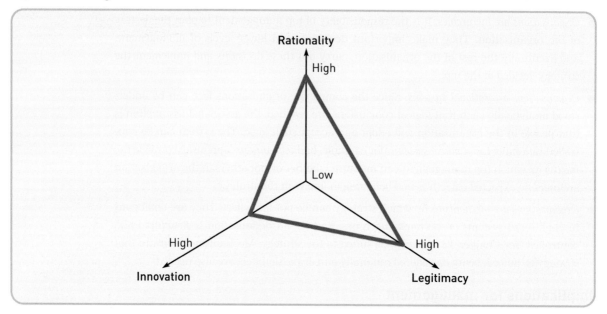

central to the management of strategy, those who see their role like this may also be seen as, or seek to position themselves as, credible, influential (and therefore legitimate) strategists.

This book argues that the design lens is indeed a useful explanation of how strategy is managed but is not sufficient. Other lenses provide insights that are also useful.

Strategy as experience

Much of the evidence from research on how strategies actually develop gives a different picture than that seen through the design lens. As early as the 1950s, Nobel prize winner Herbert Simon and management theorist Charles Lindblom[2] pointed out that rational decision-making models were unrealistic. It is not possible to obtain the information necessary to achieve the sort of exhaustive analysis required; it is not possible to predict an uncertain future; there are limits in terms of cost and time in undertaking such analysis; organisations and environments are changing continually, so it is not possible for managers to take long-term decisions at a point in time. There are also psychological limitations on managers themselves which mean that they cannot be expected to weigh the consequences of all options or be the objective analysts such rationality would expect – a point which is discussed more fully below. The best that can be expected is what Simon termed 'bounded rationality'; managers do the best they can within the limits of their circumstances, knowledge and experience. The experience lens recognises this boundedness in **viewing strategy development as the outcome of people's individual and collective taken-for-granted assumptions and ways of doing things**.

Individual experience and bias[3]

Managers make sense of their complex world by drawing on their previous experience. Human beings function in their everyday lives not least because they have the cognitive capability to make sense of problems or issues they encounter. They recognise and make sense of these on the basis of past experience and what they come to believe to be true about the world. More formally, how we interpret issues we face can be explained in terms of the mental (or cognitive) models we build over time to help make sense of our situations. Managers are no exception to this. When they face a problem they make sense of it in terms of their mental models. This has major advantages. They are able to relate such problems to prior events and therefore have comparisons to draw upon. They can interpret one issue in the light of another. Making sense of situations in this way is fast and, most often, efficient. Indeed, if managers did not have such mental models they could not function effectively; they would meet each situation as though they were experiencing it for the first time.

There are, however, downsides. Mental models simplify complexity. It is not possible for managers to operate in terms of 'perfect knowledge'. Understanding the effects of such *simplification processes* is important. Even if managers have a very rich understanding of their environment, they will not bring that complex understanding to bear for all situations and decisions. They will access part of that knowledge.[4] This is called *selective attention*: selecting from total understanding the parts of knowledge that seem most relevant. Managers also use *exemplars* and *prototypes*. For example, commonly competitors become prototypical. Television company executives came to see other television companies – even specific channels – as their competitors. They therefore readily accepted that satellite broadcasting could introduce new competition because it would introduce new television channels. However, they failed to see that the Internet and sites such as YouTube would become an alternative to watching television. There is also the risk that the 'chunk' of information most often used becomes the only information used and that stimuli from the environment are selected to fit these dominant representations of reality. Information that squares with other television channels being the competitors is taken on board, whilst information counter to that is not. Sometimes this distortion can lead to severe errors as managers miss crucial indicators because they are, in effect, scanning the environment for issues and events that are familiar or readily recognisable.[5]

In summary, there are three important points:

- *Cognitive bias is inevitable.* The idea that managers approach problems and issues of a strategic nature entirely dispassionately and objectively is unrealistic.

- *The future is likely to be made sense of in terms of the past.* Managers typically make sense of new issues in the context of past issues; so when it comes to strategic decisions they are likely to resolve a problem in much the same way as they dealt with a previous one seen as similar. This is one explanation of why strategies tend to develop incrementally from prior strategy (see section 5.2.1).

- Nonetheless, *experience may confer legitimacy and power.* Managers with extensive experience may well be seen as experts or have significant influence in an organisation.

However, managers do not operate purely as individuals; they work and interact with others in organisations, and at this collective level there are also reasons to expect similar tendencies.

Collective experience and organisational culture

How people make sense of situations and issues is not just a matter of individual cognition, but has a collective aspect to it. In this context cultural influences are important: indeed culture was defined by the anthropologist Clifford Geertz as 'socially established structures of meaning'.[6] Central to the concept of culture is the importance of what is 'taken for granted' in terms of assumptions and in terms of activities or practices – 'the way we do things around here'. In everyday life, for example, there are assumptions such as those about the role of the family in bringing up children and about behaviour within the family. These assumptions and associated ways of behaving differ between societies in different parts of the world. In organisational life, an equivalent example might be assumptions about top management, their roles and how they should behave. These also differ, for example between Western firms and Japanese firms. Taken-for-granted aspects of culture also exist at different levels: for example, within a managerial function such as marketing or finance; an organisational unit such as a business; or more widely a professional grouping, such as accountants, an industry sector or even a national culture. The important point here is that these assumptions and taken-for-granted ways of behaving influence strategy in three ways.

First, cultural influences help to explain why managers within a group – an organisation or a department, for example – may see things in similar ways and respond to situations similarly. Second, given this, they help explain why such managers may adhere to familiar strategies and be reluctant to change them. However, third, differences in culture also explain why different groups see things differently; Japanese managers may see things differently from European managers or marketing managers differently from accountants. In turn, and together with the differences in people's personal experience and biases, this helps explain why the management of strategy is often characterised by a good deal of bargaining and negotiation to reconcile such differences.

Implications for management

The experience lens, then, puts people, their experience and the culture in which they work at the centre of strategy development. Figure C.ii summarises its implications in relation to the three dimensions of strategic management. Rationality, in the sense of the careful weighing of options in a search for optimal solutions, is not the emphasis; rather strategies develop as managers try to relate their experience, individual and collective, to the strategic issues that they face. Managers' experience may, however, be seen by colleagues as relevant and important and therefore bestow a high degree of legitimacy. However, strategic change or innovation is likely to be problematic. It should not be assumed that analysis or reasoned argument necessarily

Figure C.ii Experience lens

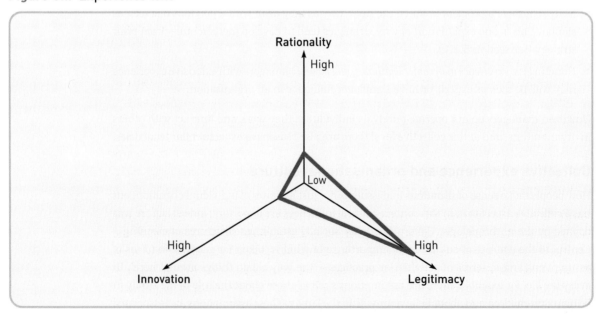

changes deeply embedded assumptions or ways of doing things; readers need only think of their own experience in trying to persuade others to rethink their religious beliefs or, indeed, allegiances to sports teams to realise this.

In turn this provides insights into two other important phenomena associated with managing strategy:

- *Strategic drift* is a risk. If managers are 'captured' by their own and their colleagues' experience the strategy of the organisation gradually drifts away from the realities of its environment and towards an internally determined view of the world. This can lead to significant perform-ance downturn and, potentially, the demise of the organisation (see section 5.2).

- *Bargaining and negotiation* may take place between managers on the basis of different inter-pretations of events according to their past experience or cultural differences. This is the more likely, since managers' personal reputation and standing are likely to be based partly on such experience. This perspective is reflected in discussions of strategy development as a political process (sections 4.5.2 and 14.4.5).

Strategy as variety

The extent to which the two lenses described so far help explain innovation is rather limited. The variety lens helps explain innovative strategies, processes and products; and how organisations faced with fast-changing environments and short decision horizons, such as those in high-technology businesses or the fashion industries, cope with the speed of change and innovation required.

The variety lens builds on complexity theory[7] and evolutionary theory.[8] McKinsey consultant Shona Brown and Stanford academic Kathy Eisenhardt[9] have shown these are helpful when it comes to explaining the conditions that help generate innovation. The basic tenets of evolutionary theory – variation, selection and retention – provide an understanding of how organisational context is important in relation to the generation of new ideas and how managers may help shape that context. The emphasis of complexity theory on how systems cope with uncertainty in non-linear ways adds to that understanding. Viewed through the variety lens, top-down design and direction of strategy is de-emphasised. Rather, strategies are seen as emerging from ideas that bubble up from the variety in and around organisations.

The importance of variety

New ideas are generated in conditions of variety whereas conditions of uniformity give rise to fewer new ideas. Whether the concern is with species, as in the natural world, people in societies or indeed ideas in organisations,[10] uniformity is not the norm; there exists variety. There is an ever-changing environment, different types of businesses, a variety of groups and individuals, a variety of their experience and ideas, and there are deviations from routine ways of doing things.[11] Evolution helps explain how any living system, including an organisation, evolves through natural selection acting upon such variation.

Variety is likely to be greatest where the environment is changing fastest. For example, in our biological world there has been the rapid development of new strains of viruses given the advances in modern medicine to fight them. There are parallels with regard to organisations. Organisations in industry sectors that are developing and fragmented tend to be more innovative than those in mature and concentrated industries,[12] because of the variety of ideas that exist in such dynamic conditions. Take the example of the microelectronics industry. It is a fast-changing industry. This has spawned many different types of businesses, from hardware manufacturers through to software boutiques and firms engaged in applications of such technology. Within these organisations, in turn, there develop new ideas as people interpret opportunities and potential applications differently.

A good deal of this variety occurs naturally and quite likely outside managers' direct control. Since sensing of its environment takes place throughout an organisation, new ideas quite likely come from low down in an organisation, not just from the top.[13] Such ideas will be more or less well informed, may not be well formulated and, at the individual level at least, they may be very diverse. Complexity theorist Bill McKelvey refers to this as the 'distributed intelligence' of an organisation.[14] Moreover, innovation in large organisations often comes from outside their boundaries, perhaps from smaller businesses.[15]

Managers may seek to generate such variety and some of the ways they do this are discussed below. Variation may not, however, always be intentional. In the natural world, change and newness come about because of *imperfections* – a mutation of a gene, for example – that may provide the basis for a 'fitter' organism in a changing environment. In organisations, ideas are also copied imperfectly between individuals, groups or organisations. Some of these will give rise to innovations better suited to the changing environment. A research chemist's idea may be taken up by a marketing executive but interpreted differently from the original idea. Managers in one organisation may seek to copy the strategy of another, but will not do things in exactly the same way. Some of these imperfect copies will not be successful; but others may be. A famous example is Post-its, which originated in an 'imperfect' glue being applied to paper, but resulted in a semi-adhesive for which the researcher saw market potential. There may also be surprises and unforeseen circumstances in the environment; for example the unexpected skills or views introduced by new appointees or unintended consequences arising from management initiatives.

Figure C.iii **Variety lens**

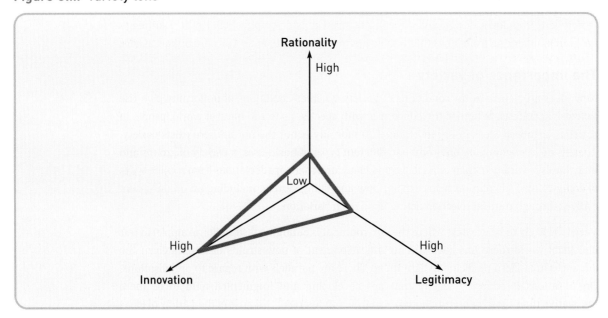

Selection and retention

The implication of the design lens is that the selection of a strategy is a matter of deliberate choice to optimise some sort of outcome, for example competitive advantage leading to enhanced profits. The variety lens and evolutionary theory in particular do not deny the deliberate acts of managers. They do suggest, however, that selection is 'blind'[16] in the sense that outcomes cannot be known. Managers may exercise judgement and choice, indeed may use or refer to management tools to do so, but the strategies that develop are also the result of other processes of selection and retention. These include:

- *Experience and culture.* People's experience and the culture of an organisation act as filters of ideas that do not 'fit'. Formal processes of control, planning and evaluation act to regularise what ideas will and will not go forward. The self-interest of powerful managers may block ideas counter to their own. So pressures for conformity may see off potential new ideas.

- *Functional benefit.* An idea may meet the needs of environmental and market forces. However, many of these (from climate changes to competitor responses) can at best be partially known. There may, however, be other functions such as serving the interests of individuals within the organisation, for example in furthering career aspirations.

- *Alignment.* An idea is likely to be more successful if it aligns with other successful ideas, for example because it is what other organisations are doing or it fits the culture and experience of the organisation itself.

- *Attraction.* Some strategic ideas, by their very nature, are more or less attractive than others.[17] For example, ideas that are altruistic tend to spread and get adopted most.[18] In line with this, complexity theory emphasises the need for sufficient support or 'positive feedback', and some ideas are more likely to attract this than others. For example, a new product idea in a science-based company persisted despite strong evidence of its lack of commercial viability because it addressed 'green' issues and its potential benefits interested colleagues in other divisions and friends and families of the managers developing it.

- *Retention.* As well as processes of selection, there are processes of retention. 'Retention occurs when selected variations are preserved, duplicated or otherwise reproduced',[19] leading to their future repetition. One key factor here is the extent to which ideas become routinised and thus retained. Routinisation varies from formal procedures (for example, job descriptions), accounting and control systems, management information systems, training, organisation structuring, to the formal or informal standardisation of work routines and the eventual embedding of such routines in the culture of the organisation.

Implications for management[20]

A key insight from the variety lens is that managers need to be wary of assuming they can directly control the generation and adoption of new ideas. However, managers can foster new ideas and innovation by *creating the context* and conditions where they are more likely to emerge.

First, they can do this by considering what the appropriate *boundaries* are for the organisation. The more the *boundaries between the organisation and its environment* are reduced, the more innovation is likely to occur. For some high-technology businesses it is difficult to see quite what their boundaries are. They are networks, intimately linked to their wider environment. As that environment changes, so do the ideas in the network. For example, in Formula One motor racing the different teams are intimately linked with the wider motor industry as well as other areas of advanced technology. As a result of this networking new ideas get imitated (but changed) very rapidly. In contrast, where people are insulated from the environment, perhaps by relying on particular ways of doing things, as in a highly rule-based bureaucracy, an organisation will generate less variety of ideas and less innovation.

Second, managers can promote behaviours likely to encourage new ideas in at least five ways:

- *Interaction and cooperation* within organisations encourage variety and the spread of ideas. There is a danger that organisational structures become too established such that people's relationships become too predictable and ordered; rather, ideas tend to be generated more where there are 'weak ties' based on less established relationships.[21] However, there may be limits to this. Too many 'connections' may lead to an over-complex system.[22] All this may help explain why so much effort is spent by managers in changing organisational structures in the search for the most appropriate working environment (see Chapter 13).

- *Questioning and challenge* of 'received wisdom' are important. For example, large organisations often move executives across businesses or divisions with the specific intention of encouraging new ideas and challenging prevailing views.

- *Experimentation* is important. This may take different forms. Some organisations have formal incentive programmes to encourage experimentation. Others have established it as part of their culture. For example, Google gives staff 20 per cent of their time to pursue their own projects. Strategic experiments at an organisational level, such as alliances and joint ventures, are also ways in which organisations may try out possible strategy developments and generate new ideas without over-commitment.

- *Adaptive tension.* Some complexity theorists argue that innovation and creativity emerge when there is sufficient order to make things happen but not when there is such rigidity of control as to prevent such innovation. This is the idea of 'adaptive tension' or 'edge of chaos'.[23] Innovation occurs most readily when the organisation never quite settles down into a steady state or equilibrium and volatility arising from variation is given sufficient rein (see Figure C.iv), though of course not to the extent that the organisation cannot function.

- *Order-generating rules.* Complexity theory also suggests there is no need for elaborate control to create sufficient order for an organisation to work effectively; that ordered patterns of behaviour can come about through just a few 'order-generating rules' or 'simple rules'. In organisations in which innovation is important, managers need to be very clear about the very few overarching requirements that have to be met, but then allow flexibility and latitude in how they are achieved. Table C.i summarises the types of rules identified as important in organisations facing fast-changing environments[24] and gives some examples of how they take form and their effects.

Finally, top management need to consider their role in developing strategy. They need to be able to discern promising ideas, monitor how they 'function' and 'fit' (see above) as they develop, be sensitive to their outcome and impact, and mould the most promising into coherent strategies. Strategy development by top management is therefore more about '*pattern recognition*' than formal analysis and planning. Managers need to develop the competences to do this rather than being over-reliant on the formal tools and techniques of the design lens.

Figure C.iv Adaptive tension

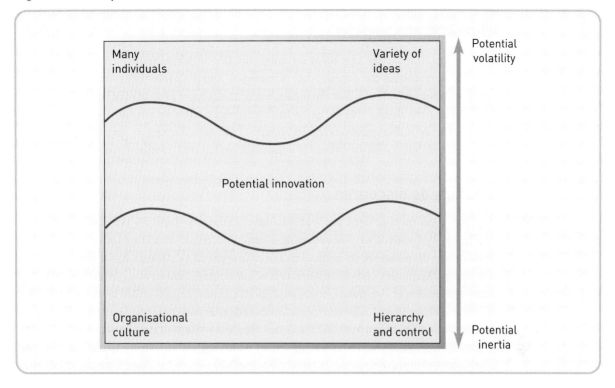

Table C.i Simple rules

Turbulent markets require strategic flexibility to seize opportunities – but flexibility can be disciplined. Different types of simple rules help.

Type	Purpose	Example
How-to rules	Spell out key features of how a process is executed – 'What makes our process unique?'	Dell focus on focused customer segments. So a Dell business must be split in two when its revenue hits $1 billion.
Boundary rules	Focus managers on which opportunities can be pursued and which should not	In Miramax movie-picking process, every movie must: i) revolve around a central human condition, such as love; ii) have a main character appealing but deeply flawed; iii) have a clear story line.
Priority rules	Help managers rank the accepted opportunities	Intel's rule for allocating manufacturing capacity: allocation is based on a product's gross margin. (See Illustration 12.5).
Timing rules	Synchronise managers with the pace of emerging opportunities and other parts of the company	Nortel's product development time must be less than 18 months, which forces it to move quickly into new opportunities.
Exit rules	Help managers decide when to pull out of yesterday's opportunities	In Oticon, the Danish hearing aid company, if a key team member – manager or not – chooses to leave a project for another within the company, the project is killed.

Source: Reprinted by permission of *Harvard Business Review*. Exhibit adapted from 'Strategy as simple rules' by K.M. Eisenhardt and D.N. Sull, January 2001. Copyright © 2001 by the Havard Business School Publishing Corporation. All rights reserved.

In addition, since new ideas are unlikely to emerge fully formed – indeed they may be the result of 'imperfect copying' – managers have to learn to tolerate such imperfection and allow for failures if they want innovation.

In summary, the variety lens helps an understanding of where innovative strategies come from. It de-emphasises the directive role of managers and their rationality and therefore poses questions about whether or not top management really have control over strategic direction to the extent the design lens suggests. In this respect and in its emphasis on the dispersed nature of ideas, it also questions the legitimacy of top management as the strategic directors and source of the success (or failure) of organisations. Figure C.iv summarises this.

Strategy as discourse

In many ways management is about discourse. Managers spend 75 per cent of their time communicating with others[25] in gathering information, persuading others of a course of action or following up decisions. In particular, the management of strategy has a high discursive component. Managers and consultants talk about strategy and strategy is written as formal plans and mission or vision statements, explained in annual reports and in newspaper releases. Efforts to get managerial colleagues, employees and other stakeholders to buy into strategy are also fundamentally discursive; and managers use the language of strategy for their own ends, to gain influence and establish their legitimacy as strategists. The ability to use discursive resources effectively can, then, be an advantage and competence for a manager (see Chapter 15 on strategy practice which discusses strategy 'conversations'). Looking at strategy development in terms of strategy as discourse therefore provides insight into how the language of strategy is used by managers to persuade others, to gain influence and power or establish their identity as strategists.[26]

Discourse and rationality

As discussion of the design lens pointed out, rationality is a central component of the orthodox language of strategy. From a management point of view, then, appearing rational is key to making strategy: 'To be rational is to make persuasive sense.'[27] Strategic management must seem more than just hunch and intuition; it should be more like science and the models like scientific models. As such, managers familiar with such logic can call on it and employ it to justify the 'rightness' of their arguments and views. Indeed typically, even when managers find themselves unable to achieve the goals of strategy – unable, for example, to achieve competitive advantage – they do not deny the logic of the strategy, merely the ability of the organisation to achieve it.[28] They may employ this language because they are themselves persuaded of the logic of a strategy, because they believe that by doing so their arguments will carry more weight with others, because it is the typical way in which strategy is communicated or because, by so doing, it positions them as an authority on the subject.

Discourse and influence

The language of strategy has characteristics that make it convincing to others.[29] Strategy is not only written about in impressive documents – strategic plans or annual reports, for example – but also written about important phenomena such as markets, competitors and customers. It is often associated with 'heroic' chief executives or successful firms. Strategy discussions take place in important places such as boardrooms or strategy away-days. There is also evidence that the employment of strategy discourse works. Managers consciously employ the vocabulary and concepts of strategy to effect change,[30] to justify and legitimise strategies that are to be followed,[31] or to ensure conformity to the right ways to manage strategy.[32] In other words, managers draw on the concepts of strategy and the apparent 'rightness' of strategy concepts to convince others they should comply.

Discourse, identity and legitimacy

How managers talk about strategy also positions them in relation to others, either by their own deliberate choice or as a result of how they are perceived. Discourse is therefore also related to the identity and legitimacy of managers. The common use of the language of rationality has been highlighted above. At other times or in other circumstances managers may also employ different discourse. For example, in trying to get a strategy implemented at an operational level down the line a manager may draw on previous experience as a 'hands-on worker'. In other circumstances reference to prior experience in turning around an organisation may matter. In other contexts the language of the 'visionary leader' or the innovative entrepreneur may be employed.

Strategy discourse may also be consciously or unconsciously employed by managers – particularly top managers – to provide certain benefits for themselves.[33] It helps legitimise a manager as a knowledgeable strategist, employing the right concepts, using the right logic, doing the right thing and being at the forefront of management thinking. It also provides the sense of centrality, of 'making a difference' to the most important aspects of organisational survival. Since over time different strategy discourses have been more or less fashionable, some elements of discourse are likely to be more effective than others at different times. In the 1960s and 1970s it was the language of corporate or strategic planning; in the 1980s there was more of an emphasis on organisational culture; and latterly strategy has become discussed and communicated more in terms of capabilities and competences.

Discourse as power

In turn the discourse of strategy is linked to power and control. By understanding the concepts of strategy, or being seen to do so, it is top managers or strategy specialists who are positioned as having the knowledge about how to deal with the really difficult problems the organisation faces. The possession of such knowledge gives them power over others who do not have it. It 'allows managers to imagine themselves as controllers of . . . economic life'.[34]

Thus the discourse of strategy can also operate as social control. Groups may adopt particular ways of thinking, behaving and speaking about strategy. For example, some organisations, especially firms of consultants, have developed their own discourse on strategy. Or there may develop ways of approaching strategic issues that are embedded in particular discourse. For example, the need to cut costs may be indisputable in certain circumstances. However, it can foster a mindset in which cutting becomes the norm such that it is difficult to propose a strategy that would not lead to reduced costs. Similarly, 'offshoring' and 'the world is flat' have become common terms amongst Western businesses, helping to legitimise the transfer of work from highly paid employees in home countries to cheaper labour in Asian countries. Such discourse may become so taken-for-granted, so difficult to question or change that it becomes a powerful influence on behaviour. In this sense discourse is associated with power when it attracts followers and is self-reproducing and self-reinforcing.

Figure C.v Discourse lens

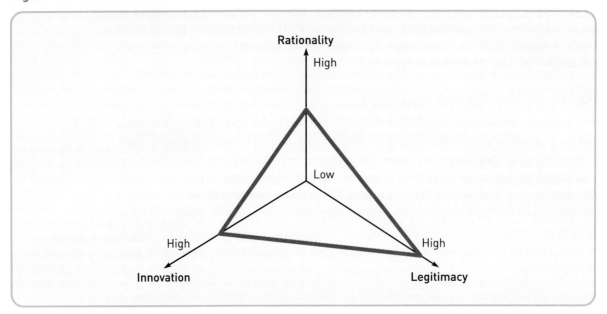

Implications for management

In summary, as shown in Figure C.v, the discourse lens raises the question of the extent to which managers rely on the appearance, rather than the reality, of rational argument. Discourse is used not only to justify strategies, but as ways of seeking power, identity, recognition (and therefore legitimacy). The extent to which such discourse promotes innovation and change will depend on the motivations of the managers and the nature of the language used, though there is evidence that language can play an important role in the management of change.

The fundamental lesson for managers is that the language of strategy they employ matters. The discourse lens highlights this, provides a way of considering how this is so and in practical terms offers concepts and cues by which managers can manage more effectively, for example:

- *Discourse and context*. Different strategy discourses are likely to be more or less effective in different contexts and circumstances. How a strategy is explained and justified to a potential investor may call for a major emphasis on logic and reason under-pinning a financial case. A similarly rational approach may be needed to persuade fellow managers, but perhaps with an additional component related to the benefits in terms of their own interests, future influence and standing. A similar explanation to the workforce of an organisation will have to address the implications for job security, but perhaps also needs to be expressed in ways that reinforce confidence in management. A press release on strategy will likely need to give thought to the main headlines or 'sound bites'. Careful thought needs to go into how strategy is explained and justified to whom.

- *Discourse and the management of strategic change*. Strategy discourse plays an especially important role in the diffusion of innovations, new management practices and the management of change.[35] In particular, different forms of language may be more or less useful in achieving the adoption and retention of new practices. Language that appeals to emotion and self-interest may help adoption, but a reliance on this may lead to the early rejection of new practices. A more rational approach may mean that it takes longer to achieve adoption but will be less likely to result in early rejection. Language that appeals to or relates to accepted ways of doing things may, however, help ensure retention.

- *Common discourse.* It may be beneficial to seek to develop a common language of strategy in an organisation. This is a common reason for management development programmes in relation to strategy. The argued benefit is that managers can then communicate on the basis of a common set of generally understood concepts, terms and tools of strategy which makes strategy debate more effective. It is also a role management educators provide in the diffusion of strategy concepts and language, of course.

- *A critical perspective for managers.* A critical perspective on the discourse of strategy should prompt managers and students alike to question just how substantial concepts and models to do with strategy really are. Are they really based on sound evidence and theory; do they really make a difference? Or are they a discourse being employed because it seems to be what is expected; because it is 'the language of strategists'; or a way for managers to gain power and influence? In this sense, seeing strategy as discourse can prompt the healthy questioning of concepts, ideas and assumptions that might otherwise be taken for granted.

Conclusion

The core assumptions and the key implications of the four lenses of design, experience, variety and discourse are summarised in Table C.ii. They are not offered here as an exhaustive list. They are an attempt to encapsulate different approaches and insights into the complex

Table C.ii A summary of the strategy lenses

	Strategy as:			
	Design	**Experience**	**Variety**	**Discourse**
Strategy develops through . . .	A logical process of analysis and evaluation	People's experience, assumptions and taken-for-granted ways of doing things	Ideas bubbling up from the variety of people in and around organisations	Managers seeking influence, power and legitimacy through the language they use
Assumptions about organisations	Mechanistic, hierarchical, rational systems	Cultures based on experience, legitimacy and past success	Complex and potentially diverse organic systems	Arenas of power and influence
Role of top management	Strategic decision-makers	Enactors of their experience	'Coaches', creators of context and pattern-recognisers	Exercising or gaining power and influence over others
Key implications	Undertake careful and thorough analysis of strategic issues	Recognise that people's experience is central and needs to be built upon but also challenged	If innovation is important look for ideas bubbling up from the bottom and periphery of the organisation	Unpick the language used by managers to uncover hidden assumptions and political interests

concept of strategy. Indeed, the suggestion is that you may usefully extend your exploration of different lenses yourself. It should be apparent in what you have read so far that the lenses presented here actually include several perspectives themselves. For example, the experience lens builds on explanations from cognition, sociology and cultural anthropology and the variety lens builds on both evolutionary theory and complexity theory. So, within these lenses there are finer-grained insights that can be gained and the references and key readings should help with that. In addition there are whole books written that provide multiple perspectives on strategy, from the four that Richard Whittington[36] offers to the ten of Henry Mintzberg and his co-authors.[37]

However, there are two overarching messages that come through consistently. The first is the one with which this commentary began: in considering a topic like strategy, it helps to take more than one perspective. The second is that, in so doing, there is a need to question the conventional wisdom of strategy encapsulated in the design lens. In particular the central tenet of managers at the top planning and directing strategy through machine-like organisations is too limited a view of what strategic management is about.

In the rest of the book the four lenses are employed in commentaries at the ends of Parts I, II and III in particular to examine critically the coverage of each part and consider the management implications.

REFERENCES

1. A useful review of the principles of rational decision making can be found in J.G. March, *A Primer on Decision Making: How Decisions Happen*, Simon & Schuster, 1994, Chapter 1, Limited liability, pp. 1–35.

2. See H.A. Simon, *The New Science of Management Decision*, Prentice Hall, 1960; and C.E. Lindblom, 'The science of muddling through', *Public Administration Review*, vol. 19 (1959), pp. 79–88.

3. For a thorough explanation of the role of psychological processes in strategy see G.P. Hodgkinson and P.R. Sparrow, *The Competent Organization*, Open University Press, 2002.

4. For a review of these points see the introduction to J. Dutton, E. Walton and E. Abrahamson, 'Important dimensions of strategic issues: separating the wheat from the chaff', *Journal of Management Studies*, vol. 26, no. 4 (1989), pp. 380–95.

5. See A. Tversky and D. Kahnemann, 'Judgments under uncertainty: heuristics and biases', *Science*, vol. 185 (1975), pp. 1124–31.

6. See C. Geertz, *The Interpretation of Culture*, Basic Books, 1973, p. 12.

7. For a fuller discussion of complexity theory in relation to strategy see R.D. Stacey, *Strategic Management and Organizational Dynamics: The Challenge of Complexity*, 3rd edition, Pearson Education, 2000; and B. Burnes, 'Complexity theories and organizational change', *International Journal of Management Reviews*, vol. 7 issue 2 (2005), 73–90.

8. For a systematic discussion of the implications of evolutionary theory on management see H. Aldrich, *Organizations Evolving*, Sage, 1999.

9. See S.L. Brown and K.M. Eisenhardt, *Competing on the Edge*, Harvard Business School Press, 1998.

10. An excellent discussion of the development of ideas (or what the authors refer to as 'memes') and the relationship of this to the role and nature of organisations can be found in J. Weeks and C. Galunic, 'A theory of the cultural evolution of the firm: the intra-organizational ecology of memes', *Organization Studies*, vol. 24, no. 8 (2003), pp. 1309–52.

11. M.S. Feldman and B.T. Pentland, 'Reconceptualizing organizational routines as a source of flexibility and change', *Administrative Science Quarterly*, vol. 48 (2003), 94–118, show how 'performative' variations from standardised (they call them ostensive) routines may create variation which creates organisational change.

12. See Z.J. Acs and D.B. Audretsch, 'Innovation in large and small firms – an empirical analysis', *American Economic Review*, vol. 78, September (1988), pp. 678–90.

13. See G. Johnson and A.S. Huff, 'Everyday innovation/everyday strategy', in G. Hamel, G.K. Prahalad, H. Thomas and D. O'Neal (eds), *Strategic Flexibility – Managing in a Turbulent Environment*, Wiley, 1998, pp. 13–27. Patrick Regner also shows how new strategic directions can grow from the periphery of organisations in the face of opposition from the centre; see 'Strategy creation in the periphery: inductive versus deductive strategy making', *Journal of Management Studies*, vol. 40, no. 1 (2003), pp. 57–82.

14. Bill McKelvey, a complexity theorist, argues that the variety within this distributed intelligence is increased because individual managers seek to become better

informed about their environment: see B. McKelvey, 'Simple rules for improving corporate IQ: basic lessons from complexity science', in P. Andriani and G. Passiante (eds), *Complexity, Theory and the Management of Networks*, Imperial College Press, 2004.

15. See E. von Hippel, *The Sources of Innovation*, Oxford University Press, 1988.

16. The concept of blind selection is explained more fully in the chapter by D. Barron on evolutionary theory in the *Oxford Handbook of Strategy*, ed. D. Faulkner and A. Campbell, Oxford University Press, 2003.

17. See Weeks and Galunic, reference 10.

18. The role of altruism and other bases of attraction is discussed by Susan Blackmore in *The Meme Machine*, Oxford University Press, 1999.

19. See Aldrich, reference 8, p. 30.

20. For other implications see some of the references above. In particular Stacey (7), Brown and Eisenhardt (9) and McKelvey (14).

21. See M.S. Granovetter, 'The strength of weak ties', *American Journal of Sociology*, vol. 78, no. 6 (1973), pp. 1360–80.

22. See McKelvey, reference 14.

23. This is the term used by Brown and Eisenhardt, reference 9, amongst others.

24. This discussion is based on research by K.M. Eisenhardt and D.N. Sull, reported in 'Strategy as simple rules', *Harvard Business Review*, vol. 79, no. 1 (2001), pp. 107–16.

25. H. Mintzberg, *The Nature of Managerial Work*, Harper & Row, 1973.

26. In the *Handbook of Discourse Analysis* (ed. D. Schiffrin and H. Hamilton, Blackwell, 2001) T.A. Van Dijk writes: 'Critical Discourse Analysis primarily studies the way social power abuse, dominance and inequality are enacted, reproduced and resisted by text and talk in the social and political context' (p. 352).

27. S.E. Green Jr, 'A rhetorical theory of diffusion', *Academy of Management Review*, vol. 29, no. 4 (2004), pp. 653–69.

28. D. Knights, 'Changing spaces: the disruptive impact of a new epistemological location for the study of management', *Academy of Management Review*, vol. 17, no. 3 (1992), pp. 514–36.

29. D. Barry and M. Elmes, 'Strategy retold: toward a narrative view of strategic discourse', *Academy of Management Review*, vol. 22, no. 2 (1997).

30. For example, see C. Hardy, I. Palmer and N. Phillips, 'Discourse as a strategic resource', *Human Relations*, vol. 53, no. 9 (2000), p. 1231 and L. Heracleous and M. Barrett, 'Organizational change as discourse: communicative actions and deep structures in the context of information technology implementation', *Academy of Management Journal*, vol. 44, no. 4 (2001), pp. 755–78.

31. R. Suddaby and R. Greenwood, 'Rhetorical strategies of legitimacy', *Administrative Science Quarterly*, vol. 50 (2005), pp. 35–67. Also J. Sillence and F. Mueller, 'Switching strategic perspective: the reframing of accounts of responsibility', *Organization Studies*, vol. 28, no. 2 (2007), pp. 175–6.

32. L. Oakes, B. Townley and D.J. Cooper, 'Business planning as pedagogy: language and institutions in a changing institutional field', *Administrative Science Quarterly*, vol. 43, no. 2 (1998), pp. 257–92.

33. D. Knights and G. Morgan 'Corporate strategy, organizations and subjectivity', *Organization Studies*, vol. 12, no. 2 (1991), pp. 251–73.

34. A. Spicer, 'Book review of *Recreating Strategy*', *Organization Studies*, vol. 25, no. 7 (2004), p. 1256.

35. For example see Hardy, Palmer and Phillips (30 above).

36. R. Whittington, *What Is Strategy – and Does it Matter?*, 2nd edition, Thomson, 2000.

37. H. Mintzberg, B. Ahlstrand and J. Lampel, *Strategy Safari*, Prentice Hall, 1998.

PART I
THE STRATEGIC POSITION

This part explains:

- How to analyse an organisation's position in the external environment.

- How to analyse the determinants of strategic capability – resources, competences and the linkages between them.

- How to understand an organisation's purposes, taking into account corporate governance, stakeholder expectations and business ethics.

- How to address the role of history and culture in determining an organisation's position.

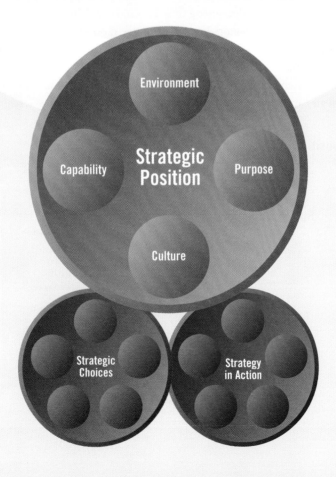

INTRODUCTION TO PART I

This part of the book is concerned with understanding the strategic position of the organisation. There are four chapters, organised around two themes. The first theme is the organisation's strategic *potential*, in other words what it *can* do. The second theme is the organisation's strategic *ambitions*, what it actually *seeks* to do, sometimes deliberately and sometimes not so deliberately (see Figure I.i).

Strategic potential is addressed as follows:

- Chapter 2 considers how different environments can be more or less rich in opportunities or hostile, imposing threats and constraints.
- Chapter 3 considers how each organisation has its own particular strategic capabilities (resources and competences), and how these can enable or constrain strategies.

Organisational ambitions are addressed in the following two chapters:

- Chapter 4 is about how the expectations of powerful groups can shape an organisation's purpose, often expressed in terms of vision and mission statements for example.
- Chapter 5 examines how an organisation's culture and history may shape the ambitions of an organisation, often in semi-conscious and hard-to-change ways.

There is an important strategic dilemma that runs through Chapters 2 and 3. How much should managers concentrate their attention on the external market position and how much should they focus on developing their internal capabilities? On the external side, many argue that environmental factors are what matter most to success: strategy development should be primarily about seeking attractive opportunities in the marketplace. Those favouring a more internal approach, on the other hand, argue that an organisation's specific strategic capabilities should drive strategy. It is from these internal characteristics that distinctive strategies and superior performance can be built. There can be a real trade-off here. Managers

Figure I.i Strategic position

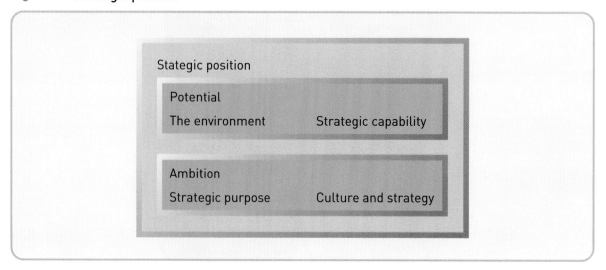

who invest time and resources in developing their external market position (perhaps through acquiring companies that are potential competitors) have less time and resources to invest in managing their internal capabilities (for example, building up research and development). The same applies in reverse. This trade-off between the internal and the external is discussed explicitly in Chapter 2's Key Debate at the end of that chapter.

Chapters 4 and 5 raise another underlying issue. To what extent should managers' ambitions for their organisations be considered as free or constrained? Chapter 4 explains how the expectations of investors, regulators, employees and customers can often influence strategy. Chapter 5 raises the constraints on managers exercised by organisational history and culture. Managers may be only partially aware of these kinds of constraints and are often in danger of underestimating the hidden limits to their ambitions.

Understanding the extent of managers' freedom to choose is fundamental to considering the issues of strategic choice that make up Part II of this book. But first Part I provides a foundation by exploring the question of strategic position.

2

THE ENVIRONMENT

Learning outcomes

After reading this chapter, you should be able to:

- Analyse the broad macro-environment of organisations in terms of political, economic, social, technological, environmental ('green') and legal factors (*PESTEL*).

- Identify key drivers in this macro-environment and use these key drivers to construct alternative *scenarios* with regard to environmental change.

- Use *Porter's five forces* analysis in order to define the attractiveness of industries and sectors and to identify their potential for change.

- Identify successful *strategic groups*, valuable *market segments* and attractive *'Blue Oceans'* within industries.

- Use these various concepts and techniques in order to recognise *threats* and *opportunities* in the marketplace.

mystrategylab

PEARSON

MyStrategyLab is designed to help you make the most of your studies.

Visit **www.pearsoned.co.uk/mystrategylab** to discover a wide range of resources specific to this chapter, including:

- A personalised **Study plan** that will help you understand core concepts
- **Audio** and **video clips** that put the spotlight on strategy in the real world
- **Online glossaries** and **flashcards** that provide helpful reminders when you're looking for some quick revision.

(2.1) INTRODUCTION

The environment is what gives organisations their means of survival. It creates opportunities and it presents threats. For example, the success of Apple's iPhone created rich market opportunities for the writers of mobile phone apps. On the other hand, the rise of electronic encyclopaedias such as Microsoft's Encarta and online Wikipedia nearly destroyed the market for the traditional print market-leader, *Encyclopaedia Britannica*, after two hundred years of existence. Although the future can never be predicted perfectly, it is clearly important that entrepreneurs and managers try to analyse their environments as carefully as they can in order to anticipate and – if possible – influence environmental change.

This chapter therefore provides frameworks for analysing changing and complex environments. These frameworks are organised in a series of 'layers' briefly introduced here and summarised in Figure 2.1.

- *The macro-environment* is the highest-level layer. This consists of broad environmental factors that impact to a greater or lesser extent on almost all organisations. Here, the PESTEL framework can be used to identify how future issues in the *political, economic, social, technological, environmental ('green') and legal* environments might affect organisations. This PESTEL analysis provides the broad 'data' from which to identify *key drivers of change*. These key drivers can be used to construct *scenarios* of alternative possible futures.

- *Industry, or sector,* forms the next layer within this broad general environment. This is made up of organisations producing the same products or services. Here the *five forces* framework

Figure 2.1 Layers of the business environment

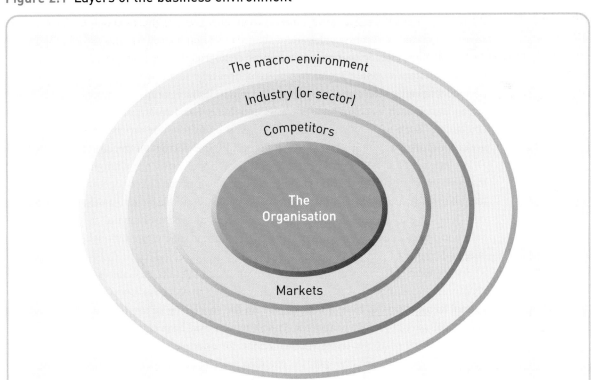

is particularly useful in understanding the attractiveness of particular industries or sectors and potential threats from outside the present set of competitors. The Key Debate at the end of this chapter addresses the importance of industry factors, rather than business-specific factors, in determining success.

● *Competitors and markets* are the most immediate layer surrounding organisations. Here the concept of *strategic groups* can help identify different kinds of competitors. Similarly, in the marketplace, customers' expectations are not all the same. They have a range of different requirements the importance of which can be understood through the concepts of *market segments* and *critical success factors*.

This chapter works through these three layers in turn, starting with the macro-environment.

2.2 THE MACRO-ENVIRONMENT

The three concepts in this section – PESTEL, key drivers and scenarios – are interrelated tools for analysing the broad macro-environment of an organisation. PESTEL provides a wide overview; key drivers help focus on what is most important; and scenarios build on key drivers to explore different ways in which the macro-environment might change.

2.2.1 The PESTEL framework

KEY CONCEPT

PESTEL framework

The **PESTEL framework** categorises environmental influences into six main types: **political, economic, social, technological, environmental and legal.** Thus PESTEL provides a comprehensive list of influences on the possible success or failure of particular strategies.[1] In particular, Politics highlights the role of governments; Economics refers to macro-economic factors such as exchange rates, business cycles and differential economic growth rates around the world; Social influences include changing cultures and demographics, for example ageing populations in many Western societies; Technological influences refer to innovations such as the internet, nano-technology or the rise of new composite materials; Environmental stands specifically for 'green' issues, such as pollution and waste; and finally Legal embraces legislative constraints or changes, such as health and safety legislation or restrictions on company mergers and acquisitions. Illustration 2.1 provides examples of PESTEL factors for the airline industry.

For managers, it is important to analyse how these factors are changing, drawing out implications for their organisations. Many of these factors are linked together. For example, technology developments may simultaneously change economic factors (for example, creating new jobs), social factors (facilitating more leisure) and environmental factors (reducing pollution). As can be imagined, analysing these factors and their interrelationships can produce long and complex lists.

Rather than getting overwhelmed by a multitude of details, it is necessary to step back eventually to identify the key drivers for change. **Key drivers for change** are the environmental factors likely to have a high impact on the success or failure of strategy. Typical key drivers will vary by industry or sector. Thus a retailer may be primarily concerned with social changes driving customer tastes and behaviour, for example forces encouraging out-of-town shopping, and economic changes, for example rates of economic growth and employment. Public-sector managers are likely to be especially concerned with social change (for example, an ageing population), political change (changing government funding and policies) and

ILLUSTRATION 2.1

PESTEL analysis of the airline industry

Environmental influences on organisations can be summarised within six categories. For the airline industry, an initial list of influences under the six PESTEL analysis categories might include the following:

Political

- Government support for national carriers
- Security controls
- Restrictions on migration

Economic

- National growth rates
- Fuel prices

Social

- Rise in travel by elderly
- Student international study exchanges

Technological

- Fuel-efficient engines and airframes
- Security check technologies
- Teleconferencing for business

Environmental

- Noise pollution controls
- Energy consumption controls
- Land for growing airports

Legal

- Restrictions on mergers
- Preferential airport rights for some carriers

Questions

1 What additional environmental influences would you add to this initial list for the airline industry?
2 From your more comprehensive list, which of these influences would you highlight as likely to be the 'key drivers for change' for airlines in the coming five years?

legislative change (introducing new requirements). Identifying key drivers for change helps managers to focus on the PESTEL factors that are most important and which must be addressed as the highest priority. Many other changes will depend on these key drivers anyway (for example, an ageing population will drive changes in public policy and funding). Without a clear sense of the key drivers for change, managers will not be able to take the decisions that allow for effective action.

2.2.2 Building scenarios

When the business environment has high levels of *uncertainty* arising from either complexity or rapid change (or both), it is impossible to develop a single view of how environmental influences might affect an organisation's strategies – indeed it would be dangerous to do so. Scenario analyses are carried out to allow for different possibilities and help prevent managers from closing their minds about alternatives. Thus scenarios offer plausible alternative views of how the business environment might develop in the future, based on key drivers for change about which there is a high level of uncertainty.[2] Scenarios typically build on PESTEL analyses and key drivers for change, but do not offer a single forecast of how the environment will change. The point is not to predict, but to encourage managers to be alert to a range of possible futures.

Illustration 2.2 shows an example of scenario planning for the global financial system to 2020. Rather than incorporating a multitude of factors, the authors focus on two key drivers which (i) have high potential impact and (ii) are uncertain: geo-economic power shifts and international coordination on financial policy. Both of these drivers may produce very different futures, which can be combined to create four internally consistent scenarios for the next decade. The authors do not predict that one will prevail over the others, nor do they allocate relative probabilities. Prediction would close managers' minds to alternatives, while probabilities would imply a spurious kind of accuracy.

Scenario analyses can be carried out as follows:[3]

- *Identifying the scope* is an important first step. Scope refers to the subject of the scenario analysis and the time span. For example, scenario analyses can be carried out for a whole industry globally, or for particular geographical regions and markets. They can be for a decade or so (as in Illustration 2.2) or for just three to five years ahead.

- *Identifying key drivers for change* comes next. Here PESTEL analysis can be used to uncover issues likely to have a major impact upon the future of the industry, region or market.

- *Selecting opposing key drivers* is crucial in order to generate a range of different but plausible scenarios. Typically scenario analyses select from the various key drivers for change two key drivers which both have high uncertainty and have the potential for producing significantly divergent or opposing outcomes. In the oil industry, for example, political stability in the oil-producing regions is one major uncertainty; another is the capacity to develop major new oilfields, thanks to new extraction technologies or oilfield discoveries.

- *Developing scenario 'stories'*: as in films, scenarios are basically stories. Having selected opposing key drivers for change, it is necessary to knit together plausible 'stories' that incorporate both key drivers and other factors into a coherent whole. Thus in Illustration 2.2, the Fragmented protectionism scenario brings together in a consistent way failure to achieve international coordination and a slow rate of geo-economic shift: nationalistic protectionist measures in the West would prevent coordination at the same time as delaying the rise of the Asian economies. But completing the 'story' of Fragmented protectionism would also involve incorporating other consistent factors: for example, slow economic growth resulting from barriers to trade; possible military conflicts due to lack of international cooperation; and illiberal domestic politics associated with nationalism.

- *Identifying impacts* of alternative scenarios on organisations is the final key stage of scenario building. Fragmented protectionism would obviously have a very negative impact for most multinational corporations. Rebalanced multilateralism on the other hand would favour multinationals, especially those from the rising Asian economies. It would be important for an organisation to carry out *robustness checks* in the face of each plausible scenario and develop *contingency plans* in case they happen.

ILLUSTRATION 2.2

Scenarios for the global financial system, 2020

Founded in 1971, the World Economic Forum (www.weforum.org) is a not-for-profit organisation based in Geneva dedicated to developing new thinking amongst political, business and society leaders from countries worldwide. Participants at its famous annual Davos meetings have included German Chancellor Angela Merkel, Microsoft founder Bill Gates and South African President Nelson Mandela. As the world wrestled with the financial crisis of 2008–9, the World Economic Forum proposed to the 2009 Davos meeting four long-range scenarios for how the global financial system might develop to 2025. These scenarios were developed through eight separate workshops involving over 250 financial executives, regulators, policy-makers and senior academics.

The scenarios were based on two key drivers, each governed by a great deal of uncertainty. The first key driver was the pace of geo-economic power shifts, in particular from the traditional centres of economic power in the United States and Europe to the emerging ones in Asia and elsewhere. The second key driver was the degree of international coordination of financial policy, referring to issues such as banking regulation and currency policies. It was the

upsides and downsides of these key drivers that defined the following four scenarios.

Re-engineered Western-centrism proposes a world in which the power-shift from the West is reasonably slow and policy-makers manage to coordinate a stable financial framework in which to navigate change. This is a comforting scenario for many Western companies. The *Rebalanced multilateralism* scenario envisages a more rapid shift from the West, but none the less policy-makers are able to co-ordinate change. For most Western companies, this is challenging but manageable, with Asia continuing to value their participation. More limiting is the *Financial regionalism* scenario. Here policy-makers are unable to find global agreement and the world splits into three major blocs, an American one, a European one and an increasingly powerful Asian one. Western companies are obliged to adopt very different strategies and structures for each of the three main blocs. The final scenario of *Fragmented protectionism* is daunting. Here nationalistic protectionism slows the shift from the West, but also reduces economic growth and leads to the collapse of the integrated Eurozone. All kinds of international business suffer from volatility, conflict and controls.

The World Economic Forum made no forecast about which scenario was more probable. But in presenting the alternatives, it aimed to get policy-makers to see the need for serious action, at the same time as warning business leaders that 'business as usual' was not a likely prospect.

Source: http://www.weforum.org/pdf/scenarios/ TheFutureoftheGlobalFinancialSystem.pdf.

	Slow geo-economic shift	Rapid geo-economic shift
Harmonised financial coordination	Re-engineered Western-centrism	Rebalanced multilateralism
Discordant financial coordination	Fragmented protectionism	Financial regionalism

Question

Over which of the two drivers – the geo-economic power shift and policy coordination – do companies have the most influence? How should they exercise this influence?

Because debating and learning are so valuable in the scenario building process, and they deal with such high uncertainty, some scenario experts advise managers to avoid producing just three scenarios. Three scenarios tend to fall into a range of 'optimistic', 'middling' and 'pessimistic'. Managers naturally focus on the middling scenario and neglect the other two, reducing the amount of organisational learning and contingency planning. It is therefore typically better to have two or four scenarios, avoiding an easy mid-point. It does not matter if the scenarios do not come to pass: the value lies in the process of exploration and contingency planning that the scenarios set off.

 ## 2.3 INDUSTRIES AND SECTORS

The previous section looked at how forces in the macro-environment might influence the success or failure of an organisation's strategies. But the impact of these general factors tends to surface in the more immediate environment through changes in the competitive forces surrounding organisations. An important aspect of this for most organisations will be competition within their industry, sector or market. **An industry is a group of firms producing products and services that are essentially the same.**[4] Examples are the automobile industry and the airline industry. Industries are also often described as 'sectors', especially in public services (for example, the health sector or the education sector). Industries and sectors are often made up of several specific markets. **A market is a group of customers for specific products or services that are essentially the same (for example, a particular geographical market).** Thus the automobile industry has markets in North America, Europe and Asia, for example.

This section concentrates on industry analysis, starting with Michael Porter's *five forces framework* and then introducing techniques for analysing the *dynamics* of industries. However, while the following section will address markets in more detail, this section will refer to markets and most of the concepts apply similarly to markets and industries.

2.3.1 Competitive forces – the five forces framework

Porter's five forces framework

Porter's five forces framework[5] **helps identify the attractiveness of an industry in terms of five competitive forces: the threat of entry, the threat of substitutes, the power of buyers, the power of suppliers and the extent of rivalry between competitors.** These five forces together constitute an industry's 'structure' (see Figure 2.2), which is typically fairly stable. For Porter, an attractive industry structure is one that offers good profit potential. His essential message is that where the five forces are high, industries are not attractive to compete in. There will be too much competition, and too much pressure, to allow reasonable profits.

Although initially developed with businesses in mind, the five forces framework is relevant to most organisations. It can provide a useful starting point for strategic analysis even where profit criteria may not apply. In the public sector, it is important to understand how powerful suppliers can push up costs; amongst charities, it is important to avoid excessive rivalry within the same market. Moreover, once the degree of industry attractiveness has been understood, the five forces can help set an agenda for action on the various critical issues that they identify: for example, what should be done to control excessive rivalry in a particular industry? The rest of this section introduces each of the five forces in more detail. Illustration 2.3 on the evolving steel industry provides examples.

Figure 2.2 The five forces framework

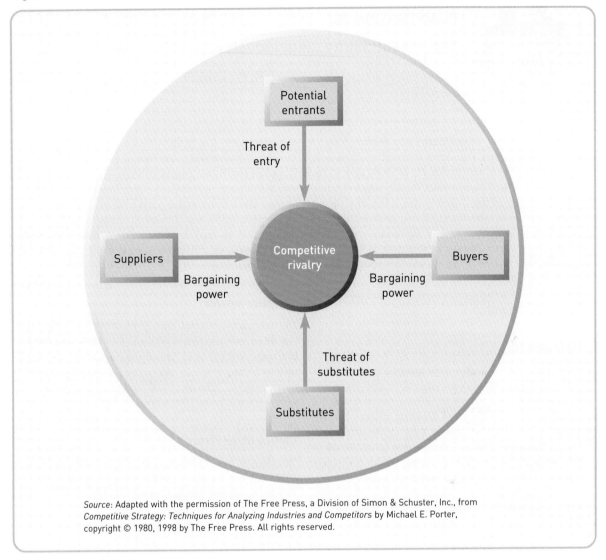

The threat of entry

How easy it is to enter the industry obviously influences the degree of competition. The greater the threat of entry, the worse it is for incumbents (existing competitors) in an industry. An attractive industry has high barriers to entry in order to reduce the threat of new competitors. **Barriers to entry are the factors that need to be overcome by new entrants if they are to compete in an industry**. Typical barriers are as follows:

- *Scale and experience*. In some industries, *economies of scale* are extremely important: for example, in the production of automobiles or the advertising of fast-moving consumer goods. Once incumbents have reached large-scale production, it will be very expensive for new entrants to match them and until they reach a similar volume they will have higher unit costs. This scale effect is increased where there are high *investment requirements* for entry, for example research costs in pharmaceuticals or capital equipment costs in automobiles. Barriers to entry also come from *experience curve* effects that give incumbents a cost

ILLUSTRATION 2.3

The consolidating steel industry

Five forces analysis helps understand the changing attractiveness of an industry.

For a long time, the steel industry was seen as a static and unprofitable one. Producers were nationally-based, often state-owned and frequently unprofitable – the early 2000s saw 50 independent steel producers going into bankruptcy in the United States alone. But recent years have seen a turnaround. During 2006, Mittal Steel paid $35bn (~€24.5bn) to buy European steel giant Arcelor, creating the world's largest steel company. The following year, Indian conglomerate Tata bought Anglo-Dutch steel company Corus for $13bn. These high prices indicated considerable confidence in the prospects of a better industry structure.

New entrants

In the last two decades, two powerful groups have entered world steel markets. First, after a period of privatisation and reorganisation, Russia had become the world's second largest steel exporting country (behind Japan) in 2009, led by giants such as Severstal and Evraz. China too had become a major force. Between the early 1990s and 2009, Chinese producers have increased their capacity six times. Although Chinese share of world capacity reached over 40% in 2009, most of this was directed at the domestic market. China was the word's fourth largest steel exporter in 2009.

Substitutes

Steel is a nineteenth century technology, increasingly substituted for by other materials such as aluminium in cars, plastics and aluminium in packaging and ceramics and composites in many high-tech applications. Steel's own technological advances sometimes work to reduce need: thus steel cans have become about one third thinner over the last few decades.

Buyer power

The major buyers of steel are the global car manufacturers. Car manufacturers are sophisticated users, often leading in the technological development of their materials. In North America at least, the decline of the once dominant 'Big Three' – General Motors, Ford and Chrysler – has meant many new domestic buyers, with companies such as Toyota, Nissan, Honda and BMW establishing local production plants. Another important user of steel is the metal packaging industry. Leading can producers such as Crown Holdings, which makes one third of all food cans produced in North America and Europe, buy in large volumes, coordinating purchases around the world.

Supplier power

The key raw material for steel producers is iron ore. The big three ore producers – Vale, Rio Tinto and BHP Billiton – control about 70% of the market for internationally traded ore. Iron ore prices had multiplied four times between 2005 and 2008, and, despite the recession, were still twice 2005's level in 2010.

Competitive rivalry

The industry has traditionally been very fragmented: in 2000, the world's top 5 producers accounted for only 14% of production. Companies such as Nucor in the US, Thyssen-Krupp in Germany as well as Mittal and Tata responded by buying up weaker players internationally. By 2009, the top 5 producers accounted for 20% of world production. New steel giant ArcelorMittal alone accounted for about 10% of world production, with one fifth of the European Union market. None the less, despite a cyclical peak in 2008 and a slump in 2009, the world steel price was basically the same in 2010 as in 2005.

Questions

1 In recent years, which of the five forces has become more positive for steel producers, which less so?

2 Explain the acquisition strategies of players such as Mittal, Tata and Nucor.

3 In the future, what might change to make the steel industry less attractive or more attractive?

advantage because they have learnt how to do things more efficiently than an inexperienced new entrant could possibly do (see section 6.3.1). Until the new entrant has built up equivalent experience over time, it will tend to produce at higher cost.

- *Access to supply or distribution channels.* In many industries manufacturers have had control over supply and/or distribution channels. Sometimes this has been through direct ownership (vertical integration), sometimes just through customer or supplier loyalty. In some industries this barrier has been overcome by new entrants who have bypassed retail distributors and sold directly to consumers through e-commerce (for example, Dell Computers and Amazon).

- *Expected retaliation.* If an organisation considering entering an industry believes that the retaliation of an existing firm will be so great as to prevent entry, or mean that entry would be too costly, this is also a barrier. Retaliation could take the form of a price war or a marketing blitz. Just the knowledge that incumbents are prepared to retaliate is often sufficiently discouraging to act as a barrier. This dynamic interaction between incumbents and potential new entrants will be discussed more fully in section 2.3.2 below.

- *Legislation or government action.* Legal restraints on new entry vary from patent protection (e.g. pharmaceuticals), to regulation of markets (e.g. pension selling), through to direct government action (e.g. tariffs). Of course, organisations are vulnerable to new entrants if governments remove such protection, as has happened with deregulation of the airline industry.

- *Differentiation.* Differentiation means providing a product or service with higher perceived value than the competition; its importance will be discussed more fully in section 6.3.2. Cars are differentiated, for example, by quality and branding. Steel, by contrast, is by-and-large a commodity, undifferentiated and therefore sold by the ton. Steel buyers will simply buy the cheapest. Differentiation reduces the threat of entry because of increasing customer loyalty.

The threat of substitutes

Substitutes are products or services that offer a similar benefit to an industry's products or services, but by a different process. For example, aluminium is a substitute for steel in automobiles; trains are a substitute for cars; television and videogames are substitutes for each other. Managers often focus on their competitors in their own industry, and neglect the threat posed by substitutes. Substitutes can reduce demand for a particular type of product as customers switch to alternatives – even to the extent that this type of product or service becomes obsolete. However, there does not have to be much actual switching for the substitute threat to have an effect. The simple risk of substitution puts a cap on the prices that can be charged in an industry. Thus, although Eurostar has no direct competitors in terms of train services from Paris to London, the prices it can charge are ultimately limited by the cost of flights between the two cities.

There are two important points to bear in mind about substitutes:

- *The price/performance ratio* is critical to substitution threats. A substitute is still an effective threat even if more expensive, so long as it offers performance advantages that customers value. Thus aluminium is more expensive than steel, but its relative lightness and its resistance to corrosion give it an advantage in some automobile manufacturing applications. It is the ratio of price to performance that matters, rather than simple price.

- *Extra-industry effects* are the core of the substitution concept. Substitutes come from outside the incumbents' industry and should not be confused with competitors' threats from within the industry. The value of the substitution concept is to force managers to look outside their own industry to consider more distant threats and constraints. The higher the threat of substitution, the less attractive the industry is likely to be.

The power of buyers

Buyers are the organisation's immediate customers, not necessarily the ultimate consumers. If buyers are powerful, then they can demand cheap prices or product or service improvements liable to reduce profits.

Buyer power is likely to be high when some of the following conditions prevail:

- *Concentrated buyers.* Where a few large customers account for the majority of sales, buyer power is increased. This is the case on items such as milk in the grocery sector in many European countries, where just a few retailers dominate the market. If a product or service accounts for a high percentage of the buyers' total purchases their power is also likely to increase as they are more likely to 'shop around' to get the best price and therefore 'squeeze' suppliers than they would for more trivial purchases.

- *Low switching costs.* Where buyers can easily switch between one supplier and another, they have a strong negotiating position and can squeeze suppliers who are desperate for their business. Switching costs are typically low for weakly differentiated commodities such as steel.

- *Buyer competition threat.* If the buyer has the capability to supply itself, or if it has the possibility of acquiring such a capability, it tends to be powerful. In negotiation with its suppliers, it can raise the threat of doing the suppliers' job themselves. This is called *backward vertical integration* (see section 7.5), moving back to sources of supply, and might occur if satisfactory prices or quality from suppliers cannot be obtained. For example, some steel companies have gained power over their iron ore suppliers as they have acquired iron ore sources for themselves.

It is very important that *buyers* are distinguished from *ultimate consumers*. Thus for companies like Procter & Gamble or Unilever (makers of shampoo, washing powders and so on), their buyers are retailers such as Carrefour or Tesco, not ordinary consumers (see discussion of the 'strategic customer' in 2.4.2). Carrefour and Tesco have much more negotiating power than an ordinary consumer would have. The high buying power of such supermarkets has become a major source of pressure for the companies supplying them.

The power of suppliers

Suppliers are those who supply the organisation with what it needs to produce the product or service. As well as fuel, raw materials and equipment, this can include labour and sources of finance. The factors increasing supplier power are the converse to those for buyer power. Thus *supplier power* is likely to be high where there are:

- *Concentrated suppliers.* Where just a few producers dominate supply, suppliers have more power over buyers. The iron ore industry is now concentrated in the hands of three main producers, leaving the steel companies, still relatively fragmented, in a weak negotiating position for this essential raw material.

- *High switching cost.* If it is expensive or disruptive to move from one supplier to another, then the buyer becomes relatively dependent and correspondingly weak. Microsoft is a powerful supplier because of the high switching costs of moving from one operating system to another. Buyers are prepared to pay a premium to avoid the trouble, and Microsoft knows it.

- *Supplier competition threat.* Suppliers have increased power where they are able to cut out buyers who are acting as middlemen. Thus airlines have been able to negotiate tough contracts with travel agencies as the rise of online booking has allowed them to create a direct route to customers. This is called *forward vertical integration*, moving up closer to the ultimate customer.

Most organisations have many suppliers, so it is necessary to concentrate the analysis on the most important ones or types. If their power is high, suppliers can capture all their buyers' own potential profits simply by raising their prices. Star football players have succeeded in raising their rewards to astronomical levels, while even the leading football clubs – their 'buyers' – struggle to make money.

Competitive rivalry

These wider competitive forces (the four arrows in the model in Figure 2.2) all impinge on the direct competitive rivalry between an organisation and its most immediate rivals. Thus low barriers to entry increase the number of rivals; powerful buyers with low switching costs force their suppliers to high rivalry in order to offer the best deals. The more competitive rivalry there is, the worse it is for incumbents within the industry.

Competitive rivals are organisations with similar products and services aimed at the same customer group (i.e. not substitutes). In the European airline industry, Air France and British Airways are rivals; trains are a substitute. As well as the influence of the four previous forces, there are a number of additional factors directly affecting the degree of competitive rivalry in an industry or sector:

- *Competitor balance.* Where competitors are of roughly equal size there is the danger of intensely rivalrous behaviour as one competitor attempts to gain dominance over others, through aggressive price cuts for example. Conversely, less rivalrous industries tend to have one or two dominant organisations, with the smaller players reluctant to challenge the larger ones directly (for example, by focusing on niches to avoid the 'attention' of the dominant companies).

- *Industry growth rate.* In situations of strong growth, an organisation can grow with the market, but in situations of low growth or decline, any growth is likely to be at the expense of a rival, and meet with fierce resistance. Low growth markets are therefore often associated with price competition and low profitability. The *industry life cycle* influences growth rates, and hence competitive conditions: see section 2.3.2.

- *High fixed costs.* Industries with high fixed costs, perhaps because requiring high investments in capital equipment or initial research, tend to be highly rivalrous. Companies will seek to spread their costs (i.e. reduce unit costs) by increasing their volumes: to do so, they typically cut their prices, prompting competitors to do the same and thereby triggering price wars in which everyone in the industry suffers. Similarly, if extra capacity can only be added in large increments (as in many manufacturing sectors, for example a chemical or glass factory), the competitor making such an addition is likely to create short-term over-capacity in the industry, leading to increased competition to use capacity.

- *High exit barriers.* The existence of high barriers to exit – in other words, closure or disinvestment – tends to increase rivalry, especially in declining industries. Excess capacity persists and consequently incumbents fight to maintain market share. Exit barriers might be high for a variety of reasons: for example, high redundancy costs or high investment in specific assets such as plant and equipment that others would not buy.

- *Low differentiation.* In a commodity market, where products or services are poorly differentiated, rivalry is increased because there is little to stop customers switching between competitors and the only way to compete is on price.

Types of industry

Five forces analysis helps to identify four main types of industry structure. In practice, particular industries are typically not pure representatives of these types, but nonetheless it is helpful to have these broad categories in mind in order to compare the attractiveness of industries and likely broad patterns of competitive behaviour within them. These four types are:

- *Monopolistic industries.* **A monopoly is formally an industry with just one firm and therefore no competitive rivalry**. Because of the lack of choice between rivals, there is potentially very great power over buyers and suppliers. This can be very profitable. In practice, pure monopolies are rare because government regulators typically prohibit them. However, firms may still have 'monopolistic power' where their dominance over other firms in the industry is very great, as for example Google which in early 2010 had 65 per cent of the American search market, against Yahoo's 17 per cent and Microsoft's 11 per cent. Such monopolistic power gives firms considerable leverage in negotiating prices with buyers and suppliers. Thus Google has strong price-setting power in the internet advertising business.

- *Oligopolistic industries.* **An oligopoly is where just a few firms dominate an industry, with the potential for limited rivalry and great power over buyers and suppliers**. The iron ore market is an oligopoly, dominated by Vale, Rio Tinto and BHP Billiton (see Illustration 2.3). Where there are just two oligopolistic rivals, as for Airbus and Boeing in the civil airline industry, the situation is a duopoly. In theory, oligopoly can be highly profitable, but much depends on the extent of rivalrous behaviour, the threat of entry and substitutes and the growth of final demand in key markets. Oligopolistic firms have a strong interest in minimising rivalry between each other so as to maintain a common front against buyers and suppliers.

- *Hypercompetitive industries.* **Hypercompetition occurs where the frequency, boldness and aggression of competitor interactions accelerate to create a condition of constant disequilibrium and change.**[6] Under hypercompetition, rivals tend to invest heavily in destabilising innovation, expensive marketing initiatives and aggressive price cuts, with negative impacts on profits. Hypercompetition often breaks out in otherwise oligopolistic industries. Thus the global mobile phone industry has some oligopolistic characteristics, with Nokia holding 35 per cent share, Samsung 21 per cent and LG 11 per cent in 2009. However, Samsung and LG are increasing their share aggressively, and there are many strong challengers, including the innovative Apple iPhone and Google's Nexus One. Competitive moves under conditions of hypercompetition are discussed in section 6.4.2.

- *Perfectly competitive industries.* **Perfect competition exists where barriers to entry are low, there are many equal rivals each with very similar products, and information about competitors is freely available**. Few markets are absolutely perfectly competitive, but many are highly so. In these conditions, firms are unable to earn more profit than the bare minimum required to survive. Competition focuses heavily on price, because competitors typically cannot fund major innovations or marketing initiatives. Minicab services in large cities often come close to perfect competition. Entrepreneurs should beware entering industries with low barriers to entry, as these are liable to be perfectly or highly competitive and good profits will be very hard to earn.

Implications of five forces analysis

The five forces framework provides useful insights into the forces at work in the industry or market environment of an organisation. It is important, however, to use the framework for more than simply listing the forces. The bottom line is an assessment of the attractiveness of the industry. The analysis should conclude with a judgement about whether the industry is a good one to compete in or not.

The analysis should next prompt investigation of the *implications* of these forces, for example:

- *Which industries to enter (or leave)?* The fundamental purpose of the five forces model is to identify the relative attractiveness of different industries: industries are attractive when the forces are weak. Entrepreneurs and managers should invest in industries where the five forces work in their favour and avoid, or disinvest from, markets where they are strongly against.

- *What influence can be exerted?* Industry structures are not necessarily fixed, but can be influenced by deliberate managerial strategies. For example, organisations can build barriers to entry by increasing advertising spend to improve customer loyalty. They can buy up competitors to reduce rivalry and increase power over suppliers or buyers. Influencing industry structure involves many issues relating to *competitive strategy* and will be a major concern of Chapter 6.

- *How are competitors differently affected?* Not all competitors will be affected equally by changes in industry structure, deliberate or spontaneous. If barriers are rising because of increased R&D or advertising spending, smaller players in the industry may not be able to keep up with the larger players, and be squeezed out. Similarly, growing buyer power is likely to hurt small competitors most. Strategic group analysis is helpful here (see 2.4.1).

Although originating in the private sector, five forces analysis can have important implications for organisations in the public sector too. For example, the forces can be used to adjust the service offer or focus on key issues. Thus it might be worth switching managerial initiative from an arena with many crowded and overlapping services (e.g. social work, probation services and education) to one that is less rivalrous and where the organisation can do something more distinctive. Similarly, strategies could be launched to reduce dependence on particularly powerful and expensive suppliers, for example energy sources or high shortage skills.

Key issues in using the five forces framework

The five forces framework has to be used carefully and is not necessarily complete, even at the industry level. When using this framework, it is important to bear the following three issues in mind:

- *Defining the 'right' industry.* Most industries can be analysed at different levels, for example different markets and even different segments within them (see 2.4.2 below). For example, the airline industry has different geographical markets (Europe, China and so on) and it also has different segments within each market (e.g. leisure, business and freight). The competitive forces are likely to be different for each of these markets and segments and can be analysed separately. It is sometimes useful to conduct industry analysis at a disaggregated level, for each distinct segment or market. The overall picture for the industry as a whole can then be assembled.

● *Converging industries*. Industry definition is often difficult too because industry boundaries are continuously changing. For example, many industries, especially in high-tech arenas, are converging. Convergence is where previously separate industries begin to overlap or merge in terms of activities, technologies, products and customers.[7] Technological change has brought convergence between the telephone and photographic industries, for example, as mobile phones have come to include camera and video functions. For a camera company like Kodak, Nokia and Samsung could even be considered direct competitors.

● *Complementary organisations*. Some analysts argue that industry analyses need to include a 'sixth force', the existence of organisations that are complementors rather than simple competitors. **An organisation is your** `complementor`: **(i) if customers value your product more when they have the other organisation's product than when they have the product alone; (ii) if it's more attractive for suppliers to provide resources to you when they are also supplying the other organisation than when they are supplying you alone.**[8] An example of the first is Microsoft Windows software and McAfee computer security: each is better because of the other. An example of the second is airlines in relationship to an aircraft supplier such as Boeing: Boeing invests more in innovation because of the existence of many airline companies as potential customers. Complementarity implies a significant shift in perspective. While Porter's five forces sees organisations as battling against each other for share of industry value, complementors may *cooperate* to increase the total value available[9]. If Microsoft and McAfee keep each other in touch with their technological developments, they increase the value of both their products. Opportunities for cooperation can be seen through a `value net`: **a map of organisations in a business environment demonstrating opportunities for value-creating cooperation as well as competition.** In Figure 2.3, Sony is a complementor, supplier and competitor to Apple's iPod. Sony and Apple have an interest in cooperating as well as competing.

2.3.2 The dynamics of industry structure

Industry structure analysis can easily become too static: after all, structure implies stablility.[10] However, the previous sections have raised the issue of how competitive forces change *over time*. The key drivers for change are likely to alter industry structures and scenario analyses can be used to understand possible impacts. An illustration of changing industry structure, and the competitive implications of this, is provided by the Illustration 2.4 on the UK charity sector. This section examines three additional approaches to understanding change in industry structure: the *industry life cycle* concept; *comparative five forces analyses*; and the notion of *hypercompetitive cycles of competition*.

The industry life cycle

The power of the five forces typically varies with the stages of the industry life cycle. The industry life cycle concept proposes that industries start small in their development stage, then go through period of rapid growth (the equivalent to 'adolescence' in the human life cycle), culminating in a period of 'shake-out'. The final two stages are first a period of slow or even

Figure 2.3 The value net

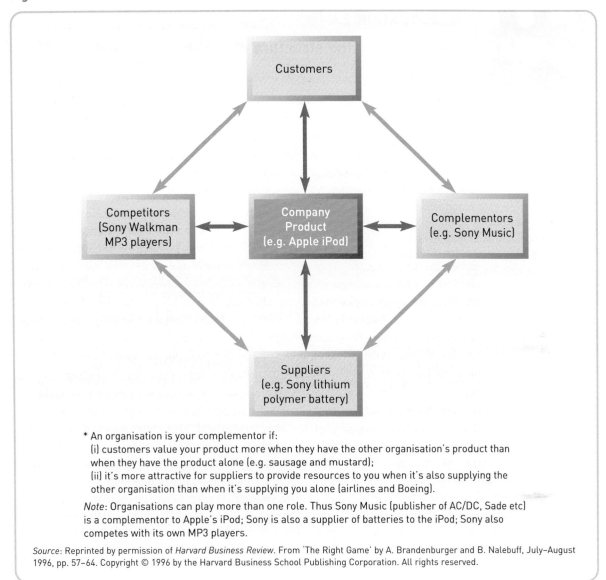

* An organisation is your complementor if:
  (i) customers value your product more when they have the other organisation's product than when they have the product alone (e.g. sausage and mustard);
  (ii) it's more attractive for suppliers to provide resources to you when it's also supplying the other organisation than when it's supplying you alone (airlines and Boeing).

Note: Organisations can play more than one role. Thus Sony Music (publisher of AC/DC, Sade etc) is a complementor to Apple's iPod; Sony is also a supplier of batteries to the iPod; Sony also competes with its own MP3 players.

zero growth ('maturity'), and then the final stage of decline ('old age'). Each of these stages has implications for the five forces.[11]

The *development stage* is an experimental one, typically with few players, little direct rivalry and highly differentiated products. The five forces are likely to be weak, therefore, though profits may actually be scarce because of high investment requirements. The next stage is one of high growth, with rivalry low as there is plenty of market opportunity for everybody. Buyers may be keen to secure supplies of the booming new product and may also lack sophistication about what they are buying, so diminishing their power. One downside of the growth stage is that barriers to entry may be low, as existing competitors have not built up much scale, experience or customer loyalty. Another potential downside is the power of suppliers if there is a shortage of components or materials that fast-growing businesses need for expansion. The *shake-out stage* begins as the growth rate starts to decline, so that increased rivalry forces the

ILLUSTRATION 2.4

Chugging and the structure of the charity sector

Industry structure contributes to inefficiency and aggression in the United Kingdom's charity sector.

The charity sector has become controversial in the United Kingdom. The aggressive fund-raising of some charities is epitomised by workers soliciting donations from shoppers on a commission basis. Such is their perceived aggression that these charity workers are known as 'chuggers', compared with the violent street-crime of 'muggers'.

In 2008, there were 189,000 charities registered in England and Wales, 95 per cent having annual incomes of less than £500,000. However, about 80 per cent of all charity income is raised by the largest twenty charities, headed by Cancer Research UK (2008 income, £355m (~€390m; ~$532m)). According to *Charity Market Monitor*, in 2008, the top 300 charities averaged a 0.9 per cent increase in income, but the largest 10 managed income growth of 2.3 per cent (excluding impact of mergers).

The United Kingdom government introduced the 2006 Charities Act with the specific intention of assisting mergers between independent charities. This had followed a report of the Charity Commission, the regulator for charities in England and Wales, that had commented on the charity sector thus:

> Some people believe that there are too many charities competing for too few funds and that a significant amount of charitable resource could be saved if more charities pooled their resources and worked together. . . .
>
> The majority of charities are relatively small, local organisations that rely entirely on the unpaid help of their trustees and other volunteers. They may have similar purposes to many other charities but they are all serving different communities. The nature of these charities suggests that there are less likely to be significant areas of overlap . . . It is the much larger, professionally run, charities which, because of their size, tend to face charges of duplication, waste and over-aggressive fund-raising. Whilst there are some clear advantages to be had from a healthy plurality of charities, which are constantly refreshed by new charities pursuing new activities, there are also big benefits of public

confidence and support to be had from showing collaborative, as opposed to over-competitive, instincts.

Local authorities in particular were frustrated by duplication and waste, as they increasingly commission local charities to deliver services. With respect to small charities, local authority budgets are relatively large. One charity sector chief executive, Caroline Shaw, told *Charity Times* as she pursued more cooperation between local charities:

> 'Without a doubt there is increased competition when it comes to [local authority] commissioning . . . Our driving force has really been to try to create a more effective service for front line organisations; to offer more projects, more diverse services, more effective services. There's a huge amount [of charities] all fighting for funding. I really think that people should be looking at working more closely together.'

During 2008, more than 230 charity mergers were registered with the Charity Commission. As the recession began to put pressure on charitable donations throughout the sector, early 2009 saw the merger of two well-established charities helping the elderly in the United Kingom, Help the Aged and Age Concern. The new charity, Age UK, has a combined income of around £160 million, including £47 million a year raised through fundraising, and over 520 charity shops.

Sources: 'RS 4a – Collaborative working and mergers: Summary', http://www.charity-commission.gov.uk/publications/rs4a.asp; *Charity Times*, 'Strength in Numbers', August 2007; *Charity Market Monitor*, 2009.

Questions

1 Which of Porter's five forces are creating problems for the United Kingdom's charity sector?

2 What type of industry structure might the charity industry be moving towards? What would be the benefits and disadvantages of that structure?

Figure 2.4 **The industry life cycle**

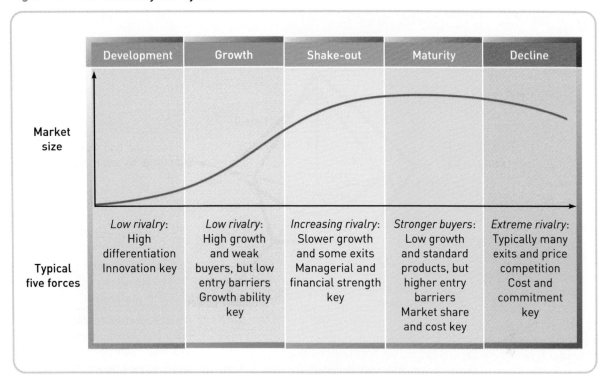

weakest of the new entrants out of the business. In the *maturity stage*, barriers to entry tend to increase, as control over distribution is established and economies of scale and experience curve benefits come into play. Products or service tend to standardise. Buyers may become more powerful as they become less avid for the industry's products or services and more confident in switching between suppliers. Market share is typically crucial at the maturity stage, providing leverage against buyers and competitive advantage in terms of cost. Finally, the *decline stage* can be a period of extreme rivalry, especially where there are high exit barriers, as falling sales force remaining competitors into dog-eat-dog competition. Figure 2.4 summarises some of the conditions that can be expected at different stages in the life cycle.

It is important to avoid putting too much faith in the inevitability of life-cycle stages. One stage does not follow predictably after another: industries vary widely in the length of their growth stages, and others can rapidly 'de-mature' through radical innovation. The telephony industry, based for nearly a century on fixed-line telephones, de-matured rapidly with the introduction of mobile and internet telephony. Anita McGahan of Toronto University warns of the 'maturity mindset', which can leave many managers complacent and slow to respond to new competition.[12] Managing in mature industries is not necessarily just about waiting for decline. However, even if the various stages are not inevitable, the life-cycle concept does remind managers that conditions are likely to change over time. Especially in fast-moving industries, five forces analyses need to be reviewed quite regularly.

Comparative industry structure analyses

The industry life cycle underlines the need to make industry structure analysis dynamic. One effective means of doing this is to compare the five forces over time in a simple 'radar plot'.

Figure 2.5 Comparative industry structure analysis

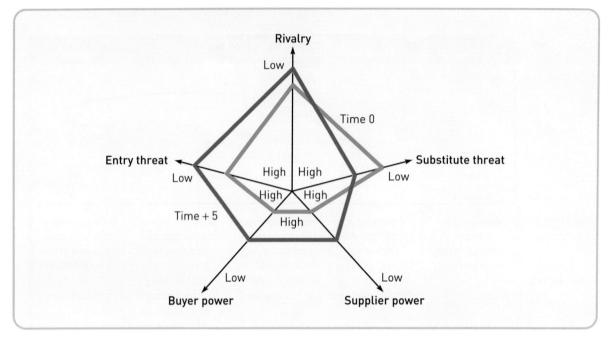

Figure 2.5 provides a framework for summarising the power of each of the five forces on five axes. Power diminishes as the axes go outwards. Where the forces are low, the total area enclosed by the lines between the axes is large; where the forces are high, the total area enclosed by the lines is small. The larger the enclosed area, therefore, the greater is the profit potential. In Figure 2.5, the industry at Time 0 (represented by the light blue lines) has relatively low rivalry (just a few competitors) and faces low substitution threats. The threat of entry is moderate, but both buyer power and supplier power are relatively high. Overall, this looks like only a moderately attractive industry to invest in.

However, given the dynamic nature of industries, managers need to look forward – here five years represented by the dark blue lines in Figure 2.5. Managers are predicting in this case some rise in the threat of substitutes (perhaps new technologies will be developed). On the other hand, they predict a falling entry threat, while both buyer power and supplier power will be easing. Rivalry will reduce still further. This looks like a classic case of an industry in which a few players emerge with overall dominance. The area enclosed by the blue lines is large, suggesting a relatively attractive industry. For a firm confident of becoming one of the dominant players, this might be an industry well worth investing in.

Comparing the five forces over time on a radar plot thus helps to give industry structure analysis a dynamic aspect. Similar plots can be made to aid diversification decisions (see Chapter 7), where possible new industries to enter can be compared in terms of attractiveness. The lines are only approximate, of course, because they aggregate the many individual elements that make up each of the forces into a simple composite measure. Notice too that if one of the forces is very adverse, then this might nullify positive assessments on the other four axes: for example, an industry with low rivalry, low substitution, low entry barriers and low supplier power might still be unattractive if powerful buyers were able to demand highly discounted prices. With these warnings in mind, such radar plots can nonetheless be both a useful device for initial analysis and an effective summary of a final, more refined analysis.

Figure 2.6 Cycles of competition

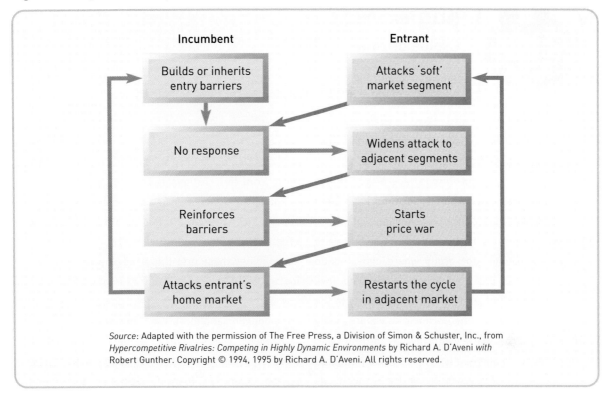

Competitive cycles[13]

In most industries, competitors constantly interact in terms of competitive moves: price cuts are matched and innovations imitated. These sequences of move and counter-move are called *cycles of competition*. If these cycles of competition become very rapid and aggressive, then industry structure becomes unstable. The industry may fall into a state of hypercompetition, implying low profitability for most competitors (see 2.3.1 above).

Figure 2.6 shows a cycle of competition involving various moves and counter-moves between competitors over time. The starting point is a new entrant attacking an incumbent's established market, apparently protected by inherited entry barriers. The new entrant sensibly attacks a particularly 'soft' (unprotected) segment of the overall market. If receiving no strong competitive response from the incumbent (i.e. no retaliation), the new entrant widens its attack to adjacent segments of the incumbent's market. There is a danger of increased industry rivalry and rapidly falling industry profits. In Figure 2.6, the incumbent finally responds by increasing entry barriers, perhaps by reinforcing customers' loyalty through increased differentiation. The new entrant counters with a price war. The final resort of the incumbent is to attack the new entrant's home market, hoping to do enough damage there to persuade the new entrant to back off. Thus rivalry increases in that home industry as well. The incumbent meanwhile does its best to raise barriers to entry at home.

Illustration 2.5 demonstrates a similar cycle of competition in an international context. Here moves and counter-moves by organisations and their competitors take place simultaneously in several locations. So a competitive move in one arena, the German company's aggressive move into France, did not trigger off a counter-move in that arena (France), but in its competitor's home territory (Germany).

ILLUSTRATION 2.5

Cycles of competition

Industry attractiveness can easily be undermined by rivalrous behaviour, setting off a cycle of move and countermove destructive of industry profitability.

Deutschespitze was a German company with a specialised consumer goods product that was wishing to become a significant Europe-wide player. It was particularly interested in the French market, where Francotop was the highly profitable dominant player.

Deutschespitze's first competitive move was to target a consumer age group where consumption and brand awareness in France were both low. Francotop had limited their marketing efforts to the over-25 age groups – the Germans saw a possibility of extending the market into the 18–25 group and aimed their promotional efforts at the group with some success. This first move was ignored by Francotop as it did not impact on its current business. However, from this bridgehead Deutschespitze's second move was to attack Francotop's key older market. This triggered Francotop to launch an advertising campaign reinforcing brand awareness in its traditional segments, hoping to confine the German company to its initial niche.

Deutschespitze responded by counter-advertising and price reductions – undermining the margins earned by its French rival. Competition then escalated with a counter-attack by Francotop into the German market. This wider competitive activity played itself out resulting in the erosion of both of the original strongholds and a progressive merger of the French and German markets. With falling barriers between the two markets, profits fell.

It is possible at this stage that this whole cycle of competition could have repeated itself in an adjacent market, such as the UK. However, what happened was that Deutschespitze saw an opportunity to move away from this *cost/quality* basis of competition by adapting the product for use by businesses. Its core competences in R&D allowed it to get the adapted product to market faster than its French rival. It then consolidated these first-mover advantages by building and defending barriers. For example, it appointed key account salesmen and gave special offers for early adoption and three-year contracts.

However, this stronghold came under attack by the French firm and a cycle of competition similar to the consumer market described above was triggered. The German firm had built up enough financial reserves to survive a price war, which they then initiated. It was willing and able to fund losses longer than the French competitor – which was forced to exit the business user market.

Questions

1 Which moves were likely to trigger intensely rivalrous behaviour and which were better calculated to minimise destructive competition?

2 How might the French firm have prevented this cycle of competition from breaking out in the first place?

(2.4) COMPETITORS AND MARKETS

An industry or sector may be too high a level to provide for a detailed understanding of competition. The five forces can impact differently on different kinds of players. To return to the earlier example, Hyundai and Porsche may be in the same broad industry (automobiles), but they are positioned differently: they are protected by different barriers to entry and competitive moves by one are unlikely to affect the other. It is often useful to disaggregate. Many industries contain a range of companies, each of which has different capabilities and competes on different bases. These competitor differences are captured by the concept of *strategic groups*. Customers too can differ significantly and these can be captured by distinguishing between different *market segments*. Thinking in terms of different strategic groups and market segments provides opportunities for organisations to develop highly distinctive positionings within broader industries. The potential for distinctiveness is further explored through '*Blue Ocean*' thinking, the last topic in this section.

2.4.1 Strategic groups[14]

Strategic groups **are organisations within an industry or sector with similar strategic characteristics, following similar strategies or competing on similar bases**. These characteristics are different from those in other strategic groups in the same industry or sector. For example, in the grocery retailing industry, supermarkets, convenience stores and corner shops each form different strategic groups. There are many different characteristics that distinguish between strategic groups but these can be grouped into two major categories (see Figure 2.7).[15]

Figure 2.7 Some characteristics for identifying strategic groups

It is useful to consider the extent to which organisations *differ* in terms of **characteristics** such as:

Scope of activities

- Extent of product (or service) diversity
- Extent of geographical coverage
- Number of market segments served
- Distribution channels used

Resource commitment

- Extent (number) of **branding**
- **Marketing effort** (e.g. advertising spread, size of salesforce)
- Extent of **vertical integration**
- Product or service **quality**
- **Technological leadership** (a leader or follower)
- **Size** of organisation

First, the *scope* of an organisation's activities (such as product range, geographical coverage and range of distribution channels used). Second, the *resource commitment* (such as brands, marketing spend and extent of vertical integration). Which characteristics are relevant differs from industry to industry, but typically important are those characteristics that separate high performers from low performers.

Strategic groups can be mapped on to two-dimensional charts – for example, one axis might be the extent of product range and the other axis the size of marketing spend. One method for choosing key dimensions by which to map strategic groups is to identify top performers (by growth or profitability) in an industry and to compare them with low performers. Characteristics that are shared by top performers, but not by low performers, are likely to be particularly relevant for mapping strategic groups. For example, the most profitable firms in an industry might all be narrow in terms of product range, and lavish in terms of marketing spend, while the less-profitable firms might be more widely spread in terms of products and restrained in their marketing. Here the two dimensions for mapping would be product range and marketing spend. A potential recommendation for the less-profitable firms would be to cut back their product range and boost their marketing.

Figure 2.8 shows strategic groups amongst Indian pharmaceutical companies, with research and development intensity (R&D spend as a percentage of sales) and overseas focus (exports and patents registered overseas) defining the axes of the map. These two axes do

Figure 2.8 Strategic groups in the Indian pharmaceutical industry

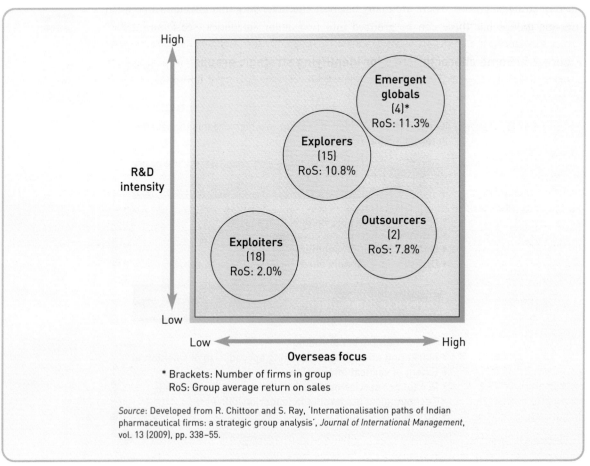

* Brackets: Number of firms in group
  RoS: Group average return on sales

Source: Developed from R. Chittoor and S. Ray, 'Internationalisation paths of Indian pharmaceutical firms: a strategic group analysis', *Journal of International Management*, vol. 13 (2009), pp. 338–55.

explain a good deal of the variation in profitability between groups. The most profitable group is the Emergent Globals (11.3 per cent average return on sales), those with high R&D intensity and high overseas focus. On the other hand, the Exploiter group spends little on R&D and is focused on domestic markets, and only enjoys 2.0 per cent average return on sales.

This strategic group concept is useful in at least three ways:

- *Understanding competition.* Managers can focus on their direct competitors within their particular strategic group, rather than the whole industry. They can also establish the dimensions that distinguish them most from other groups, and which might be the basis for relative success or failure. These dimensions can then become the focus of their action.

- *Analysis of strategic opportunities.* Strategic group maps can identify the most attractive 'strategic spaces' within an industry. Some spaces on the map may be 'white spaces', relatively under-occupied. In the Indian pharmaceutical industry, the white space is high R&D investment combined with focus on domestic markets. Such white spaces might be unexploited opportunities. On the other hand, they could turn out to be 'black holes', impossible to exploit and likely to damage any entrant. A strategic group map is only the first stage of the analysis. Strategic spaces need to tested carefully.

- *Analysis of mobility barriers.* Of course, moving across the map to take advantage of opportunities is not costless. Often it will require difficult decisions and rare resources. Strategic groups are therefore characterised by 'mobility barriers', obstacles to movement from one strategic group to another. These are similar to barriers to entry in five forces analysis. Although movement from the Exploiter group in Indian pharmaceuticals to the Emergent Global group might seem very attractive in terms of profits, it is likely to demand very substantial financial investment and strong managerial skills. Mobility into the Emergent Global group will not be easy. As with barriers to entry, it is good to be in a successful strategic group into which there are strong mobility barriers, to impede imitation.

2.4.2 Market segments

The concept of strategic groups discussed above helps with understanding the similarities and differences in terms of competitor characteristics. The concept of market segment looks at the other side, differences in customer needs. A **market segment**[16] **is a group of customers who have similar needs that are different from customer needs in other parts of the market.** Where these customer groups are relatively small, such market segments are often called 'niches'. Dominance of a market segment or niche can be very valuable, for the same reasons that dominance of an industry can be valuable following five forces reasoning. However, dominance of market segments is typically less secure than that of a whole industry, as entry from competitors in adjacent market segments is likely to be relatively easy. For long-term success, strategies based on market segments must keep customer needs firmly in mind.

Three issues are particularly important in market segment analysis, therefore:

- *Variation in customer needs.* Focusing on customer needs that are highly distinctive from those typical in the market is one means of building a secure segment strategy. Customer needs vary for a whole variety of reasons – some of which are identified in Table 2.1. Theoretically, any of these factors could be used to identify distinct market segments. However, the crucial bases of segmentation vary according to market. In industrial markets, segmentation is often thought of in terms of industrial classification of buyers: steel producers might segment

Table 2.1 Some bases of market segmentation

Type of factor	Consumer markets	Industrial/organisational markets
Characteristics of people/organisations	Age, sex, race Income Family size Life-cycle stage Location Lifestyle	Industry Location Size Technology Profitability Management
Purchase/use situation	Size of purchase Brand loyalty Purpose of use Purchasing behaviour Importance of purchase Choice criteria	Application Importance of purchase Volume Frequency of purchase Purchasing procedure Choice criteria Distribution channel
Users' needs and preferences for product characteristics	Product similarity Price preference Brand preferences Desired features Quality	Performance requirements Assistance from suppliers Brand preferences Desired features Quality Service requirements

by automobile industry, packaging industry and construction industry, for example. On the other hand, segmentation by buyer behaviour (for example, direct buying versus those users who buy through third parties such as contractors) or purchase value (for example, high-value bulk purchasers versus frequent low-value purchasers) might be more appropriate. Being able to serve a highly distinctive segment that other organisations find difficult to serve is often the basis for a secure long-term strategy.

● *Specialisation* within a market segment can also be an important basis for a successful segmentation strategy. This is sometimes called a 'niche strategy'. Organisations that have built up most experience in servicing a particular market segment should not only have lower costs in so doing, but also have built relationships which may be difficult for others to break down. Experience and relationships are likely to protect a dominant position in a particular segment. However, precisely because customers value different things in different segments, specialised producers may find it very difficult to compete on a broader basis. For example, a small local brewery competing against the big brands on the basis of its ability to satisfy distinctive local tastes is unlikely to find it easy to serve other segments where tastes are different, scale requirements are larger and distribution channels are more complex.

● *Strategic customers*. It is crucial to understand whose needs matter. **The strategic customer is the person(s) at whom the strategy is primarily addressed because they have the most influence over which goods or services are purchased**. As above, for a food manufacturer, it is the retailers' needs that matter most directly, not simply the ultimate consumers of the food. It is retailers who pay the manufacturer and decide what to stock. Retailers care about price and quality because consumers do, so the manufacturer must take these needs into account. But retailers also care about delivery convenience and reliability. For a food manufacturer, therefore, the strategic customer is the retailer: the retailer's needs, not just the ultimate consumers' needs, should shape strategy. In the public sector, the strategic customer is very often the agency that controls the funds or authorises use rather than the user of the service. In public health care, therefore, it is hospitals, not patients, that are the strategic customers of pharmaceutical companies.

2.4.3 Blue Ocean thinking

The more differentiated views of competitors and customers embodied in strategic groups and market segments can be taken a step further by 'Blue Ocean' thinking. As developed by W. Chan Kim and Renée Mauborgne at INSEAD, **Blue Oceans are new market spaces where competition is minimised**.[17] Blue Oceans contrast with 'Red Oceans', where industries are already well defined and rivalry is intense. Blue Oceans evoke wide empty seas. Red Oceans are associated with bloody competition and 'red ink', in other words financial losses.

Blue Ocean thinking therefore encourages entrepreneurs and managers to be different by finding or creating market spaces that are not currently being served. Strategy here is about finding *strategic gaps*, opportunities in the environment that are not being fully exploited by competitors. The strategy canvas is one framework that can effectively assist this kind of Blue Ocean thinking. A **strategy canvas compares competitors according to their performance on key success factors in order to develop strategies based on creating new market spaces**. Figure 2.9 shows a strategy canvas for three engineering components companies, highlighting the following three features:

- **Critical success factors** (CSFs) **are those factors that are either particularly valued by customers or which provide a significant advantage in terms of cost**. Critical success factors are therefore likely to be an important source of competitive advantage or disadvantage. Figure 2.9 identifies five established critical success factors in this engineering components

Figure 2.9 Strategy canvas for electrical components companies

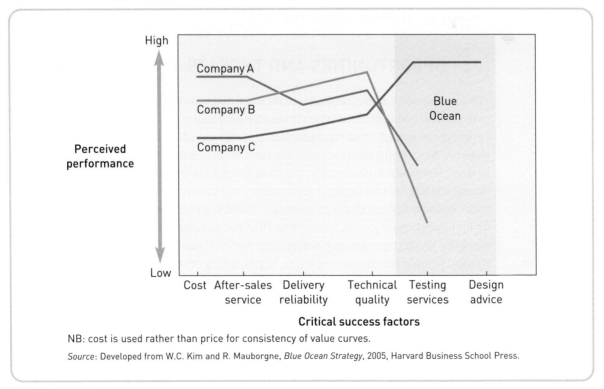

NB: cost is used rather than price for consistency of value curves.

Source: Developed from W.C. Kim and R. Mauborgne, *Blue Ocean Strategy*, 2005, Harvard Business School Press.

market (cost, after-sales service, delivery reliability, technical quality and testing facilities). Note there is also a new sixth critical success factor, design advisory services, which will be discussed under the third subhead, value innovation.

● **Value curves are a graphic depiction of how customers perceive competitors' relative performance across the critical success factors**. In Figure 2.9, companies A and B perform well on cost, service, reliability and quality, but less well on testing. They do not offer any design advice. Company C has a radically different value curve, characteristic of a 'value innovator'.

● **Value innovation is the creation of new market space by excelling on established critical success factors on which competitors are performing badly and/or by creating new critical success factors representing previously unrecognised customer wants.** Thus in Figure 2.9, company C is a value innovator in both senses. First, it excels on the established customer need of offering testing facilities for customers' products using its components. Second, it offers a new and valued design service advising customers on how to integrate their components in order for them to create better products.

Company C's strategy exemplifies two critical principles in Blue Ocean thinking: *focus* and *divergence*. First, Company C focuses its efforts on just two factors, testing and design services, while maintaining only adequate performance on the other critical success factors where its competitors are already high performers. Second, it has created a value curve that significantly diverges from its competitors' value curves, creating a substantial strategic gap, or Blue Ocean, in the areas of testing and design services. This is shrewd. For Company C, beating Companies A and B in the areas where they are performing well anyway would require major investment and likely provide little advantage given that customers are already highly satisfied. Challenging A and B on cost, after-sales service, delivery or quality would be a Red Ocean strategy. Far better is to concentrate on where a large gap can be created between competitors. Company C faces little competition for those customers who really value testing and design services, and consequently can charge good prices for them.

(2.5) OPPORTUNITIES AND THREATS

The concepts and frameworks discussed above should be helpful in understanding the factors in the macro-, industry and competitor/market environments of an organisation (see the Key Debate: just how much do such industry and market factors affect successful strategic outcomes?). However, the critical issue is the *implications* that are drawn from this understanding in guiding strategic decisions and choices. The crucial next stage, therefore, is to draw from the environmental analysis specific strategic opportunities and threats for the organisation. Identifying these opportunities and threats is extremely valuable when thinking about strategic choices for the future (the subject of Chapters 6 to 10). Opportunities and threats forms one half of the Strengths, Weaknesses, Opportunities and Threats (SWOT) analyses that shape many companies' strategy formulation (see section 3.4.4). In responding strategically to the environment, the goal is to reduce identified threats and take advantage of the best opportunities.

The techniques and concepts in this chapter should help in identifying environmental threats and opportunities, for instance:

● a *PESTEL analysis* of the macro-environment might reveal threats and opportunities presented by technological change, or shifts in market demographics and similar;

KEY DEBATE

How much does industry matter?

A good start in strategy must be to choose a profitable industry to compete in. But does simply being in the right industry matter more than having the right kinds of skills and resources?

This chapter has focused on the role of the environment in strategy-making, with particular regard to industries. But the importance of industries in determining organisational performance has been challenged in recent years. This has led to a debate about whether strategy-making should be externally-orientated, starting with the environment, or internally-orientated, starting with the organisation's own skills and resources (the focus of Chapter 3).[1]

Managers favouring an external approach look primarily *outside* the organisation, for example building market share in their industries through mergers and acquisitions or aggressive marketing. Managers favouring an internal approach concentrate their attention *inside* the organisation, fostering the skills of their people or nurturing technologies, for example. Because managerial time is limited, there is a real trade-off to be made between external and internal approaches.

The chief advocate of the external approach is Michael Porter, Professor at Harvard Business School and founder of the Monitor Consulting Group. An influential sceptic of this approach is Richard Rumelt, a student at Harvard Business School but now at University of California Los Angeles. Porter, Rumelt and others have done a series of empirical studies examining the relative importance of industries in explaining organisations' performance.

Typically, these studies take a large sample of firms and compare the extent to which variance in profitability is due to firms or industries (controlling for other effects such as size). If firms within the same industry tend to bunch together in terms of profitability, it is industry that is accounting for the greater proportion of profitability: an external approach to strategy is supported. If firms within the same industry vary widely in terms of profitability, it is the specific skills and resources of the firms that matter most: an internal approach is most appropriate.

The two most important studies in fact find that more of the variance in profitability is due to firms rather than industries – firms account for 47 per cent in Rumelt's study of manufacturing (see the figure).[2] However, when Porter and McGahan included service industries as well as manufacturing, they found a larger industry effect (19 per cent).[3,4]

Per cent of variance in profitability due to:

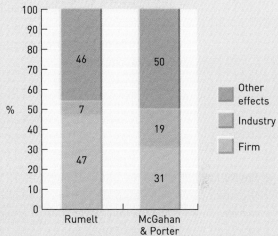

The implication from this work is that firm-specific factors generally influence profitability more than industry factors. Firms need to attend carefully to their own skills and resources. However, the greater industry effect found in Porter and McGahan's study of both manufacturing and services suggests that industry's importance varies strongly by industry. External influences can matter more in some industries than others.

References:
1. E.H. Bowman and C.E. Helfat, 'Does corporate strategy matter?', *Strategic Management Journal*, vol. 22, no. 1 (2001), pp. 1–14.
2. R.P. Rumelt, 'How much does industry matter?', *Strategic Management Journal*, vol. 12, no. 2 (1991), pp. 167–85.
3. M.E. Porter and A.M. McGahan, 'How much does industry matter really?', *Strategic Management Journal*, vol. 18, Summer Special Issue (1997), pp. 15–30.
4. M.E. Porter and A.M. McGahan, 'The emergence and sustainability of abnormal profits', *Strategic Organization*, vol. 1, no. 1 (2003), pp. 79–108.

Question

Porter and McGahan's study suggests that some industries influence member firms' profitabilities more than others: in other words, their profitabilities bunch together. Why might some industries have a larger influence on their members' profitability than others?

- identification of *key drivers for change* can help generate different scenarios for managerial discussion, some more threatening, others more favourable;

- a *Porter five forces analysis* might for example identify a rise or fall in barriers to entry, or opportunities to reduce industry rivalry, perhaps by acquisition of competitors;

- *Blue Ocean* thinking might reveal where companies can create new market spaces; alternatively it could help identify success factors which new entrants might attack in order to turn 'Blue Oceans' into 'Red Oceans'.

While all these techniques and concepts are important tools for understanding environments, it is important to recognise that any analysis is likely to be somewhat subjective. Entrepreneurs and managers often have particular blinkers with regard to what they see and prioritise.[18] Techniques and concepts can be helpful in challenging existing assumptions and encouraging broader perspectives, but they are unlikely to overcome human subjectivity and biases completely.

SUMMARY

- Environmental influences can be thought of as layers around an organisation, with the outer layer making up the *macro-environment*, the middle layer making up the *industry or sector* and the inner layer *strategic groups* and *market segments*.

- The macro-environment can be analysed in terms of the *PESTEL factors*, from which *key drivers of change* can be identified. Alternative *scenarios* about the future can be constructed according to how the key drivers develop.

- Industries and sectors can be analysed in terms of the *Porter five forces* – barriers to entry, substitutes, buyer power, supplier power and rivalry. Together, these determine industry or sector attractiveness.

- Industries and sectors are dynamic, and their changes can be analysed in terms of the *industry life cycle*, *comparative five forces radar plots* and *hypercompetitive cycles of competition*.

- In the inner layer of the environment, *strategic group* analysis, *market segment* analysis and the *strategy canvass* can help identify strategic gaps or opportunities.

- *Blue Ocean* strategies characterised by low rivalry are likely to be better opportunities than *Red Ocean* strategies with many rivals.

VIDEO ASSIGNMENT

Visit *MyStrategyLab* and watch the *Hiscox* case study.

1 Describe recent environmental changes in the insurance industry in terms of Porter's five forces. What else needs to be factored into an environmental analysis?

2 Assess Hiscox's strategic position in this environmental context.

WORK ASSIGNMENTS

* Denotes more advanced work assignments. * Refers to a case study in the Text and Cases edition.

2.1 For an organisation of your choice carry out a PESTEL analysis and identify key drivers for change. Use Illustration 2.1 as a model.

2.2* For the same organisation as in 2.1, and using Illustration 2.2 as a model, construct four scenarios for the evolution of its environment. What implications are there for the organisation's strategy?

2.3 Drawing on section 2.3, carry out a five forces analysis of the pharmaceutical industry* or Vodafone's position in the mobile phone industry*. What do you conclude about that industry's attractiveness?

2.4* Drawing on section 2.3, and particularly using the radar plot technique of Figure 2.5, choose two industries or sectors and compare their attractiveness in terms of the five forces (a) today; (b) in approximately three to five years' time. Justify your assessment of each of the five forces' strengths. Which industry or sector would you invest in?

2.5 With regard to section 2.4.1 and Figure 2.8, identify an industry (for example, the motor industry or clothing retailers) and, by comparing competitors, map out the main strategic groups in the industry according to key strategic dimensions. Try more than one set of key strategic dimensions to map the industry. Do the resulting maps identify any under-exploited opportunities in the industry?

2.6* Drawing on section 2.4.3, and particularly on Figure 2.10, identify critical success factors for an industry with which you and your peers are familiar (for example, clothing retailers or mobile phone companies). Using your own estimates (or those of your peers), construct a strategy canvas comparing the main competitors, as in Figure 2.10. What implications does your strategy canvas have for the strategies of these competitors?

Integrative assignment

2.7 Carry out a full analysis of an industry or sector of your choice (using for example PESTEL, scenarios, five forces and strategic groups). Consider explicitly how the industry or sector is affected by globalisation (see Chapter 8, particularly Figure 8.2 on drivers) and innovation (see Chapter 9, particularly Figure 9.2 on product and process innovation).

RECOMMENDED KEY READINGS

- The classic book on the analysis of industries is M.E. Porter, *Competitive Strategy*, Free Press, 1980. An updated view is available in M.E. Porter, 'The five competitive forces that shape strategy', *Harvard Business Review*, vol. 86, no. 1 (2008), pp. 58–77. An influential development on Porter's basic ideas is W.C. Kim and R. Mauborgne, *Blue Ocean Strategy: How to Create Uncontested Market Space and Make Competition Irrelevant*, Harvard Business School Press, 2005.

- For approaches to how environments change, see K. van der Heijden, *Scenarios: The Art of Strategic Conversation*, 2nd edition, Wiley, 2005, and the work of Michael Porter's colleague, A. McGahan, *How Industries Evolve*, Harvard Business School Press, 2004.

- A collection of academic articles on the latest views on PEST, scenarios and similar is the special issue of *International Studies of Management and Organization*, vol. 36, no. 3 (2006), edited by Peter McKiernan.

REFERENCES

1. PESTEL is an extension of PEST (Politics, Economics, Social and Technology) analysis, taking more account of environmental ('green') and legal issues. For an application of PEST analysis to the world of business schools, relevant also to PESTEL, see H. Thomas, 'An analysis of the environment and competitive dynamics of management education', *Journal of Management Development*, vol. 26, no. 1 (2007), pp. 9–21.

2. For a discussion of scenario planning in practice, see K. van der Hiejden, *Scenarios: The Art of Strategic Conversation*, second edition, Wiley, 2005. For how scenario planning fits with other forms of environmental analysis such as PESTEL, see P. Walsh, 'Dealing with the uncertainties of environmental change by adding scenario planning to the strategy reformulation equation', *Management Decision*, no. 43, vol. 1 (2005), pp. 113–22 and G. Burt, G. Wright, R. Bradfield and K. van der Heijden, 'The role of scenario planning in exploring the environment in view of the limitations of PEST and its derivatives', *International Studies of Management and Organization*, vol 36, no. 3 (2006), pp. 50–76.

3. Based on P. Schoemaker, 'Scenario Planning: a tool for strategic thinking'. *Sloan Management Review*, vol. 36 (1995), pp. 25–34. Variations on this approach are offered in the sources in reference 2 above.

4. See M.E. Porter, *Competitive Strategy: Techniques for Analysing Industries and Competitors*, Free Press, 1980, p. 5.

5. An updated discussion of the classic framework is M. Porter, 'The five competitive forces that shape strategy', *Harvard Business Review*, vol. 86, no. 1 (2008), pp. 58–77. C. Christensen, 'The past and future of competitive advantage', *Sloan Management Review*, vol. 42, no. 2 (2001), pp.105–9 provides an interesting critique and update of some of the factors underlying Porter's five forces.

6. This definition is from R. D'Aveni, *Hypercompetition: Managing the Dynamics of Strategic Manoeuvring*, Free Press, 1994. p. 2. In his later book, *Strategic Supremacy: How Industry Leaders Create Spheres of Influence*, Simon and Schuster International, 2002, he gives examples of strategies that can help defend a strong position in conditions of hypercompetition.

7. See: L. Van den Berghe and K. Verweire, 'Convergence in the financial services industry', *Geneva Papers on Risk and Insurance*, vol. 25, no. 2 (2000), pp. 262–72; A. Malhotra and A. Gupta, 'An investigation of firms' responses to industry convergence', *Academy of Management Proceedings*, 2001, pp. G1–6.

8. A. Brandenburger and B. Nalebuff, 'The right game', *Harvard Business Review*, July–August 1995, pp. 57–64.

9. See: K. Walley, 'Coopetition: an introduction to the subject and an agenda for research', *International Studies of Management and Organization*, vol. 37, no. 2 (2007), pp. 11–31. On the dangers of 'complementors', see D. Yoffie and M. Kwak, 'With friends like these', *Harvard Business Review*, vol. 84, no. 9 (2006), pp. 88–98.

10. There is a good discussion of the static nature of the Porter model, and other limitations, in M. Grundy, 'Rethinking and reinventing Michael Porter's five forces model', *Strategic Change*, vol. 15 (2006), pp. 213–29.

11. A classic academic overview of the industry life cycle is S. Klepper, 'Industry life cycles', *Industrial and Corporate Change*, vol. 6, no. 1 (1996), pp. 119–43. See also A. McGahan, 'How industries evolve', *Business Strategy Review*, vol. 11, no. 3 (2000), pp. 1–16.

12. A. McGahan, 'How industries evolve', *Business Strategy Review*, vol. 11, no. 3 (2000), pp. 1–16.

13. For a full discussion of the dynamics of competition see: R. D'Aveni (with R. Gunther), *Hypercompetitive Rivalries*, Free Press, 1995. For a critical overview of various recent perspectives on hypercompetition and turbulence, plus cases, see J. Slesky, J. Goes and O. Babüroglu, 'Contrasting perspectives of strategy making: applications in hyper environments, *Organization Studies*, vol. 28, no. 1 (2007), pp. 71–94.

14. For recent examples of strategic group analysis, see G. Leask and D. Parker, 'Strategic groups, competitive groups and performance in the UK pharmaceutical industry', *Strategic Management Journal*, vol. 28, no. 7 (2007), pp. 723–45; and W. Desarbo, R. Grewal and R. Wang, 'Dynamic strategic groups: deriving spatial evolutionary paths', *Strategic Management Journal*, vol. 30, no. 8 (2009), 1420–39.

15. These characteristics are based on Porter, reference 4 above.

16. A useful discussion of segmentation in relation to competitive strategy is provided in M.E. Porter, *Competitive Advantage*, Free Press, 1985, Chapter 7. See also the discussion on market segmentation in P. Kotler, G. Armstrong, J. Saunders and V. Wong, *Principles of Marketing*, 3rd European edition, Financial Times Prentice Hall, 2002, Chapter 9. For a more detailed review of segmentation methods see: M. Wedel and W. Kamakura, *Market Segmentation: Conceptual and Methodological Foundations*, 2nd edition, Kluwer Academic, 1999.

17. W.C. Kim and R. Mauborgne, 'How strategy shapes structure', *Harvard Business Review*, September 2009, 73–80.

18. P. Schoemaker and G. Day, 'How to make sense of weak signals', *Sloan Management Review*, vol. 50, no. 3 (2009), pp. 81–9.

CASE EXAMPLE

Global forces and the Western European brewing industry

Mike Blee and Richard Whittington

This case is centred on the European brewing industry in Western Europe and examines how the increasingly competitive pressure of operating within global markets is causing consolidation through acquisitions, alliances and closures within the industry. This has resulted in the growth of the brewers' reliance upon super-brands.

In the early years of the 21st century, European brewers faced a surprising paradox. The traditional centre of the beer industry worldwide and home to the world's largest brewing companies, Europe, was turning off beer. Beer consumption was falling in the largest markets of Germany and the United Kingdom, while burgeoning in emerging markets around the world. In 2008, Europe's largest market, Germany, ranked only 5th in the world, behind China, the United States, Brazil and Russia. China, with 12% annual growth between 2003 and 2008, had become the largest single market by volume, alone accounting for 23% of world consumption (Euromonitor, 2010).

Table 1 details the overall decline of European beer consumption. Decline in traditional key markets is due to several factors. Governments are campaigning strongly against drunken driving, affecting the propensity to drink

Table 1 European beer consumption by country and year (000 hectolitres)

Country	1980	2000	2003	2007
Austria	7651	8762	8979	9100
Belgium	12945	10064	9935	9137
Denmark	6698	5452	5181	4840
Finland	2738	4024	4179	4073
France	23745	21420	21168	18781
Germany‡	89820	103105	97107	91000
Greece	N/A	4288	3905	4600
Ireland	4174	5594	5315	5193
Italy	9539	16289	17452	17766
Luxembourg	417	472	373	429
Netherlands	12213	13129	12771	12910
Norway*	7651	2327	2270	2670
Portugal	3534	6453	6008	6200
Spain	20065	29151	33451	35658
Sweden	3935	5011	4969	4900
Switzerland*	4433	4194	4334	4489
UK	65490	57007	60302	51300

* Non-EU countries; ‡ 1980 excludes GDR. Figures adjusted.

Source: Based on information from www.Brewersofeurope.org.

Source: Alamy Images/Picturesbyrob.

beer in restaurants, pubs and bars. There is increasing awareness of the effects of alcohol on health and fitness. Particularly in the United Kingdom, there is growing hostility to so-called 'binge drinking', excessive alcohol consumption in pubs and clubs. Wines have also become increasingly popular in Northern European markets. However, beer consumption per capita varies widely between countries, being four times higher in Germany than in Italy, for example. Some traditionally low consumption European markets have been showing good growth.

The drive against drunken driving and binge drinking has helped shift sales from the 'on-trade' (beer consumed on the premises, as in pubs or restaurants) to the off-trade (retail). Worldwide, the off-trade increased from 63% of volume in 2000 to 67% in 2008. The off-trade is increasingly dominated by large supermarket chains such as Tesco or Carrefour, who often use cut-price offers on beer in order to lure people into their shops. More than one fifth of beer volume is now sold through supermarkets. German retailers such as Aldi and Lidl have had considerable success with their own 'private-label' (rather than brewery-branded) beers. Pubs have suffered: in the United Kingdom, an estimated 50 pubs closed per week during the recessionary year 2009. However, although on-trade volumes are falling

Table 2 Imports of beer by country

Country	Imports 2002 (% of consumption*)	Imports 2008 (% of consumption)
Austria	5.1	6.6
Belgium	4.74	12.8
Denmark	2.6	10.5
Finland	2.3	10.1
France	23	31.4
Germany	3.1	7.6
Greece	4.1	6.5
Ireland	NA	16.8
Italy	27.2	33.5
Luxembourg	NA	43.1
Netherlands	3.2	18.6
Norway	5.4	3.7
Portugal	1.1	0.6
Spain	11.7	8.6
Sweden	NA	23.4
Switzerland	15.4	17.6
United Kingdom	10.9	17.7

Note: Import figures do not include beers brewed under licence in home country; also countries vary in measuring per cent of consumption.

Source: Based on information from www.Brewersofeurope.org.

in Europe, the sales values are generally rising, as brewers introduce higher-priced premium products such as non-alcoholic beers, extra cold lagers or fruit-flavoured beers. On the other hand, a good deal of this increasing demand for premium products is being satisfied by the import of apparently exotic beers from overseas (see Table 2).

Brewers' main purchasing costs are packaging (accounting for around half of non-labour costs), raw material such as barley, and energy. The European packaging industry is highly concentrated, dominated by international companies such as Crown in cans and Owens-Illinois in glass bottles. In the United Kingdom, for example, there are just three can makers: Ball Packaging Europe, Crown Bevcan and REXAM.

Acquisition, licensing and strategic alliances have all occurred as the leading brewers battle to control the market. There are global pressures for consolidation due to over-capacity within the industry, the need to contain costs and benefits of leveraging strong brands. For example, in 2004, Belgian brewer Interbrew merged with Am Bev, the Brazilian brewery group, to create the largest brewer in the world, InBev. In 2008, the new InBev bought the second largest brewer, the American Anheuser-Busch, giving it nearly 20 per cent of the world market. In 2002, South African Breweries acquired the Miller Group (USA) and Pilsner Urquell in the Czech Republic, becoming SABMiller. SABMiller in turn bought Dutch specialist Grolsch in 2007. Smaller players in the fast-growing Chinese and Latin American markets are being snapped up by the large international brewers too: in 2010, Dutch Heineken bought Mexico's second largest brewery, FEMSA. On the other hand, medium-sized Australian brewer Fosters has withdrawn from the European market. The European Commission fined Heineken and Kronenbourg in 2004 for price-fixing in France, and Heineken, Grolsch and Bavaria in 2007 for a price-fixing cartel in the Dutch market.

Table 3 lists the world's top ten brewing companies, which accounted for about 60 per cent of world beer volumes in 2009. However, there remain many specialist, regional and microbreweries, for example Greene King (see below). Germany, with its pub-brewing tradition (the Brauhaus), still has 1319 separate breweries owned by 583 separate brewing companies. None the less, market concentration has increased in Western Europe: in 2000, the top two players (Heineken and Interbrew) had 19.3 per cent of the market; in 2009, the top two players, Heineken and Carlsberg, held 28.5 per cent of the Western European market, with A-B InBev accounting for a further 10.6 per cent.

Three brewing companies

The European market contains many very different kinds of competitor: this section introduces the world's largest brewer and two outliers.

Table 3 The world's top ten brewery companies by volume: 2000 and 2009

2000		2009	
Company	Share global volume %	Company	Share global volume %
Anheuser-Busch (US)	8.8	A-B InBev (Belgium)	19.5
AmBev (Brazil)	4.6	SABMiller (UK)	9.5
Heineken (Dutch)	4.3	Heineken (Dutch)	6.9
Interbrew (Belgium)	4.0	Carlsberg (Danish)	5.9
Miller (US)	3.6	China Resources (China)	4.5
SAB (South Africa)	3.3	Tsingtao (China)	3.1
Modelo (Mexico)	2.7	Modelo (Mexico)	2.9
Coors (US)	2.0	Molson Coors (US)	2.8
Asahi (Japan)	2.0	Beijing Yanjing (China)	2.5
Kirin (Japan)	1.9	FEMSA (Mexico)	2.3

Source: Euromonitor International, 2010.

Anheuser-Busch InBev (Belgium)

A-B InBev has roots going back to 1366, but has transformed itself in the last decade with a series of spectacular mergers. First, InBev was created in 2004 from the merger of Belgian InterBrew and Brazilian AmBev. As well as making it the second largest brewing company in the world, this merger gave it a significant position in the Latin American soft drinks market. Then in 2008 InBev acquired the leading American brewer Anheuser-Busch for $52bn (~€36.4bn), making the company indisputably the world leader. The company now has nearly 300 brands, led by such well-known international beers as Beck's, Budweiser and Stella Artois. The company has nearly 50 per cent share of the US market, and owns 50 per cent of Mexico's leading brewer, Modelo, famous for its global Corona brand. In 2008, the new A-N InBev had four of the top ten selling beers in the world, and a number one or number two position in over 20 national markets. However, the company has been reducing its stake in the Chinese market in order to raise funds to pay for the Anheuser-Busch acquisition and to meet local monopoly authority concerns. It also sold its Central and Eastern beer operations in 2009.

The company is frank about its strategy: to transform itself from the biggest brewing company in the world to the best. It aims to do this by building strong global brands and increasing efficiency. Efficiency gains will come from more central coordination of purchasing, including media and IT; from the optimisation of its inherited network of breweries; and from the sharing of best practice across sites internationally. A-B InBev is now emphasising organic growth and improved margins from its existing business. Its declared intention is to be 'The Best Beer Company in a Better World'.

Greene King (United Kingdom)

Established in 1799, Greene King is now the largest domestic British brewer, owner of famous brands such as Abbot, IPA and Old Speckled Hen. It has expanded through a series of acquisitions including Ruddles (1995), Morland (1999) and Hardys and Hansons (2006). Acquisition is typically followed by the closure of the acquired brewery, the termination of minor brands and the transfer of major brand production to its main brewery in Bury St. Edmunds. This strategy has led to critics calling the company 'Greedy King'. IPA is the UK's top cask ale, with over 20 per cent of the on-trade market, and Old Speckled Hen is the top premium UK ale with more than one eighth of the multiple retailer market. Greene King is unusual amongst contemporary breweries in operating many of its own pubs, having added to its original chain several acquisitions (notably Laurels

with 432 pubs and Belhaven with 271). Greene King now operates nearly 2000 pubs across the United Kingdom, with a particularly dominant position in its home region of East Anglia. The company is also active in restaurants. Business is effectively confined to the UK market. In 2009, Greene King raised £207m (~€228m; ~$310m) on the financial markets in order to fund further acquisitions. Greene King explains its success formula in brewing thus: 'The Brewing Company's continued out-performance is driven by a consistent, focused strategy: most importantly, we brew high quality beer from an efficient, single-site brewery; [and] we have a focused brand portfolio, minimising the complexity and cost of a multibrand strategy.'

Tsingtao (China)

Tsingtao Brewery was founded in 1903 by German settlers in China. After state ownership under Communism, Tsingtao was privatised in the early 1990s and listed on the Hong Kong Stock Exchange in 1993. In 2009, the Japanese Asahi Breweries held 19.9 per cent of the shares, purchased from A-B InBev (which also sold the remainder of its original stake – 7 per cent – to a Chinese private investor). Tsingtao has 13 per cent market share of its home market but has long had an export orientation, accounting for more than 50 per cent of China's beer exports. Tsingtao Beer was introduced to the United States in 1972 and is the Chinese brand-leader in the US market. A bottle of Tsingtao appeared in the 1982 science fiction film *Blade Runner*. Tsingtao set up its European office in 1992 and its beer is now sold in 62 countries. The company has described its ambition thus: 'to promote the continuous growth of the sales volume and income to step forward (sic) the target of becoming an international great company'.

Sources: Ernst & Young, The Contribution Made by Beer to the European Economy, 2009; Euromonitor International, Global Alcoholic Drinks: Beer – Opportunities in Niche Categories, April, 2009; Euromonitor, Strategies for Growth in an Increasingly Consolidated Global Beer Market, February 2010.

Questions

1 Using the data from the case (and any other sources available), carry out for the Western European brewing industry (i) a PESTEL analysis and (ii) a five forces analysis. What do you conclude?

2 For the three breweries outlined above (or breweries of your own choice) explain:

   (a) how these trends will impact differently on these different companies; and

   (b) the relative strengths and weaknesses of each company.

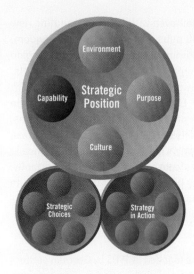

3

STRATEGIC CAPABILITIES

Learning outcomes

After reading this chapter you should be able to:

● Identify what comprises *strategic capabilities* in terms of organisational *resources* and *competences* and how these relate to the strategies of organisations.

● Analyse how strategic capabilities might provide sustainable competitive advantage on the basis of their *value, rarity, inimitability and non-substitutability (VRIN)*.

● Diagnose strategic capability by means of *benchmarking, value chain analysis, activity mapping* and *SWOT analysis*.

● Consider how managers can *develop strategic capabilities* for their organisations.

Key terms

Competences p. 84

Core competences p. 89

Dynamic capabilities p. 85

Inimitable capabilities p. 91

Organisational knowledge p. 94

Profit pools p. 102

Rare capabilities p. 90

Resource-based view p. 83

Resources p. 84

Strategic capabilities p. 84

SWOT p. 106

Threshold capabilities p. 87

Value p. 90

Value chain p. 97

Value network p. 97

PEARSON

mystrategylab

MyStrategyLab is designed to help you make the most of your studies.

Visit **www.pearsoned.co.uk/mystrategylab** to discover a wide range of resources specific to this chapter, including:

• A personalised **Study plan** that will help you understand core concepts

• **Audio** and **video clips** that put the spotlight on strategy in the real world

• **Online glossaries** and **flashcards** that provide helpful reminders when you're looking for some quick revision.

(3.1) INTRODUCTION

Chapter 2 outlined how the external environment of an organisation can create both strategic opportunities and threats. However, Nokia, Sony and Motorola have all sought to compete in the same market for mobile phones and develop their businesses within the same technological environment, but with markedly different success. Nokia has been relatively successful consistently. Sony has found it more difficult to compete effectively of late. And Motorola's performance has been such that it has considered withdrawing altogether despite being an early innovator in the market. It is not so much variations in the environment which explain these differences in performance, but the differences in their *strategic capabilities* in terms of the *resources and competences* they have or have tried to develop. It is the strategic importance of such capabilities that is the focus of this chapter.

The key issues posed by the chapter are summarised in Figure 3.1. Underlying these are two key concepts. The first is that organisations are not identical, but have different capabilities; they are 'heterogeneous' in this respect. The second is that it can be difficult for one organisation to obtain or copy the capabilities of another. For example, competitors cannot readily obtain or access Nokia's experience built up over decades of success. The implication for managers is that they need to understand how their organisations are different from their rivals in ways that may be the basis of achieving competitive advantage and superior performance. These concepts underlie what has become known as the **resource-based view** (RBV) of strategy[1] (though it might more appropriately be labelled the 'capabilities view'): **that the competitive advantage and superior performance of an organisation is explained by the distinctiveness of its capabilities**. RBV has become very influential in strategy and this chapter draws on it a good deal. It should be borne in mind, however, that there are different treatments of the topic.

Figure 3.1 Strategic capabilities: the key issues

So, whilst the terminology and concepts employed here align with RBV, readers will find different terminology used elsewhere.

The chapter has four further sections:

- Section 3.2 discusses the foundations of *strategic capability*; in particular what is meant by *resources, competences* and the related concept of *dynamic capabilities*. It also draws a distinction between *threshold capabilities* required to be able to compete in a market and *distinctive capabilities* that may be a basis for achieving competitive advantage and superior performance.

- Section 3.3 explains the ways in which distinctive capabilities may contribute to the *developing and sustaining of competitive advantage* (in a public-sector context the equivalent concern might be how some organisations sustain relative superior performance over time). In particular, the importance of the *Value, Rarity, Inimitability and Non-substitutability (VRIN)* of capabilities is explained.

- Section 3.4 moves on to consider different ways strategic capability might be analysed. These include *benchmarking, value chain analysis* and *activity system mapping*. The section concludes by explaining the use of *SWOT* analysis as a basis for pulling together the insights from the analyses of the environment (explained in Chapter 2) and of strategic capabilities in this chapter.

- Finally section 3.5 discusses some of the key issues in managing the *development of strategic capabilities* through internal and external development and the management of people.

FOUNDATIONS OF STRATEGIC CAPABILITY

Given that different writers, managers and consultants use different terms and concepts it is important to understand how concepts relating to strategic capabilities are used in this book. Here **strategic capabilities** means **the capabilities of an organisation that contribute to its long-term survival or competitive advantage.** However, to understand and to manage strategic capability it is necessary to explain its components and the characteristics of those components.

3.2.1 Resources and competences

There are two components of strategic capability: resources and competences. **Resources are the assets that organisations have or can call upon** (e.g. from partners or suppliers); **competences are the ways those assets are used or deployed effectively.** A shorthand way of thinking of this is that resources are 'what we *have*' and competences are 'what we *do well*'. Other terms are common. For example, Gary Hamel and C.K. Prahalad refer to *core competences* and many writers use the term *intangible assets* as an umbrella term to include intangible resources such as brands and business systems as well as competences.

Typically all strategic capabilities have elements of both resources and competences as Table 3.1 shows. Resources are certainly important but how an organisation employs and deploys its resources matters at least as much. There would be no point in having state-of-the-art equipment if it were not used effectively. The efficiency and effectiveness of physical or financial resources, or the people in an organisation, depend, not just on their existence, but on the systems and processes by which they are managed, the relationships and cooperation

Table 3.1 Components of strategic capabilities

Strategic capability		
Resources: what we have, e.g.		**Competences: what we do well, e.g.**
Machines, buildings, raw materials, products, patents, data bases, computer systems	Physical	Ways of achieving utilisation of plant, efficiency, productivity, flexibility, marketing
Balance sheet, cash flow, suppliers of funds	Financial	Ability to raise funds and manage cash flows, debtors, creditors etc.
Managers, employees, partners, suppliers, customers	Human	How people gain and use experience, skills, knowledge, build relationships, motivate others and innovate

Long-term survival and competitive advantage

between people, their adaptability, their innovatory capacity, the relationship with customers and suppliers and the experience and learning about what works well and what does not. Illustration 3.1 shows examples of how executives explain the importance of the resources and capabilities of their different organisations.

3.2.2 Dynamic capabilities[2]

If they are to provide a basis for long-term success, strategic capabilities cannot be static; they need to change. University of Berkeley economist David Teece has introduced the concept of **dynamic capabilities**, by which he means **an organisation's ability to renew and recreate its strategic capabilities to meet the needs of changing environments**. He argues that the capabilities that are necessary for efficient operations: 'maintaining incentive alignment, owning tangible assets, controlling costs, maintaining quality, optimizing inventories – are necessary but . . . are unlikely to be sufficient for sustaining superior performance'.[3] Moreover he acknowledges the further danger that capabilities that were the basis of competitive success may over time be imitated by competitors, become common practice in an industry or become redundant as its environment changes. Harvard's Dorothy Leonard-Barton also warns of the danger that, despite a changing environment, such capabilities can become 'rigidities'.[4] Chapter 5 deals with some of the problematic consequences of this. So, the important lesson is that if capabilities are to be effective over time they need to change; they cannot be static.

In this context, Teece suggests that there are three generic types of dynamic capabilities: those concerned with *sensing* opportunities and threats, those concerned with *seizing* opportunities and those concerned with *re-configuring* the capabilities of an organisation. This view of dynamic capabilities relates directly to the framework for this book. Sensing capabilities is to do with understanding an organisation's strategic position; seizing opportunities relates to making strategic choices; and re-configuration is to do with enacting strategies.

Dynamic capabilities may take the form of relatively formal organisational systems, such as recruitment and management development processes, or major strategic moves, such as

ILLUSTRATION 3.1

Strategic capabilities

Executives emphasise different strategic capabilities in different organisations.

The Goddard Space Center

Flight Center NASA's Goddard Space Flight Center manages many aspects of the space agency's missions and lays claim to some unique resources. For example, its 42-foot-tall acoustic test chamber can produce sounds of up to 150 decibels to allow technicians to expose payloads to launch noise. The high bay clean room, which can accommodate two space shuttle payloads, circulates nine million cubic feet of air every minute through its filters to prevent contaminants damaging spacecraft components – essential to space missions since cleaning of such contaminants in space is highly problematic. And its 120-foot-diameter high-capacity centrifuge with two 1250-horsepower motors can accelerate a 2.5-ton payload up to 30Gs.

Royal Opera House, London

Tony Hall, Chief Executive of the Royal Opera House:

'World-class' is neither an idle nor boastful claim. In the context of the Royal Opera House the term refers to the quality of our people, the standards of our productions and the diversity of our work and initiatives. Unique? Unashamedly so. We shy away from labels such as 'elite', because of the obvious negative connotations of exclusiveness. But I want people to take away from here the fact that we are elite in the sense that we have the best singers, dancers, directors, designers, orchestra, chorus, backstage crew and administrative staff. We are also amongst the best in our ability to reach out to as wide and diverse a community as possible.[2]

Maersk

Maersk is the the leading container shipping company in the world. Its fleet comprises more than 500 vessels and it has over 300 offices in 125 countries across the world. They also operate container terminals in 50 locations. Maersk emphasise the value and comparative rarity of their size, not least in terms of

it providing a reliable and comprehensive coverage for customers worldwide. Their website emphasises size in a number of novel ways: for example:

If all Maersk Line containers were placed one after the other, they would reach about 19,000 km. This is more than the distance from Copenhagen, Denmark to Perth, Australia, via Cape Town, South Africa or almost half of the earth's circumference.

However, Brian Godsafe, a Customer Service Director emphasises other capabilities. He explained that Maersk Line's stated top priority is: 'to provide you, our customers, with services you can count on to satisfy your own customers and grow your business'. Since Maersk are connected to so many markets around the world, customers are able to use them for multiple rather than singular trades. In terms of sales service, Maersk have a dedicated account manager for every regular customer, empowered to deal with their requests. Moreover this is replicated throughout the world. So, for example, there is a dedicated customer service team for each client based in the UK but this team is duplicated in locations around the world. In this way their global clients have touch points into their business all around the world. Many other companies just do not have that advantage.[3]

Sources: (1) Goddard Space Center website. (2) *Annual Review*, 2005/6, p. 11. (3) Pearson Strategy Documentaries.

Questions

1 Categorise the range of capabilities highlighted by the executives in terms of section 3.2 and Tables 3.1 and 3.2.

2 To what extent and why might these capabilities be the basis of *sustained* competitive advantage?

3 For an organisation of your choice undertake the same exercise as in questions 1 and 2 above.

acquisitions or alliances, by which new skills are learned and developed. For example, Stanford's Kathy Eisenhardt[5] has shown that successful acquisition processes can bring in new knowledge to organisations. However, this depends on high-quality pre- and post-acquisition understanding of how the acquisition can be integrated into the new organisation so as to capture synergies and bases of learning from that acquisition. As Teece acknowledges, then, dynamic capabilities are likely to have foundations in less formal, behavioural aspects of organisations, such as the way in which decisions get taken, personal relationships, and entrepreneurial and intuitive skills. Illustration 3.2 provides an example in the context of a new business venture.

3.2.3 Threshold and distinctive capabilities

A distinction also needs to be made between strategic capabilities that are at a threshold level and those that might help the organisation achieve competitive advantage and superior performance. Table 3.2 summarises these distinctions.

Threshold capabilities are those needed for an organisation to meet the necessary requirements to compete in a given market and achieve parity with competitors in that market. Without such capabilities the organisation could not survive over time. Indeed many start-up businesses find this to be the case. They simply do not have or cannot obtain the resources or competences needed to compete with established competitors. Identifying threshold requirements is, however, also important for established businesses. By the end of the first decade of the 21st century BP faced declining oil output in countries such as the US, the UK and Russia. BP's board regarded securing new sources of supply as a major challenge. In 2008/9 some high-profile financial institutions went bankrupt or were bailed out by huge government funding because they did not have the financial resources to meet their debts as recessionary pressures grew. There could also be changing *threshold resources* required to meet minimum customer requirements: for example, the increasing demands by modern multiple retailers of their suppliers mean that those suppliers have to possess a quite sophisticated IT infrastructure simply to stand a chance of meeting retailer requirements. Or they could be the *threshold competences* required to deploy resources so as to meet customers' requirements and support particular strategies. Retailers do not simply expect suppliers to have the required IT infrastructure, but to be able to use it effectively so as to guarantee the required level of service.

Identifying and managing threshold capabilities raises two significant challenges:

● *Threshold levels of capability will change* as critical success factors change (see section 2.4.3) or through the activities of competitors and new entrants. To continue the example, suppliers

Table 3.2 Threshold and distinctive capabilities

	Resources	Competences
Threshold capabilities Required to be able to compete in a market	Threshold resources	Threshold competences
Distinctive capabilities Required to achieve competitive advantage	Distinctive resources	Distinctive competences

ILLUSTRATION 3.2

Building dynamic capabilities in a new venture

Networks and partnerships can be a source of dynamic capabilities and learning for firms and for managers.

HMD Clinical is an Edinburgh-based clinical technological new venture that seeks to make large-scale clinical trials more efficient for drug development companies. HMD initially provided bespoke services using telephony technology (for example, interactive voice recognition) to monitor clinical trials. However, this was problematic, principally due to human error. HMD therefore sought to develop a product based on another technology – radiofrequency identification. HMD felt this would also offer the prospect of market diversification, especially through international expansion. However, making changes to the company's product market domain called for capabilities to expand or modify HMD's current configuration of resources and capabilities – in other words, for dynamic capabilities.

HMD decided to partner with a large established firm, which HMD saw as a potential source of legitimacy, resources and opportunities: Sun Microsystems, a multinational corporation with a significant presence in Scotland. Co-founder Ian Davison commented, 'There's a certain cachet in being associated with a big company.' Sun was interested in HMD's product idea and within months there was progress in establishing the alliance. Davison believes that considerable benefit was derived by HMD: 'We got what we wanted out of the relationship because we managed to build a prototype using the Sun technology.' HMD's experience also illustrates the building of dynamic capabilities at various levels.

Opportunities arose for mutual learning. From HMD's perspective, the venture benefited from exposure to new technological ideas. Of particular advantage was Sun's ability to tap into its widespread resources and capabilities elsewhere in the UK and beyond (for example, Western Europe). Also, Sun's reputation opened doors for HMD. When the prototype was built, HMD made a joint sales call with Sun to a prospective international customer and a demonstration was subsequently held on Sun's Scottish premises. Such activities facilitated experiential learning about processes such as product development and sales.

There were also further benefits for HMD:

- *Product development.* In developing a prototype with Sun, HMD engaged in integrating resources and capabilities to achieve synergies; for example, its own customer-centric technological knowledge in the clinical trials domain was combined with Sun's hardware technology architecture.
- *Alliancing.* Through inputs from a public sector intermediary, HMD gained vital knowledge about formal aspects of alliancing, such as the legalities of sharing intellectual property; equally, HMD came to appreciate the utility of informal social networking in ensuring the smooth progress of joint activity.
- *Strategic decision making.* HMD was able to build new thinking within the firm in terms of, for example, the identification of external knowledge sources as evident from subsequent decisions to expand the alliance to include a third partner.

At the individual level within HMD managers also learned 'new tricks' by engaging in informal routines such as brainstorming sessions and everyday activities such as negotiating. Managers claimed that such learning would help HMD approach its next alliance by replicating certain aspects while modifying others. Davison commented: 'In future we would approach this sort of relationship in a broadly similar manner [but] I think we would attempt to set some clearer company goals and boundaries at the outset.'

Prepared by Shameen Prashantham, Department of Management, University of Glasgow.

Questions

1 At what levels could dynamic capabilities benefit organisations?

2 How do network relationships, such as strategic partnerships, potentially contribute to dynamic capability development?

3 What other joint activity within, and across, organisations could give rise to dynamic capabilities? How?

4 Can dynamic capability development be deliberately planned? How?

to major retailers did not require the same level of IT and logistics support a decade ago. But the retailers' drive to reduce costs, improve efficiency and ensure availability of merchandise to their customers means that their expectations of their suppliers have increased markedly in that time and continue to do so. So there is a need for those suppliers continuously to review and improve their logistics resource and competence base just to stay in business.

● *Trade-offs* may need to be made to achieve the threshold capability required for different customers. For example, businesses have found it difficult to compete in market segments that require large quantities of standard product as well as market segments that require added-value specialist products. Typically, the first requires high-capacity, fast-throughput plant, standardised highly efficient systems and a low-cost labour force; the second a skilled labour force, flexible plant and a more innovative capacity. The danger is that an organisation fails to achieve the threshold capabilities required for either segment.

While threshold capabilities are important, they do not of themselves create competitive advantage or the basis of superior performance. These are dependent on an organisation having distinctive or unique capabilities that are of value to customers and which competitors find difficult to imitate. This could be because the organisation has *distinctive resources* that critically underpin competitive advantage and that others cannot imitate or obtain – a long-established brand, for example. Or it could be that an organisation achieves competitive advantage because it has *distinctive competences* – ways of doing things that are unique to that organisation and effectively utilised so as to be valuable to customers and difficult for competitors to obtain or imitate. Gary Hamel and C.K. Prahalad[6] argue that the distinctive competences that are especially important are likely to be: 'A bundle of constituent skills and technologies rather than a single, discrete skill or technology'. They use the term **core competences** to emphasize **the linked set of skills, activities and resources that, together, deliver customer value, differentiate a business from its competitors and, potentially, can be extended and developed.** For example as markets change or new opportunities arise. There are, then, also similarities here to Teece's conceptualisation of dynamic capabilities.

KEY CONCEPT

Core competences

Bringing these concepts together, a supplier that achieves competitive advantage in a retail market might have done so on the basis of a distinctive resource such as a powerful brand, but also by distinctive competences such as the building of excellent relations with retailers. However, it is likely that what will be most difficult for competitors to match and will therefore be the basis of competitive advantage will be the multiple and linked ways of providing products, high levels of service and building relationships – its core competence.

Section 3.3 that follows discusses in more depth the role played by distinctive resources and competences in contributing to long-term, sustainable competitive advantage. Section 3.4 then explores further the importance of linkages of activities.

3.3 'VRIN' STRATEGIC CAPABILITIES AS A BASIS OF COMPETITIVE ADVANTAGE

How, then, does a strategist consider on what bases organisational capabilities might be the foundation for sustainable competitive advantage and superior economic performance? As argued above, this is unlikely if the organisation is no different from its rivals and therefore has nothing that provides a basis for earning greater profits. Threshold capabilities may achieve parity with competitors but not advantage over those competitors. This section considers four key criteria by which capabilities can be assessed in terms of their providing a basis for achieving such competitive advantage: value, rarity, inimitability and non-substitutability – or *VRIN*.[7]

3.3.1 V – value of strategic capabilities

Strategic capabilities are of value when they provide potential competitive advantage in a market at a cost that allows an organisation to realise acceptable levels of return (in the case of the private sector).[8] There are four components here:

- *Taking advantage of opportunities and neutralising threats*: the most fundamental question is whether the capabilities provide the potential to address the opportunities and threats that arise in the organisation's environment.

- *Value to customers*: it may seem an obvious point to make that capabilities need to be of value to customers, but in practice it is often ignored or poorly understood. For example, managers may seek to build on capabilities that *they* may see as valuable but which do not meet customers' critical success factors (see section 2.4.3). Or they may see a distinctive capability as of value simply because it is distinctive. Having capabilities that are different from other organisations' is not, of itself, a basis of competitive advantage. So the discussion in sections 3.3.2 and 3.3.3 and the lessons it draws are important here.

- *Providing potential competitive advantage*: the capabilities do, nonetheless, need to be capable of delivering a product or service that competitors do not currently have or do not currently emphasise.

- *Cost*: the product or service needs to be provided at a cost that still allows the organisation to make the returns expected of it (e.g. by investors). The danger is that the cost of developing the capabilities to deliver what customers especially value is such that products or services are not profitable.

Managers should therefore consider carefully which of their organisation's activities are especially important in providing such value and which are of less value. Value chain analysis and activity mapping explained in sections 3.4.2 and 3.4.3 can help here.

3.3.2 R – rarity

If competitors have similar capabilities they can respond quickly to the strategic initiative of a rival. This has happened in competition between car manufacturers as they have sought to add more accessories and gadgets to cars. As soon as it becomes evident that these are valued by customers, they are introduced widely by competitors who typically have access to the same technology. **Rare capabilities**, on the other hand, **are those possessed uniquely by one organisation or by a few others**. Here competitive advantage might be longer-lasting. For example, a company may have patented products or services that give it advantage. Service organisations may have rare resources in the form of intellectual capital – perhaps particularly talented individuals. Some libraries have unique collections of books unavailable elsewhere; a company may have a powerful brand; or retail stores may have prime locations. In terms of competences, organisations may have unique skills developed over time or have built special relationships with customers or suppliers not widely possessed by competitors. However, there are two important points to bear in mind about the extent to which rarity might provide competitive advantage:

- *Meeting customer need*: again rarity, of itself, is of little value unless the resources or capabilities lead to outputs in the form of products or services that meet customer needs and are therefore of value to them.

- *Sustainability*: rarity could be temporary. For example, uniquely talented individuals may be an advantage but can also be a risk. In 2009 the financial press reported increasing concerns about Apple, given the health of its CEO Steve Jobs, with headlines such as: 'Can Apple survive without Steve Jobs?'[9] Moreover it may be dangerous to assume that resources and capabilities that are rare will remain so. If an organisation is successful on the basis of something distinctive, then competitors will very likely seek to imitate or obtain that distinctiveness. So it may be necessary to consider other bases of sustainability.

3.3.3 I – inimitability

It should be clear by now that the search for strategic capability that provides sustainable competitive advantage is not straightforward. Having capabilities that are valuable to customers and relatively rare is important, but this may not be enough. Sustainable competitive advantage also involves identifying inimitable capabilities – **those that competitors find difficult to imitate or obtain**. For example, the competitive advantage of some professional service organisations is built around the competence of specific individuals – such as a doctor in 'leading-edge' medicine, individual fund managers, the manager of a top sports team or the CEO of a business. However, since these individuals may leave or join competitors, this resource may be a fragile basis of advantage. More sustainable advantage may be found in capabilities that exist for recruiting, training, motivating and rewarding such individuals or be embedded in the culture that attracts them to the organisation – so ensuring that they do not defect to 'competitors'.

At the risk of over-generalisation, it is unusual for competitive advantage to be explainable by differences in the tangible resources of organisations, since over time these can usually be acquired or imitated. Advantage is more likely to be determined by the way in which resources are deployed and managed in terms of an organisation's activities; in other words on the basis of competences.[10] For example, it is unlikely an IT system will improve an organisation's competitive standing of itself, not least because competitors can probably buy something very similar in the open market. On the other hand the capabilities to manage, develop and deploy such a system to the benefit of customers may be much more difficult to imitate. This is likely to be so if two conditions are met:

- *Superior performance*: the capabilities lead to levels of performance of product or service that are significantly better than competitors';

- *Linked competences*: if the capability integrates activities, skills and knowledge both inside and outside the organisation in distinct and mutually compatible ways. It is then the *linkages* of the activities that go to make up capabilities that can be especially significant. There are four reasons why such linkages may make capabilities particularly difficult for competitors to imitate. These are summarised in Figure 3.2 and are now briefly reviewed.

Figure 3.2 Criteria for the inimitability of strategic capabilities

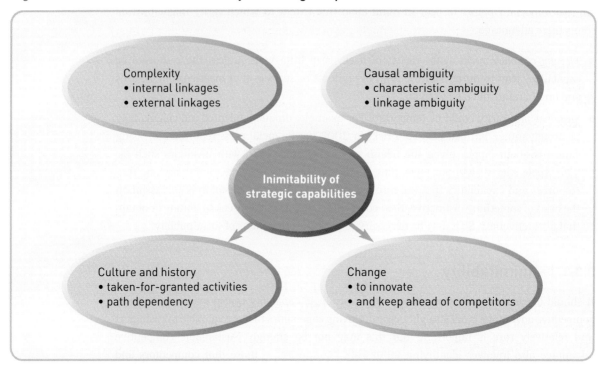

Complexity

The capabilities of an organisation may be difficult to imitate because they are complex. This may be for two main reasons.

● *Internal linkages.* There may be linked activities and processes that, together, deliver customer value. The discussion of activity systems in section 3.4.3 below explains this in more detail and shows how such linked sets of activities might be mapped so that they can be better understood. However, even if a competitor possessed such a map, it is unlikely that it would be able to replicate the sort of complexity it represents. This is not only because of the complexity itself but because, very likely, it has developed on the basis of custom and practice built up over years and is specific to the organisation concerned.

● *External interconnectedness.* Organisations can make it difficult for others to imitate or obtain their bases of competitive advantage by developing activities together with the customer such that the customer becomes dependent on them. This is sometimes referred to as *co-specialisation.* For example, an industrial lubricants business moved away from just selling its products to customers by coming to an agreement with them to manage the applications of lubricants within the customers' sites against agreed targets on cost savings. The more efficient the use of lubricants, the more both parties benefited. Similarly software businesses can achieve advantage by developing computer programs that are distinctively beneficial to specific customer needs.

Causal ambiguity[11]

Another reason why capabilities might be difficult to imitate is that competitors find it difficult to discern the causes and effects underpinning an organisation's advantage. This is called *causal ambiguity.* Causal ambiguity may exist in two different forms:[12]

● *Characteristic ambiguity.* Where the significance of the characteristic itself is difficult to discern or comprehend, perhaps because it is based on tacit knowledge or rooted in the organisation's culture. For example, the know-how of the buyers in a successful fashion retailer may be evident in the sales achieved for the ranges they buy year after year. But it may be very difficult to comprehend just what that know-how is, so competitors will find it difficult to imitate.

● *Linkage ambiguity.* Where competitors cannot discern which activities and processes are dependent on which others to form linkages that create core competences. The expertise of the fashion buyers is unlikely to be lodged in the one individual or even one function. It is likely that there will be a network of suppliers, intelligence networks to understand the market and links with designers. Indeed in some organisations the managers themselves admit that they do not fully comprehend the linkages throughout the organisation that deliver customer value. If this is so it would certainly be difficult for competitors to understand them.

Culture and history

Competences may become embedded in an organisation's culture. So coordination between various activities occurs 'naturally' because people know their part in the wider picture or it is simply 'taken for granted' that activities are done in particular ways. We see this in high-performing sports teams, in teams that work together to combine specialist skills as in operating theatres; but also, for example, in how some firms integrate different activities in their business to deliver excellent customer service. Linked to this cultural embeddedness is the likelihood that such competences have developed over time and in a particular way. The origins and history by which competences have developed over time are referred to as *path dependency.*[13] This history is specific to the organisation and cannot be imitated (see section 5.3.1). As explained in Chapter 5 there is, however, a danger that culturally embedded competences built up over time become so embedded that they are difficult to change: they become rigidities.

Change

The concept of dynamic capabilities is relevant here. If an organisation builds a basis of competitive advantage on resources or capabilities that change as the dynamics of a market or the needs of customers change, they will be more difficult for competitors to imitate. Indeed, arguably, organisations that wish to be market leaders, to innovate and create new markets must do so on the basis of dynamic capabilities. They are, in effect, continually seeking to stay ahead of their competitors by evolving new bases of doing so.

3.3.4 N – non-substitutability[14]

Providing value to customers and possessing competences that are rare and difficult to imitate may mean that it is very difficult for organisations to copy them. However, the organisation may still be at risk from substitution. Substitution could take two different forms:

● *Product or service substitution.* As already discussed in Chapter 2 in relation to the five forces model of competition, a product or service as a whole might be a victim of substitution. For example, increasingly e-mail systems have substituted for postal systems. No matter how complex and culturally embedded were the competences of the postal service, it could not avoid this sort of substitution.

Figure 3.3 **VRIN**

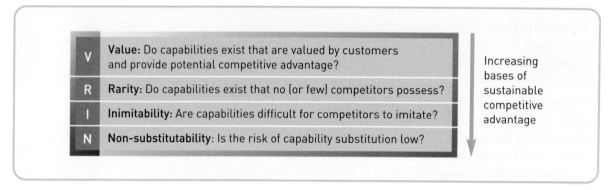

- *Competence substitution.* Substitution might, however, not be at the product or service level but at the competence level. For example, task-based industries have often suffered because of an over-reliance on the competences of skilled craft workers that have been replaced by expert systems and mechanisation.

In summary and from a resource-based view of organisations, managers need to consider whether their organisation has strategic capabilities to achieve and sustain competitive advantage. To do so they need to consider how and to what extent it has capabilities which are (i) valuable to buyers, (ii) rare, (iii) inimitable and (iv) non-substitutable.

As Figure 3.3 shows, there is an additive effect here. Strategic capabilities provide sustainable bases of competitive advantage the more they meet all four criteria. If such capabilities for competitive advantage do not exist, then managers need to consider if they can be developed. How this might be done is considered in section 3.5 below.

3.3.5 Organisational knowledge as a basis of competitive advantage

A good example of how both resources and competences may combine to produce competitive advantage for an organisation is in terms of organisational knowledge.[15] **Organisational knowledge is the collective intelligence, specific to an organisation, accumulated through both formal systems and the shared experience of people in that organisation.**

The reasons why organisational knowledge is seen as especially important illustrate many of the points made above. As organisations become larger and more complex, the need to share what people know becomes more and more important but increasingly challenging. So organisations that can share knowledge especially well may gain advantage over those that do not. Computerised information systems are available or have been developed by organisations to codify technological, financial and market data that are *valuable* to them; indeed without which they probably could not compete effectively. However, the technology which forms the basis of information systems is hardly *rare*; it is widely available or can be developed. It is therefore less likely that organisations will achieve competitive advantage through such resources and more likely that it will be achieved through the way they manage and develop organisational knowledge more broadly. This may be to do with the competences they employ to utilise and develop

ILLUSTRATION 3.3

Sandvik's rapid production capabilities

Different strategic capabilities might be valuable, rare, inimitable or non-substitutable.

Swedish-based global industrial group Sandvik manufactures products for companies operating in a wide range of industries including medical technology. In a 2009 press release, it announced it had:

invested in a technologically advanced direct metal laser sintering machine (DMLS) in order to provide rapid production capabilities to its customers, unique amongst contract manufacturers.

Sandvik is now significantly reducing the time required to cost-effectively develop working prototypes, which means its customers can bring new innovations to market far more quickly than was previously possible. Sandvik is also exploiting the powder-based technique used by the DMLS machine to manufacture to almost any design, thereby removing limitations previously imposed on design teams within medical device OEMs (original equipment manufacturers). In an industry where innovation and speed to market are crucial differentiators, these benefits represent a real commercial advantage to OEMs.

Through this investment and the enhanced capabilities it brings, Sandvik has further strengthened its position as a strategic partner to medical technology companies, helping them improve their competitiveness.

Tord Lendau, President Sandvik MedTech, explained:

'Medical device OEMs operate in a highly competitive market. We want to leverage Sandvik's long experience within powder metallurgy to deliver real value to OEMs and so must continuously introduce new manufacturing techniques, which is why we have made this significant investment. . . . Medical device manufacturers can now capitalise on enhanced capabilities and improve the speed to market of their new designs and innovations.'

The press release continued:

The new capabilities provided by the DMLS machine are ideal for the production of working prototypes of medical devices and for complex custom-made instruments.

It quoted John Reynolds, a special projects manager at Sandvik:

'Prototyping is an important stage in the creation of a new device, since it provides the opportunity to explore the design and make the necessary adjustments prior to full production. However, most rapid prototyping processes do not produce a working model while those that do are time consuming and more expensive. . . . By using the DMLS machine we can bring to bear rapid production techniques that enable us to quickly and cost-effectively manufacture a working prototype. This means our customers can present a working model to their customers in a fraction of the time it would take with conventional manufacturing techniques and bring the final design to market far quicker. . . . We can also now manufacture almost any design the OEM can create, irrespective of the complexity of the geometry. This means our customers' design teams are not constrained by the manufacturing limitations previously typical in the industry. They have the flexibility to respond with precision to the individual preferences of any one surgeon or the specific needs of a patient.'

The press release concluded:

By enhancing its capabilities through this significant investment and combining it with its materials and manufacturing expertise, Sandvik is helping OEMs achieve real competitive advantage in a challenging market.

Source: www.smt.sandvik.com/sandvik. © AB Sandvik Materials Technology.

Questions

1 Assess the bases of Sandvik's strategic capabilities using the VRIN criteria.

2 Which are the key strategic capabilities which provide, or could provide, Sandvik with sustainable competitive advantage?

information technology. But it is also likely to be about how they draw on and develop the accumulated and dispersed experience-based knowledge in the organisation.

The distinction between *explicit* and *tacit organisational knowledge* made by Ikijuro Nonaka and Hiro Takeuchi[16] helps explain why this is important in terms of achieving competitive advantage. Explicit or 'objective' knowledge is transmitted in formal systematic ways. It may take the form of a codified information resource such as a systems manual or files of market research and intelligence. In contrast, tacit knowledge is more personal, context-specific and therefore hard to formalise and communicate. For example it could be the knowledge of a highly experienced sales force or research and development team; or the experience of a top management team in making many successful acquisitions. It is therefore not only distinctive to the organisation, but likely to be *difficult to imitate* or obtain for the reasons explained in 3.3.3 above. Such knowledge may have been developed over the years by '*communities of practice*'[17] developing and sharing information because it is mutually beneficial to them. It may also be continually changing as their experience changes. It will also be difficult for competitors to comprehend precisely because it is context specific, experiential and dispersed (and therefore complex and causally ambiguous).

Many organisations that have tried to improve the sharing of knowledge by relying on IT-based systems have come to realise that, while some knowledge can usefully be codified and built into computer-based systems, it may be very difficult to codify the knowledge that truly bestows competitive advantage.

DIAGNOSING STRATEGIC CAPABILITIES

So far this chapter has been concerned with explaining concepts associated with the strategic significance of organisations' resources and capabilities. This section now provides some ways in which strategic capabilities can be understood and diagnosed.

3.4.1 Benchmarking[18]

Benchmarking is used as a means of understanding how an organisation compares with others – typically competitors. Many benchmarking exercises focus on outputs such as standards of product or service, but others do attempt to take account of organisational capabilities.

Broadly, there are two approaches to benchmarking:

- *Industry/sector benchmarking.* Insights about performance standards can be gleaned by comparing performance against other organisations in the same industry sector or between similar service providers against a set of performance indicators. Some public-sector organisations have, in effect, acknowledged the existence of strategic groups (see section 2.4.1) by benchmarking against similar organisations rather than against everybody: for example, local government services and police treat 'urban' differently from 'rural' in their benchmarking and league tables. An overriding danger of industry norm comparisons (whether in the private or the public sector) is, however, that the whole industry may be performing badly and losing out competitively to other industries that can satisfy customers' needs in different ways. Another danger with benchmarking within an industry is that the boundaries of industries are blurring through competitive activity and industry convergence. For example, supermarkets have entered retail banking and the benchmarking processes of the traditional retail banks probably need to reflect this.

- *Best-in-class benchmarking.* Best-in-class benchmarking compares an organisation's performance or capabilities against 'best-in-class' performance – wherever that is found – and therefore seeks to overcome some of the above limitations. It may also help challenge managers' mindsets that acceptable improvements in performance will result from incremental changes in resources or competences. It can therefore encourage a more fundamental reconsideration of how to improve organisational capabilities. For example, British Airways improved aircraft maintenance, refuelling and turnaround time studying the processes surrounding Formula One Grand Prix motor racing pit stops.[19] Xerox benchmarked its distribution capabilities against LL Bean, a mail order company. A police force wishing to improve the way in which it responded to emergency telephone calls studied call-centre operations in the banking and IT sectors.

The importance of benchmarking is, then, not so much in the detailed 'mechanics' of comparison but in the impact that these comparisons might have on reviewing capabilities underlying performance. But it has two major limitations:

- *Surface comparisons.* If benchmarking is limited to comparing inputs (resources) and outputs or outcomes, it does not directly identify the reasons for relative performance in terms of underlying capabilities. For example, it may demonstrate that one organisation is poorer at customer service than another but not show the underlying reasons. However, it could encourage managers to seek out these reasons and hence understand how capabilities could be improved.

- *Measurement distortion.* Benchmarking can lead to a situation where '*you get what you measure*' and this may not be what is intended strategically. It can therefore result in changes in behaviour that are unintended or dysfunctional. For example, the university sector in the UK has been subjected to rankings in league tables on research output. This has resulted in academics being 'forced' to orient their published research to certain types of academic journals that may have little to do directly with the quality of the education in universities.

3.4.2 The value chain and value network

The **value chain** describes the categories of activities within an organisation which, together, create a product or service. Most organisations are also part of a wider **value network**, the set of inter-organisational links and relationships that are necessary to create a product or service. Both are useful in understanding the strategic position of an organisation.

KEY CONCEPT

Value chain and value network

The value chain

If organisations are to achieve competitive advantage by delivering value to customers, managers need to understand which activities their organisation undertakes are especially important in creating that value and which are not. It can, then, be used to model the value system of an organisation. The important point is that the concept of the value chain invites the strategist to think of an organisation in terms of sets of activities. There are different frameworks for considering these categories: Figure 3.4 is a representation of a value chain as developed by Michael Porter.[20]

Primary activities are directly concerned with the creation or delivery of a product or service. For example, for a manufacturing business:

- *Inbound logistics* are activities concerned with receiving, storing and distributing inputs to the product or service including materials handling, stock control, transport, etc.

Figure 3.4 **The value chain within an organisation**

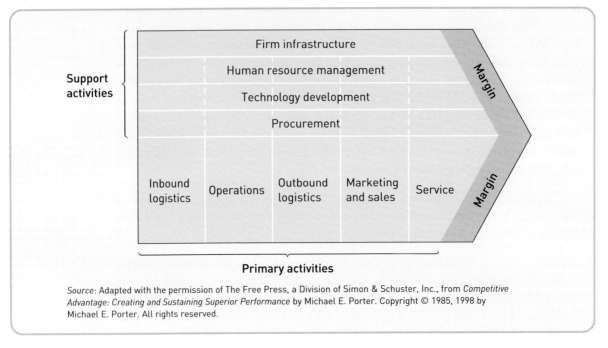

- *Operations* transform these inputs into the final product or service: machining, packaging, assembly, testing, etc.

- *Outbound logistics* collect, store and distribute the product to customers; for example, warehousing, materials handling, distribution.

- *Marketing and sales* provide the means whereby consumers or users are made aware of the product or service and are able to purchase it. This includes sales administration, advertising and selling.

- *Service* includes those activities that enhance or maintain the value of a product or service, such as installation, repair, training and spares.

Each of these groups of primary activities is linked to *support activities* which help to improve the effectiveness or efficiency of primary activities:

- *Procurement.* Processes that occur in many parts of the organisation for acquiring the various resource inputs to the primary activities. These can be vitally important in achieving scale advantages. So, for example, many large consumer goods companies with multiple businesses nonetheless procure advertising centrally.

- *Technology development.* All value activities have a 'technology', even if it is just know-how. Technologies may be concerned directly with a product (e.g. R&D, product design) or with processes (e.g. process development) or with a particular resource (e.g. raw materials improvements).

- *Human resource management.* These transcend all primary activities and are concerned with recruiting, managing, training, developing and rewarding people within the organisation.

- *Infrastructure.* The formal systems of planning, finance, quality control, information management and the structure of an organisation.

The value chain can be used to understand the strategic position of an organisation in three ways.

- As a *generic description of activities* it can help managers understand if there is a cluster of activities providing benefit to customers located within particular areas of the value chain. Perhaps a business is especially good at outbound logistics linked to its marketing and sales operation and supported by its technology development. It might be less good in terms of its operations and its inbound logistics. The value chain also prompts managers to think about the role different activities play. For example, in a local family-run sandwich bar, is sandwich making best thought of as 'operations' or as 'marketing and sales', given that its reputation and appeal may rely on the social relations and banter between customers and sandwich makers? Arguably it is 'operations' if done badly but 'marketing and sales' if done well.

- In *analysing the competitive position of the organisation* using the VRIN criteria as follows:

  V Which value creating activities are especially significant for an organisation in meeting customer needs and could they be usefully developed further?

  R To what extent and how does an organisation have bases of value creation that are *rare*? Or conversely are all elements of their value chain common to their competitors?

  I What aspects of value creation are difficult for others to *imitate*, perhaps because they are *embedded* in the activity systems of the organisation (see section 3.4.3 below)?

  N What aspects of the value chain are or are not vulnerable to substitution? For example, the production and distribution of CDs was seen as a key value-creating activity by firms such as EMI in the music industry; but the availability of music downloads via the internet has dramatically reduced the value of such activities.

- To *analyse the cost and value of activities*[21] of an organisation. This could involve the following steps:

  - *Identifying sets of value activities.* Figure 3.5 might be appropriate as a general framework here or a value chain more specific to an organisation may be needed. The important thing is to ask (a) which separate categories of activities best describe the operations of the organisation and (b) which of these are most significant in delivering the strategy and achieving advantage over competitors? For example, it is likely that in a branded pharmaceutical company research and development and marketing activities will be crucially important.

  - *Relative importance of activity costs internally.* Which activities are most significant in terms of the costs of operations? Does the significance of the costs align with the significance of the activities? Which activities most add value to the final product or service (and in turn to the customer) and which do not? It can also be important to establish which sets of activities are linked to or are dependent on others and which, in effect, are self-standing. For example, organisations that have undertaken such analyses often find that central services have grown to the extent that they are a disproportionate cost to internal sets of activities and to the customer.

  - *Relative importance of activities externally.* How does value and the cost of a set of activities compare with the similar activities of competitors? For example, although they are both global oil businesses, BP and Shell are different in terms of the significance of their value chain activities. BP has historically outperformed Shell in terms of exploration; but the reverse is the case with regard to refining and marketing.

● *Where and how can costs be reduced?* Given the picture that emerges from such an analysis it should be possible to ask some important questions about the cost structure of the organisation in terms of the strategy being followed (or that needs to be followed in the future). For example, is the balance of cost in line with the strategic significance of the elements of the value chain? Can costs be reduced in some areas without affecting the value created for customers? Can some activities be outsourced (see section 7.5.2), for example those that are relatively free-standing and do not add value significantly? Can cost savings be made by increasing economies of scale or scope; for example, through central procurement or consolidating currently fragmented activities (e.g. manufacturing units)?

The value network

A single organisation rarely undertakes in-house all of the value activities from design through to the delivery of the final product or service to the final consumer. There is usually specialisation of roles so, as Figure 3.5 shows, any one organisation is part of a wider *value network.* There are questions that arise here that build on an understanding of the value chain itself.

● *What are the activities and cost/price structures of the value network?* Just as costs can be analysed across the internal value chain, they can also be analysed across the value network: Illustration 3.4 shows this in relation to fish farming. Value network analysis

ILLUSTRATION 3.4

A value network for Ugandan chilled fish fillet exports

Even small enterprises can be part of an international value network. Analysing it can provide strategic benefits.

A fish factory in Uganda barely made any profit. Fish were caught from small motorboats owned by poor fishermen from local villages. Just before they set out they would collect ice and plastic fish boxes from the agents who bought the catch on their return. The boxes were imported, along with tackle and boat parts. All supplies had to be paid for in cash in advance by the agents. Sometimes ice and supplies were not available in time. Fish landed with insufficient ice achieved half of the price of iced fish, and sometimes could not be sold to the agents at all. The fish factory had always processed the fillets in the same way – disposing of the waste back into the lake. Once a week, some foreign traders would come and buy the better fillets; they didn't say who they sold them to, and sometimes they didn't buy very much.

By mapping the value chain it was clear that there were opportunities for capturing more value along the chain and reducing losses. Together with outside specialists, the fish factory and the fishing community developed a strategy to improve their capabilities, as indicated in the figure, until they became a flourishing international business, The Lake Victoria Fish Company, with regular air-freight exports around the world.

You can see more of their current operations at http://www.ufpea.co.ug/, and find out more about the type of analytical process applied at www.justreturn.ch.

(The approximate costs and prices given represent the situation before improvements were implemented.)

Questions

1 Draw up a value chain or value network for another business in terms of the activities within its component parts.

2 Estimate the relative costs and/or assets associated with these activities.

3 What are the strategic implications of your analysis?

Figure 3.5 The value network

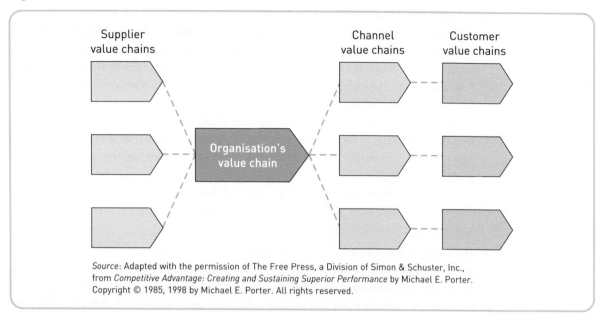

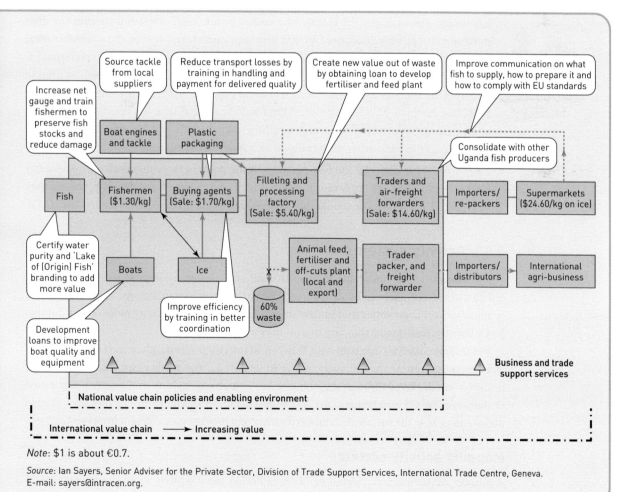

Note: $1 is about €0.7.

Source: Ian Sayers, Senior Adviser for the Private Sector, Division of Trade Support Services, International Trade Centre, Geneva. E-mail: sayers@intracen.org.

was used by Ugandan fish farmers as a way of identifying what they should focus on in developing a more profitable business model.

● *Where are the profit pools?*[22] **Profit pools refer to the different levels of profit available at different parts of the value network**. Some parts of a value network may be inherently more profitable than others because of the differences in competitive intensity (see section 2.3.1). For example, in the computer industry microprocessors and software have historically been more profitable than hardware manufacture. The strategic question becomes whether it is possible to focus on the areas of greatest profit potential? Care has to be exercised here. It is one thing to identify such potential; it is another to be successful in it given the capabilities an organisation has. For example, engineering firms may recognise the greater profit potential in providing engineering consulting services in addition to or instead of manufacturing. Nonetheless many have found it difficult to develop such services success- fully either because their staff do not have consultancy capabilities or because their clients do not recognise the firms as having them.

● *The 'make or buy'* decision for a particular activity is critical given some of the above questions. This is the *outsourcing* decision. Increasingly outsourcing is becoming common as a means of lowering costs. Of course, the more an organisation outsources, the more its ability to influence the performance of other organisations in the value network may become a critically important capability in itself and even a source of competitive advantage. For example, the quality of a cooker or a television when it reaches the final purchaser is not only influenced by the activities undertaken within the manufacturing company itself, but also by the quality of components from suppliers and the performance of the distributors. There is, of course, the converse question: which activities most need to be part of the internal value chain because they are central to achieving competitive advan- tage? For example, Howard Schultz,[23] the founder, argued that the benefit to Starbucks of owning and controlling most activities in its value chain was because its competitive advantage lay in the quality of its coffee, which it needed to guarantee.

● *Partnering*. Who might be the best partners in the parts of the value network? And what kind of *relationships* are important to develop with each partner? For example, should they be regarded as suppliers or should they be regarded as alliance partners (see section 10.4)?

3.4.3 Activity systems

The discussion so far highlights the fact that all organisations comprise sets of capabilities but that these are likely to be configured differently across organisations. It is this variable configuration of capabilities that makes an organisation and its strategy more or less unique. So for the strategist, understanding this matters a good deal.

Value chain analysis can help with this, but so too can understanding the activity systems of an organisation. As the discussion above in section 3.3 has made clear, the way in which resources are deployed through the organisation actually takes form in the activities pursued by that organisation; so it is important to identify what these activities are, why they are valuable to customers, how the various activities fit together and how they are different from competitors'.

Mapping activity systems

A number of the writers,[24] including Michael Porter, have written about the importance of mapping activity systems and shown how this might be done.

The starting point is to identify what Porter refers to as 'higher order strategic themes'. In effect these are the ways in which the organisation meets the critical success factors determining them in the market. The next step is to identify the clusters of activities that underpin each of these themes and how these do or do not fit together. The result is a picture of the organisation represented in terms of activity systems such as that shown in Illustration 3.5. This shows an activity systems map for the Scandinavian strategic communications consultancy, Geelmuyden.Kiese.[25] At the heart of its success is its knowledge, built over the years, of how effective communications can influence 'the power dynamics of decision making processes'. However, as Illustration 3.5 shows, this central theme is related to other higher-order strategic themes, each of which is underpinned by clusters of activities. Three points need to be emphasised here:

- *Relationship to the value chain.* The various activities represented in an activity map can also be seen as parts of a value chain. The in-house methodology is, in effect, part of Geelmuyden.Kiese's operations; their recruitment practices are a component of their human resource management; their stance on integrity and insistence on openness rather than suppression of the information part of their service offering; and so on. However, activity systems mapping encourages a greater understanding of the complexity of strategic capabilities – important if bases of competitive advantage are to be identified and managed.

- *The importance of linkages and fit.* An activity systems map emphasises the importance of different activities that create value to customers pulling in the same direction and supporting rather than opposing each other. So the need is to understand (a) the fit between the various activities and how these reinforce each other and (b) the fit externally with the needs of clients. There are three implications:

  - The danger of *piecemeal change* or tinkering with such systems which may damage the positive benefits of the linkages that exist.

  - The consequent *challenge of managing change.* When change is needed the implication is that change to one part of the system will almost inevitably affect another; or, put another way, change probably has to be managed to the whole system.

  - The need to understand where there is an *absence of fit* which can be extremely damaging. For example, the Institute of Public Policy Research produced a report in 2009 pointing to the way in which failures to link up different arms of government was doing potential damage to the UK's national security.[26]

- *Relationship to VRIN.* It is these linkages and this fit that can be the bases of sustainable competitive advantage. In combination they may be *valuable* to clients, truly distinctive and therefore *rare.* Moreover, whilst individual components of an activity system might be relatively easy to imitate, in combination they may well constitute the complexity and causal ambiguity rooted in culture and history that makes them *difficult to imitate.*

However, it is not just at the conceptual level that activity maps are important; they can also be directly helpful in the management of strategy.

- *Disaggregation.*[27] Useful as an activity map is, the danger is that, in seeking to explain capabilities underpinning their strategy, managers may identify capabilities at too abstract a level. If the strategic benefits of activity systems are to be understood greater disaggregation is likely to be needed. For example, managers may talk of 'innovation' or 'putting the customer first' as a basis for 'good service'. These terms are too generic; they are umbrella descriptors of activities that exist at an even more operational level than those shown in the

ILLUSTRATION 3.5

Activity systems at Geelmuyden.Kiese

The strategic capabilities of an organisation can be understood and analysed in terms of linked activities (an activity system).

Geelmuyden.Kiese is a Scandinavian strategic communications consultancy – an extension of what has traditionally been known as public relations services (PR). Their clients include organisations in the financial, oil, energy, pharmaceuticals and health care sectors. These clients typically approach Geelmuyden.Kiese when they have a problem, the solution of which critically depends on effective external or internal communication. In this context, their services include facilitation of contacts with public agencies, officials and government, investor relations, media relations, communication campaigns for new product launches, crisis management and in-company communication on key strategic issues.

At the heart of the company's success is the knowledge they have built up since their founding in 1989 of the dynamics of decision making processes, often within influential bodies such as government and, linked to this, 'how effective communication may move power within those decision making processes'. This knowledge is underpinned by some key aspects in the way in which they do business (also see Figure 3.6).

- They seek to *work at a strategic level* with their clients, prioritising those clients where such work is especially valued. Here they employ their own in-house methodology, developed on the basis of years of experience and systematically review the assignments they undertake both internally and on the basis of client surveys.

- They take a clear stance on *integrity of communication*. They always advise openness of communication rather than suppression of information and only deal with clients that will accept such principles. They often take a stance on this approach in controversial and high profile issues in the public domain.

- Staff are given high degrees of *freedom* but with some absolute criteria of *responsibility*. In this regard there are strict rules for handling clients' confidential information and strict sanctions if such rules are broken.

- *Recruitment* is based on ensuring that such responsibility can be achieved. It is largely on the basis of values of openness and integrity but also humour. The emphasis tends to be on recruiting junior personnel and developing them. Geelmuyden.Kiese has learned that this is a better way of delivering its services than recruiting established 'high profile' consultants. Combined with its mentoring system for competence development of junior staff, they therefore believe that it offers the *best learning opportunities* in Scandinavia for young communications consultants.

- Geelmuyden.Kiese also offers *strong financial incentives* for top performance within the firm. Such performance includes rewards for the development of junior personnel but is also based on the internal evaluation of leadership qualities and performance.

activity map. If an activity map is to be useful for the purposes of managing activities then managers need to identify specific activities at an operating level that are manageable. To take an example from Illustration 3.5, there is the recognition that the mentoring of junior staff by partners is important; but the map itself does not show specifically how this is done. Managers need to delve further and further into explanations of how specific activities support other activities so as to eventually 'deliver' customer benefit. There are computer programs in existence that can be used for this purpose;[28] or it may be done more basically, for example by mapping activities on a large blank wall by using Post-its.[29]

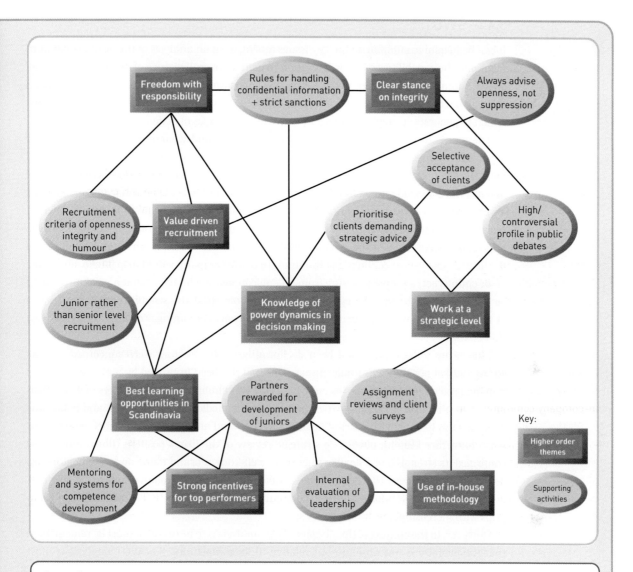

Questions

1 Assuming Geelmuyden.Kiese managers are correct that they have capabilities that provide competitive advantage:

   a What would competitors find difficult to imitate and why?

   b Are there any activities that could be done away with without threatening that advantage?

2 If disaggregation (see section 3.4.3) is important, suggest what even more specific activities underpinning those in the activity map that might be important.

● *Superfluous activities.* Just as in value chain analysis, but at a more detailed level, the question can be asked: are there activities that are not required in order to pursue a particular strategy? Or how do activities contribute to value creation? If activities do not do this, why are they being pursued by the organisation? Whether Ryanair used activity mapping or not, they have systematically identified and done away with many activities that other airlines commonly have. They are also continually seeking further activities that can be eliminated or outsourced to reduce cost.

3.4.4 SWOT[30]

It can be helpful to summarise the key issues arising from an analysis of the business environment and the capabilities of an organisation to gain an overall picture of its strategic position. **SWOT summarises the strengths, weaknesses, opportunities and threats likely to impact on strategy development** that arise from such analyses. This can also be useful as a basis against which to generate strategic options and assess future courses of action.

The aim is to identify the extent to which strengths and weaknesses are relevant to, or capable of dealing with, the changes taking place in the business environment. Illustration 3.6 takes the example of a pharmaceuticals firm (Pharmcare).[31] It assumes that key environmental impacts have been identified from analyses explained in Chapter 2 and that major strengths and weaknesses have been identified using the analytic tools explained in this chapter. A scoring mechanism (plus 5 to minus 5) is used as a means of getting managers to assess the interrelationship between the environmental impacts and the strengths and weaknesses of the firm. A positive (+) denotes that the strength of the company would help it take advantage of, or counteract, a problem arising from an environmental change or that a weakness would be offset by that change. A negative (−) score denotes that the strength would be reduced or that a weakness would prevent the organisation from overcoming problems associated with that change.

Pharmcare's share price had been declining because investors were concerned that its strong market position was under threat. This had not been improved by a merger that was proving problematic. The pharmaceutical market was changing with new ways of doing business, driven by new technology, the quest to provide medicines at lower cost and politicians seeking ways to cope with soaring health-care costs and an ever more informed patient. But was Pharmcare keeping pace? The strategic review of the firm's position (Illustration 3.6a) confirmed its strengths of a flexible salesforce, well-known brand name and new health-care department. However, there were major weaknesses, namely relative failure on low-cost drugs, competence in information and communication technology (ICT) and a failure to get to grips with increasingly well-informed users.

However, in the context of this chapter, if this analysis is to be useful, it must be remembered that the exercise is not absolute but relative to its competitors. So SWOT analysis is most useful when it is comparative – if it examines strengths, weaknesses, opportunities and threats in relation to competitors. When the impact of environmental forces on competitors was analysed (Illustration 3.6b), it showed that Pharmcare was still outperforming its traditional competitor (Company W), but potentially vulnerable to changing dynamics in the general industry structure courtesy of niche players (X and Y).

There are two main dangers in a SWOT exercise:

- *Listing.* A SWOT exercise can generate very long lists of apparent strengths, weaknesses, opportunities and threats, whereas what matters is to be clear about what is really important and what is less important. So prioritisation of issues matters.

- *A summary, not a substitute.* SWOT analysis is an engaging and fairly simple tool. It is also useful in summarising and consolidating other analysis that has been explained in Chapters 2 and 3. It is not, however, a substitute for that analysis. There are two dangers if it is used on its own. The first is that, in the absence of more thorough analysis, managers rely on preconceived, often inherited and biased views. The second is again the danger of a lack of specificity. Identifying very general strengths, for example, does not explain the underlying reasons for those strengths.

ILLUSTRATION 3.6

SWOT analysis of Pharmcare

A SWOT analysis explores the relationship between the environmental influences and the strategic capabilities of an organisation compared with its competitors.

(a) SWOT analysis for Pharmcare

	Environmental change (opportunities and threats)					
	Health care rationing	Complex and changing buying structures	Increased integration of health care	Informed patients	+	–
Strengths						
Flexible salesforce	+3	+5	+2	+2	12	0
Economies of scale	0	0	+3	+3	+6	0
Strong brand name	+2	+1	0	–1	3	–1
Health care education department	+4	+3	+4	+5	+16	0
Weaknesses						
Limited competences in biotechnology and genetics	0	0	–4	–3	0	–7
Ever lower R&D productivity	–3	–2	–1	–2	0	–8
Weak ICT competences	–2	–2	–5	–5	0	–14
Over-reliance on leading product	–1	–1	–3	–1	0	–6
Environmental impact scores	+9	+9	+9	+10		
	–6	–5	–14	–12		

(b) Competitor SWOT analyses

	Environmental change (opportunities and threats)				
	Health care rationing	Complex and changing buying structures	Increased integration of health care	Informed and passionate patients	Overall impact
Pharmcare *Big global player suffering fall in share price, low research productivity and post-mega-merger bureaucracy*	–3 Struggling to prove cost-effectiveness of new drugs to new regulators of health care rationing	+6 Well-known brand, a flexible salesforce combined with a new health care education department creates positive synergy	–3 Weak ICT and lack of integration following mergers means sales, research and admin. are all underperforming	–2 Have yet to get into the groove of patient power fuelled by the Internet	–2 Declining performance over time worsened after merger
Company W *Big pharma with patchy response to change, losing ground in new areas of competition*	–4 Focus is on old-style promotional selling rather than helping doctors control costs through drugs	–4 Traditional salesforce not helped by marketing which can be unaccommodating of national differences	+0 Alliances with equipment manufacturers but little work done across alliance to show dual use of drugs and new surgical techniques	+4 New recruits in the ICT department have worked cross-functionally to involve patients like never before	–4 Needs to modernise across the whole company
Organisation X *Partnership between a charity managed by people with venture capital experience and top hospital geneticists*	+3 Potentially able to deliver rapid advances in genetics-based illnesses	+2 Able possibly to bypass these with innovative cost-effective drug(s)	+2 Innovative drugs can help integrate health care through enabling patients to stay at home	+3 Patients will fight for advances in treatment areas where little recent progress has been made	+10 Could be the basis of a new business model for drug discovery – but all to prove as yet
Company Y *Only develops drugs for less common diseases*	+3 Partnering with big pharma allows the development of drugs discovered by big pharma but not economical for them to develop	0 Focus on small market segments so not as vulnerable to overall market structure, but innovative approach might be risky	+2 Innovative use of web to show why products still worthwhile developing even for less common illnesses	+1 Toll-free call centres for sufferers of less common illnesses Company, like patients, is passionate about its mission	+6 Novel approach can be considered either risky or a winner, or both!

Questions

1 What does the SWOT analysis tell us about the competitive position of Pharmcare with the industry as a whole?

2 How readily do you think executives of Pharmcare identify the strengths and weaknesses of competitors?

3 Identify the benefits and dangers (other than those identified in the text) of a SWOT analysis such as that in the illustration.

Prepared by Jill Shepherd, Segal Graduate School of Business, Simon Fraser University, Vancouver, Canada.

Figure 3.6 The TOWS matrix

	Internal factors	
	Strengths (S)	**Weaknesses (W)**
Opportunities (O)	**SO Strategic options** Generate options here that use srengths to take advantage of opportunities	**WO Strategic options** Generate options here that take advantage of opportunities by overcoming weaknesses
Threats (T)	**ST Strategic options** Generate options here that use srengths to avoid threats	**WT Strategic options** Generate options here that minimise weaknesses and avoid threats

External factors

SWOT can also help focus discussion on future choices and the extent to which an organisation is capable of supporting these strategies. A useful way of doing this is to use a TOWS matrix[32] as shown in Figure 3.6. This builds directly on the information in a SWOT exercise. Each box of the TOWS matrix can be used to identify options that address a different combination of the internal factors (strengths and weaknesses) and the external factors (opportunities and threats). For example, the top left-hand box prompts a consideration of options that use the strengths of the organisation to take advantage of opportunities in the business environment. An example for Pharmcare might be the re-training of the salesforce to deal with changes in pharmaceuticals buying. The bottom right-hand box prompts options that minimise weaknesses and also avoid threats; for Pharmcare this might include the need to develop their ICT systems to service better more informed patients. Quite likely this would also help take advantage of opportunities arising from changes in the buying structure of the industry (top right). The bottom left box suggests the need to use strengths to avoid threats, perhaps by building on the success of their health-care education department to also better service informed patients.

3.5 MANAGING STRATEGIC CAPABILITY

The previous section was concerned with diagnosing strategic capability. This section considers what managers might do to manage and improve resources and capabilities to the strategic benefit of their organisation.

One lesson that emerges from an understanding of the strategic importance of capabilities is that the basis of competitive advantage may lie in aspects of the organisation that are difficult to discern or be specific about. The first point is, then, to emphasise that, if managers are to manage the resources and capabilities of their organisation, the sort of analyses explained here, especially value chain analysis and activity systems mapping, are centrally important. If capabilities are not understood at these levels, there are dangers that managers may take the wrong course of action. For example, managers in an industrial cleaning company undertook an activity mapping exercise. It revealed that the way their van drivers dealt with collecting often filthy garments from industrial premises was especially valued by customers. This had developed through custom and practice, competitors did not do it and the managers themselves were not aware of it explicitly until they did the exercise. The irony was that they were just about to outsource the van delivery service! They were about to lose control of one of their bases of competitive advantage for the sake of cost reduction.

Assuming, then, that such analyses have been undertaken, what can managers do?

3.5.1 Managing activities for capability development[33]

There are different ways in which managers might develop strategic capabilities:

- *Internal capability development.* Could capabilities be added or upgraded so that they become more reinforcing of outcomes that deliver against critical success factors? This might be done, for example, by:

  - *Leveraging capabilities.*[34] Managers might identify strategic capabilities in one area of their organisation, perhaps customer service in one geographic business unit of a multi-national, that are not present in other business units. They might then seek to extend this throughout all the business units. Whilst this seems straightforward, studies[35] find it is not. The capabilities of one part of an organisation might not be easily transferred to another because of the problems of managing change (see Chapter 14).

  - *Stretching capabilities.* Managers may see the opportunity to build new products or services out of existing capabilities. Indeed, building new businesses in this way is the basis of related diversification, as explained in Chapter 7.

- *External capability development.* Similarly, there may be ways of developing capabilities by looking externally. For example, this could be by developing new capabilities by acquisition or entering into alliances and joint ventures (see Chapter 10).

- *Ceasing activities.* Could current activities, not central to the delivery of value to customers, be done away with, outsourced or reduced in cost? If managers are aware of the capabilities central to bases of competitive advantage, they can retain these and focus on areas of cost reduction that are less significant.

- *Monitor outputs and benefits* when it is not possible to fully understand capabilities. There are organisations where managers may know that there are activities that have a positive impact on competitive advantage, but may not fully understand just how such positive impact arises. For example, the delivery of value may be dependent on highly specialised skills as in a cutting-edge hi-tech firm; or on complex linkages far down in the organisation. Here managers may have to be careful about disturbing the bases of such capabilities whilst, at the same time, ensuring that they *monitor the outputs and benefits* created for customers.[36]

3.5.2 Managing people for capability development

One of the lessons of this chapter is that the bases of competitive advantage often lie in the day-to-day activities that people undertake in organisations, so developing the ability of people to recognise the relevance of what they do in terms of how that contributes to the strategy of the organisation is important. More specifically:

KEY DEBATE

The resource-based view of competitive advantage: is it useful to managers?

The view that the resource-based view explains the superior performance of firms has been questioned.

The resource-based view (RBV) of strategy has become highly influential. Much academic research has been carried out on it and managers readily talk about the importance of building on strategic capabilities or core competences to gain competitive advantage. However, some academics have raised questions about the value of RBV.

Scott Newbert[1] undertook a systematic assessment of 166 research studies employing RBV. He concluded that only 53% actually provided empirical evidence to support the claim that it explains the superior performance of firms. Others, too, have raised questions about the explanatory value of RBV.

The critique

Richard Priem and John Butler[2] raise the first two bases of the critique:

1. *The risk of tautology.* The underlying explanation of RBV is that the resource characteristics (or capabilities) that lead to competitive advantage are those that are valuable and rare. Since competitive advantage is defined in terms of value and rarity this verges on tautology. To say that a business performs better than another because it has superior resources or is better at some things than other businesses is not helpful unless it is possible to be specific about what capabilities are important, why and how they can be managed.

2. *The lack of specificity.* However, there is typically little specific in what is written about RBV. 'Top management skills' or 'innovatory capacity' mean little without being specific about the activities and processes that they comprise. And there is relatively little research that identifies such specifics or how they can be managed. Priem and Butler suggest this is particularly so with regard to the argued importance of tacit knowledge in bestowing competitive advantage: 'This may be descriptively correct, but it is likely to be quite difficult for practitioners to effectively manipulate that which is inherently unknowable.'

3. *Stability versus change.* A third critique is that RBV may only hold in relatively stable conditions where 'the rules of the game' in an industry remain relatively fixed.[3] In more unpredictable environments the value of resources can diminish, emphasising, of course, the importance of dynamic capabilities.

The response

Jay Barney,[4] one of the main proponents of RBV, accepts that there is a need to understand more about how resources are used and how people behave in bestowing competitive advantage. However, he defends the managerial relevance of RBV because he believes it highlights that managers need to identify and develop the most critical capabilities of a firm.

In his earlier writing[5] Barney argued that an organisation's culture could be a source of sustainable advantage provided it was valuable, rare and difficult to imitate. In such circumstances he suggested managers should 'nurture these cultures'. However, he went on to argue that:

> If one firm is able to modify its culture, then it is likely that others can as well. In this case the advantages associated with the culture are imitable and thus only a source of normal economic performance. Only when it is not possible to manage a firm's culture in a planned way does that culture have the potential of generating expected sustained superior financial performance.

In other words, he argues that valuable sources of competitive advantage are the intangible assets and resources or competences embedded in a culture in such a way that not only can competitors not imitate them, but managers cannot readily manage them. Priem and Butler would no doubt argue that this makes their point: that RBV is not very helpful in providing practical help to managers.

References:
1. S.L. Newbert, 'Empirical research on the Resource-based View of the Firm: an Assessment and Suggestions for Future Research', *Strategic Management Journal*, 28, 121–46, 2007.
2. R. Priem and J.E. Butler, 'Is the resource-based view a useful perspective for strategic management research?', *Academy of Management Review*, vol. 26, no. 1 (2001), pp. 22–40.
3. J. Kraaijenbrink, J.-C. Spender and A.J. Groen. 'The resource-based view: A review and assessment of its critiques', *Journal of Management*, 36, 1, 349–72, 2010.
4. J.B. Barney, 'Is the resource based view a useful perspective for strategic management research? Yes', *Academy of Management Review*, vol. 26, no. 1 (2001), pp. 41–56.
5. J.B. Barney, 'Organizational culture: can it be a source of sustained competitive advantage?', *Academy of Management Review*, vol. 11, no. 3 (1986), pp. 656–65.

Questions

1 How specific would the identification of strategic capabilities need to be to permit them to be managed to achieve competitive advantage?

2 Do you agree that if it were possible to identify and manage such capabilities they would be imitated?

3 Is the RBV useful?

- *Targeted training and development* may be possible. Often companies design training and development programmes that are very general. For strategic purposes it may be important to target the development of skills and competences which can provide competitive advantage.

- *Staffing policies* might be employed to develop particular competences. For example, an oil company that sought to build its competitive advantage around the building of close customer relationships in markets for industrial oils did so by ensuring that senior field managers with an aptitude for this were promoted and sent to different parts of the world that needed to be developed in such ways.

- *Organisational learning* may be recognised as central, particularly in fast-changing conditions. Here successful firms may be those that have grown the *dynamic capabilities* to continually readjust and refine bases of competitive advantage. In effect their competence becomes that of learning and development.

- *Develop people's awareness* that what they do in their jobs can matter at the strategic level. It is a common complaint in organisations that 'no one values what I do'. Helping people see how their work relates to the bigger strategic picture can both enhance the likelihood that they will, indeed, contribute positively to helping achieve competitive success and increase their motivation to do so.

Much of the discussion in this chapter builds on research and the writing of scholars who take a resource-based view of strategy. They therefore emphasise the central importance of managing resources and capabilities for competitive advantage. The Key Debate summarises the arguments for and against the practical value of such an approach.

SUMMARY

- *The competitive advantage* of an organisation is likely to be based on the strategic *capabilities* it has that are valuable to customers and that its rivals do not have or have difficulty in obtaining. Strategic capabilities comprise both *resources and competences*.

- The concept of *dynamic capabilities* highlights that strategic capabilities need to change as the market and environmental context of an organisation changes.

- Sustainability of competitive advantage is likely to depend on an organisation's capabilities being of at least *threshold value* in a market but also being *valuable*, relatively *rare, inimitable and non-substitutable*.

- Ways of *diagnosing organisational capabilities* include:

  - *Benchmarking* as a means of understanding the relative performance of organisations.

  - Analysing an organisation's *value chain* and *value network* as a basis for understanding how value to a customer is created and can be developed.

  - *Activity mapping* as a means of identifying more detailed activities which underpin strategic capabilities.

  - *SWOT analysis* as a way of drawing together an understanding of strengths, weaknesses, opportunities and threats an organisation faces.

- Managers need to think about how and to what extent they can manage the *development of strategic capabilities* of their organisation by internal and external capability development and by the way they manage people in their organisation.

WORK ASSIGNMENTS

*✱ Denotes more advanced work assignments. * Refers to a case study in the Text and Cases edition.*

3.1 Using Tables 3.1 and 3.2 identify the resources and competences of an organisation with which you are familiar. You can answer this in relation to Dyson, Amazon* or Formula One* if you wish.

3.2✱ Undertake an analysis of the strategic capability of an organisation with which you are familiar in order to identify which capabilities, if any, meet the criteria of (a) value, (b) rarity, (c) inimitability and (d) non-substitutability (see section 3.3). You can answer this in relation to Dyson, Amazon* or Formula One* if you so wish.

3.3✱ For an industry or public service consider how the strategic capabilities that have been the basis of competitive advantage (or best value in the public sector) have changed over time. Why have these changes occurred? How did the relative strengths of different companies or service providers change over this period? Why?

3.4 Undertake a value chain or network analysis for an organisation of your choice (referring to Illustration 3.4 could be helpful). You can answer this in relation to a case study in the book such as Tesco* or Ryanair* if you wish.

3.5✱ For a benchmarking exercise for which you have access, make a critical assessment of the benefits and dangers of the approach that was taken.

Integrative assignment

3.6 Prepare a SWOT analysis for an organisation of your choice and in relation to competitors (see Illustration 3.6). Explain why you have chosen each of the factors you have included in the analysis, in particular their relationship to other analyses you have undertaken in Chapters 2 and 3. What are the conclusions you arrive at from your analysis and how would these inform an evaluation of strategy (see Chapter 11)?

VIDEO ASSIGNMENT

Visit *MyStrategyLab* and watch the *Maersk* case study.

1 What are the strategic capabilities that Maersk claim provide them with competitive advantage in the global freight market?

2 Drawing on VRIN, suggest on what bases might these be sustainable over time.

RECOMMENDED KEY READINGS

- For an understanding of the resource-based view of the firm, an early and much cited paper is by Jay Barney: 'Firm resources and sustained competitive advantage', *Journal of Management*, vol. 17 (1991), pp. 99–120. For a review of the development of RBV and evidence of its explanatory power see: Scott Newbert, 'Empirical research on the Resource Based View of the firm: an assessment and suggestions for future research', *Strategic Management Journal*, vol. 28 (2007), pp. 121–46.

- The concept of Dynamic Capabilities is reviewed in C.L. Wang and P.K. Ahmed, 'Dynamic Capabilities: a review and research agenda', *International Journal of Management Reviews*, vol. 9, no. 1 (2007), pp. 31–52

and by Veronique Ambrosini and Cliff Bowman, 'What are dynamic capabilities and are they a useful construct in strategic management?', *International Journal of Management Reviews*, vol. 11, no. 1 (2009), pp. 29–49.

- Michael Porter explains how mapping activity systems can be important in considering competitive strategy in his article 'What is strategy?' (*Harvard Business Review*, Nov–Dec 1996, pp. 61–78).

- For a critical discussion of the use and misuse of SWOT analysis see T. Hill and R. Westbrook, 'SWOT analysis: it's time for a product recall', *Long Range Planning*, vol. 30, no. 1 (1997), pp. 46–52.

REFERENCES

1. The concept of resource-based strategies was introduced by B. Wernerfelt, 'A resource-based view of the firm', *Strategic Management Journal*, vol. 5, no. 2, pp. 171–80, 1984. A much cited paper is by Jay Barney: 'Firm resources and sustained competitive advantage', *Journal of Management*, vol. 17 (1991), no. 1, pp. 99–120. There are now many books and papers that explain and summarise the approach: for example D. Hoopes, T. Madsen and G. Walker in the special issue of the *Strategic Management Journal*, 'Why is there a resource based view?' (vol. 24, no. 10, pp. 889–902, 2003) and J. Barney and D. Clark, *Resource-Based Theory: Creating and Sustaining Competitive Advantage*, Oxford University Press, 2007.

2. For summary papers on dynamic capabilities see C.L. Wang and P.K. Ahmed, 'Dynamic Capabilities: a review and research agenda', *International Journal of Management Reviews*, 9, 1, 31–52, 2007 and V. Ambrosini and C. Bowman, 'What are dynamic capabilities and are they a useful construct in strategic management?', *International Journal of Management Reviews*, 11, 1, 29–49, 2009. Also see C. Helfat, S. Finkelstein, W. Mitchell, M. Peteraf, H. Singh, D. Teece and S. Winter, *Dynamic Capabilities: Understanding Strategic Change in Organizations*, Blackwell Publishing, 2007.

3. David Teece has written about dynamic capabilities originally in D.J. Teece, G. Pisano and A. Shuen: 'Dynamic capabilities and strategic management', *Strategic Management Journal*, vol. 18 (1997), no. 7, pp. 509–34. More recently he has expanded his explanation in D. Teece, Explicating dynamic capabilities: the nature and micro-foundations of (sustainable) enterprise performance, *Strategic Management Journal*, 28, 1319–50, 2007, pp. 1320–1.

4. D. Leonard-Barton, 'Core capabilities and core rigidities: a paradox in managing new product development', *Strategic Management Journal*, vol. 13, pp. 111–25, 1992.

5. K.M. Eisenhardt and J.A. Martin, 'Dynamic capabilities: what are they?', *Strategic Management Journal*, vol. 21 (2000), no. 10/11, pp. 1105–21.

6. Gary Hamel and C.K. Prahalad were the academics who promoted the idea of core competences. For example, G. Hamel and C.K. Prahalad, 'The core competence of the corporation', *Harvard Business Review*, vol. 68, no. 3 (1990), pp. 79–91. The idea of driving strategy development from the resources and competences of an organisation is discussed in G. Hamel and C.K. Prahalad, 'Strategic intent', *Harvard Business Review*, vol. 67, no. 3 (1989), pp. 63–76; and G. Hamel and C.K. Prahalad, 'Strategy as stretch and leverage', *Harvard Business Review*, vol. 71, no. 2 (1993), pp. 75–84.

7. The VRIN criteria were originally introduced by Jay Barney in his 1991 paper (see 1 above).

8. For a discussion of the concept of value, see C. Bowman and V. Ambrosini, 'Identifying valuable resources', *European Management Journal*, 25, 4, 320–9, 2007.

9. 'Can Apple survive without Steve Jobs', *Sunday Times*, 18 January 2009.

10. This is borne out in a meta-study of research on RBV by S.L. Newbert, 'Empirical, research on the Resource Based View of the firm: an assessment and suggestions for future research, *Strategic Management Journal*, 28, 121–46, 2007.

11. The seminal paper on causal ambiguity is S. Lippman and R. Rumelt, 'Uncertain imitability: an analysis of interfirm differences in efficiency under competition', *Bell Journal of Economics*, vol. 13 (1982), pp. 418–38.

12. The distinction between and importance of characteristic and linkage ambiguity is explained by A.W. King and C.P. Zeithaml in 'Competencies and firm performance: examining the causal ambiguity paradox', *Strategic Management Journal*, vol. 22 (2001), no. 1, pp. 75–99.

13. For a fuller discussion of path dependency in the context of strategic capabilities, see D. Holbrook, W. Cohen, D. Hounshell and S. Klepper, 'The nature, sources and consequences of firm differences in the early history of the semiconductor industry', *Strategic Management Journal*, vol. 21, nos 10–11 (2000), pp. 1017–42.

14. The importance of non-substitutability and ways of identifying possible bases of substitution are discussed in M.A. Peteraf and M.E. Bergen, 'Scanning dynamic competitive landscapes: a market and resource based framework', *Strategic Management Journal*, vol. 24, no. 10 (2003), pp. 1027–42.

15. The importance of analysing and understanding knowledge is discussed in I. Nonaka and H. Takeuchi, *The Knowledge-creating Company*, Oxford University Press, 1995. There are also collections of articles on organisational knowledge: e.g. the Special Issue of the *Strategic Management Journal* edited by R. Grant and J.-C. Spender, vol. 17, 1996 and the *Harvard Business Review on Knowledge Management*, HBR Press, 1998. More recently Mark Easterby-Smith and Isabel Prieto have explored the relationships in: 'Dynamic capabilities and knowledge management: an integrative role for learning', *British Journal of Management*, 19, 235–49, 2008.

16. See I. Nonaka and H. Takeuchi, 15 above.

17. E.C. Wenger and W.M. Snyder, 'Communities of practice: the organisational frontier', *Harvard Business Review*, vol. 73 (Jan–Feb 2000), no. 3, pp. 201–7 and E. Wenger, *Communities of Practice: Learning, Meaning and Identity*, Cambridge University Press, 1999.

18. See R. Camp, *Benchmarking: the Search for Industry Best Practices that Lead to Superior Performance*, Quality Press, 2006.

19. See A. Murdoch, 'Lateral benchmarking, or what Formula One taught an airline', *Management Today*, November 1997, pp. 64–7. See also the Formula One case study in the case study section of this book (Text and Cases version only).

20. An extensive discussion of the value chain concept and its application can be found in M.E. Porter, *Competitive Advantage*, Free Press, 1985.

21. For an extended example of value chain analysis see 'Understanding and using value chain analysis' by Andrew Shepherd in *Exploring Techniques of Analysis and Evaluation in Strategic Management* edited by Veronique Ambrosini, Prentice Hall, 1998.

22. The importance of profit pools is discussed by O. Gadiesh and J.L. Gilbert in 'Profit pools: a fresh look at strategy', *Harvard Business Review*, vol. 76 (May–June 1998), no. 3, pp. 139–47.

23. H. Schultz and D. Yang Young, *Pour your Heart Into It*, Hyperion, 1997.

24. See M. Porter, 'What is Strategy?' (*Harvard Business Review*, Nov–Dec, 61–78, 1996) and N. Siggelkow, 'Evolution towards fit', *Administrative Science Quarterly*, 47, 1, 125–59, 2002.

25. We are grateful for this example based on the doctoral dissertation of Bjorn Haugstad, Strategy as the Intentional Structuration of Practice, Translation of Formal Strategies into Strategies in Practice, submitted to the Said Business School, University of Oxford in 2009.

26. The Institute of Public Policy Research, Shared Responsibilities, National Security Strategy for the UK, 2009.

27. 'Disaggregation' is a term used by D. Collis and C. Montgomery, 'Competing on resources', *Harvard Business Review*, July–August, 140–50, 2008.

28. A good example of such computer-based systems for analysing organisational capabilities can be found in a paper by C. Eden and F. Ackermann, 'Mapping distinctive competencies: a systemic approach', *Journal of the Operational Research Society*, vol. 51 (2000), no. 1, pp. 12–20.

29. For a more comprehensive account of the use of such network mapping, see V. Ambrosini, *Tacit and Ambiguous Resources as Sources of Competitive Advantage*, Palgrave Macmillan, 2003. Also see Chapter 6 of *Making Strategy* by F. Ackermann and C. Eden with I. Brown, Sage Publications, 2005.

30. The idea of SWOT as a common-sense checklist has been used for many years: for example, S. Tilles, 'Making strategy explicit', in I. Ansoff (ed.), *Business Strategy*, Penguin, 1968. See also T. Jacobs, J. Shepherd and G. Johnson's chapter on SWOT analysis in V. Ambrosini (ed.), *Exploring Techniques of Strategy Analysis and Evaluation*, Prentice Hall, 1998. For a critical discussion of the (mis)use of SWOT, see T. Hill and R. Westbrook, 'SWOT analysis: it's time for a product recall', *Long Range Planning*, vol. 30 (1997), no. 1, pp. 46–52.

31. For background reading on the pharmaceutical industry see, for example, 'The drug industry – from bench to bedside', *The Economist*, 4 November 2006, and *Science Business* by Gary Pisano, Harvard Business School Press, 2006.

32. See H. Weihrich, 'The TOWS matrix – a tool for situational analysis', *Long Range Planning*, April 1982, pp. 54–66.

33. For a fuller discussion of how managers may manage strategic capabilities, see C. Bowman and N. Collier, 'A contingency approach to resource-creation processes', *International Journal of Management Reviews*, 8, 4, 191–211, 2006.

34. Leveraging is a term used by D. Collis and C. Montgomery (see 27 above).

35. See C.A. Maritan and T.H. Brush, 'Heterogeneity and transferring practices: implementing flow practices in multiple plants', *Strategic Management Journal*, vol. 24 (2003), no. 10, pp. 945–60.

36. This observation is made by Veronique Ambrosini in her book (see 29 above).

'Inside Dyson': a distinctive company?

Jill Shepherd, Segal Graduate School of Business, Simon Fraser University, Vancouver, Canada

Dyson is a private company, famous for its distinctive vacuum cleaners. It is not listed on a stock market and James Dyson, its founder and master inventor, has accumulated a personal fortune of over £1bn (~€1.1bn; ~$1.5bn). He is the sole owner of the company and is one of the few people to appear on Top Rich lists who has made money from his own inventions.

In 2005 the profit of the company reached £100m despite selling fewer vacuum cleaners than competitor Hoover. In terms of value rather than units sold, Dyson sells more in the US than Hoover, a company it sued for patent infringement winning around $5 (~€3.5) million. It is a global company, distributing its products in 45 countries including competitive markets such as China, the USA and Japan, as well as in its home market of the UK.

The company is built upon innovative products that are marketed as robust, presented well in bright colours and often in advertisements featuring James Dyson himself. From bag-less vacuum cleaners to energy-efficient and time-efficient hand-dryers for public places, to desk fans with no blades; all of the products are distinctive. His latest idea involves space saving kitchen appliances and even whole kitchens. All elements of the kitchens will be cubes with controls sliding into the main body so that the cubes fit and stack together into bigger cubes.

It hasn't all been straightforward success though, Dyson was about to launch a vacuum that could pick up water and dust. Customers were suspicious that such '3 in 1' products would not work and were not at all positive about wetting their carpets no matter how attractive the product design. Similarly a purple and silver washing machine with two rotating drums did not sell well and was also withdrawn.

Sir James Dyson

Dyson promote a story of their own heritage that suggests that the way the company works today is a function of the early career development path of its

Source: Getty Images.

leader. Dyson studied in art schools, rebelling against his family's tradition of reading Classics at Cambridge University. At art school he sought to apply engineering to functional problems in a way that respected design as an art. His first commercially successful vacuum product used cyclone technology. But from the beginning, he had problems convincing manufacturers both that the technology could be transferred to vacuum cleaners and could be patented. His confident answer was to set up his own firm: adopting unconventional routes and taking risks are still embedded within the organisational culture of Dyson.

Though, by 2010, the company was run by CEO Martin McCourt, James Dyson's own image and personal brand remained central to the firm's promotion. Apart from featuring in many of their adverts, he was highly visible beyond corporate boundaries. He appears to enjoy promoting engineering and design. He finances yearly design awards, collaborated with fashion designer Issey Miyake in an engineering themed fashion show and attempted to fund a Dyson School of Design Innovation. This latter endeavour was abandoned when the UK government put too many hurdles in its way thus limiting Dyson's own independence.

Engineering and design

Investment in R&D at Dyson quadrupled between 2004 and 2009. Dyson HQ is in a rural part of the west of England and is home to 350 engineers and scientists as well as the usual company personnel. It is also linked to 20 specialist laboratories all close by. Their large testing facility in Malaysia operates continually with over 120 testing stations. The operation in the UK employs 1200 varied people: some experienced, some freshly qualified, some with 'way out' ideas. James Dyson has said:

> 'We want people who are creative and courageous – unconditioned fresh-thinkers. We don't strap people into a suit and plonk them behind a desk, we like to give people the chance to make a difference.'

Success revolves around engineering ideas that are fine-tuned, not always on computer screens, but in the hands of engineers who make 100s, even 1000s of prototypes. Special computerised technology helps the engineers develop prototypes but they also use plasticine, cardboard or whatever material they wish to make prototypes in an almost child-like fashion. The engineers will tell you that the journey from prototype to prototype is an iterative journey of failures that creates new ideas. In walkabouts and feedbacks, they are encouraged to fiddle, to 'take the road less travelled' and to be 'less than sensible'. The same engineers report that, whilst competitors may have good robust engineering, they are not as inventive in terms of initial ideas and do not have the persistence and patience to make wacky ideas work in robust terms.

There is a clear corporate-level commitment to product development with half of all profit being channelled into the creation of new ideas supported by their mantra of *thinking, testing, breaking, questioning*. It is product engineering that takes centre stage on the company website and generally in all company communications. This company is obvious in its desire to promote the idea that a Dyson product means new, different, a radical change: a Dyson product whether vacuum or washing machine *is* an innovation and the bright colours help these clever products stand out from the crowd. For example,

the Dyson air multiplier™ performs the same function as a conventional air fan but in a radically different way. Conventional fans cause buffering of the air as the blades interrupt its flow. The multiplier™ 'amplifies surrounding air, giving an uninterrupted stream of flow of smooth air'. When you look at its sleek design you wonder whether it is a function of the innovation in engineering or design or the blurring of the two. Either way, design is deeply embedded in engineering and of all the capabilities at Dyson engineering is king.

Unlike Apple, another design great, who designs then subcontracts all manufacturing, Dyson believe the combination of design engineering and manufacturing is crucial in developing the most inimitable competences that can be protected through patents. Dyson believes in patents to protect its differentiated products, but this does not mean competitors do not try to imitate. Within Dyson's vacuums there is 'patented Ball technology for improved manoeuvrability'. The Miele equivalent has 'unique swivel head technology'. Hoover USA has Wind Tunnel vacuums available in 'fresh colours'. Dyson's colours are usually bright and it does launch exclusive editions based on novel colours. Dyson's hand-blade hand dryer wipes water off your hands in seconds using less energy rather than evaporating water as in standard hand dryers. The competitor product from US specialists in hand drying, the Xlerator, also claims to dry hands in seconds and with far less energy than standard hand dryers. The Dyson desk fan has 11 patent separate applications and involved every discipline within the company.

Global working

James Dyson was heavily criticised in the UK press for taking the managerial decision to place the manufacturing part of his vacuum value chain in Malaysia and later that of his hand dryers in Nanjing in China. He needed, he said, to follow competitors to lower cost manufacturing as margins were being eaten away. One hundred jobs were lost in the UK in the first move and several hundred in the second. Later, with manufacturing costs down and profits up, more engineers were hired in the UK. James Dyson says the decision to move to Malaysia was not an easy one for him. It was not solely based on cost but also his belief that he needed to have a testing facility nearer to suppliers and those were all in the East. In contrast, Miele and Excel Dryer Corporation keep their manufacturing in their home countries.

Dyson and its competitors

Company	Location of headquarters	Product range	Manufacturing locations	Relative company size (1 largest, 5 smallest) based on approximate global turnover	Distribution	Distinctive capabilities?
Dyson	UK	Vacuums, fan, hand dryers, moving into integrated kitchens and robotic vacuums following the success of iRobots	Asia	4	Own online and through retail outlets	Engineering design
Electrolux	Sweden	Range of vacuums, washing machines, fridges and ovens and a robotic vacuum	Not known	2	Retail outlets	Emphasis on energy-saving products Brand licensing of over 50 brands
Hoover (Techtronic Floor Care Technology Limited)	USA and Hong Kong for (TTI)	Vacuums and for TTI Floor Care power tools, outdoor power equipment, floor care appliances, solar-powered lighting and electronic measuring products In USA Hoover range includes patented and trade-marked 'Wind Tunnel' with no loss of suction	Not known, possibly various around Asia	1	Vacuums sold through retail outlets and own online shop in the USA	Possibly the sheer scale of its global operations rather than any particular capability gives it the edge?
Hoover Limited	UK (Italy)	Vacuums and a wide range of domestic appliances			Hoovers sold in retail outlets and online accessories only	
Miele	Germany	Domestic appliances from microwaves to wine storage	Germany ('90% of value creation within Germany')	3	Only through stores including Miele stores, Miele specialists and Miele studios Online stores also	Engineering that results in highly reliable and robust products
Excel Dryer Corporation	USA	A range of hand dryers	USA (products very much advertised as 'Made in USA')	5	Can be bought direct or through licensed distributors Sees end users (e.g. restaurants), distributors, architects and government as customers	Transformation possibly, given the choice by new owner in 1997 to collaborate with a partner – Invent Resources – that produced the Xlerator product and changed the financial profile of the company

Dyson claims to be helping national competitiveness by pulling the UK up the value chain as global competition heats up. China claims contracts like Dyson's help pull China up the manufacturing value chain too towards ever more complex products of the highest quality. Dyson himself appears to view China as a major market. He has made choices to reflect that, such as launching his hand dryers there by offering them free to the Sofitel Hotel in Nanjing. As the costs of making things seem to be an ever decreasing part of the price a consumer pays, perhaps design and development are the future.

Dyson's secrecy of success

Undoubtedly a success story, it is a firm that prefers to keep its secret of success just that – secret. So much is evident, for example in their UK HQ. Access to the building and then subsequent areas is via thumb print and even then some areas are out of bounds. They have

even developed their own sound-absorbing panels to ensure that conversations can be kept secret.

Postscript: In March 2010 James Dyson stood down as chairman, although he maintained his role as 'chief inventor'.

Questions

1 Using frameworks from the chapter, analyse the strategic capabilities of Dyson.

2 To what extent do you think any of the capabilities can be imitated by competitors?

3 Which of Dyson's distinctive capabilities may, over time, become threshold capabilities?

4 Bearing in mind your answers to questions 1 and 2, how crucial is Sir James Dyson to the future of of the company? What might be the effect of his completely leaving or selling the company?

4

STRATEGIC PURPOSE

Learning outcomes

After reading this chapter you should be able to:

● Consider appropriate ways to express the *strategic purpose* of an organisation in terms of *statements of purpose*, *values*, *vision*, *mission* or *objectives*.

● Identify the components of the *governance chain* of an organisation.

● Understand differences in *governance structures* and the advantages and disadvantages of these.

● Identify differences in the *corporate responsibility* stances taken by organisations and how *ethical issues* relate to strategic purpose.

● Undertake *stakeholder analysis* as a means of identifying the influence of different stakeholder groups in terms of their power and interest.

Key terms

Corporate governance p. 123

Corporate social responsibility p. 134

Governance chain p. 124

Mission statement p. 120

Objectives p. 121

Power p. 145

Stakeholder mapping p. 141

Stakeholders p. 119

Statements of corporate values p. 121

Vision statement p. 121

(4.1) INTRODUCTION

In September 2008 Lehman Brothers, then the fourth largest investment bank in the United States, collapsed: the biggest banking collapse in history. The view of the financial press was that the failure was avoidable. In their view central to the problem was, not only a flawed strategy, but the failure of the Lehman board to be more responsible and proactive in monitoring and constraining CEO Dick Fuld's reckless pursuit of that strategy. It was a failure of both strategy and governance.

The previous two chapters have looked respectively at the influence of the environment and capabilities on an organisation's strategic position. These were important in the downfall of Lehman Brothers, but this case also shows the importance of being clear about what purposes drive the strategy of organisations, who influences such purposes and who monitors performance against them. These are the concerns of this chapter. An important concept here is that of **stakeholders, those individuals or groups that depend on an organisation to fulfil their own goals and on whom, in turn, the organisation depends.** An underlying question is whether the strategic purpose of the organisation should be determined in response to the expectations of a particular stakeholder, for example shareholders in the case of a commercial enterprise, or to broader stakeholder interests – at the extreme society and the social good. Figure 4.1 summarises the different influences on strategic purpose discussed in the chapter:

KEY CONCEPT

Stakeholders

- The chapter begins in section 4.2 by developing the discussion in Chapter 1 about different ways in which organisations express *strategic purpose*, including statements of *values*, *vision*, *mission* and *objectives*.

- Section 4.3 considers *corporate governance* and the *regulatory framework* within which organisations operate. The concern is with the way in which formally constituted bodies

Figure 4.1 Influences on strategic purpose

such as investors or boards influence strategic purpose through the formalised processes of supervising executive decisions and actions. In turn this raises issues of *accountability*: who are strategists accountable to? Differences in the approach to corporate governance internationally are also discussed.

- Section 4.4 is concerned with issues of *social responsibility and ethics*. Here the question is which purposes an organisation *should* fulfil. How should managers respond to the expectations society has of their organisations, both in terms of *corporate responsibility* and in terms of the *behaviour of individuals* within organisations, not least themselves?

- In all this it is, then, important to understand *different stakeholder expectations* and their relative influence on strategic purpose. This requires an understanding of both the *power* and *interest* of different stakeholder groups. This is addressed through *stakeholder analysis* in section 4.5.

4.2 ORGANISATIONAL PURPOSE: VALUES, MISSION, VISION AND OBJECTIVES

It is executives who form a view on the purpose of their organisation. It can be that an explicit statement of such a purpose is expected of the organisation by one or more stakeholders; or that managers themselves decide such a statement is useful; or that a founding entrepreneur's initial purpose has an enduring legacy. The purpose of an organisation may be expressed in different ways.

4.2.1 Statements of mission, vision and value

Harvard University's Cynthia Montgomery[1] argues that defining and expressing a clear and motivating purpose for the organisation is at the core of a strategist's job. In the absence of such clarity, the strategy of an organisation is a mystery to those who work within the organisation and those who observe it from the outside. They end up having to interpret for themselves why the organisation is doing what it is doing. Montgomery's view is that the stated purpose of the organisation must address the question: what is the organisation there to do that makes a difference, and to whom? If the stakeholders of an organisation can relate to such a purpose it can be highly motivating. So Montgomery suggests that executives need to find ways of expressing strategic purpose in ways that are easy to grasp and that people can relate to. There are three ways in which executives typically attempt to do this:

Mission
statement

- A **mission statement** aims **to provide employees and stakeholders with clarity about the overriding purpose of the organisation**, sometimes referred to in terms of the apparently simple but challenging question: 'What business are we in?' A mission statement should make this clear in terms of long-term purpose. The two linked questions managers need to ask are 'What would be lost if the organisation did not exist?' and 'How do we make a difference?' Though they do not use the term 'mission statement', Jim Collins and Jerry Porras[2] suggest this can best be addressed by managers starting with a descriptive statement of what the organisation does, then repeatedly delving deeper into the purpose of what the organisation is there for by asking 'why do we do this?' They use the example of managers in a gravel and asphalt company arriving at the conclusion that its mission is to make people's lives better by improving the quality of built structures.

- A **vision statement is concerned with the desired future state of the organisation;** an aspiration that will enthuse, gain commitment and stretch performance. So here the question is: 'What do we want to achieve?' Porras and Collins suggest managers can identify this by asking: 'If we were sitting here in twenty years what do we want to have created or achieved?' They cite the example of Henry Ford's original vision in the very early days of automobile production that the ownership of a car should be within the reach of everyone.

- **Statements of corporate values communicate the underlying and enduring core 'principles' that guide an organisation's strategy and define the way that the organisation should operate.**[3] So a question to ask is: 'Would these values change with circumstances?' And if the answer is 'yes' then they are not 'core' and not 'enduring'. An example is the importance of leading-edge research in some universities. Whatever the constraints on funding, such universities hold to the enduring centrality of this.

Illustration 4.1 shows examples of mission, vision and value statements. Many critics regard such statements as bland and too wide-ranging.[4] However, they have become widely adopted, arguably because if there is substantial disagreement within the organisation or with stakeholders as to its mission or vision, there can be real problems in resolving the strategic direction of the organisation. So they can be a useful means of focusing debate on the fundamentals of the organisation.

Collins and Porras claim that the long-run success of many US corporates – such as Disney, General Electric or 3M – can be attributed (at least in part) to their clarity on such statements of purpose.[5] There are, however, potential downsides to public statements of corporate purpose and values if an organisation demonstrably fails to live them out in practice. For example, Lehman Brothers' (see Illustration 4.2) 2007 annual report included twelve principles amongst which were 'doing the right thing', 'demonstrating a commitment to excellence', 'demonstrating smart risk management', 'acting always with ownership mentality' and, of course, 'maximizing shareholder value'.

4.2.2 Objectives

Whether or not organisations use mission, vision or value statements, they use objectives. **Objectives are statements of specific outcomes that are to be achieved** and are often expressed in financial terms. They could be the expression of desired sales or profit levels, rates of growth, dividend levels or share valuation.[6] Organisations may also have market-based objectives, many of which are quantified as targets – such as market share, customer service, repeat business and so on. Increasingly organisations are also setting objectives referred to as 'the triple bottom line', by which is meant not only economic objectives such as those above, but also environmental and social objectives to do with their corporate responsibility to wider society (see section 4.4.1 below).

There are three related issues that managers need to consider with regard to setting objectives.

- *Objectives and measurement.* Some managers argue that objectives are not helpful unless their achievement can be measured. Certainly there are times when specific quantified objectives are required, for example when urgent action is needed and it becomes essential for management to focus attention on a limited number of priority requirements – as in a

ILLUSTRATION 4.1

Mission, vision and values statements

Can well-crafted statements of mission, vision or values be an important means of motivating an organisation's stakeholders?

Whirpool

Vision

Every home . . . Everywhere . . . with Pride, Passion and Performance.

Our vision reinforces that every home is our domain, every customer and customer activity our opportunity. This vision fuels the passion that we have for our customers, pushing us to provide innovative solutions to uniquely meet their needs.

Pride . . . in our work and each other.

Passion . . . for creating unmatched customer loyalty for our brands.

Performance . . . that excites and rewards global investors with superior returns.

We bring this vision to life through the power of our unique global enterprise and our outstanding people . . . working together . . . everywhere.

Mission

Everyone, passionately creating loyal customers for life.

Our mission defines our focus and what we do differently to create value. We are a company of people captivated with creating loyal customers. From every job, across every contact, we will build unmatched customer loyalty . . . one customer at a time.

Values

Our values are constant and define the way that all Whirlpool Corporation employees are expected to behave and conduct business everywhere in the world.

Respect – We must trust one another as individuals and value the capabilities and contributions of each person.

Integrity – We must conduct all aspects of business honorably – ever mindful of the longtime Whirlpool Corporation belief that there is no right way to do a wrong thing.

Diversity and Inclusion – We must maintain the broad diversity of Whirlpool people and ideas. Diversity honors differences, while inclusion allows everyone to contribute. Together, we create value.

Teamwork – We must recognize that pride results in working together to unleash everyone's potential, achieving exceptional results.

Spirit of Winning – We must promote a Whirlpool culture that enables individuals and teams to reach and take pride in extraordinary results and further inspire the 'Spirit of Winning' in all of us.

Age Concern

Our mission

Our mission is to promote the well-being of all older people and to help make later life a fulfilling and enjoyable experience.

Principles

Values and principles underpin what we do, why we do it, and guide how we work to achieve our mission. Our underlying principles are:

- Ageism is unacceptable: we are against all forms of unfair discrimination, and challenge unfair treatment on grounds of age
- All people have the right to make decisions about their lives: we help older people to discover and exercise these rights
- People less able to help themselves should be offered support: we seek to support older people to live their lives with dignity
- Diversity is valued in all that we do: we recognise the diversity of older people and their different needs, choices, cultures and values
- It is only through working together that we can use our local, regional and national presence to the greatest effect.

Values

Our work is also guided by a set of values:

- Enabling: we enable older people to live independently and exercise choice.
- Influential: we draw strength from the voices of older people, and ensure that those voices are heard.
- Dynamic: we are innovative and driven by results and constantly deliver for older people.
- Caring: we are passionate about what we do and care about each individual.
- Expert: we are authoritative, trusted and quality-orientated.

Sources: Whirlpool and Age Concern websites 2010.

Questions

1 Which of these statements do you think are likely to motivate which stakeholders? Why?

2 Could any of them have been improved? How?

3 Identify other statements of mission, vision, purpose or values that you think are especially well crafted and explain why.

turnaround situation (see section 14.5.1). If the choice is between going out of business and surviving, there is no room for latitude through vaguely stated requirements. However, it may be that in other circumstances – for example, in trying to raise the aspirations of people in the organisation – more attention needs to be paid to qualitative statements of purpose such as mission or vision statements than to quantified objectives.

● *Identifying core objectives.*[7] Managers in most companies set objectives which are financial in nature because they recognise that unless adequate profits are made to satisfy shareholders and allow for reinvestment in the business, it will not survive. It may be, however, that there are other aspects of business performance upon which survival and prosperity of the business are based. For example, how the organisation is distinctive from its rivals, or how it is to achieve competitive advantage and sustain it. As Chapter 3 pointed out, this is likely to be on the basis of capabilities that are valued by customers and distinctive from competition. Identifying objectives that capture the bases of such competitive advantage and allow monitoring of performance against it become crucial too. For example, low-cost airlines such as Southwestern in the US set an objective on turnaround time for their aircraft because this is at the core of their distinctive low-cost advantage.

● *Objectives and control.* A recurring problem with objectives is that managers and employees 'lower down' in the hierarchy are unclear as to how their day-to-day work contributes to the achievement of a higher level of objectives. This could, in principle, be addressed by a 'cascade' of objectives – defining a set of detailed objectives at each level in the hierarchy. Many organisations attempt to do this. Here consideration needs to be given to a trade-off: how to achieve required levels of clarity on strategy without being over-restrictive in terms of the latitude people have,[8] an issue discussed in section 13.3.3).

Whatever statements of mission, vision, values are employed, or whatever the objectives that are set, it is important to understand who influences what they are. The rest of the chapter examines this.

CORPORATE GOVERNANCE[9]

Corporate governance is concerned with the structures and systems of control by which managers are held accountable to those who have a legitimate stake in an organisation.[10] These are the stakeholders that, in ownership and management terms, influence an organisation. Governance has become an increasingly important issue for organisations for three main reasons.

● *The separation of ownership and management control* of organisations (which is now the norm except with very small businesses) means that most organisations operate within a hierarchy, or chain, of governance. This chain represents those groups that influence an organisation through their involvement in either ownership or management of an organisation.

● *Corporate failures and scandals*, such as that of Enron in 2001 and Lehman Brothers and the Royal Bank of Scotland in 2008, have fuelled public debate about how different parties in the governance chain should interact and influence each other. Most notable here is the relationship between shareholders and the boards of businesses, but an equivalent issue in the public sector is the relationship between government or public funding bodies and public-sector organisations.

- *Increased accountability to wider stakeholder interests* has also been increasingly advocated; in particular the argument that corporations need to be more visibly accountable and/or responsive, not only to 'owners' and 'managers' in the governance chain but to wider social interest.

4.3.1 The governance chain

KEY CONCEPT

Governance chain

The **governance chain** shows the roles and relationships of different groups involved in the governance of an organisation. In a small family business, the governance chain is simple: there are family shareholders, a board with some family members and there are managers, some of whom may be family too. Here there are just three layers in the chain. However, even in such businesses there are variations, for example, in the extent of family involvement and influence.[11] In large businesses influence on governance can be complex. Figure 4.2 shows a governance chain for a typical large, publicly quoted organisation. Here the size of the organisation means there are extra layers of management internally, while being publicly quoted

Figure 4.2 The chain of corporate governance: typical reporting structures

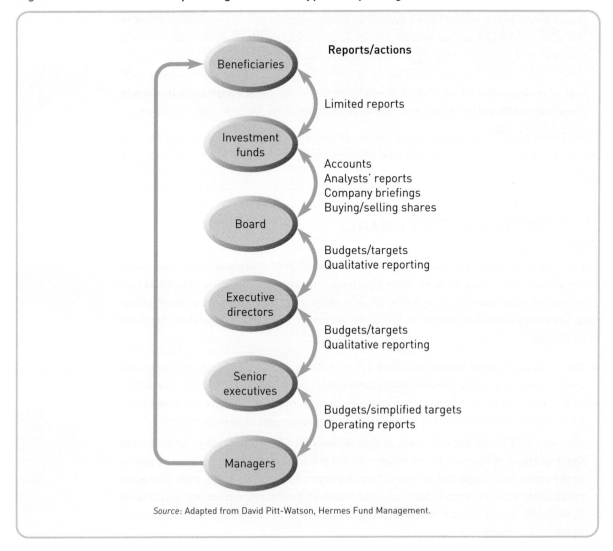

Source: Adapted from David Pitt-Watson, Hermes Fund Management.

introduces more investor layers too. Individual investors (the ultimate beneficiaries) often invest in public companies through investment funds, for example unit trusts or pension funds, which then invest in a range of companies on their behalf. Such funds are of growing importance. By 2010 they owned over 50 per cent of the equity of US corporations (19 per cent in 1970) and over 70 per cent in the UK (25 per cent in 1963), with similar growth elsewhere in Europe. Funds are typically controlled by trustees, with day-to-day investment activity undertaken by investment managers. So the ultimate beneficiaries may not even know in which companies they have a financial stake and have little power to influence the companies' boards directly.

The relationships in such governance chains can be understood in terms of the *principal–agent model*.[12] 'Principals' pay 'agents' to act on their behalf, just as homeowners employ estate agents to sell their homes. In Figure 4.2, the beneficiaries are the ultimate principals and fund trustees and investment managers are their agents in terms of achieving good returns on their investments. Further down the chain, company boards are principals too, with senior executives their agents in managing the company. There are many layers of agents between ultimate principals and the managers at the bottom, with the reporting mechanisms between each layer liable to be imperfect.

Principal–agent theory assumes that agents will not work diligently for principals unless incentives are carefully and appropriately aligned. However, it can be seen from Figure 4.2 that in large companies board members and other managers driving strategy are likely to be very remote from the ultimate beneficiaries of the company's performance. In such circumstances, the danger is twofold:

- *Self-interest*. Any agent in the chain may act out of self-interest. Managers will be striving for promotion and/or increased earnings, investment managers will be seeking to increase their bonuses, and so on.

- *Misalignment of incentives and control*. As influence passes down the governance chain, the expectations of one group are not passed on to the next appropriately. For example, ultimate beneficiaries may be mainly concerned with the long-term security of their pension fund, but the investment managers or the executives with whom they interact may place a greater emphasis on short-term growth.

The result may be that decisions are taken that are not in the best interests of the final beneficiary. This is just what has happened in the case of many of the corporate scandals of recent years, such as Lehman Brothers (see Illustration 4.2).

In this context, the governance chain helps highlight important issues that affect the management of strategy:

- *Responsibility to whom?* A fundamental question in large corporations is whether executives should regard themselves as *solely* responsible to shareholders, or as 'trustees of the assets of the corporation' acting on behalf of a wider range of stakeholders. (See the key debate at the end of the chapter.) Even in terms of formal governance structures this varies across the world, as section 4.3.3 shows.

- *Who are the shareholders?* If managers do see themselves as primarily responsible to shareholders, what does this mean in terms of the governance chain? As explained above, the final beneficiaries are far removed from the managers, so for many managers responsibility to them is notional. In practical terms, directors of a firm are likely to engage most frequently with institutional representatives of those shareholders – an investment manager or analyst from a pension fund or insurance company perhaps. Strategists within

ILLUSTRATION 4.2

The collapse of Lehman Brothers

Executive decisions may not always be in the best interest of shareholders; with disastrous results.

In 2008 Lehman Brothers was the fourth largest investment bank in the USA. Founded in the mid 1800s, its chief executive was Dick Fuld. Under his guidance the bank had been pursuing a strategy of rapid growth and, in common with other banks, up to 2008 this included the development of derivative products linked to the housing boom. The idea was to reduce their vulnerability to market fluctuations and allow them to take on higher lending risks through 'securitisation'.

The Times suggested that Lehman's strategy of investment on a huge scale in the US real estate market was 'in the hope of emulating the profitability of the big players in investment banking'. This involved: 'packaging debt into marketable instruments and selling them to investors . . . (so that) . . . risk could be diversified by spreading it across a wide investor base'. The problem was that such 'packages' included assets that were of dubious value. The result was that, when the housing boom ended and the value of housing plummeted, far from spreading risk, Lehman, together with many other banks that had followed similar strategies, found such products worthless. The banks, Lehman included, had mis-read the market and embarked on a strategy based on products that few people understood (many of the executives included). Moreover Lehman had intensi-fied its exposure in the housing market even after the onset of the credit crisis that had developed.

In September 2008 Lehman collapsed and filed for bankruptcy. The knock-on effect was felt the world over as other banks increasingly turned to govern-ments or new investors for funding to support them. *The Times* leader laid the problems of Lehman Brothers at the feet of Dick Fuld and his board:

Mr Fuld has been the imperious chief executive of Lehmans . . . since 1994. A curious cross between Gordon Gekko and Tony Soprano, Mr Fuld was an unapologetic mogul of Wall Street: he put down his colleagues in public: he was good at straight talking but not so practised at straight-listening and ultimately he deluded himself and those around him that, having seen off a brush with bankruptcy in the late 1990s, he and his bank had taken the precautions necessary to weather any financial storm. At Lehman's annual general meeting last April (2008), he said: 'The worst of the impact on the financial services industry is behind us.' Two months later his bank revealed $2.8 (~€2.0) billion in quarterly losses . . . What happened to Lehman Brothers was avoidable. Mr Fuld could have ensured more prudent management of the bank. A board other than Lehman's compliant one might have supervised him more closely or ousted him. After the failure of Bear Stearns (another major financial services business) . . . it ought to have been the prime concern of the Lehmans board to anticipate and prevent a similar outcome.

The Times went on to suggest that, given the need for capital to survive, Lehman's board might have decided to sell the business or part of the business such as its fund management arm. Instead: 'Fuld and Lehman's board proved to have wholly unrealistic expectations of the genuine value of the bank . . . (and) . . . a catastrophic failure to understand the Lehman's business model or the nature of the finan-cial market place that had changed . . .'

Source: The Times, 16 September 2008, p. 2; © The Times/The Sun/nisyndication.com.

Questions

1 Why might Fuld and the Lehman board have behaved the way they did?

2 What other mechanisms in the governance chain should (or could) have prevented what happened?

3 What changes in corporate governance are required to prevent similar occurrences?

a firm therefore face a difficult choice, even if they espouse primary responsibility to shareholders. Do they develop strategies they believe to be in the best interest of a highly fragmented group of unknown shareholders; or to meet the needs and aspirations of the investment managers? A similar problem exists for public-sector managers. They may see themselves as developing strategies in the public good, but they may face direct scrutiny from another body such as a government department or an agency appointed by the government. Is the strategy to be designed for the general public good, or to meet the scrutiny of the government department? For example, managers and doctors in the UK health service are dedicated to the well-being of their patients. But increasingly how they manage their services is governed by the targets placed upon them by a government department, which presumably also believes it is acting in the public good.

- *The role of institutional investors.* The role of institutional investors with regard to the strategy of firms differs according to governance structures around the world (see section 4.3.3). However, a common issue is the extent to which they do or should actively seek to influence strategy (see Illustration 4.3). Historically, in economies like those of the UK or US, investors have exerted their influence on firms through the buying and selling of shares rather than through an engagement with the company on strategic issues. The stock market becomes the judge of their actions through share price movements. There are signs, however, that investors are becoming more actively involved in the strategies of the firms in which they invest.[13] Such involvement varies a good deal[14] but has grown.

- *The role of boards.* Boards of directors typically consist of both executives and non-executive directors. The balance between these varies by type of organisation and by country. However, the principle is that the non-executive directors are there either to represent particular stakeholders, or to take a dispassionate view on the strategy and performance of the firm. The danger is that non-executive directors become too aligned with executives within the company. In the US and UK critics have pointed out that many non-executive directors are chosen on the basis of their previous association and links with senior executives within a firm, with the danger that this reduces the likelihood of their objectivity in performing their roles. There have been attempts to reduce these dangers with, for example, codes of conduct for the appointment of non-executive directors.

- *Scrutiny and control.* Given the concerns about governance that have grown in the last decade, there have been increasing attempts to build means of scrutinising and controlling the activities of 'agents' in the chain to safeguard the interests of the final beneficiaries. Figure 4.2 indicates the information typically available to each 'player' in the chain to judge the performance of others. There are increasing statutory requirements as well as voluntary codes placed upon boards to disclose information publicly and regulate their activities. Nonetheless managers have a great deal of discretion as to what information to provide to whom and what information to require of those who report to them. For example, how specific should a chief executive be in explaining future strategy to shareholders in public statements such as annual reports? What are the appropriate targets and measures to incentivise and control management within a firm? Should these primarily be concerned with the achievement of shareholder value? Or is more of a balanced scorecard approach appropriate to meet the needs of various stakeholders (see section 13.3.3)? Are the typical accountancy methods (such as return on capital employed) the most appropriate measures or should measures be specifically designed to fit the needs of particular strategies or particular stakeholder/shareholder expectations? There are no categoric answers to these

ILLUSTRATION 4.3

Investor interventions

To what extent and how should investors intervene in a company?

Piedmont and M&B

In 2010 M&B was the UK's largest owner of pubs, including Harvester, O'Neill's and All Bar One. It was a company that analysts saw as performing well in 2009. However in January 2010, Simon Laffin, then Chairman of M&B, was ousted by a group of shareholders headed by Joe Lewis who was reported to run Piedmont 'largely from a super yacht in the Caribbean'.

In autumn 2009 M&B had asked the takeover panel in the UK to investigate whether Piedmont was attempting to take over the company without a formal bid. This followed Piedmont's representatives on the Board blocking the appointment of two non-executive directors, Laffin taking over as Chairman and in turn ejecting the Piedmont directors from the Board. M&B management won backing from some big institutional investors such as Standard Life and Aviva on this who said it was wrong for a minority shareholder to be able to nominate so many Board members.

At the AGM in January 2010 Joe Lewis (with 23% shareholding through Piedmont), supported by Elpida, the investment vehicle of Irish racing tycoons John Magnier and J.P. Macmanus (with a 17.6% shareholding), proposed the removal of Simon Laffin from the Board. They secured the support of 66% of shareholders for this. Lewis expressed concerns about mismanagement, greed, high central overheads and pension provisions for departing directors at M&B: concerns which Laffin dismissed as 'complete nonsense'.

The new Chairman appointed was John Lovering, previously Chairman of Debenhams. In the knowledge that the recent feud had cost the group some £2 (~€2.2; ~$3) million he commented: 'Most observers think there should be more shareholder activism, and I agree with that . . . but there must be easier and less fractious ways of achieving these goals.'

The *Financial Times* commented: 'For Mr Lewis the next few months will test his supporters' contention that they are the exponents of sensible, engaged stewardship . . . (but) . . . there is one benefit of the damaging struggle over M&B: if any shareholders were asleep, they are wide awake now.'

Investor AB and Astra Zeneca

Investor AB, the Swedish investment group, is linked to the Wallenberg family and in 2009 held a 3.5% stake in Astra Zeneca. The Wallenberg policy is investment for the long term: they therefore have a strategic, not just a financial, interest in the firms in which they invest. In 2008 Boje Eckholm, the President and Chief Executive of Investor AB, questioned the long term viability of the business model of big pharmaceutical firms and in particular whether it discouraged the development of new medicines.

'You have to ask yourself: do you have economies of scale in R & D? . . . One of the fundamental ways that companies create value for shareholders is strong R & D. It raises the question: is big better? Maybe you have to split into smaller parts.'

His question, then, was whether farming out research to smaller organisations might make sense. This question came at a time when large pharmaceutical companies such as Astra Zeneca were grappling with rising research costs, intense competition from generic drugs and some high profile late stage failures in the research and development process of a promising new drug. Management at Astra Zeneca were reluctant to comment on Mr Eckholm's questions.

Sources: Financial Times, 29 January 2010 and the Observer Business Section, 24 January 2010, p. 3. The Times, 4 April 2008, p. 55.

Questions

1 Did the investors in the respective companies intervene in appropriate ways?

2 What is the role of the Chairman (or woman) in such circumstances?

3 In what ways should top management of companies behave in such circumstances?

questions. How managers answer them will depend on what they decide the strategic purpose of the organisation is, which itself will be influenced by their view on whom they see themselves responsible to.

The governance chain, then, typically operates imperfectly for at least five reasons: (i) a lack of clarity on who the end beneficiaries are; (ii) unequal division of power between the different 'players' in the chain; (iii) with different levels of access to information available to them; (iv) potentially agents in the chain pursuing their own self-interest; and (v) using measures and targets reflecting their own interests rather than those of end beneficiaries. In such circumstances it is not surprising that there are attempts to reform corporate governance and that governance structures are changing around the world.

4.3.2 Different governance structures

The governing body of an organisation is typically a board of directors. The primary statutory responsibility of a board is to ensure that an organisation fulfils the wishes and purposes of the formally recognised primary stakeholders. However, who these stakeholders are varies. In the private sector in some parts of the world it is shareholders, but in other parts of the world it is a broader or different stakeholder base. In the public sector, the governing body is accountable to the political arm of government – possibly through some intermediary such as a funding body. These differences lead to differences in how the purposes of an organisation are shaped and how strategies are developed as well as the role and composition of boards.

At the most general level there are two governance structures: the shareholder model and the stakeholder model.[15]

A shareholder model of governance

The shareholder model is epitomised by the economies of the US and UK. Here shareholding is relatively dispersed and shareholders have legitimate primacy in relation to the wealth generated by the corporations rather than, for example, the rights of other stakeholders such as employees, union representatives or banks. However, proponents argue that maximising shareholder value benefits other stakeholders too. At least in principle, the trading of shares provides a regulatory mechanism for maximising shareholder value. Dissatisfied shareholders may sell their shares, the result being a drop in share price and the threat of takeovers for under-performing firms. So the shareholder interest in a company is assumed to be largely financial.

There are arguments for and against the shareholder model. The *argued advantages* include:

● *Benefits for investors.* Relative to the stakeholder model the investor gets a higher rate of return. Shareholders can also reduce risk through diversifying their holdings in an equity market where shares can be readily traded. The system also provides for minority share-holding rights both through high disclosure of information required by companies but also in empowering them with voting rights (e.g. to appoint directors).

● *Benefits to the economy.* Since the system facilitates higher risk-taking by investors, there is a higher likelihood of the encouragement of economic growth and of entrepreneurship.

● *Benefits for management.* Arguably the separation of ownership and management makes strategic decisions more objectively related to the potentially different demands and con-straints of financial, labour and customer markets. A diversified shareholding also means that no one shareholder is likely to control management decisions, provided the firm performs well.

The *argued disadvantages* include:

● *Disadvantages for investors.* Relatively dispersed shareholdings prevent close monitoring of management. This may result in the managers sacrificing shareholder value to pursue their own agendas. For example, CEOs may further their own egos and empires with mergers that add no value to shareholders.

● *Disadvantages for the economy: the risk of short-termism.* Lack of control of management may lead to them taking decisions to benefit their own careers (for example, to gain promotion). This, combined with the threat of takeovers, may encourage managers to focus on short-term gains at the expense of long-term projects.[16]

● *Corporate reputation and top management greed.* The lack of management control allows for the huge compensations the managers reward themselves in the form of salary, bonuses and stock options. In the USA CEOs have over 500 times more compensation than their lowest-paid employees.[17]

The stakeholder model of governance

An alternative model of governance is the stakeholder model. This is founded on the principle that wealth is created, captured and distributed by a variety of stakeholders. This may include shareholders but could include family holdings, other investors such as banks, as well as employees or their union representatives. As such, management needs to be responsive to multiple stakeholders who, themselves, may be formally represented on boards. Germany, Italy and Japan are often cited as examples of the stakeholder model.

In practice, under the stakeholder model one or two large groups of investors or *block holders* often come to dominate ownership. For example, in Germany nearly three-quarters of all the German listed companies have a majority owner – very different from the UK or USA for example. Majority ownership is also common in Italy and France. There is also concentrated ownership of firms in Japan, with a small group of shareholders owning a large percentage of the company and a system of cross-shareholding, where large companies own shares of other companies and banks finance the same subgroup.

There are *argued advantages* for the stakeholder model of governance:

● *Long-term horizons.* It is argued that the major investors – banks or other companies, for example – are likely to regard their investments as long-term, thus reducing the pressure for short-term results as against longer-term performance.

● *Advantages for stakeholders.* Apart from the argument that the wider interests of stakeholders are taken into account, it is also argued that employee influence is a deterrent to high-risk decisions and investments. The long-term perspective of majority shareholders will, likely, also be in the interest of other stakeholders.

● *Advantages for investors.* Perhaps ironically it is argued that it is block investments that provide economic benefits. Given investors' concern for the strategic direction of the company, there may be a closer level of monitoring of management, with investors having greater access to information from within the firm. Further, because power may reside with relatively few block investors, intervention is easier in case of management failure.

There are also *argued disadvantages* of the stakeholder model of governance:

● *Disadvantages for management.* Close monitoring could lead to interference, slowing down of decision processes and the loss of management objectivity when critical decisions have to be made.

Table 4.1 Benefits and disadvantages of governance systems

	Shareholder model	Stakeholder model
Benefits	For investors: • Higher rate of return • Reduced risk For the economy: • Encourages entrepreneurship • Encourages inward investment For management: • Independence	For investors: • Closer monitoring of management • Longer-term decision horizons For stakeholders: • Deterrent to high-risk decisions
Disadvantages	For investors: • Difficult to monitor management For the economy: • The risk of short-termism • And top management greed	For management: • Potential interference • Slower decision-making • Reduced independence For the economy: • Reduced financing opportunities for growth • Weak market for corporate control

- *Disadvantages for investors.* There is relatively weak representation of minority shareholders. It is the dominant shareholders that tend to have the major influence, not least because they may well have representatives on boards. Due to lack of financial pressure from shareholders, long-term investments may also be made on projects where the returns may be below market expectations.

- *Disadvantage for the economy.* There are fewer alternatives for raising finance, thus limiting the possibilities of growth and entrepreneurial activity. There is also a relatively weak market for corporate control. The dominance of ownership by large block holders and the relatively high debt financing rather than equity financing can mean that firms, even when performing poorly, may be protected from takeover.

These argued advantages and disadvantages are summarised in Table 4.1.

It is also worth noting that there are implications with regard to the financing of businesses. In the shareholder model, equity is the dominant form of long-term finance and commercial banks provide debt capital, so relationships with bankers are essentially contractual. There are significant implications. Managers need to limit gearing to a prudent level, so more equity is needed for major strategy developments. It also means that the company itself has a higher degree of influence over strategic decisions since the banks are not seeking a strategic involvement with the company. However, if strategies start to fail, the organisation can become increasingly dependent on the bank as a key stakeholder. This often happens in family-owned small businesses. In the extreme banks may exercise their power by withdrawing funds, even if this liquidates the company. In contrast, in some stakeholder systems (notably Japan and to a lesser extent Germany), banks often have significant equity stakes or are part of the same parent company. They are less likely to adopt an arm's-length relationship, more likely to seek active strategic involvement and less likely to withdraw funds in difficult times.

Three qualifications to the governance models explained above need to be made in relation to ownership:

● *Family-controlled firms* can be very large indeed – such as Wal-Mart and Mars. Here share ownership may be concentrated in family hands and it may be that the board is largely family-controlled.

● *State ownership*: many large corporations are either state-owned or owned by sovereign wealth funds that are, themselves, state-controlled. Such funds include, for example, the Abu Dhabi and Kuwait Investment Authorities, the China Investment Corporation and the Government of Singapore Investment Corporation. Firms with such ownership may nominally correspond to a stakeholder model of governance in that they have a dominant block shareholder and many of the advantages and disadvantages of the stakeholder system identified above may prevail.

● *Public services* have a wide variety of arrangements for governing bodies, but there are some commonalities. Governing bodies are often 'representational' of key stakeholders, in practice even if not by regulation. This particularly applies to the place of employees and unions on governing bodies. There has also been a move in many countries to increase the proportion of (so-called) independent members on governing bodies, the nearest equivalent to non-executive directors in the private sector.

4.3.3 Changes and reforms to governance structures

International pressures but also history may influence how governance models change and there is an active debate in many countries on the relative merits of the different governance systems. For example, in many respects historically and culturally the Netherlands is close to Germany and the Nordic countries and, as such, there are those who favour the stakeholder model. There are, however, also those who advocate the shareholder model, reflecting the strong links with the UK and US politically, culturally and economically.[18] In Japan, institutional and foreign investors are gaining influence, and deregulation and liberalisation are increasing the pressure to change governance structures. In Germany, too, there are pressures for change, with arguments being made that, if German companies are to remain globally competitive, employee representation on boards needs to be reviewed, not least to reduce costs and speed decision-making. In Sweden historically firms were privately owned or in the hands of family-controlled foundations, holding companies and investment companies, but in the last decade this has significantly reduced. In India there was a high level of state protectionism. However, since 1991 there has been radical change. India is still characterised by family firms, but with increasing separation of ownership and management and a move towards a shareholder model of governance.

Many governments have also been proactive in reforming aspects of corporate governance. Reforms have taken many forms.[19] There has been legislation on tightening accounting standards and increasing auditor independence from management; on the nature of internal financial controls and external disclosure of information; on the role and independence of non-executive directors; and in the US, on the requirement for shareholder approval of stock-based compensation plans for executives. Throughout Europe there has been an attempt to increase the power and ease of voting for shareholders.

4.3.4 How boards of directors influence strategy

A central governance issue is the role of boards of directors and of directors themselves. Since boards have the ultimate responsibility for the success or failure of an organisation as well as the benefits received by shareholders or wider stakeholders, they must be concerned with strategy.

Under the shareholder model there is typically a single-tier board structure, with a majority of non-executive directors and the role of driving the company forward as well as an oversight role on behalf of shareholders. The emphasis on outside directors is intended to bring greater independence to the primary role of the board, that of oversight on behalf of shareholders. However, as explained above, this is not without its problems since how non-executives are chosen has raised questions about their independence.

The stakeholder model can involve a two-tier board structure. For example, in Germany for firms of more than 500 employees there is a supervisory board (*Aufsichtsrat*) and a management board (*Vorstand*). The supervisory board is a forum where the interest of various groups is represented, including shareholders and employees but also typically bankers, lawyers and stock exchange experts. Strategic planning and operational control are vested with the management board, but major decisions like mergers and acquisitions require approval of the supervisory board. In other European countries, notably the Netherlands and France, two-tier boards also exist.

Two issues are, then, especially significant here:

- *Delegation.* Strategic management can be entirely delegated to management, with the board receiving and approving plans and decisions. Here the 'stewardship' role of the board requires processes that ensure that an organisation's strategy is not 'captured' by management at the expense of other stakeholders. The two-tier board system seeks to do this. It is less clear how this occurs in the single-board structure typical of the shareholder model; the Lehman case (Illustration 4.2) is an example of the dangers.

- *Engagement.* The board can engage in the strategic management process. This has practical problems concerning the time and knowledge level of non-executive directors in particular to perform their role this way. This problem can be especially pronounced in organisations such as charities or public bodies with governing boards or trustees of people committed to the mission of the organisation, keen to become involved but with limited operational understanding of it.

In the guidelines increasingly issued by governments[20] or advocated by commentators there are some common themes:

- Boards must be seen to *operate 'independently' of the management* of the company. So the role of non-executive directors is heightened.

- Boards must be *competent to scrutinise the activities of managers.* So the collective experience of the board, its training and the information available to it are crucially important.

- Directors must have the *time* to do their job properly. So limitations on the number of directorships that an individual can hold are also an important consideration.

- However, it is the *behaviour of boards* and their members that is likely to be most significant[21] whatever structural arrangements are put in place. For example, respect, trust, 'constructive friction' between board members, fluidity of roles, individual as well as collective responsibility, and the evaluation of individual director and collective board performance.

SOCIAL RESPONSIBILITY AND ETHICS[22]

Underlying the discussion of corporate governance is an issue highlighted in the introduction to this chapter. Is the purpose of an organisation and its strategy for the benefit of a primary stakeholder such as the shareholders of a company, or is it there for the benefit of a wider group of stakeholders? In turn this raises the question of societal expectations placed on organisations, how these impact on an organisation's purposes and, in turn, on its strategy. This section considers, first, *corporate social responsibility*: the role businesses and other organisations might take in society. Second, it considers the *ethics* of the behaviour and actions of people in relation to the strategy of their organisations.

4.4.1 Corporate social responsibility

The sheer size and global reach of many companies means that they are bound to have significant influence on society. Further, the widely publicised corporate scandals and failures of the last two decades have fuelled a concern about the role they play. The regulatory environment and the corporate governance arrangements for an organisation determine its minimum obligations towards its stakeholders. However, such legal and regulatory frameworks pay uneven attention to the rights of different stakeholders. For example, customers, suppliers or employees are *contractual stakeholders* in that they have a legal relationship with an organisation, whereas *community stakeholders* such as local communities and pressure groups do not have the equivalent protection of the law. **Corporate social responsibility (CSR) is the commitment by organisations to 'behave ethically and contribute to economic development while improving the quality of life of the workforce and their families as well as the local community and society at large'.**[23] CSR is therefore concerned with the ways in which an organisation exceeds its minimum obligations to stakeholders specified through regulation.

Different organisations take different stances on CSR which are reflected in how they manage such responsibilities. Table 4.2 outlines four stereotypes to illustrate these differences. They represent a progressively more inclusive 'list' of stakeholder interests and a greater breadth of criteria against which strategies and performance will be judged. The discussion that follows also explains what such stances typically involve in terms of the ways companies act.[24]

The laissez-faire view (literally 'let do' in French) represents an extreme stance. Proponents argue that the only responsibility of business is to make a profit and provide for the interests of shareholders.[25] It is for government to prescribe, through legislation and regulation, the constraints which society chooses to impose on businesses in their pursuit of economic efficiency. Organisations should meet these minimum obligations but no more. Expecting companies to exercise social duties beyond this can, in extreme cases, undermine the authority of government.

This stance may be taken by executives who are persuaded of it ideologically or by smaller businesses that do not have the resources to do other than minimally comply with regulations. Insofar as social good is pursued, this is justified in terms of improving profitability.[26] This might occur, for example, if social obligations were imposed as a requirement for gaining contracts (for example, if equal opportunities employment practices were required from suppliers to public-sector customers) or to defend their reputation. Responsibility for such actions is

Table 4.2 **Corporate social responsibility stances**

	Laissez-faire	Enlightened self-interest	Forum for stakeholder interaction	Shaper of society
Rationale	Legal compliance: make a profit, pay taxes and provide jobs	Sound business sense	Sustainability or triple bottom line	Social and market change
Leadership	Peripheral	Supportive	Champion	Visionary
Management	Middle-management responsibility	Systems to ensure good practice	Board-level issue; organisation-wide monitoring	Individual responsibility throughout the organisation
Mode	Defensive to outside pressures	Reactive to outside pressures	Proactive	Defining
Stakeholder relationships	Unilateral	Interactive	Partnership	Multi-organisation alliances

likely to be with middle managers or functional heads rather than with the chief executive, who is unlikely to see this role as part of his or her brief. Relationships with stakeholders are likely to be largely unilateral and one-way rather than interactive. The problem is that society increasingly expects more than this from large organisations and the evidence is that chief executives themselves are aware of this and agree organisations should play a more proactive role.[27]

Enlightened self-interest is tempered with recognition of the long-term financial benefit to the shareholder of well-managed relationships with other stakeholders. The justification for social action is that it makes good business sense. An organisation's reputation is important to its long-term financial success. Given that employees see it as important that their employer acts in a socially responsible manner, a more proactive stance on social issues also helps in recruiting and retaining staff. So, like any other form of investment or promotion expenditure, corporate philanthropy or welfare provision might be regarded as sensible expenditure.[28] The sponsorship of major sporting or arts events by companies is an example. The avoidance of 'shady' marketing practices is also necessary to prevent the need for yet more legislation in that area. Managers here would take the view that organisations not only have responsibility to their shareholders, but also a responsibility for *relationships with* other stakeholders (as against *responsibilities to* other stakeholders). So communication with stakeholder groups is likely to be more interactive than for laissez-faire-type organisations. They may well also set up systems and policies to ensure compliance with best practice (for example, ISO 14000 certification, the protection of human rights in overseas operations, etc.) and begin to monitor their social responsibility performance. Top management may also play more of a part, at least insofar as they support the firm taking a more proactive social role.

A *forum for stakeholder interaction*[29] explicitly incorporates multiple stakeholder interests and expectations rather than just shareholders as influences on organisational purposes and strategies. Here the argument is that the performance of an organisation should be measured in a more pluralistic way than just through the financial bottom line. Companies in this category might retain uneconomic units to preserve jobs, avoid manufacturing or selling 'anti-social' products and be prepared to bear reductions in profitability for the social good. Some financial service organisations have also chosen to offer socially responsible investment 'products' to investors. These include only holdings in organisations that meet high standards of social responsibility in their activities.

In such organisations responsibility for CSR may be elevated to board-level appointments and structures may be set up for monitoring social performance across its global operations. Targets, often through balanced scorecards, may be built into operational aspects of business and issues of social responsibility managed proactively and in a coordinated fashion. The expectation is that such a corporate stance will, in turn, be reflected in the ethical behaviour of individuals within the firm. Organisations in this category inevitably take longer over the development of new strategies as they are committed to wide consultation with stakeholders and with managing the difficult political trade-offs between conflicting stakeholders' expectations.

Shapers of society regard financial considerations as of secondary importance or a constraint. These are activists, seeking to change society and social norms. The firm may have been founded for this purpose, as in the case of Traidcraft UK, a public limited company established with the specific mission of fighting world poverty. Here the social role is the *raison d'être* of the business. Such organisations may see their strategic purpose as 'changing the rules of the game' through which they may benefit but by which they wish to assure that society benefits. In this role it is unlikely that they will be operating on their own: rather they are likely to be partnering with other organisations, commercial and otherwise, to achieve their purposes.

The extent to which this is a viable stance depends upon issues of regulation, corporate governance and accountability. It is easier for a privately owned organisation to operate in this way, since it is not accountable to external shareholders. Arguably the great historical achievements of the public services in transforming the quality of life for millions of people were largely because they were 'mission-driven' in this way, supported by a political framework in which they operated. However, in many countries there have been challenges to the legitimacy of this mission-driven stance of public services and demands for citizens (as taxpayers) to expect demonstrable best value from them. Charitable organisations face similar dilemmas. It is fundamental to their existence that they have zeal to improve the interests of particular groups in society, but they also need to remain financially viable, which can lead to them being seen as over-commercial and spending too much on administration or promotional activities.

Illustration 4.4 shows different examples of company activities that have significant social impacts and Table 4.3 provides some questions against which an organisation's actions on CSR can be assessed.

Managers' increasing sympathy with CSR is not solely for ethical reasons but because there is a belief that there are advantages to businesses in so doing and dangers if they do not.[30] Social responsibility is justified in terms of the 'triple bottom line' – social and environmental benefits as well as increased profits. Indeed it is argued that socially responsible strategies should be followed because they can provide a basis of gaining competitive advantage. The need is to seek 'win–win' situations to optimise the economic return on environmental investments.[31] Fighting the AIDS pandemic in Africa is not just a matter of 'good works' for a pharmaceutical company or an African mining company, it is central to their own

ILLUSTRATION 4.4

The social impact of business strategies

The activities of businesses can have significant impacts on societies.
But what motivates such activities?

Social good or spotting the market trend?

In 2009 Pepsi Co launched a range of healthy snacks targeting 8–12-year-old schoolchildren. There were also plans to launch a children's porridge under the Quaker brand and to publish a health audit of its products. This followed Pepsi Co's decision 5 years earlier to stop promoting full-sugar Pepsi and focus on the diet and non-sugared alternatives, Pepsi Max and Diet Pepsi. The company also claimed to have reduced saturated fat in its Walkers Crisps by 70% by switching from palm oil to sunflower oil. Salman Amin, Pepsi Co's CEO in Britain, explained that, whilst it would take years: 'I think we will lick obesity as a social issue. . . . I'm a huge optimist.' Commentators also pointed out that Pepsi Co had, in the past, been good at spotting trends in food consumption and capitalising on them.[1]

Cheap medicines for the world's poor or a smart competitive move?

In early 2009 Andrew Witty, the Chief Executive of GlaxoSmithKlein (GSK) announced the decision to cut its prices in the 50 least developed countries in the world to no more than 25% of levels in the UK and the US prices on all medicines produced by GSK, re-invest 20% of any profits it made in the least developed countries into hospitals, clinics and staff and share knowledge about potential drugs currently protected by patents by making them available in a 'patent pool'. This followed repeated criticisms of drug companies for defending their patents, fighting off generic alternatives and refusing to drop prices for HIV drugs despite the HIV/AIDS crisis in Africa and Asia. Witty hoped it might 'stimulate a different behaviour' adding: 'maybe someone has to move before many people move.'

Whilst campaigners widely applauded the decisions there remained some concerns. Why shouldn't current HIV drugs be included in the patent pool?

And might the GSK decision undermine the generics industry already attempting to supply cheap drugs to poor countries? Indeed the *Guardian* (14/2/09) wrote 'GSK would love to undermine the Indian and Chinese generics companies, which sell copies of their drugs at rock bottom prices in Africa and Asian countries where patents do not apply.'[2]

Powering African homes – or cheap power for Europe?

In 2009 the World Bank announced its $80 (~€56) billion support to build the Grand Inga Dam in the Democratic Republic of Congo. This would feed electricity to South Africa, Egypt, Nigeria and other countries in Africa. At 40,000 MW it would have twice the generation capacity of the Three Gorges Dam in China. However the feasibility study also examined the possibility of extending supply to southern Europe. Critics argued it was a: 'flight of fancy that would only benefit huge Western multinationals and quite possibly feed African energy into European households' when less than 30% of Africans have access to electricity – in some African countries as low as 10%. Supporters, on the other hand, pointed out that it could bring electricity to 500 million African homes and that diverting power to Europe had the benefit of attracting additional financing, thus potentially aiding the local community.[3]

Sources: (1) The *Observer*, 23 August 2009, p. 3; (2) *Financial Times*, 4 March 2009, p. 4; (3) the *Observer* Media and Business, 23 August 2009, p. 1.

Questions

1 How would you categorise each of the decisions in terms of the stances on social responsibility in Table 4.2?

2 To what extent and how should the development of strategic options consider the impact on society?

Table 4.3 Some questions of corporate social responsibility

Should organisations be responsible for . . .

INTERNAL ASPECTS

Exployee welfare
. . . providing medical care, assistance with housing finance, extended sick leave, assistance for dependants, etc.?

Working conditions
. . . job security, enhancing working surroundings, social and sporting clubs, above-minimum safety standards, training and development, etc.?

Job design
. . . designing jobs to the increased satisfaction of workers rather than just for economic efficiency? This would include issues of work/life balance?

Intellectual property
. . . respecting the private knowledge of individuals and not claiming corporate ownership?

EXTERNAL ASPECTS

Environmental issues
. . . reducing pollution to below legal standards if competitors are not doing so?
. . . energy conservation?

Products
. . . dangers arising from the careless use of products by consumers?

Markets and marketing
. . . deciding not to sell in some markets?
. . . advertising standards?

Suppliers
. . . 'fair' terms of trade?
. . . blacklisting suppliers?

Employment
. . . positive discrimination in favour of minorities?
. . . maintaining jobs?

Community activity
. . . sponsoring local events and supporting local good works?

Human rights
. . . respecting human rights in relation to: child labour, workers' and union rights, oppressive political regimes? Both directly and in the choice of markets, suppliers and partners?

interests. Similarly, helping reduce carbon emissions provides a business opportunity for a car manufacturer.[32]

The evidence is equivocal as to whether there really are economic pay-offs to a proactive stance on CSR. There is a claim for the links of an enlightened self-interest approach to superior financial performance.[33] A more qualified view, however, is that a visible concern for CSR benefits performance most for firms where there are low levels of innovation or in industries where there are few other bases of differentiation between firms.[34]

4.4.2 The ethics of individuals and managers

Ethical issues have to be faced at the individual as well as corporate level and can pose difficult dilemmas for individuals and managers. For example, what is the responsibility of an individual who believes that the strategy of his or her organisation is unethical (for example, its trading practices) or is not adequately representing the legitimate interests of one or more stakeholder groups? Should that person leave the company on the grounds of a mismatch of values; or is *whistle-blowing* appropriate, such as divulging information to outside bodies, for example regulatory bodies or the press?

Given that strategy development can be an intensely political process with implications for the personal careers of those concerned, managers can find difficulties establishing and maintaining a position of integrity. There is also potential conflict between what strategies are in managers' own best interests and what strategies are in the longer-term interests of their organisation and the shareholders. Some organisations set down explicit guidelines they expect their employees to follow. Texas Instruments posed these questions:[35]

> Is the action legal? . . . If no, stop immediately.
>
> Does it comply with our values? . . . If it does not, stop.
>
> If you do it would you feel bad? . . . Ask your own conscience if you can live with it.
>
> How would this look in the newspaper? . . . Ask if this goes public tomorrow would you do it today?
>
> If you know it's wrong . . . don't do it.
>
> If you are not sure . . . ask; and keep asking until you get an answer.

Perhaps the biggest challenge for managers is to develop a high level of self-awareness of their own behaviour in relation to the issues raised above.[36] This can be difficult because it requires them to stand apart from often deep-rooted and taken-for-granted assumptions that are part of the culture of their organisation – a key theme of the next chapter.

STAKEHOLDER EXPECTATIONS[37]

It should be clear from the preceding sections that the decisions managers have to make about the purpose and strategy of their organisation are influenced by the expectations of stakeholders. This poses a challenge because there are likely to be many stakeholders, especially for a large organisation (see Figure 4.3), with different, perhaps conflicting, expectations. This means that managers need to take a view on (i) which stakeholders will have the greatest influence, therefore (ii) which expectations they need to pay most attention to and (iii) to what extent the expectations and influence of different stakeholders vary.

4.5.1 Stakeholder groups

External stakeholders can be usefully divided into four types in terms of the nature of their relationship with the organisation and how they might affect the success or failure of a strategy:[38]

- *Economic stakeholders*, including suppliers, competitors, distributors (whose influence can be identified using the five forces framework from Chapter 2 (Figure 2.2) and shareholders (whose influence can be considered in terms of the governance chain discussed in section 4.3.1).

Figure 4.3 Stakeholders of a large organisation

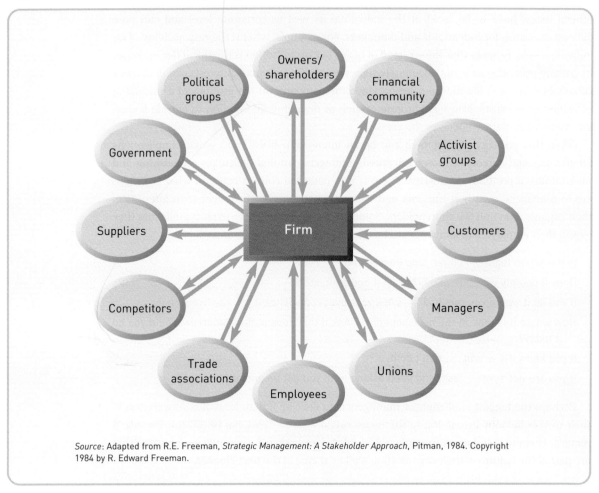

Source: Adapted from R.E. Freeman, *Strategic Management: A Stakeholder Approach*, Pitman, 1984. Copyright 1984 by R. Edward Freeman.

- *Social/political stakeholders*, such as policy makers, regulators and government agencies that may directly influence the strategy or the context in which strategy is developed.
- *Technological stakeholders*, such as key adopters, standards agencies and owners of competitive technologies that will influence the diffusion of new technologies and the adoption of industry standards.
- *Community stakeholders*, who are affected by what an organisation does; for example, those who live close to a factory or, indeed, wider society. These stakeholders have no formal relationship with the organisation but may, of course, take action (e.g. through lobbying or activism) to influence the organisation.

The influence of these different types of stakeholders is likely to vary in different situations. For example, the 'technological group' will be crucial for strategies of new product introduction whilst the 'social/political' group is usually particularly influential in the public-sector context or for companies operating in different countries with different political and legal systems.

There are also stakeholder groups internal to an organisation, which may be departments, geographical locations or different levels in the hierarchy. Individuals may belong to more than one stakeholder group and such groups may 'line up' differently depending on the issue or strategy in hand. Of course, external stakeholders may seek to influence an organisation's

Table 4.4 **Some common conflicts of expectations**

- In order to grow, short-term profitability, cash flow and pay levels may need to be sacrificed.

- 'Short-termism' may suit managerial career aspirations but preclude investment in long-term projects.

- When family businesses grow, the owners may lose control if they need to appoint professional managers.

- New developments may require additional funding through share issue or loans. In either case, financial independence may be sacrificed.

- Public ownership of shares will require more openness and accountability from the management.

- Cost efficiency through capital investment can mean job losses.

- Extending into mass markets may require a reduction in quality standards.

- In public services, a common conflict is between mass provision and specialist services (e.g. preventative dentistry or heart transplants).

- In large multinational organisations, conflict can result because of a division's responsibilities to the company and also to its host country.

strategy through their links with internal stakeholders. For example, customers may exert pressure on sales managers to represent their interests within the company.

Since the expectations of stakeholder groups will differ, it is normal for conflict to exist regarding the importance or desirability of aspects of strategy. In most situations, a compromise will need to be reached. The more companies globalise the more they add further complications as they operate in multiple arenas. For example, an overseas division is part of the parent company, which will likely have expectations about consistent global behaviour and performance, but is also part of a local community, which may well have different expectations. Table 4.4 shows some typical situations which give rise to conflicting stakeholder expectations. It may, however, also be possible in developing a strategy to look for compatible stakeholder expectations. For example, managers of the Cornish conservation tourist attraction, the Eden Project, looked for 'synergies around purpose' amongst different stakeholders to obtain support and funding for it. Both the European Union and the local economic development agency were interested in developing the economy of Cornwall, one of the poorest areas in the UK, and the Millennium Commission, a government-sponsored funding body, was interested in developing local iconic architecture.

The stakeholder concept is, then, valuable when trying to understand the political context within which strategy develops. Indeed, taking stakeholder expectations and influence into account is an important aspect of strategic choice, as will be seen in Chapter 11.

4.5.2 Stakeholder mapping[39]

There are different ways in which stakeholder mapping can be used to gain an understanding of stakeholder influence.[40] The approach to **stakeholder mapping** here **identifies stakeholder**

Figure 4.4 Stakeholder mapping: the power/interest matrix

Level of interest

Low ←————————→ High

	A Minimal effort	**B** Keep informed
Power	**C** Keep satisfied	**D** Key players

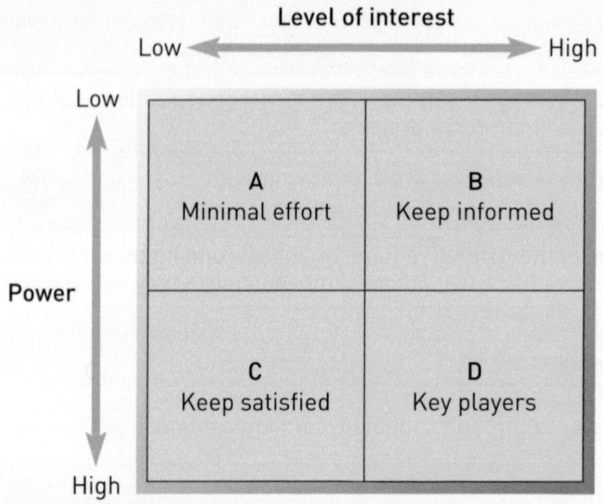

Source: Adapted from A. Mendelow, *Proceedings of the Second International Conference on Information Systems*, Cambridge, MA, 1986.

expectations and power and helps in understanding political priorities. It underlines the importance of two issues:

- The *interest* each stakeholder has in imposing its expectations on the organisation's purposes and choice of strategies.
- The *power* each stakeholder has to influence strategy.

These two dimensions form the basis of the power/interest matrix shown as Figure 4.4. The matrix classifies stakeholders in relation to the power they hold and the extent to which they are likely to show interest in supporting or opposing a particular strategy. The matrix helps in thinking through stakeholder influences on the development of strategy. However, it must be emphasised that how managers handle relationships will depend on the governance structures under which they operate (see section 4.3) and the stance taken on corporate responsibility (section 4.4.1). For example, in some countries unions may be weak but in others they may be represented on supervisory boards; banks may take an 'arm's-length' relationship with regard to strategy in some countries, but be part of the governance structures in others. A laissez-faire type of business may only pay attention to stakeholders with the most powerful economic influence (for example, investors), whereas shapers of society might seek to engage with and influence the expectations and involvement of stakeholders who would not typically see themselves as influential.

In order to show the way in which the matrix may be used, take the example of a business where managers see themselves as formulating strategy by trying to ensure the compliance of stakeholders with their own assessment of strategic imperatives. In this context the matrix indicates the type of relationship that managers might typically establish with stakeholder groups in the different quadrants. Clearly, the acceptability of strategies to *key players* (segment D) is of major importance. It could be that these are major investors or particular individuals or agencies with a lot of power – for example, a major shareholder in a family firm or a government funding agency in a public-sector organisation. Often the most difficult issues relate to stakeholders in segment C. Although these might, in general, be relatively passive, a disastrous situation can arise when their level of interest is underrated and they reposition to segment D and frustrate the adoption of a new strategy. Institutional shareholders such as pension funds or insurance firms can fall into this category. They may show little interest unless share prices start to dip, but may then demand to be heard by senior management. Managers might choose to address the expectations of stakeholders in segment B, for example community groups, through information provision. It may be important not to alienate such stakeholders because they can be crucially important 'allies' in influencing the attitudes of more powerful stakeholders: for example, through lobbying.

Stakeholder mapping can also help in understanding the following issues:

- In *determining purpose and strategy*, which stakeholder expectations need to be most considered?
- Whether the *actual levels of interest and power* of stakeholders properly reflect the corporate governance framework within which the organisation is operating, as in the examples above (institutional investors, community groups).
- Who the key *blockers* and *facilitators* of a strategy are likely to be and the appropriate response.
- Whether *repositioning* of certain stakeholders is desirable and/or feasible: for example, to lessen the influence of a key player or, in certain instances, to ensure that there are more key players who will champion the strategy (this is often critical in the public-sector context).
- *Maintaining* the level of interest or power of some key stakeholders: for example, public 'endorsement' by powerful suppliers or customers may be critical to the success of a strategy. It may also be necessary to discourage some stakeholders from repositioning themselves. This is what is meant by *keep satisfied* in relation to stakeholders in segment C, and to a lesser extent *keep informed* for those in segment B.

All this can raise difficult ethical issues for managers in deciding the role they should play in the political activity surrounding stakeholder management. This takes the debate back to the considerations of governance and ethics discussed earlier in section 4.4. For example, are managers really the honest brokers who weigh the conflicting expectations of stakeholder groups? Or should they be answerable to one stakeholder – such as shareholders – and hence is their role to ensure the acceptability of their strategies to other stakeholders? Or are they, as many authors suggest, the real power themselves, constructing strategies to suit their own purposes and managing stakeholder expectations to ensure acceptance of these strategies?

Illustration 4.5 shows some of the practical issues of using stakeholder mapping to understand the political context surrounding a new strategy. The example relates to a German bank considering the centralisation of its corporate banking services in its headquarters in Frankfurt with the implication of the closure of its Toulouse office. The example illustrates two further issues.

- *Heterogeneity of stakeholder groups*, which typically contain a variety of subgroups with different expectations and power. In the illustration, *customers* are shown divided into those who are largely supportive of the strategy (customer X), those who are actively hostile (customer Y) and those who are indifferent (customer Z). So, when using stakeholder mapping, there is a balance to be struck between describing stakeholders too generically – hence hiding important issues of diversity – and too much subdivision, making the situation confusing and difficult to interpret.

ILLUSTRATION 4.5

Stakeholder mapping at Tallman GmbH

Stakeholder mapping can be a useful tool for determining the political priorities for specific strategic developments or changes.

Tallman GmbH was a German bank providing both retail and corporate banking services throughout Germany, Benelux and France. There were concerns about its loss in market share in the corporate sector which was serviced from two centres – Frankfurt (for Germany and Benelux) and Toulouse (for France). It was considering closing the Toulouse operation and servicing all corporate clients from Frankfurt. This would result in significant job losses in Toulouse, some of which would be replaced in Frankfurt alongside vastly improved IT systems.

Two power/interest maps were drawn up by the company officials to establish likely stakeholder reactions to the proposed closure of the Toulouse operation. Map A represents the likely situation and map B the preferred situation – where support for the proposal would be sufficient to proceed.

Referring to map A, it can be seen that, with the exception of customer X and IT supplier A, the stakeholders in box B are currently opposed to the closure of the Toulouse operation. If Tallman was to have any chance of convincing these stakeholders to change their stance to a more supportive one, the company must address their questions and, where possible, alleviate their fears. If such fears were overcome, these people might become important allies in influencing the more

Map A: The likely situation

	Shareholder M (−) Toulouse office (−) Customer X (+) French minister (−) Marketing (−) IT supplier A (+)
A	B
Customer Z German minister	Customer Y (+) Frankfurt office (+) Corporate finance (+)
C	D

Map B: The preferred situation

French minister	Shareholder M (−) Toulouse office (−) Marketing (−) IT supplier A (+)
A	B
Customer Z German minister	Customer X (+) Customer Y (+) Frankfurt office (+) Corporate finance (+)
C	D

- *The role and the individual* currently undertaking that role need to be distinguished. It is useful to know if a new individual in that role would shift the positioning. Serious misjudgements can be made if care is not paid to this point. In the example, it has been concluded that the German minister (segment C) is largely indifferent to the new development. However, a change of minister might change this situation. Although removing such uncertainties entirely is impossible, there are implications for political priorities. For example, permanent officials advising the minister need to be kept satisfied, since they will outlive individual ministers and provide a continuity which can diminish uncertainty. It is also possible, of course, that the German minister's level of interest will be raised by lobbying from her French counterpart. This would have implications for how the company handles the situation in France.

powerful stakeholders in boxes C and D. The supportive attitude of customer X could be usefully harnessed in this quest. Customer X was a multinational with operations throughout Europe. It had shown dissatisfaction with the inconsistent treatment that it received from Frankfurt and Toulouse.

The relationships Tallman had with the stakeholders in box C were the most difficult to manage since, whilst they were considered to be relatively passive, largely due to their indifference to the proposed strategy, a disastrous situation could arise if their level of interest was underrated. For example, if the German minister were replaced, her successor might be opposed to the strategy and actively seek to stop the changes. In this case they would shift to box D.

The acceptability of the proposed strategy to the current players in box D was a key consideration. Of particular concern was customer Y (a major French manufacturer who operated only in France – accounting for 20 per cent of Toulouse corporate banking income). Customer Y was opposed to the closure of the Toulouse operation and could have the power to prevent it from happening, for example by the withdrawal of its business. The company clearly needed to have open discussions with this stakeholder.

By comparing the position of stakeholders in map A and map B, and identifying any changes and mismatches, Tallman could establish a number of tactics to change the stance of certain stakeholders to a more positive one and to increase the power of certain stakeholders. For example, customer X could be encouraged to champion the proposed strategy and assist Tallman by providing media access, or even convincing customer Y that the change could be beneficial.

Tallman could also seek to dissuade or prevent powerful stakeholders from changing their stance to a negative one: for example, unless direct action were taken, lobbying from her French counterpart may well raise the German minister's level of interest. This would have implications for how the company handled the situation in France. Time could be spent talking the strategy through with the French minister and also customer Y to try to shift them away from opposition at least to neutrality, if not support.

Activity

To ensure that you are clear about how to undertake stakeholder mapping, produce your own complete analysis for Tallman GmbH against a different strategy, that is *to service all corporate clients from Toulouse*. Ensure that you go through the following steps:

1 Plot the most likely situation (map A) – remembering to be careful to *reassess* interest and power for each stakeholder in relation to this *new* strategy.

2 Map the preferred situation (map B).

3 Identify the mismatches – and hence the political priorities. Remember to include the need to *maintain* a stakeholder in its 'opening' position (if relevant).

4 Finish off by listing the actions you would propose to take and give a final view of the degree of political risk in pursuing this new strategy.

4.5.3 Power[41]

In considering stakeholder expectations the previous section highlighted the importance of power and how it is shared unequally between various stakeholders. For the purposes of this discussion, **power is the ability of individuals or groups to persuade, induce or coerce others into following certain courses of action**. As Table 4.5 shows, there are different sources of power. It is not only derived from people's hierarchical position within an organisation or formal corporate governance arrangements. It could be a function of the resources or know-how they control or the networks they have built up, for example.

The relative importance of these sources of power will vary over time. Indeed changes in the business environment can significantly shift the power balance between organisations and

Table 4.5 Sources and indicators of power

Sources of power	
Within organisations	**For external stakeholders**
• Hierarchy (formal power), e.g. autocratic decision-making • Influence (informal power), e.g. charismatic leadership • Control of strategic resources, e.g. strategic products • Possession of knowledge and skills, e.g. computer specialists • Control of the human environment, e.g. negotiating skills • Involvement in strategy implementation, e.g. by exercising discretion	• Control of strategic resources, e.g. materials, labour, money • Involvement in strategy implementation, e.g. distribution outlets, agents • Possession of knowledge or skills, e.g. subcontractors, partners • Through internal links, e.g. informal influence
Indicators of power	
Within organisations	**For external stakeholders**
• Status • Claim on resources • Representation • Symbols	• Status • Resource dependence • Negotiating arrangements • Symbols

their stakeholders. For example, consumers' knowledge of different companies' offerings through internet browsing has increased their power as they compare different offerings and reduce their traditional loyalty to a particular supplier. The distribution of power will also vary in relation to the strategy under consideration. For example, a corporate finance function will be more powerful in relation to developments requiring new capital or revenue commitments than in relation to ones which are largely self-financing or within the financial authority of separate divisions or subsidiaries.

Since there are a variety of different sources of power, it is useful to look for *indicators of power*, the visible signs that stakeholders have been able to exploit sources of power. These include: the *status* of the individual or group (such as job grade or reputation); the *claim on resources* (such as budget size); *representation* in powerful positions; and *symbols* of power (such as office size or use of titles and names). For external stakeholders a key indicator is *resource dependence*; for example, the relative size of shareholdings or loans, or the proportion of a company's business tied up with any one customer, or a similar dependence on suppliers. One way of assessing resource dependence is to consider the ease with which a supplier, financier or customer could switch or *be switched* at short notice.

An underlying theme in this chapter has been that strategists have to consider the overall strategic purpose of their organisations. However, a central question that arises is what stakeholder expectations they should respond to in so doing. The key debate provides three views on this in the context of publicly quoted large commercial organisations.

KEY DEBATE

Three views on the purpose of a business

Since there is no one categoric view of the overarching purpose of a business, stakeholders, including managers, have to decide.

Milton Friedman and profit maximisation

Milton Friedman,[1] the renowned economist, wrote:

> In a free enterprise, private property system, a corporate executive is an employee of the owners of the business. He has direct responsibility to his employers. That responsibility is to conduct the business in accordance with their desires, which generally will be to make as much money as possible while conforming to the basic rules of society. . . . What does it mean to say that the corporate executive has a 'social responsibility'? . . . If the statement is not pure rhetoric, it must mean that he is to act in some way that is not in the interests of his employers. . . . Insofar as his actions in accord with his 'social responsibility' reduce returns to stockholders, he is spending their money. Insofar as his actions raise the price to customers, he is spending the customers' money. Insofar as his actions lower the wages of some employees he is spending their money.

Milton Friedman's maxim was that 'the business of business is business', that the 'only social responsibility of business is to increase its profit'. Market mechanisms are then adequate in themselves. If customers are not satisfied, they take their business elsewhere. If employees are not satisfied they work elsewhere. It is the job of government to ensure that there is a free market to allow those conditions to take effect.

Charles Handy's stakeholder view

Citing the corporate scandals of the last decade, Charles Handy[2] argues that the driving for shareholder value linked to stock options for executives, especially in the USA, has resulted in the system 'creating value where none existed'. He accepts

> that there is, first, a clear and important need to meet the expectations of a company's theoretical owners: the shareholders. It would, however, be more accurate to call them investors, perhaps even gamblers. They have none of the pride or responsibility of ownership and are . . . only there for the money. . . . But to turn shareholders' needs into a purpose is to be guilty of a logical confusion. To mistake a necessary condition for a sufficient one. We need to eat to live; food is a necessary condition of life. But if we lived mainly to eat, making food a sufficient or sole purpose of life, we would become gross. The purpose of a business, in other words, is not to make a profit. It is to make a profit so that the business can do something more or better. That 'something' becomes the real justification for the business.

The new capitalists' argument: 'Society and share owners are becoming one and the same'

In their book *The New Capitalists*,[3] the authors also recognise that 'a corporation is the property of its stock owners and should serve their interests'. However, it is the 'millions of pension holders and other savers . . . [who] . . . own the world's giant corporations'. These 'new capitalists are likely to be highly diversified in their investments'. Investment funds, such as pension funds, are their representatives and 'hold a tiny share in hundreds, perhaps even thousands, of companies around the world'. They then argue:

> Imagine that all your savings were invested in one company. The success of that company alone would be your only interest. You would want it to survive, prosper and grow, even if that did damage to the economic system as a whole. But your perspective would change if you had investments in lots of companies. [Then] it is to your disadvantage that any business should seek to behave socially irresponsibly towards other businesses, the customers, employees or society generally. By so doing they will damage the interests of other firms in which you have an interest. The new capitalist has an interest in all the firms in which he or she is investing behaving responsibly: 'in creating rules that lead to the success of the economic system as a whole, even if, in particular circumstances, those rules may tie the hands of an individual company' . . . . managers of a business should quite properly 'concentrate single mindedly on the success of their own organisations . . . however they will not be serving their share owners' interest if they undertake activities that may be good for them individually, but damaging to the larger economic system.

References:
1. M. Friedman, 'The social responsibility of business is to increase its profits', *New York Times. Magazine*, 13 September (1970).
2. C. Handy, 'What's a business for?', *Harvard Business Review*, vol. 80, no. 12, December (2002), pp. 49–55.
3. S. Davies, J. Lukommik and D. Pitt-Watson, *The New Capitalists*, Harvard Business School Press, 2006.

Questions

1 Which view do you hold:
   (a) as a manager?   (b) as a shareholder?

2 What are the implications of the different views for managers' development of organisational strategy?

SUMMARY

- An important managerial task is to decide how the organisation should express its strategic purpose through statements of *mission, vision, values* or *objectives*.
- The purpose of an organisation will be influenced by the expectations of its *stakeholders*.
- The influence of some key stakeholders will be represented formally within the *governance structure* of an organisation. This can be represented in terms of a *governance chain*, showing the links between ultimate beneficiaries and the managers of an organisation.
- There are two generic governance structure systems: the *shareholder model* and the *stakeholder model*, though there are variations of these internationally.
- Organisations adopt different stances on *corporate social responsibility* depending on how they perceive their role in society. Individual managers may also be faced with ethical dilemmas relating to the purpose of their organisation or the actions it takes.
- Different stakeholders exercise different influence on organisational purpose and strategy, dependent on the extent of their power and interest. Managers can assess the influence of different stakeholder groups through *stakeholder analysis*.

VIDEO ASSIGNMENT

Visit *MyStrategyLab* and watch the *Eden* case study.

1 Write a statement of Eden's mission, vision and values.

2 Explain how Eden's management developed its strategy on the basis of aligning stakeholder interests.

WORK ASSIGNMENTS

✳ *Denotes more advanced work assignments. * Refers to a case study in the Text and Cases edition.*

4.1   Write mission and vision statements for an organisation of your choice and suggest what strategic objectives managers might set. Explain why you think these are appropriate.

4.2   * For an organisation of your choice, map out a governance chain that identifies the key players through to the beneficiaries of the organisation's good (or poor) performance. To what extent do you think managers are:

(a) knowledgeable about the expectations of beneficiaries;
(b) actively pursuing their interests;
(c) keeping them informed?

4.3   What are your own views of the strengths and weaknesses of the stakeholder and shareholder models of governance?

4.4   Identify organisations that correspond to the overall stances on corporate social responsibility described in Table 4.2.

4.5   Identify the key corporate social responsibility issues which are of major concern in an industry or public service of your choice (refer to Table 4.3). Compare the approach of two or more organisations in that industry, and explain how this relates to their competitive standing.

4.6   Using Illustration 4.5 as a worked example, identify and map out the stakeholders for RED, Manchester United* or an organisation of your choice in relation to:

(a) current strategies;
(b) different future strategies of your choice.

What are the implications of your analysis for the strategy of the organisation?

Integrative assignment

4.7   Using specific examples suggest how changes in corporate governance and in expectations about corporate social responsibility may require organisations to develop new capabilities (Chapter 3) and influencing the choice of strategies they follow (Chapter 11).

RECOMMENDED KEY READINGS

- The case for the importance of clarity of strategic values and vision is especially strongly made by J. Collins and J. Porras, *Built to Last: Successful Habits of Visionary Companies*, Harper Business, 2002 (in particular see chapter 11).

- For books providing a fuller explanation of corporate governance: R. Monks and N. Minow (eds), *Corporate Governance*, 4th edition, Wiley-Blackwell, 2008; and J. Solomon, *Corporate Governance and Accountability*, 2nd edition, Wiley, 2007. For a provocative critique and proposals for the future of corporate governance linked to issues of social responsibility see S. Davies, J. Lukomnik and D. Pitt-Watson, *The New Capitalists*, Harvard Business School Press, 2006.

- For a review of different stances on corporate social responsibility see P. Mirvis and B. Googins, 'Stages of corporate citizenship', *California Management Review*, vol. 48, no. 2 (2006), pp. 104–26. Also see A.B. Carroll and K.M. Shabana, 'The business case for Corporate Social Responsibility, *International Journal of Management Reviews*, vol. 12, no. 1 (2010), pp. 85–105.

- For more about the stakeholder concept and analysis see K. Scholes's chapter in V. Ambrosini with G. Johnson and K. Scholes (eds), *Exploring Techniques of Analysis and Evaluation in Strategic Management*, Prentice Hall, 1998. Also J.M. Bryson, 'What to do when stakeholders matter: stakeholder identification and analysis techniques', *Public Management Review*, vol. 6, no. 1 (2004), pp. 21–53.

REFERENCES

1. Cynthia A. Montgomery, 'Putting leadership back into strategy', *Harvard Business Review*, Jan 2008, pp. 54–60.
2. J. Collins and J. Porras, 'Building your company's vision', *Harvard Business Review*, Sept-Oct, 1996, pp. 65–77.
3. P. Lencioni, 'Make your values mean something', *Harvard Business Review*, vol. 80, no. 7 (2002), pp. 113–17.
4. For example, see B. Bartkus, M. Glassman and B. McAfee, 'Mission statements: are they smoke and mirrors?', *Business Horizons*, vol. 43, no. 6 (2000), pp. 23–8; and B. Bartkus, M. Glassman and B. McAfee, 'Mission statement quality and financial performance', *European Management Journal*, vol. 24, no. 1 (2006), pp. 86–94.
5. See J. Collins and J. Porras, *Built to Last: Successful Habits of Visionary Companies*, Harper Business, 2002.
6. Communicating effectively with the investing community is essential, as discussed by A. Hutton, 'Four rules', *Harvard Business Review*, vol. 79, no. 5 (2001), pp. 125–32.
7. See Sayan Chatterjee, 'Core objectives: clarity in designing strategy', *California Management Review*, 47, 2, 2005, 33–49.
8. See A. Neely, 'Measuring performance in innovative firms', in R. Delbridge, L. Grattan and G. Johnson (eds), *The Exceptional Manager*, Oxford University Press, 2006, chapter 6.
9. Useful general references on corporate governance are: R. Monks and N. Minow (eds), *Corporate Governance*, 4th edition, Blackwell, 2008; and J. Solomon, *Corporate Governance and Accountability*, 2nd edition, Wiley, 2007. Also see Ruth Aguilera and Gregory Jackson, 'The cross-national diversity of corporate governance: dimensions and determinants', *Academy of Management Review*, vol. 28, no. 3 (2003), pp. 447–65.
10. This definition is based on, but adapted from, that in S. Jacoby, 'Corporate governance and society', *Challenge*, vol. 48, no. 4 (2005), pp. 69–87.
11. M.K. Fiegener, 'Locus of ownership and family involvement in small private firms', *Journal of Management Studies*, vol. 47, no. 2 (2010), pp. 296–321.
12. The principal–agent model is part of agency theory which developed within organisational economics but is now widely used in the management field as described here. Two useful references are: K. Eisenhardt, 'Agency theory: an assessment and review', *Academy of Management Review*, vol. 14, no. 1 (1989), pp. 57–74; J.-J. Laffont and D. Martimort, *The Theory of Incentives: The Principal–Agent Model*, Princeton University Press, 2002.
13. For a strong advocacy of this position see S. Davies, J. Lukomnik and D. Pitt-Watson, *The New Capitalists*, Harvard Business School Press, 2006.
14. For a typology and examples of ways in which investors engage with firms, see N. Amos and W. Oulton, 'Approaching and engaging with CR', *Corporate Responsibility Management*, vol. 2, no. 3 (2006), pp. 34–7.
15. Within this broad classification there are other models. For further explanation see, for example, A. Murphy and K. Topyan, 'Corporate governance: a critical survey of key concepts, issues, and recent reforms in the US', *Employee*

Responsibility and Rights Journal, vol. 17, no. 2 (2005), pp. 75–89.
16. See J.A. McCahery, P. Moerland, T. Raijmakers and L. Renneboog, *Corporate Governance Regimes: Convergence and Diversity*, Oxford University Press, 2002.
17. See S. Jacoby (2005) (see reference 10).
18. We are grateful to Rob Pieters for this background to governance systems in the Netherlands.
19. For a discussion of corporate governance reforms in continental Europe see L. Anriques and P. Volpin, 'Corporate governance reforms in continental Europe', *Journal of Economic Perspectives*, vol. 21, no. 1 (2007), pp. 117–40.
20. In the USA: the Sarbanes–Oxley Act (2002). In the UK: D. Higgs, 'Review of the role and effectiveness of non-executive directors', UK Department of Trade and Industry, 2003.
21. See D. Norburn, B. Boyd, M. Fox and M. Muth, 'International corporate governance reform', *European Business Journal*, vol. 12, no. 3 (2000), pp. 116–33; J. Sonnenfeld, 'What makes great boards great', *Harvard Business Review*, vol. 80, no. 9 (2002), pp. 106–13.
22. Practising managers might wish to consult B. Kelley, *Ethics at Work*, Gower, 1999, which covers many of the issues in this section and includes the Institute of Management guidelines on ethical management. Also see M.T. Brown, *Corporate Integrity: Rethinking Organisational Ethics and Leadership*, Cambridge University Press, 2005.
23. This definition is based on that by the World Business Council for Sustainable Development.
24. Based on research undertaken at the Center for Corporate Citizenship at the Boston College, reported in P. Mirvis and B. Googins, 'Stages of corporate citizenship', *California Management Review*, vol. 48, no. 2 (2006), pp. 104–26.
25. Often quoted as a summary of Milton Friedman's argument is M. Friedman: 'The social responsibility of business is to increase its profits', *New York Times Magazine*, 13 September 1970.
26. See A. McWilliams and D. Seigel, 'Corporate social responsibility: a theory of the firm perspective', *Academy of Management Review*, vol. 26 (2001), pp. 117–27.
27. See *The State of Corporate Citizenship in the US: A View from Inside, 2003–2004*, Center for Corporate Citizenship, Boston College; also reported in Mirvis and Googins, reference 24.
28. See M. Porter and M. Kramer, 'The competitive advantage of corporate philanthropy', *Harvard Business Review*, vol. 80, no. 12 (2002), pp. 56–68.
29. H. Hummels, 'Organizing ethics: a stakeholder debate', *Journal of Business Ethics*, vol. 17, no. 13 (1998), pp. 1403–19.
30. D. Vogel, 'Is there a market for virtue? The business case for corporate social responsibility', *California Management Review*, vol. 47, no. 4 (2005), pp. 19–45.
31. S.A. Waddock and C. Bodwell, 'Managing responsibility: what can be learned from the quality movement', *California Management Review*, vol. 47, no. 1 (2004), pp. 25–37; and R. Orsato, 'Competitive environmental strategies: when

does it pay to be green?', *California Management Review*, vol. 48, no. 2 (2006), pp. 127–43.

32. These examples are given by Porter and Kramer, reference 28.

33. K. Schnietz and M. Epstein, 'Does a reputation for corporate social responsibility pay off?', *Social Issues in Management Conference Papers*, Academy of Management Proceedings, 2002. This paper shows that the Fortune 500 firms that were also in the Domini Social Index outperformed the others in terms of stock return.

34. Clyde E. Hull and Sandra Rothenberg, 'Firm performance: the interactions of corporate social performance with innovation and industry differentiation', *Strategic Management Journal*, vol. 29 (2008), pp. 781–9.

35. We are grateful to Angela Sutherland of Glasgow Caledonian University for this example.

36. M.R. Banaji, M.H. Bazerman and D. Chugh, 'How (UN)ethical are you?', *Harvard Business Review*, vol. 81, no. 12 (2003), pp. 56–64.

37. Early writings about stakeholders are still worthy of note. For example, the seminal work by R.M. Cyert and J.G. March, *A Behavioral Theory of the Firm*, Prentice Hall, 1964; and R.E. Freeman, *Strategic Management: A Stakeholder Approach*, Pitman, 1984. Also see J. Bryson, 'What to do when stakeholders matter: stakeholder identification and analysis techniques', *Public Management Review*, vol. 6, no. 1 (2004), pp. 21–53.

38. A fuller explanation of how these three groups interact with organisations can be found in J. Cummings and J. Doh, 'Identifying who matters: mapping key players in multiple environments', *California Management Review*, vol. 42, no. 2 (2000), pp. 83–104.

39. This approach to stakeholder mapping has been adapted from A. Mendelow, *Proceedings of the 2nd International Conference on Information Systems*, Cambridge, MA, 1991. See also K. Scholes's chapter, 'Stakeholder analysis', in V. Ambrosini with G. Johnson and K. Scholes (eds), *Exploring Techniques of Analysis and Evaluation in Strategic Management*, Prentice Hall, 1998. For a public-sector explanation, see K. Scholes, 'Stakeholder mapping: a practical tool for public sector managers', in G. Johnson and K. Scholes (eds), *Exploring Public Sector Strategy*, Financial Times Prentice Hall, 2001, chapter 9; and J. Bryson, 'What to do when stakeholders matter: stakeholder identification and analysis techniques', *Public Management Review*, vol. 6, no. 1 (2004), pp. 21–53.

40. For example, see Ronald K. Mitchell, Bradley R. Agle and Donna J. Wood, 'Toward a theory of stakeholder identification and salience: defining the principle of who and what really counts', *The Academy of Management Review*, vol. 22, no. 4 (1997), pp. 853–86, and Kalle Pajunen, 'Stakeholder influences in organizational survival', *Journal of Management Studies*, vol. 43, no. 6 (2006), pp. 1261–88.

41. D. Buchanan and R. Badham, *Power, Politics and Organisational Change: Winning the Turf Game*, Sage, 1999, provide a useful analysis of the relationship between power and strategy.

CASE EXAMPLE

(RED)™

Phyl Johnson, Strategy Explorers

'We can shop to help end Aids in Africa' Oprah Winfrey

(RED)™ sometimes referred to as (Product)RED, was created in 2006 as a form of creative capitalism: an organisation that collaborates with some of the world's best known corporate brands but for a charitable purpose. (RED) is global organisation that administers and promotes an umbrella brand ((RED)™) that member corporations may use for their products and then pay back into the Global Fund to fight Aids, tuberculosis and malaria in Africa. Its set-up was funded by leading players in the world's corporate markets such as Bill Gates of Microsoft and the financier George Soros but was inspired and is led by U2 front-man Bono and US political activist Bobby Shriver. (See the (RED) manifesto.)

Rwanda was selected as the initial country to benefit from sales of the (RED)™ products but by 2010 they were active in Swaziland, Ghana and Lesotho. The early corporate members included American Express with a (RED)™ credit card, Apple with a (RED)™ iPod, Motorola with a (RED)™ phone and Gap with a series of (RED)™ T-shirts. Later, baby buggy manufacturer Bugaboo, Hallmark (greetings cards), Dell, Nike, Starbucks and Diptyque candles all joined the initiative.

The sole recipient of monies raised by the (RED)™ initiative is The Global Fund, which, since its start in 2002, rose to become the dominant funder of programmes to fight Aids, tuberculosis and malaria. It has been estimated that with more than 600 programmes running, The Global Fund has saved in excess of 4.5 million lives by providing Aids treatment for 2.3 million people, anti-tuberculosis treatment for 5.4 million people and the distribution of 88 million insecticide-treated bed nets for the prevention of malaria. The percentage that (RED)™ donates to this Global Fund is unclear.

Support for the (RED)™ campaign repeatedly comes from Microsoft's Bill Gates; writing in *Time Magazine*:[1]

It's a great thing: the companies make a difference while adding to their bottom line, consumers get to

> THE (RED)™ MANIFESTO
>
> ALL THINGS BEING EQUAL, THEY ARE NOT.
>
> AS FIRST WORLD CONSUMERS, WE HAVE TREMENDOUS POWER. WHAT WE COLLECTIVELY CHOOSE TO BUY, OR NOT TO BUY, CAN CHANGE THE COURSE OF LIFE AND HISTORY ON THIS PLANET.
>
> (RED) IS THAT SIMPLE AN IDEA. AND THAT POWERFUL. NOW, YOU HAVE A CHOICE. THERE ARE (RED) CREDIT CARDS, (RED) PHONES, (RED) SHOES, (RED) FASHION BRANDS. AND NO, THIS DOES NOT MEAN THEY ARE ALL RED IN COLOR. ALTHOUGH SOME ARE.
>
> IF YOU BUY A (RED) PRODUCT OR SIGN UP FOR A (RED) SERVICE, AT NO COST TO YOU, A (RED) COMPANY WILL GIVE SOME OF ITS PROFITS TO BUY AND DISTRIBUTE ANTI-RETROVIRAL MEDICINE TO OUR BROTHERS AND SISTERS DYING OF AIDS IN AFRICA.
>
> WE BELIEVE THAT WHEN CONSUMERS ARE OFFERED THIS CHOICE, AND THE PRODUCTS MEET THEIR NEEDS, THEY WILL CHOOSE (RED). AND WHEN THEY CHOOSE (RED) OVER NON-(RED), THEN MORE BRANDS WILL CHOOSE TO BECOME (RED) BECAUSE IT WILL MAKE GOOD BUSINESS SENSE TO DO SO. AND MORE LIVES WILL BE SAVED.
>
> (RED) IS NOT A CHARITY. IT IS SIMPLY A BUSINESS MODEL. YOU BUY (RED) STUFF. WE GET THE MONEY. BUY THE PILLS AND DISTRIBUTE THEM. THEY TAKE THE PILLS. STAY ALIVE. AND CONTINUE TO TAKE CARE OF THEIR FAMILIES AND CONTRIBUTE SOCIALLY AND ECONOMICALLY IN THEIR COMMUNITIES.
>
> IF THEY DON'T GET THE PILLS, THEY DIE. WE DON'T WANT THEM TO DIE. WE WANT TO GIVE THEM THE PILLS. AND WE CAN. AND YOU CAN. AND IT'S EASY.
>
> ALL YOU HAVE TO DO IS UPGRADE YOUR CHOICE.

Source: http://www.joinred.com/manifesto.asp.

show their support for a good cause, and – most important – lives are saved.

In other articles he has acknowledged that governments also need to be more generous in the battle against life-threatening and preventable disease in Africa, but believes that as consumers, most people would want to *'associate themselves with saving lives'* and that Gap with their T-shirts or Armani with their sunglasses offer this opportunity through (RED).

Perhaps as a result of the fame of its leaders, in particular Bono who is highly active on behalf of (RED), it has maintained a high profile amongst the glitterati of world society. This is especially the case in the USA. Vocal supporters have included the US chat show host Oprah Winfrey, Hollywood star Scarlett Johansson and the music industry's Lady Gaga. All of these will offer interviews, talk-show time and concert appearances as either fund or awareness raising endeavours.

However, the international response to (RED) has not been universally positive. The moot point being that at its heart, is this endeavour about philanthropy or exploitation: should you use an illness to market a product?

Environmental arguments against (RED) focus on the downside of linking consumerism to charitable giving. Instead of supporting (RED)'s own phrase *Buying Red Saves Lives*, environmental groups make the argument: buy less and give money to charity instead; save the planet *and* its people.

Arguments against (RED) also come from other quarters and suggest that weak campaigns, as they see (RED) to be, dilute international will and skill to make a genuine difference to people's suffering. In an article published in the UK's leading medical journal *The Lancet*, a socio-political argument is made against (RED) as a mask or '*charitainment*' that hides the true complexity and seriousness of Africa's position in relation to the west. For instance, (RED) is about consumers making *connections* from the prosperous west to the third world of Africa. But there always have been socio-political *connections* between the west and Africa. At first it was slavery, then more complicated forms of economic relationships normally ending with African states coming off the worst, e.g. being crippled by debts to the international community that cleared countries of their health resources just at the time when the Aids epidemic began to take hold. The *Lancet* article argues that the (RED) initiative is fluff, window dressing that hides the real issue and distracts us from higher impact solutions such as major government sponsored and tax funded coordinated and sustained funding. In short, it allows western consumers to feel better about what is ultimately the maintenance of an unhealthy status quo.

Quite apart from challenges as to the purpose of (RED), questions have been raised as to its effectiveness as a business model, its governance and transparency of the percentages of sales donated to The Global Fund. A 2007 article in *Advertising Age*[2] claimed that the campaign had raised only $18m (~€12.6m) in a year despite a marketing outlay by companies involved in the scheme of $100 million. Whereas Bill Gates suggested in 2008 that between January 2007 and July 2008 (RED) had raised $100 million. Gap was the biggest spender on advertising in the 2007 period with a budget of $7.8 million. Critics ask, if the purpose of (RED) is to raise money then a crucial challenge is why not cut out the product and get Gap etc. to donate their 7.8 million direct to The Global Fund: why is (RED) needed and for whom does it really exist?

A spokeswoman for (RED) claimed that the *Ad Age* figure of 100 million was merely a 'phantom number pulled out of thin air'. Yet it refuses to go away, appearing in most commentaries that are critical of (RED).

However, an article in the *Independent*[3] went on to do its own mathematics: 'I believe the money raised in six months since the product range was launched is $25 million on an advertising investment of $40 million. As such, arguably this is a good rate of return on an advertising investment in the time available.' They went on to argue:

> What the (RED) initiative has set out to do – and with some success if $25 million in six months is half the profits (RED) products would have made – is create a stream of revenue for the fight against AIDS in Africa which will far exceed one-off payments from corporate philanthropy budgets. It looks set to create a major source of cash for the global fund, and one which is sustainable. It is an entirely new model for fund raising.

But wouldn't it be better if people simply gave the money that they spend on the products directly to charity? 'If only that were the choice. But most people wouldn't give the cost of a new iPod to the global fund.' They continued: 'The money (RED) has raised means that some 160,000 Africans will be put on life-saving anti-retrovirals in the coming months, orphans are being fed and kept in school in Swaziland and a national HIV treatment and prevention programme has begun in Rwanda.'

Moving the spotlight from the governance, purpose and model of (RED) and toward its collection of corporate collaborators does not simplify the issue. If the purpose of business is to be in business, then why would American Express for example donate 1% of its customers' spend on their (RED)™ credit cards to (RED) and ultimately The Global Fund? Does it make shareholder sense? Taking the example of Gap, on their website, their head of social responsibility states

> Acting in an ethical way is not only the right thing to do – it also unlocks new ways for us to do business better.

Hence they find themselves at the forefront of the (RED) campaign. *The Times*[4] newspaper offered a stinging critique of Gap's position.

> My problem here is with what this ((Red)™) does for the very idea of capitalism, for companies pursuing their real and entirely wholesome responsibility of making money. Free market capitalism, untrammelled by marketing people in alliance with special interest groups on a mission to save the world, has done more to alleviate poverty than any well-intentioned anti-poverty campaign in the history of the globe.

By concentrating on selling quality, low-priced goods, some of them made with labour that would otherwise lie idle (and dying) in the developing world, Gap saves lives. By helping to keep prices down and generating profits, Gap ploughs money back into the pockets of people in the US, the UK and elsewhere. This creates the demand for imports of products from the developing world, which keeps the poor of those countries from suffering even more than they do now.

In a complex world, we all operate in a division of labour. Companies make profits. It is what they are designed to do. It is what they do best. When they depart from that mission, they lead their employees and their shareholders down a long, slow route to perdition.

You think that is over the top? What is most troubling about campaigns such as (Product)RED is that they represent an accommodation with groups who think the business of capitalism is fundamentally evil. By appeasing people who regard globalisation as a process of exploitation, companies such as Gap are making the world much worse for all of us. They are implicitly acknowledging that their main business – selling things that people want for a profit – is inherently immoral and needs to be expiated by an occasional show of real goodness.

Rather than resisting it, they are nurturing and feeding an anti-business sentiment that will impoverish us all. What's more, this encroachment by companies is fundamentally undemocratic. Companies should not collude with interest groups and non-governmental organisations to decide on public priorities. That is for free people, through their elected governments, to do.

None of this is to say companies – or the people who run them – should not behave morally. They should observe not only the law, but the highest ethical standards, which means honesty, straight dealing and openness. It might even at times be in their corporate interests (i.e. longer-term profitability) to contribute to political or charitable causes – in those cases shareholders can and should vote on the appropriation of funds for such purposes.

Whether (RED) is good or bad for charity and business alike or a new path continues to be debated. Meanwhile, Bono and co. continue to sign up new corporate partners and generate new headlines, but all done in the glossiest magazines possible.

References:
1. *Time Magazine*, Thursday 31 July 2008.
2. Frazier, Mya, 'Costly Red Campaign reaps meager $18m', *Advertising Age*, 78, 10, 5 March 2007.
3. Vallely, P. 'The big question: does RED campaign help big Western brands more than Africa?', *Independent*, p. 50, 9 March 2007.
4. From Baker, Gerrard, 'Mind the Gap – With this attack on Globalization', *The Times*, 24 October 2006. © The Times/The Sun/nisyndication.com.

Source: (Product)RED website http://joinred.blogspot.com.

Questions

1 Drawing on the three perspectives in the Key Debate or the four stances in Table 4.2, what is the rationale of:

(a) The founders of (Product)RED?

(b) The Director of Social Responsibility for Gap?

(c) The author of the article in *The Times*?

2 What views might shareholders of Gap have of (Product)RED?

3 In your view is (Product)RED an appropriate corporate activity?

5

CULTURE AND STRATEGY

Learning outcomes

After reading this chapter you should be able to:

- Identify organisations that have experienced *strategic drift* and the symptoms of strategic drift.

- Analyse how *history* influences the strategic position of organisations.

- Analyse the influence of an *organisation's culture* on its strategy using the *cultural web*.

- Recognise the importance of strategists questioning the *taken-for-granted aspects of a culture*.

PEARSON
mystrategylab

MyStrategyLab is designed to help you make the most of your studies.

Visit **www.pearsoned.co.uk/mystrategylab** to discover a wide range of resources specific to this chapter, including:

- A personalised **Study plan** that will help you understand core concepts
- **Audio** and **video clips** that put the spotlight on strategy in the real world
- **Online glossaries** and **flashcards** that provide helpful reminders when you're looking for some quick revision.

(5.1) INTRODUCTION

Chapters 2, 3 and 4 have considered the important influences of the environment, organisational capabilities and stakeholder expectations on the development of strategy. Vital as these are to understand, there is a danger that managers fail to take into account other significant issues. One of these is the culture of the organisation. By 2010 Marks & Spencer had been wrestling with a strategic change for almost a decade; yet commentators still cited its cultural heritage of over a century as a major influence on its strategic direction. This highlights the danger of failing to take in how the past influences current and future strategy. Many organisations have long histories. The large Japanese Mitsui Group was founded in the 17th century; Daimler was founded in 19th century; managers in the UK retailer Sainsbury's still refer to the founding principles of the Sainsbury family in the 19th century. All these and many public-sector organisations – government departments, the police, universities, for example – are strongly influenced by their historical legacies that have become embedded in their cultures.

Figure 5.1 summarises the chapter structure. The chapter begins by explaining the phenomenon of *strategic drift* that highlights the importance of history and culture in relation to strategy development and identifies important challenges managers face in managing that development. The chapter then considers the two important and linked perspectives of *history and culture*. Section 5.3 examines the influence of the history of an organisation on its current and future strategy and goes on to consider how that history can be analysed. Section 5.4 then explains what is meant by culture and how cultural influences at the national, institutional and organisational levels influence current and future strategy. It then suggests how a culture can be analysed and its influence on strategy understood.

Historical and cultural perspectives can help an understanding of both opportunities and constraints that organisations face. The business environment (Chapter 2) cannot be

Figure 5.1 The influence of history and culture

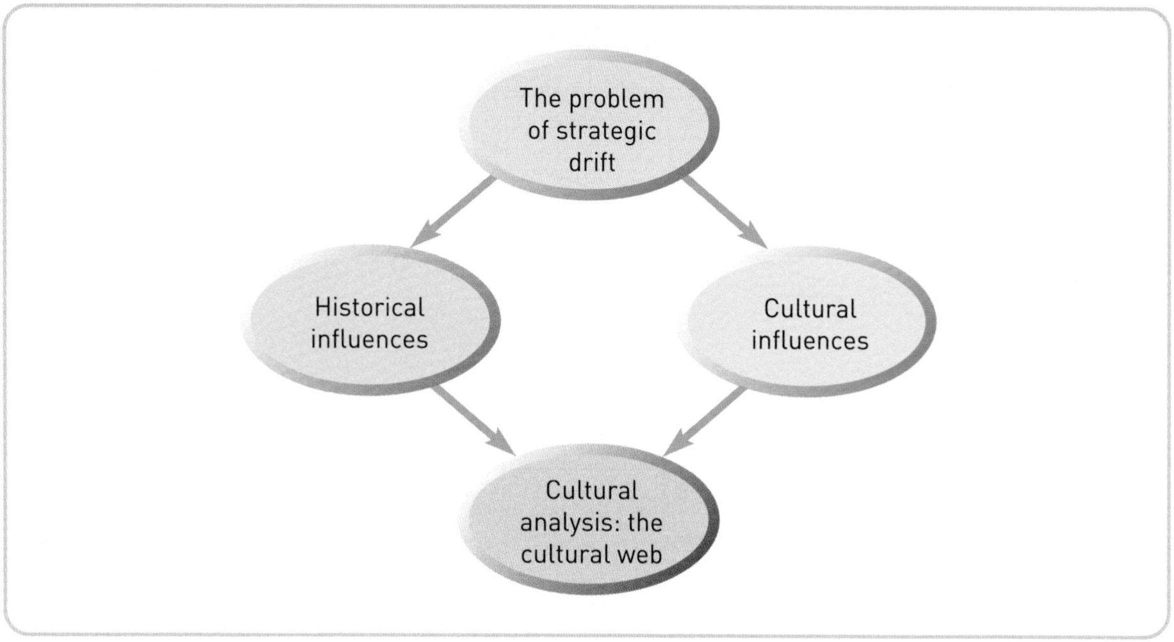

understood without considering how it has developed over time. The capabilities of an organisation (Chapter 3), especially those that provide organisations with competitive advantage, may have built up over time in ways unique to that organisation. In so doing such capabilities may become part of the culture of an organisation – the taken-for-granted way of doing things, therefore difficult for other organisations to copy. However, they may also be difficult to change. The power and influence of different stakeholders (Chapter 4) are also likely to have historical origins that are important to understand. The theme of this chapter is, then, that understanding the strategic position of an organisation includes understanding that its culture sometimes has deep historical roots. Such an understanding also informs the evaluation of the feasibilty of a strategy (Chapter 11), helps explain how strategies develop (Chapter 12) and informs the challenges of strategic change (Chapter 14).

 STRATEGIC DRIFT

Historical studies of organisations have shown a pattern that is represented in Figure 5.2. **Strategic drift**[1] **is the tendency for strategies to develop incrementally on the basis of historical and cultural influences, but fail to keep pace with a changing environment.** An example of strategic drift is given in Illustration 5.1. The reasons and consequences of strategic drift are important to understand, not only because it is common, but also because it helps explain why organisations often seem to stagnate in their strategy development. Strategic drift also highlights some significant challenges for managers which, in turn, point to some important lessons.

5.2.1 Strategies change incrementally

Strategies of organisations most often change gradually. This is discussed more fully in Chapter 11. Here it is sufficient to summarise by explaining that there is a tendency for strategies to develop

Figure 5.2 Strategic drift

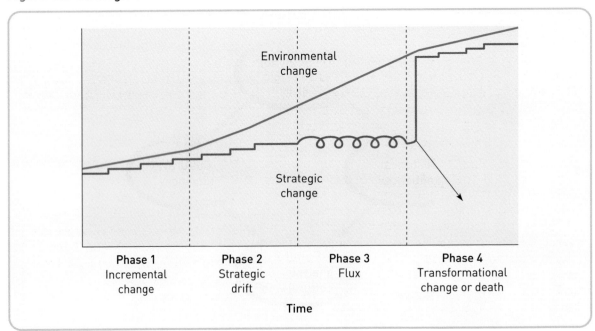

ILLUSTRATION 5.1

Motorola: Does history repeat itself?

The bases of a firm's success may persist over time but be the cause of strategic drift.

Founded in 1928, from the beginning, Motorola was known for its technological innovation. It introduced the 2-way walkie-talkie radio device widely used in the Second World War; and it marketed the first television for under $200 (€140). By the 1950s it had developed capabilities in printed circuit, ceramic substrate technology and electronic systems design. By the 1970s it was a leading producer of microprocessors and regarded as world leader in terms of technology.

By the mid 1980s Motorola was also the leading producer of cell phones using analogue technology. Indeed by the mid 1990s Motorola held over 60% of the US mobile telephone market and had experienced 27% year on year growth. At that time, however, these phones were bulky, expensive and targeted at business managers. In the mid 1990s digital technology was being developed. This overcame some of the shortcomings of analogue technology, reducing interference and allowing greater security, reduction in the size and weight of handsets, and more subscribers than analogue. It was technology supporting mass market development in a consumer market and demand grew rapidly.

Motorola claimed to be at the 'forefront of the development of digital technology'. However it chose to stay with analogue technology for many years, licensing its digital capabilities to Nokia and Eriksson. Indeed Motorola launched a new analogue phone, Star-TAC supported by an aggressive marketing campaign to promote it. This was despite the fact that wireless carrier customers were lobbying Motorola to develop digital phones.

By 1998 Motorola's market share had dropped to 34% and it was forced to lay off 20,000 people. Over the next decade, despite launching digital phones, Motorola faced an uphill battle to regain market share against competitors such as Eriksson and Nokia.

In 2005 Motorola launched its Razr V3 cell phone. Widely applauded for its technology and design, the initial selling price was $500. Motorola experienced initial success but by 2007 the price of a Razr had dropped to $30, Motorola's profits had plunged again, as had its share price; and once again it was planning to lay off workers. This was despite a market for more than 1 billion mobile phones per year.

What Motorola had overlooked was that the market had changed significantly. Consumers were replacing phones faster, typically every two years or less; in effect it was becoming a fashion market. Motorola on the other hand continued to focus on advancing technology in microchips, screen size and data speed. Moreover, just as in other fashion markets, competitors rapidly replicated the design benefits of the Razr.

By 2010 it was smartphones that were showing most growth in the market. Motorola's co-chief executive Sanjay Jha was confident in the development of the company's smartphone based on Google Inc's Android software. But some industry experts were worried that Motorola's sale of smartphones was relatively slow, together with continued decline in sales of their cheaper phones, their biggest selling product.

Even in Motorola's early days, critics suggested that the firm risked putting technology before market trends. The worry was that the same problem remained in 2010.

Sources: S. Finkelstein, 'Why smart executives fail: four case histories of how people learn the wrong lessons from history', *Business History*, 48, 2 (2006), pp. 153–70, and Brad Stone, *New York Times*, 3 February 2007.

Questions

1 Given that in the 1980s Motorola had the technology and knew the digital market was developing, give reasons why it persisted with analogue technology. (See Chapter 12 and the commentaries to help with this question.)

2 Update the illustration. Has Motorola learned its lessons?

on the basis of what the organisation has done in the past – especially if that has been successful.[2] For example, for many years UK retailer HMV had quite successfully developed its business by adapting to changing technology and tastes in the entertainment market. They had moved from vinyl to CDs; introduced DVDs and computer games when they arrived on the market; and increased the space allocation to them as demand increased. This is shown in phase 1 of the figure. In most successful businesses there are usually long periods of relative *continuity* during which established strategy remains largely unchanged or changes very *incrementally*. There are three main reasons for this:

- *Alignment with environmental change.* It could be that the environment, particularly the market, is changing gradually and the organisation is keeping in line with those changes by such incremental change. It would make no sense for the strategy to change dramatically when the market is not doing so.

- *The success of the past.* There may be a natural unwillingness by managers to change a strategy significantly if it has been successful in the past, especially if it is built on capabilities that have been shown to be the basis of competitive advantage (see Chapters 3 and 6) or of innovation (see Chapter 9). Managers quite understandably will argue that they should stick to what they know and do best.

- *Experimentation around a theme.* Managers may have learned how to build variations around their successful formula; in effect experimenting without moving too far from their capability base. (This is akin to what some writers have referred to as 'logical incrementalism'; see section 12.3.1).

This poses challenges for managers, however. For how long and to what extent can they rely on incremental change being sufficient? When should they make more fundamental strategic changes? And how can they detect when this is necessary?

5.2.2 The tendency towards strategic drift

HMV persisted in the conviction that there was a market for the sale of music and DVDs through specialist retail outlets. They continued to adjust their retail formats and extended product ranges in the search for a sustainable competitive position. They had difficulty, however, reconciling themselves to the need for more fundamental change to their business model given the shifts in the first decade of this century to the way in which people accessed music through the internet or bought through supermarkets.

Whilst an organisation's strategy may continue to change incrementally, the problem is that there do not need to be sudden or dramatic environmental changes for the strategy to become less aligned with the environment. Phase 2 of Figure 5.2 shows environmental change accelerating, but it is not sudden. For HMV it was not as if changes in buyer behaviour or the growth in supermarket sales of CDs and DVDs happened overnight. These changes took place over years. The problem that gives rise to strategic drift is that, as with many organisations, HMV's strategy was not keeping pace with these changes. There are at least five reasons for this:

- *Steady as you go.* Chapter 2 has provided ways to analyse the environment and such analyses may yield insights. But how are managers to be sure of the direction and significance of such changes? Or changes may be seen as temporary. Managers may be understandably wary of changing what they are likely to see as a winning strategy, on the basis of what might only be a fad in the market, or a temporary downturn in demand, especially if it is built on capabilities that have been the basis of competitive advantage. It may be easy to see major changes with hindsight, but it may not be so easy to see their significance as they are happening.

- *Building on the familiar.* Managers may see changes in the environment about which they are uncertain or which they do not entirely understand. In these circumstances they may try to minimise the extent to which they are faced with such uncertainty by looking for answers that are familiar, which they understand and which have served them well in the past. This will lead to a bias towards continued incremental strategic change.

- *Core rigidities.* As Chapter 3 explains, success in the past may well have been based on capabilities that are unique to an organisation and difficult for others to copy. However, the capabilities that have been bases of advantage can become difficult to change; in effect *core rigidities.*[3] There are two reasons. First, over time, the ways of doing things that have delivered past success may become taken for granted. This may well have been an advantage in the past because it was difficult for competitors to imitate them. However, taken-for-granted capabilities rarely get questioned and therefore tend to persist beyond their usefulness. Second, ways of doing things develop over time and become more and more embedded in organisational routines that reinforce and rely on each other and are difficult to unravel; this is discussed further in section 5.3.1 below.

- *Relationships become shackles.*[4] Success has probably been built on the basis of excellent relationships with customers, suppliers and employees. Maintaining these may very likely and quite rightly be seen as fundamental to the long-term health of the organisation. Yet these relationships may make it difficult to make fundamental changes to strategy that could entail changing routes to market or the customer base, developing products requiring different suppliers or changing the skill base of the organisation with the risk of disrupting relationships with the workforce.

- *Lagged performance effects.* The effects of such drift may not be easy to see in terms of the performance of the organisation. Financial performance may continue to hold up in the early stages of strategic drift. Customers may be loyal and the organisation, by becoming more efficient, cutting costs or simply trying harder, may continue to hold up its performance. So there may not be internal signals of the need for change or pressures from managers, or indeed external observers, to make major changes.

However, over time, if strategic drift continues, there will be symptoms that become evident: a downturn in financial performance, a loss in market share to competitors perhaps; a decline in the share price. Indeed such a downturn may happen quite rapidly once external observers, not least competitors and financial analysts, have identified that such drift has occurred. Even the most successful companies may drift in this way. Indeed, there is a tendency – which Danny Miller has called the Icarus Paradox[5] – for businesses to become victims of the very success of their past. They become captured by the formula that has delivered that success.

5.2.3 A period of flux

The next phase (phase 3) may be a period of *flux* triggered by the downturn in performance. Strategies may change but in no very clear direction. There may also be management changes, often at the very top as the organisation comes under pressure from its stakeholders to make changes, not least shareholders in the case of a public company. There may be internal rivalry as to which strategy to follow, quite likely based on differences of opinion as to whether future strategy should be based on historic capabilities or whether those capabilities are becoming redundant. Indeed, there have been highly publicised boardroom rows when this has happened. All this may result in a further deterioration of confidence in the organisation: perhaps a further drop in performance or share price, a difficulty in recruiting high-quality management, or a further loss of customers' loyalty.

5.2.4 Transformational change or death

As things get worse it is likely that the outcome (phase 4) will be one of three possibilities. (i) The organisation may die; in the case of a commercial organisation it may go into receivership for example. (ii) It may get taken over by another organisation. (iii) Or it may go through a period of *transformational change*. Such change could take form in multiple changes related to the organisation's strategy. For example, a change in products, markets or market focus, changes of capabilities on which the strategy is based, changes in the top management of the organisation and perhaps the way the organisation is structured.

Transformational change does not take place frequently in organisations and is usually the result of a major downturn in performance. Often it is transformational changes that are heralded as the success stories of top executives; this is where they most visibly make a difference. The problem is that, from the point of view of market position, shareholder wealth and jobs, it may be rather late. Competitive position may have been lost, shareholder value has probably already been destroyed and, very likely, many jobs will have been lost too. The time when 'making a difference' really matters most is in Phase 2 in Figure 5.2, when the organisation is beginning to drift. However, a study of 215 major UK firms identified just 28 that could be said to have avoided drift and consequent performance decline over the 20-year period 1983–2003 and only 6 of these had effected major transformational change.[6] The problem is that, very likely, such drift is not easy to see before performance suffers. So, to avoid the damaging effects of strategic drift, it is vital to take seriously the extent to which historical tendencies in strategy development tend to persist in the cultural fabric of organisations. The rest of this chapter focuses on this. The challenge is, then, how to manage change in such circumstances and this challenge is taken up in Chapter 14 on managing strategic change.

(5.3) WHY IS HISTORY IMPORTANT?

If the reasons for strategic drift are to be understood and addressed, the history of organisations needs to be taken seriously. There are also other reasons why understanding history can help in the management of strategy. First, it needs to borne in mind that managers may have spent many years in an organisation or in an industry such that the experience on which they base their decisions may be heavily influenced by that history (see the discussion on the 'Experience Lens' in the Commentary). It is therefore helpful if managers can 'stand apart' from that history so as to understand the influence it has on them and the extent to which the strategy they are seeking to develop is usefully informed by that history as distinct from being constrained by it. The discussion on the influence of organisational culture in section 5.4 below is relevant here.

Taking history seriously can also have at least four positive benefits:

1   *Avoiding recency bias.* There can be a tendency for managers to focus on the short term given the pressure of current events. Understanding the current situation in terms of the past can provide useful lessons. For example: have there been historical trends that may repeat themselves? How have competitors responded to strategic moves in the past? A historical perspective may also help managers see what gave rise to events that were seen as surprises in the past and learn from how their organisation dealt with them.

2   *'What if' questions.* History can also encourage managers to ask 'what if' questions. Asking what might have happened had there been other influences in the environment, different responses from customers or competitors or different initiatives or leadership within their organisation makes the present more evidently a product of circumstances. The current strategic position may then be seen as less fixed and possibilities for changes in the future more possible.

3   *History as legitimisation.* History can be used as a resource to *legitimise* future strategies or strategic change as shown in Illustration 5.2. Past changes may also be referred to as evidence of the organisational potential for making changes happen. Past successes in innovation or product or market development may be used as a basis for encouraging commitment to future changes.

4   *Innovation based on historic capabilities.* In the BMW museum in Munich there is a quote: 'Anyone who wants to design for the future has to leaf through the past'.[7] The museum may be about the history of BMW, but it is also about how the lessons of the past can give rise to new ideas and innovation. Indeed the Innovation and Technology Division of BMW is sited next to the museum and the archives of BMW. Innovation may build on historic capabilities in at least two ways. First, as technologies change, firms with experience and skills built over time that are most appropriate to those changes tend to innovate more than those that don't.[8] Or it could be that there are new combinations of knowledge as capabilities built up in adjacent technologies are adapted in innovative ways to new technological opportunities. For example, the development of lighting systems was derived from the way gas was distributed.[9] Similarly, successful firms that created the TV industry were previously radio manufacturers and it was they who exhibited greater innovation as the industry developed than the non-radio producers.[10] If managers seek to build future strategy on historic capabilities they do, however, need to ask themselves the extent to which the environment is changing in such a way that such capabilities will still be relevant. In other words if strategy is to evolve on the back of such capabilities, it can only do so if simultaneously the changes in markets, technologies and other aspects of the environment discussed in Chapter 2 are potentially converging with those capabilities. They need to develop a sensitivity, not only to the historic capabilities that matter but the relationship of these to an evolving environment.

5.3.1 Path dependency

A useful way of thinking of the role and influence of history is through the concept of *path dependency* and the associated notion of historical *lock-in*. **Path dependency is where early events and decisions establish 'policy paths' that have lasting effects on subsequent events and decisions.**[11] Organisational decisions are therefore historically conditioned. Path dependency's origins, its impact and how it can be understood are therefore important.

Examples often relate to technology. There are many instances where the technology we employ is better explained by path dependency than by the optimisation of such technology.

ILLUSTRATION 5.2
Building on Pringle's Scottish heritage

Managers may employ an organisation's history and heritage to support its strategy.

Pringle of Scotland are designers and manufacturers of luxury knitwear. They were founded in 1815 by Robert Pringle and grew to become a well recognised brand across the UK, USA and Japan. Pringle traded on a combination of its quality and highly recognisable plaids such as the iconic Argyle Pringle pattern. In the 1940s Pringle was favoured by the British Royal family and movie stars and saw their designs feature on a *Vogue* magazine front cover. A very traditional company, Pringle's knitwear had a strong connection with tartan and golf, two of Scotland's great exports [another being whisky]. Pringle's longest serving brand champion was UK golf champion Nick Faldo who promoted their sweaters from 1981 to 2001.

By the new millennium Pringle's fortunes were in decline and it was acquired in 2000 by the Hong Kong based Fang Brothers for just £6 (~€6.6, ~$9) million. They recruited a new CEO, Kim Winser from Marks and Spencer. She decided to reposition Pringle away from a staid, middle aged image towards a designer fashion brand. She recruited new young designers and moved the design function from Scotland to London. Nick Faldo was 'out' and super model Sophie Dahl was 'in' starring in a series of sexed-up ad campaigns. However, Winser decided to retain manufacturing in the long established Hawick mill in the Scottish Borders which she saw as a key part of the firm's heritage and the brand was re-launched as 'Pringle of Scotland': 'I have added Scotland to the name because in a lot of countries worldwide, it is definitely a bonus – people trust Scottish cashmere.'

But the new Pringle didn't attract the new trendy customers they hoped for and fortunes fell. The Fangs had invested more than £50m into the company since acquiring it, but losses continued. Given these losses the manufacturing base in Hawick in Scotland was eventually closed in 2006.

In 2008 Mary-Adair Macaire replaced Kim Winser. Macaire joined from Chanel and planned to reconnect further with the history of the brand. Her view was that to succeed Pringle had to make a clearer connection between their new collections, the work of former Gucci designer Clare Waight Keller, and its core product offer, such as cashmere twinsets. 'There has to be a connection, otherwise there is schizophrenia. . . . Here was a company that invented the twinset, yet didn't sell them in its stores.'

Her plan was to return to the old Hollywood glamour of Grace Kelly in a petite pastel twinset. She was quoted as saying; 'I'm not trying to turn Pringle into something that it wasn't already. I'm trying to revive its reputation and identity as a house that makes luxurious garments with a focus on knitwear and style.' Moreover, despite the closure of the factory, she still saw the Scottish heritage as vital: 'The Fangs tried hard to keep [the Hawick mill] going, but after eight years of investment, felt the funds could be better used elsewhere. We are actually producing more goods in Scotland now than when we had the factory.'

Between 2008 and 2010 the Fangs invested a further £18million, but the accounts reported a loss of £9.3million in the year to March 2009.

Questions

1 Why do you think successive CEOs of Pringle decided to employ the heritage of their businesses to support the strategy?

2 Identify other organisations that have employed their organisational histories to support their strategy.

3 What are the benefits and potential problems of legitimising a strategy on the basis of an organisation's history?

A famous one is the system used for typewriter keyboards in most English-speaking countries around the world: QWERTY. This originated in the 19th century because it was a layout that reduced the problem of the keys on mechanical typewriters getting tangled when sales people demonstrated the machine at maximum speed by typing the word 'typewriter'. There are more optimal layouts, but QWERTY has remained with us for over 150 years despite changes in typewriter technology and the eventual development of personal computers.[12] There are countless other examples ranging from technologies in nuclear power stations through to automobile engines.

Path dependency is not just about technology. It also relates to any form of behaviour that has its origins in the past and becomes entrenched. In an organisational context it could begin with a decision which, of itself, may or may not be especially significant and where consequential succeeding events are unforeseeable. If successful, this initial decision can lead to positive feedback in the form of self-reinforcing mechanisms. Within an organisation these could include the development of behavioural routines supported by hardware and technology that make up systems of selling, marketing, recruiting, accounting and so on;[13] and externally these could be reinforced by repeated usage of a product or service by networks of customers and suppliers who come to see it as the dominant or standard offering. The result could be '*lock-in*' around that product or service.

There are many examples in the business world of such patterns of development, both at an organisational level and beyond. Take the example of accounting systems. The lock-in of these has occurred at multiple levels involving networks comprising what people do, those with whom they interact within and outside their organisation, the skills, standards and systems in which they are trained and objects and technologies they generate or use. All these have developed over time and mutually reinforce each other, as Figure 5.3 shows. Rather like QWERTY, the 'rightness' or at least inevitability of such systems tends to be taken for granted. They also strongly influence decision-making, not least in relation to strategic analysis and strategic choice. Historic accounting systems also persist despite increasing numbers of experts, both in the accountancy profession and elsewhere,[14] who point to fundamental weaknesses in such systems, not least the failure of accounting systems to provide measures for many of the factors that account for the market value of firms.

Given such lock-in, path dependency has sometimes been described as like the 'furrows in a road' that become deeper and deeper as more and more traffic goes along. Once that happens the traffic has no option but to go along those furrows. Hence, for example, capabilities, once the bases of competitive advantage and success, become core rigidities leading to the phenomenon of strategic drift explained in section 5.2 above.

Path dependency is, then, a way of thinking about how historical events and decisions, within and around an organisation, have an effect on that organisation for good or ill in at least three ways:

- *Building strategy around the path-dependent capabilities* that may have developed within an organisation. This is at the root of much of the argument put forward for the building of competitive advantage discussed in Chapter 3 and further developed in Chapter 6. Indeed there is evidence that this is so. Path dependency has been shown to explain organisational strategies.[15] Firms tend to enter markets, focus on market segments and diversify in line with the previous path-dependent capabilities they have developed. In so doing they tend to focus on types of customers that they have serviced or capabilities on which their success has been based. This may be a basis for success but can also be dangerous as the Motorola example in Illustration 5.1 shows.

Figure 5.3 **Path dependency and lock-in**

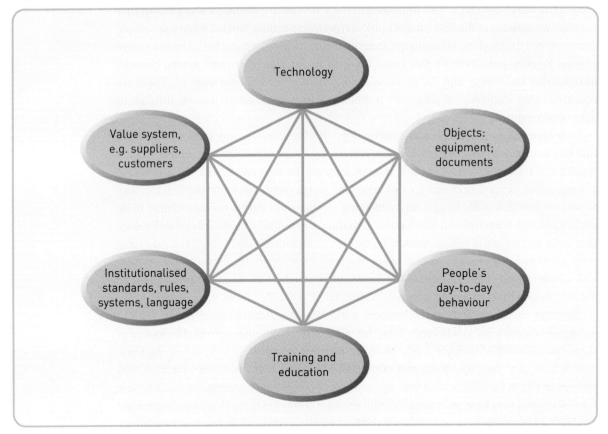

- *Path creation* suggests that some managers, whilst acknowledging the relevance and potential benefits of history, may actively seek to amend and deviate from path-dependent ways of doing things. In so doing, they may be sensitive enough to history to recognise what they can and cannot change. Going too far may be risky (see the discussion on 'legitimacy' in section 5.4.2 below), but setting in motion changes that are accepted as appropriate and beneficial by others in the network may be a way of achieving advantage. Arguably this is what new players in the insurance market such as the retailer Tesco have done. They have not tried to change basic principles of insurance provision; but they have significantly changed the way in which insurance is sold and distributed. In such circumstances managers need to see the past in relation to the future and ask what is relevant from the past that can help with the future and what the future demands but also does not require from the past.

- *Management style* may also have its roots in history. This may not only be in terms of the values of the founder, which indeed may have a strong influence, but also in the interplay between past ways of doing things and the lessons learned from the organisation's evolving environment.[16] Take Tesco as an example again. It is now one of the most successful international retailers. In its early days it was a family firm run by founder Jack Cohen, renowned for his authoritative and confrontational style. This gave rise to internal conflicts within the firm and between suppliers and Tesco. Things are different in Tesco now but the historic conflict has evolved into productive challenge and rivalry between managers and different parts of the firm that, arguably, have substantially contributed to its innovation and success.[17] Again, however, there is another side to these potential benefits. Just as capabilities that are path dependent and rooted in history may become entrenched, so might management style and this too may not be in line with the needs of a changing environment, giving rise to problems of change (see Chapter 14).

5.3.2 Historical analysis

How then might managers undertake a historical strategic analysis of their organisation? There are four ways this may be done.[18]

- *Chronological analysis.* At the most basic level this involves setting down a chronology of key events showing changes in the organisation's environment – especially its markets – how the organisation's strategy itself has changed and with what consequences – not least financial. Some firms have done this much more extensively by commissioning extensive corporate histories. These may sometimes be little more than public relations exercises, but the better ones are serious exercises in documenting history[19] and can help sensitise managers to the sort of questions raised above.

- *Cyclical influences.* Is there evidence of cyclical influences? Certainly these have been shown to exist in terms of economic cycles, but also in terms of cycles of industry activity, such as periods when there are many mergers and acquisitions. Understanding when these cycles might occur and how industry and market forces might change during such cycles can inform decisions on whether to build strategy in line with those cycles or in a counter-cyclical fashion.

- *Anchor points.* History may be regarded as continuous but historical events can also be significant for an organisation at particular points in time: these are sometimes known as 'anchor points'. They could be particularly significant events, either in terms of industry change or an organisation's strategic decisions. Or they might be policies laid down by a founder or by powerful senior executives. Or major successes or failures; or defining periods of time that have informed received wisdom or which managers have come to see as especially important. Such anchor points may be traced to many years ago in the organisation's history, yet may have profound effects on current organisational strategy and strategic thinking or exercise significant constraints on future strategy. This could, of course, be for the good: they may provide a very clear overall direction strategically that contributes to the sort of vision discussed in the previous chapter. They could, on the other hand, be a major barrier to challenging existing strategies or changing strategic direction. A famous example is Henry Ford's maxim 'You can have any color provided it's black', which set a trajectory for mass production and low variety in the car industry for decades. Currently government (and political opposition) health policy in the UK is constrained by the historical mantra that health provision should be 'free at point of delivery' when it clearly is not. Apple's 1984 advertising campaign marked its clear positioning against the domination of bland, standard products as then epitomised by IBM: the peak-time television ad featured a young female athlete hurling a sledgehammer at a TV image of an Orwellian Big Brother.

- *Historical narratives.* How do people in an organisation talk about and explain its history? In trying to understand the foundations of the strategy of an organisation a new chief executive or an external consultant will typically spend a good deal of time talking with people to try and understand the meaning and gain insights from their personal accounts of history.[20] What do they have to say about the way they see their organisation and its past, not least in terms of anchor points and origins of success? In turn, what are the implications for future strategy development? For example, historical accounts can be significant as the basis and legitimation of future strategy; indeed this is so even in a new firm where, for example, stories of its founding may play such a role. Does what people say suggest an organisation with the historic capabilities of relevance to particular markets and customers; one capable of innovation and change or one so rooted in past ways of doing things that there are risks of strategic drift?

History, then, is important in terms of how it influences current strategy for better or worse. As suggested here, there are ways in which history can be analysed. It is not always easy, however, to trace the links to the organisation as it currently exists. It is here that understanding the organisation's culture becomes important. The current culture of an organisation is, to a great extent, the legacy of its history; history becomes 'encapsulated in culture'.[21] So understanding an organisation's culture is one way of understanding the historical influences, which as we have seen, can be very powerful. The next section goes on to explain what culture is and how it can be analysed.

5.4 WHAT IS CULTURE AND WHY IS IT IMPORTANT?

There are many definitions of culture. In the Commentary on the Experience Lens it is defined as 'socially established structures of meaning'.[22] Edgar Schein defines *organisational culture* as the 'basic *assumptions and beliefs* that are shared by members of an organisation, that operate unconsciously and define in a basic taken-for-granted fashion an organisation's view of itself and its environment'.[23] Related to this are taken-for-granted *ways 'we do things around here'*[24] that accumulate over time. So **organisational culture is the taken-for-granted assumptions and behaviours that make sense of people's organisational context** and therefore contributes to how groups of people respond and behave in relation to issues they face. It therefore has important influences on the development and change of organisational strategy.

Organisational culture

Different cultural contexts are likely to influence individuals, as Figure 5.4 shows. The sections that follow will identify the important factors and issues in terms of different cultural frames of reference and then show how culture can be analysed and characterised as a means of understanding its influences on both current and future organisational purposes and strategies. The Key Debate at the end of the chapter then raises some questions about the feasibility of undertaking such analysis.

5.4.1 National and regional cultures

Many writers, perhaps the most well known of whom is Geert Hofstede,[25] have shown how attitudes to work, authority, equality and other important factors differ from one country to another. Such differences have been shaped by powerful cultural forces concerned with history, religion and even climate over many centuries. Organisations that operate internationally need to understand and cope with such differences, which can manifest themselves in terms of different standards, values and expectations in the various countries in which they operate.[26] For example, Euro Disney's attempt to replicate the success of the Disney theme parks in the US was termed 'cultural imperialism' in the French media and has experienced difficulties. Wal-Mart failed to develop its retail presence in Germany because it failed to understand how German shopping

Figure 5.4 Cultural frames of reference

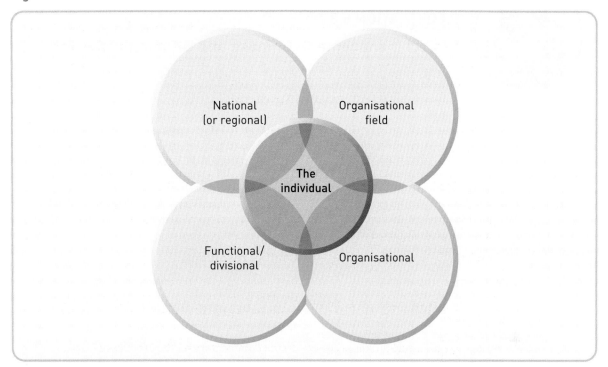

behaviour differed from US. Illustration 5.3 also shows how cultural differences underpin different conceptions of management between Chinese and Western managers.

Although they are not shown separately in Figure 5.4 (for reasons of simplification), it may also be important to understand *subnational* (usually regional) cultures. For example, attitudes to some aspects of employment and supplier relationships may differ at a regional level even in a relatively small and cohesive country like the UK, and quite markedly elsewhere in Europe (e.g. between northern and southern Italy). There may also be differences between urban and rural locations.

5.4.2 The organisational field[27]

The culture of an organisation is also shaped by 'work-based' groupings such as an industry (or sector), a profession or what is sometimes known as 'an organisational field'. An **organisational field is a community of organisations that interact more frequently with one another than with those outside the field and that have developed a shared meaning system**.[28] Such organisations may share a common technology, set of regulations or education and training. In turn this can mean that they tend to cohere around a **recipe**:[29] **a set of assumptions, norms and routines held in common within an organisational field about the appropriate purposes and strategies of field members**: in effect a 'shared wisdom'. For example, there are many organisations in the organisational field of 'justice', such as lawyers, police, courts, prisons and probation services. The roles of each are different and their detailed prescriptions as to how justice should be achieved differ. However, they are all committed to the principle that justice is a good thing which is worth striving for, they interact frequently on this issue, have developed shared ways of understanding and debating issues that arise and operate common routines or readily accommodate the routines of others in the field. Similar

ILLUSTRATION 5.3

Project management: Chinese and UK perspectives

A study of how project management is viewed in China and the UK surfaced significant different perspectives on management.

Project management can be important in the implementation of strategy and since the 1980s has become increasingly recognised in China as a useful management tool. Researchers have, however, found different conceptions of project management between managers in China and managers in the UK. These findings, in turn, inform an understanding of some underlying differences of the wider conception of management itself.

Relationship with the company

Chinese managers saw their personal career development as strongly linked to the company's development: none of those studied had changed their company since the start of their career in the construction industry. UK managers, on the other hand, were more individualistic and most had changed companies several times.

Team work

Both Chinese and UK managers placed a high value on team work, relationships with clients and with subcontractors but interpreted these differently. Chinese managers saw the team like a family where the team leader was like the father of the family and team members should support each other. So Chinese managers preferred to stay with their established teams and select new team members introduced to them by other members of the team. UK managers placed an emphasis on respect and trust but much more within the work context and with much less concern for how long people had worked in the team.

Relationship with clients

Chinese managers saw the client as: 'like your parents; you need to do whatever they instruct you . . . you need to do all you can to make them happy'. It was also important to build strong personal relationships with the client. UK managers saw the client as the provider of project funds, with a greater emphasis on contractual relationships: 'we deliver what the client wants, based on the contract'.

Relationship with subcontractors

For Chinese managers, subcontractors were like brothers and sisters of their project team family. They recognised that there could be competition with subcontractors but saw the answer to this as the building of long-term relationships. UK managers also saw subcontractors as members of the project team but with an emphasis on their specialised techniques and skills. Again they preferred to keep a more impersonal, contractual distance.

Conflict resolution

Both groups of managers acknowledged that conflict with clients or subcontractors could be a possibility. For Chinese managers negotiation was the basis of conflict resolution. Failure to resolve problems which might end with a claim against a subcontractor was regarded as a loss of 'face' and reputation. Conflicts needed to be resolved amicably. Though they too preferred to settle things amicably, UK managers again emphasised contractual conditions. Claims on clients or contractual penalties on subcontractors were normal project management practice.

Attitudes to uncertainty

Both Chinese and UK managers accepted uncertainty as inherent in project management. However, Chinese managers found this more stressful and problematic than UK managers, who, rather, enjoyed the challenges that arose: 'I am very lucky in my job in that I have numerous different challenges every day and it's full of change.'

Source: Ping Chen and David Partington, An interpretive comparison of Chinese and Western conceptions of relationships in construction project management work, *International Journal of Project Management*, 22, 5, 397–406 (2004).

Questions

1 In what other aspects of managing strategy might the differences identified here be important?

2 If you are seeking to operate in a country with a very different culture, how would you set about trying to understand that culture and its underlying assumptions?

coherence around a recipe is common in other organisational fields; for example professional services such as accountancy (see Illustration 5.4) and many industries.

This links to the concept of path dependency discussed above. The different parties in an organisational field form a self-reinforcing network built on such assumptions and behaviours that, quite likely, will lead to behavioural lock-in. Indeed professions, or trade associations, often attempt to formalise an organisational field where the membership is exclusive and the behaviour of members is regulated. Such cultural influences can be advantageous – say to customers – in maintaining standards and consistency between individual providers. Managers can, however, become 'institutionalised' such that they do not see the opportunities or indeed threats from outside their organisational field and the recipes they inherit become difficult to change.

Just as previous chapters have shown the importance of environmental forces (Chapter 2), strategic capabilities (Chapter 3) and stakeholder expectations (Chapter 4), within an organisational field *legitimacy* is an important influence. **Legitimacy is concerned with meeting the expectations within an organisational field in terms of assumptions, behaviours and strategies.** Strategies can be shaped by the need for legitimacy in several ways. For example, through *regulation* (e.g. standards and codes of behaviour specified, perhaps by a professional body), *normative expectations* (what is socially expected), or simply that which is taken for granted as being appropriate (e.g. the *recipe*). Over time, there tends to develop a consensus within an organisational field about strategies that will be successful or acceptable – so strategies themselves become legitimised. By conforming to such norms, organisations may secure approval, support and public endorsement, thus increasing their legitimacy. Stepping outside that strategy may be risky because important stakeholders (such as customers or bankers) may not see such a move as legitimate. Therefore, organisations tend to mimic each other's strategies. There may be differences in strategies between organisations but within bounds of legitimacy.[30] This is shown in the discussion of strategy in Illustration 5.4. Of course, some fringe players may actually represent successful future strategies (e.g. internet providers of downloadable music), but *initially* this may not be seen – customers may remain loyal to established companies; investors and bankers may be reluctant to fund such ventures; and existing players in the market may dismiss what they see as aberrations.

Because recipes vary from one field to another, the transition of managers between sectors can prove difficult. For example, private-sector managers have been encouraged to join public services in an attempt to inject new ways of doing things into the public sector. Many have expressed difficulties in gaining acceptance of their ways of working and in adjusting their management style to the different traditions and expectations of their new organisation, for example in issues like consensus building as part of the decision-making process. Or, to take the example in Illustration 5.4, Michael Jones's different career background means he has some quite different views on strategy from his accountant colleagues.

5.4.3 Organisational culture

As the different definitions of culture provided at the beginning of this section suggest, culture can be conceived as consisting of different layers: the four proposed by Edgar Schein[31] are (see Figure 5.5):

- *Values* may be easy to identify in terms of those formally stated by an organisation since they are often explicit, perhaps written down (see section 4.2 in Chapter 4). For example,

ILLUSTRATION 5.4

Strategy debate in an accounting firm

The perceived legitimacy of a strategy may have different roots.

Edward Gray, the managing partner of QDG, one of the larger accountancy firms in the world, was discussing its global development with two of his senior partners. Global development had been the main issue at the firm's international committee in the US the previous week. Like most accountancy firms, QDG was organised along national lines. Its origins were in auditing but it now offered tax and financial advice, corporate recovery and information systems services. International co-operation was based on personal contacts of partners across the world. However, large clients were beginning to demand a 'seamless global service'. At the meeting was Alan Clark, with 20 years' experience as a partner and high reputation in the accountancy profession, and Michael Jones, new to QDG and unlike the others not an accountant, who headed up the information systems arm of QDG, having been recruited from a consultancy firm.

Gray: 'Unless we move towards a more global form of business, QDG could lose its position as one of the leading accountancy firms in the world. Our competitors are moving this way, so we have to. The issue is how?'

Clark was sympathetic but cautionary. He pointed out that clients were entering growing economies such as China. 'Governments there will insist on international standards of practice, but they have difficulties. For example, in China there is often no real concept of profit, let alone how to measure it. If there is to be a market economy, the need for the services we provide is high. There are however major problems, not least, the enormous number of people required. It is not possible to churn out experienced accountants overnight. Our professional standards would be compromised. The firm cannot be driven by market opportunity at the expense of standards. There is another issue. Our business is based on personal relationships and trust; this must not be compromised in the name of "global integration".'

Michael Jones suggested that the problem was more challenging: 'All our competitors are going global. They will be pitching for the same clients, offering the same services and the same standard of service. Where is the difference? To achieve any competitive advantage we need to do things differently and think beyond the obvious. For example why not a two-tier partnership, where smaller countries are non-equity partners. That would allow us to make decisions more quickly, allow us to enforce standards and give formal authority to senior partners looking after our major international clients.'

Alan Clark had expected this: 'This is not an opportunity to make money; it's about the development of proper systems for the economies of previously closed countries. We need to co-operate with other firms to make sure that there are compatible standards. This cannot be helped by changing a partnership structure that has served well for a hundred years.'

Gray: 'The view at last week's meeting was certainly that there is a need for a more internationally co-ordinated firm, with a more effective client management system, less reliance on who knows whom and more on drawing on the best of our people when we need them.'

Clark: 'I could equally argue that we have an unparalleled network of personal relationships throughout the world which we have been building for decades. That what we have to do is strengthen this using modern technology and modern communications.'

Edward Gray reconciled himself to a lengthy discussion.

Source: Adapted from the case study in G. Johnson and R. Greenwood, 'Institutional Theory and Strategic Management', in *Strategic Management: A Multiple-Perspective Approach*, edited by Mark Jenkins and V. Ambrosini, Palgrave, 2007.

Questions

1 What are the underlying assumptions of the arguments being advanced by the three partners?

2 What may be the origins of these assumptions?

3 How do the different views correspond to the discussions of strategic capabilities (Chapter 3) and competitive strategy (Chapter 6)?

Figure 5.5 Culture in four layers

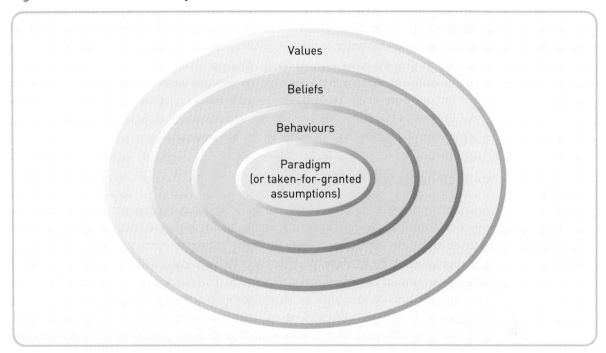

in the last decade, many banks espoused values of shareholder value creation, careful risk management and, of course, high levels of customer service. But they indulged in highly risky lending, resulting in the need for huge government financial support in 2009. Clearly the values that drove the strategies were different. It is therefore important to delve beneath espoused values to uncover underlying, perhaps taken-for-granted, values that can help explain the strategy actually being pursued by an organisation (see 5.4.7 below).

● *Beliefs* are more specific. They can typically be discerned in how people talk about issues the organisation faces; for example, a belief that the company should not trade with particular countries or, as with Michael Clark in Illustration 5.4, a belief in the rightness of accountancy systems and standards.

With regard to both values and beliefs it is important to remember that in relation to culture, the concern is with the collective rather than individuals' values and beliefs. Indeed it may be that individuals in organisations have values and beliefs that at times run counter to their organisation's, which can give rise to the sort of ethical tensions and problems discussed in section 4.4.2 of Chapter 4.

● *Behaviours* are the day-to-day way in which an organisation operates and can be seen by people both inside and often outside the organisation. This includes the work routines, how the organisation is structured and controlled and 'softer' issues around symbolic behaviours (see section 5.4.6 below). These behaviours may become the taken-for-granted 'ways we do things around here' that are potentially the bases for inimitable strategic capabilities (see section 3.3.3) but also significant barriers to achieving strategic change if that becomes necessary (see Chapter 14).

● *Taken-for-granted assumptions* are the core of an organisation's culture. They are the aspects of organisational life which people find difficult to identify and explain. In this book we refer to them as the 'organisational paradigm'. The **paradigm is the set of assumptions held in common and taken for granted in an organisation**. For an organisation to operate effectively there is bound to be such a generally accepted set of assumptions. As mentioned above, these assumptions represent *collective experience* without which people would have to 'reinvent their world' for different circumstances that they face. The paradigm can underpin successful strategies by providing a basis of common understanding in an organisation, but can also be a major problem, for example when major strategic change is needed (see Chapter 14), or when organisations try to merge and find they are incompatible. The importance of the paradigm is discussed further in section 5.4.6.

5.4.4 Organisational subcultures

In seeking to understand the relationship between culture and an organisation's strategies, it may be possible to identify some aspects of culture that pervade the whole organisation. However, there may also be important *subcultures*. These may relate directly to the structure of the organisation: for example, the differences between geographical divisions in a multinational company, or between functional groups such as finance, marketing and operations. Differences between divisions may be particularly evident in organisations that have grown through acquisition. Also different divisions may be pursuing different types of strategy that require or foster different cultures. Indeed, aligning strategic positioning and organisational culture is a critical feature of successful organisations. Differences between business functions can also relate to the different nature of work in different functions. For example, in an oil company like Shell or BP differences are likely between those functions engaged in 'upstream' exploration, where time horizons may be in decades, and those concerned with 'downstream' retailing, with much shorter market-driven time horizons. Arguably, this is one reason why both Shell and BP pay so much attention to trying to forge a corporate culture that crosses such functions.

5.4.5 Culture's influence on strategy

George Davis, the founder of clothing retailers Next and GIVe, who also established the highly successful Per Una brand in Marks & Spencer, sees culture as central to management: 'Culture is the thing that that makes us do things and stops us doing things.'[32] The taken-for-granted nature of culture is what makes it centrally important in relation to strategy and the management of strategy. There are three primary reasons for this.

- *Cultural 'glue'.* There are benefits in the taken-for-granted nature of culture. Josephine Rydberg-Dumont, president of IKEA, argues that, because all employees take as given the way the firm operates, it reduces the need for constant supervision. Moreover, since an aspect of the culture is to constantly question the status quo, it 'fuels' innovation. There are then benefits to the taken-for-granted aspect of culture.

- *Captured by culture.* Organisations can, however, be 'captured' by their culture. Managers, faced with a changing business environment, are more likely to attempt to deal with the situation by searching for what they can understand and cope with in terms of the existing culture. The result is likely to be the incremental strategic change with the risk of eventual strategic drift explained in section 5.2. Culture is, in effect, an unintended driver of strategy.

Figure 5.6 Culture's influence on strategy development

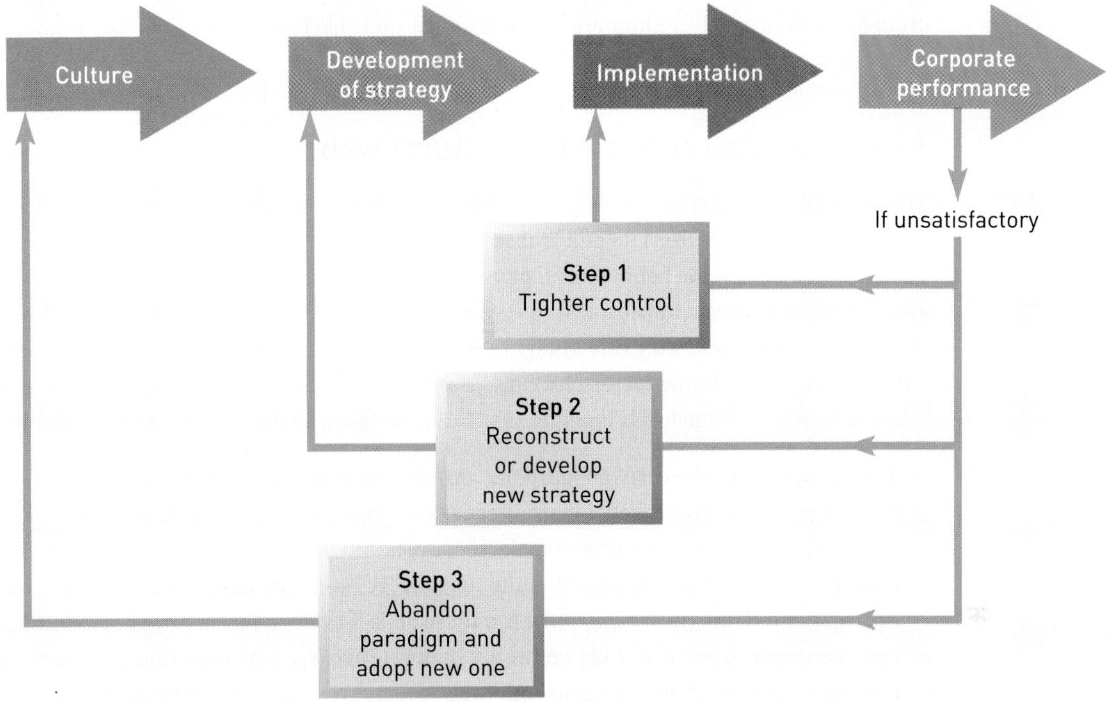

Source: Adapted from P. Gringer and J.-C. Spender, *Turnaround: Managerial Recipes for Strategic Success*, Associated Business Press, 1979, p. 203.

- *Managing culture.* Because it is difficult to observe, identify and control that which is taken for granted, it is also difficult to manage. This is why having a way to analyse culture so as to make it more evident is important – the subject of the next section. (However, see the key debate at the end of the chapter.)

The effect of culture on strategy is shown in Figure 5.6.[33] Faced with a stimulus for action, such as declining performance, managers first try to improve the implementation of existing strategy. This might be through trying to lower cost, improve efficiency, tighten controls or improve accepted way of doing things. If this is not effective, a change of strategy may occur, but a change in line with the existing culture. For example, managers may seek to extend the market for their business, but assume that it will be similar to their existing market, and therefore set about managing the new venture in much the same way as they have been used to. Alternatively, even where managers know intellectually that they need to change strategy, indeed know technologically how to do so, they find themselves constrained by path-dependent organisational routines and assumptions or political processes, as seems likely in Illustration 5.1. This often happens, for example, when there are attempts to change highly bureaucratic organisations to be customer-oriented. Even if people who accept the need to change a culture's emphasis on the importance of conforming to established rules, routines and reporting relationships, they do not readily do so. It is a fallacy to assume reasoned argument necessarily changes deeply embedded assumptions rooted in collective experience built up over long periods of time. Readers need only think of their own experience in trying to persuade others to rethink their religious beliefs, or indeed, allegiances to sports teams, to realise this. So it is with groups and organisations: people prefer the familiar and typically minimise uncertainty or ambiguity. They are likely to continue to do so until there is, perhaps, dramatic evidence of the redundancy of the culture, quite likely as the result of the organisation entering phases 3 or 4 of strategic drift (see Figure 5.2).

5.4.6 Analysing culture: the cultural web

KEY CONCEPT
www.pearsoned.co.uk/mystrategylab

Cultural web

In order to understand the existing culture and its effects it is important to be able to analyse an organisation's culture. The cultural web[34] is a means of doing this (see Figure 5.7). The **cultural web shows the behavioural, physical and symbolic manifestations of a culture** that inform and are informed by the taken-for-granted assumptions, or paradigm, of an organisation. It is in effect the inner two ovals in Figure 5.5. The cultural web can be used to understand culture in any of the frames of reference discussed above but is most often used at the organisational and/or functional levels in Figure 5.4.[35] The elements of the cultural web are as follows:

- The *paradigm* is at the core of Figure 5.7. As previously defined it is the set of assumptions held in common and taken for granted in an organisation: in effect it is the *collective experience* applied to a situation to make sense of it and inform a likely course of action. The assumptions of the paradigm are, quite likely, very basic but may or may not align with the logic of a strategy. For example, it may seem self-evident that a newspaper business's core assumptions are about the centrality of news coverage and reporting. However, from a strategic point of view, increasingly newspapers' revenues are reliant on advertising income and the strategy may need to be directed to this. The paradigm of a charity may be

Figure 5.7 The cultural web of an organisation

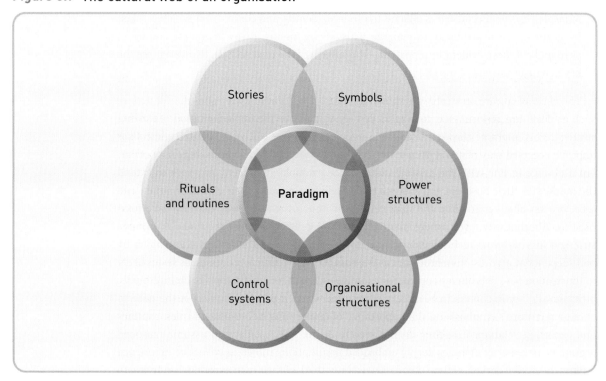

about doing good works for the needy, but this cannot be achieved if it is not run effectively for the purpose of raising money. It is quite likely that, even if the rational view is to build a strategy around revenue generation for the newspaper or the charity, people in those organisations may still interpret issues and behave in line with its paradigm. So understanding what the paradigm is and how it informs debate on strategy matters. The problem is that, since it is unlikely to be talked about, or even be something that people are conscious of, trying to identify it can be difficult; especially if you are part of that organisation. Outside observers may find it easier to identify simply by listening to what people say and watching what they do and emphasise; but this may not be so easy for insiders who are part of the culture. One way of 'insiders' getting to see the assumptions they take for granted is to focus initially on other aspects of the cultural web because these are to do with more visible manifestations of culture. Moreover these other aspects are likely to act to reinforce the assumptions within that paradigm.

- **Routines are 'the way we do things around here' on a day-to-day basis**. These may have a long history and may well be common across organisations (see section 5.3 above). At their best, these lubricate the working of the organisation, and may provide a basis for distinctive organisational capabilities. However, they can also represent a taken-for-grantedness about how things should happen which, again, can guide how people respond to issues and be difficult to change.

- The **rituals** of organisational life are particular **activities or special events that emphasise, highlight or reinforce what is important in the culture**. Examples include training programmes, interview panels, promotion and assessment procedures, sales conferences and so on. An extreme example, of course, is the ritualistic training of army recruits to prepare them for the discipline required in conflict. However, rituals can also be informal activities such as drinks in the pub after work or gossiping around photocopying machines. A checklist of rituals is provided in Chapter 14 (see Table 14.2).

- The *stories*[36] told by members of an organisation to each other, to outsiders, to new recruits and so on, may act to embed the present in its organisational history and also flag up important events and personalities. They typically have to do with successes, disasters, heroes, villains and mavericks (who deviate from the norm). They can be a way of letting people know what is conventionally important in an organisation.

- **Symbols**[37] **are objects, events, acts or people that convey, maintain or create meaning over and above their functional purpose**. For example, offices and office layout, cars and job titles have a functional purpose, but are also typically signals about status and hierarchy. Particular people may come to represent specially important aspects of an organisation or historic turning points. The form of language used in an organisation can also be particularly revealing, especially with regard to customers or clients. For example, the head of a consumer protection agency in Australia described his clients as 'complainers'. In a major teaching hospital in the UK, consultants described patients as 'clinical material'. Whilst such examples might be amusing, they reveal an underlying assumption about customers (or patients) that might play a significant role in influencing the strategy of an organisation. Although symbols are shown separately in the cultural web, it should be remembered that many elements of the web are symbolic. So, routines, control and reward systems and structures are not only functional but also symbolic.

- **Power** was defined in Chapter 4 as **the ability of individuals or groups to persuade, induce or coerce others into following certain courses of action**. So *power structures* are distributions of power to groups of people in an organisation. The most powerful individuals or groups are likely to be closely associated with the paradigm. For example, in firms that experience strategic drift, it is not unusual to find powerful executives who have long association with long-established ways of doing things. In analysing power the guidance given in Chapter 4 (section 4.5.2) is useful.

- **Organisational structures are the roles, responsibilities and reporting relationships in organisations.** These are likely to reflect power structures and how they manifest themselves emphasises which roles and relationships really matter in an organisation. Formal hierarchical, mechanistic structures may emphasise that strategy is the province of top managers and everyone else is 'working to orders'. Structures with less emphasis on formal reporting relationships might indicate more participative strategy making. Highly devolved structures (as discussed in Chapter 13) may signify that collaboration is less important than competition and so on.

- **Control systems are the formal and informal ways of monitoring and supporting people within and around an organisation** and tend to emphasise what is seen to be important in the organisation. They include measurements and reward systems. For example, public-service organisations have often been accused of being concerned more with stewardship of funds than with quality of service. This is reflected in their control systems, which are more about accounting for spending rather than with quality of service. Individually based bonus schemes related to volume are likely to signal a culture of individuality, internal competition and an emphasis on sales volume rather than teamwork and an emphasis on quality.

Illustration 5.5 shows a cultural web drawn up by the partners of a medium-sized law firm as part of a strategic review. The key point to emerge was that the culture of the firm was dominated by their personalities and personal styles linked to an expectation of collective commitment and the need to 'fit in'. This was an issue for the firm as they faced a strategic choice of whether to try to sell their firm on to a much larger one or attempt to grow the firm with themselves at the helm. The problem for either choice was the dominance of these senior executives in the firm's culture: they were seen as 'the brotherhood; the heart of the firm'. If they were to sell the firm, they each would leave and so take away a significant element of the firm's formula for success. If they were to try to grow the firm, how would they duplicate themselves and develop the leadership potential of others to fill the expanding roles?

5.4.7 Undertaking cultural analysis

If an analysis of the culture of an organisation is to be undertaken, there are some important issues to bear in mind:

- *Questions to ask.* Figure 5.8 outlines some of the questions that might help build up an understanding of culture using the cultural web. However, analysing a culture is not straightforward, as the Key Debate at the end of the chapter explains.

- *Statements of cultural values.* As section 4.2 in Chapter 4 and 5.4.3 above explained, organisations may make public statements of their values, beliefs and purposes – for example, in annual reports, mission or values statements and business plans. There is a danger that these are seen as useful descriptions of the organisational culture. But this is likely to be at

ILLUSTRATION 5.5

The cultural web of a law firm

The cultural web can be used to identify the behaviours and taken-for-granted assumptions of an organisation.

This is an adapted version of a cultural web produced by partners and managers of a law firm.

Heroic commitment to the firm:
if you don't fit, don't share
the right principles,
you exit

Unity, inclusivity and
conformity

Stories
- Heroes
- Epic travel
- Commitment to the firm
- Wrong/bad people being sacked
- The salvation – our big money making deal

Symbols
- No one has offices
- All desks same size
- Being made a partner
- Dispersed share ownership
- Heading up major client accounts

Rituals/routines
- We celebrate long service to the firm
- We have routines that are about 'us leader, you follower'
- We don't really celebrate the success of the firm

Paradigm
- Almost a secret society element to it
- A brotherhood
- Like pioneers of our way of doing business
- Evangelising

Power
- The CEO and like minded senior executives
- Energy, drive, assertiveness
- Egotism
- Male

Rituals are about
being the right kind of
person.
*'We do leaving very well,
Sinatra tours for long
service.'*

Controls
- Lots of measurement
- Anxiety about control
- Overly anxious about monitoring

Structure
- Meetings; lots of them
- Absence of guiding principles
- Segmented structure

Power is the property
of individuals, manifest
in their visible energy.
*'Bursting into a room
with an armful of papers
is power, noise is power.'*

We are concerned about control,
but paradoxically we love a crisis
to rush in and solve

Meetings dominate the
structure

Questions

1 How would you characterise the dominant culture here?

2 How do the various elements of the web inter-relate?

3 Draw up a cultural web for an organisation of your choice.

Figure 5.8 The cultural web: some useful questions

Stories
- What core beliefs do stories reflect?
- What stories are commonly told e.g. to newcomers?
- How do these reflect core assumptions and beliefs?
- What norms do the mavericks deviate from?

Symbols
- What objects, events or people do people in the organisation particularly identify with?
- What are these related to in the history of the organisation?
- What aspects of strategy are highlighted in publicity?

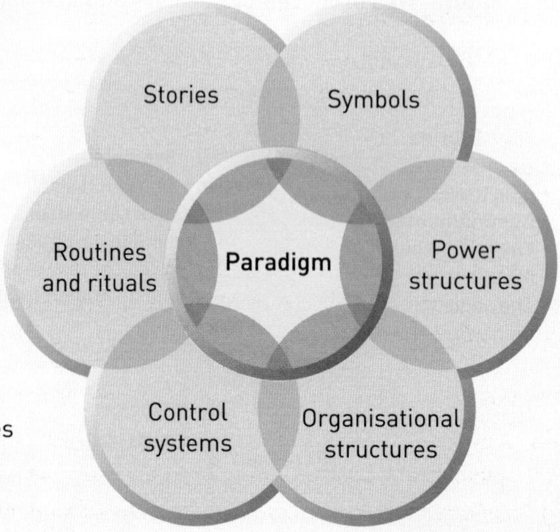

Routines and rituals
- Which routines are emphasised?
- Which are embedded in history?
- What behaviour do routines encourage?
- What are the key rituals?
- What assumptions and core beliefs do they reflect?
- What do training programmes emphasise?
- How easy are rituals/routines to change?

Power structures
- Where does power reside? Indicators include:
  (a) status
  (b) claim on resources
  (c) symbols of power
- Who 'makes things happen'?
- Who stops things happening?

Stories · Symbols · Routines and rituals · Paradigm · Power structures · Control systems · Organisational structures

Control systems
- What is most closely monitored/controlled?
- Is emphasis on reward or punishment?
- Are controls rooted in history or current strategies?
- Are there many/few controls?

Organisational structures
- How formal/informal are the structures?
- Do structures encourage collaboration or competition?
- What types of power structure do they support?

Overall
- What do the answers to these questions suggest are the (few) fundamental assumptions that are the paradigm?
- How would you characterise the dominant culture?
- How easy is this to change?

best only partially true, and at worst misleading. This is not to suggest that there is any organised deception. It is simply that the statements of values and beliefs are often carefully considered and carefully crafted statements of the aspirations of a particular stakeholder (such as the CEO) rather than descriptions of the actual culture. For example, an outside observer of a police force might conclude from its public statements of purpose and priorities that it had a balanced approach to the various aspects of police work – catching criminals, crime prevention, community relations. However, a deeper probing might quickly reveal that (in cultural terms) there is the 'real' police work (catching criminals) and the 'lesser work' (crime prevention, community relations).

- *Pulling it together*. The detailed 'map' produced by the cultural web can be a rich source of information about an organisation's culture, but it is useful to be able to characterise the culture that the information conveys. Sometimes this is possible by means of graphic descriptors. For example, the managers who undertook a cultural analysis in the UK National Health Service (NHS) summed up their culture as 'The National Sickness Service'. Although this approach is rather crude and unscientific, it can be powerful in terms of organisational members seeing the organisation as it really is – which may not be immediately apparent from all of the detailed points in the cultural web. It can also help people to understand that culture drives strategies; for example, a 'national sickness service' would clearly prioritise strategies that are about developments in curing sick people above strategies of health promotion and prevention. So those favouring health promotion strategies need to understand that they are facing the need to change a culture and that in doing so they may not be able to assume that rational processes like planning and resource allocation will be enough (see Chapter 14).

If managers are to develop strategies that are different from those of the past, they need to be able to challenge, question and potentially change the organisational culture that under-pins the current strategy. In this context, the cultural analysis suggested in this chapter can inform aspects of strategic management discussed in other parts of this book.

- *Strategic capabilities*. As Chapter 3 makes clear, historically embedded capabilities are, very likely, part of the culture of the organisation. The cultural analysis of the organisa-tion therefore provides a complementary basis of analysis to an examination of strategic capabilities (see Chapter 3). In effect, such an analysis of capabilities should end up digging into the culture of the organisation, especially in terms of its routines, control systems and the everyday way in which the organisation runs, very likely on a 'taken-for-granted' basis.

- *Strategy development*. An understanding of organisational culture sensitises managers to the way in which historical and cultural influences will likely affect future strategy for good or ill. It therefore relates to the discussion on strategy development in Chapter 12.

- *Managing strategic change*. An analysis of the culture also provides a basis for the manage-ment of strategic change, since it provides a picture of the existing culture that can be set against a desired strategy so as to give insights as to what may constrain the development of that strategy or what needs to be changed in order to achieve it. This is discussed more extensively in Chapter 14 on managing strategic change.

- *Leadership and management style*. Chapter 14 also raises questions about leadership and management style. If one of the major requirements of a strategist is to be able to encourage the questioning of that which is taken for granted, the sort of analytical tools covered in this chapter and in this book can be an aid. However, it is also likely to require a management style – indeed a culture – that allows and encourages such questioning. If the leadership style is such as to discourage such questioning, it is unlikely that the lessons of history will be learned and more likely that the dictates of history will be followed.

- *Culture and experience*. There have been repeated references in this section to the role culture plays as a vehicle by which meaning is created in organisations. This is discussed more fully in the Commentary on the Experience Lens and provides a useful way in which many aspects of strategy can be considered (see the commentaries throughout the book).

KEY DEBATE
Understanding organisational culture

If organisational culture is so important an influence on strategy, then understanding just what it is and what its influences are is of key importance. But is this possible to do?

In this chapter, in particular section 5.4, it is argued that understanding an organisation's culture is important for the strategist and ways of doing this such as the cultural web are proposed. There are also a variety of other tools and techniques for analysing organisational cultures, such including survey instuments (for example see Kim Cameron and Robert Quinn, *Diagnosing and Changing Organizational Culture*, Jossey Bass, 2006) that are employed by managers and consultants.

However, in his book *Understanding Organizational Culture* Mats Alvesson suggests that there are dangers and problems in understanding organisational culture, in particular the temptation to simplify and trivialise what is meant by organisational culture. He suggests that managers often fall victim to 'seven sins':

Reifying culture: Seeing culture as an 'it'. So the need is to avoid the idea of 'culture' as something 'thing-like' that, for example, directly links to performance or can be readily managed. What really matters is the meaning shared by a collective and that is a more complex idea.

Essentializing culture: Describing culture in terms of a few essential traits, such as 'service minded, adaptable, personnel-oriented, open, individualistic, etc'. The danger again is a 'too strongly ordered and superficial view on culture'. The need is for a more careful interpretation of what culture means and recognition of variations within a culture.

Unifying culture: 'Equating cultural boundaries with formal or legal ones, as implied by terms such as corporate culture or national culture ... Cultural orientations may not follow established social differentiation criteria.' Avoid treating organizations as homogeneous groups based on such categories.

Idealizing culture: Focusing on the levels of ideas, symbols and meanings 'in a social and material vacuum'. Such ideas are actually shaped and reshaped in the context of material reality and behaviours which themselves are 'loaded with meaning and symbolism and affect cultural patterns and processes'.

Consensualizing culture: Assuming that culture means a unity of shared values. 'Shared meanings do not necessarily imply consensus and harmony ... an organization may be characterized by shared ideas and beliefs about the significance of self interest, fierce internal competition and a view of corporate life as fairly harsh and jungle-like.'

Totalizing culture: Assuming that a culture can be captured 'once and for all' when 'it is the shared meanings on a specific topic that is of interest to pay attention to' such as core competences or the future of an industry.

Otherizing culture: The danger of contrasts, for example comparing one culture against another, which might be seen as superior or inferior. The danger of 'otherizing' is, again, that it tends to trivialize and prevent a more nuanced view of culture.

Alvesson concludes his warning against the seven sins by adding that there are 'sometimes pragmatic reasons ... for simplifications and the expression of something accessible – which often leads to some of the sins above. ... My point is, however, that the traps and temptations should be handled with great care. Caution should taken not to theorize culture in a way giving the seven sins privilege'.

Source: M. Alvesson, *Understanding Organizational Culture*, Sage, 2002, pp. 186–9.

Questions

1 Undertake a cultural analysis of an organisation. To what extent did you find yourself committing any of the 'seven sins'?

2 If, as Alvesson suggests, pragmatically some of the sins are difficult to avoid, how can managers avoid 'privileging' them?

3 Managers often talk about the need to 'manage organisational culture'. How feasible is this given the complex nature of organisational culture that Alvesson describes? (Reference to Chapter 14 may be helpful here.)

SUMMARY

● The history and culture of an organisation may contribute to its strategic capabilities, but may also give rise to strategic drift as its strategy develops incrementally on the basis of such influences and fails to keep pace with a changing environment.

● Historical, path-dependent processes play a significant part in the success or failure of an organisation and need to be understood by managers. There are historical analyses that can be conducted to help uncover these influences.

● Cultural and institutional influences both inform and constrain the strategic development of organisations.

● Organisational culture is the basic assumptions and beliefs that are shared by members of an organisation, that operate unconsciously and define in a basic taken-for-granted fashion an organisation's view of itself and its environment.

● An understanding of the culture of an organisation and its relationship to organisational strategy can be gained by using the cultural web.

WORK ASSIGNMENTS

✻ *Denotes more advanced work assignments.* * *Refers to a case study in the Text and Cases edition.*

5.1 Identify four organisations that, in your view, are in the different phases of strategic drift (see Figure 5.2). Justify your selection.

5.2✻ In the context of section 5.3, undertake a historical analysis of the strategy development of Club Med or an organisation of your choice and consider the question: 'Does history matter in managing strategy?'

5.3 Map out an organisational field (see section 5.4.2) within which an organisation of your choice operates. (As a basis for this you could for example use accountancy, an organisation operating in the public sector such as Cordia* or Formula One*.)

5.4 Identify (a) an organisation where its publicly stated values correspond with your experience of it and (b) one where they do not. Explain why (a) and (b) might be so.

5.5 Use the questions in Figure 5.8 to plot a cultural web for ClubMed, Cordia* or an organisation of your choice.

5.6✻ By using a number of the examples from above and taking into account the issues raised in the Key Debate, critically appraise the assertion that 'culture can only really be usefully analysed by the symptoms displayed in the way the organisation operates'. (You may wish to refer to Schein's book in the recommended key readings to assist you with this task.)

Integrative assignment

5.7✻ What is the relationship between competitive advantage, strategic capabilities, organisation culture, strategy development and the challenge of managing strategic change? (Refer to Chapters 3, 5, 6, 12 and 14.) Consider this in relation to a major change in strategy.

VIDEO ASSIGNMENT

Visit *MyStrategyLab* and watch the *IKEA* case study.

1 What does Josephine Rydburg-Dumont mean when she says: 'The importance of IKEA culture is, in a way, everything'?

2 What aspects of IKEA's cultural web can be identified from the video? What do you think the other aspects of the web might include?

RECOMMENDED KEY READINGS

- For a more thorough explanation of the phenomenon of strategic drift see Gerry Johnson, 'Rethinking incrementalism', *Strategic Management Journal*, vol. 9 (1988), pp. 75–91, and 'Managing strategic change – strategy, culture and action', *Long Range Planning*, vol. 25, no. 1 (1992), pp. 28–36. (These papers also explain the cultural web.) Also see Donald S. Sull: 'Why good companies go bad', *Harvard Business Review*, July/August 1999, pp. 42–52.

- For a historical perspective on strategy see: I. Greener, 'Theorizing path dependency: how does history come to matter in organizations?', *Management Decision*, vol. 40, no. 6 (2002), pp. 614–19; and Jorg Sydow, George

Schraeyogg and Jochen Koch, 'Organisational path dependence: opening the black box', *Academy of Management Review*, vol. 34, no. 4 (2009), pp. 689–708.

- For a summary and illustrated explanation of institutional theory see Gerry Johnson and Royston Greenwood, 'Institutional theory and strategy', in *Strategic Management: A Multiple-Perspective Approach*, edited by Mark Jenkins and V. Ambrosini, Palgrave, 2007.

- For a comprehensive and critical explanation of organisational culture see Mats Alvesson, *Understanding Organizational Culture*, Sage, 2002.

REFERENCES

1. For an explanation of strategic drift see G. Johnson, 'Rethinking incrementalism', *Strategic Management Journal*, vol. 9, pp. 75–91, 1988 and 'Managing strategic change – strategy, culture and action', *Long Range Planning*, vol. 25, no. 1, pp. 28–36, 1992. Also see E. Romanelli and M.T. Tushman, 'Organizational transformation as punctuated equilibrium: an empirical test', *Academy of Management Journal*, vol. 7, no. 5, pp. 1141–66, 1994. They explain the tendency of strategies to develop very incrementally with periodic transformational change.

2. See D. Miller and P. Friesen, 'Momentum and revolution in organisational adaptation', *Academy of Management Journal*, vol. 23, no. 4, pp. 591–614, 1980.

3. See D. Leonard-Barton, 'Core capabilities and core rigidities: a paradox in managing new product development', *Strategic Management Journal*, vol. 13, pp. 111–25, 1992.

4. This is a term used by Donald S. Sull in accounting for the decline of high-performing firms (see 'Why good companies go bad', *Harvard Business Review*, July/August, 1999, pp. 42–52).

5. In *The Icarus Paradox* (D. Miller, Harper-Collins, 1990) Danny Miller makes a convincing case that organisations' success leads to a number of potentially pathological tendencies, not least of which are the tendencies to inflate the durability of bases of success and to build future strategies relatively uncritically. Hence the idea of the Icarus paradox, building on the Greek mythological character, Icarus, who successfully built himself wings to fly but then flew too close to the sun such that they melted.

6. This research, known as the Successful Strategic Transformers (SST) project, was in progress at the time of writing. It was part of the UK Advanced Institute of Management Research initiative. For an explanation of stage 1 of the research, on which these findings are based, see: G. Yip, T. Devinney and G. Johnson, 'Measuring long-term superior performance: the UK's long term superior performers 1984–2003', *Long Range Planning*, vol. 43, no. 3, 2009, pp. 390–413.

7. This quote by André Malroux and the story of the BMW museum was provided by the business historian Mary Rose.

8. See D. Holbrook, W. Cohen, D. Hounshell and S. Klepper, 'The nature, sources and consequences of firm differences in the early history of the semiconductor industry', *Strategic Management Journal*, vol. 21, no. 10–11, pp. 107–42, 2000.

9. Private correspondence with Mary Rose who suggests that: 'it links to Schumpeter and his notion of boundary crossing which may be between sectors, between technologies or informing the development and application of old technology with new knowledge'.

10. S. Klepper and K.L. Simons, 'Dominance by birthright: entry of prior radio producers and competitive ramifications in the US television receiver industry', *Strategic Management Journal*, vol. 21, no. 10–11, pp. 987–1016, 2000.

11. W.B. Arthur, Competing technologies, increasing returns and lock in by historical events', *Economic Journal*, vol. 99, pp. 116–31, 1989.

12. P.A. David, Clio and the economics of QWERTY, *Economic History*, 75 (2), 332–7, 1985.

13. For discussions of path dependency in an organisational context see: I. Greener, 'Theorizing path dependency: how does history come to matter in organizations?', *Management Decision*, 40 (6), 614–19, 2002 and Jorg Sydow, George Schraeyogg and Jochen Koch, 'Organisational path dependance: opening the black box', *Academy of Management Review*, 34 (4), 2009, 689–708.

14. The world's biggest accounting firms have called for radical reform; 'Big four in call for real time accounts', page 1, *Financial Times*, 8 Nov 2006.

15. Holbrook et al. (ref. 8 above).

16. See J.R. Kimberley and H. Bouchikhi, 'The dynamics of organizational development and change: how the past shapes the present and constrains the future', *Organization Science*, 6, 1, 9–18, 1995.

17. This example is also taken from stage 2 of the SST research project referred to in ref. 6 above. At the time of writing there are no published results from this stage of the research.

18. Also see D.J. Jeremy, 'Business history and strategy', in *The Handbook of Strategy and Management*, pp. 436–60, eds A. Pettigrew, H. Thomas and R. Whittington, Sage, 2002.

19. For good examples of corporate histories see G. Jones, *Renewing Unilever: Transformation and Tradition*, Oxford University Press, 2005; R. Fitzgerald, *Rowntrees and the Marketing Revolution, 1862–1969*, Cambridge University Press, 1995; T.R. Gourvish, *British Railways 1948–73*, Cambridge University Press, 1986.

20. Walsh and Ungson make the point that 'organisational memory' is stored in a number of ways but these include shared interpretations and individual recollections. See J.P. Walsh and G.R. Ungson, 'Organizational memory', *The Academy of Management Review*, vol. 16, no. 1, pp. 57–91, January 1991.

21. This quote is from S. Finkelstein, 'Why smart executives fail: four case histories of how people learn the wrong lessons from history', *Business History*, 48, 2, 153–70, 2006.

22. See Clifford Geertz, *The Interpretation of Culture*, Basic Books, 1973, p. 12 and see Mats Alvesson, *Understanding Organizational Culture*, Sage, 2002, p. 3.

23. This definition of culture is taken from E. Schein, *Organisational Culture and Leadership*, 2nd edition, Jossey-Bass, 1992, p. 6.

24. This is how Terrence Deal and Alan Kennedy define organisational culture in *Corporate Cultures: the Rites and Rituals of Corporate Life*, Addison-Wesley, 1982.

25. See G. Hofstede, *Culture's Consequences*, Sage, 2nd edn, 2001. For critiques of Hofstede's work, see B. McSweeney, 'Hofstede's model of national cultural differences and their consequences: a triumph of faith – a failure of analysis', *Human Relations*, vol. 55, no. 1, 89–118 (2002) and A.M. Soares, M. Farhangmeher and A.S. Shoham, 'Hofstede's dimensions of culture in international marketing studies', *Journal of Business Research*, 60, 3, 277–84, 2007.

26. On cross-cultural managerment also see R. Lewis, *When Cultures Collide: Managing Successfully across Cultures*, 2nd edition, Brealey, 2000, a practical guide for managers. It offers an insight into different national cultures, business conventions and leadership styles. Also S. Schneider and J.-L. Barsoux, *Managing across Cultures*, 2nd edition, Financial Times Prentice Hall, 2003. T. Jackson, 'Management ethics and corporate policy: a cross-cultural comparison', *Journal of Management Studies*, vol. 37, no. 3 (2000), pp. 349–70 looks at how national culture influences management ethics.

27. A useful review of research on this topic is: T. Dacin, J. Goodstein and R. Scott, 'Institutional theory and institutional change: introduction to the special research forum', *Academy of Management Journal*, vol. 45, no. 1 (2002), pp. 45–57. For a more general review see G. Johnson and R. Greenwood, 'Institutional theory and strategy', in *Strategic Management: a Multiple-Perspective Approach*, edited by Mark Jenkins and V. Ambrosini, Palgrave, 2007.

28. This definition is taken from W. Scott, *Institutions and Organizations*, Sage, 1995.

29. The term 'recipe' was introduced to refer to industries by J.-C. Spender, *Industry Recipes: the Nature and Sources of Management Judgement*, Blackwell, 1989. We have broadened its use by applying it to *organisational fields*. The fundamental idea that behaviours are driven by a collective set of norms and values remains unchanged.

30. D. Deephouse, 'To be different or to be the same? It's a question (and theory) of strategic balance', *Strategic Management Journal*, vol. 20, no. 2 (1999), pp. 147–66.

31. E. Schein (see reference 23) and A. Brown, *Organisational Culture*, Financial Times Prentice Hall, 1998, are useful in understanding the relationship between organisational culture and strategy. For a useful critique of the concept of organisational culture see M. Alvesson, *Understanding Organizational Culture*, Sage, 2002.

32. *Observer*, 7.2.10 Business section, p. 3.

33. Figure 5.4 is adapted from the original in P. Grinyer and J.-C. Spender, *Turnaround: Managerial Recipes for Strategic Success*, Associated British Press, p. 203, 1979.

34. A fuller explanation of the cultural web can be found in G. Johnson, *Strategic Change and the Management Process*, 1987, and G. Johnson, 'Managing strategic change: strategy, culture and action', *Long Range Planning*, vol. 25, Blackwell, no. 1 (1992), pp. 28–36.

35. A practical explanation of cultural web mapping can be found in G. Johnson, 'Mapping and re-mapping organisational culture', in V. Ambrosini with G. Johnson and K. Scholes (eds), *Exploring Techniques of Analysis and Evaluation in Strategic Management*, Prentice Hall, 1998.

36. See J. Martin and A.L. Wilkins, 'Organisational stories as symbols which control the organisation', in L.R. Pondy, P.J. Frost, G. Morgan and T.C. Dandridge (eds), *Organisational Symbolism*, JAI Press, 1983.

37. The significance of organisational symbolism is explained in G. Johnson, 'Managing strategic change: the role of symbolic action', *British Journal of Management*, vol. 1, no. 4 (1990), pp. 183–200.

Cultural turnaround at Club Med

Frédéric Fréry, ESCP Europe

In 2010, the repositioning of Club Med as an 'upscale, friendly and multicultural' tour operator was supposed to be achieved, through the complete renovation of its portfolio of vacation villages. However, the outcome of this strategy, implemented since the early 2000s, when Club Med had faced the loss of impetus of its historical model, was still unclear. Such a repositioning clearly clashed with Club Med's history and culture, generally associated with a relaxed atmosphere, rough and ready amenities and an open-minded lifestyle.

The 2009 results showed that, even if operating profits were finally up after several years of decrease, revenues were still declining. Club Med's Chairman and CEO Henri

Source: Shutterstock.

Figure 1 Club Med revenues
(million euros)

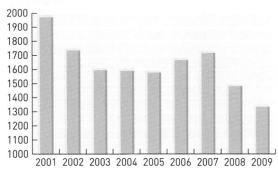

€1m is about $1.4m.

Figure 2 Club Med net profits
(million euros)

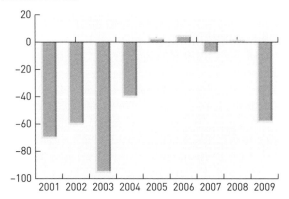

€1m is about $1.4m.

Giscard d'Estaing explained that the net loss (€58m; ~$81m) resulted from four elements: (1) the overall economic crisis, (2) the H1N1 flu virus and its impact on tourism, (3) the renovation cost of the villages, and (4) a 'limited number of property transactions, due to the mortgage crisis'. He also announced the opening of five new villages in China between 2010 and 2015. His promise was to 'deliver a new profitable Club Med for 2010'.

However, the break with Club Med's history and culture had to succeed: since 2004, this strategic turnaround had cost around €1bn.

Club Med's history: the years of growth

Club Med was founded after the Second World War by Gérard Blitz and Gilbert Trigano.

Coming from a Belgian diamond merchant family, Gérard Blitz was a world-class athlete in swimming and water-polo. In 1950, he spent some days of vacation in a tent village close to Calvi, Corsica. This gave him the idea to create a 'vacation camp' under the sun. He founded the Belgian association 'Club Méditerranée' in April 1950 and opened his first village on a desert beach on the island of Mallorca, Spain.

Blitz bought his tents from a French supplier, Gilbert Trigano. Apart from owning a family tent business, Trigano was a former resistance fighter and a reporter for the French Communist newspaper *L'Humanité*. Attracted by the vacation village concept, fascinated by

Blitz's personality, Trigano became the treasurer of the association in 1953, then president in 1963. The same year, Club Méditerranée was incorporated.

In 1955, Club Méditerranée opened a second tent village in Tahiti (Blitz's wife was of Tahitian origin). In 1956, a winter village was opened in Leysin, Switzerland, and in 1965, Club Méditerranée opened its first permanent village in Agadir, Morocco.

In 1966, in order to finance a vast international expansion plan in Northern Africa, Europe, America and Asia, the company was listed at the Paris stock exchange. During the next twenty years, dozens of villages opened, including two giant sailing ships, *Club Med 1* and *Club Med 2*.

First difficulties

In 1991, the year Blitz died, Operation Desert Storm strongly impacted the tourist industry and Club Med suffered heavy losses. In 1993, Gilbert Trigano was replaced as chairman and CEO by his son, Serge. In spite of his turnaround plan, Serge Trigano did not manage to put the situation right. In 1997, upset shareholders replaced him with an external manager, Philippe Bourguignon, the former CEO of EuroDisney.

Bourguignon's ambition was to 'transform a vacation villages company into a service company'. He implemented a growth strategy, both organic (new concepts such as a low-cost village for young people) and external (takeover of another tour operator and of a gym clubs chain). This ambitious expansion strategy came with a severe cost-cutting plan, a shift in human resource management (in the villages, many Club Med employees were replaced with local suppliers) and the implementation of a real IT infrastructure (many processes were still done manually). Club Med became profitable in 1998. In 1999, net profits grew by 48%. In 2000, revenues and profits soared again (+28% and +51% respectively). In three years, Club Med attracted more than 300,000 new customers. In 2001, when Gilbert Trigano died, Club Med had 127 villages, 24,200 employees and 1.8 million customers.

However, the terrorist attacks of 9/11 caused an immediate collapse of the tourist market. Bourguignon's volume strategy was no longer sustainable. Since he was disowned by Club Med's employees – who criticised his autocratic management and were used to Trigano's paternalism – he resigned from the chairmanship in 2002. He was replaced by the CEO he had recruited himself from Danone, Henri Giscard d'Estaing. Giscard d'Estaing was also the elder son of the former President of the French Republic.

The repositioning plan

When Giscard d'Estaing became chairman and CEO, Club Med was facing two external threats:

- The tourist industry was heavily affected by the terrorist threat.
- Thanks to the Internet, new low-cost entrants were rapidly expanding, and incumbents were offered vacation villages, similar to the Club Med concept, but at lower prices.

All this convinced Giscard d'Estaing to implement an upscale repositioning: the closing down of approximately 50 low-end villages, renovation of the existing infrastructure, opening of new prestigious establishments, a significant rise in services (all-inclusive package, open-bar policy, more comfortable rooms), but also a significant price rise. The number of villages decreased to 80 and a much more sophisticated advertising campaign was launched. Between 1998 and 2008, the proportion of high-end villages went from 18% to 47%, whereas low-end villages were disappearing. The clientele also evolved significantly: households with a high revenue accounted for 63% of customers in 2003, and 82% in 2005.

This repositioning was mainly financed by selling property, which reduced financial costs and amortisation, limited debt, and allowed Club Med to offer an acceptable balance sheet for investors to finance the renovation of its villages. However, two external events weakened this strategy: the market was still in a downturn (on top of terrorist threats, the 2004 tsunami in Asia also had an impact), and from 2007 the mortgage crisis brutally reduced the opportunity for property profits.

In 2010, analysts were still uncertain about the results of this profound strategic reorientation, which was disrupting Club Med's historical culture.

The roots of Club Med's culture

For more than fifty years, Club Med exhibited a distinct culture. Gilbert Trigano used to say that he had created a 'profoundly psychological industry'.

Marked by the Second World War, Blitz had created Club Med because he thought that all Europeans deserved vacations on the seaside and under the sun. He defined his concept as the 'antidote against civilisation'. According to Gilbert Trigano: 'More than Gérard, I tried to reconcile capitalism with utopia. I remember these early mornings when we were boldly building the world with a total madness, but we knew perfectly what we were doing: we knew we wanted to influence people's life and future.' Blitz was an idealist and

Trigano a pragmatist, but they agreed on 'gathering people hurt by modern society in a peaceful and soft place where they could regain their forces, an artificial environment to teach people to smile again'.

To do so, they built up a culture with rich symbols, rituals and myths. Villages were isolated from their local environment in order to break from day-to-day life. Amenities were limited: tents at first, then huts – often without electricity – with shared bathrooms. In this closed world, as of 1951, customers were named GMs (Gracious Members) and coordinators GOs (Gracious Organisers). On arrival, welcomed by GOs, GMs had to ban professional jargon and social origins. At the restaurant, there were only eight-people tables, in order to force GMs to make new acquaintances. As of 1956, Club Med banned money from the villages and implemented a payment system based on plastic pearl necklaces.

GOs were the keystone of the whole system. They were expected to maintain a permanent festive atmosphere through shows, village dances and sport competitions. During the first years, Blitz personally recruited them with his wife, Claudine. Gilbert Trigano insisted: 'Claudine informally played the role of head of personnel, which was a key role because everything relies on GOs. She and Gérard were the tutelary parents of the Club, they choose children in their image and maintain family relations with them.'

From an organisational point of view, the best GOs could become general managers of a village, in charge of all the operational aspects, from animation to hospitality and security. The best general managers – a job it was difficult to cope with after the age of 45, because it required an almost permanent night-and-day presence with GMs – could access administrative positions at Club Med headquarters in Paris, even if these coordinators were not necessarily good executives.

Under the trident logo (a reference to Poseidon and the Mediterranean Sea), Club Med generated a 'sea, sex and sun' alchemy which reached its apogee in the 1970s.

Towards a new culture

In the 1990s, this life in a community was no longer in line with social evolution. Loose morals were unacceptable for families. Villages were more and more considered as ghettos, without any contact with local cultures. Undue familiarity between GOs and GMs repelled some customers and the obligation to participate in all activities was seen as brigading.

As a consequence, as of 2002, after having asked Serge Trigano about Club Med's historical culture, Giscard d'Estaing attempted deep cultural change. An ambiance charter was produced. It highlighted the core values of the company: multicultural, pioneer, kindness, freedom, responsibility. It also spelled out inappropriate behaviours for GOs: cronyism, hasty judgement, individualism. As thick as a phone book, it also explained new procedures and limited 'vulgar' activities such as water games or roles played by a member of the opposite sex. A school village opened in Vittel in France, in order to train 10,000 employees (out of a total of 16,000). The goal was to reconsider relational behaviours, ways of dressing and attitudes. The organisation of the village was also modified. General managers – who used to supervise directly 15 services – were now assisted by two deputies (one in charge of hospitality, the other in charge of leisure).

A transformation in progress

This evolution was still in progress by 2010. Even if customer satisfaction had increased, the occupancy rate had not. Nothing indicated that shareholders would give Giscard d'Estaing enough time to complete Club Med's transformation: the share price plummeted from €54 in August 2007 to €13 in January 2010.

Even if Giscard d'Estaing maintained that his strategy was beginning to bear fruit, in mid-2009 he had had to react to the potential threat of a hostile takeover bid from external investors, who estimated that an upscale repositioning was inconsistent with Club Med's values and business model. An increase in capital dispelled this threat, but analysts were still cautious about the result of such a strategic and cultural turnaround.

Sources: clubmed.net; psychologies.com; *Les Echos*, 10 September 2007, 17 September 2007, 14 December 2009; *Challenges*, 11 December 2009; *Le Monde*, 16 December 2007; ESCP Europe monograph by J. de Florival and C. Hamard, 2007.

Questions

1 Analyse Club Med's culture before 2000.

2 Explain the reasons for Club Med's success between the 1950s and the 1990s.

3 How do you explain Club Med's difficulties in the early 1990s?

4 Why did Bourguignon's plan fail? Do you think that Giscard d'Estaing's plan will be more successful?

COMMENTARY ON PART I

Part I of the book has discussed some of the main influences that managers in organisations have to take into account in developing the strategies of their organisations. The underlying theme here is that reconciling these different forces is problematic. Not only are there many of them, but also their effects are difficult to predict and they are likely to change, creating potentially high levels of uncertainty. The forces may also be in conflict with one another, or pulling in different directions. Understanding the strategic position of an organisation is therefore challenging for managers. In this Commentary the four strategy lenses introduced in the initial

Design lens

The concepts and analytic tools of strategy can be used to understand the complex and uncertain world managers face in developing strategy. So it makes sense to:

- Undertake rigorous and extensive analysis, drawing largely on principles of economics, to understand environmental forces, strategic capabilities and the power and influence of stakeholders.
- Integrate the insights from such analyses into a clear view of the strategic position of the organisation,
- Thus ensure that top management can take a rational approach to the development of future strategy by considering how the issues identified might be addressed by different strategic options.
- Involve managers in such analysis through systematic strategic planning.

Experience lens

The experience lens focuses attention on trying to understand why people make sense of influences on their organisations the way they do in terms of their individual or collective experience and how this shapes and constrains their responses. It highlights that such experience is *both* useful because it provides short cuts in sense making, and also dangerous because it becomes fixed and biases responses. It suggests that an uncertain future is likely to be understood in terms of past experience that acts as an 'uncertainty reduction mechanism'. It also warns that strategic capabilities (especially core competences) that have driven past success may become embedded in organisational culture, giving rise to strategic drift.

The experience lens suggests that it is important to:

- Understand the cultural influences on the organisations's strategic position.
- Encourage the questioning and challenging of that which is taken for granted.
- Surface the assumptions that managers have because it is likely to be such assumptions that drive strategic decisions.
- Use the frameworks of analysis described in Part I to challenge such taken-for-granted assumptions; e.g. by building scenarios to sensitise managers to possible futures.

THE STRATEGIC POSITION

Commentary are used to reconsider how managers can and do make sense of the strategic position they face. Note that:

- There is no suggestion here that one of these lenses is better than another, but they do provide different insights into the problems faced and the ways managers cope with the challenge.
- If you have *not* read the Commentary following Chapter 1 that explains the four lenses, you should now do so.

Variety lens

The variety lens highlights that new ideas and insights into the strategic position of an organisation are likely to arise by:

- The ambiguity and uncertainty of the future giving rise to different perspectives that can stimulate new ideas from within and around the organisation.
- Such ideas just as likely bubbling up from below as being originated at the top of an organisation.

So, if innovation is important, managers need to learn how to foster and harness the variety of views and ideas in an organisation by:

- Welcoming, being sensitive to and cultivating such variety rather than seeking to foster conformity and uniformity.
- Looking for ideas and views arising from anywhere in the organisation.
- Being wary of seeking to identify *the* strategic position of the organisation such as to foster conformity and a 'right way' of seeing things.

Discourse lens

The strategic position of an organisation is not so much a matter of objective 'fact' as that which is represented and privileged in the discourse of major stakeholders and powerful people, for example a CEO, senior managers, investors or government. What such stakeholders say shows how influential people seek to frame an explanation of the strategic position of an organisation. In this context, three points suggest there is a need to take a critical, even sceptical, view of discourse on strategy:

- Strategy discourse has as much to do with stakeholders (managers included) seeking to influence a situation as it has to do with objective fact. Nonetheless such discourse can have a very real influence on organisations' strategies.
- The concepts and tools associated with strategy can be employed by managers so that they can (a) look as though they have insights that give them a special place with regard to the destiny of the organisation and (b) justify a perspective on strategy that is in their own interest. In this sense strategy discourse is linked to power.
- People get locked into their ways of talking about strategy. It can be difficult to change this. In this sense dominant discourse can contribute to strategic drift.

PART II
STRATEGIC CHOICES

This part explains strategic choices in terms of:

- How organisations relate to competitors in terms of their competitive business strategies.

- How broad and diverse organisations should be in terms of their corporate portfolios.

- How far organisations should extend themselves internationally.

- How organisations are created and innovate.

- How organisations pursue strategies through organic development, acquisitions or strategic alliances.

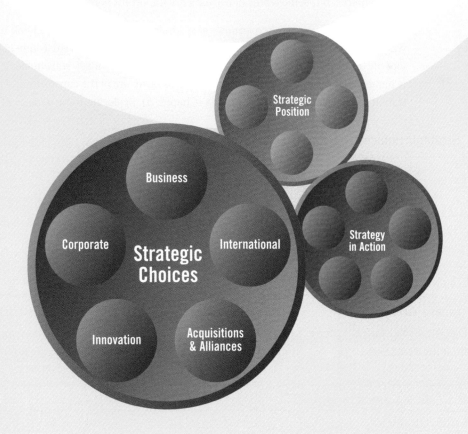

INTRODUCTION TO PART II

This Part is concerned with the palette of strategic choices, or options, potentially available to an organisation for responding to the positioning issues discussed in Part I of the book. There are three overarching choices to be made as shown in Figure II.i. These are:

- Choices as to *how an organisation at a business level positions itself in relation to competitors.* This is a matter of deciding how to compete in a market. For example, should the business compete on the basis of cost or differentiation? Or is competitive advantage possible through being more flexible and fleet-of-foot than competitors? Or is a more cooperative approach to competitors appropriate? These *business strategy* questions are addressed in Chapter 6.

- Choices of *strategic direction*, in other words, which products, industries and markets to pursue. Should the organisation be very focused on just a few products and markets? Or should it be much broader in scope, perhaps very diversified both in terms of products (or services) and markets? Should it create new products or should it enter new countries? These questions relate to corporate strategy, addressed in Chapter 7, international strategy in Chapter 8 and innovation and entrepreneurial strategy, as discussed in Chapter 9.

- Choices about *methods by which to pursue strategies.* For any of these choices, should they be pursued independently by organic development, by acquisitions or by strategic alliances with other organisations? This is the theme of Chapter 10.

The discussion in these chapters provides frameworks and rationales for a wide range of strategic choices. But some words of warning are important here:

- *Strategic choices relate back to analysis of strategic position.* Part I of the book has provided ways in which strategists can identify forces at work in the business environment (Chapter 2), identify and build on strategic capabilities (Chapter 3), meet stakeholder expectations (Chapter 4) and build on the benefits, as well as be aware of the constraints, of their organisation's historical and cultural context (Chapter 5). Exploring these issues will provide the

Figure II.i Strategic choices

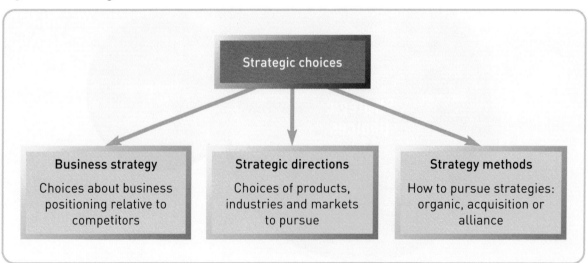

foundation for considering strategic options. However, working through the choices of Part II is also likely to feed back into the initial analysis of strategic position. Given particular strategic options, aspects of strategic position may need to be explored more deeply or revised.

- *Key strategic issues*. Choices have to be made in the context of an organisation's strategic position, of course. But here it is important that the analysis of strategic position distinguishes the *key strategic issues* from all the many positioning issues that are likely to arise. Analysis needs to avoid producing a very long list of observations without any clarity of what such key issues are. There is no single 'strategy tool' for this. Identifying key strategic issues is a matter of informed judgement and, because managers usually work in groups, of debate. The analytic tools provided can help, but are not a substitute for judgement.

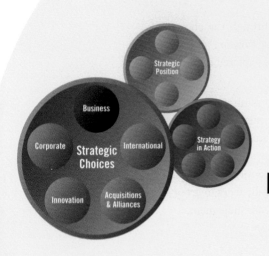

6

BUSINESS STRATEGY

Learning outcomes

After reading this chapter you should be able to:

● Identify *strategic business units* (SBUs) in organisations.

● Assess business strategy in terms of the generic strategies of *cost leadership*, *differentiation* and *focus*.

● Identify business strategies suited to *hypercompetitive* conditions.

● Assess the benefits of *cooperation* in business strategy.

● Apply principles of *game theory* to business strategy.

Key terms

Competitive advantage p. 199

Competitive strategy p. 199

Cost-leadership strategy p. 200

Differentiation p. 203

Focus strategy p. 205

Game theory p. 217

Strategic business unit p. 198

Strategic lock-in p. 210

mystrategylab

MyStrategyLab is designed to help you make the most of your studies. Visit www.pearsoned.co.uk/mystrategylab to discover a wide range of resources specific to this chapter, including:

• A personalised **Study plan** that will help you understand core concepts

• **Audio** and **video clips** that put the spotlight on strategy in the real world

• **Online glossaries** and **flashcards** that provide helpful reminders when you're looking for some quick revision.

(6.1) INTRODUCTION

This chapter is about a fundamental strategic choice: what strategy should a business unit adopt in its market? Business strategy questions are fundamental both to stand-alone small businesses and to all the many business units that typically make up large diversified corporations. Thus a restaurant business has to decide a range of issues such as menus, décor and prices in the light of competition from other restaurants locally. Similarly, in a large diversified corporation such as Unilever or Nestlé, every business unit must decide how it should operate in its own particular market. For example, Unilever's ice-cream business has to decide how it will compete against Nestlé's ice-cream business on a range of dimensions including product features, pricing, branding and distribution channels. These kinds of *business* strategy issues are distinct from the question as to whether Unilever should own an ice-cream business in the first place: this is a matter of *corporate* strategy, the subject of Chapter 7.

Figure 6.1 shows the main themes that provide the structure for the rest of the chapter. Starting from a definition of *strategic business units (SBUs)*, the chapter has two main themes:

● *Generic competitive strategies*, including *cost leadership*, *differentiation* and *focus*, and considering the *strategy clock*. An important theme here will be how far these strategies are sustainable over time and here *strategic lock-in* is often important.

● *Interactive strategies*, building on the notion of generic strategies to consider interaction with competitors, especially in *hypercompetitive environments*, and including both *cooperative strategies* and *game theory*. Business strategy often involves avoiding counter-productive competition in favour of explicit or tacit cooperation.

Business strategy is not relevant just to the private business sector. Charities and public-sector organisations both cooperate and compete. Thus charities compete between each other for support from donors. Public-sector organisations also need to be 'competitive' against comparable organisations in order to satisfy their stakeholders and secure their funding. Schools compete in terms of examination results, while hospitals compete in terms of waiting times, treatment survival rates and so on. Although some of the detailed implications may vary

Figure 6.1 **Business strategy**

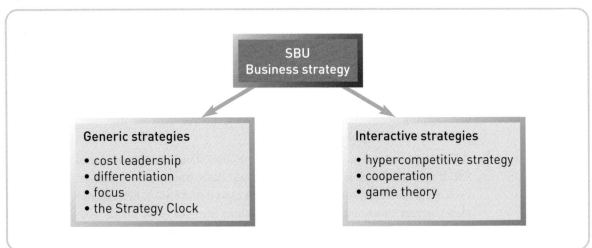

between sectors, wherever comparison is possible with other similar organisations, basic principles of business strategy are likely to be relevant. Very few organisations can afford to be demonstrably inferior to peers, and almost all have to make choices on key competitive variables such as costs, prices and quality.

6.2 IDENTIFYING STRATEGIC BUSINESS UNITS

KEY CONCEPT

Strategic business unit (SBU)

The starting point for business strategy is identifying the relevant business unit. A **strategic business unit (SBU) supplies goods or services for a distinct domain of activity**. A small business focused on a single market, such as a restaurant or specialist retailer, would count as a strategic business unit. More commonly, though, SBUs refer to the distinct businesses within a large diversified corporation (sometimes these SBUs are called 'divisions' or 'profit centres'). For example, the Japanese entertainment group Namco Bandai is divided into four SBUS: Toys and Hobby (Power Rangers, Tamagotchi and similar), Game Contents (arcade games and similar), Visual and Music (animation and music publishing) and Amusement (theme parks). Typically within a large diversified corporation, each SBU will have responsibility for its own business strategy. In a large public-sector organisation, such as a local authority, individual schools might be considered too as SBUs, with their domain of activity being education in a geographical area.

Thus the SBU concept has three effects within large organisations. First, SBUs decentralise initiative to smaller units within the corporation as a whole. In Namco Bandai, Toys and Hobby can pursue its business strategy without continuously seeking permission from central headquarters for minor adjustments (see also section 7.6 on the role of the centre). Second, SBUs allow large corporations to vary their business strategies according to the different needs of the various external markets they serve. Namco Bandai does not have to impose the same business strategy (for example, a focus on low prices) across all its SBUs. Finally, the SBU concept encourages accountability. If managers determine the business strategy for their own SBU, then they can be held accountable for the success or failure of that strategy.

Identifying the right boundaries for SBUs is often complex.[1] Distinct markets can be defined at different levels of analysis: for example, Namco Bandai's Toys and Hobbies business could be further segmented by target age-group, distribution channel or geography. In many corporations, SBU boundaries change frequently as well: the computer company Dell is well known for reorganising its SBUs continuously, as market conditions change and units get too big. There are two basic criteria that can help in identifying appropriate SBUs:

- *Market-based criteria.* Different parts of an organisation might be regarded as the same SBU if they are targeting the same *customer types*, through the same sorts of *channels* and facing similar *competitors*. On the other hand, it would usually be sensible to distinguish a unit tailoring products or services to specific local needs from one that offers standardised products or services globally.

- *Capabilities-based criteria.* Parts of an organisation should only be regarded as the same SBU if they have similar strategic capabilities. Many traditional retailers or financial services companies operate their internet services as distinct SBUs. Even though they may be targeting very similar customers, the capabilities involved in the internet-based businesses are typically too different to the original physical stores or outlets to manage within the same unit.

(6.3) GENERIC COMPETITIVE STRATEGIES

This section introduces the competitive element of business strategy, with cooperation addressed particularly in section 6.4. **Competitive strategy is concerned with how a strategic business unit achieves competitive advantage in its domain of activity.** In turn, **competitive advantage is about how an SBU creates value for its users both greater than the costs of supplying them and superior to that of rival SBUs.** There are two important features of competitive advantage here. To be *competitive* at all, the SBU must ensure that users (customers or funders) see sufficient value that they are prepared to pay more than the costs of supply. To have an *advantage*, the SBU must be able to create greater value than competitors. In the absence of a competitive advantage, the SBU is always vulnerable to attack by competitors with better products or services or offering lower prices, and could be driven out of business.

Michael Porter[2] argues that there are two fundamental means of achieving competitive advantage. An SBU can have lower costs than its competitors. Or it can have products or services that are so exceptionally valuable to customers that it can charge higher prices than competitors. In defining competitive strategies, Porter adds a further dimension based on the scope of customers that the business chooses to serve. Businesses can choose to focus on narrow customer segments, for example a particular demographic group such as the youth market. Alternatively they can attempt to target a broad range of customers, across a range of characteristics such as age, wealth or geography.

Porter's distinctions define three 'generic' strategies: in other words, basic types of strategy that hold across many kinds of business situations. These three generic strategies are illustrated in Figure 6.2. In the top left-hand corner is a strategy of *cost leadership*, as exemplified in the British women's clothing market by retailers such as Matalan. Matalan seeks to use large economies of scale and tight cost discipline to serve a wide range of women with reasonably fashionable clothing at a good price. Monsoon's shops pursues a strategy of *differentiation*, offering

Figure 6.2 Three generic strategies

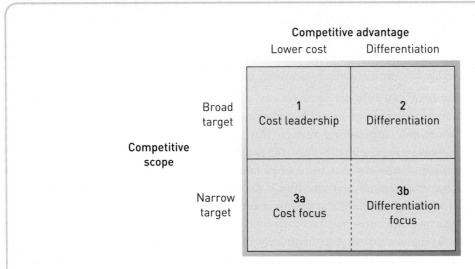

arty styles to women across a range of ages at significantly higher prices. The third generic strategy is *focus*, involving a narrow competitive scope. Porter distinguishes between cost focus and differentiation focus, but for him narrow scope is such a distinctive fundamental principle that these two are merely variations on the same basic theme of narrowness. For example, Evans targets only women needing larger-sized clothing, achieving a higher price for its distinctive products through a *differentiation focus* strategy. On the other hand, the clothing lines of the major supermarkets target shoppers who are simply looking for good-value standard clothing for their families, a *cost focus* strategy. The rest of this section discusses these three generic strategies in more detail.

6.3.1 Cost-leadership

Cost-leadership strategy involves becoming the lowest-cost organisation in a domain of activity. There are four key *cost drivers* that can help deliver cost leadership, as follows:

- *Input costs* are often very important, for example labour or raw materials. Many companies seek competitive advantage through locating their labour-intensive operations in countries with low labour costs. Examples might be service call-centres in India or manufacturing in China. Location close to raw material sources can also be advantageous, as for example the Brazilian steel producer CSN which benefits from its own local iron-ore facilities.

- *Economies of scale* refer to how increasing scale usually reduces the average costs of operation over a particular time period, perhaps a month or a year. Economies of scale are important wherever there are high fixed costs. Fixed costs are those costs necessary for at level of output: for example, a pharmaceutical manufacturer typically needs to do extensive R&D before it produces a single pill. Economies of scale come from spreading these fixed costs over high levels of output: the average cost due to an expensive R&D project halves when output increases from one million to two million units. Economies of scale in purchasing can also reduce input costs. The large airlines, for example, are able to negotiate steep discounts from aircraft manufacturers. For the cost-leader, it is important to reach the output level equivalent to the *minimum efficient scale*. Note, though, that *diseconomies of scale* are possible. Large volumes of output that require special overtime payments to workers or involve the neglect of equipment maintenance can soon become very expensive. As in Figure 6.3, therefore, the economies of scale curve is typically somewhat U-shaped, with the average cost per unit actually increasing beyond a certain point.

- *Experience*[3] can be a key source of cost efficiency. The *experience curve* implies that the cumulative experience gained by an organisation with each unit of output leads to reductions in unit costs (see Figure 6.3). There is no time limit: simply the more experience an organisation has in an activity, the more efficient it gets at doing it. The efficiencies are basically of two sorts. First, there are gains in labour productivity as staff simply learn to do things more cheaply over time (this is the specific *learning curve* effect). Second, costs are saved through more efficient designs or equipment as experience shows what works best. The experience curve has three important implications for business strategy. First, entry timing into a market is important: early entrants into a market will have experience that late entrants do not yet have and so will gain a cost advantage. Second, it is important to gain and hold market share, as companies with higher market share have more 'cumulative experience' simply because of their greater volumes. Finally, although the gains from experience are typically greatest at the start, as indicated by the steep initial curve in

Figure 6.3 Economies of scale and the experience curve

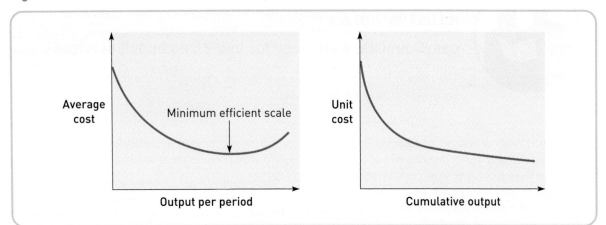

Figure 6.3, improvements normally continue over time. Opportunities for cost reduction are theoretically endless. Figure 6.3 compares the experience curve and economies of scale in order to underline the contrast here. Unlike scale, where diseconomies appear beyond a certain point, the experience curve implies at worst a flattening of the rate of cost reduction. Cost savings due to accumulated experience are continuously available.

- *Product/process design* also influences cost. Efficiency can be 'designed in' at the outset. For example, engineers can choose to build a product from cheap standard components rather than expensive specialised components. Organisations can choose to interact with customers exclusively through cheap web-based methods, rather than via telephone or stores. Organisations can also tailor their offerings in order to meet the most important customer needs, saving money by ignoring others: this, arguably, is the strategy of Barnet, the 'easyCouncil' (Illustration 6.1). In designing a product or service, it is important to recognise *whole-life costs*, in other words, the costs to the customer not just of purchase but of subsequent use and maintenance. In the photocopier market, for example, Canon eroded Xerox's advantage (which was built on service and a support network) by designing a copier that needed far less servicing.

Porter underlines two tough requirements for cost-based strategies. First of all, the principle of competitive advantage indicates that a business's cost structure needs to be *lowest* cost, i.e. lower than all competitors'. Having the second lowest cost structure implies a competitive disadvantage against somebody. Competitors with higher costs than the cost-leader are always at risk of being undercut on price, especially in market downturns. For businesses competing on a cost basis, cost leadership is always more secure than being second or third in terms of costs.

Porter's second requirement is that low cost should not be pursued in total disregard for quality. To sell its products or services, the cost-leader has to be able to meet market standards. For example, low-cost Chinese car producers seeking to export into Western markets not only need to offer cars that are cheap, but cars that meet acceptable norms in terms of style, service network, reliability, resale value and other important characteristics. Cost-leaders have two options here:

- *Parity* (in other words, equivalence) with competitors in product or service features valued by customers. Parity allows the cost-leader to charge the same prices as the average competitor in the marketplace, while translating its cost advantage wholly into extra profit (as

ILLUSTRATION 6.1

easyCouncils: a strategy for low-cost council services

The London Borough of Barnet has chosen a budget airline model for its services, on the lines of easyJet.

In 2008–09, with pressures on budgets increasing, Conservative Party-controlled councils in the United Kingdom were looking to save costs by adopting the low-cost model pioneered by airlines such as Ryanair and easyJet. Barnet, a borough council in North London with a population of over 300,000, is one of the pioneers.

The Conservative borough council is led by a former PwC management consultant, Mike Freer. In a context of falling central government subsidies, and wanting to save local taxes, the council is looking to cut costs by £15m (~€16.5; ~$22.5) a year. In 2008, the council launched a consultation process on radical reform called 'Future Shape'. In 2009, they declared their intention to adopt a budget airline model, which council officials dubbed 'easyCouncil'.

Mike Freer gave some examples. Just as budget airlines allow passengers to pay extra for priority boarding, in future householders will be able to pay extra to jump the queue in order to get faster responses on planning applications for new buildings or house extensions. Similarly, as airline passengers can choose whether to have a meal or not (and pay accordingly), users of adult social care will be allowed to choose their own options. Freer explained to the *Guardian*:

> 'In the past we would do things for our residents rather than letting them choose for themselves. We would tell them they need one hour help shopping, or one hour cleaning, meals-on-wheels, and they would get it, like it or not. Instead, we will assess what level of personal care they need, place a value on it and give them the budget. If they say, "Frankly, I'd like a weekend in Eastbourne [a holiday resort]", they can have it.'

Opposition Labour leader Alison Moore warned in the *Guardian*:

> 'There is a real danger of problems in the local community and that vulnerable people will lose out. People who are dependent on care services may find that they aren't there at the same quality as before.'

John Burgess, branch secretary of the main local government services trade union, commented:

> 'Democratically accountable public services are the best way to ensure quality services and value for money. Comparing public services to gimmicks used by a cheap airline company beggars belief.'

Barnet citizens differed on the new approach. 87-year-old Sarah Walker broke a bone in an accident, forcing her to spend three weeks in hospital. When she returned home, she was initially badly disabled and feared being sent to a local authority care home, from which she would never return. The council's new policy of avoiding expensive care homes and instead offering a burst of intensive help to ease the disabled into independence worked for her:

> 'I had three carers a day for the first week. One in the morning, one at lunchtime and one in the evening. They gave me the confidence to get back to doing things for myself. At the end of six weeks, I was managing quite well and I'm independent now. It would be a waste of money if they were sending someone once a week for ever more, so this was the right approach for me.'

On the other hand, 68-year-old Bill Kelly compared the Council's logic to electronic tagging in order to save the costs of prison for criminals: 'I can see Mr Freer giving us all ankle tags so they know where we are.'

Sources: R. Booth, 'Tory-Controlled Borough of Barnet adopts budget airline model', *Guardian*, 27 August 2009; J. Burgess, 'The budget airline model won't work for councils', *Guardian*, 2 September 2009.

Questions

1 What are the advantages and disadvantages of this approach to low-cost council services?

2 In what sense do borough councils 'compete'?

Figure 6.4 Costs, prices and profits for generic strategies

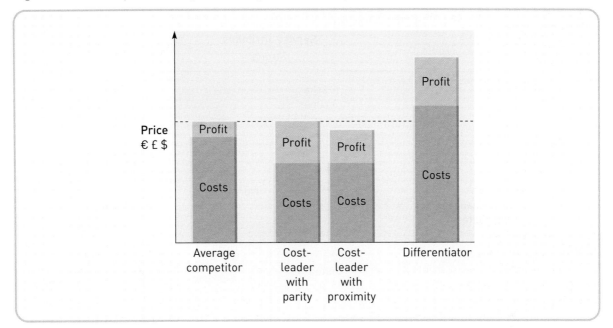

in the second column of Figure 6.4). The Brazilian steel producer CSN, with its cheap iron-ore sources, is able to charge the average price for its steel, and take the cost difference in greater profit.

● *Proximity* (closeness) to competitors in terms of features. Where a competitor is sufficiently close to competitors in terms of product or service features, customers may only require small cuts in prices to compensate for the slightly lower quality. As in the third column in Figure 6.4, the proximate cost-leader still earns better profits than the average competitor because its lower price eats up only a part of its cost advantage. This proximate cost-leadership strategy might be the option chosen initially by Chinese car manufacturers in export markets, for example.

6.3.2 Differentiation strategies

For Porter, the principal alternative to cost-leadership is differentiation.[4] **Differentiation involves uniqueness along some dimension that is sufficiently valued by customers to allow a price premium.** Relevant points of differentiation vary between markets. Within each market too, businesses may differentiate along different dimensions. Thus in clothing retail, competitors may differentiate by store size, locations or fashion. In cars, competitors may differentiate by safety, style or fuel efficiency. Where there are many alternative dimensions that are valued by customers, it is possible to have many different types of differentiation strategy in a market. Thus, even at the same top end of the car market, BMW and Mercedes differentiate in different ways, the first typically with a sportier image, the second with more conservative values. The strategy canvas provides one means of mapping these various kinds of differentiation (see section 2.4.3).

Managers can identify potential for differentiation by using perceptual mapping of their products or services against those of competitors. For example, Figure 6.5 maps customer perceptions of American airline companies along two bundles of attributes: flight performance

Figure 6.5 Mapping differentiation in the US airline industry

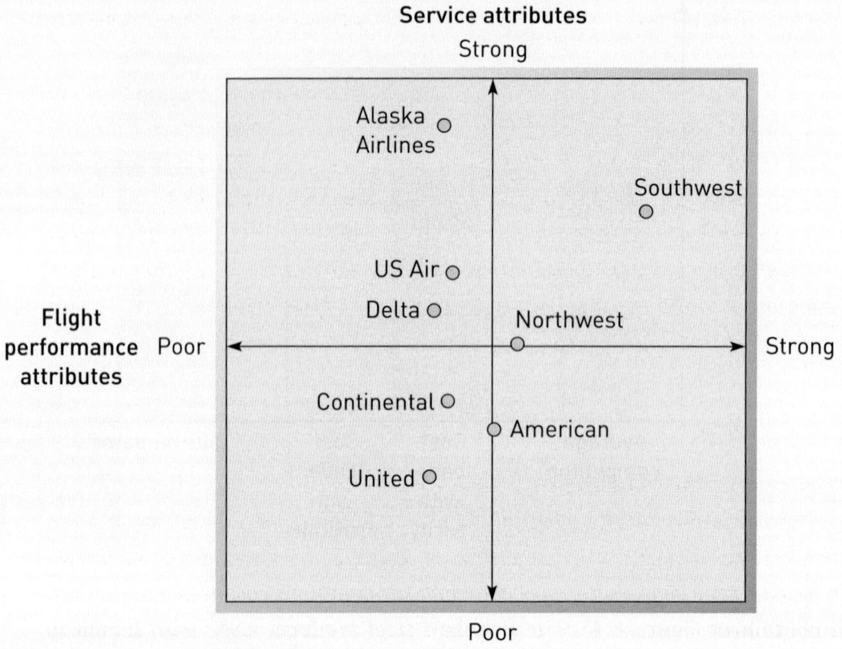

Source: Simplified from Figure 1, in D. Gursoy, M. Chen and H. Kim (2005), 'The US airlines relative positioning', *Tourism Management*, 26, 5, 57–67: p. 62.

attributes such as delays, and service attributes such as baggage problems or boarding complaints. Most of the larger airlines are quite closely bunched together. For example, US Air and Delta are not significantly differentiated from each other in terms of on-time flights, and they are perceived similarly in terms of service elements such as boarding, ticketing and reservations. One airline that does stand out as a differentiator is Southwest, which does well in terms of both flight delays and service. In the period studied, Southwest was also the most profitable of these airlines. It seems that Southwest was able to differentiate on attributes that were highly valued by its customers.

However, the attributes on which to differentiate need to be chosen carefully. Differentiation strategies require clarity about two key factors:

● *The strategic customer.* It is vital to identify clearly the strategic customer on whose needs the differentiation is based. This is not always straightforward, as discussed in section 2.4.2. For example, for a newspaper business, the strategic customers could be readers (who pay a purchase price), advertisers (who pay for advertising), or both. Finding a distinctive means of prioritising customers can be a valuable source of differentiation.

● *Key competitors.* It is very easy for a differentiator to draw the boundaries for comparison too tightly, concentrating on a particular niche. Thus specialist Italian clothing company Benetton originally had a strong position with its specialist knitwear shops. However, it lost ground because it did not recognise early enough that general retailers such as Marks & Spencers could also compete in the same product space of colourful pullovers and similar products.

There is an important condition for a successful differentiation strategy. Differentiation allows higher prices, but usually comes at a cost. To create a point of valuable differentiation typically involves additional investments, for example in R&D, branding or staff quality. The differentiator can expect that its costs will be higher than those of the average competitor. But, as in column 4 in Figure 6.4, the differentiator needs to ensure that the additional costs of differentiation do not exceed the gains in price. It is easy to pile on additional costs in ways that are not valued sufficiently by customers. The failures under British ownership of the luxury car companies Rolls-Royce and Bentley against top-end Mercedes cars are partly attributable to the expensive crafting of wood and leather interiors, the full cost of which even wealthy customers were not prepared to pay for. Just as cost-leaders should not neglect quality, so should differentiators attend closely to costs, especially in areas irrelevant to their sources of differentiation. As in Illustration 6.2, Volvo's differentiation strategy in the Indian bus market seems to have involved keeping an eye on costs as well.

6.3.3 Focus strategies

Porter distinguishes focus as the third generic strategy, based on competitive scope. A **focus strategy targets a narrow segment of domain of activity and tailors its products or services to the needs of that specific segment to the exclusion of others.** Focus strategies come in two variants, according to the underlying sources of competitive advantage, cost or differentiation. In air travel, Ryanair follows a *cost-focus strategy*, targeting price-conscious holiday travellers with no need for connecting flights. In the domestic detergent market, the Belgian company Ecover follows a *differentiation focus* strategy, gaining a price premium over rivals on account of its ecological cleaning products.

The focuser achieves competitive advantage by dedicating itself to serving its target segments better than others which are trying to cover a wider range of segments. Serving a broad range of segments can bring disadvantages in terms of coordination, compromise or inflexibility. Focus strategies are able to seek out the weak spots of broad cost-leaders and differentiators:

- *Cost focusers* identify areas where broader cost-based strategies fail because of the added costs of trying to satisfy a wide range of needs. For instance, in the United Kingdom food retail market, Iceland Foods has a cost-focused strategy concentrated on frozen and chilled foods, reducing costs against generalist discount food retailers such as Aldi which have all the complexity of fresh foods and groceries as well as their own frozen and chilled food ranges.

- *Differentiation focusers* look for specific needs that broader differentiators do not serve so well. Focus on one particular need helps to build specialist knowledge and technology, increases commitment to service and can improve brand recognition and customer loyalty. For example, ARM Holdings dominates the world market for mobile phone chips, despite being only a fraction of the size of the leading microprocessor manufacturers, AMD and Intel, which also make chips for a wide range of computers.

Successful focus strategies depend on at least one of three key factors:

- *Distinct segment needs.* Focus strategies depend on the distinctiveness of segment needs. If segment distinctiveness erodes, it becomes harder to defend the segment against broader competitors. For example, now that the boundaries are blurring between smartphones used by general consumers and smartphones used by business people, it has become easier for

ILLUSTRATION 6.2
Volvo's different Indian buses

Volvo has a strategy to sell buses at nearly four times the prevailing market price.

The Indian bus market has long been dominated by two home-players, subsidiaries of major Indian conglomerates: Tata Motors and Ashok Leyland. The two companies made simple coaches on a design that had hardly changed for decades. On top of a basic truck chassis, the two companies bolted a rudimentary coach body. Engines were a meagre 110–120 horse-power, and roared heartily as they hauled their loads up the steep mountain roads of India. Mounted at the front, the heat from the over-strained engines would pervade the whole bus. Air conditioning was a matter of open windows, through which the dust and noise of the Indian roads would pour. Suspension was old-fashioned, guaranteeing a shaky ride on pot-holed roads. Bags were typically slung on the top of the bus, where they were easily soiled and at high risk of theft. But at least the buses were cheap, selling to local bus companies at around Rs 1.2m (€15,000; $21,000).

In 1997, Swedish bus company Volvo decided to enter the market, with buses prices at Rs 4m, nearly four times as much as local products. Akash Passey, Volvo's first Indian employee, commissioned a consultancy company to evaluate prospects. The consultancy company recommended that Volvo should not even try. Passey told the *Financial Times*: 'My response was simple – I took the report and went to the nearest dustbin and threw it in'. Passey entered the market in 2001 with the high-priced luxury buses.

Passey used the time to develop a distinctive strategy. His basic product had superior features. Volvo's standard engines were 240–250 hp and mounted at the back, ensuring a faster and quieter ride. Air conditioning was standard of course. The positioning of the engine and the specific bus design of the chassis meant a more roomy interior, plus storage for bags internally. But Passey realised this would not be enough. He commented to the *Financial Times*: 'You had to do a lot of things to break the way business is done normally'.

Volvo offered post-sale maintenance services, increasing life expectancy of buses from three to ten years, and allowing bus operating companies to dispense with their own expensive maintenance workshops. Free training was given to drivers, so they drove more safely and took more care of their buses. The company advertised the benefits of the buses direct to customers in cinemas, rather than simply promoting them to the bus operators. To kick-start the market, Volvo supplied about 20 subsidised trial units to selected operators. Volvo trainees rode these buses, alerting the company immediately when something went wrong so Volvo could immediately send its engineers. Faster, smoother and more reliable travel allowed the bus operators to increase their ticket prices for the luxury Volvo buses by 35 per cent.

Business people and the middle classes were delighted with the new Volvo services. Speedier, more comfortable journeys allowed them to arrive fresh for meetings and potentially to save the costs of overnight stays. Tata and Ashok Leyland both now produce their own luxury buses, with Mercedes and Isuzu following Volvo into the market. None the less, the phrase 'taking a Volvo' has become synonymous with choosing a luxury bus service in India, rather as 'hoover' came to refer to any kind of vacuum cleaner.

In 2008, Volvo opened a new state-of-the-art bus factory in Bangalore. It is Volvo's most efficient bus factory worldwide, producing a fully-built bus in 20–25 days. Annual capacity is 1000 buses per year.

Source: J. Leahy, 'Volvo takes a lead in India', *Financial Times*, 31 August 2009.

Questions

1 Rank the elements of Passey's strategy for Volvo in order of importance. Could any have been dispensed with?

2 How sustainable is Volvo's luxury bus strategy?

Nokia and Apple to attack the traditional distinctive niche of Research in Motion (RIM) with its BlackBerry business phones.

● *Distinct segment value chains.* Focus strategies are strengthened if they have distinctive value chains that will be difficult or costly for rivals to construct. If the production processes and distribution channels are very similar, it is easy for a broad-based differentiator to push a specialised product through its own standardised value chain at a lower cost than a rival focuser. In detergents, Procter & Gamble cannot easily respond to Ecover because achieving the same ecological friendliness would involve transforming its purchasing and production processes.

● *Viable segment economics.* Segments can easily become too small to serve economically as demand or supply conditions change. For example, changing economies of scale and greater competition have eliminated from many smaller cities the traditional town-centre department stores, with their wider ranges of different kinds of goods from hardware to clothing.

6.3.4 'Stuck in the middle'?

Porter claims that managers face a crucial choice between the generic strategies of cost-leadership, differentiation and focus. According to him, it is unwise to blur this choice. As earlier, the lowest-cost competitor can always undercut the second lowest-cost competitor. For a company seeking advantage through low costs, therefore, it makes no sense to add extra costs by half-hearted efforts at differentiation. For a differentiator, it is self-defeating to make economies that jeopardise the basis for differentiation. For a focuser, it is dangerous to move outside the original specialised segment, because products or services tailored to one set of customers are likely to have inappropriate costs or features for the new target customers. This was a risk for RIM as it moved its BlackBerry business phones into the broader consumer market, for whom e-mail encryption was not so important. Porter's argument is that managers are generally best to choose which generic strategy they are pursuing and then stick rigorously to it. Otherwise there is a danger of being *stuck in the middle*, doing no strategy well.

Porter's warning about the danger of being stuck in the middle provides a useful discipline for managers. It is very easy for them to make incremental decisions that compromise the basic generic strategy. As profits accumulate, the successful cost-leader will be tempted to stop scrimping and saving. In hard times, a differentiator might easily cut back the R&D or advertising investments essential to its long-term differentiation advantage. Consistency with generic strategy provides a valuable check for managerial decision-making.

However, Porter's argument for pure generic strategies is controversial.[5] He himself acknowledges there are circumstances in which the strategies can be combined:[6]

● *Organisational separation.* It is possible for a company to create separate strategic business units each pursuing different generic strategies and with different cost structures. The challenge, however, is to prevent negative spill-overs from one SBU to another. For example, a company mostly pursuing differentiated strategies is liable to have high head-office costs that the low-cost SBUs will also have to bear. On the other hand, a cheap cost-leader might damage the brand-value of a sister SBU seeking differentiation. As illustrated by the failures of British Airways with its low-cost subsidiary Go, and Delta with its low-cost Song airline, in practice it can be very difficult to pursue different generic strategies within a single set of related businesses.

● *Technological or managerial innovation.* Sometimes technological innovations allow radical improvements in both cost and quality. Internet retailing reduces the costs of book-selling, at the same time as increasing product stock and, through online book reviews, improving advice. Managerial innovations are capable of such simultaneous improvements too. The Japanese car manufacturers' introduction of Total Quality Management led to reductions in production-line mistakes that both cut manufacturing costs and improved car reliability, a point of successful differentiation.

● *Competitive failures.* Where competitors are also stuck in the middle, there is less competitive pressure to remove competitive disadvantage. Equally, where a company dominates a particular market, competitive pressures for consistency with a single competitive strategy are reduced.

6.3.5 The Strategy Clock

The **Strategy Clock** provides another way of approaching the generic strategies (see Figure 6.6).[7] The Strategy Clock has two distinctive features. First, it is more market-focused than the generic strategies, being focused on prices to customers rather than costs to the organisation. Second, the circular design of the clock allows for more continuous choices than Michael Porter's sharp contrast between cost-leadership and differentiation: there is a full range of incremental adjustments that can be made between the 7 o'clock position at the bottom of the low-price strategy and the 2 o'clock position at the bottom of the differentiation

Figure 6.6 The Strategy Clock

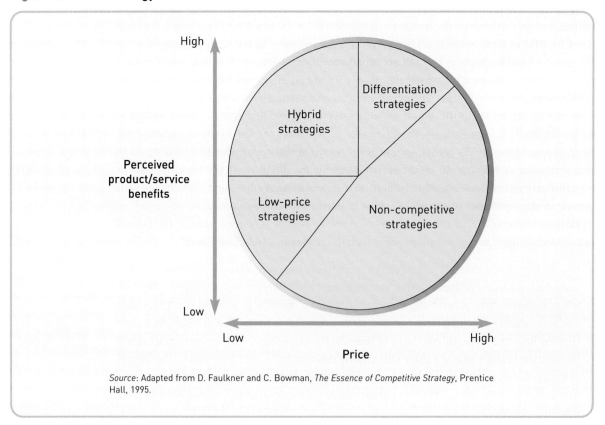

Source: Adapted from D. Faulkner and C. Bowman, *The Essence of Competitive Strategy*, Prentice Hall, 1995.

strategy. Organisations often travel around the clock, as they adjust their pricing and benefits over time.

The Strategy Clock identifies three zones of feasible strategies, and one zone likely to lead to ultimate failure:

- *The differentiation zone.* This zone contains a range of feasible strategies for building on high perceptions of product or service benefits amongst customers. Close to the 12 o'clock position is a strategy of *differentiation without price premium*. Differentiation without a price premium combines high perceived benefits and moderate prices, typically used to gain market share. If high benefits also entail relatively high costs, this moderate pricing strategy would only be sustainable in the short term. Once increased market share had been achieved, it might be logical to move to *differentiation with price premium* closer to a 1 or 2 o'clock position. Movement all the way towards the 2 o'clock position is likely to involve a focus strategy, in Michael Porter's terms. Such a *focused differentiation* strategy targets a niche where the higher prices and reduced benefits are sustainable, for instance because of a lack of competition in a particular geographical area.

- *The low-price zone.* This zone allows for different combinations of low prices and low perceived value. Close to the 9 o'clock position, a standard *low price* strategy would gain market share, by combining low prices with reasonable value (at parity with competitors). Again, if reasonable benefits are associated with higher costs, this position is unlikely to be sustainable for long. Either cuts in benefits or increases in prices would be desirable over time. A variation on the standard low price strategy is the *no frills* strategy, close to the 7 o'clock position. No frills strategies involve both low benefits and low prices, similar to low-cost airlines such as Ryanair (which even proposed to charge for use of its on-board toilets).

- *The hybrid strategy zone.* A distinctive feature of the Strategy Clock are the possibilities it allows between low-price and differentiation strategies.[8] Hybrid strategies involve both lower prices than differentiation strategies, and higher benefits than low-price strategies. Hybrid strategies are often used to make aggressive bids for increased market-share. They can also be an effective way of entering a new market, for instance overseas. Even in the case of innovations with high benefits, it can make sense to price low initially in order to gain experience curve efficiencies or lock-in through network effects (see section 6.3.6). Some companies sustain hybrid strategies over long periods of time: for example, furniture store IKEA, which uses scale advantages to combine relatively low prices with differentiated Swedish design.

- *Non-competitive strategies.* The final set of strategies occupy a zone of infeasible economics, with low benefits and high prices. Unless businesses have exceptional strategic lock-in, customers will quickly reject these combinations. Typically these strategies lead to failure.

The Strategy Clock's focus on price, and its scope for incremental adjustments in strategy, provide a more dynamic view on strategy than Porter's generic strategies. Instead of organisations being fairly fixed in terms of either a cost or a differentiation strategy, they can move around the clock. For example, an organisation might start with a *low price* strategy to gain market-share, later shift to a higher-priced *differentiation with premium* strategy in order to reap profits, and then move back to a *hybrid strategy* in order to defend itself from new entrants. However, Porter's generic strategies do remind managers that costs are critical. Unless an organisation has some secure cost advantage (such as economies of scale), a hybrid strategy of high perceived benefits and low prices is unlikely to be sustainable for long.

6.3.6 Lock-in and sustainable business strategies

Business strategies should ideally be sustainable over time. This may involve having competitive advantages that rivals cannot match. Thus, as in section 3.3, strategies are more likely to be sustained if underpinned by capabilities that combine all the VRIN characteristics of value, rarity, inimitability and non-substitutability. Another approach to sustaining business strategies is creating 'lock-in'.

Strategic lock-in is where users become dependent on a supplier and are unable to use another supplier without substantial switching costs.[9] Strategic lock-in is related to the concept of path dependency (see section 5.3.1) and essentially extends the principles of inimitability and non-substitutability. Under conditions of lock-in, imitators and substitutes are unable to attract customers. This is particularly valuable to differentiators. With customers securely locked in, it becomes possible to keep prices well above costs.

Lock-in can be achieved in two main ways:

● *Controlling complementary products or services.* Opportunities for lock-in to a particular product or service arise where other products or services are necessary for customers using it. This is often known as the 'razor and blade' strategy: once a customer has bought a particular kind of razor, they are obliged to buy compatible blades to use it. Apple originally applied a similar strategy when it used Digital Rights Management to ensure that music bought on its iTunes store could only be played on its own iPod players. To switch to a Sony player would mean losing access to all the iTunes music previously purchased.

● *Creating a proprietary industry standard.* Sometimes companies are so successful that they create an industry standard under their own control. Similar to the razor-and-blade effect, as customers invest in training and systems using that standard, it becomes more expensive to switch to another product or service. However, with industry standards, *network effects* also operate: as other members of the network also adopt the same standard, it becomes even more valuable to stay within it. Microsoft built this kind of proprietary standard with its Windows operating system, which holds more than 90 per cent of the market. For a business to switch to another operating system would mean retraining staff and translating files onto the new system, while perhaps creating communications problems with network members (such as customers or suppliers) who had stuck with Windows.

(6.4) INTERACTIVE STRATEGIES

Generic strategies need to be chosen, and adjusted, in the light of competitors' strategies. If everybody else is chasing after cost leadership, then a differentiation strategy might be sensible. Thus business strategy choices *interact* with those of competitors. This section starts by considering business strategy in the light of competitor moves, especially in hypercompetition. It then addresses the option of cooperation and closes with game theory, which helps managers choose between competition and more cooperative strategies.

6.4.1 Interactive price and quality strategies

Richard D'Aveni depicts competitor interactions in terms of movements against the variables of price (the vertical axis) and perceived quality (the horizontal axis), similar to the Strategy Clock: see Figure 6.7.[10] Although D'Aveni applies his analysis to the very fast-moving environments

Figure 6.7 Interactive price and quality strategies

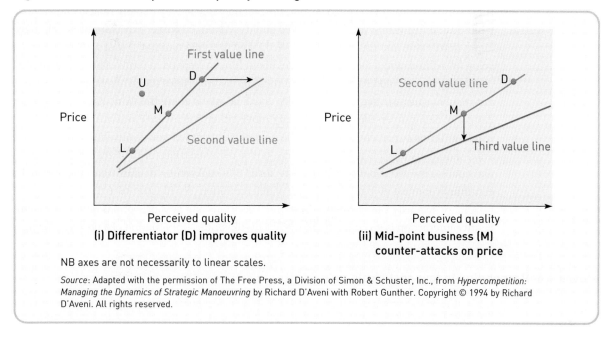

(i) Differentiator (D) improves quality

(ii) Mid-point business (M) counter-attacks on price

NB axes are not necessarily to linear scales.

Source: Adapted with the permission of The Free Press, a Division of Simon & Schuster, Inc., from *Hypercompetition: Managing the Dynamics of Strategic Manoeuvring* by Richard D'Aveni with Robert Gunther. Copyright © 1994 by Richard D'Aveni. All rights reserved.

he terms 'hypercompetitive' (see section 2.3.1), similar reasoning applies wherever competitors' moves are interdependent.

Figure 6.7 shows different organisations competing by emphasising either low prices or high quality or some mixture of the two. Graph i. starts with a 'first value line', describing various trade-offs in terms of price and perceived quality that are acceptable to customers. The cost-leading firm (here L) offers relatively poor perceived quality, but customers accept this because of the lower price. While the relative positions on the graph should not be taken exactly literally, in the car market this cost-leading position might describe some of Hyundai's products. The differentiator (D) has a higher price, but much better quality. This might be Mercedes. In between, there are a range of perfectly acceptable combinations, with the mid-point firm (M) offering a combination of reasonable prices and reasonable quality. This might be Ford. M's strategy is on the first value line and therefore entirely viable at this stage. On the other hand, firm U is uncompetitive, falling behind the value line. Its price is higher than M's, and its quality is worse. U's predicament is typical of the business that is 'stuck in the middle', in Porter's terms. U no longer offers acceptable value and must quickly move back onto the value line or fail.

In any market, competitors and their moves or counter-moves can be plotted against these two axes of price and perceived value. For example, in graph i of Figure 6.7, the differentiator (D) makes an aggressive move by substantially improving its perceived quality while holding its prices. This improvement in quality shifts customer expectations of quality right across the market. These changed expectations are reflected by the new, second value line (in green). With the second value line, even the cost-leader (L) may have to make some improvement to quality, or accept a small price cut. But the greatest threat is for the mid-point competitor, M. To catch up with the second value line, M must respond either by making a substantial improvement in quality while holding prices, or by slashing prices, or by some combination of the two.

However, mid-point competitor M also has the option of an aggressive counter-attack. Given the necessary capabilities, M might choose to push the value line still further outwards, wrong-footing differentiator D by creating a third value line that is even more demanding in terms of the price-perceived quality trade-off. The starting point in graph ii. of Figure 6.7 is all three competitors

L, M and D successfully reaching the second value line (uncompetitive U has disappeared). However, M's next move is to go beyond the second value line by making radical cuts in price while sustaining its new level of perceived quality. Again, customer expectations are changed and a third value line (in red) is established. Now it is differentiator D that is at most risk of being left behind, and it faces hard choices about how to respond in terms of price and quality.

Plotting moves and counter-moves in these terms underlines the dynamic and interactive nature of business strategy. Economically viable positions along the value line are always in danger of being superseded as competitors move either downwards in terms of price or outwards in terms of perceived quality. The generic strategies of cost-leadership and differentiation should not be seen as static positions, but as dynamic trajectories along the axes of price and quality. The movement towards more 'local' Starbucks stores demonstrates the need to be continually moving along the trajectory of differentiation (see Illustration 6.3).

A more detailed example of the sequence of decisions and possible options involved in competitive interaction is given in Figure 6.8.[11] This illustrates the situation of a business facing a

Figure 6.8 Responding to low-cost rivals

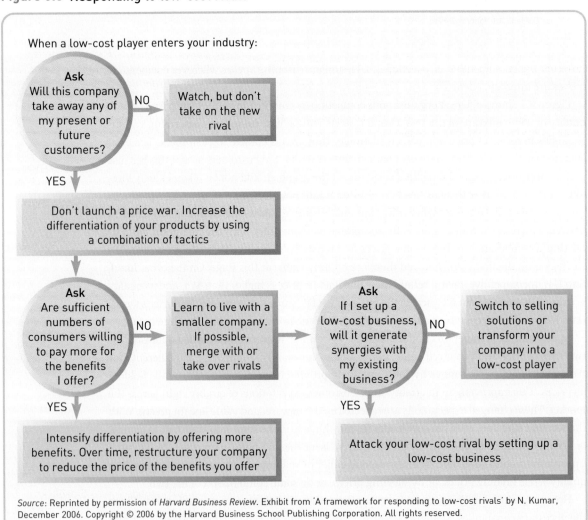

ILLUSTRATION 6.3

McCafés challenge Starbucks

Starbucks coffee chain is having to change its strategy in response to McDonald's.

In 2009, Starbucks was in trouble. With 16,000 outlets and operating in 49 countries, Starbucks was the world's largest coffee chain. But economic recession was taking its toll, with 2009 sales 5 per cent down on the previous year's. And fast-food chain McDonald's was pushing hard its cheap coffee concept, McCafés.

The McCafé concept had emerged in Australia in the 1990s. McCafés typically operate within or next to regular McDonald's outlets. They use high-quality coffee machines and sell different blends of coffee according to the tastes of local markets. The coffee is priced substantially lower than Starbucks' traditional prices. By 2009, nearly half of Germany's 1200 McDonald's restaurants operated a McCafé, and McCafés were spreading rapidly across Europe. The target was 1200 McCafés in Europe by the end of 2009, against Starbucks' 1300.

Starbucks' response to recession and competition was vigorous. Company founder and CEO Howard Schultz proclaimed:

'We are laser-focused on delivering the finest quality coffee and getting the customer experience right every time. We have . . . been putting our feet into the shoes of our customers and are responding directly to their needs. Our customers are telling us they want value and quality and we will deliver that in a way that is meaningful to them and authentic to Starbucks.'

The company announced a $500m ($700m) cost reduction programme, with investments in operational efficiencies and new technologies. Starbucks also entered the $17bn instant coffee market, launching its Starbucks Via™ Ready Brew coffee head-to-head against brands such as Nestlé and Maxwell House. In particular, it began to transform the format of its stores.

Traditionally, all Starbucks stores have been designed on the basis of a standard palette of colours and furniture, worldwide. Now, in Seattle – the very city where Starbucks had originally started – the company opened a new store without any of the usual branding. Named '15th Ave. Coffee and Tea', the new store was based on close study of local independent coffee stores. One local store-owner complained about Starbucks'

researchers: 'They spent the last 12 months in our store up on 15th [Avenue] with these obnoxious folders that said "Observation" '. The 15th Ave. Coffee and Tea store is a radical departure. Starbucks' logo is completely absent, and wine and beer are available. Table tops come from a landscaper's stone yard and the shop uses discarded theatre seats. Evenings offer live music and poetry readings.

In the United Kingdom, Starbucks' largest European market, the same thinking is being applied. Facing competition from companies like Costa Coffee, McDonald's and Wetherspoons, Darcy Willson-Rymer, Starbucks' local managing director, commented to the *Independent*: 'What we did was set the standard, then we allowed people to catch us up'. The UK's Starbucks chain is abandoning the old identikit format. Local artefacts, bolder colours, bigger community noticeboards and even second-hand furniture will all be used to create more individual stores. Carrot sticks and porridge are joining the usual high-calorie cakes and paninis. Willson-Rymer explained: 'In every store, there will be something that is locally relevant. The thing that needs to be the same in every store is the latte, the cappuccino, the product and the culture of coffee tastings and the knowledge.' He commented on past mistakes thus: 'The business is run 80 per cent heart and 20 per cent head, and we tried to flip it on its head. I don't know what the right proportion is, but I believe that the heart is back in the company.'

Sources: 'Starbucks tests new names for stores', *Seattle Times*, 16 July 2009; 'Starbuck chief admits: our shops are all wrong', *Independent*, 18 September 2009; 'McDonald's set to mug Starbucks in Europe', *Financial Times*, 26 May 2009.

Questions

1 Plot the moves of McDonald's and Starbucks on the axes of price and perceived quality, as in Figure 6.7.

2 What should be the response of a company with a similar original position as Starbucks (for example, Costa Coffee in the UK)?

low-price competitor, for example a high-cost Western manufacturer facing possible attack by cheap imports from Asia. There are three key decisions:

- *Threat assessment.* The first decision point is whether the threat is substantial or not. If there is a threat, the high-cost organisation should not automatically respond to a low-price competitor by trying to match prices: it is likely to lose a price war with its existing cost structure. The high-cost organisation needs a more sophisticated response.

- *Differentiation response.* If there are enough consumers who value them, the high-cost organisation can seek out new points of differentiation. For example, a Western manufacturer may exploit its closeness to local markets by improving service levels. At the same time, unnecessary costs should be stripped out. If increased differentiation is not possible, then more radical cost solutions should be sought.

- *Cost response.* Merger with other high-cost organisations may help reduce costs and match prices through economies of scale. If a low-cost business is synergistic with (in other words, has benefits for) the existing business, this can be an effective platform for an aggressive cost-based counter-attack. If there is neither scope for further differentiation nor synergy between the existing business and a possible new low-cost business, then the existing business must sooner or later be abandoned. For a Western manufacturer, one option might be to outsource all production to low-cost operators, simply applying its design and branding expertise. Another option would be to abandon manufacturing in favour of becoming a 'solutions provider', aggregating manufactured components from different suppliers and adding value through whole-systems design, consultantcy or service.

Equivalent decisions would have to be made, of course, by a low-price competitor facing a differentiator. When Apple entered the phone market with its expensive touchscreen iPhone, established handset manufacturers had first to decide whether Apple was a serious long-term threat, and then choose how far they should either match the iPhone's features or increase the price differential between their products and Apple's expensive ones.

6.4.2 Interactive strategies in hypercompetition

According to Richard D'Aveni, the kinds of move and counter-move outlined in the preceding section are a constant feature of hypercompetitive environments. As in section 2.3.1, hypercompetition describes markets with continuous disequilibrium and change, for example popular music or consumer electronics. In these conditions, it may no longer be possible to plan for sustainable positions of competitive advantage. Indeed, planning for long-term sustainability may actually destroy competitive advantage by slowing down response. Managers have to be able to act faster than their competitors.

Successful competitive interaction in hypercompetition demands speed and initiative rather than defensiveness. Richard D'Aveni highlights four key principles:

- *Cannibalise bases of success*: sustaining old advantages distracts from developing new advantages. An organisation has to be willing to cannibalise the basis of its own success.

- *Series of small moves rather than big moves*: smaller moves create more flexibility and give a series of temporary advantages. At the same time, smaller moves make it harder for competitors to detect and counter the overall strategic direction.

- *Be unpredictable*. If competitors can see a pattern they can predict the next competitive moves and quickly learn how to imitate or outflank an organisation. So surprise, unpredictability, even apparent irrationality can be important. Managers must learn ways of appearing to be unpredictable to the external world whilst, internally, thinking strategies through.

- *Mislead the competition*. Drawing on the lessons of game theory (see section 6.4.4), the organisation might signal particular moves, but then do something else (for example, talk about alliances, and then make an acquisition). Or the organisation might disguise initial success in a market, until ready to respond to competitor retaliation.[12]

6.4.3 Cooperative strategy

So far the emphasis has been on competition and competitive advantage. However, the competitive moves and counter-moves in section 6.4.1 make it clear that sometimes competition can escalate in a way that is dangerous to all competitors. It can be in the self-interest of organisations to restrain competition. Moreover, advantage may not always be achieved just by competing. Collaboration between some organisations in a market may give them advantage over other competitors in the same market, or potential new entrants. Collaboration can be explicit in terms of formal agreements to cooperate, or tacit in terms of informal mutual understandings between organisations. In short, business strategy has to include cooperative options as well as competitive ones.[13]

Figure 6.9 illustrates various kinds of benefits from cooperation between firms in terms of Michael Porter's five forces of buyers, suppliers, rivals, entrants and substitutes (section 2.3.1). Key benefits of cooperation are as follows:

- *Suppliers*. In Figure 6.9, cooperation between rivals A and B in an industry will increase their purchasing power against suppliers. Moreover, cooperation between rivals A and B may enable them to standardise requirements, enabling suppliers to make cost reductions to all parties' benefit. For example, two car manufacturers might agree on common component specifications, allowing their supplier to gain economies through production of the standardised part on a greater scale.

- *Buyers*. Conversely, cooperation between rivals A and B will increase their power as suppliers vis-à-vis buyers. It will be harder for buyers to shop around. Such *collusion* between rivals can help maintain or raise prices, as for example in the South African airline industry (see Illustration 6.4). On the other hand, buyers may benefit if their inputs are standardised, again enabling reductions in costs that all can share. For example, if food manufacturers supplying a retailer agree on common pallet sizes for deliveries, the retailer can manage its warehouses much more efficiently.

- *Rivals*. If cooperative rivals A and B are getting benefits with regard to both buyers and suppliers, other competitors without such agreements – in Figure 6.9, rival C – will be at a competitive disadvantage. Rival C will be in danger of being squeezed out of the industry.

- *Entrants*. Similarly, potential entrants will likely lack the advantages of the combined rivals A and B. Moreover, A and B can coordinate their retaliation strategies against any new entrant, for example by cutting prices by the same proportions in order to protect their own relative positions while undermining the competitiveness of the new entrant.

- *Substitutes*. Finally, the improved costs or efficiencies that come from cooperation between rivals A and B reduces the incentives for buyers to look to substitutes. Steel companies have cooperated on research to reduce the weight of steel used in cars, in order to discourage car manufacturers from switching to lighter substitutes such as aluminium or plastics.

Further kinds of cooperation will be considered under alliance strategy in section 10.4.

ILLUSTRATION 6.4

Cup-winners: competition and collusion in South Africa

Were South Africa's airlines cooperating to take advantage of the 2010 World Cup?

The 2010 Football World Cup was a great opportunity to put South Africa on the world tourism map. Up to three million international visitors were expected to visit the country during the month of June, many of whom might be encouraged to come back in the future. It was of course also a great opportunity for South African business. But in February 2010, the major domestic airlines were accused of exploiting the surge of demand by trying to fix prices together.

Domestic airline travel between matches would be important, as the World Cup involves 10 stadiums scattered around a large country. From Cape Town to Johannesburg is 880 miles, or 17 hours of hard driving. There are 2000 domestic flights a day.

The dominant player in both the domestic and international market is South African Airways (SAA), the national flag-carrier. Another major domestic player is Comair, which is part owned by British Airways, operator of many services between South Africa and Europe. However, many new airlines have entered the market in recent years. Significant low-cost airlines in South Africa are SA Express (founded 1994), SA Airlink (founded 1996), Kulula (founded 2001 by Comair), 1Time (founded 2004) and Mango (founded 2006). SA Airlink, SA Express and SAA had been part of a strategic alliance until 2006. Competition is a challenge for airlines: a half-full flight costs nearly as much as a full one, but of course earns half the money. It is not surprising then that SAA has made persistent losses in recent years.

The accusation of price-fixing had come in December 2009 from SAA itself, when the company offered cooperation with the competition authority in return for leniency. The accusation centred on a November e-mail sent by Comair's chief executive Erik Venter to SAA, 1Time, SA Airlink, Mango and SA Express regarding pricing strategy during the World Cup. The e-mail said: 'airlines have the option to either not provide any inventory [seats] for sale until such time [as they knew where matches would be played and when] or price all inventory at peak-time rates until such time as they have greater certainty'.

The *Sunday Times* reported the head of the competition authority as saying of Comair: 'they have set out a methodology to influence the pricing outcome'. CEO Venter riposted that the e-mail

'reflected textbook airline pricing principles that any commercial airline would implement, based on supply and demand and cost recovery . . . The email clearly states that Comair expects airline prices to fall once the airlines have implemented their extra capacity for the World Cup, and that the pricing is anticipated to average out at the level experienced over a typical South African peak holiday season.'

SAA and the other airlines had some history with regard to price-fixing. For example, in 2006, SAA, Kulula, SA Express and SA Airlink had been fined for agreeing a simultaneous standard increase in fuel surcharges. SAA had also been accused of offering travel agents inducements to recommend its flights to customers even when they knew cheaper flights were available. One low-cost competitor, Nationwide, had allegedly been driven out of business by this practice. The *Guardian* reported the England Football Supporters' Federation as warning:

'England's regular travellers are having to take a long and sober look at the costs involved in following the team. It would be a mistake for South Africa to regard the World Cup as a four-week opportunity to rip off fans.'

Sources: 'Airlines Investigated for Price-Fixing during World Cup', *Guardian*, 30 January 2010; 'Probes into Airlines to Proceed', *Sunday Times*, 31 January 2010; 'South African body probes claims of over-pricing', *BBC*, 15 February 2010.

Questions

1 What would be the advantages *and* the disadvantages of raising prices artificially during the World Cup?

2 Suggest three reasons why it may make sense that SAA raised the price-fixing accusation, rather than any other airline.

Figure 6.9 Cooperating with rivals

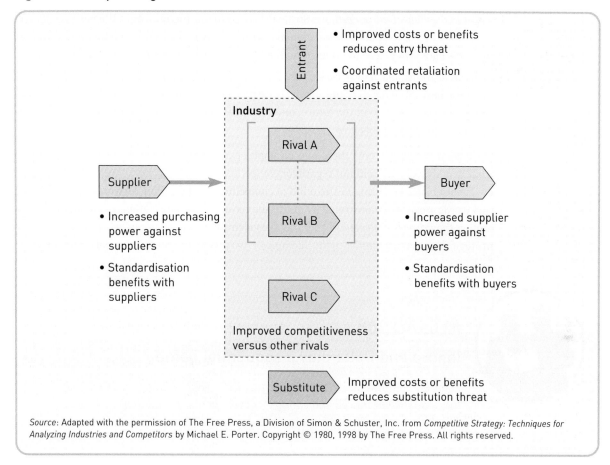

6.4.4 Game theory

Game theory provides important insights into competitor interaction.[14] The 'game' refers to the kinds of interactive moves two players make in a game of chess. **Game theory encourages an organisation to consider competitors' likely moves and the implications of these moves for its own strategy.** Game theorists are alert to two kinds of interaction in particular. First, game theorists consider how a *competitor response* to a strategic move might change the original assumptions behind that move: for example, challenging a competitor in one area might lead to a counter-attack in another. Second, game theorists are sensitive to the *strategic signals*, or messages, their moves might convey to competitors, for example with regard to how fiercely they seem willing to defend their position in a particular market. In the light of possible attacks and counter-attacks, game theorists often advise a more cooperative approach than head-to-head competition.

Game theory is particularly relevant where competitors are *interdependent*. Interdependence exists where the outcome of choices made by one competitor is dependent on the choices made by other competitors. For example, the success of price cuts by a retailer depends on the responses of its rivals: if rivals do not match the price cuts, then the price-cutter gains market-share; but if rivals follow the price cuts, nobody gains market-share and all players suffer from the lower prices. Anticipating competitor counter-moves is clearly vital to deciding whether to go forward with the price-cutting strategy.

There are two important guiding principles that arise from interdependence:

- *Get in the mind of the competitors.* Strategists need to put themselves in the position of competitors, take a view about what competitors are likely to do and choose their own strategy in this light. They need to understand their competitors' game-plan to plan their own.

- *Think forwards and reason backwards.* Strategists should choose their competitive moves on the basis of understanding the likely responses of competitors. Think forwards to what competitors might do in the future, and then reason backwards to what would be sensible to do in the light of this now.

Illustration 6.5 shows how these two principles can lead to exactly the opposite strategy to what would be chosen without regard for competitors.

The principles of getting in the mind of competitors and thinking forwards and reasoning backwards are also demonstrated by one of the most famous illustrations of game theory reasoning: the *prisoner's dilemma*. Game theorists identify many situations where organisations' strategic decisions are similar to the dilemma of two prisoners accused of serial crimes together

ILLUSTRATION 6.5

Innova and Dolla play a sequential game

Many competitive situations are 'sequential', where outcomes depend on the sequence of moves and counter-moves. In these situations, thinking forwards and reasoning backwards is crucial.

Innova and Dolla, competitors in the market for games consoles, face a decision on investment in research and development. Innova has highly innovative designers but is short of the finance required to invest heavily in rapid development of products. Dolla is strong financially but relatively weak in terms of its research and development. Thinking forwards then reasoning backwards can help Innova determine its move and when to make it.

The two companies know that high investment in R&D would shorten the development time, but they are also concerned about costs. Indeed, high levels of investment by both is the worst outcome. The expected pay-off is low for Innova because raising finance will be expensive for it; the expected pay-off is low for Dolla because, with equal investment, Innova has better chances of winning given its design capabilities.

Being short of funds, Innova particularly wants to keep its investment low. If Dolla were to invest low as well, Innova would expect a better pay-off because of its innovative capabilities. But Dolla knows that if it

goes for a low level of investment, it has no advantage over Innova's superior innovative capabilities. The likelihood therefore is that Dolla will counter Innova's low investment strategy with high investment.

Innova's situation can be seen as a series of sequential decisions, as in Figure 1. If Innova decides to invest low, it knows that Dolla is likely to respond high and gain the advantage simply by outspending its rival (pay-off C is 2:4). However, if Innova moves first and invests high, it places Dolla in a difficult position. If Dolla also invests high, it ends up with a low pay-off, as does Innova (pay-off A is just 1:1): they both have high expenses. In these circumstances, Dolla might well reject that strategy and economise by investing low. The resultant pay-off B (3:2) is better than pay-off A (1:1) for both parties, but particularly for Innova.

Working through these different game logics, Innova should realise that, despite its shortage of finance, it does not necessarily make sense to invest low. If it moves first and invests high, Dolla's own self-interest in responding low gives Innova both the

and being interrogated in separate prison cells without the possibility of communicating with each other. The prisoners have to decide on the relative merits of: (i) loyally supporting each other by refusing to divulge any information to their interrogators; and (ii), seeking an advantage by betraying the other. If both stay silent, they might get away with most of their crimes and only suffer some lesser punishment, perhaps on just one or two offences. The interrogators, though, will tempt each of them to divulge full information by offering them their freedom if only they betray their fellow criminal. However, if both betray, then the judge is unlikely to be grateful for the confessions, and will punish them for all their crimes. The dilemma for each of the prisoners is how much to trust in their mutual loyalty: if they both refuse the temptation to divulge, they can both get away with the lesser punishment; on the other hand, if one is sure that the other will not betray, it makes even more sense to betray the loyal one as that allows the betrayer to go totally free. The two prisoners are clearly interdependent. But because they cannot communicate, they each have to get in the mind of the other, think forwards to what they might do, and then reason backwards in order to decide what their own strategy should be – stay silent or betray.

Figure 1 A sequential move game

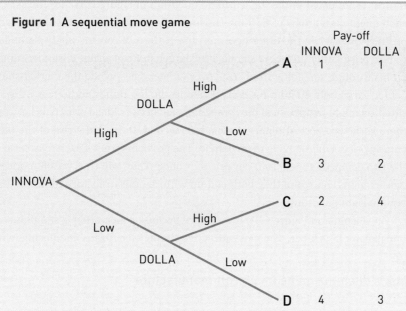

Source: From *Thinking Strategically: The Competitive Edge in Business, Politics and Everyday Life* by Avinash K. Dixit and Barry J. Nalebuff. Copyright © 1991 by Avinash K. Dixit and Barry J. Natebuff. Used by permission of W.W. Norton & Company, Inc.

advantage of higher investment and that of superior designers. Of course, if there is some way of Innova signalling a decision to invest high whilst actually investing low, thus persuading Dolla to invest low too, then Innova achieves its most attractive outcome (pay-off D).

Question

Given the clear incentive to Innova to move first with a high investment strategy, what should Dolla do and what might be the sequence of decisions and pattern of outcomes then?

The prisoner's dilemma has its equivalence in business where there are two major players competing head-to-head against each other in a situation of tight interdependence. This is the position of Airbus and Boeing in the aircraft business, Sony and Microsoft in the games market, or British Airways and Virgin in transatlantic travel. It would be relevant to the strategic decisions of two such interdependent companies in a range of situations: for example, if one company was thinking about making a major investment in an innovative new product that the other company could match; if one company was pondering an attack on the home market of the other company; or if the two companies were contemplating making competing takeover bids for a third company. For two such competitors to communicate directly about their strategies in these situations would likely be judged illegal by the competition authorities. They therefore have to get into each other's minds, think forwards and reason backwards. How will the other company act or react, and in the light of that, what strategy is best?

The kind of situation two interdependent competitors could get into is represented in the prisoner's dilemma matrix of Figure 6.10. Suppose the two main aircraft manufacturers Airbus and Boeing were both under pricing pressure, perhaps because of falling demand. They each have to decide whether to announce radical price cuts or to hold their prices up. If both choose to hold their prices, neither gets an advantage over the other and they both get the returns represented in the top left-hand quadrant of Figure 6.10: for the sake of illustration, each might earn profits of €500m. However, if one competitor pursues the radical price cuts on their own while the other does not, the pattern of returns might be quite different: the radical price-cutter attracts a significantly larger share of airline customers and earns €700m profits through spreading fixed costs over greater sales, while the market-share-losing competitor earns only €100m (as represented in the top-right and bottom-left quadrants). This situation might tempt one of the competitors to choose radical price cuts for two reasons: first, there is the prospect of higher profits; but, second, there is the risk of the other competitor cutting prices while leaving them behind. The problem is that if each reasons in the same way, the two competitors will *both* cut prices at once. They will thus set off a price war in which neither gains share and they both end up with the unsatisfactory return of just €300m (the bottom-right quadrant).

The dilemma in Figure 6.10 is awkward because cooperation is simultaneously attractive and difficult to achieve. The most attractive strategy for Airbus and Boeing jointly is for them

Figure 6.10 Prisoner's dilemma game in aircraft manufacture

		Boeing	
		Hold prices	Cut prices
Airbus	Hold prices	500 500	700 100
	Cut prices	100 700	300 300

Hypothetical data constructed for illustration purposes only

both to hold their prices, yet in practice they are likely to cut prices because they must expect the other to do so anyway. A distinctive feature of game theory is that it frequently highlights the value of a more cooperative approach to competitor interaction, rather than aggressive competition. The cooperation need not be in the form of an explicit agreement: cooperation can be tacit, supported by the recognition of mutual self-interest in not attacking each other head-to-head. Game theory therefore encourages managers to consider how a 'game' can be transformed from lose–lose competition to win–win cooperation. There are four principles that can help here:

- *Ensure repetition*. The prisoner's dilemma above assumes just one interaction. The thinking forwards is quite limited. In many circumstances, though, it is easier to achieve tacit co-operation if the two players know that they will be making similar interdependent decisions over time. Ensuring repetition makes cooperation much more likely. In a repetitive game, starting with a cooperative approach, and only making more aggressive moves in *response* to the aggression of the other player, has been shown generally to help players maintain a mutually satisfactory position of tacit cooperation. In this approach, both Airbus and Boeing would start by holding their prices; if one cut its prices, the other would simply cut its prices for one period, hoping that the first would move back to the higher price-level; if the first company did move back to the higher prices, the second would follow. The idea is that in repeated interactions over time, players can learn from each other's moves and counter-moves the benefits of cooperation.

- *Signalling*. Another insight from game theory is that strategic moves are also signals to com-petitors. Strategists need to be aware of the messages that their moves convey and read the messages of their competitors' moves. If Airbus failed to punish a price cut of Boeing with its own price cut, then Boeing might decide that Airbus was not serious about the market and would continue its price-cutting strategy. Responding aggressively to an initial price cut may actually support long-term cooperation in a repeated game.

- *Deterrence*. As above, signalling can clearly be about deterring unwanted strategic moves by competitors. During the Cold War, game theorists attribute the lack of direct warfare between the United States and the Soviet Union to the fact that both possessed nuclear deterrents: if one country attacked the other, then the second country would retaliate with a nuclear attack. This was known as Mutually Assured Destruction (MAD), but it worked. In a similar vein, interdependent competitors have to demonstrate that the costs of an unwanted move will be very high. Two effective forms of deterrent would be maintaining extra capacity that could be used to flood the market, or holding a minor position in a com-petitor's key market that could easily be expanded. Even if these investments in deterrence are expensive, they may be worthwhile if they encourage cooperation.

- *Commitment*. It is important also to signal commitment. When the Roman invader Julius Caesar burnt his ships on the shores of England, the message was to his adversaries as much as his own invading army. The Ancient Britons knew that Caesar would fight to the death: they had strong incentives to negotiate a peace with him. Caesar's signal of commitment was credible because it was costly and irreversible. Similarly, if a company invests heavily in developing its brand in a market, or building up a portfolio of patents, then competitors will know that it is highly committed, and be less likely to attack head-on. Again, additional investments have a signalling value that can help cooperation long-term.

KEY DEBATE

To be different or the same?

Can differentiation strategies rebound, making an organisation seem dangerously eccentric rather than delivering competitive advantage?

This chapter has introduced the potential value of differentiation strategies, in which the organisation emphasises its uniqueness. This is consistent also with the argument of the resource-based view (Chapter 3) in favour of the distinctiveness and inimitability of an organisation's resources. But how far should an organisation push its uniqueness, especially if there is a danger of it beginning to be seen as simply eccentric?

McKinsey & Co. consultant Philipp Natterman makes a strong case for differentiation.[1] He tracks the relationship between profitability and differentiation (in terms of pricing and product features) over long periods in both the personal computer and mobile phone industries. He finds that as differentiation falls over time, so too do industry profit margins. Natterman blames management techniques such as benchmarking (Chapter 3), which tend to encourage convergence on industry 'best practices'. The trouble with best practices is that they easily become standard practices. There is no competitive advantage in following the herd.

However, 'institutional theorists' such as Paul DiMaggio and Walter Powell point to some advantages in herd-like behaviour.[2] They think of industries as 'organisational fields' in which all sorts of actors must interact – customers, suppliers, employees and regulators. The ability of these actors to interact effectively depends upon being legitimate in the eyes of other actors in the field. Over time, industries develop institutionalised norms of legitimate behaviour, which it makes sense for everybody to follow. It is easier for customers and suppliers to do business with organisations that are more or less the same as the others in the industry. It is reassuring to potential employees and industry regulators if organisations do not seem highly eccentric. Especially when there is high uncertainty about what drives performance – for example, in knowledge-based industries – it can be a lot better to be legitimate than different. To the extent that customers, suppliers, employees and regulators value conformity, then it is valuable in itself. Being a 'misfit' can be costly.

This institutionalist appreciation of conformity makes sense of a lot of strategic behaviour. For example, merger waves in some industries seem to be driven by bandwagons, in which organisations become panicked into making acquisitions simply for fear of being left behind. Likewise, many management initiatives, such as business process re-engineering, e-business or outsourcing, are the product of fads and fashions as much as hard objective analysis. The insight from institutionalist theory, however, is that following the fashion is not necessarily a bad thing.

Thus institutional theory and the resource-based view appear to have opposing perspectives on the value of differentiation. David Deephouse has investigated this apparent trade-off between differentiation and conformity in the American banking industry and found a curvilinear relationship between differentiation and financial performance.[3] Strong conformity led to inferior performance; moderate differentiation was associated with improved performance; extreme differentiation appeared to damage performance.

Deephouse concludes in favour of 'balance' between differentiation and conformity. He also suggests that the value of differentiation depends on the extent to which key actors in the industry – customers, suppliers, employees, and so on – have converged on institutionalised norms of appropriate strategy. It seems that strategies can be too differentiated, but that how much 'too differentiated' is depends on the kind of industry that one is in.

References:
1. P.M. Natterman, 'Best practice does not equal best strategy', *McKinsey Quarterly*, no. 2 (2000), pp. 22–31.
2. P. DiMaggio and W. Powell, 'The iron cage revisited: institutional isomorphism and collective rationality in organizational fields', *American Sociological Review*, vol. 48 (1983), pp. 147–60.
3. D. Deephouse, 'To be different or to be the same? It's a question (and theory) of strategic balance', *Strategic Management Journal*, vol. 20 (1999), pp. 147–66.

Questions

1 To what extent do (a) universities and (b) car manufacturers compete by being different or the same?

2 Considering the nature of their industries, and key players within them, why might these organisations adopt these approaches to conformity or differentiation?

SUMMARY

- Business strategy is concerned with seeking competitive advantage in markets at the *business* rather than *corporate* level.

- Business strategy needs to be considered and defined in terms of *strategic business units* (SBUs).

- Different *generic strategies* can be defined in terms of cost-leadership, differentiation and focus.

- Managers need to consider how business strategies can be sustained through strategic capabilities and/or the ability to achieve a '*lock-in*' position with buyers.

- In *hypercompetitive* conditions sustainable competitive advantage is difficult to achieve. Competitors need to be able to cannibalise, make small moves, be unpredictable and mislead their rivals.

- *Cooperative strategies* may offer alternatives to competitive strategies or may run in parallel.

- Game theory encourages managers to *get in the mind of competitors* and *think forwards and reason backwards*.

WORK ASSIGNMENTS

* *Denotes more advanced work assignments.* * *Refers to a case study in the Text and Case edition.*

6.1 What are the advantages and what are the disadvantages of applying principles of business strategy to public-sector or charity organisations? Illustrate your argument by reference to a public-sector organisation of your choice.

6.2 Using either Porter's generic strategies or the Strategy Clock, identify examples of organisations following strategies of differentiation, low cost or low price, and stuck-in-the-middle or hybrid. How successful are these strategies?

6.3＊ You have been appointed personal assistant to the chief executive of a major manufacturing firm, who has asked you to explain what is meant by 'differentiation' and why it is important. Write a brief report addressing these questions.

6.4＊ Choose an industry or sector which is becoming more and more competitive (for example, financial services or fashion retailing). How might the principles of hypercompetitive strategies apply to that industry?

6.5＊ Drawing on section 6.4 (on cooperative strategies) write a report for the chief executive of a business in a competitive market (for example, pharmaceuticals* or Formula One*) explaining when and in what ways cooperation rather than direct competition might make sense.

Integrative assignment

6.6＊ Applying game theory ideas from section 6.4.4 to issues of international strategy (Chapter 8), how might a domestic player discourage an overseas player from entering into its home market?

VIDEO ASSIGNMENT

Visit **MyStrategyLab** and watch the *Land Rover* case study.

1 Identify Land Rover's generic strategy, in terms of Porter's generic strategies or the Strategy Clock, or both.

2 Given its competition, how sustainable is Land Rover's strategy?

RECOMMENDED KEY READINGS

- The foundations of the discussions of generic competitive strategies are to be found in the writings of Michael Porter, which include *Competitive Strategy* (1980) and *Competitive Advantage* (1985), both published by Free Press. Both are recommended for readers who wish to understand the background to discussions in section 6.3 on competitive strategy and competitive advantage.

- Hypercompetition, and the strategies associated with it, are explained in Richard D'Aveni, *Hypercompetitive*

Rivalries: Competing in Highly Dynamic Environments, Free Press, 1995.

- There is much written on game theory but a good deal of it can be rather inaccessible to the lay reader. Exceptions are R. McCain, *Game Theory: a Non-technical Introduction to the Analysis of Strategy*, South Western, 2003, and A. Dixit and B. Nalebuff, *The Art of Strategy: a Game Theorist's Guide to Success in Business and Life*, Norton, 2008.

REFERENCES

1. For a detailed discussion as to how organisational structures might 'address' an organisation's mix of SBUs see M. Goold and A. Campbell, *Designing Effective Organizations: How to Create Structured Networks*, Jossey-Bass, 2002. Also K. Eisenhardt and S. Brown, 'Patching', *Harvard Business Review*, vol. 77, no. 3 (1999), p. 72.

2. This section draws heavily on M. Porter, *Competitive Advantage*, Free Press, 1985. For a more recent discussion of the generic strategies concept, see J. Parnell, 'Generic strategies after two decades: a reconceptualisation of competitive strategy', *Management Decision*, vol. 48, no. 8 (2006), pp. 1139–54.

3. P. Conley, *Experience Curves as a Planning Tool*, available as a pamphlet from the Boston Consulting Group. See also A.C. Hax and N.S. Majluf, in R.G. Dyson (ed.), *Strategic Planning: Models and Analytical Techniques*, Wiley, 1990.

4. B. Sharp and J. Dawes, 'What is differentiation and how does it work?', *Journal of Marketing Management*, vol. 17, nos 7/8 (2001), pp. 739–59, reviews the relationship between differentiation and profitability.

5. See, for example, D. Miller, 'The generic strategy trap', *Journal of Business Strategy*, vol. 13, no. 1 (1992), pp. 37–42; C.W.L. Hill, 'Differentiation versus low cost or differentiation and low cost: a contingency framework', *Academy of Management Review*, vol. 13, no. 3 (1998), pp. 401–12; and S. Thornhill and R. White, 'Strategic purity: a multi-industry evaluation of pure vs hybrid business strategies',

Strategic Management Journal, vol. 28, no. 5 (2007), pp. 553–61.

6. C. Markides and C. Charitou, 'Competing with dual business models: a contingency approach', *Academy of Management Executive*, vol. 18, no. 3 (2004), pp. 22–36.

7. See D. Faulkner and C. Bowman, *The Essence of Competitive Strategy*, Prentice Hall, 1995.

8. For empirical support for the benefits of a hybrid strategy, see E. Pertusa-Ortega, J. Molina-Azorín and E. Claver-Cortés, 'Competitive strategies and firm performance: a comparative analysis of pure, hybrid and "stuck-in-the-middle" strategies in Spanish firms', *British Journal of Management*, vol. 20, no. 4 (2008), pp. 508–23.

9. W.B. Arthur, 'Increasing returns and the new world of business', *Harvard Business Review*, July–August (1996), pp. 100–9. See also the concept of system lock-in in A. Hax and D. Wilde, 'The Delta Model – discovering new sources of profitability in a networked economy', *European Management Journal*, vol. 19, no. 4 (2001), pp. 379–91.

10. R. D'Aveni, *Hypercompetition: the Dynamics of Strategic Maneuvering*, Free Press, New York.

11. This analysis is based on N. Kumar, 'Strategies to fight low cost rivals', *Harvard Business Review*, vol. 84, no. 12 (2006), pp. 104–13.

12. For other examples of misleading signals see G. Stalk Jr, 'Curveball: strategies to fool the competition', *Harvard Business Review*, September (2006), pp. 115–22.

13. Useful books on collaborative strategies are Y. Doz and G. Hamel, *Alliance Advantage: The Art of Creating Value through Partnering*, Harvard Business School Press, 1998; *Creating Collaborative Advantage*, ed. Chris Huxham, Sage, 1996; and D. Faulkner, *Strategic Alliances: Cooperating to Compete*, McGraw-Hill, 1995.

14. For readings on game theory see B. Nalebuff and A. Brandenburger, *Co-opetition*, Profile Books, 1997; R. McCain, *Game Theory: A Non-technical Introduction to the Analysis of Strategy*, South Western, 2003; and, for a summary, S. Regan, 'Game theory perspective', in M. Jenkins and V. Ambrosini (eds), *Advanced Strategic Management: a Multi-Perspective Approach*, 2nd edition, Palgrave Macmillan, 2007, pp. 83–101. A recent practical example is in H. Lindstädt and J. Müller, 'Making game theory work for managers', *McKinsey Quarterly*, December (2009).

Madonna: the reigning queen of pop?

Phyl Johnson, Strategy Explorers

She's the highest-ever paid female singer, in 2009 had the highest-earning tour of any artist and is second only to the Beatles in her haul of 11 UK number one albums. But the music industry has always been the backdrop for one-hit wonders and brief careers. Pop-stars who have remained at the top for decades are very few. Madonna is one such phenomenon; the question is, after almost thirty years at the top, how much longer can it last?

Described by *Billboard Magazine* as the smartest business woman in show business, Madonna Louise Ciccone began her music career in 1983 with the hit single 'Holiday' and in 2008, enjoyed success with the album *Hard Candy* featuring the hit single '4 Minutes' with Justin Timberlake. In the meantime, she had consistent chart success with many singles and eighteen albums, multiple sell-out world tours, major roles in six films, picked up numerous music awards, was inducted into the Rock and Roll Hall of Fame and has been the style icon behind a range of products (Pepsi, Max Factor, Gap, H&M and Louis Vuitton), and become a worldwide bestselling children's author.

The foundation of Madonna's business success has been her ability to sustain her reign as the 'queen of pop'. Phil Quattro, the President of Warner Brothers, said 'she always manages to land on the cusp of what we call contemporary music. Every established artist faces the dilemma of maintaining their importance and relevance, Madonna never fails to be relevant'. Madonna's chameleon-like ability to change persona, change her music genre with it and yet still achieve major record sales has been the hallmark of her success and is seemingly not replicable by other male and female artists.

Madonna's early poppy style was targeted at young 'wannabe' girls. The image that she portrayed through hits such as 'Holiday' and 'Lucky Star' in 1983 was picked up by Macy's, the US-based department store. They produced a range of Madonna lookalike clothes that mothers were happy to purchase for their daughters. One year later in 1984, Madonna underwent her first image change and in doing so offered the first hint of the smart cookie behind the media image. In the video for her hit *Material Girl*, she deliberately mirrored the glamour-based, sexual pussycat image of Marilyn

Source: Rex Features/Lehtikuva OY.

Monroe whilst simultaneously mocking both the growing materialism of the late eighties and the men fawning after her. Media analysts Sam and Diana Kirschner commented that with this kind of packaging, Madonna allowed the record companies to keep hold of a saleable 'Marilyn image' for a new cohort of fans, but also allowed her original fan base of now growing up wannabe girls to take the more critical message from the music. The theme of courting controversy but staying marketable enough has been recurrent throughout her career.

Madonna's subsequent image changes were more dramatic. First she took on the Catholic Church in her 1989 video *Like a Prayer* where, as a red-dressed 'sinner', she kissed a black saint easily interpreted as a Jesus figure. Her image had become increasingly sexual whilst also holding on to a critical social theme: e.g. her pointed illustration of white-only imagery in the Catholic Church. At this point in her career, Madonna took full control of her image in the $60 (~€42) million deal with Time-Warner that created her record company Maverick. In 1991, she published a coffee-table soft porn book entitled *Sex* that exclusively featured pictures of herself in erotic poses. Her image and music also reflected this erotic theme. In her 'Girlie' tour, her singles 'Erotica' and 'Justify my Love' and her fly-on-the wall movie *In Bed with Madonna* she played out scenes of sadomasochistic and lesbian fantasies. Although allegedly a period of her career she would rather forget, Madonna more than survived it. In fact, she gained a whole new demographic of fans who not only respected her artistic courage but also did not miss the fact that Madonna was consistent in her message: her sexuality was her own and not in need of a male gaze.

Changing gear in 1996, Madonna finally took centre stage in the lead role in the film *Evita* which she had chased for over five years. She achieved the image transition from erotica to saint-like persona of Eva Peron and won critical acclaim to boot. Another vote of confidence from the 'establishment' came from Max Factor, who in 1999 signed her up to front their relaunch campaign which was crafted around a glamour theme. Proctor & Gamble (owners of the Max Factor make-up range) argued that they saw Madonna as 'the closest thing the 90s has to an old-style Hollywood star . . . she is a real woman'.

Madonna's album *Ray of Light* was released in 1998. Radio stations world-wide were desperate to get hold of the album which was billed as her most successful musical voyage to date. In a smart move, Madonna had teamed up with techno pioneer William Orbit to write and produce the album. It was a huge success, taking Madonna into the super-trendy techno sphere, not the natural environment for a pop-star from the early 80s. Madonna took up an 'earth mother / spiritual' image and spawned a trend for all things eastern in fashion and music. This phase may have produced more than just an image as it is the time in Madonna's life that locates the beginning of her continued faith in the Kabbalah tradition of eastern spiritual worship.

By 2001, her next persona was unveiled with the release of her album *Music*. Here her style had moved on again to 'acid rock'. With her marriage to her second husband, British movie director Guy Ritchie, the ultimate 'American Pie' had become a fully-fledged Brit babe earning the endearing nickname of 'Madge' in the British press.

By 2003 some commentators were suggesting that an interesting turn of events hinted that perhaps 'the cutting edge' Madonna, 'the fearless', was starting to think about being part of, rather than beating, the establishment. When she launched her new Che Guevara-inspired image, instead of maximising the potential of this image in terms of its political and social symbolism during the second Gulf War, in April 2003 she withdrew her militaristic image and video for the album *American Life*. That action, timed with the publication of her children's book *The English Roses* based on the themes of compassion and friendship, sparked questions in the press around the theme 'has Madonna gone soft?'

By late 2003 she negotiated a glitzy high profile ad campaign for the Gap clothing retailer in which she danced around accompanied by rapper Missy Elliot to a retrospective re-mix of her eighties track 'Get into the Groove'. Here Madonna was keeping the 'thirty-somethings', who remembered the track from first time around, happy. They could purchase jeans for themselves and their newly teenage daughters whilst also purchasing the re-released CD (on sale in-store).

Late 2005 saw the release of the world record breaking, Grammy and Brit Award winning *Confessions on a Dance Floor* album which was marketed as her comeback album after her lowest selling *American Life*. Here Madonna focused on the high selling principle of re-mix, choosing samples of the gay-iconic disco favourites of Abba and Giorgio Moroder to be at the heart of her symbolic reinvention of herself from artist to DJ. The 'Confessions' world tour achieved the highest-selling peak of her career with the album breaking the world record for solo female artists when it debuted at number one in over 40 countries.

Throughout 2008 Madonna lived through a mixed period in her personal and professional lives. In the wake of her divorce from her second husband, she attracted large amounts of negative publicity for the adoption of her youngest children from Malawi. There was also mixed media reaction to the publicity shots for her *Hard Candy* album as Madonna was back to her erotic best: wearing thigh-high boots and little else but with her highly toned body used to full effect. At 51 years of age some commentators questioned: is this sexy or smutty; does Madonna need dignity? Either way, her image, undeniably sultry and alluring, was still hitting the high notes.

Crucially, in 2009, as the music world moved into a phase where its highest earners were not those with the most record sales but those with the best-selling tours, Madonna reigned supreme. Her world record breaking 'Sticky and Sweet' world tour topped *Billboard*'s money-makers chart with a reported $242 million in revenue. This level of revenue was $100 million ahead of her nearest competitor Bon Jovi and showed her razor-sharp appreciation that her records were simply advertisements for her tours. Madonna, along with all artists, had seen record sales falling, and with online

Table 1

Releases	Year	Image	Target audience
Lucky Star	1982	Trashy pop	Young wannabe girls, dovetailing from fading disco to emerging 'club scene'
Like a Virgin Like a Prayer	1984	Originally a Marilyn glamour image, then became a Saint & Sinner	More grown-up rebellious – fan base, more critical female audience and male worshippers
Vogue Erotica Bedtime Stories	1990 1992 1994	Erotic porn star, sadomasochistic, sexual control, more Minelli in *Cabaret* than Monroe	Peculiar mix of target audiences: gay club scene, 90s women taking control of their own lives, also pure male titillation
Something to Remember Evita	1995	Softer image, ballads preparing for glamour image of Evita film role	Broadest audience target, picking up potential film audiences as well as regular fan base. Most conventional image. Max Factor later used this mixture of Marilyn and Eva Peron to market their glamour image.
Ray of Light	1998	Earth mother, eastern mysticism, dance music fusion	Clubbing generation of the 90s, new cohort of fans plus original fan base of now 30-somethings desperately staying trendy
Music	2000	Acid rock, tongue-in-cheek Miss USA/cowgirl, cool Britannia	Managing to hit the changing club scene and 30-something Brits
American Life	2003	Militaristic image Che Guevara Anti-consumerism of American dream	Unclear audience reliant on existing base
Confessions on a Dance Floor	2005	Retro-80s disco imagery, high motion dance-pop sound	Strong gay-icon audience, pop-disco audience, danced-based audience
Hard Candy	2008	Pop, dance, electro-pop urban	Deliberate move toward a more urban R&B direction with collaborations with Justine Timberlake and Kayne West pulling in a new young audience
Celebration	2009	Queen of pop	Compilation of hits from her entire career targeted at enduring/touring fan base

music sales still relatively small, had realised that live music, endorsements and merchandising were her best revenue generating avenues going forward. She signed a new ten year record deal with Live Nation, the largest concert promotion company in the world, ensuring that she retains 90% of gross touring revenues as well as 50% of endorsements.

Sell-out tours crucially rely on a return and return again fan base. Madonna used the 2009 release of *Celebration* (her definitive collection of hit singles) to keep her fan base warm until her next world trek. But at 50 plus, how long can Madonna keep it up? A positive indicator is that The Eagles, Neil Diamond, The Police and Billy Joel all appeared in the tour-earning top 20 of 2008. A negative indicator is that they are all male and selling nostalgia rather than their own sexually-charged image: an ageing female image may well be harder to sell and Madonna, with no female benchmarks to measure up to, found herself in uncharted territory. Yet again Madonna pioneers and currently endures as one of the most influential celebrity women on the planet.

Sources: 'Bennett takes the reins at Maverick', *Billboard Magazine*, 7 August 1999; 'Warner Bros expects Madonna to light up international markets', *Billboard Magazine*, 21 February 1998; 'Maverick builds on early success', *Billboard Magazine*, 12 November 1994; Jardine, A. (1999) 'Max Factor strikes gold with Madonna', *Marketing*, vol. 29, pp. 14–15; Kirschner, S. and Kirschner, D. (1997) 'MTV, adolescence and Madonna: a discourse analysis', in *Perspectives on Psychology and the Media*, American Psychological Association, Washington, DC; 'Warner to buy out maverick co-founder', *Los Angeles Times*, 2 March 1999; 'Why Madonna is back in Vogue', *New Statesman*, 18 September 2000; 'Madonna and Microsoft', *Financial Times*, 28 November 2000; 'Power of Goodbye: Madonna's Split May Herald Record Industry's Death', *The Times Online*, 12 October 2007.

Questions

1 Describe and explain the strategy being followed by Madonna in terms of the explanation of competitive strategy given in Chapter 6.

2 Why has she experienced sustained success over three decades?

3 Can Madonna sustain her success?

7

CORPORATE STRATEGY AND DIVERSIFICATION

Learning objectives

After reading this chapter, you should be able to:

- Identify alternative strategy options, including *market penetration*, *product development*, *market development* and *diversification*.

- Distinguish between different diversification strategies (*related* and *conglomerate* diversification) and evaluate *diversification drivers*.

- Assess the relative benefits of *vertical integration* and *outsourcing*.

- Analyse the ways in which a *corporate parent* can add or destroy value for its portfolio of business units.

- Analyse *portfolios* of business units and judge which to invest in and which to divest.

PEARSON
mystrategylab

MyStrategyLab is designed to help you make the most of your studies.

Visit **www.pearsoned.co.uk/mystrategylab** to discover a wide range of resources specific to this chapter, including:

- A personalised **Study plan** that will help you understand core concepts
- **Audio** and **video clips** that put the spotlight on strategy in the real world
- **Online glossaries** and **flashcards** that provide helpful reminders when you're looking for some quick revision.

(7.1) INTRODUCTION

Chapter 6 was concerned with choices at the level of single business or organisational units, for instance through pricing strategies or differentiation. This chapter is about choices of *products and markets* for an organisation to enter or exit (see the figure in the Part II introduction). Organisations often choose to enter many new product and market areas. For example, the Virgin Group started out in the music business, but is now highly diverse, operating in the holiday, cinema, retail, air-travel and rail markets. Sony began by making small radios, but now produces games, music and movies, as well as a host of electronic products. As organisations add new units, their strategies are no longer concerned just with the business-level, but with the *corporate-level* choices involved in having many different businesses or markets.

Figure 7.1 indicates the basic themes of this chapter. First of all, there are questions to do with the *scope*, or breadth, of the corporate whole. **Scope is concerned with how far an organisation should be diversified in terms of products and markets.** Here a basic framework is provided by Ansoff's two axes, indicating different diversification strategies according to novelty of products or markets. Another way of increasing the scope of an organisation is through *vertical integration*, where the organisation acts as an internal supplier or a customer to itself (as for example an oil company supplies its petrol to its own petrol stations). Here we also consider the possibility of *outsourcing*, where an organisation 'dis-integrates' by subcontracting an internal activity to an external supplier.

Scope raises the two other key themes of the chapter. First, given that an organisation has decided to operate in different areas of activity, what should be the role of the 'corporate-level' (head-office) executives that act as 'parents' to the individual business units that make up their organisation's portfolio? How do corporate-level activities, decisions and resources add value to the actual businesses? As will be seen in the Key Debate at the end of this chapter, there is considerable scepticism about the value-adding role of corporate-level strategy. The second theme is, within an overall diversification strategy, which specific business units should be included in the corporate *portfolio*, and how should they be managed financially? Here portfolio matrices help structure corporate-level choices about which businesses to invest in and which to divest.

Figure 7.1 **Strategic directions and corporate-level strategy**

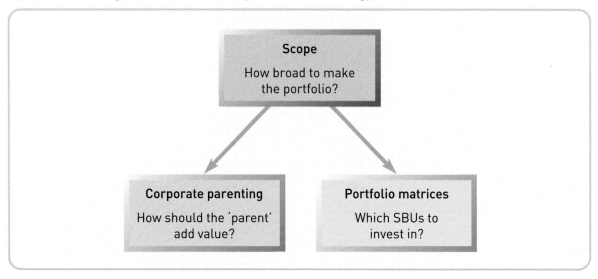

This chapter is not just about large commercial businesses. Even small businesses may consist of a number of business units. For example, a local builder may be undertaking contract work for local government, work for industrial buyers and for local homeowners. Not only are these different market segments, but the mode of operation and capabilities required for competitive success are also likely to be different. Moreover, the owner of that business has to take decisions about the extent of investment and activity in each segment. Public-sector organisations such as local government or health services also provide different services, which correspond to business units in commercial organisations. Corporate-level strategy is highly relevant to the appropriate drawing of organisational boundaries in the public sector, and privatisation and outsourcing decisions can be considered as responses to the failure of public-sector organisations to add sufficient value by their parenting.

(7.2) STRATEGY DIRECTIONS

The Ansoff product/market growth matrix[1] provides a simple way of generating four basic directions for corporate strategy: see Figure 7.2 for an adapted version. An organisation typically starts in the zone around point A, the top left-hand corner of Figure 7.2. According to Ansoff, the organisation basically has a choice between *penetrating* still further within its existing sphere (staying in zone A) or increasing its diversity along the two axes of increasing novelty of markets or increasing novelty of products. **Diversification involves increasing the range of products or markets served by an organisation. Related diversification involves diversifying into products or services with relationships to the existing business.** Thus on Ansoff's axes the organisation has two related diversification strategies available: moving rightwards by *developing new products* for its existing markets (zone B) or moving downwards

Figure 7.2 Corporate strategy directions

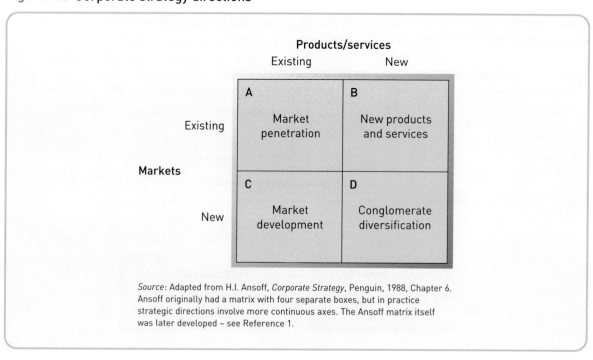

Source: Adapted from H.I. Ansoff, *Corporate Strategy*, Penguin, 1988, Chapter 6. Ansoff originally had a matrix with four separate boxes, but in practice strategic directions involve more continuous axes. The Ansoff matrix itself was later developed – see Reference 1.

ILLUSTRATION 7.1

Corporate strategy choices for Axel Springer

This German publishing company has many opportunities, and the money to pursue them.

In 2007, Mathias Döpfner, chairman and chief executive of Axel Springer publishers, had about €2bn ($2.8bn) to invest in new opportunities. The previous year, the competition authorities had prohibited his take-over of Germany's largest television broadcaster, ProSiebenSat.1 . . . Now Döpfner was looking for alternative directions.

Founded in 1946 by Axel Springer himself, by 2007 the company was already Germany's largest publisher of newspapers and magazines, with more than 10,000 employees and over 150 titles. Famous print titles included *Die Welt*, the *Berliner Morgenpost*, *Bild* and *Hörzu*. Outside Germany, Axel Springer was strongest in Eastern Europe. The company also had a scattering of mostly small investments in German radio and television companies. Axel Springer described its strategic objectives as market leadership in the German language core business, internationalisation and digitalisation of the core business.

Döpfner had opportunities for further penetration with his existing markets and products. Increased digitalisation of the core newspapers and magazines business was clearly important and would require substantial funding. There were also opportunities for the launch of new print magazine titles in the German market.

However, Döpfner was considering expanding also into new markets and new products. Such moves would likely involve acquisitions: 'it goes without saying', he told the *Financial Times*, 'that whenever a large international media company comes on to the market (i.e. is up for sale), we will examine it very closely – whether in print, TV or the online sector'. Döpfner mentioned several specific kinds of acquisition opportunity. For example, he was still interested in buying a large European television broadcaster, even if it would probably have to be outside Germany. He was also attracted by the possibility of buying under-valued assets in the old media (i.e. print), and turning them around in the style of a private-equity investor: 'I would love to buy businesses in need of restructuring, where we can add value by introducing our management and sector expertise'. However, Döpfner reassured his shareholders by affirming that he felt no need 'to do a big thing in order to do a big thing'.

Main source: Financial Times Deutschland, 2 April 2007.

Questions

1 Referring to Figure 7.2, classify the various strategic directions Mattias Döpfner is considering for Axel Springer.

2 Using the Ansoff axes, what other options could Döpfner pursue?

by bringing its existing products into *new markets* (zone C). In each case, the further along the two axes, the more diversified is the strategy. Alternatively, the organisation can move in both directions at once, following a *conglomerate diversification* strategy with altogether new markets and new products (zone D). Thus **conglomerate (unrelated) diversification involves diversifying into products or services with no relationships to the existing businesses**.

Ansoff's axes can be used effectively in brainstorming strategic options, checking that options in all four zones have been properly considered. This section will consider each of Ansoff's four main directions in some detail. Section 7.5 will examine the additional option of *vertical integration*.

7.2.1 Market penetration

For a simple, undiversified business, the most obvious strategic option is often increased penetration of its existing market, with its existing products. **Market penetration implies increasing share of current markets with the current product range**. This strategy builds on established strategic capabilities and does not require the organisation to venture into uncharted territory. The organisation's scope is exactly the same. Moreover, greater market share implies increased power vis-à-vis buyers and suppliers (in terms of Porter's five forces), greater economies of scale and experience curve benefits.

However, organisations seeking greater market penetration may face two constraints:

- *Retaliation from competitors.* In terms of the five forces (section 2.3.1), increasing market penetration is likely to exacerbate industry rivalry as other competitors in the market defend their share. Increased rivalry might involve price wars or expensive marketing battles, which may cost more than any market-share gains are actually worth. The dangers of provoking fierce retaliation are greater in low-growth markets, as any gains in volume will be much more at the expense of other players. Where retaliation is a danger, organisations seeking market penetration need strategic capabilities that give a clear competitive advantage. In low-growth or declining markets, it can be more effective simply to acquire competitors. Some companies have grown quickly in this way. For example, in the steel industry the Indian company LNM (Mittal) moved rapidly in the 2000s to become the largest steel producer in the world by acquiring struggling steel companies around the world. Acquisitions can actually reduce rivalry, by taking out independent players and controlling them under one umbrella.

- *Legal constraints.* Greater market penetration can raise concerns from official competition regulators concerning excessive market power. Most countries have regulators with the powers to restrain powerful companies or prevent mergers and acquisitions that would create such excessive power. In the United Kingdom, the Competition Commission can investigate any merger or acquisition that would account for more than 25 per cent of the national market, and either halt the deal or propose measures that would reduce market power. The European Commission has an overview of the whole European market and can similarly intervene. For example, when the German T-Mobile and French Orange companies proposed to merge their UK mobile phone operations in 2010, the European Commission insisted that the merged companies should divest a quarter of their combined share of the key mobile phone 1800 MHz spectrum.[2]

Market penetration may not be an option too where economic constraints are severe, for instance during a market downturn or public-sector funding crisis. Here organisations will need to consider the strategic option of *retrenchment*, withdrawal from marginal activities in order to concentrate on the most valuable segments and products within their existing business. However, where growth is still sought after, the Ansoff axes suggest further directions, as follows.

7.2.2 Product development

Product development is where organisations deliver modified or new products (or services) to existing markets. This can involve varying degrees of diversification along the rightward axis of Figure 7.2. For Sony, developing its Walkman products from the original tape-based product, through CDs and recently to MP3s involved little diversification: although the technologies differed, Sony was targeting the same customers and using very similar production processes and distribution channels. A more radical form of product development would be Axel Springer's move into the online media businesses: effectively the same consumer markets are involved as for its existing newspaper and magazine businesses, but the production technologies and distribution channels are radically different (see Illustration 7.1). This form of product diversification would typically be described as *related diversification*, as Axel Springer's online business would be related through similar customers to its existing newspaper and magazine customers.

Despite the potential for relatedness, product development can be an expensive and high-risk activity for at least two reasons:

- *New strategic capabilities*. Product development strategies typically involve mastering new processes or technologies that are unfamiliar to the organisation. For example, many banks entered online banking at the beginning of this century, but suffered many setbacks with technologies so radically different from their traditional high-street branch means of delivering banking services. Success frequently depended on a willingness to acquire new technological and marketing capabilities, often with the help of specialised information technology and e-commerce consultancy firms. Thus product development typically involves heavy investments and high risk of project failures.

- *Project management risk*. Even within fairly familiar domains, product development projects are typically subject to the risk of delays and increased costs due to project complexity and changing project specifications over time. An extreme example is Boeing's Dreamliner 787 plane: making innovative use of carbon-fibre composites, the Dreamliner had incurred two and a half years of delay by launch in 2010, and required $2.5bn (~€1.75bn) write-offs due to cancelled orders.

Strategies for product development are considered further in Chapter 9.

7.2.3 Market development

If product development is risky and expensive, an alternative strategy is market development. **Market development** involves offering existing products to new markets. Again, the degree of diversification varies along Figure 7.2's downward axis. Typically, of course, market development entails some product development as well, if only in terms of packaging or service. Nonetheless, market development remains a form of related diversification given its origins in similar products. Market development takes two basic forms:

- *New users*. Here an example would be aluminium, whose original users, packaging and cutlery manufacturers, are now supplemented by users in aerospace and automobiles.

- *New geographies*. The prime example of this is internationalisation, but the spread of a small retailer into new towns would also be a case.

In all cases, it is essential that market development strategies be based on products or services that meet the *critical success factors* of the new market (see section 2.4.3). Strategies based on simply off-loading traditional products or services in new markets are likely to fail. Moreover, market development faces similar problems to product development. In terms of strategic capabilities, market developers often lack the right marketing skills and brands to

ILLUSTRATION 7.2

Zodiac deflates: diversification and de-diversification

The Zodiac Group has managed a portfolio of related business for the best part of a century, with both diversification and de-diversification.

The Zodiac Group is probably best known for its Zodiac inflatable boats, used by Jacques Cousteau and seen in harbours around the world. But in 2007, Zodiac sold all its marine and leisure businesses and concentrated on aerospace.

The Zodiac company was founded in 1896 by Maurice Mallet just after his first hot-air balloon ascent. For 40 years, Zodiac manufactured only dirigible airships. In 1937, the German Zeppelin *Hindenburg* crashed near New York, which abruptly stopped the development of the market for airships. Because of the extinction of its traditional activity, Zodiac decided to leverage its technical expertise and moved from dirigible airships to inflatable boats. This diversification proved to be very successful: by 2004, over one million Zodiac rubber inflatables had sold worldwide.

However, because of increasing competition, especially from Italian manufacturers, Zodiac had been diversifying its business interests. In 1978, it took over Aerazur, a company specialising in parachutes, but also in life vests and inflatable life rafts. These products had strong market and technical synergies with rubber boats and their main customers were aircraft manufacturers. Zodiac confirmed this move to a new market in 1987 by the takeover of Air Cruisers, a manufacturer of inflatable escape slides for aeroplanes. As a consequence, Zodiac became a key supplier to Boeing, McDonnell Douglas and Airbus. Zodiac strengthened this position through the takeover of the two leading manufacturers of aeroplane seats: Sicma Aero Seats from France and Weber Aircraft from the USA. In 1997, Zodiac also took over, for €150m (~$210m), MAG Aerospace, the world leader for aircraft vacuum waste systems. In 1999, Zodiac took over Intertechnique, a leading player in active components for aircraft (fuel circulation, hydraulics, oxygen and life support, electrical power, flight-deck controls and displays, systems monitoring, etc.). By combining these competences with its traditional expertise in inflatable products, Zodiac launched a new business unit: airbags for the automobile industry.

In parallel to these diversifications, Zodiac strengthened its position in inflatable boats by the takeover of several competitors: Bombard-L'Angevinière in 1980, Sevylor in 1981, Hurricane and Metzeler in 1987. The company also developed a swimming-pool business. The first product line, back in 1981, was based on inflatable structure technology, and Zodiac later moved – again through takeovers – to rigid above-ground pools, modular in-ground pools, pool cleaners and water purification systems, inflatable beach gear and air mattresses.

However, by 2007, aircraft products accounted for 80 per cent of the total turnover of the group. Zodiac held a 40 per cent market share of the world market for some airline equipment: for instance, the electrical power systems of the new Airbus A380 and Boeing 787 were Zodiac products. Zodiac had even reached Mars: NASA Mars probes *Spirit* and *Opportunity* were equipped with Zodiac equipment, developed by its US subsidiary Pioneer Aerospace.

Chief Executive Jean-Louis Gérondeau explained the sale of the marine and leisure businesses thus: 'The proposed transaction . . . would allow the Zodiac Group . . . to reinforce its acquisition capabilities in the aerospace sector'. However, the sale was also a response to pressure from financial analysts, who considered Zodiac too diversified. The sale was rapidly followed in 2008 by three further acquisitions of aircraft cabin equipment companies: Driessen, Adder and TIA.

Source: Based on an illustration by Frédéric Fréry, ESCP Europe Business School.

Questions

1 Explain the ways in which relatedness informed Zodiac's diversification strategy over time.

2 What are the advantages and potential dangers of its decision to focus on the aircraft products market?

make progress in a market with unfamiliar customers. On the management side, the challenge is coordinating between different users and geographies, which might all have different needs. *International* market development strategy is considered in Chapter 8.

7.2.4 Conglomerate diversification

Conglomerate (or unrelated) diversification takes the organisation beyond both its existing markets and its existing products (i.e. zone D in Figure 7.2). In this sense, it radically increases the organisation's scope. Conglomerate diversification strategies are not trusted by many observers, because there are no obvious ways in which the businesses are better off for being together, while there is a clear cost in the managers at headquarters who control them. For this reason, conglomerate companies' share prices often suffer from what is called the 'conglomerate discount' – in other words, a lower valuation than the individual constituent businesses would have if stand-alone. In 2009, the French conglomerate Vivendi, with wide interests in mobile telephony and media, was trading at an estimated discount of 24 per cent on the value of its constituent assets. Naturally, shareholders were pressurising management to sell off its more highly valued parts on the open market.

However, it is important to recognise that the distinction between related and unrelated conglomerate diversification is often a matter of degree. Also relationships might turn out not to be so valuable as expected. Thus the large accounting firms have often struggled in translating their skills and client contacts developed in auditing into effective consulting practices. Similarly, relationships may change in importance over time, as the nature of technologies or customers change: see for example the decision by Zodiac to divest itself of its iconic boat business (Illustration 7.2).

 ## 7.3   DIVERSIFICATION DRIVERS

Diversification might be chosen for a variety of reasons, some more value-creating than others.[3] Growth in organisational size is rarely a good enough reason for diversification on its own: growth must be profitable. Indeed, growth can often be merely a form of 'empire building', especially in the public sector. Diversification decisions need to be approached sceptically.

Four potentially value-creating drivers for diversification are as follows.

- *Exploiting economies of scope.* **Economies of scope refers to efficiency gains through applying the organisation's existing resources or competences to new markets or services.**[4] If an organisation has under-utilised resources or competences that it cannot effectively close or sell to other potential users, it is efficient to use these resources or competences by diversification into a new activity. In other words, there are economies to be gained by extending the scope of the organisation's activities. For example, many universities have large resources in terms of halls of residence, which they must have for their students but which are under-utilised out of term-time. These halls of residence are more efficiently used if the universities expand the scope of their activities into conferencing and tourism during vacation periods. Economies of scope may apply to both *tangible* resources, such as halls of residence, and *intangible* resources and competences, such as brands or staff skills.

- *Stretching corporate management competences ('dominant logics').* This is a special case of economies of scope, and refers to the potential for applying the skills of talented corporate-level managers (referred to as 'corporate parenting skills' in section 7.6) to new businesses. The **dominant logic is the set of corporate-level managerial competences applied across the portfolio of businesses.**[5] Corporate-level managers may have competences that can be applied even to businesses which do not share resources at the operating-unit level. Thus the French luxury-goods conglomerate LVMH includes a wide range of businesses – from champagne, through fashion and perfumes, to financial media – that share very few operational resources or business-level competences. However, LVMH creates value for these specialised companies by applying corporate-level competences in developing classic brands and nurturing highly creative people that are relevant to all its individual businesses. See also the discussion of dominant logic at Berkshire Hathaway in Illustration 7.4 later.

- *Exploiting superior internal processes.* Internal processes within a diversified corporation can often be more efficient than external processes in the open market. This is especially the case where external capital and labour markets do not yet work well, as in many developing economies. In these circumstances, well-managed conglomerates can make sense, even if their constituent businesses do not have operating relationships with each other. For example, China has many conglomerates because they are able to mobilise investment, develop managers and exploit networks in a way that stand-alone Chinese companies, relying on imperfect markets, cannot. For example, China's largest privately owned conglomerate, the Fosun Group, owns steel mills, pharmaceutical companies and China's largest retailer, Yuyuan Tourist Mart.[6]

- *Increasing market power.*[7] Being diversified in many businesses can increase power vis-à-vis competitors in at least two ways. First, having the same wide portfolio of products as a competitor increases the potential for *mutual forbearance*. The ability to retaliate across the whole range of the portfolio acts to discourage the competitor from making any aggressive moves at all. Two similarly diversified competitors are thus likely to forbear from competing aggressively with each other. Second, having a diversified range of businesses increases the power to *cross-subsidise* one business from the profits of the others. On the one hand, the ability to cross-subsidise can support aggressive bids to drive competitors out of a particular market. On the other hand, knowing this power to cross-subsidise a particular business, competitors without equivalent power will be reluctant to attack that business.

Where diversification creates value, it is described as 'synergistic'.[8] **Synergy refers to the benefits gained where activities or assets complement each other so that their combined effect is greater than the sum of the parts** (the famous $2 + 2 = 5$ equation). Thus a film company and a music publisher would be synergistic if they were worth more together than separately. However, synergies are often harder to identify and more costly to extract in practice than managers like to admit.[9]

Indeed, some drivers for diversification involve negative synergies, in other words value destruction. Three potentially value-destroying diversification drivers are:

- *Responding to market decline* is one common but doubtful driver for diversification. Rather than let the managers of a declining business invest spare funds in a new business, conventional finance theory suggests it is usually best to let shareholders find new growth investment opportunities for themselves. For example, it is arguable that Microsoft's diversification into electronic games such as the Xbox – whose launch cost $500m (~€350m) in marketing alone – is a response to declining prospects in its core Windows operating systems business. But if future profits in the core business are likely to be low, shareholders might prefer Microsoft simply to hand back the surplus directly to them, rather than spending it on attacking strong companies such as Sony and Nintendo. If shareholders had wanted to invest in the games business, they could have invested in the original dominant companies themselves.

- *Spreading risk* across a range of markets is another common justification for diversification. Again, conventional finance theory is very sceptical about risk-spreading by diversification. Shareholders can easily spread their risk by taking small stakes in dozens of very different companies themselves. Diversification strategies, on the other hand, are likely to involve a limited range of fairly related markets. While managers might like the security of having more than one market, shareholders typically do not need each of the companies they invest in to be diversified as well – they would prefer managers to concentrate on managing their core business as well as they can. However, conventional finance theory does not apply to private businesses, where the owners have a large proportion of their assets tied up in their company: here it can make sense to diversify risk across a number of distinct activities, so that if one part is in trouble, the whole business is not pulled down.

- *Managerial ambition* can sometimes drive inappropriate diversification. It is argued that the managers of British banks such as Royal Bank of Scotland (at one point the fifth largest bank in the world) and HBOS (Britain's largest housing-lender) promoted strategies of excessive growth and diversification into new markets during the first decade of the 21st century. Such growth and diversification gave the managers short-term benefits in terms of managerial bonuses and prestige. But going beyond their areas of true expertise soon brought financial disaster, leading to the nationalisation of RBS and the takeover of HBOS by rival Lloyds bank.

(7.4) DIVERSIFICATION AND PERFORMANCE

Because most large corporations today are diversified, but also because diversification can sometimes be in management's self-interest, many scholars and policy-makers have been concerned to establish whether diversified companies really perform better than undiversified companies. After all, it would be deeply troubling if large corporations were diversifying simply to spread risk for managers, to save managerial jobs in declining businesses or to generate short-term growth, as in the case of RBS and HBOS.

Research studies of diversification have particularly focused on the relative benefits of related diversification and conglomerate or unrelated diversification. Researchers generally find that related or limited diversifiers outperform both firms that remain specialised and those which have unrelated or extensively diversified strategies.[10] In other words, the diversification–performance relationship tends to follow an inverted (or upside-down) U-shape, as in Figure 7.3. The implication is that some diversification is good – but not too much.

However, these performance studies produce statistical averages. Some related diversification strategies fail – as in the case of some accounting firms' ventures in consulting – while some conglomerates succeed – as in the case of LVMH. The case against unrelated diversification is not solid, and effective dominant logics or particular national contexts can play in its favour. The conclusion from the performance studies is that, although on average related diversification pays better than unrelated, any diversification strategy needs rigorous questioning on its particular merits.

Figure 7.3 Diversity and performance

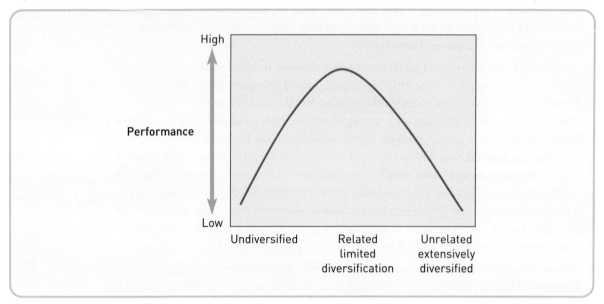

(7.5) VERTICAL INTEGRATION

As well as diversification, another direction for corporate strategy can be vertical integration. **Vertical integration describes entering activities where the organisation is its own supplier or customer.** Thus it involves operating at another stage of the value network (see section 3.4.2). This section considers both vertical integration and vertical dis-integration, particularly in the form of outsourcing.

7.5.1 Forward and backward integration

Vertical integration can go in either of two directions:

● **Backward integration refers to development into activities concerned with the inputs into the company's current business** (i.e. they are further back in the value network). For example, the acquisition by a car manufacturer of a component supplier would be a backward integration move.

● **Forward integration refers to development into activities concerned with the outputs of a company's current business** (i.e. are further forward in the value network). For a car manufacturer, forward integration would be into car retail, repairs and servicing.

Thus vertical integration is like diversification in increasing corporate scope. The difference is that it brings together activities up and down the same value network, while diversification typically involves more or less different value networks. However, because realising synergies involves bringing together different value networks, diversification (especially related diversification) is sometimes also described as *horizontal integration.* For example, a company diversified in cars, trucks and buses could find benefits in integrating aspects of the various design or component-sourcing processes. The relationship between horizontal integration and vertical integration is depicted in Figure 7.4.

Figure 7.4 **Diversification and integration options: car manufacturer example**

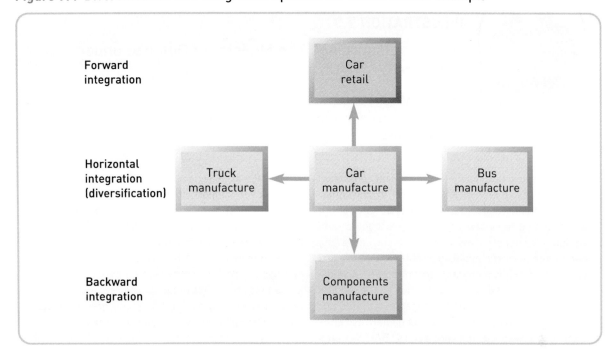

Vertical integration is often favoured because it seems to 'capture' more of the profits in a value network. The car manufacturer gains the retailer's profits as well. However, it is important to be aware of two dangers. First, vertical integration involves investment. Expensive investments in activities that are less profitable than the original core business will be unattractive to shareholders because they are reducing their *average* or overall rate of return on investment. Second, even if there is a degree of relatedness through the value network, vertical integration is likely to involve quite different strategic capabilities. Thus car manufacturers who forwardly integrate into car service and repair have found that managing networks of small service outlets is very different to managing large manufacturing plants. Growing appreciation of both the risks of diluting overall returns on investment and the distinct capabilities involved at different stages of the value network has led many companies in recent years to vertically *dis*-integrate.

7.5.2 To integrate or to outsource?

As above, it is often proposed to replace vertically integrated operations by outsourcing or subcontracting. **Outsourcing is the process by which activities previously carried out internally are subcontracted to external suppliers**. Outsourcing can refer to the subcontracting of components in manufacturing, but is now particularly common for services such as information technology, customer call centres and human resource management. The argument for outsourcing to specialist suppliers is often based on strategic capabilities. Specialists in a particular activity are likely to have superior capabilities than an organisation for which that particular activity is not a central part of their business. A specialist IT contractor is usually better at IT than the IT department of a steel company.

However, Nobel prize-winning economist Oliver Williamson has argued that the decision to integrate or outsource involves more than just relative capabilities. His *transaction cost*

ILLUSTRATION 7.3

Deadly outsourcing? The Ministry of Defence under pressure

The UK's Ministry of Defence faces a dilemma over whether to outsource more of its support services, possibly at the expense of the safety of its own personnel.

Under pressure from budget cuts, and still committed to an expensive war in Afghanistan, in November 2009 the United Kingdom's Ministry of Defence (MoD) was planning to outsource more of its logistics and equipment support. This announcement came just one month after the publication of the official report on the 2006 Nimrod military aircraft crash, in which 14 personnel had died. The chairman of the inquiry, Charles Haddon-Cave, had castigated the MoD for 'lamentable' safety procedures. But he had also criticised two private-sector contractors, BAE Systems and Qinetiq, who had been involved in the safety checks for the doomed Nimrod aircraft. Haddon-Smith complained: 'there has been a shift in culture and priorities at the MoD towards business and financial targets at the expense of. . . . safety and airworthiness'.

But now the Ministry of Defence was launching its Defence Support Review (DSR), where it announced: 'past efficiencies have . . . been delivered from a range of increasingly innovative arrangements with industry. . . . The cost base has, and will continue to, migrate to industry.' The Defence Support Review claimed its recommendations could save £474m (~€521m; ~$711m) in the first four years of its plan, and up to £2.4bn over the subsequent six years. The BAE Systems contract for the support of Tornado fighter aircraft had already delivered savings of £1.3bn. The main MoD civil service union replied that it was '. . . concerned that the DSR is premature and will damage the MoD's ability to support the front-line'.

The Royal Air Force is the most committed of the three armed services to outsourcing support work to contractors. Minor repairs on aircraft are done in-theatre by RAF mechanics. However, more substantial maintenance is done by contractors such as BAE Systems, Rolls-Royce and Qinetiq at main operating bases distributed around the world. Contracts typically guarantee that aircraft will be available to fly a certain number of hours over an agreed period.

The Royal Navy relies on BAE Systems and Babcock for support of its submarine and surface fleets. It leases fishery protection vessels from BAE Systems as well. Availability contracts work less well for ships than for aircraft because there are fewer of them, making it harder to keep a contracted number of ships in service over an agreed period. The Army is the most reluctant to outsource repair and maintenance work, relying more on the in-house Defence Support Group. However, in 2008, it signed a contract with BAE Systems to sustain about 400 Panther command and liaison vehicles.

BAE Systems is the second largest defence contractor in the world, behind the American Lockheed-Martin. It makes and supports aircraft, missiles, ships, submarines and armoured vehicles. In 2009, BAE Systems employed over 30,000 people in the UK, about 10 per cent of all UK defence industry jobs. The 2006 Parliamentary Select Committee on Defence had established that about 5 per cent of all MoD defence contracts by value go to BAE Systems each year, while BAE Systems derived 28 per cent of their sales from the MoD. BAE Systems was effectively a monopoly supplier in the UK of air systems and aircraft support.

Sources: House of Commons Defence Committee, 7th Report, 2006; J. Lerner, 'MoD considers call for rise of outsourcing', Financial Times, 17 November 2009; 'Learning from the Nimrod Disaster', Financial Times, 30 October 2009.

Questions

1 Compare the arguments for defence outsourcing from strategic capabilities and transaction costs points of view.

2 If you were outsourcing aircraft maintenance, what might you be concerned about and how might you design the contract and the tendering process to reduce those concerns?

framework helps analyse the relative costs and benefits of managing ('transacting') activities internally or externally (see also the Key Debate at the end of this chapter).[11] In assessing whether to integrate or outsource an activity, he warns against underestimating the long-term costs of *opportunism* by external subcontractors (or indeed any other organisation in a market relationship). Subcontractors are liable over time to take advantage of their position, either to reduce their standards or to extract higher prices. Market relationships tend to fail in controlling subcontractor opportunism where:

- there are *few alternatives* to the subcontractor and it is hard to shop around;
- the product or service is *complex and changing*, and therefore impossible to specify fully in a legally binding contract;
- investments have been made in *specific assets*, which the subcontractor knows will have little value if they withhold their product or service.

Both capabilities and transaction cost reasoning have influenced the outsourcing decisions of the Ministry of Defence, see Illustration 7.3.

This transaction cost framework suggests that the costs of opportunism can outweigh the benefits of subcontracting to organisations with superior strategic capabilities. For example, mining companies in isolated parts of the Australian outback typically own and operate housing for their workers. The isolation creates specific assets (the housing is worth nothing if the mine closes down) and a lack of alternatives (the nearest town might be a hundred miles away). Consequently, there would be large risks to both partners if the mine subcontracted housing to an independent company specialising in worker accommodation, however strong its capabilities. Transaction cost economics therefore offers the following advice: if there are few alternative suppliers, if activities are complex and likely to change, and if there are significant investments in specific assets, then it is likely to be better to vertically integrate rather than outsource.

In sum, the decision to integrate or subcontract rests on the balance between two distinct factors:

- *Relative strategic capabilities.* Does the subcontractor have the potential to do the work significantly better?
- *Risk of opportunism.* Is the subcontractor likely to take advantage of the relationship over time?

(7.6) VALUE CREATION AND THE CORPORATE PARENT

Given the doubt over diversification and integration strategies, it is clear that sometimes corporate parents are not adding value to their constituent businesses. Where there is no added value, it is usually best to divest the relevant businesses from the corporate portfolio. Thus when Carphone Warehouse recognised that its businesses would be more valuable separate rather than together, it decided in 2010 to break itself up entirely, creating a specialised retail business (including Best Buy, Europe's largest phone retailer) on the one hand, and a specialised home broadband service (TalkTalk) on the other. In the public sector too, units such as schools or hospitals are increasingly being given freedom from parenting authorities, because independence is seen as more effective. Some theorists even challenge the notion of corporate-level strategy altogether, the subject of the Key Debate at the end of this chapter.

This section examines how corporate parents can both add and destroy value, and considers three different parenting approaches that can be effective.

7.6.1 Value-adding and value-destroying activities of corporate parents[12]

Any corporate parent needs to demonstrate that they create more value than they cost. This applies to both commercial and public-sector organisations. For public-sector organisations, privatisation or outsourcing is likely to be the consequence of failure to demonstrate value. Companies whose shares are traded freely on the stock markets face a further challenge. They must demonstrate they create more value than any other rival corporate parent could create. Failure to do so is likely to lead to a hostile takeover or break-up. Rival companies that think they can create more value out of the business units can bid for the company's shares, on the expectation of either running the businesses better or selling them off to other potential parents. If the rival's bid is more attractive and credible than what the current parent can promise, shareholders will back them at the expense of incumbent management.

In this sense, competition takes place between different corporate parents for the right to own and control businesses. In the competitive market for the control of businesses, corporate parents must show that they have *parenting advantage*, on the same principle that business units must demonstrate competitive advantage. They must demonstrate that they are the best possible parent for the businesses they control. Parents therefore must have a very clear approach to how they create value. In practice, however, many of their activities can be value-destroying as well as value-creating.

Value-adding activities[13]

There are four main types of activity by which a corporate parent can add value.

- *Envisioning.* The corporate parent can provide a clear overall vision or *strategic intent* for its business units.[14] This vision should guide and motivate the business unit managers in order to maximise corporation-wide performance through commitment to a common purpose. The vision should also provide stakeholders with a *clear external image* about what the organisation as a whole is about: this can reassure shareholders about the rationale for having a diversified strategy in the first place. Finally, a clear vision provides a *discipline* on the corporate parent to stop it wandering into inappropriate activities or taking on unnecessary costs.

- *Coaching and facilitating.* The corporate parent can help business unit managers *develop strategic capabilities*, by coaching them to improve their skills and confidence. They can also facilitate cooperation and sharing across the business units, so improving the *synergies* from being within the same corporate organisation. Corporate-wide management courses are one effective means of achieving these objectives, as bringing managers across the business to learn strategy skills also provides an opportunity for them to build relationships between each other and see opportunities for cooperation.

- *Providing central services and resources.* The centre is obviously a provider of capital for *investment*. The centre can also provide central services such as treasury, tax and human resource advice, which if centralised can have *sufficient scale* to be efficient and to build up *relevant expertise*. Centralised services often have greater *leverage*: for example, combining the purchases of separate business units increases their bargaining power for shared inputs such as energy. This leverage can be helpful in *brokering* with external bodies, such as government regulators, or other companies in negotiating alliances. Finally, the centre can have an important role in managing expertise within the corporate whole, for instance by *transferring managers* across the business units or by creating shared *knowledge management* systems via corporate intranets.

- *Intervening*. Finally, the corporate parent can also intervene within its business units in order to ensure appropriate performance. The corporate parent should be able to closely *monitor* business unit performance and *improve performance* either by replacing weak managers or by assisting them in turning around their businesses. The parent can also *challenge and develop* the strategic ambitions of business units, so that satisfactorily performing businesses are encouraged to perform even better.

Value-destroying activities

However, there are also three broad ways in which the corporate parent can inadvertently destroy value:

- *Adding management costs*. Most simply, the staff and facilities of the corporate centre are expensive. The corporate centre typically has the best-paid managers and the most luxurious offices. It is the actual businesses that have to generate the revenues that pay for them. If their costs are greater than the value they create, then the corporate centre's managers are net value-destroying.

- *Adding bureaucratic complexity*. As well as these direct financial costs, there is the 'bureaucratic fog' created by an additional layer of management and the need to coordinate with sister businesses. These typically slow down managers' responses to issues and lead to compromises between the interests of individual businesses.

- *Obscuring financial performance*. One danger in a large diversified company is that the under-performance of weak businesses can be obscured. Weak businesses might be cross-subsidised by the stronger ones. Internally, the possibility of hiding weak performance diminishes the incentives for business unit managers to strive as hard as they can for their businesses: they have a parental safety-net. Externally, shareholders and financial analysts cannot easily judge the performance of individual units within the corporate whole. Diversified companies' share prices are often marked down, because shareholders prefer the 'pure plays' of stand-alone units, where weak performance cannot be hidden.[15]

These dangers suggest clear paths for corporate parents that wish to avoid value destruction. They should keep a close eye on centre costs, both financial and bureaucratic, ensuring that they are no more than required by their corporate strategy. They should also do all they can to promote financial transparency, so that business units remain under pressure to perform and shareholders are confident that there are no hidden disasters.

Overall, there are many ways in which corporate parents can add value. It is, of course, difficult to pursue them all and some are hard to mix with others. For example, a corporate parent that does a great deal of top-down intervening is less likely to be seen by its managers as a helpful coach and facilitator. Business unit managers will concentrate on maximising their own individual performance rather than looking out for ways to cooperate with other business unit managers for the greater good of the whole. For this reason, corporate parenting roles tend to fall into three main types, each coherent within itself but distinct from the others.[16] These three types of corporate parenting role are summarised in Figure 7.5.

ILLUSTRATION 7.4

Eating its own cooking: Berkshire Hathaway's parenting

A portfolio manager may seek to manage a highly diverse set of business units on behalf of its shareholders.

Berkshire Hathaway's chairman and CEO is Warren Buffett, one of the world's richest men – and also one of the most plain-spoken about how to run a business. With annual sales now over $100bn (€70bn), Buffet founded this conglomerate with a small textile business in the early 1960s. Berkshire Hathaway's businesses now are highly diverse. They include large insurance businesses (GEICO, General Re, NRG), manufacturers of carpets, building products, clothing and footwear, retail companies and NetJets, the private jet service. The company also has significant long-term minority stakes in businesses such as Coca-Cola and General Electric. Aged 79, Buffett remains highly active: in 2008, he took a 10 per cent stake in Goldman Sachs, the world's leading investment bank, and in 2009 he completed the purchase of BNSF, the second largest railway company in the United States. Since the mid-1960s, Berkshire has averaged a growth in book value of 20.3% each year.

The 2009 Berkshire Hathaway annual report explains how Buffet and his deputy chairman Charlie Munger run the business. With regard to shareholders, Buffet writes:

> Charlie Munger and I think of our shareholders as owner-partners, and of ourselves as managing partners. (Because of the size of our shareholdings we are also, for better or worse, controlling partners.) We do not view the company itself as the ultimate owner of our business assets but instead view the company as a conduit through which our shareholders own the assets. . . . In line with Berkshire's owner-orientation, most of our directors have a major portion of their net worth invested in the company. We eat our own cooking.

Berkshire has a clear 'dominant logic':

> Charlie and I avoid businesses whose futures we can't evaluate, no matter how exciting their products may be. In the past, it required no brilliance for people to foresee the fabulous growth that awaited such industries as autos (in 1910), aircraft (in 1930) and television sets (in 1950). But the future then also included competitive dynamics

that would decimate almost all of the companies entering those industries. Even the survivors tended to come away bleeding. Just because Charlie and I can clearly see dramatic growth ahead for an industry does not mean we can judge what its profit margins and returns on capital will be as a host of competitors battle for supremacy. At Berkshire we will stick with businesses whose profit picture for decades to come seems reasonably predictable. Even then, we will make plenty of mistakes.

Buffett also explains how they manage their subsidiary businesses:

> Charlie and I are the managing partners of Berkshire. But we subcontract all of the heavy lifting in this business to the managers of our subsidiaries. In fact, we delegate almost to the point of abdication: Though Berkshire has about 257,000 employees, only 21 of these are at headquarters. Charlie and I mainly attend to capital allocation and the care and feeding of our key managers. Most of these managers are happiest when they are left alone to run their businesses, and that is customarily just how we leave them. That puts them in charge of all operating decisions and of dispatching the excess cash they generate to headquarters. By sending it to us, they don't get diverted by the various enticements that would come their way were they responsible for deploying the cash their businesses throw off. Furthermore, Charlie and I are exposed to a much wider range of possibilities for investing these funds than any of our managers could find in his or her own industry.

Questions

1 In what ways does Berkshire Hathaway conform (and not conform) to the archetypal portfolio manager described in section 7.6.2?

2 Suggest some industries and businesses, or types of industries and businesses, that Warren Buffett is likely never to invest in.

Figure 7.5 Portfolio managers, synergy managers and parental developers

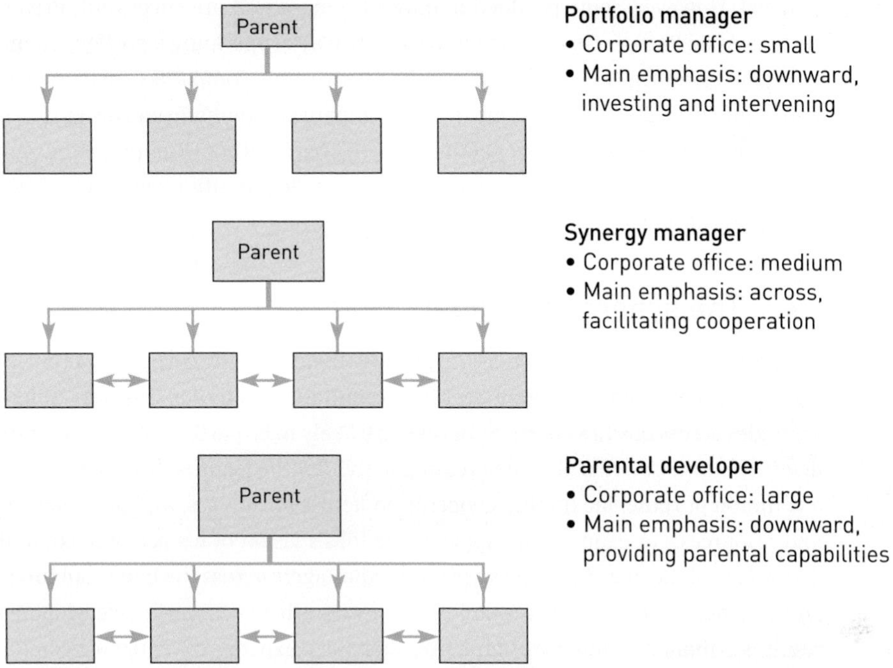

Portfolio manager
- Corporate office: small
- Main emphasis: downward, investing and intervening

Synergy manager
- Corporate office: medium
- Main emphasis: across, facilitating cooperation

Parental developer
- Corporate office: large
- Main emphasis: downward, providing parental capabilities

Source: Adapted from M. Goold, A. Campbell and M. Alexander, *Corporate Level Strategy*, Wiley, 1994.

7.6.2 The portfolio manager

The **portfolio manager** operates as an active investor in a way that shareholders in the stock market are either too dispersed or too inexpert to be able to do. In effect, the portfolio manager is acting as an agent on behalf of financial markets and shareholders with a view to extracting more value from the various businesses than they could achieve themselves. Its role is to identify and acquire under-valued assets or businesses and improve them. The portfolio manager might do this, for example, by acquiring another corporation, divesting low-performing businesses within it and intervening to improve the performance of those with potential. Such corporations may not be much concerned about the relatedness (see section 7.2) of the business units in their portfolio, typically adopting a conglomerate strategy. Their role is not to get closely involved in the routine management of the businesses, only to act over short periods of time to improve performance. In terms of the value-creating activities identified earlier, the portfolio manager concentrates on intervening and the provision (or withdrawal) of investment.

Portfolio managers seek to keep the cost of the centre low, for example by having a small corporate staff with few central services, leaving the business units alone so that their chief executives have a high degree of autonomy. They set clear financial targets for those chief executives, offering high rewards if they achieve them and likely loss of position if they do not. Such corporate parents can, of course, manage quite a large number of such businesses because they are not directly managing the everyday strategies of those businesses. Rather they are acting from above, setting financial targets, making central evaluations about the well-being and future prospects of such businesses, and investing, intervening or divesting accordingly.

Some argue that the days of the portfolio manager are gone. Improving financial markets mean that the scope for finding and investing cheaply in under-performing companies is much reduced. However, some portfolio managers remain and are successful. Private equity firms such as Apax Partners or Blackstone are a new way of operating a portfolio management style, typically investing in, improving and then divesting companies in loosely knit portfolios. For example, in 2010, Blackstone owned companies ranging from Hilton Hotels to the China BlueStar chemicals company, totalling more than 990,000 employees around the world. Illustration 7.4 includes a description of the portfolio parenting approach of Warren Buffet at Berkshire Hathaway.

7.6.3 The synergy manager

Obtaining synergy is often seen as the prime rationale for the corporate parent.[17] The **synergy manager is a corporate parent seeking to enhance value for business units by managing synergies across business units.** Synergies are likely to be particularly rich in the case of related diversification. In terms of value-creating activities, the focus is threefold: envisioning to build a common purpose; facilitating cooperation across businesses; and providing central services and resources. For example, at Apple, Steve Jobs's vision of his personal computers being the digital hub of the new digital lifestyle guides managers across the iMac computer, iPod, iPhone and iPad businesses to ensure seamless connections between the fast-developing offerings. The result is enhanced value through better customer experience. A metals company diversified into both steel and aluminium might centralise its energy procurement, gaining synergy benefits through increased bargaining power over suppliers.

However, achieving such synergistic benefits involves at least three challenges:

- *Excessive costs.* The benefits in sharing and cooperation need to outweigh the costs of undertaking such integration, both direct financial costs and opportunity costs. Managing synergistic relationships tends to involve expensive investments in management time.

- *Overcoming self-interest.* Managers in the business units have to want to cooperate. Especially where managers are rewarded largely according to the performance of their own particular business unit, they are likely to be unwilling to sacrifice their time and resources for the common good.

- *Illusory synergies.* It is easy to overestimate the value of skills or resources to other businesses. This is particularly common when the corporate centre needs to justify a new venture or the acquisition of a new company. Claimed synergies often prove illusory when managers actually have to put them into practice.

The failure of many companies to extract expected synergies from their businesses has led to growing scepticism about the notion of synergy. Synergistic benefits are not as easy to achieve as would appear. For example, in 2007 Daimler sold most of its stake in mass-market car manufacturer Chrysler after ten years of trying to extract synergies with its luxury Mercedes business. However, synergy continues to be a common theme in corporate-level strategy, as Illustration 7.2 on Zodiac exemplifies.

7.6.4 The parental developer[18]

The **parental developer seeks to employ its own central capabilities to add value to its businesses.** This is not so much about how the parent can develop benefits *across* business units or transfer capabilities between business units, as in the case of managing synergy. Rather parental developers focus on the resources or capabilities they have as parents which they can transfer *downwards* to enhance the potential of business units. For example, a parent could have a valuable brand or specialist skills in financial management or product development. If such parenting capabilities exist, corporate managers then need to identify a '*parenting opportunity*': a business which is not fulfilling its potential but which could be improved by applying the parenting capability, such as branding or product development. Such parenting opportunities are therefore more common in the case of related rather than unrelated diversified strategies and are likely to involve exchanges of managers and other resources across the businesses. Key value-creating activities for the parent will be the provision of central services and resources. For example, a consumer products company might offer substantial guidance on branding and distribution from the centre; a technology company might run a large central R&D laboratory.

There are two crucial challenges to managing a parental developer:

- *Parental focus.* Corporate parents need to be rigorous and focused in identifying their unique value-adding capabilities. They should always be asking what others can do better than them, and focus their energy and time on activities where they really do add value. Other central services should typically be outsourced to specialist companies that can do it better.

- *The 'crown jewel' problem.* Some diversified companies have business units in their portfolios which are performing well but to which the parent adds little value. These can become 'crown jewels', to which corporate parents become excessively attached. The logic of the parental development approach is if the centre cannot add value, it is just a cost and therefore destroying value. Parental developers should divest businesses they do not add value to, even profitable ones. Funds raised by selling a profitable business can be reinvested in businesses where the parent can add value.

PORTFOLIO MATRICES

Section 7.6 discussed rationales for corporate parents of multi-business organisations. This section introduces models by which managers can determine financial investment and divestment within their portfolios of business. Each model gives more or less attention to one of three criteria:

- the *balance* of the portfolio, e.g. in relation to its markets and the needs of the corporation;

- the *attractiveness* of the business units in terms of how strong they are individually and how profitable their markets or industries are likely to be; and

- the '*fit*' that the business units have with each other in terms of potential synergies or the extent to which the corporate parent will be good at looking after them.

7.7.1 The BCG (or growth/share) matrix[19]

One of the most common and long-standing ways of conceiving of the balance of a portfolio of businesses is the Boston Consulting Group (BCG) matrix (see Figure 7.6). The **BCG matrix uses market share and market growth criteria for determining the attractiveness and balance of a business portfolio.** High market share and high growth are, of course, attractive. However, the

BCG matrix

Figure 7.6 The growth share (or BCG) matrix

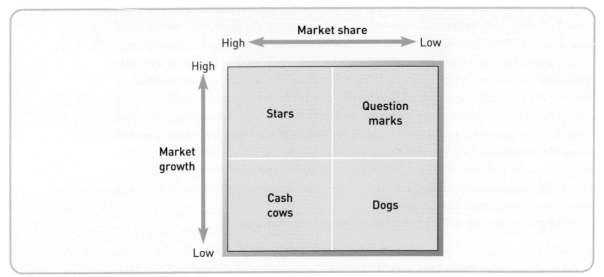

BCG matrix also warns that high growth demands heavy investment, for instance to expand capacity or develop brands. There needs to be a balance within the portfolio, so that there are some low-growth businesses that are making sufficient surplus to fund the investment needs of higher-growth businesses.

The growth/share axes of the BCG matrix define four sorts of business:

- A **star is a business unit within a portfolio which has a high market share in a growing market**. The business unit may be spending heavily to keep up with growth, but high market share should yield sufficient profits to make it more or less self-sufficient in terms of investment needs.

- A **question mark (or problem child) is a business unit within a portfolio that is in a growing market, but does not yet have high market share**. Developing question marks into stars, with high market share, takes heavy investment. Many question marks fail to develop, so the BCG advises corporate parents to nurture several at a time. It is important to make sure that some question marks develop into stars, as existing stars eventually become cash cows and cash cows may decline into dogs.

- A **cash cow is a business unit within a portfolio that has a high market share in a mature market**. However, because growth is low, investments needs are less, while high market share means that the business unit should be profitable. The cash cow should then be a cash provider, helping to fund investments in question marks.

- **Dogs are business units within a portfolio that have low share in static or declining markets** and are thus the worst of all combinations. They may be a cash drain and use up a disproportionate amount of managerial time and company resources. The BCG usually recommends divestment or closure.

The BCG matrix has several advantages. It provides a good way of visualising the different needs and potential of all the diverse businesses within the corporate portfolio. It warns corporate parents of the financial demands of what might otherwise look like a desirable portfolio of high-growth businesses. It also reminds corporate parents that stars are likely eventually to wane. Finally, it provides a useful discipline to business unit managers, underlining the fact

ILLUSTRATION 7.5

ITC's diverse portfolio: smelling sweeter

What was once the Imperial Tobacco Company of India now has a portfolio stretching from cigarettes to fragrances.

ITC is one of India's largest consumer good companies, with an increasingly diversified portfolio of products. Its chairman, Y.C. Deveshwar describes its strategy thus: 'It is ITC's endeavour to continuously explore opportunites for growth by synergising and blending its multiple core competences to create new epicentres of growth. The employees of ITC are inspired by the vision of growing ITC into one of India's premier institutions and are willing to go the extra mile to generate value for the economy, in the process creating growing value for the shareholders.'

ITC was founded in 1910 as the Imperial Tobacco Company of India, with brands such as Wills, Gold Cut and John Players. ITC now holds about two thirds of the market for cigarettes in India, with Philip Morris and BAT affiliated companies distant seconds with about 13 per cent each. However, cigarettes in India are highly discouraged by the Indian government, and increasingly heavily taxed.

ITC has a long diversification history. The company's original activities in the growth of leaf tobacco developed into a range of agricultural businesses within India, including edible oils, fruit pulp, spices and frozen foods. ITC had set up a packaging and printing business in the 1920s, originally to supply its cigarette business. By 2009, this was India's largest packaging solutions provider. In 1975, ITC had entered the hotel business, becoming the country's second largest operator with over 100 hotels by 2009, ranging from de luxe to economy. In 1979, the company also entered the paperboard industry, and three decades later was the country's largest producer, accounting for 29% of the market by value.

The early 21st century had seen many new diversification initiatives, especially in the booming Fast Moving Consumer Goods (FMCG) sector. Initially it started in the food business, with Kitchens-of-India ready-to-eat gourmet foods, the *Aashirvaad* wheat-flour business, Sunfeast biscuits and Bingo snacks. ITC's own agri-businesses were an important source of supply for these initiatives. *Aashirvaad* reached over 50 per cent Indian market share, while Sunfeast gained 12 per cent market share and Bingo 11 per cent by 2008. At the same time, ITC took advantage of the strong brand values of its Wills cigarettes to launch Wills Lifestyle, a range of upmarket clothing stores, with its own designs. In 2009, Wills Lifestyle was recognised as India's 'Most Admired Fashion Brand of the Year'. In 2005, ITC launched its personal care business, again using its cigarette brandnames: for example, 'Essenza Di Wills' (fragrances) and 'Fiama Di Wills' (hair and skin care).

ITC segmental sales and profits (Rs in Crores)

Segment	2005 sales	2005 profits	2009 sales	2009 profits
Cigarettes	10,002	2,288	15,115	4,184
Other FMCG	563	(195)	3,010	(483)
Hotels	577	141	1,014	316
Agribusiness	1,780	96.4	2,284	256
Paperboard, paper and packaging	1,565	280	1,719	509

5 Rs in Crores ~ US $1,000,000 ~€700,000. Profits are before interest and tax. Figures in brackets are losses.

Sources: ITC annual reports; M. Balaji, 2006, *ITC: Adding Shareholder Value through Diversifications*, IBSCDC; B. Gopal and S. Kora, 2009, *Indian Conglomerate ITC*, IBS Research Center.

Questions

1 How well does ITC's portfolio fit in terms of the BCG matrix?

2 Identify and evaluate the various synergies in ITC's business.

that the corporate parent ultimately owns the surplus resources they generate and can allocate them according to what is best for the corporate whole. Cash cows should not hoard their profits.

However, there are at least three potential problems with the BCG matrix:

- *Definitional vagueness.* It can be hard to decide what high and low growth or share mean in particular situations. Managers are often keen to define themselves as 'high-share' by defining their market in a particularly narrow way (for example, ignoring relevant international markets).

- *Capital market assumptions.* The notion that a corporate parent needs a balanced portfolio to finance investment from internal sources (cash cows) assumes that capital cannot be raised in external markets, for instance by issuing shares or raising loans. The notion of a balanced portfolio may be more relevant in countries where capital markets are under-developed or in private companies that wish to minimise dependence on external shareholders or banks.

- *Unkind to animals.* Both cash cows and dogs receive ungenerous treatment, the first being simply milked, the second terminated or cast out of the corporate home. This treatment can cause *motivation problems*, as managers in these units see little point in working hard for the sake of other businesses. There is also the danger of the *self-fulfilling prophecy*. Cash cows will become dogs even more quickly than the model expects if they are simply milked and denied adequate investment. Finally, the notion that a dog can be simply sold or closed down also assumes that there are *no ties to other business units* in the portfolio, whose performance might depend in part on keeping the dog alive. This portfolio approach to dogs works better for conglomerate strategies, where divestments or closures are unlikely to have knock-on effects on other parts of the portfolio.

7.7.2 The directional policy (GE–McKinsey) matrix

Another way to consider a portfolio of businesses is by means of the *directional policy matrix*[20] which categorises business units into those with good prospects and those with less good prospects. The matrix was originally developed by McKinsey & Co. consultants in order to help the American conglomerate General Electric manage its portfolio of business units. Specifically, the directional policy matrix positions business units according to (a) how attractive the relevant market is in which they are operating, and (b) the competitive strength of the SBU in that market. Attractiveness can be identified by PESTEL or five forces analyses; business unit strength can be defined by competitor analysis (for instance the strategy canvas): see section 2.4.3. Some analysts also choose to show graphically how large the market is for a given business unit's activity, and even the market share of that business unit, as shown in Figure 7.7. For example, managers in a firm with the portfolio shown in Figure 7.7 will be concerned that they have relatively low shares in the largest and most attractive market, whereas their greatest strength is in a market with only medium attractiveness and smaller markets with little long-term attractiveness.

The matrix also offers strategy guidelines given the positioning of the business units, as shown in Figure 7.8. It suggests that the businesses with the highest growth potential and the greatest strength are those in which to invest for growth. Those that are the weakest and in the least attractive markets should be divested or 'harvested' (i.e. used to yield as much cash as possible before divesting).

The directional policy matrix is more complex than the BCG matrix. However, it can have two advantages. First, unlike the simpler four-box BCG matrix, the nine cells of the directional

Figure 7.7 Directional policy (GE–McKinsey) matrix

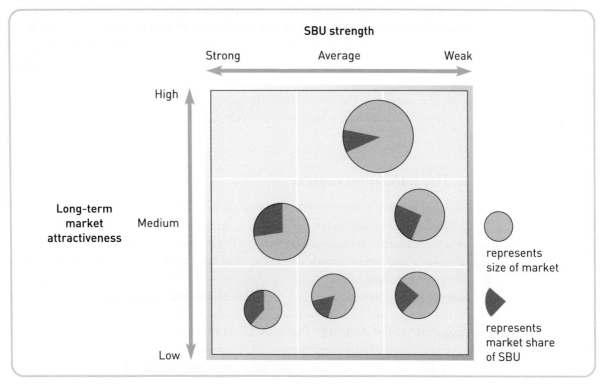

Figure 7.8 Strategy guidelines based on the directional policy matrix

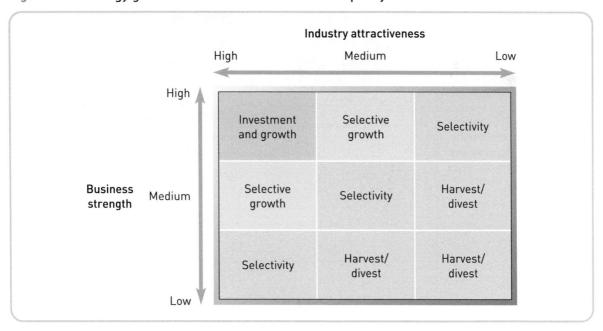

policy matrix acknowledge the possibility of a difficult middle ground. Here managers have to be carefully selective. In this sense, the directional policy matrix is less mechanistic than the BCG matrix, encouraging open debate on less clear-cut cases. Second, the two axes of the directional policy matrix are not based on single measures (i.e. market share and market growth).

Business strength can derive from many other factors than market share, and industry attractiveness does not just boil down to industry growth rates. On the other hand, the directional policy matrix shares some problems with the BCG matrix, particularly about vague definitions, capital market assumptions, motivation and self-fulfilling prophecy. Overall, however, the value of the matrix is to help managers invest in the businesses which are most likely to pay off.

So far the discussion has been about the logic of portfolios in terms of balance and attractiveness. The third logic is to do with 'fit' with the particular capabilities of the corporate parent.

7.7.3 The parenting matrix

The *parenting matrix* (or Ashridge Portfolio Display) developed by consultants Michael Goold and Andrew Campbell introduces parental fit as an important criterion for including businesses in the portfolio.[21] Businesses may be attractive in terms of the BCG or directional policy matrices, but if the parent cannot add value, then the parent ought to be cautious about acquiring or retaining them.

There are two key dimensions of fit in the parenting matrix (see Figure 7.9):

Figure 7.9 **The parenting matrix: the Ashridge Portfolio Display**

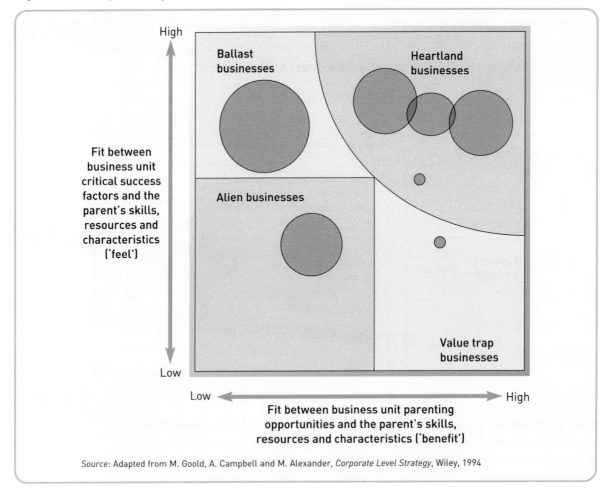

Source: Adapted from M. Goold, A. Campbell and M. Alexander, *Corporate Level Strategy*, Wiley, 1994

- *'Feel'*. This is a measure of the fit between each business unit's *critical success factors* (see section 2.4.3) and the capabilities (in terms of competences and resources) of the corporate parent. In other words, does the corporate parent have the necessary 'feel', or understanding, for the businesses it will parent?

- *'Benefit'*. This measures the fit between the *parenting opportunities*, or needs, of business units and the capabilities of the parent. Parenting opportunities are about the upside, areas in which good parenting can benefit the business (for instance, by bringing marketing expertise). For the benefit to be realised, of course, the parent must have the right capabilities to match the parenting opportunities.

The power of using these two dimensions of fit is as follows. It is easy to see that a corporate parent should avoid running businesses that it has no *feel* for. What is less clear is that parenting should be avoided if there is no *benefit*. This challenges the corporate parenting of even businesses for which the parent has high feel. Businesses for which a corporate parent has high feel but can add little benefit should either be run with a very light touch or be divested.

Figure 7.9 shows four kinds of business along these two dimensions of feel and benefit:

- *Heartland* business units are ones which the parent understands well and can continue to add value to. They should be at the core of future strategy.

- *Ballast* business units are ones the parent understands well but can do little for. They would probably be at least as successful as independent companies. If not divested, they should be spared as much corporate bureaucracy as possible.

- *Value-trap* business units are dangerous. They appear attractive because there are opportunities to add value (for instance, marketing could be improved). But they are deceptively attractive, because the parent's lack of feel will result in more harm than good (i.e. the parent lacks the right marketing skills). The parent will need to acquire new capabilities if it is to be able to move value-trap businesses into the heartland. It might be easier to divest to another corporate parent which could add value, and will pay well for the chance.

- *Alien* business units are clear misfits. They offer little opportunity to add value and the parent does not understand them anyway. Exit is definitely the best strategy.

This approach to considering corporate portfolios places the emphasis firmly on how the parent benefits the business units. It requires careful analysis of both parenting capabilities and business-unit parenting needs. The parenting matrix can therefore assist hard decisions where either high feel or high parenting opportunities tempt the corporate parent to acquire or retain businesses. Parents should concentrate on actual or potential heartland businesses, where there is both high feel and high benefit.

The concept of fit has equal relevance in the public-sector. The implication is that public-sector managers should control directly only those services and activities for which they have special managerial expertise. Other services should be outsourced or set up as independent agencies (see section 7.5).

KEY DEBATE

Why have corporate-level strategies anyway?

Do we really need diversified corporations?

The notion of corporate strategy assumes that corporations should own and control businesses in a range of markets or products. But 'transaction cost' economist Oliver Williamson believes that diversified corporations should only exist in the presence of 'market failures' (see also section 7.5.2). If markets worked well, there would be no need for business units to be coordinated through managerial structures. Business units could be independent, coordinating where necessary by simple transactions in the marketplace. The 'invisible hand' of the market could replace the 'visible hand' of managers at corporate headquarters. There would be no 'corporate strategy'.

Market failures favouring the diversified corporation occur for two reasons:

- *'Bounded rationality'*: people cannot know everything that is going on in the market, so perfectly rational market transactions are impossible. Information, for instance on quality and costs, can sometimes be better inside the corporate fold.
- *'Opportunism'*: independent businesses trading between each other may behave opportunistically, for example by cheating on delivery or quality promises. Cheating can sometimes be policed and punished more easily within a corporate hierarchy.

According to Williamson, activities should only be brought into the corporation when the 'transaction costs' of coping with bounded rationality (gaining information) and opportunism (guarding against cheats) are lower inside the corporate hierarchy than they would be if simply relying on transactions in the marketplace.

This comparison of the transaction costs of markets and hierarchies has powerful implications for trends in product diversification:

- Improving capital markets may reduce the relative information advantages of conglomerates in managing a set of unrelated businesses. As markets get better at capturing information there will be less need for conglomerates, something that may account for the recent decline in conglomerates in many economies.

- Improving protection of intellectual property rights may increase the incentives for corporations to license out their technologies to companies, rather than trying to do everything themselves. If the prospect of collecting royalties improves, there is less advantage for corporations keeping everything in-house.

Thus fewer market failures also means narrower product scope.

Williamson's 'transaction cost' view puts a heavy burden on corporations to justify themselves. Two justifications are possible. First, knowledge is hard to trade in the market. Buyers can only know the value of new knowledge once they have already bought it. Because they can trust each other, colleagues in sister business units within the same corporation are better at transferring knowledge than independent companies are in the open market. Second, corporations are not just about minimising the costs of information and cheating, but also about maximising the value of the combined resources. Bringing creative people together in a collective enterprise enhances knowledge exchange, innovation and motivation. Corporations are value creators as well as cost minimisers.

References:
1. O.E. Williamson, 'Strategy Research: Governance and Competence Perspectives', *Strategic Management Journal*, vol. 12, pp. 75–94 (1998).
2. B. Kogut and U. Zander, 'What Firms Do? Coordination, Identity and Learning', *Organization Science*, vol. 7, no. 5 (1996), 502–19.
3. S. Ghoshal, C. Bartlett and P. Moran, 'A New Manifesto for Management', *Sloan Management Review*, Spring (1999), pp. 9–20.

Question

Consider a diversified corporation such as Unilever (food, personal care and household): what kinds of hard-to-trade knowledge might it be able to transfer between product and country subsidiaries and is such knowledge likely to be of increasing or decreasing importance?

SUMMARY

- Many corporations comprise several, sometimes many, business units. Decisions and activities above the level of business units are the concern of what in this chapter is called the *corporate parent*.

- Organisational *scope* is often considered in terms of *related* and *unrelated* diversification.

- Corporate parents may seek to add value by adopting different parenting roles: the *portfolio manager*, the *synergy manager* or the *parental developer*.

- There are several portfolio models to help corporate parents manage their businesses, of which the most common are: the *BCG matrix*, the *directional policy matrix* and the *parenting matrix*.

- *Divestment* and *outsourcing* should be considered as well as diversification, particularly in the light of relative strategic capabilities and the transaction costs of *opportunism*.

WORK ASSIGNMENTS

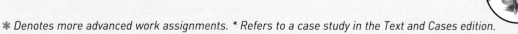

✳ *Denotes more advanced work assignments.* * *Refers to a case study in the Text and Cases edition.*

7.1 Using the Ansoff axes (Figure 7.2), identify and explain corporate strategic directions for any one of these case organisations: CRH*, Ferrovial*, SAB Miller*.

7.2 Go to the website of any large multi-business organisation (for example, Google, Tata Group, Siemens) and assess the degree to which its corporate-level strategy is characterised by (a) related or unrelated diversification and (b) a coherent 'dominant logic' (see section 7.3).

7.3 For any large multi-business corporation (as in 7.2), explain how the corporate parent should best create value for its component businesses (as portfolio manager, synergy manager or parental developer: see section 7.6). Would all the businesses fit equally well?

7.4✳ For any large multi-business corporation (as in 7.2), plot the business units on a portfolio matrix (for example, the BCG matrix: section 7.7.1). Justify any assumptions about the relative positions of businesses on the relevant axes of the matrix. What managerial conclusions do you draw from this analysis?

Integrative assignment

7.5 Take a case of a recent merger or acquisition (see Chapter 10), and assess the extent to which it involved related or unrelated diversification (if either) and how far it was consistent with the company's existing dominant logic. Using share price information (see www.bigcharts.com or similar), assess shareholders' reaction to the merger or acquisition. How do you explain this reaction?

VIDEO ASSIGNMENT

Visit *MyStrategyLab* and watch the *Fridays* case study.

1 What are the benefits and disadvantages of Fridays' relationship with the supermarkets? Relatively how strong is Fridays vis-à-vis other competitors in this relationship?

2 Explain Fridays' diversification strategy in terms of the Ansoff axes and strategic relatedness (Chapter 7: Figure 7.2).

RECOMMENDED KEY READINGS

- An accessible discussion of corporate strategy is provided by A. Campbell and R. Park, *The Growth Gamble: When Leaders Should Bet on Big New Businesses*, Nicholas Brealey, 2005.

- M. Goold and K. Luchs, 'Why diversify: four decades of management thinking' in D. Faulkner and A. Campbell (eds), *The Oxford Handbook of Strategy*, vol. 2, Oxford University Press, pp. 18–42, provides an authoritative overview of the diversification option over time.

- A summary of different portfolio analyses is provided in D. Faulkner, 'Portfolio matrices', in V. Ambrosini (ed.), *Exploring Techniques of Analysis and Evaluation in Strategic Management*, Prentice Hall, 1998.

REFERENCES

1. This figure is an extension of the product/market matrix: see I. Ansoff, *Corporate Strategy*, 1988, Chapter 6. The Ansoff matrix was later developed into the one shown below.

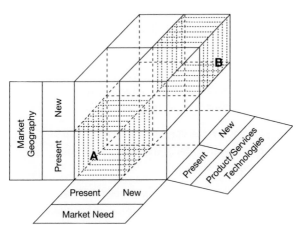

Source: H. Ansoff, *The New Corporate Strategy*, Wiley, 1988.

2. For the European Commission competition authority, http://ec.europa.eu/comm/competition; for the UK Competition Commission, see http://www.competition-commission.org.uk/.

3. For discussions of the challenge of sustained growth and diversification, see A. Campbell and R. Parks, *The Growth Gamble*, Nicholas Brearly (2005) and D. Laurie, Y. Doz and C. Sheer, 'Creating new growth platforms', *Harvard Business Review*, vol. 84, no. 5, (2006), 80–90.

4. On economies of scope, see D.J. Teece, 'Towards an economic theory of the multi-product firm', *Journal of Economic Behavior and Organization*, vol. 3 (1982), pp. 39–63.

5. See C.K. Prahalad and R. Bettis, 'The dominant logic: a new link between diversity and performance', *Strategic Management Journal*, vol. 6, no. 1 (1986), pp. 485–501; R. Bettis and C.K. Prahalad, 'The dominant logic: retrospective and extension', *Strategic Management Journal*, vol. 16, no. 1 (1995), pp. 5–15.

6. See C. Markides, 'Corporate strategy: the role of the centre' in A. Pettigrew, H. Thomas and R. Whittington (eds), *Handbook of Strategy and Management*, Sage, 2002. For a discussion of recent Chinese diversification patterns, see A. Delios, N. Zhou and W.W. Xu, 'Ownership structure and the diversification and performance of publicly-listed companies in China', *Business Horizons*, vol. 51, no. 6 (2008), pp. 802–21.

7. These benefits are often discussed in terms of 'multimarket' or 'multipoint' competition: see J. Anand, L. Mesquita and R. Vassolo, 'The dynamics of multimarket competition in exploration and exploitation activities', *Academy of Management Journal*, vol. 52, no. 4 (2009), pp. 802–21.

8. M. Goold and A. Campbell, 'Desperately seeking synergy', *Harvard Business Review*, vol. 76, no. 2 (1998), pp. 131–45.

9. A. Pehrson, 'Business relatedness and performance: a study of managerial perceptions', *Strategic Management Journal*, vol. 27, no. 3 (2006), pp. 265–82.

10. L.E. Palich, L.B. Cardinal and C. Miller, 'Curvilinearity in the diversification-performance linkage: an examination of over three decades of research', *Strategic Management*

Journal, vol. 21 (2000), pp. 155–74. The inverted-U relationship is the research consensus, but studies often disagree, particularly finding variations over time and across countries. For recent context-sensitive studies, see M. Mayer and R. Whittington, 'Diversification in context: a cross national and cross temporal extension', *Strategic Management Journal*, vol. 24 (2003), pp. 773–81 and A. Chakrabarti, K. Singh and I. Mahmood, 'Diversification and performance: evidence from East Asian firms', *Strategic Management Journal*, vol. 28 (2007), pp. 101–20.

11. For a discussion and cases on the relative guidance of transaction cost and capabilities thinking, see R. McIvor, 'How the transaction cost and resource-based theories of the firm inform outsourcing evaluation', *Journal of Operations Management*, vol. 27, no. 1 (2009), pp. 45–63. See also T. Holcomb and M. Hitt, 'Toward a model of strategic outsourcing', *Journal of Operations Management*, vol. 25, no. 2 (2007), pp. 464–81.

12. For a good discussion of corporate parenting roles, see Markides in reference 6 above. A recent empirical study of corporate headquarters is D. Collis, D. Young and M. Goold, 'The size, structure and performance of corporate headquarters', *Strategic Management Journal*, vol. 28, no. 4 (2007), pp. 383–406.

13. M. Goold, A. Campbell and M. Alexander, *Corporate Level Strategy*, Wiley, 1994, is concerned with both the value-adding and value-destroying capacity of corporate parents.

14. For a discussion of the role of a clarity of mission, see A. Campbell, M. Devine and D. Young, *A Sense of Mission*, Hutchinson Business, 1990.

15. E. Zuckerman, 'Focusing the corporate product: securities analysts and de-diversification', *Administrative Science Quarterly*, vol. 45, no. 3 (2000), pp. 591–619.

16. The first two rationales discussed here are based on M. Porter, 'From competitive advantage to corporate strategy', *Harvard Business Review*, vol. 65, no. 3 (1987), pp. 43–59.

17. See A. Campbell and K. Luchs, *Strategic Synergy*, Butterworth/Heinemann, 1992.

18. The logic of parental development is explained extensively in Goold, Campbell and Alexander (see reference 13 above).

19. For a more extensive discussion of the use of the growth share matrix see A.C. Hax and N.S. Majluf in R.G. Dyson (ed.), *Strategic Planning: Models and Analytical Techniques*, Wiley, 1990; and D. Faulkner, 'Portfolio matrices', in V. Ambrosini (ed.), *Exploring Techniques of Analysis and Evaluation in Strategic Management*, Prentice Hall, 1998; for source explanations of the BCG matrix see B.D. Henderson, *Henderson on Corporate Strategy*, Abt Books, 1979.

20. A. Hax and N. Majluf, 'The use of the industry attractiveness-business strength matrix in strategic planning', in R. Dyson (ed.), *Strategic Planning: Models and Analytical Techniques*, Wiley, 1990.

21. The discussion in this section draws on M. Goold, A. Campbell and M. Alexander, *Corporate Level Strategy*, Wiley, 1994, which provides an excellent basis for understanding issues of parenting.

Virgin: the global entrepreneur

John Treciokas

Introduction

Richard Branson founded Virgin in 1970 and has effectively used his personality to bring the Virgin brand to the attention of the consumer. Virgin's businesses are portrayed in an exciting light with a personal touch and this gives the Virgin brand a softer feel than other large multinational companies. The Virgin Group has grown over the last 40 years to become one of the largest private companies in the UK. Virgin currently has more than 200 branded companies worldwide, employing in the region of 50,000 employees in 29 countries with revenues in excess of £11 billion (approx. €12bn; $16 bn) in 2008.

The largest and most celebrated business, Virgin Atlantic celebrated 25 years of flying people across the Atlantic in 2009 with a striking advertising campaign which portrayed the excitement and fun of flying with, or working at, Virgin. Branson believes in the value of careful brand enhancement and the benefits of transferring this brand image across a diverse portfolio. Research has shown that the Virgin name is associated with words such as: 'fun', 'innovative', 'daring' and 'successful'.

However, does such a portfolio of businesses make strategic sense and will Virgin's conglomerate group of diverse companies survive after Richard Branson departs? These are the key questions facing the company in 2010, the start of a new decade.

Growth and strategy

Virgin began selling music records in 1970 when Branson was just twenty years old and its rapid growth led to an Oxford Street shop a year later. Further expansion into the music industry followed with the Virgin record label in 1973. From an early stage in the business Virgin courted controversy by signing the Sex Pistols, a 'punk rock group' whose rude and anti-establishment behaviour quickly brought them and Virgin high public exposure. Risk-taking and courting publicity epitomised Branson's philosophy from the outset.

Source: Steve Bell/Rex Features.

Virgin Atlantic was founded in 1984 and a year after Virgin Holidays began. These became the core of the Virgin group. In 1987 Virgin Records America was established: Branson commented, 'we were flying there a lot so it made sense to expand there too'. In 1988 Virgin Megastores (retail outlets with a huge selection of recorded music and related products) were opened in Glasgow and Paris, followed by numerous other British, European, American, Japanese and Pacific Basin cities. Virgin was becoming an international company.

Virgin at this stage of its existence was involved largely in two industries: travel/holidays and music. From the 1990s onwards there followed numerous acquisitions, divestments and joint ventures that resulted in a highly diversified group. Chief amongst these were:

● In 1992 the sale of Virgin Records to EMI for £510m, mainly to raise funds for Branson to invest further in his favourite business (Virgin Atlantic).
● The acquisition of the Our Price chain of shops in 1994, making Virgin Retail the UK's largest music retailer.
● The launch of a low-cost airline, Virgin Express in 1996.
● The acquisition in 1997 of the ailing West Coast rail franchise in the UK. Virgin Trains set about trying to improve its services and five years later introduced the tilting Pendolino trains, allowing faster services.

- The start of Branson's interest in the media business with the launch of Virgin One, a tabloid TV channel, in 1997.
- In 1999 the launch of Virgin Mobile, using other providers' networks via a joint venture with what is now T-mobile.
- The launch of a network of health clubs in 1999 and, in 2006, the acquisition of the Holmes Place health chain to give it a significant market share in the UK.
- The sale in 2000 Virgin of 49 per cent of Virgin Atlantic to Singapore Airlines – perhaps accepting that this was a risky and expensive business. Branson insisted, however, that Virgin would not lose its majority control in this core business.
- In 2008 Virgin Mobile in India was launched, in partnership with the Tata group. Tata Teleservices provided the network service, though it is marketed under the Virgin brand. The offering included music, entertainment and news on India's film industry, sports and stock market. The target market was the younger population – some 51 per cent of the 1.1 billion people in India are under 25 and two-thirds are under 35.
- In 2007, Virgin had tried a major move into the financial industry, with the attempted takeover of Northern Rock, a troubled British mortgage bank. The move was resisted by the press and some politicians – Branson has never quite been accepted by the establishment. However, at the beginning of 2010, Virgin continued this strategy with the purchase of a little-known private bank (Church House Trust) which enabled it to apply for a full banking licence and to offer its own mortgages and current accounts. Will this be the next major plank in the Virgin empire?

A move to merge several of its offerings occurred in 2006, when four Virgin companies combined to become one media company providing television, broadband, telephone and mobile phone services in partnership with NTL-Telewest. This company, trading as Virgin Media, had a total of nine million subscribers, giving it a strong position to compete with, and aggressively challenge, its major rival BSkyB. Virgin began to offer complete packages for the family, including a broad range of television packages, broadband at home and away, home telephone services and mobile phone services. This package often included free hardware to lock customers in for up to two years on a contract.

Since 2000 Virgin has also set up a rather futuristic attempt to launch a passenger service into suborbital space (Virgin Galactic) as well as more down to earth businesses like Virgin Comics and Virgin Healthcare.

Table 1 Other strategic developments: 1990–2010

1993	Virgin Radio commences broadcasting.
1994	Launch of Virgin Vodka and Virgin Cola.
1995	Launch of Virgin Direct, an investment product.
1996	Launch of Virgin Net, an internet service provider.
1997	Virgin Trains is founded to run a rail franchise in the UK.
1997	Virgin Cosmetics launches with four flagship stores.
1997	Virgin One commences operations in tabloid TV.
2000	Nine new companies are launched, including a new low-cost airline and mobile phone service, both in Australia.
2006	Virgin Express airline merged with SN Brussels Airline.
2006	Launch of airline in Nigeria.

The table also shows other strategic developments during this time.

Branson has also become increasingly interested in environmental issues, with the launch of the Virgin Earth Challenge. In 2007, he announced this challenge to produce practical designs that can remove large amounts of carbon dioxide from the atmosphere and offered a $25m (about €17.5m) prize. This initiative was part of a number of initiatives brought together by Branson under the banner of 'World Citizen'. These included 'People & Planet,' with the aim of ensuring that Virgin companies contribute to a sustainable society; Virgin Unite, a not-for-profit entrepreneurial foundation, with the aim of partnering to develop new ways to improve social and environmental issues; and the Virgin Green Fund to invest in companies in renewable energy and resource efficiency sectors in Europe and the US. Richard Branson also joined 'The Elders' – a group of leaders brought together by Nelson Mandela to promote peace and tackle humanitarian problems. It seems that Branson, like Microsoft's Bill Gates, was turning his attention to non-profit and CSR issues.

Corporate rationale

Branson's 2008 book, *Business Stripped Bare*, had the subtitle: 'the adventures of a global entrepreneur'. Virgin states on its own website that it is a 'leading branded venture capital organisation' and companies are part of a family rather than a hierarchy. It has minimal layers of management, no bureaucracy and a small global HQ.

Branson sees Virgin as adding value in three main ways in addition to the brand. These are: its public relations and marketing skills; its experience with 'green-field' start-ups; and its understanding of the opportunities presented by 'institutionalised' markets – by this he means those dominated by a few competitors who are not giving good value to customers because they have become inefficient, complacent or preoccupied with rivals.

The key criterion for whether Virgin backs a new venture is 'does an opportunity exist for restructuring a market and creating competitive advantage?' Each business is 'ring-fenced', so that lenders to one company have no rights over the assets of another and financial results are not consolidated. Virgin has a mix of privately owned and public-listed companies, as well as a mix of start-up small businesses and very large corporate ventures. Each may have very different strategic reasoning: some may be an attempt to keep Virgin in the public consciousness or possibly a method of training and developing managers. Some larger start-ups are serious strategic moves into new industries.

Increasingly large financial pockets and a proven track record in highly competitive industries have also enabled Virgin to enter into business opportunities with joint venture partners.

The future

Not all of Virgin's companies are successful and not all meet the standards of customer service that Virgin would like to see – both Virgin Media and Virgin Rail have had many customer complaints. None the less, Branson has created an image with the British public of a 'cheeky entrepreneur' who has battled the mighty 'monopoly' of British Airways and whose Virgin brand has grown into a business empire. The other lesser-known image – according to Branson-watcher and journalist Tom Bower – is one of a ruthless, crafty businessman always trying to get one over on his rivals.

It is difficult to discover the overall financial position of Virgin as it is made up of so many individual companies (many private) and there are no consolidated accounts. However, Bower states (2008) that the financial accounts show that the Virgin holding company lost £3.9m, even as its mainstay air-travel subsidiary made a profit of £123m. Sir Richard has argued that he pursues growth, not profits, and builds companies for the long term. With the aviation industry in crisis in 2009/10 and Virgin's dependence on airlines, this must raise concerns for the future of the organisation.

Richard Branson does not mention his departure in interviews but states that the company has been carefully groomed to continue without him, and that the brand is now globally well known, thus implying that his publicity stunts are no longer required. However, can Virgin survive as an entity without Branson?

Notes

Some parts of this case are based on the previous cases on Virgin in earlier editions of this text, originally written by Urmilla Lawson and revised by Aidan McQuade.

References and sources
www.Virgin.com.
Bower, Tom *Branson*, Harper Perennial, 2008.
www.businessweek.com/November 2007.
www.reuters.com, 16 December 2009.
The Economist, 'Virgin rebirth', 12 September 2008.
The Economist, 'Toyota slips up', 12 December 2009.
Goff, Sharlene, *Financial Times*, 8 January 2010.

Questions

1 Describe Virgin's various diversification moves in terms of Ansoff's axes (Figure 7.2).

2 How does Virgin add value as a corporate parent? Is there anything more it should do to add value?

3 Assess whether moving further into the banking industry is the right strategic option for Virgin. Does the continued pursuit of this industry suggest a more careful hidden strategic plan that is not revealed to outsiders?

4 What would be the challenges faced by a successor to Richard Branson, and what might he or she do?

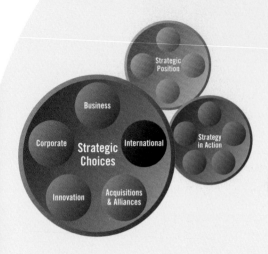

8

INTERNATIONAL STRATEGY

Learning outcomes

After reading this chapter, you should be able to:

● Assess the *internationalisation potential* of different markets.

● Identify sources of competitive advantage in international strategy, through both *global sourcing* and exploitation of *local factors*.

● Distinguish between four main types of international strategy.

● *Rank markets* for entry or expansion, taking into account attractiveness, cultural and other forms of distance and competitor retaliation threats.

● Assess the relative merits of different *market entry modes*, including joint ventures, licensing and foreign direct investment.

mystrategylab

MyStrategyLab is designed to help you make the most of your studies.

Visit **www.pearsoned.co.uk/mystrategylab** to discover a wide range of resources specific to this chapter, including:

• A personalised **Study plan** that will help you understand core concepts

• **Audio** and **video clips** that put the spotlight on strategy in the real world

• **Online glossaries** and **flashcards** that provide helpful reminders when you're looking for some quick revision.

8.1 INTRODUCTION

The last chapter introduced market development as a strategy, in relation to the Ansoff axes. This chapter focuses on a specific but important kind of market development, operating in different geographical markets. This is a challenge for all kinds of organisations nowadays. There are of course the large traditional multinationals such as Nestlé, Toyota and McDonald's. But recent years have seen the rise of emerging-country multinationals from Brazil, Russia, India and China. New small firms are increasingly 'born global', building international relationships right from the start. Public-sector organisations too are having to make choices about collaboration, outsourcing and even competition with overseas organisations. European Union legislation requires public-service organisations to accept tenders from non-national suppliers.

Figure 8.1 identifies five main themes of this chapter, with international strategy as the core. The themes are as follows:

- *Internationalisation drivers*. Drivers include market demand, the potential for cost advantages, government pressures and inducements and the need to respond to competitor moves. Given the risks and costs of international strategy, managers need to know that the drivers are strong to justify adopting an international strategy in the first place.

- *Geographical advantage*. In international competition, advantages might come from both geographic location of the original business and from the international configuration of their value network. Managers need to appraise these potential sources of competitive advantage carefully: if there are no competitive advantages, international strategy is liable to fail.

KEY CONCEPT

Four international strategies

- *International strategy*. If drivers and advantages are sufficiently strong to merit an international strategy, then a range of strategic approaches are opened up, from the simplest export strategies to the most complex global strategies.

Figure 8.1 International strategy framework

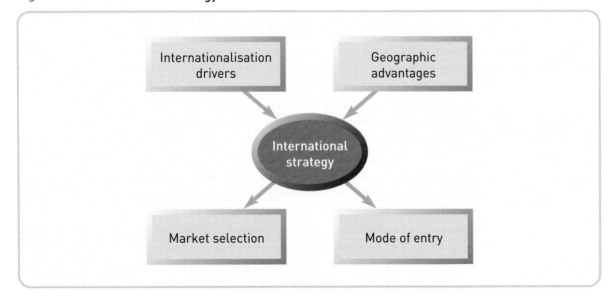

- *Market selection.* Having adopted the broad approach to international strategy, the question next is which country markets to prioritise and which to steer clear of. The issues here range from the economic to the cultural and political.

- *Entry mode.* Finally, once target countries are selected, managers have to determine how they should enter each particular market. Again, export is a simple place to start, but there are licensing, franchising, joint-venture and wholly owned subsidiary alternatives to consider as well.

The chapter takes a cautious view on international strategy. Despite the fashionable talk of increasing 'globalisation', there are many challenges and many pressures for localisation as well.[1] The chapter will therefore also consider the financial performance implications of growing internationalisation and the Key Debate at the end of this chapter considers the controversy around global, local and regional strategies.

The chapter distinguishes between international strategy and global strategy. **International strategy refers to a range of options for operating outside an organisation's country of origin.** Global strategy is only one kind of international strategy. **Global strategy involves high coordination of extensive activities dispersed geographically in many countries around the world.** This chapter keeps open alternative options to full global strategy.

 ## 8.2 INTERNATIONALISATION DRIVERS

There are many general pressures increasing internationalisation. Barriers to international trade, investment and migration are all now much lower than they were a couple of decades ago. Better international legal frameworks means that it is less risky to deal with unfamiliar partners. Improvements in communications – from cheaper air travel to the internet – make movement and the spread of ideas much easier around the world. Not least, the success of new economic powerhouses such as the so-called BRICs – Brazil, Russia, India and China – is generating new opportunities and challenges for business internationally.[2]

However, not all these internationalisation trends are one-way. Nor do they hold for all industries. For example, migration is now becoming more difficult between some countries. Trade barriers still exist for some products, especially those relating to defence technologies. Many countries protect their leading companies from takeover by overseas rivals. Markets vary widely in the extent to which consumer needs are standardising – compare computer operating systems to the highly variable national tastes in chocolate. Some so-called multinationals are in fact concentrated in very particular markets, for example North America and Western Europe, or have a quite limited set of international links, for example supply or outsourcing arrangements with just one or two countries overseas. In short, managers need to beware 'global baloney', by which economic integration into a single homogenised and competitive world is wildly exaggerated (see the Key Debate at the end of this chapter). As in the Chinese retail market (Illustration 8.1), international drivers are usually a lot more complicated than that: Chinese markets are not only very different from Western ones, but vary widely within China itself.

Given internationalisation's complexity, international strategy should be underpinned by a careful assessment of trends in each particular market. Erasmus University's George Yip provides a framework for analysing 'drivers of globalisation'. In the terms of this chapter, these globalisation drivers can be thought of as 'internationalisation drivers' more generally. In this

ILLUSTRATION 8.1

Chinese retail: global or local?

Internationalisation is not a simple process, as supermarket chains Carrefour and Wal-Mart have found in China.

China is a magnet for ambitious Western supermarket chains. With an annual growth rate of 13 per cent a year, the Chinese market is predicted by Business Monitor International to grow in value by $1.2 (~€0.84) trn. between 2009 and 2014. 520 million people are expected to join the Chinese upper middle class by 2025.

Two leading Western companies in the Chinese retail market are French supermarket chain Carrefour and the world's largest retailer, the American Wal-Mart. The two companies have had very different strategies. French supermarket chain Carrefour was the first to enter the Chinese market in a substantial fashion, entering in 1995, after six years' experience in neighbouring Taiwan. Carrefour is following a decentralised strategy: except in Shanghai, where it has several stores, Carrefour allows its local store managers, scattered across the many different regions of China, to make their own purchasing and supply decisions. By 2009, Carrefour was the fifth largest retailer in China, though this meant only 0.6% overall market share. Wal-Mart was close behind with 0.5% share. Wal-Mart's initial approach had been based on its standard centralised purchasing and distribution strategy, supplying as much as it can from its new, state-of-the-art distribution centre in Shenzen. In 2009, however, Wal-Mart experimented with a smaller-scale local store format, which it intends to roll-out nationally. It is also integrating the Chinese operations of a budget Taiwanese retailer.

One early discovery for Wal-Mart was that Chinese consumers prefer frequent shopping trips, buying small quantities each time. While Wal-Mart assumed that Chinese consumers would drive to out-of-town stores and fill their cars with large frozen multi-packs on a once-a-week shop like Americans, in fact Chinese customers would break open the multi-packs to take just the smaller quantities they required. Now Wal-Mart supplies more of its frozen foods loose, offering customers a scoop so they can take exactly the amount they want. Wal-Mart also now allows trade unions into its stores, in marked contrast to its policy in the rest of the world.

Another discovery for Western retailers is the amount of regional variation in this vast and multi-ethnic country. In the north of China, soya sauces are important; in central China, chilli pepper sauces are required; in the south, it is oyster sauces that matter. For fruit, northerners must have dates; southerners want lychees. In the north, the cold means more demand for red meat and, because customers are wearing layers of clothing, wider store aisles. Northerners don't have much access to hot water, so they wash their hair less frequently, meaning that small sachets of shampoo sell better than large bottles. And, unlike other Chinese, apparently the citizens of Zhejiang province like their toilet paper as 'rough as sandpaper'.

The growth of companies such as Carrefour and Wal-Mart demonstrates that there is a substantial market for the Western retail model. Carrefour, for example, was a pioneer of 'private label' goods in China, while Wal-Mart brings logistical expertise. But progress has been slow and Chinese companies such as market-leader GOME have imitated. Wal-Mart has yet to make a profit in China; Carrefour finally is, but its 2–3% margins are significantly below the nearly 5% margins it enjoys in France. In 2008, Carrefour suffered from a Chinese boycott after a Parisian protest over Tibet associated with the Beijing Olympics and in 2009 Carrefour was obliged to deny that it was considering leaving China.

Sources: Financial Times, Wall Street Journal and Euromonitor (various).

Questions

1 What are the pros and cons of the different China strategies pursued by Carrefour and Wal-Mart?

2 What might be the dangers for a large Western retailer in staying out of the Chinese market?

Figure 8.2 **Drivers of internationalisation**

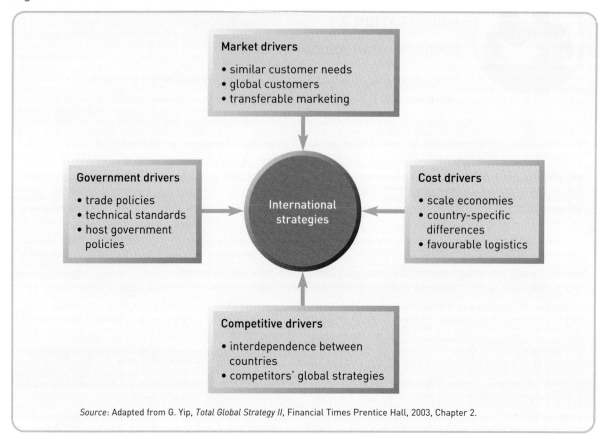

Source: Adapted from G. Yip, *Total Global Strategy II*, Financial Times Prentice Hall, 2003, Chapter 2.

KEY CONCEPT

Yip's globalisation framework

book, therefore, **Yip's globalisation framework** sees international strategy potential as determined by market drivers, cost drivers, government drivers and competitive drivers (see Figure 8.2).[3] In more detail, the four drivers are as follows:

● *Market drivers.* A critical facilitator of internationalisation is standardisation of market characteristics. There are three components underlying this driver. First, the presence of *similar customer needs and tastes*: for example, the fact that in most societies consumers have similar needs for easy credit has promoted the worldwide spread of a handful of credit card companies such as Visa. Second is the presence of *global customers*: for example, car component companies have become more international as their customers, such as Toyota or Ford, have internationalised, and required standardised components for all their factories around the world. Finally, *transferable marketing* promotes market globalisation: brands such as Coca-Cola are still successfully marketed in very similar ways across the world.

● *Cost drivers.* Costs can be reduced by operating internationally. Again, there are three main elements to cost drivers. First, increasing volume beyond what a national market might support can give *scale economies*, both on the production side and in purchasing of supplies. Companies from smaller countries such as the Netherlands and Switzerland tend therefore to become proportionately much more international than companies from the United States, which have a vast market at home. Scale economies are particularly important in industries with high product-development costs, as in the aircraft industry, where initial costs need to be spread over the large volumes of international markets. Second, internationalisation is promoted where it is possible to take advantage of variations in *country-specific differences*. Thus it makes sense to locate the manufacture of clothing in China or Africa, where labour is still considerably cheaper, but to keep design activities in cities such as New York, Paris, Milan or London, where fashion expertise is concentrated. The third element is *favourable logistics*, or the costs of moving products or services across borders relative to their final value. From this point of view, microchips are easy to source internationally, while bulky materials such as assembled furniture are harder.

- *Government drivers.* These can both facilitate and inhibit internationalisation. The relevant elements of policy are numerous, including tariff barriers, technical standards, subsidies to local firms, ownership restrictions, local content requirements, controls over technology transfer, intellectual property (patenting) regimes and currency and capital flow controls. No government allows complete economic openness and openness typically varies widely from industry to industry, with agriculture and high-tech industries related to defence likely to be particularly sensitive. Nevertheless, the World Trade Organization continues to push for greater openness and the European Union and the North American Free Trade Agreement have made significant improvements in their specific regions.[4]

- *Competitive drivers.* These relate specifically to globalisation as an integrated worldwide strategy rather than simpler international strategies. These have two elements. First, *interdependence* between country operations increases the pressure for global coordination. For example, a business with a plant in Mexico serving both the US and the Japanese markets has to coordinate carefully between the three locations: surging sales in one country, or a collapse in another, will have significant knock-on effects on the other countries. The second element relates directly to competitor strategy. The presence of *globalised competitors* increases the pressure to adopt a global strategy in response because competitors may use one country's profits to cross-subsidise their operations in another. A company with a loosely coordinated international strategy is vulnerable to globalised competitors, because it is unable to support country subsidiaries under attack from targeted, subsidised competition. The danger is of piecemeal withdrawal from countries under attack, and the gradual undermining of any overall economies of scale that the international player may have started with.[5]

The key insight from Yip's drivers framework is that the internationalisation potential of industries is variable. There are many different factors that can support or inhibit it, and an important step in determining an internationalisation strategy is a realistic assessment of the true scope for internationalisation in the particular industry. In the Chinese retail case (Illustration 8.1), it may be that the drivers for Western entry are as much competitive as market.

GEOGRAPHIC SOURCES OF ADVANTAGE

As is clear from the earlier discussion of cost drivers in international strategy, the geographical location of activities is a crucial source of potential advantage and one of the distinguishing features of international strategy relative to other diversification strategies. As INSEAD's Bruce Kogut has explained, an organisation can improve the configuration of its *value chain and network*[6] by taking advantage of country-specific differences (see section 3.4.2). There are two principal opportunities available: the exploitation of particular *locational advantages*, often in the company's home country, and sourcing advantages overseas via an *international value network*.

8.3.1 Locational advantage: Porter's Diamond[7]

As for any strategy, internationalisation needs to be based on strategic capabilities providing a sustainable competitive advantage. This competitive advantage has usually to be substantial. After all, a competitor entering a market from overseas typically starts with considerable *dis*advantages relative to existing home competitors, who will usually have superior market knowledge, established relationships with local customers, strong supply chains and the like. A foreign entrant must have significant competitive advantages to overcome such disadvantages. The example of the American giant retailer Wal-Mart provides an illustration: Wal-Mart has been successful in many Asian markets with relatively under-developed retail markets, but was forced to withdraw from Germany's more mature market after nearly a decade of failure in 2006. In Germany, unlike in most Asian markets, Wal-Mart had no significant competitive advantage over domestic retailers.

The sources of sustainable competitive advantage in general are considered in Chapters 3 and 6. However, the international context specifically raises the potential of locational sources of advantage. Countries, and regions within them, often become associated with specific types of enduring competitive advantage: for example, the Swiss in private banking, the northern Italians in leather and fur fashion goods, and the Taiwanese in laptop computers. Michael Porter has proposed a four-pointed 'diamond' to explain why some locations tend to produce firms with sustained competitive advantages in some industries more than others (see

Figure 8.3 Porter's Diamond – the determinants of national advantages

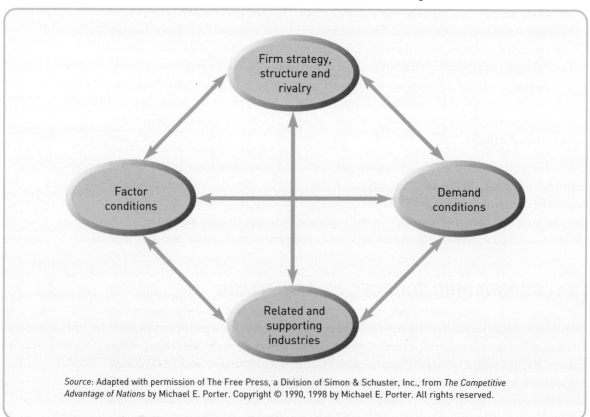

Figure 8.3). Specifically, **Porter's Diamond** suggests that locational advantages may stem from local factor conditions; local demand conditions; local related and supporting industries; and from local firm strategy structure and rivalry. These four interacting determinants of locational advantage work as follows:

Porter's
Diamond

- *Factor conditions.* These refer to the 'factors of production' that go into making a product or service (i.e. raw materials, land and labour). Factor condition advantages at a national level can translate into general competitive advantages for national firms in international markets. For example, the linguistic ability of the Swiss has provided a significant advantage to their banking industry. Cheap energy has traditionally provided an advantage for the North American aluminium industry.

- *Home demand conditions.* The nature of the domestic customers can become a source of competitive advantage. Dealing with sophisticated and demanding customers at home helps train a company to be effective overseas. For example, Japanese customers' high expectations of electrical and electronic equipment provided an impetus for those industries in Japan, leading to global dominance of those sectors. Sophisticated local customers in France and Italy have helped keep their local fashion industries at the leading edge for many decades.

- *Related and supporting industries.* Local 'clusters' of related and mutually supporting industries can be an important source of competitive advantage. These are often regionally based, making personal interaction easier. In northern Italy, for example, the leather footwear industry, the leatherworking machinery industry and the design services which underpin them group together in the same regional cluster to each other's mutual benefit. Silicon Valley forms a cluster of hardware, software, research and venture-capital organisations which together create a virtuous circle of high-technology enterprise.

- *Firm strategy, industry structure and rivalry.* The characteristic strategies, industry structures and rivalries in different countries can also be bases of advantage. German companies' strategy of investing in technical excellence gives them a characteristic advantage in engineering industries and creates large pools of expertise. A competitive local industry structure is also helpful: if too dominant in their home territory, local organisations can become complacent and lose advantage overseas. Some domestic rivalry can actually be an advantage, therefore. For example, the long-run success of the Japanese car companies is partly based on government policy sustaining several national players (unlike in the United Kingdom, where they were all merged into one) and the Swiss pharmaceuticals industry became strong in part because each company had to compete with several strong local rivals.

Porter's Diamond has been used by governments aiming to increase the competitive advantage of their local industries. The argument that rivalry can be positive has led to a major policy shift in many countries towards encouraging local competition rather than protecting home-based industries. Governments can also foster local industries by raising safety or environmental standards (i.e. creating sophisticated demand conditions) or encouraging cooperation between suppliers and buyers on a domestic level (i.e. building clusters of related and supporting industries in particular regions).

For individual organisations, however, the value of Porter's Diamond is to identify the extent to which they can build on home-based advantages to create competitive advantage in relation to others on a global front. For example, Dutch brewing companies – such as Heineken – had an advantage in early internationalisation due to the combination of sophisticated consumers and limited room to grow at home. Benetton, the Italian clothing company, has achieved global success by using its experience of working through a network of largely independent, often family-owned manufacturers to build its network of franchised retailers. Before embarking on an internationalisation strategy, managers should seek out sources of general locational advantage to underpin their company's individual sources of advantage.

8.3.2 The international value network

However, the sources of advantage need not be purely domestic. For international companies, advantage can be drawn from the international configuration of their *value network* (see section 3.4.2). Here the different skills, resources and costs of countries around the world can be systematically exploited in order to locate each element of the value chain in that country or region where it can be conducted most effectively and efficiently. This may be achieved both through foreign direct investments and joint ventures but also through **global sourcing, i.e. purchasing services and components from the most appropriate suppliers around the world, regardless of their location.** For example, in the UK, the National Health Service has been sourcing medical personnel from overseas to offset a shortfall in domestic skills and capacity.

Different locational advantages can be identified:

- *Cost advantages* include labour costs, transportation and communications costs and taxation and investment incentives. Labour costs are important. American and European firms, for example, are increasingly moving software programming tasks to India where a computer programmer costs an American firm about one-quarter of what it would pay for a worker with comparable skills in the USA. As wages in India have risen, Indian IT firms have already begun moving work to even more low-cost locations such as China, with some predicting that subsidiaries of Indian firms will come to control as much as 40 per cent of China's IT service exports.

- *Unique local capabilities* may allow an organisation to enhance its competitive advantage. For example, leading European pharmaceuticals company GSK has R&D laboratories in Boston and the Research Triangle in North Carolina in order to establish research collaborations with the leading universities and hospitals in those areas. Internationalisation, therefore, is increasingly not only about exploiting an organisation's existing capabilities in new national markets, but about developing strategic capabilities by drawing on capabilities found elsewhere in the world.

- *National market characteristics* can enable organisations to develop differentiated product offerings aimed at different market segments. American guitar-maker Gibson, for example, complements its US-made products with often similar, lower-cost alternatives produced in South Korea under the Epiphone brand. However, because of the American music tradition, Gibson's high-end guitars benefit from the reputation of still being 'made in the USA'.

Of course, one of the consequences of organisations trying to exploit the locational advantages available in different countries' organisations can be that they create complex networks of intra- and inter-organisational relationships. Boeing, for example, has developed a global web of R&D activities through its subsidiaries and partnerships with collaborating organisations (see Illustration 8.2).

ILLUSTRATION 8.2

Boeing's global nightmare

Boeing's decision to outsource production of its new Dreamliner aircraft turns into a logistical nightmare.

Work on Boeing's 787 Dreamliner aircraft began in 2003. Test flights did not begin until 2009, two years late. Airlines had cancelled orders and the company had had to pay compensation to customers for delivery delays. The company's CEO, Jim McNerney, admitted in 2009: 'We wouldn't do it exactly the same way. There's plenty of blame to go round. It's not just our suppliers' fault. It's equally our fault in many cases.'

Modern aircraft are tricky to develop. Boeing had experienced delays on its earlier 737 and 747 programmes, and more recently Airbus, the market leader, had significant problems with its giant A380 aircraft. But for Boeing the 787 was crucial to recapturing the lead from Airbus. Boeing was taking a radically different route to its European rival, going for a long-range 250–300, seat jet, by contrast to Airbus's flagship A380 with its potential 853 seats. The project was due to cost Boeing $10bn (~€7bn) in development and involve radically new technologies that would provide 20 per cent gains in fuel efficiency. Most radical of all, however, was the decision to subcontract 70 per cent of production to suppliers around the world.

The roll-call of 50 subcontractors was impressive. For example, in Japan, Mitsubishi would make the wings, Kawasaki would do the forward fuselage, while Fuji would take responsibility for the centre wing box. Sweden's Saab would make the cargo doors, while Italy's Alenia would produce the horizontal stabiliser and central fuselage. More suppliers came from France, Germany, South Korea and the United Kingdom. Back in the United States there were more than ten subcontractors, including such respected names as General Electric and Moog. Three 747 cargo planes, named 'Dreamlifters', were dedicated to transporting the various components from around the world to Boeing's assembly plant in the United States.

There were several potential advantages to this outsourcing. Boeing would get access to the technological expertise of specialists around the world. These specialist subcontractors would supply some of the development funding. The fact that parts of the plane would be made in different countries was likely to help in the sale of aircraft to the respective national airlines. Costs of labour were likely to be lower outside the US and Boeing would have a smaller workforce of its own to manage during the inevitable downturns of the boom-and-bust aircraft industry.

But there were some unanticipated problems. Alenia found itself obliged to replant a 300-year-old olive grove before it could build its factory in southern Italy. Vought, an American supplier, in turn subcontracted some work to an Israeli company, who neglected to supply assembly instructions in English. Boeing had to send its engineers around the world to smooth out technical problems. Back in the United States, Boeing's own workers were unhappy to see so much work go overseas and imposed a 58-day strike during 2008.

Despite all these problems, the Dreamliner looks set for commercial success. Even after cancellations, its launch order book was for a record-breaking 892 aircraft, at $145m a piece. CEO Jim McNerney reflected none the less: 'we have learned a lot and have the scars to prove it'. He promised that Boeing would build later variants of the 787 more in-house.

Source: Flight International, 12 September 2008; *Financial Times*, 14 July 2008; *Reuters*, 22 September 2009.

Questions

1 What are the pros and cons of specifically *international* outsourcing?

2 Boeing will still subcontract some production work for later variants of the 787. What criteria should guide its choice of subcontractors?

(8.4) INTERNATIONAL STRATEGIES

Given the ability to obtain sources of international competitive advantage through home-based factors or international value networks, organisations still face difficult questions about what kinds of strategies to pursue in their markets. Here the key problem is typically the so-called global–local dilemma. **The global–local dilemma relates to the extent to which products and services may be standardised across national boundaries or need to be adapted to meet the requirements of specific national markets.** For some products and services – such as televisions – markets appear similar across the world, offering huge potential scale economies if design, production and delivery can be centralised. For other products and services – such as television programming – tastes still seem highly national-specific, drawing companies to decentralise operations and control as near as possible to the local market. This global–local dilemma can evoke a number of responses from companies pursuing international strategies, ranging from decentralisation to centralisation, with positions in between.

This section introduces four different kinds of international strategy, based on choices about the international *configuration* of the various activities an organisation has to carry out and the degree to which these activities are then *coordinated* internationally (see Figure 8.4). More precisely, configuration refers to the geographical dispersion or concentration of activities such as manufacturing and R&D, while coordination refers to the extent to which operations in different countries are managed in a decentralised way or a centrally coordinated way. The four basic international strategies are:[8]

● *Simple export.* This strategy involves a concentration of activities (particularly manufacturing) in one country, typically the country of the organisation's origin. At the same time, marketing of the exported product is very loosely coordinated overseas, perhaps handled by independent sales agents in different markets. Pricing, packaging, distribution and even branding policies may be determined locally. This strategy is typically chosen by organisations

Figure 8.4 Four international strategies

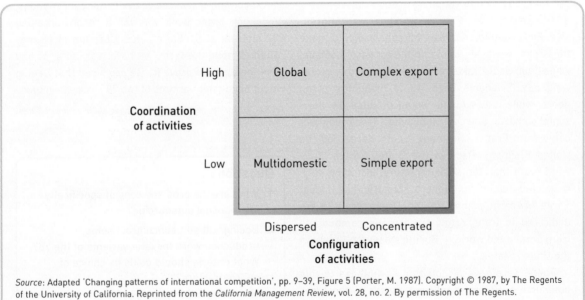

Source: Adapted 'Changing patterns of international competition', pp. 9–39, Figure 5 (Porter, M. 1987). Copyright © 1987, by The Regents of the University of California. Reprinted from the *California Management Review*, vol. 28, no. 2. By permission of The Regents.

with a strong locational advantage – as determined by the Porter Diamond, for example – but where the organisation either has insufficient managerial capabilities to coordinate marketing internationally or where coordinated marketing would add little value, for example in agricultural or raw material commodities.

- *Multidomestic*. This strategy is similarly loosely coordinated internationally, but involves a dispersion overseas of various activities, including manufacturing and sometimes product development. Instead of export, therefore, goods and services are produced locally in each national market. Each market is treated independently, with the needs of each local domestic market given priority – hence 'multidomestic'. Local adaptations can make the overall corporate portfolio increasingly diversified. This strategy is appropriate where there are few economies of scale and strong benefits to adapting to local needs. This multidomestic strategy is particularly attractive in professional services, where local relationships are critical, but it carries risks towards brand and reputation if national practices become too diverse.

- *Complex export*. This strategy still involves location of most activities in a single country, but builds on more coordinated marketing. Economies of scale can still be reaped in manufacturing and R&D, but branding and pricing opportunities are more systematically managed. The coordination demands are, of course, considerably more complex than in the simple export strategy. This is a common stage for companies from emerging economies, as they retain some locational advantages from their home country, but seek to build a stronger brand and network overseas with growing organisational maturity.

- *Global strategy*. This strategy describes the most mature international strategy, with highly coordinated activities dispersed geographically around the world. Using international value networks to the full, geographical location is chosen according to the specific locational advantage for each activity, so that product development, manufacturing, marketing and headquarters functions might all be located in different countries. For example, Detroit-based General Motors designed its Pontiac Le Mans at the firm's German subsidiary, Opel, with its high engineering skills; developed its advertising via a British agency with the creativity strengths of London; produced many of its more complex components in Japan, exploiting the sophisticated manufacturing and technological capabilities; and assembled the car in South Korea, a location where a lower-cost, yet skilled, labour force was available. All this, of course, required high investments and skill in coordination (see also the discussion of the transnational structure in section 13.2.4).

In practice, these four international strategies are not absolutely distinct. Managerial coordination and geographical concentration are matters of degree rather than sharp distinctions. Companies may often oscillate within and between the four strategies. Their choices, moreover, will be influenced by changes in the internationalisation drivers introduced earlier. Where, for example, tastes are highly standardised, companies will tend to favour complex export or global strategies. Where economies of scale are few, the logic is more in favour of multidomestic strategies.

MARKET SELECTION AND ENTRY

Having decided on an international strategy built on significant sources of competitive advantage and supported by strong internationalisation drivers, managers need next to decide which countries to enter. Not all countries are equally attractive. To an extent, however, countries can initially be compared using standard environmental analysis techniques, for example along the dimensions identified in the PESTEL framework (see section 2.2.1) or according to the industry five forces (section 2.3). However, there are specific determinants of market attractiveness that need to be considered in internationalisation strategy, and they can be analysed under two main headings: the intrinsic characteristics of the market and the nature of the competition. A key point here is how initial estimates of country attractiveness can be modified by various measures of *distance* and the likelihood of competitor *retaliation*. The section concludes by considering different *entry modes* into national markets.

8.5.1 Market characteristics

At least four elements of the PESTEL framework are particularly important in comparing countries for entry:

- *Political.* Political environments vary widely between countries and can alter rapidly. Russia since the fall of Communism has seen frequent swings for and against private foreign enterprise. Governments can of course create significant opportunities for organisations. For example, the British government has traditionally promoted the financial services industry in the City of London by offering tax advantages to high-earning financiers from abroad and providing a 'light-touch' regulatory environment. It is important, however, to determine the level of *political risk* before entering a country. Carrefour, for example, found itself the subject of an unexpected consumer boycott in China because of political tensions surrounding Tibet (see Illustration 8.1).

- *Economic.* Key comparators in deciding entry are levels of Gross Domestic Product and disposable income which help in estimating the potential size of the market. Fast-growth economies obviously provide opportunities, and in developing economies such as China and India growth is translating into an even faster creation of a high-consumption middle class. However, companies must also be aware of the stability of a country's currency, which may affect its income stream. There can be considerable *currency risk*: thus British companies that relied on international subcontractors faced increased costs as the value of sterling fell during the economic crisis of 2009–10.

- *Social.* Social factors will clearly be important, for example the availability of a well-trained workforce or the size of demographic market segments – old or young – relevant to the strategy. Cultural variations need to be considered, for instance in defining tastes in the marketplace.

- *Legal.* Countries vary widely in their legal regime, determining the extent to which businesses can enforce contracts, protect intellectual property or avoid corruption. Similarly, policing will be important for the security of employees, a factor that in the past has deterred business in some South American countries.

A common procedure is to rank country markets against each other on criteria such as these and then to choose the countries for entry that offer the highest relative scores. However, Pankaj Ghemawat from Spain's IESE business school has pointed out that what matters is not just the attractiveness of different countries relative to each other, but also the compatibility of the countries with the internationalising firm itself.[9]

Thus Ghemawat underlines the importance of *match* between country and firm. For firms coming from any particular country, some countries are more 'distant' – or mismatched – than

ILLUSTRATION 8.3

Vale – a Brazilian giant in different cultures

Rapid overseas expansion brings this Brazilian multinational some contrasting experiences.

Until the late 1990s, Brazil's Vale mining company was a state-owned sleeping giant. 2001 brought the appointment as CEO of 42-year-old former investment banker Roger Agnelli, since when the company has transfomed itself into a dynamic conglomerate. Agnelli commented in 2010: 'Vale used to be fundamentally an iron-ore company. We used to operate essentially in Brazil. Now we are in 36 countries.' Vale is the world's largest producer of iron ore, the second largest producer of nickel and has a declared ambition of being one of the world's largest fertiliser producers. It has copper operations in South Africa, steel in California and coal in Australia.

Nevertheless, iron ore remains the driver of the business. The booming Chinese market has been a gift. Between 2001 and 2009, Vale's iron ore production increased from 122m tonnes to 300m tonnes, with China alone accounting for approaching half of all sales. In the recession year of 2009, iron ore was still profitable, while its non-ferrous and coal activities were by and large unprofitable. However, the nickel business in Canada and the coal business in Mozambique offer very contrasting insights into the challenges of Vale's new international businesses.

Vale's $17.6bn (~€12.3bn) takeover in 2006 of Inco, the world's largest nickel producer, was its first major overseas acquisition. Canada's largest national newspaper, the *Globe and Mail*, described Vale's arrival as 'The great Canadian mining disaster'. Many Canadians resented this takeover by what they regarded as a business from a developing country. The first top manager sent over by Vale spoke poor English. Of 29 senior Canadian managers in early 2007, three years later 23 had departed, mostly voluntarily. The Canadians regarded nickel, which requires underground mining and goes into many high-tech businesses, as technically much more complex than iron ore, a surface-mined basic commodity. According to the *Financial Times*, one Canadian manager said that iron ore was a high

school diploma business, nickel was a PhD business. At one tense meeting a Brazilian manager riposted: 'How come, if you're so smart, you didn't take *us* over?'. In July 2009, Inco's Canadian workers went on strike, remaining so into 2010.

A contrast so far has been Vale's experience in Mozambique. Like many Brazilian companies, Vale has been attracted to the two African countries of Angola and Mozambique because of the shared cultural and linguistic heritage of Portuguese colonialism. About half the 3m black African slaves sent to Brazil between 1700 and 1850 came from Angola and in the 1820s, settlers in Angola and Mozambique applied to join the newly independent Brazil in a federation. Mozambique has some of the largest coal reserves in the world, but rudimentary infrastructure. Vale is working with Odebrecht, a Brazilian construction company, to develop not only the coal reserves, but to build a power station and the rail and port infrastructure necessary to get the coal to international markets. So vast is the task that Odebrecht has become Mozambique's largest single employer. Vale is planning £830m (€950m) of investment in Mozambique over the next couple of years. Agnelli is enthusiastic about long-term African prospects: 'The thing about Africa is that sooner or later it will become a reality . . . Africa is the future of the world's natural resources – along with South America.'

Sources: 'Vale's transformation', *Financial Times*, 25 February 2010; 'Brazil accelerates investment in Africa'. *Financial Times*, 9 February 2010; 'Heading in opposite directions', *Financial Times*, 11 February 2010.

Questions

1 Is there any downside to Vale's ties to the Chinese market, and what should Vale do to mitigate this?

2 Suggest three reasons for Vale's different reception in Canada and Mozambique.

others. For example, a Spanish company might be 'closer' to a South American market than an East Asian market and might therefore prefer that market even if it ranked lower on standard criteria of attractiveness. As well as a relative ranking of countries, therefore, each company has to add its assessment of countries in terms of closeness of match.

Ghemawat's 'CAGE framework' measures the match between countries and companies according to four dimensions of distance, reflected by the letters of the acronym. Thus the **CAGE framework emphasises the importance of cultural, administrative, geographical and economic distance**, as follows:

● *Cultural distance*. The distance dimension here relates to differences in language, ethnicity, religion and social norms. Cultural distance is not just a matter of similarity in consumer tastes, but extends to important compatibilities in terms of managerial behaviours. Here, for example, US firms might be closer to Canada than to Mexico, which Spanish firms might find relatively compatible. Figure 8.5 draws on the GLOBE survey of 17,000 managers from 62 different societal cultures around the world to contrast specifically the orientations of American and Chinese managers on some key cultural dimensions. According to this

Figure 8.5 International cross-cultural comparison

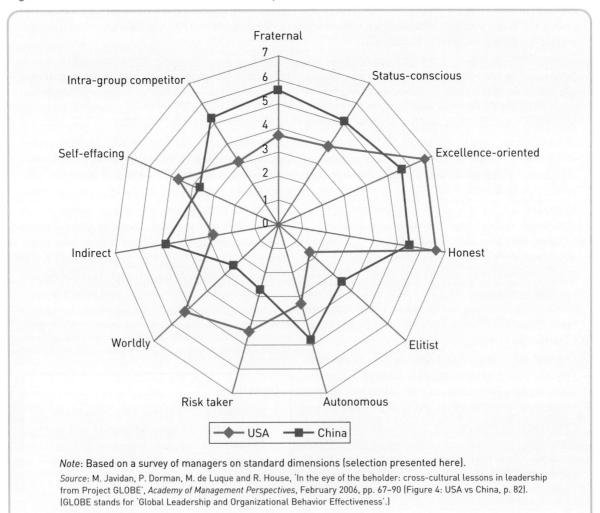

Note: Based on a survey of managers on standard dimensions (selection presented here).

Source: M. Javidan, P. Dorman, M. de Luque and R. House, 'In the eye of the beholder: cross-cultural lessons in leadership from Project GLOBE', *Academy of Management Perspectives*, February 2006, pp. 67–90 (Figure 4: USA vs China, p. 82). (GLOBE stands for 'Global Leadership and Organizational Behavior Effectiveness'.)

GLOBE survey, American managers appear to be typically more risk-taking, while Chinese managers are more autonomous.

- *Administrative and political distance.* Here distance is in terms of incompatible administrative, political or legal traditions. Colonial ties can diminish difference, so that the shared heritage of France and its former West African colonies creates certain understandings that go beyond linguistic advantages. See also, for example, the experience of the Brazilian Vale company in Mozambique, where shared Portuguese heritage made a difference (Illustration 8.3). Institutional weaknesses – for example slow or corrupt administration – can open up distance between countries. So too can political differences: Chinese companies are increasingly able to operate in parts of the world that American companies are finding harder, for example parts of the Middle East and Africa.

- *Geographical distance.* This is not just a matter of the kilometres separating one country from another, but involves other geographical characteristics of the country such as size, sea-access and the quality of communications infrastructure. For example, Wal-Mart's difficulties in Europe relate to the fact that its logistics systems were developed in the geographically enormous space of North America, and proved much less suitable for the smaller and denser countries of Europe. Transport infrastructure can shrink or exaggerate physical distance. France is much closer to large parts of Continental Europe than to the United Kingdom, because of the barrier presented by the English Channel and Britain's relatively poor road and rail infrastructure.

- *Economic.* The final element of the CAGE framework refers particularly to wealth distances. There are of course huge disparities in wealth internationally: around the world, there are 4–5 billion people in 2010 beneath the poverty threshold of income less than $2 a day.[10] Multinationals from rich countries are typically weak at serving such very poor consumers. However, these rich-country multinationals are losing out on large markets if they only concentrate on the wealthy elites overseas. University of Michigan academic C.K. Prahalad points out that the aggregated wealth of those at the 'base of the pyramid' in terms of income distribution is very substantial: simple mathematics means that those 4–5 billion below the poverty threshold represent a market of more than $2000bn per year. If rich-country multinationals can develop new capabilities to serve these numerically huge markets, they can bridge the economic distance, and thereby both significantly extend their presence in booming economies such as China and India and bring to these poor consumers the benefits that are claimed for Western goods. See Illustration 8.4 for examples of innovative base-of-the-pyramid strategies in India.

8.5.2 Competitive characteristics

Assessing the relative attractiveness of markets by PESTEL and CAGE analyses is only the first step. The second element relates to competition. Here, of course, Michael Porter's five forces framework can help (see section 2.3). For example, country markets with many existing competitors, powerful buyers (perhaps large retail chains such as in much of North America and Northern Europe) and low barriers to further new entrants from overseas would typically be unattractive. However, an additional consideration is the likelihood of retaliation from other competitors.

In the five forces framework, retaliation potential relates to rivalry, but managers can extend this by using insights directly from 'game theory' (see section 6.4.4). Here the likelihood and

ILLUSTRATION 8.4

Base of the Pyramid strategies

In India, Base of the Pyramid strategy means more than just low prices. Base of the Pyramid involves reshaping distribution channels, designing new products and forming partnerships.

Distribution channels

Procter & Gamble, the global consumer goods company, generates $20bn (~€14bn) worth of sales from developing markets. To reach poorer communities, however, it has to rely on tiny, crowded and often chaotic retail stores. Its strong brands and expensive packaging were often hidden from view underneath a ramshackle counter. Procter & Gamble has therefore hired a team of local sales agents in order to build ties with store owners, to educate them in the importance of display and to negotiate better shelf space for its products.

Product design

Nokia, the world's largest mobile phone company, has three R&D facilities in India. In order to serve markets where electricity is hard to find, they have produced a mobile phone that can operate for more than two weeks on a single charge – and which comes with a flashlight. Recognising that phones are often too costly on an individual basis, Nokia's phone allows friends and families to share a device by maintaining as many as five separate phone books and providing controls on how much any individual user can talk or spend.

Partnerships

Coca-Cola has developed an orange-flavoured fortified beverage called Vitingo, which will sell in 18 gram packets at Rs 2.50 (€0.04) each. The beverage has added nutrients (iron, vitamin C, folic acid and so on) to compensate for deficiencies in many poor people's diet, a problem called 'Hidden Hunger'. After a successful pilot project, during 2009 Coca-Cola is entering 30 Orissa districts in partnership with the local non-governmental organisation and micro-finance insitution BISWA.

Sources: The Economic Times, 11 January 2010; People and Strategy, 1 April 2009.

Questions

1 Can you imagine any risks or dangers that Western companies might face in pursuing Base of the Pyramid strategies?

2 Is there anything that Western companies might learn from Base of the Pyramid strategies in emerging markets that might be valuable in their home markets?

---

ferocity of potential competitor reactions are added to the simple calculation of relative country market attractiveness. As in Figure 8.6, country markets can be assessed according to three criteria:[11]

- *Market attractiveness* to the new entrant, based on PESTEL, CAGE and five forces analyses, for example. In Figure 8.6, countries A and B are the most attractive to the entrant.

- *Defender's reactiveness*, likely to be influenced by the market's attractiveness to the defender but also by the extent to which the defender is working with a globally integrated, rather than multidomestic, strategy. A defender will be more reactive if the markets are important to it and it has the managerial capabilities to coordinate its response. Here, the defender is highly reactive in countries A and D.

Figure 8.6 International competitor retaliation

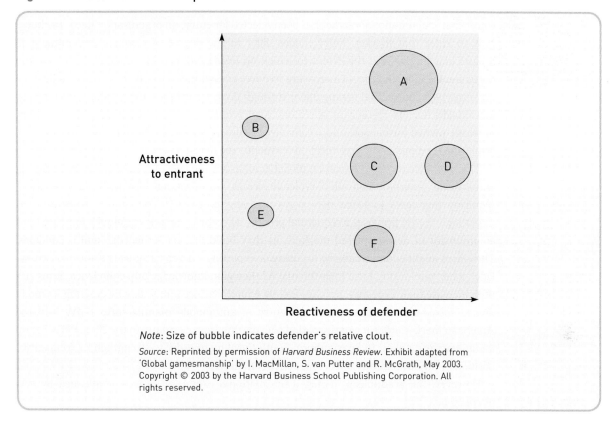

Note: Size of bubble indicates defender's relative clout.

- *Defender's clout*, i.e. the power that the defender is able to muster in order to fight back. Clout is typically a function of share in the particular market, but might be influenced by connections to other powerful local players, such as retailers or government. In Figure 8.6, clout is represented by the size of the bubbles, with the defender having most clout in countries A, C, D and F.

Choice of country to enter can be significantly modified by adding reactiveness and clout to calculations of attractiveness. Relying only on attractiveness, the top-ranked country to enter in Figure 8.6 is country A. Unfortunately, it is also one in which the defender is highly reactive, and the one in which it has most clout. Country B becomes a better international move than A. In turn, country C is a better prospect than country D, because, even though they are equally attractive, the defender is less reactive. One surprising result of taking defender reactiveness and clout into account is the re-evaluation of country E: although ranked fifth on simple attractiveness, it might rank overall second if competitor retaliation is allowed for.

This sort of analysis is particularly fruitful for considering the international moves of two interdependent competitors, such as Unilever and Procter & Gamble or British Airways and Singapore Airlines. In these cases the analysis is relevant to any aggressive strategic move, for instance the expansion of existing operations in a country as well as initial entry. Especially in the case of globally integrated competitors, moreover, the overall clout of the defender must be taken into account. The defender may choose to retaliate in other markets than the targeted one, counter-attacking wherever it has the clout to do damage to the aggressor. Naturally, too, this kind of analysis can be applied to interactions between diversified competitors as well as international ones: each bubble could represent different products or services.

8.5.3 Entry modes

Once a particular national market has been selected for entry, an organisation needs to choose how to enter that market. Entry modes differ in the degree of resource commitment to a particular market and the extent to which an organisation is operationally involved in a particular location. In order of increasing resource commitment, the four key entry mode types are: *exporting*; contractual arrangement through *licensing and franchising* to local partners, as McDonald's does to restaurant operators; *joint ventures*, in other words the establishment of jointly owned businesses; and *wholly owned subsidiaries*, either through the acquisition of established companies or 'greenfield' investments, the development of facilities from scratch.

The *staged international expansion* model emphasises the role of experience in determining entry mode. Internationalisation typically brings organisations into unfamiliar territory, requiring managers to learn new ways of doing business.[12] The **staged international expansion model proposes a sequential process whereby companies gradually increase their commitment to newly entered markets, as they build market knowledge and capabilities.** Thus firms might enter initially by licensing or exporting, thereby acquiring some local knowledge while minimising local investments. As they gain knowledge and confidence, firms can then increase their exposure, perhaps first by a joint venture and finally by creating a wholly owned subsidiary. An example is the entry of automobile manufacturer BMW into the American market. After a lengthy period of exporting from Germany to the USA, BMW set up a manufacturing plant in Spartanburg, South Carolina in order to strengthen its competitive position in the strategically important American market.

However, the gradualism of staged international expansion is now challenged by two phenomena:

- *'Born-global firms'*, in other words new small firms that internationalise rapidly at early stages in their development.[13] New technologies now help small firms link up to international sources of expertise, supply and customers worldwide. For such firms, waiting till they have enough international experience is not an option: international strategy is a condition of existence. GNI, the mini-multinational in Illustration 8.5, illustrates this born-global process.

- *Emerging-country multinationals* also often move quickly through entry modes. Prominent examples are the Chinese white-goods multinational Haier, the Indian pharmaceuticals company Ranbaxy Laboratories and Mexico's Cemex cement company.[14] Such companies typically develop *unique capabilities* in their home market that then need to be rolled out quickly worldwide before competitors catch up. For example, Haier became skilled at very efficient production of simple white goods, providing a cost advantage that is transferable outside its Chinese manufacturing base. Haier now has factories in Italy and the United States, as well as the Philippines, Malaysia, Indonesia, Egypt, Nigeria and elsewhere round the world.

Where the demands and pace of international competition rule out more gradualist staged expansion, two fundamental principles can help guide choice of market entry mode:

- *The breadth of competitive advantage* in the target market. This determines whether entry into the market can be done relying upon the company's own capabilities, or whether it must draw on the capabilities of local partners, for instance to access distribution channels or to manufacture locally.

ILLUSTRATION 8.5

The mini-multinational

GNI, a biotechnology start-up, has fewer than one hundred employees, but operates in five countries in four continents.

Christopher Savoie is a US entrepreneur who originally studied medicine in Japan, becoming fluent in Japanese and adopting Japanese citizenship. In 2001, he founded GNI, a biotechnology company that by 2006 had raised ¥3bn (€20m; $14m) in investment funds, including a stake from famed global investment bank Goldman Sachs. The company already has operations in Tokyo and Fukuoka, Japan; in Shanghai, China; in Cambridge and London, UK; and in San Jose in California. There is also collaboration with a laboratory in Auckland, New Zealand. Savoie comments: 'We take the best in each country and put them together'.

GNI's strategy is to focus on Asian ailments that have been neglected by big Western pharmaceutical companies, for example stomach cancer and hepatitis. According to Savoie: 'Asia has been getting the short end of the stick. As a small company, we had to choose a niche, and we thought that half of humanity was an acceptable place to start.'

GNI's scientists work on umbilical cords, providing genetic tissue that has been virtually unaffected by the environment. However, Japanese parents traditionally keep their children's umbilical cords. GNI therefore works with the Rosie Maternity Hospital in Cambridge to source its basic genetic materials. On the other hand, GNI in Japan has ready access to supercomputers, and Japanese scientists have worked out the algorithms required to analyse the genetic codes. Japan also has been the main source of investment funds, where regulations on start-ups are relaxed. China comes in as an effective place to test treatments on patients. Regulatory advantages mean that trials can be carried out more quickly in China, moreover for one tenth of the cost of Japan. In 2005, GNI merged with Shanghai Genomics, a start-up run by two US-educated entrepreneurs. Meanwhile, in San Jose, there is a business development office seeking out relationships with the big American pharmaceutical giants.

Savoie describes the business model as essentially simple: 'We have a Chinese cost structure, Japanese supercomputers and, in Cambridge, access to ethical materials (umbilical cords) and top clinical scientists. This is a network we can use to take high-level science and turn it into molecules to compete with the big boys.'

Sources: D. Pilling, 'March of the Mini-Multinational', *Financial Times*, 4 May 2006; www.gene-networks.com.

Questions

1 Analyse GNI's value network in terms of cost advantages, unique capabilities and national characteristics.

2 What managerial challenges will GNI face as it grows?

- *Tradability*, in other words the ability to rely on trading relationships, rather than the firm's own presence. Tradability is determined by two factors: ease of transport from home country to target country, and the quality of legal protection in the target country. Legal protection refers for example to the ability to enforce contracts, to safeguard performance standards or to protect intellectual property such as patented technologies. Tradability is low where it is unsafe to trade through market-based contracts with local partners.

Other case-specific factors are liable to enter the calculation of appropriate entry mode as well, not least the availability of suitable local partners. Nonetheless, the two principles of

Figure 8.7 **Modes of international market entry**

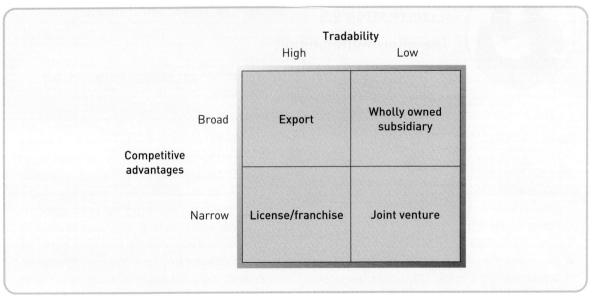

competitive advantage and tradability do suggest the following broad guidelines for entry mode (Figure 8.7):

- *Export* is the baseline option, and is suitable where the product or services are easily transported from country to country and where the home-based competitive advantages are sufficiently broad to minimise reliance on local companies.

- *License or franchise* the product or service where competitive advantages are too narrow to go it alone, but the legal environment is such that licensees and franchisees can be relied on not to abuse their contracts, under-perform on standards or steal the intellectual property.

- *Joint ventures* work where competitive advantages are narrow, but local licensees or franchisees cannot be trusted with intellectual property or long-term performance. A joint venture involving shared ownership gives the foreign company more direct control and ensures that the local partner has an interest in maximising the value of the common enterprise rather than solely their own stand-alone interests.

- *Wholly owned subsidiary* is an attractive route where competitive advantages are sufficiently broad not to depend on local partners, but where nonetheless transport difficulties rule out simple export. Such wholly owned subsidiaries can be via new 'greenfield' investments (as for example many Japanese car companies have entered European markets) or via acquisition, where the integration of a local firm completes the breadth of competitive advantage required.

(8.6) INTERNATIONALISATION AND PERFORMANCE

Just as for product and service diversity discussed in section 7.4 the relationship between internationalisation and performance has been extensively researched.[15] Some of the main findings from such research are these:

● *An inverted U-curve.* While the potential performance benefits of internationalisation are substantial, in that it allows firms to realise economies of scale and scope and benefit from the locational advantages available in countries around the globe, the combination of diverse locations and diverse business units also gives rise to high levels of organisational complexity. After a point, the costs of organisational complexity may exceed the benefits of internationalisations. Accordingly, theory and the balance of evidence suggest an inverted U-shaped relationship between internationalisation and performance (similar to the findings on product/service diversification shown in section 7.4), with moderate levels of internationalisation leading to the best results. However, Yip's recent research on large British companies suggests that managers may be getting better at internationalisation, with substantially internationalised firms actually seeing performance improving at the point where international sales are above about 40 per cent of total sales.[16] Experience and commitment to internationalisation may be able to deliver strong performance for highly internationalised firms.

● *Service-sector disadvantages.* A number of studies have suggested that, in contrast to firms in the manufacturing sector, internationalisation may not lead to improved performance for service-sector firms. There are three possible reasons for such an effect. First, the operations of foreign service firms in some sectors (such as accountants or banks) remain tightly regulated and restricted in many countries; second, due to the intangible nature of services, they are often more sensitive to cultural differences and require greater adaptation than manufactured products which may lead to higher initial learning costs; third, the services typically require a significant local presence and reduces the scope for the exploitation of economies of scale in production compared to manufacturing firms.[17]

● *Internationalisation and product diversity.* An important question to consider is the interaction between internationalisation and product/service diversification. Compared to single-business firms it has been suggested that product-diversified firms are likely to do better from international expansion because they have already developed the necessary skills and structures for managing internal diversity.[18] At the other end of the spectrum there is general consensus that firms that are highly diversified both in terms of product and international markets are likely to face excessive costs of coordination and control leading to poor performance. As many firms have not yet reached levels of internationalisation where negative effects outweigh possible gains and because of current scepticism with regard to the benefits of high levels of product diversification, many companies currently opt for reducing their product diversity whilst building their international scope. Unilever, for example, has been combining a strategy of growing internationalisation with de-diversification.

(8.7) ROLES IN AN INTERNATIONAL PORTFOLIO

Just as for product diversification, international strategies imply different relationships between subsidiary operations and the corporate centre. The complexity of the strategies followed by organisations such as General Electric or Unilever can result in highly differentiated networks of subsidiaries with a range of distinct strategic roles. Subsidiaries may play different roles according to the level of local resources and capabilities available to them and the strategic importance of their local environment (see Figure 8.8).[19]

Figure 8.8 Subsidiary roles in multinational firms

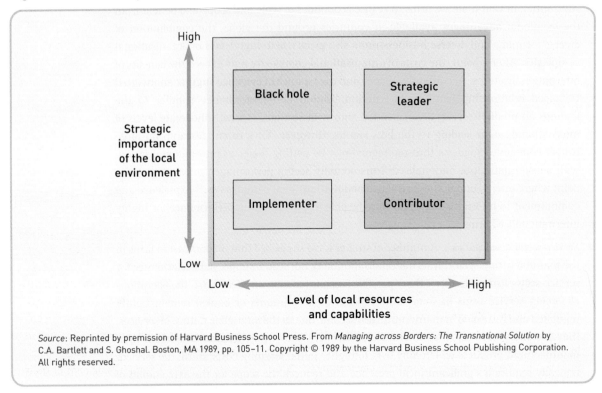

Source: Reprinted by premission of Harvard Business School Press. From *Managing across Borders: The Transnational Solution* by C.A. Bartlett and S. Ghoshal. Boston, MA 1989, pp. 105–11. Copyright © 1989 by the Harvard Business School Publishing Corporation.

- *Strategic leaders* are subsidiaries that not only hold valuable resources and capabilities but are also located in countries that are crucial for competitive success because of, for example, the size of the local market or the accessibility of key technologies. Japanese and European subsidiaries in the United States often play this role.

- *Contributors* are subsidiaries located in countries of lesser strategic significance, but with sufficiently valuable internal capabilities to nevertheless play key roles in a multinational organisation's competitive success. The Australian subsidiary of the Swedish telecommunications firm Ericsson played such a role in developing specialised systems for the firm's mobile phone business.

- *Implementers*, though not contributing substantially to the enhancement of a firm's competitive advantage, are important in the sense that they help generate vital financial resources. In this sense, they are similar to the 'cash cows' of the Boston Consulting Group matrix. The danger is that they turn into the equivalent of 'dogs'.

- *Black holes* are subsidiaries located in countries that are crucial for competitive success but with low-level resources or capabilities. This is a position many subsidiaries of American and European firms found themselves in over long periods in Japan. They have some of the characteristics of 'question marks' in the Boston Consulting Group matrix, requiring heavy investment (like an astrophysicist's black hole, sucking matter in). Possibilities for overcoming this unattractive position include the development of alliances and the selective and targeted development of key resources and capabilities.[20]

These various subsidiary roles relate to how these subsidiaries are generally controlled and managed, and this is discussed in Chapter 13.

KEY DEBATE

Global, local or regional?

Debate rages over whether companies are really becoming more global, or whether local or indeed regional pressures remain strong.

Ted Levitt, Harvard Business School professor and former non-executive director of the international advertising firm Saatchi & Saatchi, has provocatively made the case for deep commitment to global strategies in all kinds of markets. He argues that modern communications technologies are creating homogeneous market needs, while manufacturing technologies are increasing the benefits of scale. Given the cost advantages of scale, and the diminishing importance of consumer differences, companies that commit to truly global strategies will be able to use low prices to sweep out all competitors still focused on local needs. He argues: 'The global company will seek to standardize its offering everywhere . . . Companies that do not adapt to the new global realities will become victims of those that do.' He cites Coca-Cola, Rolex, Sony and McDonald's as exemplars of the trend. Companies should not hanker over detailed differences left over from the past, but recognise the big picture of coming globalisation.

Levitt's sweeping argument brought a spirited response from American academics Gerry Wind and Susan Douglas, warning of 'the Myth of Globalization'. They challenge both the trend to homogenisation and the growing role of scale economies. Even apparently global companies adapt to country needs: for example Coca-Cola sells local products in Japan alongside its classic Coke, and its Dasani bottled water is a success in the United States, but a failure in Europe. As to scale, new flexible automation technologies may even be reducing economic order sizes, allowing short production runs adapted to local needs. Besides, as the world gets richer, consumers will be less price-sensitive and more ready to spend on indulging their local tastes. Wind and Douglas warn that blind confidence in the inevitability of globalisation will surely lead to business disappointment.

Between the two poles of global and local there is a third position: regional. Pankaj Ghemawat points out that most international trade is intra-regional.

European countries trade predominantly with each other. The trend towards intra-regional trade is actually growing, from about 40 per cent of all trade forty years ago to 55 per cent at the beginning of the 21st century. This is reflected in the nature of multinational companies as well. Alan Rugman calculates that in the early years of the 21st century over 300 out of the world's largest corporations still have more than half their sales in their home region. An apparently global company like McDonald's is effectively bi-regional, with eighty per cent of its sales concentrated in North America and Europe. Established multinationals such as General Electric and Procter & Gamble have 60 per cent and 55 per cent of their sales respectively back home in North America.

Ted Levitt might be impatient with these empirical details. The essential issue for him is: where are things going in the future? Certainly there are still local differences in taste, but are these declining overall? Maybe there is a growth of intra-regional trade, but is this just the result of transitional events such as the creation of the North American Free Trade Association or the sucking-in of imports by China? We should not be distracted by temporary blips on the grand highway to global integration.

Sources: T. Levitt, 'The globalization of markets', *Harvard Business Review*, May–June (1983), pp. 92–102; Wind and Douglas, Columbia; P. Ghemawat, 'Regional strategies for global leadership', *Harvard Business Review*, December (2005), 98–108; A. Rugman, *The Regional Multinationals* (2005), Cambridge University Press.

Questions

1 Make a list of products and services which are getting more 'global' over time; then make a list of products and services which are still very 'local'.

2 How many countries in the world have you visited in your lifetime? How many countries had your parents visited by the same age?

SUMMARY

● Internationalisation potential in any particular market is determined by Yip's four drivers: market, cost, government and competitors' strategies.

● Sources of advantage in international strategy can be drawn from both global sourcing through the international value network and national sources of advantage, as captured in Porter's Diamond.

● There are four main types of international strategy, varying according to extent of coordination and geographical configuration: simple export, complex export, multidomestic and global.

● Market selection for international entry or expansion should be based on attractiveness, multidimensional measures of distance and expectations of competitor retaliation.

● Modes of entry into new markets include export, licensing and franchising, joint ventures and overseas subsidiaries.

● Internationalisation has an uncertain relationship to financial performance, with an inverted U-curve warning against over-internationalisation.

● Subsidiaries in an international firm can be managed by portfolio methods just like businesses in a diversified firm.

WORK ASSIGNMENTS

✱ *Denotes more advanced work assignments.* * *Refers to a case study in the Text and Case edition.*

8.1 Using Figure 8.2 (Yip's internationalisation drivers), compare two markets you are familiar with and analyse how strong each of the drivers is for increased international strategy.

8.2✱ Taking an industry you are familiar with that is strong in your home country (for example, fashion in France, cars in Germany), use the four determinants of Porter's Diamond (Figure 8.3) to explain that industry's national advantage.

8.3 Using the four international strategies of Figure 8.4, classify the international strategy of Tesco*, Ekomate* or any other multinational corporation with which you are familiar.

8.4✱ Using the CAGE framework (section 8.5.1), assess the relative 'distance' of the United States, China, India and France for a British company (or a company from a country of your choice).

8.5✱ Take any part of the public or not-for-profit sector (for example, education, health) and explain how far internationalisation has affected its management and consider how far it may do so in the future.

Integrative assignment

8.6 As in 8.3, use the four international strategies of Figure 8.4 to classify the international strategy of Tesco*, Ekomate* or any other multinational corporation with which you are familiar. Drawing on section 13.2, how does this corporation's organisational structure fit (or not fit) this strategy?

VIDEO ASSIGNMENT

Visit **MyStrategyLab** and watch the *Electrolux* case study.

1 Describe Electrolux's changing international strategy in terms of the four strategies of Figure 8.4. Why is it changing in this way?

2 What roles could a large subsidiary such as the Italian Zanussi play in the Electrolux international portfolio (see Figure 8.8.)?

RECOMMENDED KEY READINGS

- An eye-opening introduction to the detailed workings – and inefficiencies – of today's global economy today is P. Rivoli, *The Travels of a T-Shirt in the Global Economy: an Economist Examines the Markets, Power and Politics of World Trade*, Wiley, 2006. A more optimistic view is in T. Friedman, *The World Is Flat: the Globalized World in the Twenty-First Century*, Penguin, 2006.

- An invigorating perspective on international strategy is provided by G. Yip, *Total Global Strategy II*, Prentice Hall, 2003. A comprehensive general textbook is S. Segal-Horn and D. Faulkner, *Understanding Global Strategy*, Southwestern, 2010.

- A useful collection of academic articles on international business is in A. Rugman and T. Brewer (eds), *The Oxford Handbook of International Business*, Oxford University Press, 2003.

REFERENCES

1. For another cautious view, see M. Alexander and H. Korine, 'Why you shouldn't go global', *Harvard Business Review*, December (2008), pp. 70–7.

2. T. Friedman, *The World Is Flat: the Globalized World in the Twenty-First Century*, Penguin, 2006 and P. Rivoli, *The Travels of a T-Shirt in the Global Economy: an Economist Examines the Markets, Power and Politics of World Trade*, Wiley, 2006.

3. G. Yip, *Total Global Strategy II*, Prentice Hall, 2003.

4. Useful industry-specific data on trends in openness to trade and investment can be found at the World Trade Organization's site, www.wto.org.

5. G. Hamel and C.K. Prahalad, 'Do you really have a global strategy?', *Harvard Business Review*, vol. 63, no. 4 (1985), pp. 139–48.

6. B. Kogut, 'Designing global strategies: comparative and competitive value added changes', *Sloan Management Review*, vol. 27 (1985), pp. 15–28.

7. M. Porter, *The Competitive Advantage of Nations*, Macmillan, 1990.

8. This typology builds on the basic framework of M. Porter, 'Changing patterns of international competition', *California Management Review*, vol. 28, no. 2 (1987), pp. 9–39, but adapts its terms for the four strategies into more readily understandable terms: note particularly that here 'global' strategy is transposed to refer to the top left box, and the top right box is described as 'complex export'.

9. P. Ghemawat, 'Distance still matters', *Harvard Business Review*, September (2001), 137–47.

10. C.K. Prahalad and A. Hammond, 'Serving the world's poor, profitably', *Harvard Business Review*, September (2002), 48–55; Economist Intelligence Unit, 'From subsistence to sustainable: a bottom-up perspective on the role of business in poverty alleviation', 24 April 2009.

11. This framework is introduced in I. MacMillan, A. van Putten and R. McGrath, 'Global Gamesmanship', *Harvard Business Review*, vol. 81, no. 5 (2003), pp. 62–71.

12. For detailed discussions about of the role of learning and experience in market entry see: M.F. Guillén, 'Experience, imitation, and the sequence of foreign entry: wholly owned and joint-venture manufacturing by South Korean firms and business groups in China, 1987–1995', *Journal of International Business Studies*, vol. 83 (2003), pp. 185–98; and M.K. Erramilli, 'The experience factor in foreign market entry modes by service firms', *Journal of International Business Studies*, vol. 22, no. 3 (1991), pp. 479–501.

13. G. Knights and T. Cavusil, 'A taxonomy of born-global firms', *Management International Review*, vol. 45, no. 3 (2005), pp. 15–35.

14. For analyses of emerging-country multinationals, see T. Khanna and K. Palepu, 'Emerging giants: building world-class companies in developing countries', *Harvard Business Review*, October (2006), pp. 60–9 and the special

issue on 'The internationalization of Chinese and Indian firms – trends, motivations and strategy', *Industrial and Corporate Change*, vol. 18, no. 2 (2009).

15. A useful review of the international dimension is: M. Hitt and R.E. Hoskisson, 'International diversification: effects on innovation and firm performance in product-diversified firms', *Academy of Management Journal*, vol. 40, no. 4 (1997), pp. 767–98.

16. For detailed results on British companies, see G. Yip, A. Rugman and A. Kudina, 'International success of British companies', *Long Range Planning*, vol. 39, no. 1 (2006), pp. 241–64.

17. See N. Capar and M. Kotabe, 'The relationship between international diversification and performance in service firms', *Journal of International Business Studies*, vol. 34 (2003), pp. 345–55; F.J. Contractor, S.K. Kundu and C. Hsu, 'A three-stage theory of international expansion: the link between multinationality and performance in the service sector', *Journal of International Business Studies*, vol. 34 (2003), pp. 5–18.

18. S.C. Chang and C.-F. Wang, 'The effect of product diversification strategies on the relationship between international diversification and firm performance', *Journal of World Business*, vol. 42, no. 1 (2007), pp. 61–79.

19. C.A. Bartlett and S. Ghosal, *Managing across Borders: the Transnational Solution*, The Harvard Business School Press, 1989, pp. 105–11; A.M. Rugman and A. Verbeke, 'Extending the theory of the multinational enterprise: internalization and strategic management perspectives', *Journal of International Business Studies*, vol. 34 (2003), pp. 125–37.

20. For a more far-reaching exploration of the role of subsidiaries in multinational corporations, see J. Birkinshaw, *Entrepreneurship and the Global Firm*, Sage, 2000.

CASE EXAMPLE

Lenovo computers: East meets West

Introduction

In May 2005, the world's thirteenth largest personal computer company, Lenovo, took over the world's third largest personal computer business, IBM's PC division. Lenovo, at that time based wholly in China, was paying $1.75bn (~€1.23bn) to control a business that operated all over the world and had effectively invented the personal computer industry back in 1981. Michael Dell, the creator of the world's largest PC company, commented simply: 'it won't work'.

Lenovo had been founded back in 1984 by Liu Chuanzhi, a 40-year-old researcher working for the Computer Institute of the Chinese Academy of Sciences. His early career had included disassembling captured American radar systems during the Vietnam War and planting rice during the Chinese Cultural Revolution. Liu Chuanzhi had started with $25,000 capital from the Computer Institute and promised his boss that he would build a business with revenues of $250,000. Working in the Computer Institute's old guardhouse, and borrowing its office facilities, one of Liu's first initiatives was reselling colour televisions. But real success started to come in 1987, when Lenovo was one of the first to package Chinese-character software with imported PCs.

Lenovo began to take off, with Liu using the support of his father, well placed in the Chinese government, to help import PCs cheaply through Hong Kong. During 1988, Lenovo placed its first job advertisement, and recruited 58 young people to join the company. Whilst the founding generation of Lenovo staff were in their forties, the new recruits were all in their twenties, as the Cultural Revolution had prevented any university graduation for a period of 10 years in China. Amongst the new recruits was Yang Yuanqing, who would be running Lenovo's PC business before he was 30, and later become Chairman of the new Lenovo–IBM venture at the age of 41. It was this new team which helped launch the production of the first Lenovo PC in 1990, and drove the company to a 30 per cent market share within China by 2005. The company had partially floated on the Hong Kong Stock Exchange in 1994.

Lenovo's Chairman, Yang Yuanqing
Source: Press Associated Images/Kin Cheung/AP.

The deal

Work on the IBM PC deal had begun in 2004, with Lenovo assisted by management consultancy McKinsey & Co. and investment banker Goldman Sachs. IBM wanted to dispose of its PC business, which had only 4 per cent market share in the USA and suffered low margins in a competitive market dominated by Dell and Hewlett-Packard. Higher-margin services and mainframe computers would be IBM's future. As well as Lenovo, IBM had private equity firm Texas Pacific Group in the bidding. Lenovo offered the better price, but Texas Pacific was persuaded enough to take a stake in the new group, while IBM took 13 per cent ownership. The government-owned Chinese Academy of Sciences still owned 27 per cent of the stock, the largest single shareholder.

The new Chairman, Yang Yuanqing, had a clear vision of what the company was to achieve, while recognising some of the challenges:

'In five years, I want this (Lenovo) to be a very famous PC brand, with maybe double the growth of the industry. I want to have a very healthy profit margin, and maybe some other businesses beyond PCs, worldwide. We are at the beginnings of this new company, so we can define some fundamentals about the culture. The three words I use to describe this are "trust, respect, compromise".'

He continued:

'As a global company maybe we have to sacrifice some speed, especially during our first phase. We need more communication. We need to take time to understand each other. But speed was in the genes of the old Lenovo. I hope it will be in the genes of the new Lenovo.'

IBM was not leaving its old business to sink or swim entirely on its own. Lenovo had the right to use the IBM brand for PCs for five years, including the valuable ThinkPad name. IBM's salesforce would be offered incentives to sell Lenovo PCs, just as they had had with IBM's own-brand machines. IBM Global Services was contracted to provide maintenance and support. IBM would have two non-voting observers on the Lenovo board. Moreover, Stephen Ward, the 51-year-old former head of IBM's PC division, was to become Lenovo's Chief Executive Officer.

Managing the new giant

Having an IBM CEO was not entirely a surprise. After all, the $13bn business was nearly 80 per cent ex-IBM and customers and employees had to be reassured of continuity. But there were some significant challenges for the new company to manage none the less.

Things had not started well. When the Chinese team first flew to New York to meet the IBM team, they had not been met at the airport as they had expected and was normal polite practice in China. Yang and Ward had disagreed about the location of the new headquarters, Yang wishing it to be shared between Beijing and near New York. Ward had prevailed, and Yang moved his family to the USA. The new organisation structure kept the old IBM business and the original Lenovo business as separate divisions. But still the new company needed considerable liaison with China, a 13-hour flight away, across 12 time zones. Teleconferencing between the East Coast and China became a way of life, with the Americans calling typically at either 6.00 in the morning or 11.00 at night to catch their Chinese colleagues. Calls were always in English, with many Chinese less than fluent and body language impossible to observe.

The Chinese nature of the company was an issue for some constituencies. IBM had had a lot of government business, and populist members of the US Congress whipped up a scare campaign about Chinese computers entering sensitive domains. In Germany, labour laws allowed a voluntary transition of IBM employees to Lenovo, and many German workers chose not to transfer, leaving the company short-staffed. There was some discomfort amongst former IBM employees in Japan about Chinese ownership. Between the two dominant cultures, American and Chinese, there were considerable differences. Qiao Jian, Vice President for Human Resources, commented:

'Americans like to talk; Chinese people like to listen. At first we wondered why they kept talking when they had nothing to say. But we have learnt to be more direct when we have a problem, and the Americans are learning to listen.'

Cultural differences were not just national. Lenovo was a new and relatively simple company – basically one country, one product. Multinational giant IBM Corporation, founded in 1924, was far more complex. The Lenovo management team, mostly in their thirties, were much younger than IBM's, and the average age of the company as a whole was just 28. IBM was famous for its management processes and routines. Qiao Jian commented: 'IBM people set a time for a conference call and stick to it every week. But why have the call if there is nothing to report?' On the other hand, IBM people had a tendency for being late for meetings, something that was strictly discouraged within Lenovo.

Some results

At first, the response to the new Lenovo was positive. IBM customers stayed loyal and the stock price began to climb (see Figure 1). Remaining IBM executives recognised that at least they were part of a business committed to PCs, rather than the Cinderella in a much larger IBM empire. The fact that a Lenovo PC manufactured in China had a labour cost of just $3.00 offered a lot of opportunity.

However, market leader Dell responded to the new company with heavy price cuts, offering $100 savings on the average machine. With market share in the crucial American market beginning to slip, ex-IBM CEO Stephen Ward was replaced in December 2005 by William Amelio. This was a coup for Lenovo, as Amelio had been running Dell's Asia–Pacific region. As well as knowing Lenovo's competitor from the inside, Amelio, based for several years in Singapore, had a good understanding of Asian business:

Figure 1 Lenovo Group's stock price, 2001–2006, compared with NASDAQ index

Week of Jun 3, 2002: ▬ LHL.F 0.42   ▬ ^IXIC 1,535.48

© [type Function] Yahoo! Inc.

20% 10% 0% −10% −20% −30% −40% −50% −60%

2002   Jul   Oct 2003 Apr   Jul   Oct 2004 Apr   Jul   Oct 2005 Apr   Jul   Oct 2006 Apr   Jul   Oct2007

Source: http://finance.yahoo.com/echarts.

'In the five years I have been in Asia, one thing I have learned . . . is to have a lot more patience. I have to be someone who has a high sense of urgency and drive, but I have also learned how to temper that in the various cultures that I have dealt with in order to be more effective.'

Amelio started by addressing costs, removing 1,000 positions, or 10 per cent, from Lenovo's non-China workforce. He integrated the IBM business and the old Lenovo business into a single structure. The company launched a new range of Lenovo-branded PCs for small and medium-sized American businesses, a market traditionally ignored by IBM. To improve its reach in this segment, Lenovo expanded sales to big American retailers such as Office Depot. US market share began to recover, pushing beyond 4 per cent again. Lenovo began to consider entry into the Indian market.

Amelio's actions seemed to pay off. After a precipitous slide during the first half of 2006, the stock price turned up. But there was no disguising that the stock price in the autumn of 2006 was still below where

it was five years earlier, and that it continued to trail the hi-tech American NASDAQ index.

Sources: L. Zhijun, *The Lenovo Affair*, Wiley, Singapore, 2006; *Business Week*, 7 August (2006), 20 April (2006), 22 December (2005) and 9 May (2005); *Financial Times*, 8 November (2005), 9 November (2005) and 10 November (2005).

Questions

1 What national sources of competitive advantage might Lenovo draw from its Chinese base? What disadvantages derive from its Chinese base?

2 In the light of the CAGE framework and the MacMillan *et al.* competitor retaliation framework (Figure 8.6), comment on Lenovo's entry into the American market.

3 Now that Lenovo is international, what type of generic international strategy should it pursue – simple export, multidomestic, complex export or global?

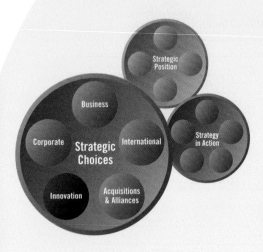

9

INNOVATION AND ENTREPRENEURSHIP

Learning outcomes

After reading this chapter you should understand how to:

● Identify and respond to key *innovation dilemmas*, such as the relative emphases to place on technologies or markets, product or process innovations, open versus closed innovation, and the underlying business model.

● Anticipate and to some extent influence the *diffusion* (or spread) of innovations.

● Decide when being a *first-mover* or a *follower* is most appropriate in innovation, and how an incumbent organisation should respond to innovative challengers.

● Anticipate key issues facing entrepreneurs as they go through the *stages of growth*, from start-up to exit.

● Evaluate opportunities and choices facing *social entrepreneurs* as they create new ventures to address social problems.

Key terms

Business model p. 301

Diffusion p. 303

Disruptive innovation p. 309

Entrepreneurial life cycle p. 311

First-mover advantage p. 307

Innovation p. 296

Open innovation p. 300

Platform leadership p. 300

S-curve p. 304

Social entrepreneurs p. 315

Tipping point p. 304

(9.1) INTRODUCTION

This chapter is about creating the new – both new products or services and new organisations. Such innovation and entrepreneurship are fundamental to today's economy. But they also pose hard choices. For example, should a company look always to be a pioneer in new technologies, or rather be a fast follower, as Apple typically is? How should a company react to radical innovations that threaten to destroy their existing revenues, as the Kodak film business had to with the rise of electronic cameras? How should entrepreneurs handle takeover bids from powerful rich companies: was social networking site MySpace right to sell out to media giant News Corporation (see Illustration 1.1)?

The chapter focuses particularly on the choices involved in innovation and entrepreneurship. Entrepreneurship is a fundamental organisational process. All businesses start with an act of entrepreneurship, and, in the form of 'social entrepreneurship', entrepreneurship is extending beyond purely commercial markets. Innovation is a key aspect of business-level strategy as introduced in Chapter 6, with implications for cost, price and sustainability. As such, it too is relevant in both public and private spheres. Promoting greater innovation and entrepreneurship is crucial to the improvement of public services.

The two main themes that link innovation and entrepreneurship are *timing* and *relationships* (see Figure 9.1). Timing decisions include when to be first-mover or fast second in innovation; when, and if, an innovation will reach its tipping point, the point where demand takes off; and, for an entrepreneurial new venture, when founders should finally exit their enterprise. The other theme is relationships. Creating innovations or new organisations is very rarely done alone. Successful innovation and entrepreneurship are typically done through relationships. These relationships come in many forms: sometimes relationships between organisations and their customers; sometimes relationships between big business and small start-ups; sometimes between business and 'social entrepreneurs'.

Figure 9.1 The innovation–entrepreneurship framework

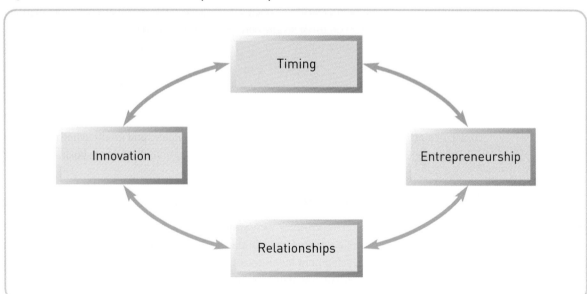

Within Figure 9.1's broad framework, this chapter will examine first innovation, then entrepreneurship:

- Section 9.2 starts with four fundamental *innovation dilemmas*: technology push as against market pull; product innovation rather than process innovation; open versus closed innovation; and, finally, technological as opposed to broader business model innovation. None of these are absolute 'either-or' dilemmas, but managers and entrepreneurs must choose where to concentrate their limited resources.

- Section 9.3 considers issues surrounding the *diffusion*, or spread, of innovations in the marketplace. Diffusion processes often follow *S-curve patterns*, raising further typical issues for decision, particularly with regard to tipping points and tripping points.

- Section 9.4 completes the discussion of innovation by considering choices with regard to timing. This includes *first-mover* advantages and disadvantages, the advantages of being '*fast second*' into a market, and the issue of how established *incumbents* should respond to innovative challengers.

- Section 9.5 addresses *entrepreneurship*. The section discusses typical choices facing entrepreneurs as their ventures progress through the uncertain *stages of growth*, from start-up to exit. It also examines the kinds of *relationships* that entrepreneurs may have to form, particularly with larger firms practising 'open innovation'.

- Section 9.6 finally introduces *social entrepreneurship*, by which individuals and small groups can launch innovative and flexible new initiatives that larger public agencies are often unable to pursue. Again, social entrepreneurs face choices with regard to relationships, particularly with big business.

The Key Debate at the end of this chapter brings entrepreneurship and innovation together again by considering the issue of whether small or large firms are better at innovation.

INNOVATION DILEMMAS

Innovation raises fundamental strategic dilemmas for strategists. Innovation is more complex than just invention. *Invention* involves the conversion of new knowledge into a new product, process or service. **Innovation involves the conversion of new knowledge into a new product, process or service** *and* **the putting of this new product, process or service into actual use.**[1] The strategic dilemmas stem from this more extended process. Strategists have to make choices with regard to four fundamental issues: how far to follow technological opportunity as against market demand; how much to invest in product innovation rather than process innovation; how far to open themselves up to innovative ideas from outside; and finally whether to focus on technological innovation rather than extending innovation to their whole business model.[2]

9.2.1 Technology push or market pull

People often see innovation as driven by technology. In the pure version of this *technology push* view, it is the new knowledge created by technologists or scientists that pushes the innovation process. Research and development laboratories produce new products, processes or services and then hand them over to the rest of the organisation to manufacture, market and distribute. According to this push perspective, managers should listen primarily to their scientists and technologists, let them follow their hunches and support them with ample resources. Generous R&D budgets are crucial to making innovation happen.

An alternative approach to innovation is *market pull*. Market pull reflects a view of innovation that goes beyond invention and sees the importance of actual use. The role of market pull has been promoted since MIT professor Eric von Hippel's discovery that in many sectors users, not producers, are common sources of important innovations.[3] In designing their innovation strategies, therefore, organisations should listen in the first place to users rather than their own scientists and technologists. Von Hippel refines this focus on users to point out that in many markets it is not ordinary users that are the source of innovation, but *lead-users*. In medical surgery, top surgeons often adapt existing surgical instruments in order to carry out new types of operation. In extreme sports such as snowboarding or windsurfing, it is leading sportspeople who make the improvements necessary for greater performance. In this view, then, it is the pull of users in the market that is responsible for innovation. Managers need to build close relationships with lead-users such as the best surgeons or sporting champions. Marketing and sales functions identify the lead-users of a field and then scientists and technologists translate their inventive ideas into commercial products, processes or services that the wider market can use.

There are merits to both the technology push and market pull views. Relying heavily on existing users can make companies too conservative, and vulnerable to disruptive technologies that uncover needs unforeseen by existing markets (see section 9.4.3). On the other hand, history is littered with examples of companies that have blindly pursued technological excellence without regard to real market needs. Technology push and market pull are best seen as extreme views, therefore, helping to focus attention on a fundamental choice: relatively how much to rely on science and technology as sources of innovation, rather than what people are actually doing in the marketplace. In practice, most organisations find a compromise between the two views, with the balance varying both between industries and over time. As at the skateboarding company Sole Technology, users may be key at start-up, but internally led innovation can become more important with growth (see Illustration 9.1). The key issue for managers is to be aware of the dilemma and to review their organisation's balance between the two extremes consciously rather than relying on habit or prejudice.

9.2.2 Product or process innovation

Just as managers must find a balance between technological push and market pull, so must they determine the relative emphasis to place on product or process innovation. *Product innovation* relates to the final product (or service) to be sold, especially with regard to its features; *process innovation* relates to the way in which this product is produced and distributed, especially with regard to improvements in cost or reliability. Some firms specialise more in product innovation, others more in process innovation. For example, in computers, Apple has generally concentrated its efforts on designing attractive product features (for instance the MacBook Air), while Dell has innovated in terms of efficient processes, for instance direct sales, modularity and build-to-order.

The relative importance of product innovation and process innovation typically changes as industries evolve over time. Usually the first stages of an industry are dominated by product innovation based on new features. Thus the early history of the automobile was dominated by competition as to whether cars should be fuelled by steam, electricity or petrol, have their engines at the front or at the rear, and have three wheels or four.[4] Industries eventually

ILLUSTRATION 9.1

Shoes for skateboarders

Innovation at Sole Technologies is driven by both users and technology.

After taking a degree in industrial software, Pierre André Senizergues started his career as a professional skateboarder in France. In less than twenty years, he created an action shoe and apparel business with $200m (~€140m) sales, and seven brands, including Etnies with its famous distinctive 'E' and the big snowboarding boot brand ThirtyTwo. He also created the first skateboard shoe research laboratory in the world.

Things had not started out so promisingly for Senizergues. In 1988 he signed to ride for the skateboard brand of a new French venture. The very next year he was forced to retire from professional skateboarding with back problems. Although he spoke poor English and had little business experience, he persuaded his employers to grant him the licence to sell its Etnies shoes in the United States. The first five years were very hard, but Senizergues introduced his own designs and from the mid-1990s Etnies began to take off. In 1996, Senizergues bought the Etnies brand from the French venture and incorporated it and other brands – including éS, Emerica and ThirtyTwo – under the Sole Technology umbrella. Growth over the next ten years ran at double digits per annum.

From the first, Senizergues had been able to use his expertise as a professional skateboarder in his designs. He told the *Financial Times*: 'In this market, you have to be authentic, you have to come from skateboarding.' For example, in the 1990s he had noticed that skateboarders were buying unsuitable low-top shoes for their looks, rather than high-top shoes with the proper performance characteristics. Senizergues responded by designing low-top shoes that had the necessary durability. His company has

stayed close to its sports, sponsoring more than 100 athletes around the world. It listens closely to customers. The company's website has a design-your-own-shoe facility and it often releases potential specifications for its new products through blogs, in order to solicit feedback and ideas. The average age of Sole Technology's 400 employees is 28, with many still involved in action sports.

However, Senizergues has also built the world's first skateboarding research facility, the Sole Technology Institute. With 10,000 square feet, it reproduces typical skateboarding obstacles such as rails, stairs and ledges. Senizergues believes that it is time for skateboarding to do its own biomechanical research, instead of borrowing technologies developed in other sports. One of the outputs of the Sole Technology Institute has been the G202 gel-and-air technology. As the trend for girls' shoes moved towards slim silhouettes during 2006, this gel-and-air technology has allowed Sole Technology to keep right abreast of fashion.

Sources: *Financial Times*, 23 August 2006; *Footwear News*, 20 February 2006; www.soletechnology.com.

Questions

1 For what reasons is it important to be 'authentic' in the skateboarding shoe market?

2 If a big company like Nike or Adidas was looking to grow in this market, what would you advise them to do?

Figure 9.2 **Product and process innovation**

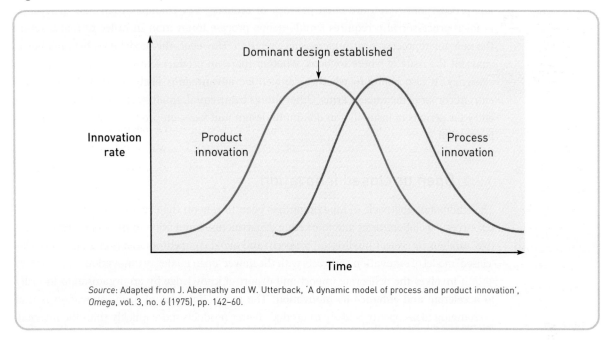

Source: Adapted from J. Abernathy and W. Utterback, 'A dynamic model of process and product innovation', *Omega*, vol. 3, no. 6 (1975), pp. 142–60.

coalesce around a *dominant design*, the standard configuration of basic features: after Henry Ford's 1908 Model T, cars generally became petrol-driven, with their engines at the front and four wheels. Once such a dominant design is established, innovation switches to process innovation, as competition shifts to producing the dominant design as efficiently as possible. Henry Ford's great process innovation was the moving assembly line, introduced in 1913. Finally, the cycle is liable to start again, as some significant innovation challenges the dominant design: in the case of cars recently, the emergence of electric power.[4]

Figure 9.2 provides a general model of the relationship between product and process innovation over time. The model has several strategic implications:

- *New developing industries* typically favour product innovation, as competition is still around defining the basic features of the product or service.

- *Maturing industries* typically favour process innovation, as competition shifts towards efficient production of a dominant design of product or service.

- *Small new entrants* typically have the greatest opportunity when dominant designs are either not yet established or beginning to collapse. Thus, in the early stages of the automobile industry, before Ford's Model T, there were more than one hundred mostly small competitors, each with their own combination of product features. The recent challenge to the petrol-based dominant design has provided opportunities to small companies such as the Californian start-up Tesla Motors, which had produced more than 1000 electric Roadsters by the beginning of 2010.

- *Large incumbent firms* typically have the advantage during periods of dominant design stability, when scale economies and the ability to roll out process innovations matter most. With the success of the Model T and the assembly line, by the 1930s there were just four large American automobile manufacturers, Ford, General Motors, Chrysler and American Motors, all producing very similar kinds of cars.

This sequence of product to process innovation is not always a neat one. In practice, product and process innovation are often pursued in tandem.[5] For example, each new generation of microprocessor also requires simultaneous process innovation in order to manufacture the new microprocessor with increasing precision. However, the model does help managers confront the issue of where to focus, whether more on product features or more on process efficiency. It also points to whether competitive advantage is likely to be with small new entrants or large incumbent firms. Other things being equal, small start-ups should time their entry for periods of instability in dominant design and focus on product rather than process innovation.

9.2.3 Open or closed innovation

The traditional approach to innovation has been to rely on the organisation's own internal resources – its laboratories and marketing departments. Innovation in this approach is secretive, anxious to protect intellectual property and avoid competitors free-riding on ideas. This 'closed' model of innovation contrasts with the newer 'open model' of innovation.[6] **Open innovation involves the deliberate import and export of knowledge by an organisation in order to accelerate and enhance its innovation.** The motivating idea of open innovation is that exchanging ideas openly is likely to produce better products more quickly than the internal, closed approach. Speedier and superior products are what are needed to keep ahead of the competition, not obsessive secrecy.

Open innovation is being widely adopted. For example, technology giant IBM has established a network of ten 'collaboratories' with other companies and universities, in countries ranging from Switzerland to Saudi Arabia. Last.fm, the online music service, hosts special 'hack days', when it invites its users for a day of free food, drink and work on developing new applications together. The American InnoCentive company has a network of 64 knowledge 'seekers', including giants Procter & Gamble, Eli Lilly and Dow Chemical, which set 'challenges' for which prizes of up to $1m are given for solutions: so far, more than 348 challenges have been solved with the participation of over 165,000 'solvers'.

Open innovation typically requires careful support of collaborators. In particular, dominant firms may need to exercise platform leadership. **Platform leadership refers to how large firms consciously nurture independent companies through successive waves of innovation around their basic technological 'platform'.**[7] Video games console companies such as Microsoft and Sony have to manage relationships with a host of large and small video games publishers in order to ensure that their consoles are supported by an attractive set of games, making full use of the latest technological possibilities. Similarly, mobile phone companies such as Nokia and Apple have to encourage and support the thousands of independent producers of 'apps' for their phones.

The balance between open and closed innovation depends on three key factors:

- *Competitive rivalry*. In highly rivalrous industries, partners are liable to behave opportunistically and steal advantages. Closed innovation is better where such rivalrous behaviours can be anticipated.

- *One-shot innovation*. Opportunistic behaviour is more likely where innovation involves a major shift in technology, likely to put winners substantially ahead and losers permanently behind. Open innovation works best where innovation is more continuous, so encouraging more reciprocal behaviour over time.

● *Tight-linked innovation*. Where technologies are complex and tightly interlinked, open innovation risks introducing damagingly inconsistent elements, with knock-on effects throughout the product range. Apple, with its smoothly integrated range of products from computers to phones, has therefore tended to prefer closed innovation in order to protect the quality of the user experience.

9.2.4 Technological or business-model innovation

Many successful innovations do not rely simply upon new science or technology, but involve reorganising into new combinations all the elements of a business. Here innovators are creating whole new *business models*, bringing customers, producers and suppliers together in new ways, with or without new technologies.[8] A **business model** describes how an organisation **manages incomes and costs through the structural arrangement of its activities**. For Ryanair, business-model innovation involved the generation of revenues via direct sales through the internet, thereby cutting out intermediary travel agents, while also using cheap secondary airports. Internet sales and cheaper airports were much more important than technological innovation. The internet technology itself was not Ryanair's creation and it had the same aeroplanes as most of its competitors. Thus it can be as effective to innovate in terms of business model as in technology.

Opportunities for business-model innovation can be analysed in terms of the value chain, value net or activity systems frameworks introduced in sections 3.4.2 and 3.4.3[9]. These frameworks point managers and entrepreneurs to two basic areas for potential innovation:

● *The product*. A new business model may redefine what the product or service is and how it is produced. In terms of the value chain specifically, this concerns technology development, procurement, inbound logistics, operations and procurement. For example, when Nucor pioneered electric-arc mini-mill technology in the steel industry, it was able to use scrap metal as its raw material rather than pure iron, employ non-unionised labour and outsource a lot of its product development to its equipment supplier Voest Alpine.

● *The selling*. A new business model may change the way in which the organisation generates its revenues, with implications for selling and distribution. In terms of the value chain, this concerns outbound logistics, marketing, sales and service. Nucor, for example, sold its cheap but low-quality steel at standard prices on the internet, by contrast to the traditional steel producers' reliance on elaborate negotiations with individual customers on prices and specifications.

The business model concept emphasises the fundamental features of how business activities are organised. In terms of business models, mature industries therefore often have a lot of standardisation. For example, most accounting firms are organised in similar ways, earning the majority of their income from audit and relying on a high ratio of junior staff to partners. Business strategy within an industry characterised by standardised business models is mostly about differentiation. Thus accounting firms might differentiate themselves within the same model by emphasising particular kinds of sectoral expertise or international networks.

However, the fundamental nature of business models means that business-model innovation tends to imply radical change. Business-model innovation is not just a matter of technology, but involves a wide range of the firm's activities. Thus the business model concept

ILLUSTRATION 9.2

Blockbuster's busted business model

Blockbuster's store rental model is challenged by new business models for movie and game distribution.

There are a lot of ways for people to see a movie nowadays. They can go to the cinema. They can buy a DVD from specialist retailers such as HMV or large supermarkets such as Tesco or Lidl. They can order a DVD online and receive it through the post. They can download movies via the internet. They can rent via a kiosk or vending machine. Or they can do it the old-fashioned way and rent it from a video store.

Blockbuster, of course, is famous for its stores: in 2010 it had 7000 stores in 18 countries around the world. The first Blockbuster store opened in 1985 in Texas. Soon Blockbuster was the world's largest movie rental company, and in 1994 was bought by media conglomerate Viacom for $7.6bn (~€5.3bn). Ten years later, as Blockbuster's growth stalled, Viacom spun it off as an independent company again, now valued at $7.5bn.

Blockbuster's business model had been an attractive one at first. Two decades ago, in a period of limited television channels, movie rental had given customers unheard-of choice of viewing. Blockbuster used its huge buying power to obtain the latest releases from the film studios at little cost. Blockbuster would give 40 per cent of the rental income to the studios and supply them with information on usage for market research purposes. Studios typically would hold back from releasing the movie to other rental companies or to retailers for an initial period, making Blockbuster the essential outlet for the latest hits. Blockbuster was able to leverage this business model into rapid growth, using a mixture of its own stores, franchising and acquisitions. It also extended the model to the rental of video games.

However, the market is now much more complex. For a start, television channels began to proliferate. In the United States, Netflix emerged in 1997, originally using a rental-by-mail model. By 2009, Netflix had mailed its two billionth DVD. In the United Kingdom, DVD mail-rental company Lovefilm

was founded in 2002, and by 2010 had 50 per cent of the national market, as well as a strong position in Scandinavia. The mail-rental model offers customers a far greater choice (Lovefilm has 70,000 titles, against the few hundred in a typical Blockbuster store) and needs only a few centralised distribution centres, as against a labour-intensive network of retail stores. Moreover, as internet capacity has improved, both Netflix and Lovefilm have also begun to stream movies straight to customers' computers. Another rental model was pioneered by 2003 start-up Redbox, which had established a network of 22,000 DVD vending machines across the United States by the end of 2009.

Blockbuster responded in several ways. In 2004, it launched its own on-line rental service, with customers able to return their DVDs simply through a local store. In 2009, Blockbuster launched its own vending machines in the United States. The company closed more than 1800 stores. It withdrew from some national markets altogether, for example Spain, Portugal, Ecuador and Peru. But still 2009 was a year of heavy financial losses. The Blockbuster shareprice, which had peaked at over $30 in 2002, had fallen to 41 cents in 2010.

Sources: Financial Times, 24 February 2010; The Times, 28 December 2009; The Express on Sunday, 28 February 2010.

Questions

1 Compare the pros and cons of the various business models for movie consumption.

2 What potential competitive advantages did Blockbuster have as a company as the new business models emerged in the last decade or so?

helps managers and entrepreneurs consider science and technology as just one part of the whole package that contributes to innovation. Innovation can be drawn from all parts of the value chain, not just technology development. Indeed, radical technological innovation often requires business-model innovation too. For example, in order to promote adoption of its innovative electric cars in France, Toyota has formed a partnership with electricity supplier EDF and local authorities to create networks of subsidised public charging points. Illustration 9.2 describes the radical repercussions of business-model innovation in the movie rental business.

(9.3) INNOVATION DIFFUSION

So far, this chapter has been concerned with sources and types of innovation, for example technology push or market pull. This section moves to the diffusion of innovations after they have been introduced.[10] **Diffusion is the process by which innovations spread amongst users.** Since innovation is typically expensive, its commercial attractiveness can hinge on the pace – extent and speed – at which the market adopts new products and services. This pace of diffusion is something managers can influence from both the supply and demand sides, and which they can also model using the S-curve.

9.3.1 The pace of diffusion

The pace of diffusion can vary widely according to the nature of the products concerned. It took 38 years for the television to reach 150 million units sold; it took just 7 years for Apple's iPod to reach the same number. The pace of diffusion is influenced by a combination of supply-side and demand-side factors, over which managers have considerable control. On the *supply side*, pace is determined by product features such as:

- *Degree of improvement* in performance above current products (from a customer's perspective) that provides incentive to change. For example, 3G mobile phones did not provide sufficient performance improvement to prompt rapid switch in many markets. Managers need to make sure innovation benefits sufficiently exceed costs.

- *Compatibility* with other factors, e.g. digital TV becomes more attractive as the broadcasting networks change more of their programmes to that format. Managers and entrepreneurs therefore need to ensure appropriate complementary products and services are in place.

- *Complexity*, either in the product itself or in the marketing methods being used to commercialise the product: unduly complex pricing structures, as with many financial service products such as pensions, discourage consumer adoption. Simple pricing structures typically accelerate adoptions.

- *Experimentation* – the ability to test products before commitment to a final decision – either directly or through the availability of information about the experience of other customers. Free initial trial periods are often used to encourage diffusion.

- *Relationship management*, in other words how easy it is to get information, place orders and receive support. Google's 2010 launch of its first phone, the Android Nexus One, was hampered because the company was not used to providing the access to help staff that mobile phone customers generally expect. Managers and entrepreneurs need to put in place an appropriate relationship management processes to assist new users.

On the *demand side*, three key factors tend to drive the pace of diffusion:

- *Market awareness.* Many potentially successful products have failed through lack of consumer awareness – particularly when the promotional effort of the innovator has been confined to 'push' promotion to its intermediaries (e.g. distributors).

- *Network effects* refer to the way that demand growth for some products accelerates as more people adopt the product or service. Once a critical mass of users have adopted, it becomes of much greater benefit, or even necessary, for others to adopt it too. Facebook enjoyed network effects as its usage raced to 150 million in just four years. Likewise, people use Microsoft PowerPoint because almost all their collaborators are likely to use it too (see also section 6.3.6).

- *Customer innovativeness.* The distribution of potential customers from early-adopter groups (keen to adopt first) through to laggards (typically indifferent to innovations). Innovations are often targeted initially at early-adopter groups – typically the young and the wealthy – in order to build the critical mass that will encourage more laggardly groups – the poorer and older – to join the bandwagon. Clothing fashion trends typically start with the wealthy and then are diffused to the wider population. Managers and entrepreneurs therefore need to target innovations initially at likely early-adopters.

9.3.2 The diffusion S-curve

The pace of diffusion is typically not steady. Successful innovations often diffuse according to a broad *S-curve* pattern.[11] The shape of the **S-curve reflects a process of initial slow adoption of innovation, followed by a rapid acceleration in diffusion, leading to a plateau representing the limit to demand** (Figure 9.3). The height of the S-curve shows the extent of diffusion; the shape of the S-curve shows the speed.

Diffusion rarely follows exactly this pattern, but nonetheless the S-curve can help managers and entrepreneurs anticipate upcoming issues. In particular, the S-curve points to four likely decision points:

- *Timing of the 'tipping point'.* Demand for a new product or service may initially be slow but then reaches a tipping point when it explodes onto a rapid upwards path of growth.[12] A **tipping point is where demand for a product or service suddenly takes off, with explosive growth.** Tipping points are particularly explosive where there are strong *network effects*: in other words, where the value of a product or service is increased the more people in a network use them. Being aware of a possible tipping point ahead can help managers plan investment in capacity and distribution. Companies can easily underestimate demand. In the mid-1980s, American companies predicted that by 2000 there would be 900,000 mobile phones worldwide. That year came, and 900,000 phones were sold every 19 hours. The Finnish company Nokia was able to seize worldwide leadership.[13] Failing to anticipate a tipping point leads to missed sales and easy opportunities for competitors.

- *Timing of the plateau.* The S-curve also alerts managers to a likely eventual slowdown in demand growth. Again, it is tempting to extrapolate existing growth rates forwards, especially when they are highly satisfactory. But heavy investment immediately before growth turns down is likely to leave firms with over-capacity and carrying extra costs in a period of industry shake-out.

Figure 9.3 **The diffusion S-curve**

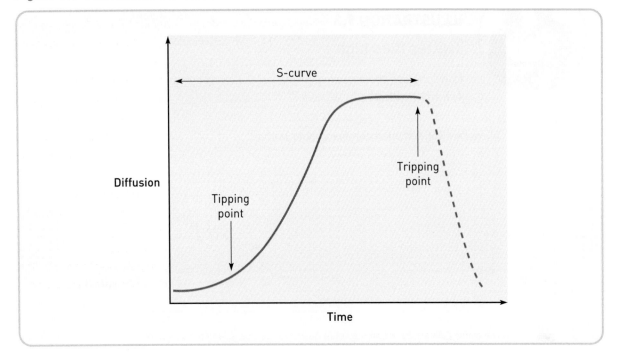

- *Extent of diffusion.* The S-curve does not necessarily lead to one hundred per cent diffusion amongst potential users. Most innovations fail to displace previous-generation products and services altogether. For example, in music, traditional turntables and LP discs are still preferred over CD and MP3 players by many disc jockeys and music connoisseurs. A critical issue for managers then is to estimate the final ceiling on diffusion, being careful not to assume that tipping point growth will necessarily take over the whole market.

- *Timing of the 'tripping point'.* The tripping point is the opposite of the tipping point, referring to when demand suddenly collapses.[14] Of course, decline is usually more gradual. However, the presence of network effects can lead to relatively few customer defections setting off a market landslide. Such landslides are very hard to reverse. This is what happened to social networking site Friendster, as American and European users defected to MySpace and Facebook. The tripping point concept warns managers all the time that a small dip in quarterly sales could presage a rapid collapse.

To summarise, the S-curve is a useful concept to help managers and entrepreneurs avoid simply extrapolating next year's sales from last year's sales. However, the tripping point also underlines the fact that innovations do not follow an inevitable process, and their diffusion patterns can be interrupted or reversed at any point. Most innovations, of course, do not even reach a tipping point, let alone a tripping point. The Segway Human Transporter, launched in 2001 as the environmentally friendly technology that would replace the car, sold 6,000 units in its first two years, despite launch production capacity of nearly 500,000 a year.

ILLUSTRATION 9.3

Twitter flies high

How long can the explosive growth of the microblogger Twitter continue? And what is its business model?

Alexa.com estimation of numbers using Twitter

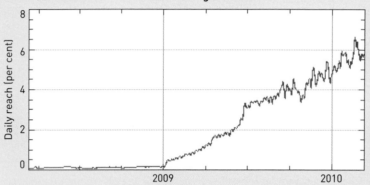

The traffic data are based on the set of Alexa toolbar users, which may not be a representative sample of the global Internet population.

Source: Alexa.com.

Twitter was founded in 2006 by Jack Dorsey, Biz Stone and Evan Williams, all in their early 30s. The original idea for Twitter was conceived during a brainstorming day, and implemented in just two weeks. Biz Stone recalls a dialogue with Evan Williams: 'Early on someone said: "Twitter is fun, but it isn't useful". Ev said: "Neither is icecream".'

A lot of people soon began to think Twitter fun. A key moment was the Spring 2007 South by Southwest film and music festival in Austin, Texas. Twitter hired two large plasma screens streaming Twitter messages from festival-goers. During the event, Twitter usage went from 20,000 'tweets' (messages) per day to 60,000 per day. Then Barack Obama used Twitter publicly during the 2008 US presidential elections. By early 2010, Alexa.com was estimating that more than 6 per cent of global internet users were visiting twitter.com per day ('daily reach').

Twitter usage is free, so a persistent question as Twitter grows is about its business model – how it would earn revenues. Twitter raised $135m (~€94.5m) in venture capital during 2009, but was cautious about how to make the venture pay. Ev Williams said: 'We think Twitter will make money. I just think it will take some time to figure it out.' The founders rejected the use of advertising. However, they were considering

how they could get companies to pay for referrals from Twitter to their own websites. At the start of 2010, Biz Stone told the *Financial Times*: 'We need to build a business out of Twitter – that needs to start happening in 2010'.

Meanwhile, social networking site Facebook was developing Twitter-like features and new imitators were springing up. In Japan, for instance, start-up Ameba Now was gaining users by signing up Japanese celebrities, offering Japanese characters and supporting 'smiley' icons, something that Twitter lacks. Within three months of its December 2009 launch, Ameba Now had one million users, against Twitter's 4.7 million in Japan. Twitter also has a high wastage rate – only 40 per cent of those who sign on are retained as regular users.

Sources: *New York Times*, 25 March 2009; www.eweek.com, 20 October 2009; *Financial Times*, 1 January 2010 and 12 March 2010.

Questions

1 How should investors in Twitter interpret Alexa.com's daily reach data?

2 Propose three ways that Twitter could make money and consider their respective pros and cons.

(9.4) INNOVATORS AND FOLLOWERS

A key choice for managers is whether to lead or to follow in innovation. The S-curve concept seems to promote leadership in innovation. First-movers get the easy sales of early fast growth and can establish a dominant position. There are plenty of examples of first-movers who have built enduring positions on the basis of innovation leadership: Coca-Cola in drinks and Hoover in vacuum cleaners are powerful century-old examples. On the other hand, many first-movers fail. Even Apple failed with its pioneering Personal Digital Assistant, the Newton, launched in 1993. Hewlett-Packard and Palm captured the PDA market nearly a decade later. This late-entry success is not unusual. Amazon entered the online bookselling market in 1995, four years after the real online pioneer, the Computer Literacy bookstore of Silicon Valley, California.

9.4.1 First-mover advantages and disadvantages

A **first-mover advantage** exists where an organisation is better off than its competitors as a result of being first to market with a new product, process or service. Fundamentally, the first-mover is a monopolist, theoretically able to charge customers high prices without fear of immediate undercutting by competitors. In practice, however, innovators often prefer to sacrifice profit margins for sales growth and, besides, monopoly is usually temporary. There are five potentially more robust first-mover advantages:[15]

KEY CONCEPT

First-mover advantage

- *Experience curve benefits* accrue to first-movers, as their rapid accumulation of experience with the innovation gives them greater expertise than late entrants still relatively unfamiliar with the new product, process or service (see section 6.3.1).

- *Scale benefits* are typically enjoyed by first-movers, as they establish earlier than competitors the volumes necessary for mass production and bulk purchasing, for example.

- *Pre-emption of scarce resources* is an opportunity for first-movers, as late movers will not have the same access to key raw materials, skilled labour or components, and will have to pay dearly for them.

- *Reputation* can be enhanced by being first, especially since consumers have little 'mind-space' to recognise new brands once a dominant brand has been established in the market.

- *Buyer switching costs* can be exploited by first-movers, by locking in their customers with privileged or sticky relationships that later challengers can only break with difficulty. Switching costs can be increased by establishing and exploiting a *technological standard* (see section 6.3.6).

Experience curve benefits, economies of scale and the pre-emption of scarce resources all confer cost advantages on first-movers. It is possible for them to retaliate against challengers with a price war. Superior reputation and customer lock-in provide a marketing advantage, allowing first-movers to charge high prices, which can then be reinvested in order to consolidate their position against late-entry competitors.

But the experience of Apple with its Newton shows that first-mover advantages are not necessarily overwhelming. Late movers have two principal potential advantages:[16]

- *Free-riding*. Late movers can imitate technological and other innovation at less expense than originally incurred by the pioneers. Research suggests that the costs of imitation are only 65 per cent of the cost of innovation.

- *Learning*. Late movers can observe what worked well and what did not work well for innovators. They may not make so many mistakes and be able to get it right first time.

9.4.2 First or second?

Given the potential advantages of late movers, managers and entrepreneurs face a hard choice between striving to be first or coming in later. London Business School's Costas Markides and Paul Geroski argue that the most appropriate response to innovation, especially radical innovation, is often not to be a first-mover, but to be a '*fast second*'.[17] A fast second strategy involves being one of the first to imitate the original innovator. Thus fast second companies may not literally be the second company into the market, but they dominate the second generation of competitors. For example, the French Bookeen company pioneered the e-book market in the early 2000s, but was followed by Sony's eReader in 2006 and Amazon's Kindle in 2007.

There are three contextual factors to consider in choosing between innovating and imitating:

- *Capacity for profit capture*. David Teece emphasises the importance of innovators being able to capture for themselves the profits of their innovations.[18] This depends on the ease with which followers can imitate. The likelihood of imitation depends on two primary factors. First, imitation is likely if the innovation is in itself *easy to replicate*: for example, if there is little tacit knowledge involved or if it is embedded in a product that is sold in the external marketplace (unlike many process technologies) and is therefore easy to 'reverse-engineer' (see section 3.3). Second, imitation is facilitated if *intellectual property rights* are weak, for example where patents are hard to define or impractical to defend.[19] It is unwise for companies to invest in first-moves if imitators are likely to be able quickly to seize their share of innovation profits.

- *Complementary assets*. Possession of the assets or resources necessary to scale up the production and marketing of the innovation is often critical.[20] Many small European bio-tech start-up companies face this constraint in the pharmaceuticals industry, where marketing and distribution channels in the United States, the world's largest market, are essential complementary assets, but are dominated by the big established pharmaceutical companies. Small European start-ups can find themselves obliged either to sell out to a larger company with the complementary marketing and distribution assets, or to license their innovation to them on disadvantageous terms. For organisations wishing to remain independent and to exploit their innovations themselves, there is little point in investing heavily to be first-mover in the absence of the necessary complementary assets.

- *Fast-moving arenas*. Where markets or technologies are moving very fast, and especially where both are highly dynamic, first-movers are unlikely to establish a durable advantage. The American electronics company Magnavox was the first to launch an electronic video game console in 1972, the Odyssey. But both the market and the technologies were evolving quickly. Magnavox only survived into the second generation of video game consoles, finally exiting in 1984. The seventh generation is now firmly dominated by Microsoft (entered in 2001), Sony (entered in 1994) and Nintendo (entered in 1983). In slower-moving markets and technologies, such as Coca-Cola's drinks arena, durable first-mover advantages are more probable. Managers and entrepreneurs need, therefore, to assess future market and technological dynamism in calculating the likely value of first-mover advantage.

9.4.3 The incumbent's response

For established companies in a market, innovation is often not so much an opportunity as a threat. Kodak's dominance of the photographic film market was made nearly worthless by the sudden rise of digital photography. Likewise, Blockbuster's network of video stores became redundant with the rise of internet film downloads (see Illustration 9.2).

As Harvard Business School's Clay Christensen has shown, the problem for incumbents can be twofold.[21] First, managers can become too attached to existing assets and skills. After all, these are what their careers have been built on. Second, relationships between incumbent organisations and their customers can become too close. Existing customers typically prefer incremental improvements to current technologies, and are unable to imagine completely new technologies. Incumbents are reluctant to 'cannibalise' their existing business by introducing something radically different. After all, as in Figure 9.4, incumbents usually have some scope for improving their existing technology, along the steady upwards trajectory described as Technology 1. Innovations on this trajectory are termed 'sustaining innovations', because they at least allow the existing technology to meet existing customer expectations.

The challenge for incumbents, however, is disruptive innovation. A **disruptive innovation creates substantial growth by offering a new performance trajectory that, even if initially inferior to the performance of existing technologies, has the potential to become markedly superior.** This superior performance can produce spectacular growth, either by creating new sets of customers or by undercutting the cost base of rival existing business models. Such disruptive innovation involves the shift from Technology 1 in Figure 9.4 to Technology 2. Disruptive innovations are hard for incumbents to respond to because their initial poor performance is likely to upset existing customer relationships and because they typically involve changing their whole business model. Thus, in the music industry, the major record companies were long content to keep on selling traditional CDs through retailers, marketing them through promotions and radio-plugging. They responded to MP3 online music simply by prosecuting operators such as Napster for breach of copyright and highlighting the relatively poor sound quality of peer-to-peer file sharing. However, the British band Arctic Monkeys, and its small independent record company Domino, radically disrupted the majors' marketing

Figure 9.4 Disruptive innovation

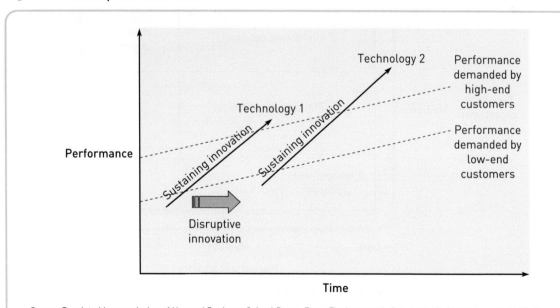

model by giving away MP3 tracks free over the internet in order to create an independent fan-base. In 2006, the Arctic Monkeys' debut CD ended up selling nearly 400,000 copies in its first week, a record for the top 20 United Kingdom album chart.

Incumbents can follow two policies to help keep them responsive to potentially disruptive innovations:

● *Develop a portfolio of real options.* Companies that are most challenged by disruptive innovations tend to be those built upon a single business model and with one main product or service. Columbia's Rita McGrath and Wharton's Ian MacMillan recommend that companies build portfolios of *real options* in order to maintain organisational dynamism.[22] Real options are limited investments that keep opportunities open for the future (for a more technical discussion, see section 11.3.2). Establishing an R&D team in a speculative new technology or acquiring a small start-up in a nascent market would both be examples of real options, each giving the potential to scale-up fast should the opportunity turn out to be substantial. McGrath and MacMillan's portfolio identifies three different kinds of options (Figure 9.5). Options where the market is broadly known, but the technologies are still uncertain, are *positioning options*: a company might want several of these, to ensure some position in an important market, by one technology or another. On the other hand, a company might have a strong technology, but be very uncertain about appropriate markets, in which case it would want to bet on several *scouting options* to explore which markets are actually best. Finally, a company would want some *stepping stone* options, very unlikely in themselves to work, but possibly leading to something more promising in the future. Even if they do not turn a profit, stepping stones should provide valuable learning opportunities. An important principle for options is: 'Fail fast, fail cheap, try again'.

Figure 9.5 Portfolio of innovation options

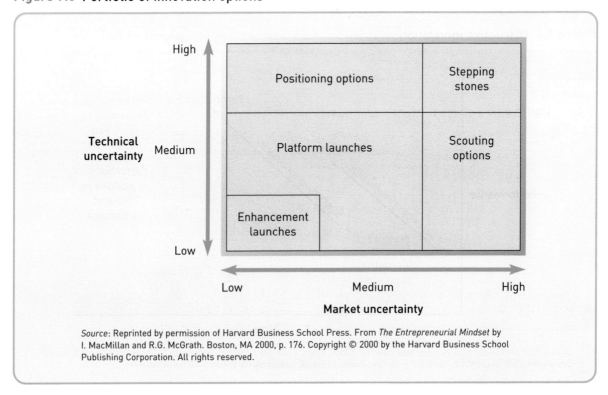

● *Develop new venture units.* New ventures, especially when undertaken from a real options perspective, may need protection from the usual systems and disciplines of a core business. It would make no sense to hold the managers of a real option strictly accountable for sales growth and profit margin: their primary objective is preparation and learning. For this reason, large incumbent organisations often set up innovative businesses as relatively autonomous 'new venture units', sometimes called new venture divisions, typically with managers hired specially from outside.[23] For example, in 2003 Delta Airlines, the American international airline dating from the 1920s, responded to the threat of low-cost airlines in its domestic markets by establishing Song Airlines as a stand-alone competitor. Song adopted the low-cost airline business model but also innovated with free personal entertainment systems at every seat, including audio MP3 selections, trivia games that could be played against other passengers and satellite television. In-flight safety instructions would be sung in different musical styles, by request. The risks of such autonomous venture units are twofold.[24] First, the new units may be denied resources that the core business could easily supply, such as branding or management information systems. Second, innovation becomes isolated from the core business: for the core organisation, innovation is something that somebody else does. Delta responded to the second risk threat by reabsorbing Song into its main operations, at the same time incorporating several of Song's innovations such as satellite television.

ENTREPRENEURSHIP AND RELATIONSHIPS

Given the difficulties of large incumbent firms in fostering innovation, many would conclude that the best approach is to start up a new venture. Independent entrepreneurs such as James Dyson, the pioneer of bagless vacuum cleaners, and Larry Page and Sergey Brin of Google are exemplars of this entrepreneurial approach to innovation (see case examples for Chapters 3 and 12).[25] This section introduces some key issues for entrepreneurial innovators, and then points to a more complex set of relationships with large firms, raising further choices for entrepreneurs. It concludes by considering the opportunities of social entrepreneurship.

9.5.1 Stages of entrepreneurial growth

Entrepreneurial ventures are often seen as going through four stages of a life cycle: see Figure 9.6. The **entrepreneurial life cycle progresses through start-up, growth, maturity and exit.**[26] Of course, most ventures do not make it through all the stages – the estimated failure rate of new businesses in their first year is more than one fifth, with two thirds going out of business within six years.[27] However, each of these four stages raises key questions for entrepreneurs:

● *Start-up.* There are many challenges at this stage, but one key question with implications for both survival and growth are sources of capital. Loans from family and friends are common sources of funds, but these are typically limited and, given the new-business failure rate, likely to lead to embarrassment. Bank loans and credit cards can provide funding too, and there is often government funding especially for new technologies or economically disadvantaged social groups or geographical areas. *Venture capitalists* are specialised investors in new ventures, especially when there is some track-record. Venture capitalists usually insist on a seat on the venture's board of directors and may install their preferred managers. Venture capitalist backing has been shown to significantly increase the chances of a

Figure 9.6 Stages of entrepreneurial growth and typical challenges

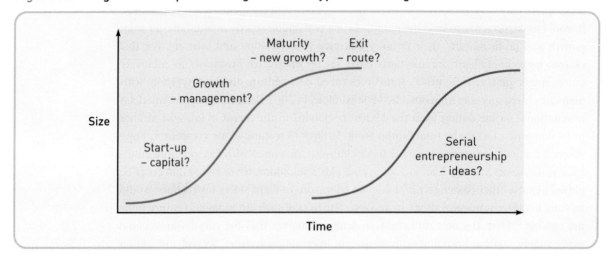

venture's success, but venture capitalists typically accept only about one in four hundred propositions put to them.[28]

- *Growth.* A key challenge for growth ventures is management. Entrepreneurs have to be ready to move from doing to managing. Typically this transition occurs as the venture grows beyond about twenty employees. Many entrepreneurs make poor managers: if they had wanted to be managers, they would probably be working in a large corporation in the first place. The choice entrepreneurs have to make is whether to rely on their own managerial skills or to bring in professional managers. In 2001, the youthful founders of Google, Larry Page and Sergey Brin, responded to pressure from their venture capitalists by recruiting 46-year-old Eric Schmidt, former Chief Executive of the large software company Novell, to run their company.

- *Maturity.* The challenge for entrepreneurs at this stage is retaining their enthusiasm and commitment and generating new growth. This is a period when entrepreneurship changes to *intrapreneurship*, the generation of new ventures from inside the organisation. An important option is usually *diversification* into new business areas, a topic dealt with in Chapter 7. Amazon.com in the United States has moved from book-selling to automotive parts, groceries and clothing. When generating new ventures at this stage, it is critical to recall the odds on success. Research suggests that many small high-tech firms fail to manage the transition to a second generation of technology, and that it is often better at this point simply to look for exit.[29]

- *Exit.* Exit refers to departure from the venture, either by the founding entrepreneurs, or by the original investors, or both. At the point of exit, entrepreneurs and venture capitalists will seek to release capital as a reward for their input and risk-taking. Entrepreneurs may consider three prime routes to exit. A simple *trade sale* of the venture to another company is a common route. Thus social networking site MySpace.com was bought by the News Corporation just two years after foundation (Illustration 1.1). Some entrepreneurs may sell to their own managers, in the form of a *management buy-out* (MBO). Another exit route for highly successful enterprises is an *initial public offering* (IPO), the sale of shares to the public, for instance on the American NASDAQ exchange. IPOs usually involve just a portion of the total shares available, and may thus allow entrepreneurs to continue in the business and provide funds for further growth. Google raised $1.67bn (~€1.17bn) with its 2004 IPO, selling only 7 per cent of its shares. It is often said that good entrepreneurs plan for their exit right from start-up, and certainly venture capitalists will insist on this.

ILLUSTRATION 9.4

Fatima's dignified gowns

A business administration degree is just the starting point for this entrepreneurial venture.

Fatima Ba-Alawi graduated in business administration from the University of Portsmouth in 2005. Less than one year later, seven National Health Service hospitals were trialling her innovative hospital gowns, with interest from private sector hospital operator Bupa too. Her new company, DCS Designs (Dignity, Comfort and Safety), had got off to a flying start.

Ba-Alawi had arrived in the United Kingdom in 1998, as a refugee from Somalia speaking no English. After studying for English GCSEs and A Levels, she says: 'I applied to the University of Portsmouth to read business administration because the idea of going into business always appealed to me'. She was keen to be have her own business after finding it 'deeply unpleasant working for somebody else at a fast food outlet as a teenager'.

It was while working in a local hospital as a care assistant that her business idea came to her. Conventional hospital gowns require patients to lift off the whole garment for medical examinations, which was undignified for wearers and awkward for carers. Ba-Alawi designed a new type of gown which provided extra coverage for the back and gave easy access points for examinations. The gowns also had an anti-microbial finish combating microbes such as the dangerous MRSA and C-Diff bugs. DCS gowns were more dignified, more comfortable and more safe.

While still studying, Ba-Alawi approached the University of Portsmouth's Centre for Enterprise for support. She won £500 (~€550; $750) in the University's Enterprise Challenge competition, which she used to fund an initial prototype and carry out some market research. The University's enterprise mentoring service provided her with one-to-one coaching,

which helped her develop her business plan. This business plan won a further University prize, worth £2000, which she used to fund a patent application and register her company, DCS Designs Ltd. She next put in a bid to the University's Student SEED Fund, gaining more support plus an office in the University's Centre for Enterprise and access to virtual office facilities. The SEED fund allowed Ba-Alawi to manufacture sample gowns and distribute them to hospitals, at the same time as launching the DCS Designs website, which had a facility for user feedback. The local Enterprise Hub also provided access to a local patent attorney to help protect her intellectual property.

Progress was slow, though. It was not until 2007 that DCS gained its first sales. NHS hospitals typically preferred to rent gowns, outsourcing the problems of laundering and repair. However, Ba-Alawi was recognised as an official 'Dignity Champion' by the Department of Health, and the company slowly progressed. In 2009, Ba-Alawi commented that her venture was 'a journey of sacrifices, sleepless nights and sometimes foodless nights! But it was worth it. . . . What pays is persistence, patience and perseverance.'

Sources: *Financial Times*, 12 April 2006; *Evening Standard*, 13 September 2005; *Independent*, 4 September 2008; http://www.sehta.co.uk/files/Fatima%20Ba-AlawiSellingtotheNHS.pdf.

Questions

1 What challenges would you anticipate for Ba-Alawi's DCS Designs company if it takes off? How should she deal with them?

2 What does your university or college do to support student entrepreneurship?

Entrepreneurs who have successfully exited a first venture often become *serial entrepreneurs*. Serial entrepreneurs are people who set up a succession of enterprises, investing the capital raised on exit from earlier ventures into new growing ventures. For example, British retailer George Davies set up first the Next fashion chain, then George, then Per Una and most recently GIVe. For serial entrepreneurs, the challenge often is no longer so much funding but good ideas.

9.5.2 Entrepreneurial relationships

For many, entrepreneurship is about independence, working for oneself. This pride in independence is reinforced by a common stereotype of entrepreneurs as heroic individuals, starting their businesses at night in a university laboratory, or in the spare room at home or in a local lock-up garage. William Hewlett and David Packard, founders of the famous computing and printer company, and Steve Jobs of Apple, are oft-quoted examples of the garage stereotype. But digging beneath the stereotype soon reveals a more complex story, in which relationships with large companies can be important right from the start. Often entrepreneurs have worked for large companies beforehand, and continue to use relationships afterwards.[30] While Hewlett came fairly directly out of Stanford University's laboratories, Packard worked at General Electric and Litton Industries. The Hewlett-Packard company used Litton Industries' foundries early on, and later used relationships at General Electric to recruit experienced managers. Steve Jobs worked for William Hewlett for a summer job aged 12, and later was the fortieth employee at video games company Atari.

Thus entrepreneurship often involves managing relationships with other companies, especially big companies. Three concepts are particularly influential here:

- *Corporate venturing*. Many large corporations, such as Intel, Nokia and Shell, have developed corporate venture units that invest externally in new ventures as safeguards against disruptive innovations and potential drivers of future growth.[31] Large corporations gain by increasing the range of ideas they are exposed to, by protecting early-stage ventures from internal bureaucracy and by spreading their risk. Entrepreneurs gain by accessing not just capital but also knowledge of large-company thinking in their domain and contacts with other members of the large company's network. It is crucial that both entrepreneurs and corporate venture capitalists continuously monitor the set of expectations behind the investment: is the investment more profit-driven in terms of expecting good financial returns or is it more strategic, in the sense of being about technological or market development? Shifting expectations on the part of the corporate venture capitalist can lead to the disruption of longer-term plans by the entrepreneurial new venture. In recent years, companies such as Siemens and Nokia have sold or diluted their stakes in some of their corporate venture units, and companies such as Ericsson and Diageo have had to close them down entirely.

- *Spin-offs (or spin-outs)*. These in a sense go in the opposite direction to corporate venturing, involving the generation of small innovative units *from* larger organisations.[32] Companies such as Fairchild Semiconductor are famous for generating many successful spin-offs, including Intel, AMD and LSI Logic, typically as the result of internal disagreements over the appropriate direction for technological innovation. However, spin-off relationships can be more amicable, with the larger parent organisation offering the new venture seed capital and access to its marketing or technological resources. The spin-off gains the flexibility of being independent, while the parent retains a stake in any future success. Sometimes parents will seek to buy out the spin-off entrepreneurs, and reintegrate the venture into the original organisation.[33] For entrepreneurial spin-off companies, therefore, there are potential benefits to managing a constructive relationship with their original parent.

- *Ecosystems.* Following the 'open innovation' approach (section 9.2.3), high-technology companies such as Cisco, IBM and Intel often foster 'ecosystems' of smaller companies. These ecosystems are communities of connected suppliers, agents, distributors, franchisees, technology entrepreneurs and makers of complementary products.[34] Apple for example has created an ecosystem around its iPod, in which more than one hundred companies manufacture accessories and peripherals such as cases, speakers and docking units. Large firms get the benefits of increased customer satisfaction through the provision of complementary products. Ecosystem members get the benefit of a large and often lucrative market: iPod accessories get plenty of retail shelf space and superior margins. Small entrepreneurial firms wishing to participate in such ecosystems have to be skilled in managing relationships with powerful technological leaders.

9.5.3 Social entrepreneurship

Entrepreneurship is not just a matter for the private sector. The public sector has seen increasing calls for a more entrepreneurial approach to service creation and delivery. Recently too the notion of social entrepreneurship has become common. **Social entrepreneurs are individuals and groups who create independent organisations to mobilise ideas and resources to address social problems, typically earning revenues but on a not-for-profit basis.**[35] Independence and revenues generated in the market give social entrepreneurs the flexibility and dynamism to pursue social problems that pure public-sector organisations are often too bureaucratic, or too politically constrained, to tackle. Social entrepreneurs have pursued a wide range of initiatives, including small loans ('micro-credit') to peasants by the Grameen bank in Bangladesh, employment creation by the Mondragon cooperative in the Basque region of Spain, and fair trade by Traidcraft in the United Kingdom. This wide range of initiatives raises at least three key choices for social entrepreneurs.

- *Social mission.* For social entrepreneurs, the social mission is primary. The social mission can embrace two elements: end-objectives and operational processes. For example, the Grameen bank has the end-objective of reducing rural poverty, especially for women. The process is empowering poor people's own business initiatives by providing micro-credit at a scale and to people that conventional banks would ignore.

- *Organisational form.* Many social enterprises take on cooperative forms, involving their employees and other stakeholders on a democratic basis and thus building commitment and channels for ideas. This form of organisation raises the issue of which stakeholders to include, and which to exclude. Cooperatives can also be slow to take hard decisions. Social enterprises therefore sometimes take more hierarchical charity or company forms of organisation. Cafédirect, the fair-trade beverages company, even became a publicly listed company, paying its first dividend to shareholders in 2006.

- *Business model.* Social enterprises typically rely to a large extent on revenues earned in the marketplace, not just government subsidy or charitable donations. Housing associations collect rents, micro-credit organisations charge interest and fair-trade organisations sell produce. Social entrepreneurs are no different to other entrepreneurs, therefore, in having to design an efficient and effective business model. This business model might involve innovative changes in the value chain. Thus fair-trade organisations have often become much

ILLUSTRATION 9.5

Sociable rats in search of a model

Rats have proved they can detect landmines in Africa. The problem now is how to make them pay.

There are 70 countries around the world affected by landmines left behind from earlier wars. In 2008, these landmines caused 5,200 casualties worldwide. Large areas of land are too dangerous to use for agriculture. But traditional mine-detecting equipment or mine-detecting dogs are very expensive.

Belgian Bart Weetjens had an idea: use rats. Rats have a very sensitive sense of smell, well able to detect the TNT in landmines. As Weetjens told the *Boston Globe*: 'Rats are organized, sensitive, sociable and smart'. In 1998, Weetjens established APOPO as a social enterprise dedicated to developing the potential for rats in de-mining. In 2003, Weetjens began field-testing African giant pouched rats in Mozambique, a country with 3 million landmines. The following year, APOPO's first eleven rats passed their offical test on a real minefield and were ready for action.

The rats work on a Pavlovian basis: for each detected mine, they get a banana or some peanuts. Rats are cheap to train: $4000 (~€2800) per rat, compared to $40,000 for dogs. They are easier to house and transport than dogs, and also less susceptible to tropical diseases. Because they are lighter than dogs, they don't trip off landmines themselves. Finally, rats are more sociable than dogs: they will work with anyone who rewards them, while dogs are inflexible, only working with those to whom they have formed an attachment. A single rat can inspect 1,000 square feet in about 30 minutes, something that would take a human a whole day working with an electronic mine-detector.

Initial funding for APOPO's development phase had come from the University of Antwerp and the Belgian Directorate for International Co-operation. By 2008, more than half of its funding was coming from various government grants, over a third from philanthropic foundations and corporate gifts, some 6 per cent from technical and research institutes and about 5 per cent from APOPO's own fundraising. Principal amongst these fundraising initiatives is the 'Hero Rat' scheme. For €5 ($7) a month, supporters can adopt a rat, each with a name and picture on APOPO's website.

The problem for APOPO is securing its viability. Because grants are typically just to cover costs, APOPO has never made the kinds of profits necessary to build financial reserves. Now that the rats are a proven concept, research funding is harder to get. As yet, there is no secure business model.

In 2010, financial adviser Alvin Hall visited APOPO on behalf of the BBC. He advised Weetjens to increase the minimum donation for adopting a 'Hero Rat'. He also proposed the creation of an endowment fund, allowing large donations to give APOPO some permanent capital. Hall also encouraged APOPO to think about diversification ventures.

One promising avenue for diversification is tuberculosis (TB) detection. APOPO is running trials in Tanzania using the rats to detect TB in the saliva of sick patients. TB is responsible for 1.7 million deaths each year, mainly in poor countries. Apparently these sensitive rats can process as many saliva samples in a few minutes as a human lab technician can in a whole day. The rats have even detected TB in samples that had been missed by conventional tests. APOPO's 2010 mission statement reflects this widening role: 'to become the centre of excellence in detection rat technologies, to enhance the impact of life-saving actions'.

Sources: www.apopo.org; *Boston Globe*, 23 November 2008; www.bbc.co.uk, 5 March 2010.

Questions

1 What are the advantages and disadvantages of a social enterprise approach in this kind of domain?

2 What would be your advice to Bart Weetjens as he searches for a secure long-term business model?

more closely involved with their suppliers than commercial organisations, for example advising farmers on agriculture and providing education and infrastructure support to their communities. Illustration 9.5 shows how mine-clearing venture APOPO is struggling to find a viable business model.

Social entrepreneurs, just like other entrepreneurs, often have to forge relationships with large commercial companies. For example, a new social enterprise called Ten Senses established Bulgaria's first fair-trade shop with assistance from the multinational bank Citigroup and the oil company Royal Dutch Shell. Harvard Business School's Rosabeth Moss Kanter points out that the benefits to business of involvement with social enterprise can go beyond a feel-good factor and attractive publicity.[36] She shows that involvement in social enterprise can help develop new technologies and services, access new pools of potential employees, and create relationships with government and other agencies that can eventually turn into new markets. Kanter concludes that large corporations should develop clear strategies with regard to social entrepreneurship, not treat it as ad hoc charity.

SUMMARY

AUDIO SUMMARY
www.pearsoned.co.uk/mystrategylab

- Strategists face four fundamental dilemmas in innovation: the relative emphasis to put on technology push or market pull; whether to focus on product or process innovation; how much to rely on 'open innovation'; and finally how far to concentrate on technological innovation as opposed to broader business-model innovation.

- Innovations often diffuse into the marketplace according to an S-curve model in which slow start-up is followed by accelerating growth (the tipping point) and finally a flattening of demand. Managers should watch out for 'tripping points'.

- Managers have a choice between being first into the marketplace and entering later. Innovators can capture first-mover advantages. However, 'fast second' strategies are often more attractive.

- Established incumbents' businesses should beware disruptive innovations. Incumbents can stave off inertia by developing portfolios of real options and by organising autonomous new venture units.

- Entrepreneurs face characteristic dilemmas as their businesses go through the entrepreneurial life cycle of start-up, growth, maturity and exit. Entrepreneurs also have to choose how they relate to large firms, particularly as they may become involved in their ecosystems or strategies for open innovation.

- Social entrepreneurship offers a flexible way of addressing social problems, but raises issues about appropriate missions, organisational forms and business models.

KEY DEBATE

Are large firms better innovators than small firms?

The famous Austrian economist Joseph Schumpeter proposed that large firms are proportionately more innovative than small firms. This proposition is a controversial one. If true, it would discourage laboratory scientists and engineers from leaving their large firm employers to set up their own ventures. It would encourage large firms like Google and Cisco to keep on buying up small innovative firms and absorbing them into their own corporate strategies. It would make government policy makers more tolerant of huge, domineering firms like Microsoft who claim that their large scale is important to continued innovation in computer software.

Schumpeter's proposition for the advantages of large firms in innovation has several points in its favour:

● Large firms have greater and more diverse resources, helping them to bring together all the various necessary elements for innovation.
● Large firms may have a greater propensity for innovation risk, knowing that they can absorb the costs of innovation failure.
● Large firms have better incentives to innovate, because they are more likely to be able to capitalise on innovation, having all the required complementary assets (distribution channels and so on) to roll it out fast and under their control.

On the other hand, there are good reasons why small firms might be more innovative:

● Small firms are typically more cohesive, so that knowledge is more easily shared.
● Small firms are typically more flexible and less bureaucratic, so that they can innovate faster and more boldly.
● Small firms are more motivated to innovate simply to survive, while large firms can simply defend and exploit their dominance of existing markets.

There has been plenty of research on whether small or large firms are proportionately more innovative. Some researchers have focused on the input side, for example measuring whether large firms are more research intensive in terms of R&D expenditure as a percentage of sales. Other researchers have focused on the output side, for example counting whether large firms have proportionately greater numbers of patents for innovations. There is no final consensus on the overall patterns of innovation. However, recent research findings suggest that in general:

● Large firms are relatively less research intensive in high technology industries, for example electronics and software.
● Large firms are relatively more innovative in service industries than in manufacturing industries.

It seems that the research so far cannot provide any firm rules about whether large or small firms are better innovators in general. However, research scientists, acquisitive large firms and government policy makers need to consider carefully the specifics of particular industries.

References:
C. Camisón-Zornosa, R. Lapiedra-Alcani, M. Segarra-Ciprés and M. Boronat-Navarro, 'A Meta-Analysis of Innovation and Organizational Size', *Organization Studies*, vol. 25, no. 3 (2004), pp. 331–61.
C-Y Lee and T. Sung, 'Schumpeter's Legacy: a New Perspective on the Relationship between Firm Size and R&D', *Research Policy*, vol. 34 (2005), pp. 914–31.

Question

What kinds of managerial action might you consider if you were trying to increase the innovativeness of a large firm in a high technology manufacturing industry?

WORK ASSIGNMENTS

✱ Denotes more advanced work assignments. * Refers to a case study in the Text and Cases edition.*

9.1✱ For a new product or service that you have recently experienced and enjoyed, investigate the strategy of the company responsible. With reference to the dilemmas of section 9.2, explain whether the innovation was more technology push or market pull, product or process driven, or technological or more broadly business model based.

9.2 Go to a web traffic site (such as alexa.com) and compare over time trends in terms of 'page views' or 'reach' for older sites (such as Amazon.com) and newer sites (such as spotify.com, or any that has more recently emerged). With reference to section 9.3, how do you explain these trends and how would you project them forward?

9.3✱ With regard to a new product or service that you have recently experienced and enjoyed (as in 9.1), investigate the strategic responses of 'incumbents' to this innovation. To what extent is the innovation disruptive for them (see section 9.4.3)?

9.4 With reference to the entrepreneurial life cycle, identify the position of either Dyson (Chapter 3), Google (Chapter 12), Web Reservations*, Ekomate* or Leax *. What managerial issues might this case company anticipate in the coming years?

9.5 Use the internet to identify a social entrepreneurial venture that interests you (via www.skollfoundation.org, for example), and, with regard to section 9.5.3, identify its social mission, its organisational form and its business model.

Integrative assignment

9.6 Consider a for-profit or social entrepreneurial idea that you or your friends or colleagues might have. Drawing on section 15.4.4, outline the elements of a strategic plan for this possible venture. What more information do you need to get?

RECOMMENDED KEY READINGS

- P. Trott, *Innovation Management and New Product Development*, 4th edition, Financial Times Prentice Hall, 2008, provides a comprehensive overview of innovation strategy issues. A lively and accessible survey of many innovation issues, together with a wealth of examples, is C. Markides and P. Geroski, *Fast Second: How Smart Companies Bypass Radical Innovation to Enter and Dominate New Markets*, Jossey-Bass, 2005.

- A good collection of accessible articles on specialised innovation topics by leading academics is J. Fagerberg, D. Mowery and R. Nelson (eds), *The Oxford Handbook of*

Innovation, Oxford University Press, 2005. An equivalent collection on entrepreneurship is M. Casson, B. Yeung, A. Basu and N. Wadeson (eds), *The Oxford Handbook of Entrepreneurship*, Oxford University Press, 2006.

- P.A. Wickham, *Strategic Entrepreneurship*, 4th edition (2008) is becoming the standard European text with regard to entrepreneurial strategy.

- Social entrepreneurship is discussed usefully in A. Nicholls (ed.), *Social Entrepreneurship: New Paradigms of Sustainable Social Change*, Oxford University Press, 2006.

REFERENCES

1. This definition adapts, in order to include the public sector, the definition in P. Trott, *Innovation Management and New Product Development*, 3rd edition, Financial Times Prentice Hall, 2005.

2. A good discussion of the academic theories that underpin these dilemmas is in R. Rothwell, 'Successful industrial innovation: critical factors for the 1990s', *R&D Management*, vol. 22, no. 3 (1992), pp. 221–39.

3. J. Abernathy and W. Utterback, 'A dynamic model of process and product innovation', *Omega*, vol. 3, no. 6 (1975), pp. l42–60.

4. P. Anderson and M.L. Tushman, 'Technological discontinuities and dominant designs: a cyclical model of technological change', *Administrative Science Quarterly*, vol. 35 (1990), pp. 604–33.

5. J. Tang, 'Competition and innovation behaviour', *Research Policy*, vol. 35 (2006), pp. 68–82.

6. H. Chesbrough and M. Appleyard, 'Open innovation and strategy', *California Management Review*, vol. 50, no. 1 (2007), pp. 57–73; O. Gasman, E. Enkel and H. Chesbrough, 'The future of open innovation', *R&D Management*, vol. 38, no. 1 (2010), pp. 1–9.

7. A. Gawer and M. Cusumano, *Platform Leadership: How Intel, Microsoft and Cisco Drive Industry Innovation*, Harvard Business School Press (2002).

8. See the special issue on business models in *Long Range Planning*, 2010, especially D.J. Teece, 'Business models, business strategy and innovation', *Long Range Planning*, vol. 43, nos 3/4 (2010).

9. J. Magretta 'Why business models matter', *Harvard Business Review*, vol. 80, no. 5 (2002), pp. 86–92; H. Chesbrough, 'Business model innovation: it's not just about technology anymore', *Strategy & Leadership*, vol. 35, no. 6 (2007), pp. 12–17.

10. Innovation diffusion is discussed in the classic E. Rogers, *Diffusion of Innovations*, Free Press, 1995; C. Kim and R. Maubourgne, 'Knowing a winning idea when you see one', *Harvard Business Review*, vol. 78, no. 5 (2000), pp. 129–38; and J. Cummings and J. Doh, 'Identifying who matters: mapping key players in multiple environments', *California Management Review*, vol. 42, no. 2 (2000), pp. 83–104 (see especially pp. 91–7).

11. J. Nichols and S. Roslow, 'The S-curve: an aid to strategic marketing', *The Journal of Consumer Marketing*, vol. 3, no. 2 (1986), pp. 53–64 and F. Suarez and G. Lanzolla, 'The half-truth of first-mover advantage', *Harvard Business Review*, vol. 83, no. 4 (2005), pp. 121–7. This S-curve refers to innovation diffusion. However, the S-curve effect sometimes also refers to the diminishing performance increases available from a maturing technology: A. Sood and G. Tellis, 'Technological evolution and radical innovation', *Journal of Marketing*, vol. 69, no. 3 (2005), pp. 152–68.

12. M. Gladwell, *The Tipping Point*, Abacus, 2000. Tipping points are also important in public policy and can help anticipate emerging problems, for example crime waves and epidemics.

13. www.bbcnews.com. 12 January 2007.

14. S. Brown, 'The tripping point', *Marketing Research*, vol. 17, no. 1 (2005), pp. 8–13.

15. C. Markides and P. Geroski, *Fast Second: How Smart Companies Bypass Radical Innovation to Enter and Dominate New Markets*, Jossey-Bass, 2005; R. Kerin, P. Varadarajan and R. Peterson, 'First-mover advantage: a synthesis, conceptual framework and research propositions', *Journal of Marketing*, vol. 56, no. 4 (1992), pp. 33–47; and P.F. Suarez and G. Lanzolla, 'The half-truth of first-mover advantage', *Harvard Business Review*, vol. 83, no. 4 (2005), pp. 121–7.

16. F. Suarez and G. Lanzolla, 'The half-truth of first-mover advantage', *Harvard Business Review*, vol. 83, no. 4 (2005), pp. 121–7. See also S. Min, U. Manohar and W. Robinson, 'Market pioneer and early follower survival risks: a contingency analysis of really new versus incrementally new product-markets', *Journal of Marketing*, vol. 70, no. 1 (2006), pp. 15–33.

17. C. Markides and P. Geroski, *Fast Second: How Smart Companies Bypass Radical Innovation to Enter and Dominate New Markets*, Jossey-Bass, 2005.

18. David Teece, the academic authority in this area, refers to the capacity to capture profits as 'the appropriability regime': see D. Teece, *Managing Intellectual Capital*, Oxford University Press, 2000.

19. An excellent survey of intellectual property rights is in *The Economist Magazine*, Survey: Patents and Technology, 25 October 2005.

20. D. Teece, *Managing Intellectual Capital*, Oxford University Press, 2000.

21. See J. Bower and C. Christensen, 'Disruptive technologies: catching the wave', *Harvard Business Review*, vol. 73, no. 1 (1995), pp. 43–53 and C. Christensen and M.E. Raynor, *The Innovator's Solution*, Harvard Business School Press, 2003.

22. R.G. McGrath and I. MacMillan, *The Entrepreneurial Mindset*, Harvard Business School Press, 2000.

23. C. Christensen and M.E. Raynor, *The Innovator's Solution*, Harvard Business School Press, 2003.

24. V. Govindarajan and C. Trimble, 'Organizational DNA for strategic innovation', *California Management Review*, vol. 43, no. 3 (2005), pp. 47–75.

25. Excellent textbooks on strategic entrepreneurship include J.A. Timmons, *New Venture Creation: Entrepreneurship in the 21st Century*, 6th edition, Irwin (2004) and P.A. Wickham, *Strategic Entrepreneurship*, 4th edition (2008).

26. D. Flynn and A. Forman, 'Life cycles of new venture organizations: different factors affecting performance', *Journal of Developmental Entrepreneurship*, vol. 6, no. 1 (2001), pp. 41–58.

27. D. Flynn and A. Forman, 'Life cycles of new venture organizations: different factors affecting performance',

Journal of Developmental Entrepreneurship, vol. 6, no. 1 (2001), pp. 41–58.

28. D. Flynn and A. Forman, 'Life cycles of new venture organizations: different factors affecting performance', *Journal of Developmental Entrepreneurship*, vol. 6, no. 1 (2001), pp. 41–58.

29. For a detailed account of Cisco's policy of taking over high-technology firms, see D. Mayer and M. Kenney, 'Economic action does not take place in a vacuum: understanding Cisco's acquisition and development strategy', *Industry and Innovation*, vol. 11, no. 4 (2004), pp. 293–325.

30. P. Audia and C. Rider, 'A garage and an idea: what more does an entrepreneur need?', *California Management Review*, vol. 40, no. 1 (2005), pp. 6–28.

31. H. Chesbrough, 'Making sense of corporate venture capital', *Harvard Business Review*, vol. 80, no. 3 (2002), pp. 4–11; A. Campbell, J. Birkinshaw, A. Morrison and R. van Basten Batenburg, 'The future of corporate venturing', *MIT Sloan Management Review*, vol. 45, no. 1 (2003), pp. 33–41.

32. S. Klepper, 'Spinoffs: a review and synthesis', *European Management Review*, vol. 6 (2009), pp. 159–71.

33. A. Parhankangas and P. Arenius, 'From a corporate venture to an independent company: a base for a taxonomy for corporate spin-off firms', *Research Policy*, vol. 32 (2003), pp. 463–81.

34. B. Iyer, C.-H. Lee and N. Venkatraman, 'Managing in a "Small World Ecosystem"', *California Management Review*, 48, 3 (2006), 28–47.

35 A. Nicholls (ed.) *Social Entrepreneurship: New Paradigms of Sustainable Social Change*, Oxford University Press (2006); J. Austin, H. Stevenson and J. Wei-Skillern. 'Social and commercial entrepreneurship: same, different, or both?' *Entrepreneurship Theory and Practice*, 30, no. 1 (2006).

36 R. Moss Kanter, 'From spare change to real change', *Harvard Business Review*, May-June 1999.

CASE EXAMPLE

Skype: innovators and entrepreneurs

Introduction

Niklas Zennström and Janus Friis have been a golden pair in the Internet business. For a period during the early 2000s, their Kazaa peer-to-peer file sharing business was the world's largest music sharing site. After selling that business to Sharman Networks, they moved quickly to establish Skype in 2003, which quickly became the dominant player in the world's VoIP (Voice over Internet Protocol) telephone market. Skype's free Internet-based VoIP service was an attractive alternative to the expensive traditional land-line and mobile telephone services, gaining 60 million users by 2005. That same year, they sold Skype to eBay for $2.6bn (~€1.8bn) – an impressive figure for a business whose total revenues were just $60m and had still not turned a profit. The eBay deal, however, turned out not to be an unblemished success.

Two entrepreneurs

Zennström is the older of the two, aged 40 at the sale to eBay. He took a first degree in business and then an MSc in engineering and computer science from Uppsala University in Sweden. He then entered the telecom-munications industry, spending nine years in Tele2, a fast-expanding European telecoms group. He met Friis in 1997, hiring him to manage a help-desk. Friis, a Dane, is 11 years younger and failed even to graduate from high school. But from the late 1990s the two worked closely together on a series of new ventures: as well as Kazaa and Skype, these included Altnet, claimed to be the world's first secure peer-to-peer wholesale network, Joltid, a company in traffic optimisation technologies, and the portal everyday.com.

The pair were committed to disruptive innovation. Zennström told the *Financial Times*: 'It's everyone's obligation to fight against monopolies and also com-panies that provide bad services.' Of the traditional landline and mobile telephone companies, he declares: 'They deserve to be challenged. They provide bad and expensive service.'

Co-founders of Skype – Niklas Zennström (left) and Janus Friis (right)

Source: Rex Features/Steve Forrest.

The Skype business model

Skype's software allows people to use the Internet to make free calls to other Skype users all over the world. Given the cost of traditional international calls, this was an exciting idea. Initial funding, however, was not easy to find as the music industry was still pursuing a lawsuit against the two founders regarding the illegal fileshar-ing their earlier Kazaa venture appeared to facilitate. For fear of legal action, Zennström and Friis dared not even enter the USA. Most traditional venture capitalists gave the new venture a wide berth. Moreover, it was not easy to see how to make money out of free calls.

The business model is more complicated than that, of course. Most users have free calls, certainly. However, Skype has very low costs, as customers download the software off the Internet and it is the customers' com-puters and Internet connections that make the network. It costs nothing to keep connections open continuously. Marketing is cheap, because customers naturally invite others to join. Skype has no telephone help-desk, citing the overwhelming number of customers and the effectiveness of its standard Internet queries services. Skype makes its money from its ancillary services, such as SkypeOut, which allows customers to call traditional landline or mobile numbers for a fee, often very small.

Zennström explains the model: 'We want to make as little money as possible per user. We don't have any cost per user, but we want a lot of them.'

This overturns the traditional landline and mobile phone business model. Traditional telephone companies of both types face high costs of both marketing and capacity building. Customers are typically charged according to distance and by the minute. The traditional principle is to maximise revenues per customer, completely the opposite to Skype. Zennström summarised to *Business Week*:

> When you're a phone company, you have marketing and customer-acquisition costs. When you have a customer, you have an operational cost of running the network. Then you have a cost for billing systems. That's an operator business model.
>
> The business model of Skype is completely different. Skype has a software business model. We don't have any distribution or marketing costs for each user – our software is spread virally. And when we have a new user, we have zero cost for serving that user because they're using P2P (peer-to-peer) software and their own bandwidth. So we have zero costs of getting new users and zero costs of running traffic. Our costs are only business development and software development.

Comparing the positions of the two types of companies, he added: 'Something that is a great business model for us is probably a terrible model for them.'

As shown in the figure, Skype's service has been attracting snowballing usage. The tipping point came towards the end of 2004, and by March 2010 Skype was achieving more than 23 million users in a single day. Of course, this success raised an awkward paradox. If Skype became near universal, who would be left for people to call using the paid service of SkypeOut to access traditional phones?

eBay's move

Skype was always likely to be for sale. Zennström and Friis had sold Kazaa quickly and their initial funders would want a profitable early exit too. It was not surprising that rumours started during 2005 of possible acquisition from technology giants such as Google, Microsoft and Yahoo!. In the end, however, it was online auctioneer eBay who did the deal, slightly surprisingly as it was not seen as a communications company.

There are similarities in the underlying business models of the two companies. Both benefit from 'network effects', where value rises disproportionately fast with increasing members of the network. One more precise rationale from eBay's point of view was that

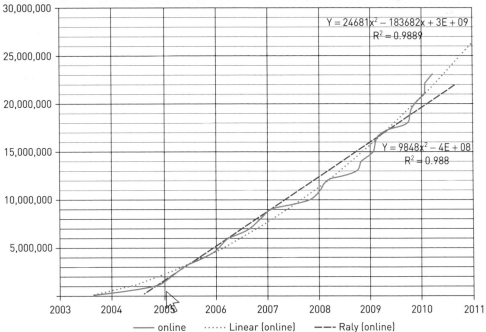

Skype Dialtone – Peak Number of Accounts Logged in during One Day

$$Y = 24681x^2 - 183682x + 3E + 09$$
$$R^2 = 0.9889$$

$$Y = 9848x^2 - 4E + 08$$
$$R^2 = 0.988$$

——— online   · · · · · · Linear (online)   — – – Raly (online)

Source: Phil Wolff, *Skype Journal*, 8 March 2010; reproduced with permission.

Skype connections could be placed directly on the eBay site, allowing customers potentially to phone sellers with a single click of the button. Also, sellers could place voice links directly on their eBay sites, so that customers could click directly to a message, paying eBay a fee every time they did. On the other hand, Skype would strengthen its links with eBay's subsidiary PayPal, which Skype already used for managing payments for its SkypeOut service.

For Zennström, however, one major attraction of eBay was that it looked likely to leave Skype more alone. Companies like Yahoo! and Microsoft tend to integrate their acquisitions closely into their existing operations, extinguishing autonomy. Zennström and Friis might be working with eBay for some time. The deal included an 'earn-out' arrangement which would push Skype's final sale price to over $4bn if they managed to meet revenue and profit targets over the coming years. Anyway, the two had an exciting vision for the future: to become the world's biggest and best platform for all communication – text, voice or video – from any Internet-connected device, whether a computer or a mobile phone.

eBay's role

eBay had a lot to offer an ambitious company like Skype. Founded only in 1995, it had reached revenues of $4.55bn and 11,600 employees in the space of 10 years. Zennström commented of Meg Whitman, eBay's Chief Executive since 1998: 'I think I can learn a lot of things from Meg. We want to see things through, but we also have some other ideas.' Skype would still have its own strategy, budgets, culture and brands. Zennström insisted to the *Financial Times*:

> One of the important things for us, but also one of the great things with eBay, is that we wanted to make sure that we could merge with a bigger company, but that Skype stays as one company. Meg said: 'Take advantage of the resources we have, but we are not going to tell you what to do because you're the best in the world to run your own business.'

The managerial demands of rapid growth were considerable. Staff quadrupled to 300 between 2005 and 2006, and included 30 nationalities scattered all over the world. eBay introduced five of its own senior managers to help, including a new president responsible for day-to-day operations, a chief financial officer and a new human resource director. But Skype was keen to preserve its own culture. According to Zennström, still the CEO, Skype's passionate, pioneering culture had to be both protected and nurtured: 'It's how you operate, how you behave. It starts when we are hiring people. They need to be really thrilled about Skype as a movement, rather than a place to work.'

eBay's exit

While Skype protected its culture, synergies were hard to find. Skype's sales in 2007 had reached $383m, but eBay users were not making the hoped-for use of Skype connections. Targets were missed. In October 2007, Zennström was obliged to step down as CEO and eBay wrote down the value of its investment by $1.4bn. In March 2008, after a 30 per cent slide in share price, Meg Whitman resigned as CEO of eBay. The new CEO, John Donahue, commented on Skype: 'If the synergies are strong, we'll keep it in our portfolio. If not, we'll reassess it.' In September 2009, eBay announced that it was selling 65 per cent of its interest to the Silver Lake group of investors for $2bn. However, it transpired that eBay had neglected to acquire the source-code for Skype software back in 2005. To buy off the threat of legal action and close the deal with Silver Lake, eBay was obliged to give Zennström and Friis 14 per cent of their company back.

Sources: 'Phone Service the "Zero Cost" Way', *Business Week online*, 7 January 2004; www.wikipedia.org; *The Economist*, 15 September 2005; *Financial Times*, 17 and 19 April 2006; *Financial Times*, 17 September 2009.

Questions

1 What are the advantages, and what are the possible limits, of Skype's business model?

2 What went wrong with eBay's acquisition of Skype?

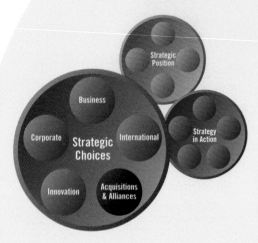

10

MERGERS, ACQUISITIONS AND ALLIANCES

Learning outcomes

After reading this chapter you should be able to:

● Establish the potential role of *organic* (stand-alone) strategies.

● Identify key issues in the successful management of *mergers and acquisitions.*

● Identify the key issues in the successful management of *strategic alliances.*

● Determine the appropriate choices between *organic* development, *mergers and acquisitions* and *strategic alliances.*

● Compare *key success factors* in mergers, acquisitions and alliances.

Key terms

Acquisition p. 329

Collaborative advantage p. 338

Collective strategy p. 338

Corporate entrepreneurship p. 328

Merger p. 329

Organic development p. 328

Organisational justice p. 337

Strategic alliance p. 338

mystrategylab

MyStrategyLab is designed to help you make the most of your studies. Visit **www.pearsoned.co.uk/mystrategylab** to discover a wide range of resources specific to this chapter, including:

• A personalised **Study plan** that will help you understand core concepts

• **Audio** and **video clips** that put the spotlight on strategy in the real world

• **Online glossaries** and **flashcards** that provide helpful reminders when you're looking for some quick revision.

(10.1) INTRODUCTION

Mergers, acquisitions and alliances are often in the news. For example in 2009, Italian carmaker Fiat formed an alliance with the American Chrysler as part of its internationalisation strategy. In 2010, the American foods conglomerate Kraft acquired the British Cadbury confectionery company in pursuit of its diversification strategy. Acquisition by one company of another, complete merger between two companies, and strategic alliance between different companies are all very common methods for carrying out strategies.

This chapter therefore addresses mergers, acquisitions and alliances as key methods for pursuing strategic options. It will consider them alongside the principal alternative of 'organic' development, in other words the pursuit of a strategy relying on the company's own resources. Figure 10.1 shows how the main strategic options considered in the previous three chapters – diversification, internationalisation and innovation – can all be achieved through mergers and acquisitions, alliances and organic development. Of course, these three methods can also be used for many other strategies, for example consolidating markets or building scale advantages.

The chapter starts with organic development. Organic development is the default option: relying on the organisation's internal resources is the natural first option to consider. The chapter then introduces the two principal external options: first mergers and acquisitions (often abbreviated as M&A) and then strategic alliances. The final section systematically compares the two external options against the internal option of organic development. Given the frequent failures of acquisitions and alliances, the fundamental issue is when to acquire, when to ally or when is it better to 'do it yourself'? The final section also considers key success factors in M&A and alliances. The problematic success record of acquisitions in particular is the subject of the Key Debate at the end of this chapter.

Figure 10.1 Three strategy methods

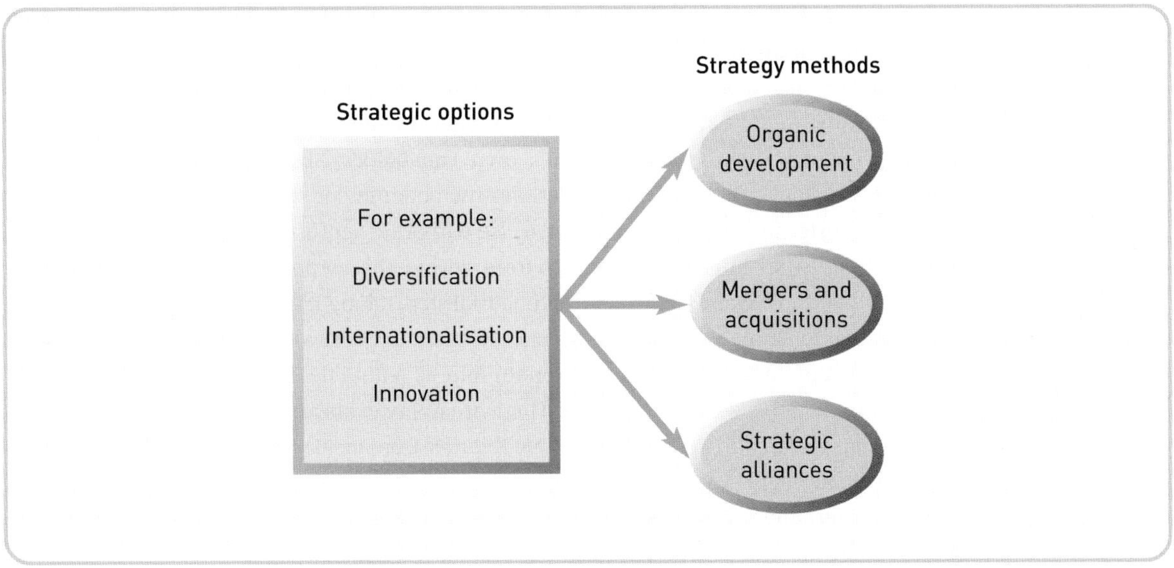

(10.2) ORGANIC DEVELOPMENT

The default method for pursuing a strategy is to 'do it yourself', relying on internal capabilities. Thus **organic development is where a strategy is pursued by building on and developing an organisation's own capabilities**. For example, Amazon's entry into the e-books market with its Kindle product was principally organic, relying on its own subsidiary Lab126 and drawing on its expertise in book retailing, internet retail and software. For Amazon, this do-it-yourself (DIY) diversification method was preferable to allying with an existing e-book producer such as Sony or buying a relevant hi-tech start-up such as the French pioneer Bookeen.

There are four principal advantages to relying on organic development:

- *Knowledge and learning.* Using the organisation's existing capabilities to pursue a new strategy can enhance organisational knowledge and learning. Direct involvement in a new market or technology is likely to promote the acquisition and internalisation of deeper knowledge than a hands-off strategic alliance, for example.

- *Spreading investment over time.* Acquisitions typically require an immediate upfront payment for the target company. Organic development allows the spreading of investment over the whole time span of the strategy's development. This reduction of upfront commitment may make it easier to reverse or adjust a strategy if conditions change.

- *No availability constraints.* Organic development has the advantage of not being dependent on the availability of suitable acquisition targets or potential alliance partners. There are few acquisition opportunities for foreign companies wanting to enter the Japanese market, for example. Organic developers also do not have to wait until the perfectly matched acquisition target comes on to the market.

- *Strategic independence.* The independence provided by organic development means that the organisation does not need to make the same compromises as might be necessary if it made an alliance with a partner organisation. For example, partnership with a foreign collaborator is likely to involve constraints on marketing activity in their home market.

The reliance of organic development on internal capabilities can be limiting. It is not easy to use existing capabilities as the platform for major leaps in terms of innovation, diversification or internationalisation, for example. However, as in the example of Amazon's Kindle, organic development can sometimes be sufficiently radical to merit the term 'corporate entrepreneurship'. **Corporate entrepreneurship refers to radical change in the organisation's business, driven principally by the organisation's own capabilities.**[1] Bringing together the words 'entrepreneurship' and 'corporate' underlines the potential for significant change or novelty not only by external entrepreneurship (see also corporate venture units in section 9.5.2), but also by reliance on internal capabilities from within the corporate organisation. Thus for Amazon, the Kindle was a radical entrepreneurial step, taking it from retailing into the design of innovative consumer electronic products.

The concept of corporate entrepreneurship is valuable because it encourages an entrepreneurial attitude inside the firm. There are many examples of corporate entrepreneurship, such as the creation of low-cost airline Ryanair from inside the aircraft leasing company Guinness Peat. Often, however, organisations have to go beyond their own internal capabilities and look externally for methods to pursue their strategies. The main themes of this chapter, therefore, are first mergers and acquisitions and second strategic alliances.

(10.3) MERGERS AND ACQUISITIONS

Mergers and acquisitions

Mergers and acquisitions (M&A) frequently grab the headlines, as they involve large sums of money and very public competitions for shareholder support. They can also provide a speedy means of achieving major strategic objectives. However, they can also lead to spectacular failures too. A famous case is that of the Royal Bank of Scotland, whose 2007 takeover of the Dutch ABN AMRO ended in commercial disaster and the bank's nationalisation by the British government.

10.3.1 Types of mergers and acquisitions

An **acquisition** **involves one firm taking over the ownership ('equity') of another, hence the alternative term 'takeover'.** Most acquisitions are ultimately *friendly*, where the acquirer and the target firm agree the terms together, and the target's management recommends acceptance to its shareholders. Sometimes acquisitions are *hostile*: here the would-be acquirer offers a price for the target firm's shares without the agreement of the target's management and the outcome is decided by which side wins the support of shareholders. Thus Cadbury's management initially rejected the hostile bid by Kraft, seeking more friendly alternative partners such as Hershey. On the other hand, **a merger is the combination of two previously separate organisations, typically as more or less equal partners.** For example, in 2009, the French Banque Populaire and Caisse d'Epargne merged to form a new bank called Groupe BPCE, which became the second largest in France. In practice, the terms 'merger' and 'acquisition' are often used interchangeably, hence the common shorthand M&A or just acquisitions.

Mergers and acquisitions can also happen in the public and non-profit sectors: for example, the Finnish government created the new Aalto University in 2010 by merging the Helsinki School of Economics, the Helsinki University of Art and Design and the Helsinki University of Technology. Even if the government is the ultimate owner of the organisations involved, as in this case, it can be appropriate to use the term 'merger' rather than simply 'reorganisation' (see Chapter 13). Publicly owned institutions frequently build up highly distinctive cultures or systems of their own, as if they were in fact independent organisations. Where there are major cultural or systems differences between organisations, the scale and depth of the managerial issues approximate to those that would be involved in a change of ownership. 'Merger' is therefore often used in such cases as that better reflects the scale of the task involved than simply 'reorganisation'.

Mergers and acquisitions are typically cyclical phenomena, involving high peaks and deep troughs. Thus 2007 was a record year for global mergers and acquisitions, involving a value of nearly $6.6bn (~€4.6bn), four times the amount of the previous trough in 2002. As the worldwide recession took hold, the value of global M&A in 2009 fell to $3.6bn (~€2.5bn).[2] These cycles are driven by over-optimism on the part of managers, shareholders and bankers during upturns, and by an exaggerated loss of confidence during downturns. This cyclical pattern should warn managers that M&A may have a strong fashion or bandwagon element. Especially in an upturn, managers should ask very carefully whether acquisitions are really justified. In an upturn too, the laws of supply and demand suggest that the price of target firms is very likely to be excessively high.

Global activity in mergers has traditionally been dominated by North America and Western Europe, whereas it has been much less common in other economies, for example Japan. Many national governance systems put barriers in the way of acquisitions, especially hostile acquisitions (see section 4.3.2). However, companies from fast-developing economies such as China and India have recently undertaken many large-scale acquisitions in order to access Western markets or technology, or to secure material resources needed for growth. For example, the Chinese computer company Lenovo bought IBM Computers and the Indian company Tata bought the car companies Jaguar and Land Rover in the United Kingdom and the Anglo-Dutch steel company Corus (see Illustration 10.2 later).

10.3.2 Motives for mergers and acquisitions

There are three broad types of motive for M&A: strategic, financial and managerial.[3]

Strategic motives for M&A

Strategic motives for M&A involve improving the actual business of the organisation in some way. These motives are often related to the reasons for diversification in general (see section 7.3). Strategic motives can be categorised in three main ways:[4]

- *Extension*. Mergers and acquisitions can be used to extend the reach of a firm in terms of geography, products or markets. Acquisitions can be speedy ways of extending international reach. Thus in 2010 the Chinese Geely car company bought the Swedish Volvo car company in order to build its global presence. Acquisitions can also be an effective way of extending into new markets, as in diversification (see Chapter 7).

- *Consolidation*. Mergers and acquisitions can be used to consolidate the competitors in an industry. Bringing together two competitors can have at least three beneficial effects. In the first place, it increases market power by reducing competition: this might enable the newly consolidated company to raise prices for customers. Second, the combination of two competitors can increase efficiency through reducing surplus capacity or sharing resources, for instance head-office facilities or distribution channels. Finally, the greater scale of the combined operations may increase production efficiency or increase bargaining power with suppliers, forcing them to reduce their prices.

- *Capabilities*. The third broad strategic motive for mergers and acquisitions is to increase a company's capabilities. High-tech companies such as Cisco and Microsoft regard acquisitions of entrepreneurial technology companies as a part of their R&D effort. Instead of researching a new technology from scratch, they allow entrepreneurial start-ups to prove the idea, and then take over these companies in order to incorporate the technological capability within their own portfolio (see section 9.5.2). Capabilities-driven acquisitions are often useful where industries are converging (see section 2.3.1). Thus the telephone company AT&T bought computer company NCR as it perceived industry convergence between telephony and computing.

Financial motives for M&A

Financial motives concern the optimal use of financial resources, rather than directly improving the actual businesses. There are three main financial motives:

- *Financial efficiency*. It is often efficient to bring together a company with a strong balance sheet (i.e. it has plenty of cash) with another company that has a weak balance sheet (i.e. it has high debt). The company with a weak balance sheet can save on interest payments by using the stronger company's assets to pay off its debt, and it can also get investment funds from the stronger company that it could not have accessed otherwise. The company with the strong balance sheet may be able to drive a good bargain in acquiring the weaker company. Also, a company with a booming share price can purchase other companies very efficiently by offering to pay the target company's shareholders with its own shares (equity), rather than paying with cash upfront.

- *Tax efficiency.* Sometimes there may be tax advantages from bringing together different companies. For example, one company may be operating in a low-taxation country, and profits from the other company in a higher-tax area can be transferred to be taxed there. Or a company that is making high profits may buy a company that has accumulated losses in order to reduce its own tax liability. Naturally, there are legal restrictions on this strategy.

- *Asset stripping or unbundling.* Some companies are effective at spotting other companies whose underlying assets are worth more than the price of the company as a whole. This makes it possible to buy such companies and then rapidly sell off ('unbundle') different business units to various buyers for a total price substantially in excess of what was originally paid for the whole. Although this is often dismissed as merely opportunistic profiteering ('asset stripping'), if the business units find better corporate parents through this unbundling process, there can be a real gain in economic effectiveness.

Managerial motives for M&A

As for diversification (see section 7.3), acquisitions may sometimes serve managers' interests better than shareholders' interests. 'Managerial' motives are so called, therefore, because they are self-serving rather than efficiency-driven. M&A may serve managerial self-interest for two types of reason:

- *Personal ambition.* There are three ways that acquisitions can satisfy the personal ambition of senior managers, regardless of the real value being created. First, senior managers' personal financial incentives may be tied to short-term growth targets or share-price targets that are more easily achieved by large and spectacular acquisitions than the more gradualist and lower-profile alternative of organic growth. Second, large acquisitions attract media attention, with opportunities to boost personal reputations through flattering media interviews and appearances. Here there is the so-called 'managerial hubris' (vanity) effect: managers who have been successful in earlier acquisitions become over-confident and embark on more and more acquisitions, each riskier and more expensive than the one before.[5] Finally, acquisitions provide opportunities to give friends and colleagues greater responsibility, helping to cement personal loyalty by developing individuals' careers.

- *Bandwagon effects.* As noted earlier, acquisitions are highly cyclical. In an upswing, there are three kinds of pressure on senior managers to join the acquisition bandwagon. First, when many other firms are making acquisitions, financial analysts and the business media may criticise more cautious managers for undue conservatism. Second, shareholders will fear that their company is being left behind, as they see opportunities for their business being snatched by rivals. Lastly, employees will worry that if their company is not acquiring, it will become the target of a hostile bid itself. For managers wanting a quiet life during a 'merger boom', the easiest strategy may be simply to join in. But the danger is of paying too much for an acquisition that the company does not really need in the first place.

In sum, there are bad reasons as well as good reasons for acquisitions and mergers. The average performance of acquisitions is unimpressive, with some suggesting that half of acquisitions fail (see Key Debate at the end of the chapter). It is therefore well worth asking sceptical questions of any M&A strategy. The converse can be true of course: there can be bad reasons for resisting a hostile takeover. Senior managers may resist being acquired because they fear losing their jobs, even if the price offered represents a good deal for their shareholders.

10.3.3 M&A processes

Acquisitions take time. First there is the search to identify an acquisition target with the best possible fit. Then there is the process of negotiating the right price. Finally managers will have to integrate the new and old businesses together, in order to realise the full value of their purchase. In other words, acquisition should be seen as a process over time. Each step in this process imposes different tasks on managers. This section will consider three key steps: target choice, valuation and integration.

Target choice in M&A

Here there are two main criteria to apply: strategic fit and organisation fit.[6]

- *Strategic fit* refers to the extent to which the target firm strengthens or complements the acquiring firm's strategy. Strategic fit will relate to the original strategic motives for the acquisition: extension, consolidation and capabilities. Managers need to assess strategic fit very carefully. The danger is that potential synergies (see section 7.3) in M&A are often exaggerated in order to justify high acquisition prices. Also, negative synergies ('contagion') between the companies involved are easily neglected.[7] An example of negative synergy was when the Bank of America bought the aggressive investment bank Merrill Lynch for $47bn (~€33bn) in 2008. Under its new owner, Merrill Lynch lost business because it was no longer allowed to advise on deals targeting the extensive list of corporations that were already lending clients of Bank of America. Consequently Merrill Lynch was a less valuable business with its new parent than when free to chase any deal it wanted.

- *Organisational fit* refers to the match between the management practices, cultural practices and staff characteristics between the target and the acquiring firms. Large mismatches between the two are likely to cause significant integration problems. The acquisition of Californian genetic engineering company Genentech by Swiss pharmaceutical company Roche raises many questions of organisational fit (see Illustration 10.1). International acquisitions are particularly liable to organisational misfits, because of cultural and language differences between countries.[8] A comparison of the two companies' cultural webs (section 5.4.6) might be helpful here.

Together, strategic and organisational fit determine the potential for the acquirer to add value, the parenting issue raised in section 7.6. Where there is a bad organisational fit, the acquirer is likely to destroy value through its corporate parenting regardless of how well the target fits strategically.

The two criteria of strategic and organisational fit can be used to create a screen according to which potential acquisition targets can be ruled in or ruled out. Note that, because the set of firms that meet the criteria *and* that are actually available for purchase is likely to be small, it is very tempting for managers to relax the criteria too far in order to build a large enough pool

ILLUSTRATION 10.1

Swiss in the Valley

Swiss pharmaceutical giant Roche faced strong resistance to its takeover of Californian biotech company Genentech.

Founded in 1896, by 2009 Swiss pharmaceutical company Roche had 80,000 employees worldwide, sales of $33.6bn (~€23.5bn) and a 56 per cent stake in the San Francisco biotechnology company Genentech. Genentech, however, was jealous of its autonomy, and regarded data on its experiments and trials as not Roche's property. Taking advantage of Genentech's fall in relative value because of a weak dollar, the Swiss company launched a bid for full control, at $89 a share, valuing the company at $44bn. Genentech's management refused the offer.

Genentech had been founded in 1976 by a young venture capitalist and an assistant professor at the San Francisco campus of the University of California. In 1977, the Silicon Valley start-up was the first in the world to express a human gene in bacteria, and in the following year it was the first to produce synthetic human insulin. Roche had bought its stake in the successful young company in 1990, but taken a hands-off approach. By 2009, Genentech was the second largest biotechnology company in the United States, with 11,000 employees. Many of these employees were top scientists, lured to the company by a combination of good salaries, stock options and a large amount of academic freedom. Genentech allowed its scientists to pursue their own research projects one day a week, and to publish articles in scientific journals. In 2008, Genentech had been awarded more patents in molecular biology than the U.S. government and the ten campuses of the University of California combined. *Science* magazine named Genentech as the best employer for scientists seven years in a row. In 2008, former biotech researcher Dr. Art Levinson, Genentech's CEO since 1995 and a supporter of the company's traditional Friday 'beer fests', had been voted by another magazine as America's 'nicest' CEO.

Roche was obliged to raise its bid, to $94 per share. Genentech's management reluctantly accepted. They had originally hoped for $112 per share, but the economic crisis of the time made that unrealistic. As shareholders themselves, however, Roche's bid had made the top management and many of Genentech's scientists very wealthy people.

Although now in full control of Genentech, the management challenges for Roche were substantial. Laurence Lasky, a Silicon Valley venture capitalist and former scientist at Genentech, commented of Roche: 'They're Swiss, and Genentech is a bunch of California cowboys'. Roche indeed had a different culture. Based in the staid town of Basel, it was still half-owned by descendants of the founding families. Its products are typically based upon chemical compounds, very different to Genentech's genetic engineering. Like many other 'big pharma' companies, moreover, the stream of new products from its research laboratories was drying up. Roche hoped to replenish its product portfolio by getting full access to Genentech's research, while also saving costs by merging its U.S. headquarters with that of Genentech in California.

Roche chairman Franz Humer, a Swiss lawyer, was none the less very positive, telling the *Wall Street Journal*: 'I am delighted that the intensive negotiations have led to a successful conclusion. . . . I have spoken with Art (Levinson) and he's extremely committed to make a success of the new company.' However, a close observer of Genentech remarked: 'the assets of Genentech walk out in tennis shoes every night, and you hope they walk back in next morning'.

Sources: *San Francisco Chronicle*, 13 March 2009, 17 August 2008; *International Herald Tribune*, 13 March 2009; *Wall Street Journal*, 17 March 2009.

Questions

1 Assess the strategic and organisational fits of Roche and Genentech

2 What must Roche do to ensure the success of this takeover?

of possible acquisitions. Strict strategic and organisational fit criteria are particularly liable to be forgotten after the failure of an initial acquisition bid. Once having committed publicly to an acquisition strategy, senior managers are susceptible to making ill-considered bids for other targets 'on the rebound'.

Valuation in M&A

Negotiating the right price for an acquisition target is absolutely critical. Offer the target too little, and the bid will be unsuccessful: senior managers will lose credibility and the company will have wasted a lot of management time. Pay too much, though, and the acquisition is unlikely ever to make a profit net of the original acquisition price.

Valuation methods include financial analysis techniques such as payback period, discounted cash flow and shareholder value analysis (see Chapter 11).[9] For acquisition of publicly quoted companies, there is the additional guide of the market value of the target company's shares. However, acquirers typically do not simply pay the current market value of the target, but have to pay a so-called *premium for control*. This premium is the additional amount that the acquirer has to pay to win total control compared to the ordinary valuation of the target's shares as an independent company. Depending on the state of the financial markets, this premium might involve paying at least 30 per cent more for the shares than normal. Especially where the target resists the initial bid, or other potential acquirers join in with their own bids, it is very easy for bid prices to escalate beyond the true economic value of the target.

It is therefore very important for the acquirer to be strictly disciplined with regard to the price that it will pay. Acquisitions are liable to the *winner's curse* – in order to win acceptance of the bid, the acquirer may pay so much that the original cost can never be earned back.[10] This winner's curse effect operated when the Royal Bank of Scotland's consortium competed with Barclays Bank to acquire the Dutch bank ABN AMRO: the Royal Bank of Scotland won, but the excessive price of €70bn (~$98bn) soon drove the victor into financial collapse and government ownership. The negative effects of paying too much can be worsened if the acquirer tries to justify the price by cutting back essential investments in order to improve immediate profits. In what is called the *vicious circle of overvaluation*, over-paying firms can easily undermine the original rationale of the acquisition by imposing savings on exactly the assets (e.g. brand-marketing, product R&D or key staff) that made up the strategic value of the target company in the first place.

Integration in M&A

The ability to extract value from an acquisition will depend critically on the approach to integrating the new business with the old. Integration is frequently challenging because of problems of organisational fit. For example, there might be strong cultural differences between the two organisations (see section 5.4) or they might have incompatible financial or information technology systems (see section 13.3). Illustration 10.2 describes some integration issues for British car company Jaguar-Land Rover after acquisition by Indian conglomerate Tata. Poor integration can cause acquisitions to fail. It is crucial to choose the correct approach to integration of merged or acquired companies.

INSEAD's Philippe Haspeslagh and David Jemison[11] argue that the most suitable approach to integration depends on two key criteria:

● *The extent of strategic interdependence.* Where there is high interdependence, the presumption is in favour of tight integration. If the acquisition is driven by the need to transfer capabilities

Figure 10.2 Acquisition integration matrix

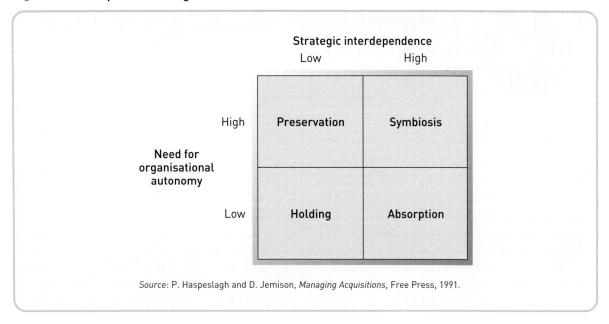

Source: P. Haspeslagh and D. Jemison, *Managing Acquisitions*, Free Press, 1991.

(for example, technology) or to share resources (for example, distribution channels), the value can only be extracted through integrating the businesses thoroughly. Of course, some acquisitions take the form of unrelated or conglomerate diversification (see section 7.2). In unrelated acquisitions, the lack of strategic interdependence means there is little need for integration beyond financial systems.

- *The need for organisational autonomy.* The nature of the organisations involved might modify the logic of strategic interdependence, however. An acquired firm that has a very distinct culture, or is geographically distant, or is dominated by prima donna professionals or star performers might be better left only loosely or gradually integrated. Sometimes an acquisition can be made precisely because the distinctiveness of the acquired organisation is valuable to the acquirer:[12] in this case, of course, it is best to learn gradually from the distinct culture, rather than risk spoiling it by clumsy integration.

As in Figure 10.2, therefore, these two criteria drive three main approaches to integration, plus a fourth residual approach:

- *Absorption* is preferred where there is strong strategic interdependence and little need for organisational autonomy. Absorption implies rapid adjustment of the acquired company's old strategies to the needs of the new owner, and corresponding changes to the company's culture and systems.

- *Preservation* is appropriate where there is little interdependence and a high need for autonomy – as in a conglomerate, perhaps. Preservation allows old strategies, cultures and systems to continue much as before, with changes confined to the essential minimum such as the financial reporting procedures needed for control.

- *Symbiosis* is indicated where there is strong strategic interdependence, but a high need for autonomy – perhaps in a professional services organisation dependent on the creativity of its staff. Symbiosis implies that both acquired firm and acquiring firm learn the best qualities from the other. Symbiosis takes time and is the most complex of the integration approaches.

ILLUSTRATION 10.2

From Nano to Jaguar

In 2008, the Indian Tata group, makers of the ultra-cheap Nano car, bought two iconic British car brands, Jaguar and Land Rover. It had to integrate these in the most demanding times.

The Tata Group is the largest privately-owned company in India, with interests spanning from steel to hotels. Its chairman, Ratan Tata, has embarked on an internationalisation strategy that included the takeover of the Anglo-Dutch Corus steel company in 2007. In January 2008, Tata Motors, already producing a range of cars and SUVs, launched the revolutionary Nano, the world's cheapest car, selling for less than $2000 (~€1400). Two months later, Tata Motors acquired its first prestige marques, Jaguar and Land Rover, from the struggling Ford Motors for $2.3bn.

With 16,000 employees in the UK, based at three manufacturing sites and two design and engineering centres, the takeover caused alarm. Would Tata save money by closing sites? Might it transfer production to its low cost base in India? Ratan Tata was quick to reassure. On a personal visit to the company, he recalled that his father had bought a classic Jaguar more than half a century ago. He talked about reviving the revered British Daimler brand and returning Jaguar to racing. Jaguar-Land Rover then announced its intention to hire 600 more skilled staff to support a £700m project to develop environmentally-friendly cars. And Tata was well-placed to sell Jaguars and Land Rovers in the booming Indian market.

Jaguar-Land Rover still faced challenges. As a subsidiary of Ford, Jaguar-Land Rover had relied on Ford Credit to finance its operations and sales. Now Jaguar-Land Rover needed its own relationships with the banks. All its information technology was based on Ford systems. Jaguar-Land Rover CEO David Smith commented: 'We're pulling companies that were embedded in Ford back out again and switching our financing to other providers. And the IT is an absolute hydra. It's going to be the most difficult part.'

However, Tata did not insist on tight integration into the Indian parent. Oversight is provided by a three-man strategy board, meeting every two months and comprising Ratan Tata, the head of Tata Automotive and David Smith himself. Smith commented: 'Tata wants us to be autonomous – I've got all the executive authority I need. . . . We can make decisions quickly – that's what will be most different from life at Ford.' The Jaguar-Land Rover executive committee, directly responsible for the company's operations, had no Tata representatives. Nevertheless, Jaguar-Land Rover would be making use of Tata Motors' expertise in cost control and the Tata Consultancy Division's skills in information technology.

A year after the takeover, David Smith commented again: 'We are still learning how the relationship with Tata will work. It's clearly more personal and based on individual relationships.' Of Ratan Tata, who had been a passionately-involved champion of the Nano and had trained as an architect and engineer, David Smith remarked: '[He] is very interested in the business. The designers love him, because he's an architect and is not only quite capable of telling them what he thinks, he can say it in the right language too.'

By Spring 2009, relationships were being tested by the economic crisis. Jaguar-Land Rover's sales had fallen by more than 30 per cent and the company had plunged into losses. The British government was refusing a financial bail-out. What would Tata do now?

Sources: Management Today, 1 May 2009; *Financial Times*, 4 August 2008.

Questions

1 In the light of Haspeslagh and Jemison's matrix, assess Tata's initial approach to the integration of Jaguar-Land Rover

2 How might Tata's approach change in the economic crisis?

- *Holding* is the residual category where there is very little to gain by integration and it is envisaged that the acquisition will be 'held' temporarily before being sold to another company. It is best in these cases simply to leave the acquired unit largely alone.

Especially for the more active absorption and symbiosis forms of integration, the ultimate success of the acquisition will depend upon how well the integration process is managed. Here methods of managing strategic change explained in Chapter 14 will be relevant. However, because acquisitions often involve the loss of jobs, sudden career changes, management relocations and the cancellation of projects, it is argued that organisational justice is particularly important for successful integration.[13] **Organisational justice refers to the perceived fairness of managerial actions, in terms of distribution, procedure and information.** Thus:

- *Distributive justice* refers to the distribution of rewards and posts: for example, it will be seen as unfair in a merger between equals if the large majority of senior management posts go to one of the partners, and not the other.

- *Procedural justice* refers to the procedures by which decisions are made: for example, if integration decisions are made through appropriate committees or task forces with representation from both sides, then the perception of fair procedures is likely to be high.

- *Informational justice* is about how information is used and communicated in the integration: if decisions are explained well to all those involved, they are more likely to be accepted positively.

Kraft offended principles of both procedural and informational justice when it assured investors and employees before its 2010 takeover of Cadbury that it would keep open the Somerdale chocolate factory near Bristol, with its 400 workers. Within a month of completing the takeover, Kraft informed its workers that production would be transferred to Poland, causing political controversy and a loss of trust amongst all its newly acquired staff.

10.3.4 M&A strategy over time

M&A strategies evolve over time. First, mergers and acquisitions will rarely be one-off events for an organisation. Organisations often make many acquisitions as their strategy develops: in this sense, they become *serial acquirers*. Second, over time some acquired units are liable to lose their fit with an organisation's evolving strategy: these units become candidates for *divesture*. This subsection examines serial acquisitions and divesture in turn:

- *Serial acquirers* are companies that make multiple acquisitions, often in parallel. Working on simultaneous acquisitions is very demanding of managerial time and skills. However, repeating the acquisition process does provide an opportunity for acquiring companies to accumulate experience about how to do M&A better. Serial acquirers therefore often develop specialist teams for managing the acquisition process, from target selection through negotiation of a price and then integration. Specialist teams can build up expertise and procedures for dealing effectively with selection, negotiation and integration. IBM for example made 50 software acquisitions in the period 2002–8. In order to make these 50 acquisitions, the company had to assess around 500 different potential acquisition targets, choosing not to proceed in the vast majority of cases. But for those 50 that the company did finally buy, IBM had to establish 50 different integration teams, with 10 or more teams each working in parallel at any one time.[14]

● *Divesture* (or divestment) is the process of selling a business that no longer fits the corporate strategy.[15] This is obviously a central part of an 'asset stripping' strategy (see section 10.3.2), but ought to be on the agenda of every diversified corporation. The key determinant of divesture is whether the corporate parent has 'parenting advantage': in other words, the corporate parent can add more value to the business unit than other potential owners of the business (see section 7.4). A corporate parent that does not have parenting advantage should divest the business for the best price it can obtain. Corporate parents are often reluctant to divest businesses, seeing it as an admission of failure. However, a dynamic perspective on M&A would encourage managers to view divestures positively. Funds raised by the sale of an ill-fitting business can be used either to invest in retained businesses or to buy other businesses that fit the corporate strategy better. Obtaining a good price for the divested unit can recoup any losses it may have originally made. Sometimes, however, a less positive reason for divesture is pressure from competition authorities, which may force the sale of businesses to reduce companies' market power. For example, in 2007 the European Commission obliged Tui, the powerful German tour operator, to sell its Irish tour business Budget Travel in order to increase competition in the fast-consolidating European tourism industry.

Acquisitions, therefore, are an important method for pursuing strategies. However, they are not easy to carry out and they are sometimes adopted for misguided reasons. It is important to consider the alternative of strategic alliances.

STRATEGIC ALLIANCES

Strategic alliances

Mergers and acquisitions bring together companies through complete changes in ownership. However, companies also often work together in strategic alliances that involve only partial changes in ownership, or no ownership changes at all. The companies remain distinct. Thus **a strategic alliance is where two or more organisations share resources and activities to pursue a strategy**. This is a common method in strategy: Andersen Consulting has estimated that the average large corporation is managing around 30 alliances.[16]

Alliance strategy challenges the traditional organisation-centred approach to strategy in at least two ways. First, practitioners of alliance strategy need to think about strategy in terms of the collective success of their networks as well as their individual organisations' self-interest.[17] **Collective strategy is about how the whole network of alliances of which an organisation is a member competes against rival networks of alliances.** Thus for Microsoft, competitive success for its Xbox games console relies heavily on the collective strength of its network of independent games developers such as Bungie Studios (makers of Halo), Bizarre Creations (Project Gotham Racing) and Team Ninja (Dead or Alive). Part of Microsoft's strategy must include having a stronger network of games developers than its rivals such as Sony and Nintendo. Collective strategy also challenges the individualistic approach to strategy by highlighting the importance of effective collaboration. Thus success involves collaborating as well as competing. **Collaborative advantage is about managing alliances better than competitors.**[18] Microsoft needs not only to have a stronger network than rivals such as Sony and Nintendo. If it wants to maximise the value of the Xbox, Microsoft must be better at working with its network in order to ensure that its members keep on producing the best games. The more effectively it collaborates, the more successful it will be. Illustration 10.3 describes Apple's approach to collective strategy and collaboration for the iPod.

ILLUSTRATION 10.3

Apple's iPod network

Does Apple manage its network of collaborators well?

By 2009, Apple had sold 200 million iPods. But this success was not Apple's alone. And Apple's relationship with its network of subcontractors and licensees was controversial.

When Apple had first launched the iPod in 2001, it needed help. The iPod combines different kinds of technologies in a uniquely small format. Apple relied substantially on external component suppliers. For example, the fifth generation iPod hard-drive – accounting for about half the total components costs – was sourced from Toshiba in Japan. The multimedia processor came from American Broadcom. The mobile memory came from the Korean Samsung. The lithium battery was Sony's. Assembly was carried out in Taiwan. The success of the iPod attracted a swarm of companies into the iPod accessory market, with companies such as Griffin from the United States and Logitech from Switzerland supplying attractive add-ons such as docking stations, cases and speakers.

Apple is at the heart, therefore, of a network spanning many companies across the world. However, the company has always been protective of its intellectual property. During the 1980s, Apple had tightly controlled the licensing of its Macintosh computer operating system, restricting independent companies from creating compatible software applications for the mass market. Meanwhile, Microsoft had opened up its operating systems, allowing a flood of independent applications that had helped give it dominance of the market.

Apple somewhat modified its strategy for the iPod. Initially the iPod was a completely closed system that worked only with the Macintosh and iTunes music warehouse. Gradually it allowed other audio file formats to be played on the system, but by 2009 Apple was still resisting Microsoft's WMA format. The company licensed none of its hardware, ensuring control of its production and maintenance of its premium pricing policy. It was impossible for any independent company to manufacture cheap iPods, in the way for instance Taiwanese manufacturers had produced cheap IBM/Microsoft-compatible personal computers during the 1980s. However, the company did license to accessory-producers the technology needed to access iPod ports. Apple benefited from royalties from its licensees, as well as the development of attractive complementary products. But the relationship with accessory-producers was arm's-length, with no information about new iPod products released ahead. A spokesman at accessory-producer Griffin commented: 'It's very much a hands-off relationship. We do not know what [new product] is coming down the pipe ahead of time.'

Apple's strategy seems to be paying off. Microsoft's rival music-player, the Zune, has been a comparative failure. However, Apple's position at the heart of a network can be seen another way: it is also surrounded by some powerful players. For example, Sony is a supplier of lithium batteries. Sony builds iPod accessories such as car adaptors and boom-boxes. Sony Music supplies its artists, such as Leona Lewis and Michael Jackson, via the iTunes site. And finally, of course, Sony has its own MP3 music-player, the Walkman, plus its own media download site, mystore (see also Figure 2.3).

Sources: M. Cusumano, 'The Puzzle of Apple', *Communications of the ACM*, vol. 51, no. 9 (2008), pp. 22–4; G. Linden, K. Kraemer, and J. Dedrick, 'Who Captures Value in a Global Innovation Network? Apple's iPod', *Communications of the ACM*, vol. 52, no. 3 (2009), pp. 140–5; P. Taylor, 'iPod ecosystem offers rich pickings', *Financial Times*, 25 January 2006, p. 15.

Questions

1 What are pros and cons of Apple's tight control of licensing?

2 What are the pros and cons of maintaining a 'hands-off' relationship with accessory-producers such as Griffin?

10.4.1 Types of strategic alliance

In terms of ownership, there are two main kinds of strategic alliance:

● *Equity alliances* involve the creation of a new entity that is owned separately by the partners involved. The most common form of equity alliance is the *joint venture*, where two organisations remain independent but set up a new organisation jointly owned by the parents. For example, General Motors and Toyota have operated the NUMMI joint venture since 1984, producing cars from both companies in the same plant in California. A *consortium alliance* involves several partners setting up a venture together. For example, IBM, Hewlett-Packard, Toshiba and Samsung are partners in the Sematech research consortium, working together on the latest semiconductor technologies.

● *Non-equity alliances* are typically looser, without the commitment implied by ownership. Non-equity alliances are often based on contracts. One common form of contractual alliance is *franchising*, where one organisation (the franchisor) gives another organisation (the franchisee) the right to sell the franchisor's products or services in a particular location in return for a fee or royalty. Kall-Kwik printing, 7-Eleven convenience stores and McDonald's restaurants are examples of franchising. *Licensing* is a similar kind of contractual alliance, allowing partners to use intellectual property such as patents or brands in return for a fee. *Long-term subcontracting* agreements are another form of loose non-equity alliance, common in automobile supply. For example, the Canadian subcontractor Magna has long-term contracts to assemble the bodies and frames for car companies such as Ford, Honda and Mercedes.

The public and voluntary sectors often get involved in both equity and non-equity strategic alliances. Governments have increasingly encouraged the public sector to contract out the building and maintenance of capital projects such as hospitals and schools under long-term contracts. Individual public organisations often band together to form purchasing consortia as well. A good example of this is university libraries, which typically negotiate collectively for the purchase of journals and books from publishers. Voluntary organisations pool their resources in alliance too. For example, relief organisations in areas suffering from natural or man-made disasters typically have to cooperate in order to deliver the full range of services in difficult circumstances. Although public- and voluntary-sector organisations might often be seen as more naturally cooperative than private-sector organisations, many of the issues that follow apply to all three kinds of organisation.

10.4.2 Motives for alliances

The definition of strategic alliances puts the stress on sharing, of resources or activities. Although sharing is the key motivator for most alliances, there may be less obvious reasons as well. Four broad rationales for alliances can be identified, as summarised in Figure 10.3:

● *Scale alliances*. Here organisations combine in order to achieve necessary scale. The capabilities of each partner may be quite similar (as indicated by the similarity of the A and B organisations in Figure 10.3), but together they can achieve advantages that they could not easily manage on their own. Thus combining together can provide economies of scale in the production of *outputs* (products or services). Combining might also provide economies of scale in terms of *inputs*, for example by reducing purchasing costs of raw materials or

Figure 10.3 Strategic alliance motives

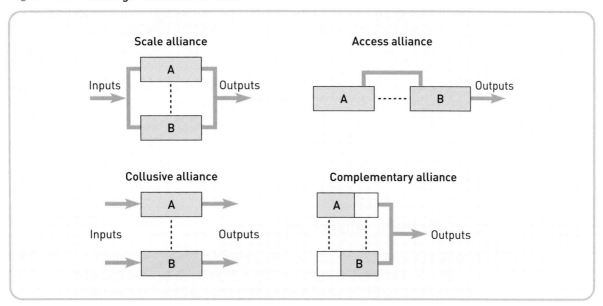

services. Thus health management organisations often combine together to negotiate better prices with pharmaceutical companies. Finally, combining allows the partners to *share risk* as well. Instead of organisations stretching themselves to find enough resources on their own, partnering can help each partner avoid committing so many resources of its own that failure would jeopardise the existence of the whole organisation.

- *Access alliances.* Organisations frequently ally in order to access the capabilities of another organisation that are required in order to produce or sell its products and services. For example, in countries such as China and India, a Western company (in Figure 10.3, organisation A) might need to partner with a local distributor (organisation B) in order to access effectively the national market for its products and services. Here organisation B is critical to organisation A's ability to sell. Access alliances can work in the opposite direction. Thus organisation B might seek a licensing alliance in order to access inputs from organisation A, for example technologies or brands. Here organisation A is critical to organisation B's ability to produce or market its products and services. Access can be about not only tangible resources such as distribution channels or products, but also about intangible resources such as knowledge.

- *Complementary alliances.* These can be seen as a form of access alliance, but involve organisations at similar points in the value network combining their distinctive resources so that they bolster each partner's particular gaps or weaknesses. Figure 10.3 shows an alliance where the strengths of organisation A (indicated by the darker shading) match the weaknesses of organisation B (indicated by the lighter shading); conversely, the strengths of organisation B match the weaknesses of organisation A. By partnering, the two organisations can bring together complementary strengths in order to overcome their individual weaknesses. An example of this is the General Motors–Toyota NUMMI alliance: here the complementarity lies in General Motors getting access to the Japanese car company's manufacturing expertise, while Toyota obtains the American car company's local marketing knowledge.

- *Collusive alliances.* Occasionally organisations secretly collude together in order to increase their market power. By combining together into cartels, they reduce competition in the marketplace, enabling them to extract higher prices from their customers or lower prices from suppliers. Such collusive cartels are generally illegal, so there is no public agreement (hence the absence of brackets joining the two collusive organisations in Figure 10.3). Mobile phone operators are often accused of collusive behaviour and in 2005 France Telecom and two other French operators were fined over €500m ($700m) for illegal market-sharing.

It can be seen that strategic alliances, like mergers and acquisitions, have mixed motives. Cooperation is often a good thing, but it is important to be aware of collusive motivations. These are likely to work against the interests of other competitors, customers and suppliers.

10.4.3 Strategic alliance processes

Like mergers and acquisitions, strategic alliances need to be understood as processes unfolding over time. Alliances are often last for very long periods. For example, the American General Electric and French SNECMA have been partners since 1974 in a continuous alliance for the development and production of small aero-engines. The needs and capabilities of the partners in a long-standing alliance such as this are bound to change over time. However, the absence of full ownership means that emerging differences cannot simply be reconciled by managerial authority; they have to be negotiated between independent partners. This lack of control by one side or the other means that the managerial processes in alliances are particularly demanding. The management challenges, moreover, will change over time.

The fact that neither partner is in control, while alliances must typically be managed over time, highlights the importance of two themes in the various stages of the alliance process:

- *Co-evolution.* Rather than thinking of strategic alliances as fixed at a particular point of time, they are better seen as co-evolutionary processes.[19] The concept of co-evolution underlines the way in which partners, strategies, capabilities and environments are constantly changing. As they change, they need realignment so that they can evolve in harmony. A co-evolutionary perspective on alliances therefore places the emphasis on flexibility and change. At completion, an alliance is unlikely to be the same as envisaged at the start.

- *Trust.* Given the probable co-evolutionary nature of alliances, and the lack of control of one partner over the other, trust becomes highly important to the success of alliances over time.[20] All future possibilities cannot be specified in the initial alliance contract. Each partner will have made investments that are vulnerable to the selfish behaviour of the other. This implies the need for partners to behave in a trustworthy fashion through the whole lifetime of the alliance. Trust in a relationship is something that has to be continuously earned. Trust is often particularly fragile in alliances between the public and private sectors, where the profit motive is suspect on one side, and sudden shifts in political agendas are feared on the other.

Oxfam's partnership principles explicitly address issues of co-evolution and trust: see Illustration 10.4.

The themes of trust and co-evolution surface in various ways at different stages in the lifespan of a strategic alliance. Figure 10.4 provides a simple stage model of strategic alliance

ILLUSTRATION 10.4

Oxfam's partnership principles: co-evolution and trust

Oxfam, an international non-governmental organisation dedicated to the overcoming of poverty, has developed principles that are relevant to private-sector alliances too.

Founded in 1942 as the Oxford Committee for Famine Relief, Oxfam was originally intended to help civilians in Nazi-occupied Europe suffering from starvation. By 2009, it was working against poverty in more than 70 countries, drawing on 3000 local partnerships. These partnerships vary in nature. In some, the local partner is essentially a sub-contractor, spending funds provided by Oxfam on an agreed programme. Other partnerships are more in the nature of joint ventures. For example, in Senegal, Oxfam has established and works with a network of six community agricultural organisations on a long-term basis to help small local farmers get access to markets for their rice.

Oxfam's reliance on local partners has led it to define five principles of partnership:

1. *Complementary purpose and added value.* Here Oxfam commits itself to partnerships that add value to its objectives of empowering and benefiting the poor. At the same time, it recognises that both sides have their own distinct capacities and resources and that each partner should be explicit about these different contributions and limitations.
2. *Mutual respect for values and beliefs.* By this Oxfam insists that partners should have common ground in terms of shared values and beliefs, while respecting differences.

3. *Clarity about roles, responsibilities and decision-making.* Oxfam believes that effective relationships rely upon good communication, reliability and agreed decision-processes. Partners should celebrate their successes and be committed to learning together from their failures.
4. *Transparency and accountability.* Oxfam recognises it should be accountable to its partners, but at the same time underlines that both it and its partners are ultimately accountable to the people and communities for whom they work.
5. *Commitment and flexibility.* Oxfam looks for long-term partnerships. Recognising that it may not be a permanent donor, it promises to be open about its funding plans and to help partners build their capacity to raise funds from other sources.

Source: www.oxfam.org/uk/resources.

Questions

1 How does Oxfam approach the issues of co-evolution and trust in its alliances?

2 To what extent do Oxfam's principles apply to private-sector business, and how might they be adapted to increase their relevance?

---

evolution. The amount of committed resources changes at each stage, but issues of trust and co-evolution recur throughout:

- *Courtship.* First there is the initial process of courting potential partners, where the main resource commitment is managerial time. This courtship process should not be rushed, as the willingness of both partners is required. Similar criteria apply to alliances at this stage as to acquisitions. Each partner has to see a strategic fit, according to the rationales in section 10.3.2. Equally, each partner has to see an organisational fit. Organisational fit can be considered as for acquisitions (section 10.3.4). However, because alliances do not entail the same degree of control as acquisitions, mutual trust between partners will need to be particularly strong right from the outset.

Figure 10.4 Alliance evolution

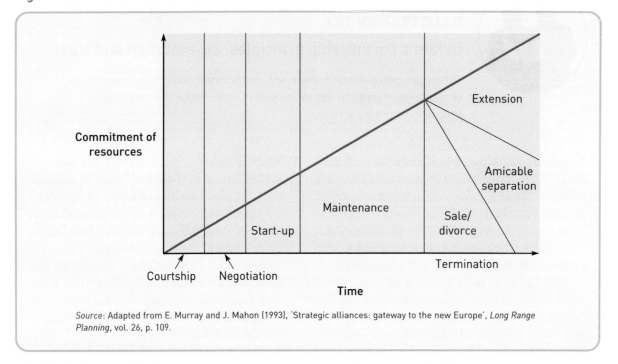

Source: Adapted from E. Murray and J. Mahon (1993), 'Strategic alliances: gateway to the new Europe', *Long Range Planning*, vol. 26, p. 109.

- *Negotiation.* Partners need of course to negotiate carefully their mutual roles at the outset. In equity alliances, the partners also have to negotiate the proportion of ownership each will have in the final joint venture. Again there is likely to be a significant commitment of managerial time at this stage, as it is important to get initial contracts clear and correct. In the case of the Areva–Siemens joint venture (Illustration 10.5), Siemens regretted the low share that it originally agreed. Although the negotiation of ownership proportions in a joint venture is similar to the valuation process in acquisitions, strategic alliance contracts generally involve a great deal more. Key behaviours required of each partner need to be specified upfront. However, a ruthless negotiation style can also damage trust going forward. Moreover, co-evolution implies the need to anticipate change. In an acquired unit, it is possible to make adjustments simply by managerial authority. In alliances, initial contracts may be considered binding even when starting conditions have changed. It is wise to include an option for renegotiating initial terms right at the outset.

- *Start-up.* Start-up is the next stage, with considerable investment of material and human resources normally involved. Trust is very important at this stage. First, the initial operation of the alliance puts the original alliance agreements to the test. Informal adjustments to working realities are likely to be required. Also, people from outside the original negotiation team are typically now obliged to work together on a day-to-day basis. They may not have the same understanding of the alliance as those who initiated it. Without the mutual trust to make adjustments and smooth misunderstandings, the alliance is liable to break up. This early period in an alliance's evolution is the one with the highest rate of failure.

- *Maintenance.* This refers to the ongoing operation of the strategic alliance, with increasing resources likely to be committed. The lesson of co-evolution is that alliance maintenance is not a simple matter of stability. Alliances have to be actively managed to allow for changing external circumstances. The internal dynamics of the partnership are likely to evolve as

ILLUSTRATION 10.5

Nuclear fission: Areva and Siemens break up

Co-evolution is not easy, as two leading French and German companies discover.

In 2001, Siemens, the German industrial conglomerate, and Areva, the French nuclear industry giant, merged their nuclear reactor businesses into a new joint venture called Areva NP. The joint venture was 34 per cent owned by Siemens, 66 per cent owned by Areva. As the German government had promised to exit nuclear power altogether for environmental reasons, Siemens no longer saw nuclear power as central to its strategy. The joint venture agreement gave the French a right-to-buy option for the Siemens minority stake.

In 2009, the new Siemens CEO, Peter Löscher, sent Areva's CEO Ann Lauvergeon a short email announcing that the Germans would be exercising their right to sell their stake to the French. The email took Madame Lauvergeon completely by surprise: 'It made me think of those men who abandon their wives by leaving a note on the kitchen table'. What had gone wrong in the eight years? Areva NP had been a success. It was the global leader in a market for nuclear reactors that was booming again. Rising oil prices and alarm over global warming made nuclear power increasingly attractive. By 2009, after many years of minimal construction, 51 plants were being built around the world, with 171 more planned. Areva NP was active not only in Europe but in the United States and China.

The recovery of the nuclear industry was in fact one source of the problem: with a new CEO, Siemens wanted back in. Siemens was frustrated by its lack of control as a minority shareholder, and by the slow decision-making in Areva NP generally. Moreover, it wanted to get a larger slice of the business than just the nuclear reactors – the big profits were elsewhere in the value chain, in fuel and recycling. Areva, the French parent company, already had a significant presence through the whole value chain.

During 2007, Siemens looked either to increase its stake in Areva NP to 50:50 or to take a direct stake in the French parent, Areva. But, more than 80 per cent owned by the French government, Areva was not easily for sale. Moreover, Nicolas Sarkozy, then a senior French government minister and soon French President, told German Chancellor Angela Merkel that France could not tolerate a role for Siemens while the German government refused to back nuclear power in its own country. Siemens had to enrol Merkel's support to prevent Areva from exercising its right-to-buy option and forcing Siemens to sell.

In late 2008, Siemens began talks with the Russian nuclear power giant Rosatom. Rosatom had a presence through the whole value chain, including the highly profitable fuel business. With memories of the Soviet nuclear disaster at Chernobyl still live, Rosatom needed Siemens' high reputation for quality. In March 2009, Siemens and Rosatom announced a joint venture with the ambition of displacing Areva NP as world leader.

Ending the Areva NP joint venture was not simple, however. Siemens' strength was in hardware, but Areva owned the software that made it work. Areva was obliged to buy Siemens' stake (~€4bn; ~$5.6bn), but lacked the funds to do so. Also, the original joint venture agreement had included a non-compete clause in case of break-down. So far as Areva was concerned, Siemens' new joint venture put it in breach of the contract, and so not entitled to the full value of its stake. And the two companies were still working together on various nuclear power stations. Indeed, Areva and Siemens were being jointly sued for €2bn for cost and time over-runs on a project in Finland. It was going to be a messy divorce.

Sources: L'Expansion, 1 April 2009; Financial Times, 28 April 2009.

Question

In what respects did co-evolution break down in the Areva NP joint venture?

well as the partners build experience. Here again trust is extremely important. Gary Hamel has warned that alliances often become *competitions for competence.*[21] Because partners are interacting closely, they can begin to learn each other's particular competences. This learning can develop into a competition for competence, with the partner that learns the fastest becoming the more powerful. The more powerful partner may consequently be able to renegotiate the terms in its favour or even break up the alliance and go it alone. If on the other hand the partners wish to maintain their strategic alliance, trustworthy behaviour that does not threaten the other partner's competence is essential to maintaining the cooperative relationships necessary for the day-to-day working of the alliance.

● *Termination.* Eventually, there will be some kind of *termination* of the alliance. Often an alliance will have had an agreed time span or purpose right from the start, so termination is a matter of completion rather than failure. Here separation is amicable. Sometimes the alliance has been so successful that the partners will wish to extend the alliance by agreeing a new alliance between themselves, committing still more resources. Sometimes too the alliance will have been a success in another sense, with one partner wishing to buy the other's share in order to commit fully to a particular market, while the other partner is happy to sell. The sale of one half of a joint venture need not be a sign of failure. However, occasionally alliances end in bitter divorces, as when Areva threatened to take Siemens to court (see Illustration 10.5). Termination needs to be managed carefully, therefore. Co-evolution implies that mutual trust is likely to be valuable after the completion of any particular partnership. Partners may be engaged in several different joint projects at the same time. For example, Cisco and IBM are partners on multiple simultaneous projects in wireless communications, IT security, data centres and data storage. The partners may need to come together again for new projects in the future. Thus Nokia, Ericsson and Siemens have had mobile telephone technology joint projects since the mid-1990s. Maintaining mutual trust in the termination stage is vital if partners are to co-evolve through generations of multiple projects.

(10.5) COMPARING ACQUISITIONS, ALLIANCES AND ORGANIC DEVELOPMENT

It will be clear so far that all three methods of M&A, strategic alliances and organic development have their own advantages and disadvantages. There are also some similarities. This section first considers criteria for choosing between the three methods, and then draws together some key success factors for M&A and alliances.

10.5.1 Buy, ally or DIY?

Acquisitions and strategic alliances have high failure rates. As in the Key Debate at the end of this chapter, acquisitions are thought to fail about half the time. Acquisitions can go wrong because of excessive initial valuations, exaggerated expectations of strategic fit, underestimated problems of organisational fit and all the other issues pointed to in this chapter. But strategic alliances too have roughly 50 per cent failure rates.[22] Alliances also suffer from miscalculations in terms of strategic and organisational fit, but, given the lack of control on either side, have their own particular issues of trust and co-evolution as well. With these high failure rates, acquisitions and alliances need to be considered cautiously alongside the default option of organic development (Do-It-Yourself).

Figure 10.5 Buy, ally or DIY matrix

	Buy	**Ally**	**DIY**
High urgency	Fast	Fast	Slow
High uncertainty	Failures potentially saleable	Share losses and retain buy option	Failures likely unsaleable
Soft capabilities important	Culture and valuation problems	Culture and control problems	Cultural consistency
Highly modular capabilities	Problem of buying whole company	Ally just with relevant partner unit	Develop in new venture unit

The best approach will differ according to circumstances. Figure 10.5 presents a 'buy, ally or DIY' matrix summarising four key factors that can help in choosing between acquisitions, alliances and organic development:[23]

- *Urgency.* Acquisitions can be a relatively short-cut method for pursuing a strategy. It would probably take decades for Tata to build up on its own two international luxury car brands equivalent to Jaguar and Land Rover (Illustration 10.2). Tata's purchase of the two brands gave an immediate kick-start to its strategy. Alliances too may accelerate the strategy by accessing additional resources or skills, though usually less quickly than a simple acquisition. Typically organic development (DIY) is slowest: everything has to be made from scratch.

- *Uncertainty.* It is often better to choose the alliance route where there is high uncertainty in terms of the markets or technologies involved. On the upside, if the markets or technologies turn out to be a success, it might be possible to turn the alliance into a full acquisition, especially if a buy option has been included in the initial alliance contract. If the venture turns out a failure, then at least the loss is shared with the alliance partner. Acquisitions also have merit if things do not turn out well: acquired units can usually be resold, even if at a lower price than the original purchase. On the other hand, a failed organic development might have to be written off entirely, with no sale value, because the business unit involved has never been on the market beforehand.

- *Type of capabilities.* Acquisitions work best when the desired capabilities (resources or competences) are '*hard*', for example physical investments in manufacturing facilities. Hard resources such as factories are easier to put a value on in the bidding process than '*soft*' resources such as people or brands. Hard resources are also typically easier to control post-acquisition than people and skills. As with the Roche takeover of Genentech (see Illustration 10.1), acquisitions pose the risk of significant cultural problems. Sometimes too the acquiring company's own image can tarnish the brand image of the target company. Acquisition of soft resources and competences should be approached with great caution. Indeed, the DIY organic method is typically the most effective with sensitive soft capabilities such as people. Internal ventures are likely to be culturally consistent at least. Even alliances can involve culture clashes between people from the two sides, and it is harder to control an alliance partner than an acquired unit.

● *Modularity of capabilities.* If the sought-after capabilities are highly *modular*, in other words they are distributed in clearly distinct sections or divisions of the proposed partners, then an alliance tends to make sense. A joint venture linking just the relevant sections of each partner can be formed, leaving each to run the rest of its businesses independently. There is no need to buy the whole of the other organisation. An acquisition can be problematic if it means buying the whole company, not just the modules that the acquirer is interested in. The DIY organic method can also be effective under conditions of modularity, as the new business can be developed under the umbrella of a distinct 'new venture division' (see section 9.5.2), rather than embroiling the whole organisation.

Of course, the choice between the three options of buy, ally and DIY is not unconstrained. Frequently there are no suitable acquisition targets or alliance partners available. One problem for voluntary organisations and charities is that the changes of ownership involved in mergers and acquisitions are much harder to achieve than in the private sector, so that their options are likely to be restricted to alliances or organic development in any case. The key message of Figure 10.5 remains nonetheless: it is important to weigh up the available options systematically and to avoid favouring one or the other without careful analysis.

10.5.2 Key success factors

Figure 10.5 indicates that, despite high failure rates, M&A and strategic alliances can still be the best option in certain circumstances. The question then is how to manage M&A and alliances as effectively as possible. Figure 10.6 provides a summary checklist of key factors, stemming from the discussion so far in this chapter. Many of the factors are similar across both M&A and alliances, but there are differences as well.

Naturally, *strategic fit* is critical in both M&A and alliances. The target or the partner should suit the desired strategy. As in section 10.3.4, it is very easy to overestimate synergies – and neglect negative synergies – in alliances as well as M&A. However, *organisational fit* is vital as well, in both cases. In particular, cultural differences are hard to manage, especially where people resources are important. Because of the lack of control, organisational fit issues are liable to be even harder to manage in alliances than in acquisitions, where the ownership rights of the buyer at least provide some managerial authority. *Valuation* likewise is a crucial issue in both M&A and alliances, especially equity alliances. Acquisitions are liable to the 'winner's curse' (section 10.3.4) of excessive valuation, particularly where there have been bid battles between competitors. But even alliance partners need to assess their relative contributions accurately in order to ensure that they do not commit too many resources with too little return and too little control.

However, M&A and alliances each raise some very distinct issues to manage. At the start of the process, alliances rely on courtship between willing partners, whereas that need not be the same for M&A. Mergers do require mutual willingness of course, but, if negotiations go poorly,

Figure 10.6 Key success factors in mergers, acquisitions and alliances

	M&A	Alliances
Similar	Strategic fit Organisational fit Valuation	Strategic fit Organisational fit Valuation
Different	Hostile option Integration Divesture	Courtship Co-evolution Termination

there often remains the option of the *hostile takeover* bid. The process of a hostile bid is principally about persuading shareholders rather than talking with the target's managers. In M&A, a crucial issue is the right approach to *integration*: absorption, preservation or symbiosis. In strategic alliances, the option to fully integrate the two partners into a single whole does not exist. Rather the task is the continued maintenance of a partnership between independent organisations which must *co-evolve*. Finally, *divesture* of acquired units and the *termination* of alliances tend to differ. Divestures are typically one-off transactions with purchasers, with few consequences for future relationships. On the other hand, the way in which alliances are terminated may have repercussions for important future relationships, as new projects and simultaneous projects often involve the same partners. In sum, it can be seen that the necessity for courtship, co-evolution and sensitive termination frequently makes the strategic alliance process a much more delicate one than simple acquisition.

SUMMARY

- There are three broad *methods* for pursuing strategy: *mergers and acquisitions, strategic alliances* and *organic development*.
- Organic development can be either continuous or radical. Radical organic development is termed *corporate entrepreneurship*.
- Acquisitions can be *hostile* or *friendly*. Motives for mergers and acquisitions can be *strategic, financial* or *managerial*.
- The acquisition process includes *target choice, valuation* and *integration*.
- Strategic alliances can be *equity* or *non-equity*. Key motives for strategic alliances include *scale, access, complementarity* and *collusion*.
- The strategic alliance process relies on *co-evolution* and *trust*.
- The choice between acquisition, alliance and organic methods is influenced by four key factors: *urgency, uncertainty, type of capabilities* and *modularity of capabilities*.

KEY DEBATE

Merger madness?

Mergers and acquisitions involve huge sums of money, but how wisely is it being spent?

This chapter has introduced the importance of mergers and acquisitions as a method of development, but also pointed to some challenges. There have been some spectacular failures. When in 2001 media company Time Warner merged with Internet company AOL, Time Warner shares were worth a total of $90bn (€63bn). Just under three years later, Time Warner investors' holdings in the merged company were worth only $36bn, a loss of over $50bn (in the same period, media companies' valuations had fallen on average 16 per cent).

Harvard Business School professor Michael Porter has been a prominent sceptic of mergers and acquisitions, noting that half of all acquired companies are sold off again within a few years.[1] The figure shows the aggregate dollar return (that is, the change in stock price associated with the acquisition announcement) of acquiring companies in the USA between 1996 and 2001.[2] In 2000, acquiring firms' shareholders lost, in all, more than $150bn. The authors of this study calculate that in the whole period of 1991 to 2001, acquiring firms' shareholders lost more than $7 for every $100 spent on acquisitions.

One interpretation of these large losses is that mergers and acquisitions represent a reckless waste of money by managers who are careless of investors' interests. Indeed there is evidence that CEOs suffer the consequences, over half being replaced within a relatively short time period.[3] It might be appropriate therefore to make mergers and acquisitions more difficult by legislating to help target companies resist or refuse hostile bids. If the law restricted hostile bids, wasteful acquisitions could be cut.

There are drawbacks to restricting mergers and acquisitions, however.[4] Even if acquiring companies often fail to make money for their shareholders, they can improve the profitability of the system as a whole in at least two ways:

- The threat of being taken over if they do not satisfy their shareholders helps keep managers focused on performance. The financial press reports just such threats regularly.
- Mergers and acquisitions can be an effective way of restructuring stagnant firms and industries. The absence of hostile takeovers in Japan is often blamed for the slow restructuring of Japanese industry since the early 1990s.

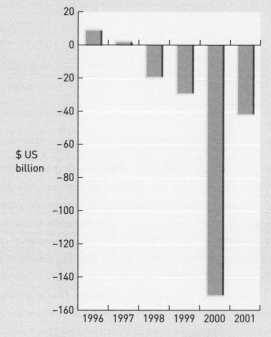

$ US billion

■ Aggregate dollar return (US $billion)

References:
1. M. Porter, 'From competitive advantage to corporate strategy', *Harvard Business Review*, May–June (1987), pp. 43–60.
2. S.B. Moeller, F.P. Schlingemann and R.M. Stulz, 'Wealth destruction on a massive scale? A study of acquiring firm returns in the recent merger wave', *Journal of Finance*, vol. 60, no. 2 (2005), pp. 757–82.
3. K.M. Lehn and M. Zhao, 'CEO turnover after acquisitions: are bad bidders fired?', *Journal of Finance*, vol. LXI, no. 4 (2006), pp. 1759–810.
4. 'Hostile bids are back again: who should rejoice?', *The Economist*, 21 February 2004.

Questions

1 For a recent large merger or acquisition, track the share prices of the companies involved (using www.bigcharts.com, for instance), for several weeks both before and after the announcement. What do the share price movements suggest about the merits of the deal?

2 Identify a hostile takeover threat from press reports. What action did the company's management do to resist the takeover?

WORK ASSIGNMENTS

✳ *Denotes more advanced work assignments.* * *Refers to a case study in the Text and Cases edition.*

10.1 Write a short (about ten lines) statement to a chief executive who has asked you to advise whether or not the company should develop through M&A. Write a similar statement to a chief executive of a hospital who is considering possible mergers with other hospitals.

10.2✳ For a recently announced acquisition, track the share prices (using www.bigcharts.com for example) of both the acquiring firm and the target firm in the period surrounding the bid? What do you conclude from the behaviour of the share prices about how investors regard the bid. Which company's investors are likely to benefit more?

10.3✳ Compare the M&A integration processes in the case studies Ferrovial* and Mergers in Education*. What do you conclude about effective and less effective practice?

10.4✳ Critically evaluate the proposition that alliance strategy is ethically superior to competitive strategy because it involves cooperation and the mutual creation of value.

10.5 Explain why family-owned companies might prefer organic development to either alliance or acquisitions.

Integrative assignment

10.6✳ Systematically compare the advantages of corporate entrepreneurship with independent entrepreneurship (section 9.5). What are the skills and personality characteristics the independent entrepreneurs and corporate entrepreneurs need most, and how do they differ between the two types of entrepreneur?

VIDEO ASSIGNMENT

Visit **MyStrategyLab** and watch the *Prêt-à-Manger* case study.

1 Assess the motives for McDonald's acquisition of a stake in Prêt-à-Manger (section 10.3.3) and assess the strategic and organisational fit (section 10.3.4).

2 In terms of the Haspeslagh and Jemison integration model (section 10.3.4), how *did* McDonald's approach integration and how *should* it have approached integration?

RECOMMENDED KEY READINGS

- A comprehensive book on mergers and acquisitions is: P. Gaughan, *Mergers, Acquisitions and Corporate Restructurings*, 4th edition, Wiley, 2007. For some alternative perspectives, see the collection by D. Angwin (ed.), *Mergers and Acquisitions*, Blackwell, 2007.

- A useful book on strategic alliances is J. Child, D. Faulkner and S. Tallman, *Cooperative Strategy: Managing Alliances, Networks and Joint Ventures*, Oxford University Press, 2005.

REFERENCES

1. P. Sharma and J. Chrisman, 'Towards a reconciliation of the definitional issues in the field of corporate entrepreneurship', *Entrepreneurial Theory and Practice*, Spring 1998, pp. 11–27; D. Garvin and L. Levesque, 'Meeting the challenge of corporate entrepreneurship', *Harvard Business Review*, October 2006, pp. 102–12.

2. Zephyr *Annual Global M&A Report 2009*, Bureau van Dijk, 2010.

3. R. Schoenberg, 'Mergers and acquisitions', in D.O. Faulkner and A. Campbell (eds), *The Oxford Handbook of Strategy: Vol. II*, Oxford University Press, 2005.

4. This adapts J. Bower, 'Not all M&As are alike – and that matters', *Harvard Business Review*, March 2001, pp. 93–101.

5. M. Hayward and D. Hambrick, 'Explaining the premiums paid for large acquisitions: evidence of CEO hubris', *Administrative Science Quarterly*, vol. 42 (1997), pp. 103–27.

6. This builds on D. Jemison and S. Sitkin, 'Corporate acquisitions: a process perspective', *Academy of Management Review*, vol. 11, no. 1 (1986), pp. 145–63.

7. J.M. Shaver, 'A paradox of synergy: contagion and capacity effects in mergers and acquisitions', *Academy of Management Review*, vol. 31, no. 4 (2006), pp. 962–78.

8. See J. Child, D. Faulkner and R. Pitkethly, *The Management of International Acquisitions*, Oxford University Press, 2001.

9. A useful discussion of valuation methods in acquisitions is in Chapter 9 of D. Sadtler, D. Smith and A. Campbell, *Smarter Acquisitions*, Prentice Hall, 2008.

10. N. Varaiya and K. Ferris, 'Overpaying in corporate takeovers: the winner's curse', *Financial Analysts Journal*, vol. 43, no. 3 (1987), pp. 64–70.

11. P. Haspeslagh and D. Jemison, *Managing Acquisitions: Creating Value through Corporate Renewal*, Free Press, 1991; P. Puranam, H. Singh and S. Chaudhuri, 'Integrating acquired capabilities: when structural integration is (un)necessary', *Organization Science*, vol. 20, no. 2 (2009), pp. 313–28.

12. G. Stahl and A. Voigt, 'Do cultural differences matter in mergers and acquisitions? A tentative model and examination', *Organization Science*, vol. 19, no. 1 (2008), pp. 160–78.

13. K. Ellis, T. Reus and B. Lamont, 'The effects of procedural and informational justice in the integration of related acquisitions', *Strategic Management Journal*, vol. 30 (2009), pp. 137–61.

14. R. Uhlaner and A. West, 'Running a winning M&A shop', *McKinsey Quarterly*, March 2008, pp. 106–12.

15. L. Dranikoff, T. Koller and A. Schneider, 'Divesture: strategy's missing link', *Harvard Business Review*, May 2002, pp. 75–83 and M. Brauer, 'What have we acquired and what should we acquire in divesture research? A review and research agenda', *Journal of Management*, vol. 32, no. 6 (2006), pp. 751–85.

16. Andersen Consulting, *Dispelling the Myths of Strategic Alliances*, 1999.

17. R. Bresser, 'Matching collective and competitive strategies', *Strategic Management Journal*, vol. 9, no. 4 (1988), pp. 375–85.

18. J. Dyer, *Collaborative Advantage*, Oxford University Press, 2000.

19. A. Inkpen and S. Curral, 'The coevolution of trust, control, and learning in joint ventures', *Organization Science*, vol. 15, no. 5 (2004), pp. 586–99; R. ul-Huq, *Alliances and Co-evolution in the Banking Sector*, Palgrave, 2005.

20. A. Arino and J. de la Torre, 'Relational quality: managing trust in corporate alliances', *California Management Review*, vol. 44, no. 1 (2001), pp. 109–31.

21. G. Hamel, *Alliance Advantage: the Art of Creating Value through Partnering*, Harvard Business School Press, 1998.

22. Andersen Consulting, *Dispelling the Myths of Strategic Alliances*, 1999.

23. This draws on J. Dyer, P. Kale and H. Singh, 'When to ally and when to acquire?', *Harvard Business Review*, vol. 82, no 7/8 (2004), pp. 108–15, and X. Yin and M. Shanley, 'Industry determinants of the merger versus alliance decision', *Academy of Management Review*, vol. 31, no. 2 (2008), pp. 473–91.

CASE EXAMPLE

Final Fantasy captures Lara Croft: acquisitions and alliances in electronic games

During 2009, Japanese games maker Square Enix launched a series of radical strategic initiatives. Famous for its role-playing games such as the *Final Fantasy* series, Square Enix established strategic alliances with the strategy games developers Double Helix and Gas Powered Games in the United States and Wargaming.net in the United Kingdom. Most radically, it also acquired the British Eidos Group, famous for the Lara Croft games. Square Enix President Yōichi Wada commented: 'Our goal is to become one of the top ten players in the world's media and entertainment industry. Since the games market is global, both our contact with our customers and our game development must become global too'.

Source: iStockphoto.

The Japanese games industry

Square Enix's strategic moves came at a challenging time for the Japanese games industry. The Japanese had enjoyed two decades of domination built on the worldwide success of Japanese consoles such as the Sony PlayStation. But the growing success of Microsoft's Xbox gave an opportunity to American games developers to return to the console market. Indeed, American games developers found that their development skills were more transferable in the new cross-over markets, where games needed to be developed for PCs, consoles and mobile phones alike. Moreover, the Americans had the advantage of proximity to Hollywood, bringing in new creative talent and offering opportunities for film tie-ins. At the same time, Japan's ageing population was shrinking the market for traditional electronic games.

Square Enix's Yōichi Wada recognised the predicament of the Japanese industry vis-à-vis the Americans:

> In the last five to ten years, the Japanese games industry has become a closed environment, with no new people coming in, no new ideas, almost xenophobic ... The lag with the US is very clear. The US games industry was not good in the past but it has now attracted people from the computer industry and from Hollywood, which has led to strong growth.[1]

At the same time, the basic economics of the games industry are changing, with rising costs due to growing technological sophistication. A typical modern game can cost from $3,000,000 (about €2,000,000) to over $20,000,000 to develop.[2] Games generally take from one to three years to develop. Yet only one in twenty games is estimated ever to make a profit. In other words, the risks are very high and the necessary scale to compete is rising.

Square Enix's strategy

Square Enix itself is the creation of a merger. Square had been founded in 1983, and in 1987 launched the first of its famous *Final Fantasy* role-playing game series. Enix had been founded in 1975, and launched its role-playing *Dragon Quest* series in 1986. The two companies merged in 2003, after the financial failure of Square's film-venture, *Final Fantasy: the Spirit Within*. Yōichi Wada, President of Square, became the president of the new merged company.

Square Enix's strategy is based on the idea of 'polymorphic content'. Its various franchises (*Final Fantasy*, *Dragon Quest* and so on) are developed for all possible hardware or media rather than any single gaming platform. Square Enix games can be played on consoles, PCs, mobile phones or online, and spin-offs include TV series, films, comics and novels. In 2005,

Square Enix bought the Japanese arcade-game company Taito Corporation, famous for its *Space Invaders* game. *Space Invaders* versions have appeared on PlayStation, Xbox and Wii consoles, as well as PCs.

By 2008, Yōichi Wada was presiding over a company that was increasingly diversified, with sales of ¥136bn (about €1 bn) and just over 3,000 employees. However, it was still overwhelmingly Japanese (85 per cent of sales at home) and lacked scale by comparison with competitors such as Electronic Arts and Activision, respectively four and three times as large. On the plus side, Square Enix was reportedly cash rich, with a 'war-chest' available for acquisitions of about ¥40bn (about €300m).[3] During the summer of 2008, Square Enix made a friendly bid for the Japanese game developer Tecmo, whose fighting games *Ninja Garden* and *Dead or Alive* were popular in North America and Europe. Tecmo rejected the bid. Wada began to look overseas.

Lara Croft falls

Eidos is a British games company best-known for the action-adventure games series, *Tomb Raider*, starring the extraordinary Lara Croft. However, during 2008, disappointing sales for *Tomb Raider: Underworld* drove its share-price down from £5 (~€5.5; ~$7.5) to around 30 pence. Eidos' founder and chief executive, Jane Cavanagh, was forced to resign. The company declared losses of £136m (about €149m), on sales of £119m (down from £179m two years earlier). In April 2009, Square Enix bought the company for £84m (about €92.4m), a premium of 129% over Eidos' current market value. Given the declining success of the *Tomb Raider* franchise, many speculated that Square Enix had overpaid for its first overseas acquisition.

The acquisition of Eidos did offer Square Enix global reach, however. About one third of Eidos' sales were in the United States and 40 per cent in Europe, excluding the United Kingdom. Eidos also brought Square Enix its first studios outside Japan, with studios in the United Kingdom, Denmark, Hungary, the United States, Canada and China. Yōichi Wada commented: 'It is significant that we have opened a window for creative talents worldwide.'

Wada chose to keep Phil Rogers, the new Eidos chief executive, in place, along with the rest of his management team. Wada described a new Group structure, in which Square Enix, the arcade business Taito and Eidos would each be stand-alone divisions: 'Our aim is to implement a hybrid management structure which avoids the extremes of being either too global or too local'.[4] He continued: 'The Group's management and administration departments will be integrated, while our product and service delivery will be established locally in each territory to maximise our business opportunities through better understanding of local customers' tastes and commercial practices.' Wada also recognised the new strength that Eidos brought in action-adventure games, by contrast with Square Enix's traditional core of role-playing games. He declared his commitment both to sharing technologies across the businesses and to sustaining particular strengths: 'While promoting shared technology and expertise amongst our studios, we will also develop products which reflect the unique identity of each studio, regardless of locality.' Wada also commented on the nature of the skilled games developers he was acquiring: 'It is always difficult to manage creatives anywhere in the world. We want to cherish the Eidos studio culture but change it where it is necessary.'[5]

One thing that Square Enix was quick to do was to end the Eidos distribution agreement with Warner Bros for its products in the United States. Square Enix regarded itself as strong enough to do that itself.

Strategic alliances

At the same time as acquiring Eidos, Square Enix cemented three significant strategic alliances. In the United Kingdom, Square Enix tied up with the strategy game developer Wargaming.net (famous for the *Massive Assault* series) in order to produce the World War II game *Order of War*. This would enter the market at the end of 2009 as Square Enix's first global product release. In the United States, Square Enix formed partnerships with Gas Powered Games (producer of the *Supreme Commander* strategy game) and with Double Helix (producer of the *Front Mission* strategy series). Together with the Eidos acquisition, these partnerships significantly extended Square Enix's range beyond its traditional core in role-playing games. They also extended the company's geographical reach. Yōichi Wada commented: 'We see great opportunities in North American and European markets, both of which are expected to be maintaining sustainable growth over these coming years. Therefore it is crucial that we create alliances with proven developers such as Gas Powered Games in order to serve these significant markets better by providing products and services in tune with customer tastes.'[6]

All three of these new partners were relatively small (around 100 employees each), privately-owned and had their origins as start-ups during the 1990s. To take one example, Gas Powered Games had been founded in 1998 by Chris Taylor and colleagues from the games developer Cavedog Entertainment. Chris Taylor had spent his whole career in games, with his first game *Hardball II* released in 1989. In an interview, Chris Taylor explained his motivation for setting up his own company, Gas Powered Games:

> I had that dream really from the day I first walked into my first full time job as a games programmer. I wanted to be the guy running the company. . . . We've created our own original IPs (intellectual properties) consistently. Some are great, some are not so great, but the fact is you have to keep throwing darts at the board. You have to keep trying to make great stuff, and you can't do that if you're inside of a large megalithic corporation to the same degree . . .[7]

Chris Taylor described how Square Enix, traditionally a role-playing company, and Gas Powered Games, more a strategy game developer, were working together on their first venture, *Supreme Commander 2*:

> One of the things that we took as a cue from Square Enix was the way they embrace character and story. We were all into that, so that was easy. When we asked them, 'How should we develop our game to work with their philosophy?', they said, 'Don't do that because we want you to do what you do. You make games for the Western market, and we're interested in making games for the Western market.' So if we changed, we would be missing the point. Which was terrific, because that meant we could do what we loved to do, make great RTS (real-time strategy) games . . . and if we tried to change them in any way, we'd be moving away from the goal.[8]

A games enthusiast's view

In the space of a few months, Square Enix had transformed its profile. From its base in Japanese-style role-playing games, it was developing a significant presence in strategy and action adventure. It had studios across the world. Its various games titles were big across Asia, Europe and America. Games enthusiast Randy commented on a gamers' website:

> Square Enix publishing a western-developed game? Is the far-reaching JRPG (Japanese role-playing game) developer dumping the androgynous boy-heroes and shovel-wide swords for WWII fatigues and M1 Carbines? No, not entirely. But they *are* bringing Wargaming.net into the fold to do it for them. First, Square Enix buys out the house that Lara Croft built, and now they're into real-time strategy war games. *Nothing in this life makes sense anymore.*[9]

References:
1. M. Palmer, 'Square Enix views Eidos as a jump to next level', *Financial Times*, 28 April 2009.
2. 'Cost of making games set to soar', www.bbcnews.co.uk, 17 November 2005.
3. 'Square Enix needs to show growth scenario to market', *Nikkei*, 9 October 2007.
4. Joint interview with Yoichi Wada and Phil Rogers, www.square-enix.com, 26 May 2009.
5. M. Palmer, 'Square Enix views Eidos as a jump to next level', *Financial Times*, 28 April 2009.
6. 'Square Enix and Gas Powered Games announce strategic partnership', *Newswire Association*, 12 November 2008.
7. P. Elliott, 'Foot on the gas', *gamesindustry.biz*, 19 August 2008.
8. X. de Matos, 'Interview: Chris Taylor on Supreme Commander 2', *joystiq.com*, 9 June 2009.
9. Randy, 'Square Enix tries hand at WWI RTS with Order of War', *Gaming Nexus*, 17 April 2009. Italics in original.

Questions

1 Explain why Square Enix chose alliances in some cases and acquisitions in others.

2 How should Square Enix manage its Eidos acquisition in order to maximise value creation, and how might that management approach change over time?

3 What are the strengths and weaknesses of the alliance strategy, and what problems might Square Enix anticipate over time?

COMMENTARY ON PART II

In Part II of the book the central concern is the strategic choices available to organisations. The chapters offer a range of such strategic choices, their rationales and evidence as to why some seem more effective than others. But this raises three linked questions on which the four lenses provide differing insights:

- How do such options get generated?
- What form are they likely to take?
- How should they be dealt with or addressed?

Design lens

High value is placed on extensive information search and analysis of the wide range of factors, both internal and external, that might influence future strategy. So it can be expected that an extensive range of strategic options will be available for managers to consider. These should be justified in terms of an objective assessment of the extent to which they address the strategic issues facing the organisation, in particular how they:

- Meet the goals and objectives of the organisation;
- Address key opportunities and threats arising from the organisation's changing environment and its strategic capabilities;
- Might achieve competitive advantage.

Indeed it is important that managers provide such a convincing rationale since it is unlikely that strategic options will be considered unless they are supported in this way.

Experience lens

Strategy develops incrementally based on past strategy, past experience and the culture of the organisation within a political context. So those strategic options considered are heavily influenced by such factors. Indeed managers may have ready-made solutions on the basis of past experience and search for opportunities and circumstances to put them into effect. The strategies of successful organisations are also likely to be mimicked by others. So managers in different organisations tend to consider similar strategic options. The result is that the strategic options that surface are not likely to be innovative but, rather, build on current strategy.

Analytic tools do not give rise to the strategies under consideration. They may, however, be used as a way of checking why a strategy might be worth considering; or convincing other managers and stakeholders that they should be.

Managers faced with assessing strategic options should seek to understand their origins in terms of the history of organisations, the expectations and biases of managers and other stakeholders who influence strategy development. Challenging the experience bases of such options may not be straightforward. Objective analysis of the viability of strategic options may be disregarded or not taken seriously. It may be important to emphasise more the surfacing and challenging of managers' assumptions underlying the options they advance.

STRATEGIC CHOICES

Note that:

- There is no suggestion here that one of these lenses is better than another, but they do provide different insights into the problems faced and the ways managers cope with the challenge.
- If you have *not* read the Commentary following Chapter 1 which explains the four lenses, you should now do so.

Variety lens

The emphasis here is on the variety of potential ideas throughout an organisation. Given such variety, it is possible that innovative strategic options could originate from anywhere in the organisation rather than be planned from the top. However, the options that do develop are likely to be ill-formed and only partially address the strategic issues facing the organisation.

Managers looking to generate strategic options will:

- Help create an organisational context that encourages open exchange of information, experimentation and trial and error behaviour and discourages a reliance on established ways of doing things;
- Actively seek and encourage ideas and suggestions from people at all levels in the organisation;
- Be prepared to entertain innovative and partially formed ideas rather than rely on well-formed strategic options articulated from the top of the organisation;
- Discern patterns in such ideas and synthesise them into coherent strategies.

Discourse lens

Strategic options surfaced will be based on the discourse of which managers are part or which is in their self-interest. So:

- Strategic options that are favoured or gain most support are likely to be those that fit within the generally accepted discourse on strategy that prevails inside an organisation or in its organisational field/industry; or strategy discourse which is currently fashionable.
- The use of the language of strategy in the advocacy of a strategic option may be one way in which a manager may seek to gain political influence or legitimacy within an organisation.

Managers should therefore exercise a healthy scepticism in relation to the strategic options being advanced. They should understand that *how* a strategy is talked about can be seen as an important influence on *which* strategies are advocated and favoured and which are not. Moreover they should be concerned to probe the personal motivations and self-interest of those advancing them.

PART III
STRATEGY IN ACTION

This part explains:

- Criteria and techniques that can be used to evaluate possible strategic options.

- How strategies develop in organisations; in particular, the processes that may give rise to intended strategies or to emergent strategies.

- The way in which organisational structures and systems of control are important in organising for strategic success.

- The leadership and management of strategic change.

- Who strategists are and what they do in practice.

INTRODUCTION TO PART III

The first two Parts of the book have been concerned with how a strategist can think through the strategic position of an organisation and the strategic choices available to it. In this Part of the book the focus moves to strategy in action. It is concerned with how a strategy actually takes shape in an organisation and what strategists actually do.

The next chapter explains ways in which the strategic choices explained in Part II can be evaluated. In particular it suggests three criteria that can be applied. *Suitability* asks whether a strategy addresses the key issues relating to the opportunities and constraints an organisation faces. *Acceptability* asks whether a strategy meets the expectations of stakeholders. And *feasibility* invites an explicit consideration of whether a strategy could work in practice. In each case tools and techniques of evaluation are provided, explained and illustrated.

Chapter 12 examines two broadly different explanations *of how strategies actually develop* in organisations. Do strategies come about in organisations by first being conceived analytically and then implemented? In other words, do strategies develop on the basis of deliberate intent? Or is strategy more emergent, for example on the basis of people's experience or as a result of responses to competitive action? Or are elements of both explanations evident in organisations? And what are the implications of these different explanations for managing strategy?

Chapter 13 considers the relationship between strategy and how an organisation functions in terms of people working with each other within different *structures and systems*. These may be formally established by management or may be more informal relationships; but they will all affect the organisation's ability to deliver its strategy. The chapter considers how successful organising requires these various elements to work together in order to create mutually reinforcing *configurations* of structures and systems that are matched to an organisation's strategies.

The development of a new strategy may also require significant change for an organisation and this is the theme of Chapter 14. The *leadership of strategic change* is examined, first by acknowledging that managing change is not the same in all organisations; that the change context matters. The chapter then examines different approaches to managing change, including styles of managing change and the variety of levers employed to manage strategic change. The chapter concludes by revisiting the importance of context to consider how different levers might be employed in different change contexts.

This Part of the book then concludes by discussing *what strategists themselves actually do*. It examines three issues in the practice of strategy. First, who are included in strategy-making activities, often not just top management but middle managers, consultants and planners too. Second, the kinds of activities strategists are involved in, from selling strategic issues to communicating chosen strategies. Third, the kinds of methodologies that strategists use, including strategy workshops, projects, hypothesis testing and business planning.

11

EVALUATING STRATEGIES

Learning outcomes

After reading this chapter you should be able to:

● Employ three *success criteria* for evaluating strategic options:

  – *Suitability*: whether a strategy addresses the key issues relating to the *opportunities and constraints* an organisation faces.

  – *Acceptability*: whether a strategy meets the *expectations* of stakeholders.

  – *Feasibility*: whether a strategy could *work in practice*.

● For each of these use a range of different *techniques for evaluating strategic options*, both financial and non-financial.

PEARSON
mystrategylab™

MyStrategyLab is designed to help you make the most of your studies.

Visit **www.pearsoned.co.uk/mystrategylab** to discover a wide range of resources specific to this chapter, including:

● A personalised **Study plan** that will help you understand core concepts

● **Audio** and **video clips** that put the spotlight on strategy in the real world

● **Online glossaries** and **flashcards** that provide helpful reminders when you're looking for some quick revision.

(11.1) INTRODUCTION

Part II of the book introduced an array of strategic options and choices. The strategist has therefore to decide between these options; to decide what the organisation is actually going to do. This can be a challenge. It is not unusual for managers in a business – or indeed a group of students analysing a case study – to generate a long list of options. How is a decision to be made between them? This chapter and the next explain different ways in which this may occur. In this chapter the focus is on systematic criteria and techniques that can be used to evaluate strategic options against those criteria. It provides tools that managers can use to approach such decisions from a rational design perspective (see the Commentary following Chapter 1). This begs the question, of course, as to how such choices are made in practice; that is the focus of Chapter 12 which follows.

This chapter is structured around three key evaluation criteria (see Table 11.1), summarised by the acronym **SAF**e. They are:

- *Suitability*, which is concerned with assessing which proposed strategies address the key issues relating to the *opportunities and constraints* an organisation faces. To what extent and how does it take advantage of opportunities, build on strengths or overcome threats and weaknesses that may have been identified in understanding the strategic position of the organisation?
- *Acceptability*, which is concerned with whether the expected *performance outcomes* of a proposed strategy meets the *expectations of stakeholders*.
- *Feasibility* is concerned with whether a strategy could *work in practice*; therefore whether an organisation has or can obtain the capabilities to deliver a strategy.

SAFe can be used to assess the viability of strategic options. In effect the criteria pose the question as to why some strategies might succeed better than others. The chapter is therefore about moving towards making a strategy happen. In the rest of the chapter each of the criteria

Table 11.1 The SAFe criteria and techniques of evaluation

Suitability	• Does a proposed strategy address the *key opportunities and constraints* an organisation faces?
Acceptability	• Does a proposed strategy meet the *expectations of stakeholders*? • Is the level of risk acceptable? • Is the likely return acceptable? • Will stakeholders accept the strategy?
Feasibility	• Would a proposed strategy *work in practice*? • Can the strategy be financed? • Do people and their skills exist or can they be obtained? • Can the required resources be obtained and integrated?

is introduced, followed by explanations, with illustrations, of techniques of evaluation and key questions appropriate to each of them.

(11.2) SUITABILITY

Part I explained how the strategic position of an organisation can be understood in terms of key drivers and expected changes in its *environment* and its *strategic capabilities* in the context of *historical* and *cultural influences*. These factors provide opportunities but also place constraints on the future direction of an organisation. **Suitability is concerned with assessing which proposed strategies address the *key opportunities and constraints* an organisation faces** through an understanding of the strategic position of an organisation: it is therefore concerned with the overall *rationale* of a strategy. At the most basic level, the need is to assess the extent to which a proposed strategy:

- Exploits the opportunities in the environment and avoids the threats;
- Capitalises on the organisation's strength and strategic capabilities and avoids or remedies the weaknesses.

So the concepts and frameworks already discussed in Chapters 2 to 5 can be especially helpful in understanding suitability. Some examples are shown in Table 11.2. However, there is an

Table 11.2 Suitability of strategic options in relation to strategic position

Concept	Figure/Table/ Illustration	Helps with understanding	Suitable strategies address (examples)
PESTEL	Ill. 2.1	Key environmental drivers Changes in industry structure	Industry cycles Industry convergence Major environmental changes
Scenarios	Ill. 2.2	Extent of uncertainty/risk Extent to which strategic options are mutually exclusive	Need for contingency plans or 'low-cost probes'
Five forces	Fig. 2.2 Ill. 2.3	Industry attractiveness Competitive forces	Reducing competitive intensity Development of barriers to new entrants
Strategic groups	Fig. 2.8	Attractiveness of groups Mobility barriers Strategic spaces	Need to reposition to a more attractive group or to an available strategic space
Strategic capabilities	Figs 3.2, 3.5 Ill. 3.5	Industry threshold standards Bases of competitive advantage	Eliminating weaknesses Exploiting strengths
Value chain	Figs 3.5, 3.6	Opportunities for vertical integration or outsourcing	Extent of vertical integration or possible outsourcing
Cultural web	Fig. 5.5 Ill. 5.4	The links between organisational culture and the current strategy	The strategic options most aligned with the prevailing culture

Table 11.3 Some examples of suitability

Strategic option	Why this option might be suitable in terms of:	
	Environment	Capability
Directions		
Retrenchment	Withdraw from declining markets Maintain market share	Identify and focus on established strengths
Market penetration	Gain market share for advantage	Exploit superior resources and capabilities
Product development	Exploit knowledge of customer needs	Exploit R&D
Market development	Current markets saturated New opportunities for: geographical spread, entering new segments or new uses	Exploit current products and capabilities
Diversification	Current markets saturated or declining	Exploit strategic capabilities in new arenas
Methods		
Organic development	Partners or acquisitions not available or not suitable	Building on own capabilities Learning and competence development
Merger/acquisition	Speed Supply/demand P/E ratios	Acquire capabilities Scale economies
Joint development	Speed Industry norm Required for market entry	Complementary capabilities Learning from partners

important point to bear in mind. It is likely that a great many issues will have been raised if the concepts and tools discussed in Part I have been employed. It is therefore important that the really important issues are identified from amongst all these. Indeed a major skill of a strategist is to be able to discern these *key strategic issues*. Evaluating the suitability of a strategy is very difficult unless the key strategic issues have been clearly sorted out from the less important issues.

The discussions about possible strategic choices in Part II were concerned not only with understanding what choices might be 'available' to organisations but also providing reasons why each might be considered. So the examples in those sections also illustrate why strategies might be regarded as *suitable*. Table 11.3 summarises these points from earlier sections and provides examples of reasons why strategies might be regarded as suitable. There are, however, also a number of screening techniques that can be used to assess the suitability of proposed strategies by reviewing their relative merits against key opportunities and constraints.

11.2.1 Ranking

Here possible strategies are assessed against key factors relating to the strategic position of the organisation and a score (or ranking) established for each option. Illustration 11.1 gives an

ILLUSTRATION 11.1

Ranking options for SRR Consulting

Ranking can usefully provide an initial view of the suitability of strategic oprions by comparing strategic options against the key strategic factors from the SWOT analysis.

Simon and Ruth were both IT specialists who returned to their companies after completing their MBAs. Raj, a friend of theirs, had been an IT consultant who did the same MBA course a year later. His MBA project looked at the feasibility of setting up an IT consultancy partnership with Simon and Ruth. SRR was established in 2008. Their strategy was initially to build on 'outsourcing' the IT needs of the organisations they worked for. Raj had worked on IT assignments for business start-ups for a consultancy: 'It was not big business for them and they were delighted to have me operate as an associate; in effect outsourcing that work'. Simon worked for a medium-sized local engineering business and Ruth for a retailer with a small chain of local shops. As Simon explained: 'Neither of our employers really needed IT specialists full-time: an outsourced facility made good economic sense.'

Ruth continued: 'Our first year went well. We provided a good service to our previous employers together with developing business with some other contacts. We are both the owners and the consultants of SRR and our overheads are pretty low so we have made a reasonable living. Our problem now is, where from here? We are keen to grow the business, not just because we would like a higher income, but because with our rather limited client base we are vulnerable. We have built on our IT expertise and the sectors we know, but we have reached something of a ceiling with regard to our personal contacts. We can see a number of possible options. There is an opportunity on the management development aspects of IT; how can IT be used to aid better management? Most of our clients don't understand

this. Our problem is that we are not trainers so we would need to develop those skills or hire someone who has them. Another option is to actively go out and develop new contacts. The problems here are that it means branching out into sectors unfamiliar to us and that will take our time – which won't be fee earning – so it would reduce our income at least in the short term. Linked to this is the possibility of going for much bigger clients. This might get us bigger fees, perhaps, but it would quite possibly mean competition with some big competitors. In the last year our business has also been very local. We could stick with the same sectors we know but broaden the geographic area. The problem there, of course, is we are not known. Finally we have been approached by another IT consultancy about the possibility of a merger. They operate in complementary sectors and do have training capabilities, but it is bigger than us and I don't know if we are ready to lose our own identity yet.'

Simon, Ruth and Raj had begun a ranking exercise to look at these options as shown below.

Questions

1 Are there other options or factors that you think Simon, Ruth and Raj should consider?

2 How could you improve the ranking analysis?

3 Consider the most favoured options in terms of acceptability and feasibility criteria.

Ranking exercise

Strategic options	Key strategic factors								
	Fit with technical competences	Fit with sector know how	Builds on our known reputation	Increases non fee earning management time	Reached our 'contact ceiling'	Builds on client need	Higher fee income	Increased competition	Ranking
1. Develop new contacts	✓	✗	✓	✗	✓	?	?	?	3–2 (B)
2. Develop bigger clients	✓	?	✗	✗	✓	✗	✓	✗	3–3 (C)
3. Geographic market development	✓	✓	✓	✗	✓	✓	✗	✗	5–3 (B)
4. Develop IT training	✗	✓	✓	✗	✓	✓	✓	✓	6–2 (A)
5. Merger	✓	✓	?	✓	✓	?	?	✓	5–0 (A)

✓ = favourable; ✗ = unfavourable; ? = uncertain or irrelevant.
A = most suitable; B = possible; C = unsuitable.

example. One of the advantages of this approach is that it forces a debate about the implications and impacts of specific key factors on specific strategic proposals. It therefore helps overcome a potential danger in strategy evaluation; namely that managers are likely to interpret the impact of particular factors, or have preferences for proposed strategies, in terms of their own subjectivity.

More sophisticated approaches to ranking can assign weightings to factors in recognition that some will be of more importance in the evaluation than others. It should, however, be remembered that assigning numbers, of itself, is not a basis of evaluation; any scoring or weighting is only a reflection of the quality of the analysis and debate that goes into the scoring.

A similar approach can be adopted in relation to examining proposed strategies in terms of the responses of competitors. Section 6.4.4 on game theory emphasised that the viability of a strategy should take into account the likely response of competitors to any strategy an organisation might consider. Ranking can be used for this purpose. In effect the key factors become the key competitors. Each proposed strategy is then considered in terms of the likely responses of each competitor to that strategy. Suitability is then assessed in terms of which proposed strategy would be most likely to be effective in competitive terms.

11.2.2 Screening through scenarios

Here strategic options are considered against a range of future scenarios (see section 2.2.2 and Illustration 2.2). This is especially useful where a high degree of uncertainty exists. Suitable options are ones that make sense in terms of the various scenarios. As a result of such analysis it may be that several strategic options need to be 'kept open', perhaps in the form of contingency plans, developed as 'low-cost probes' or further evaluated in terms of their feasibility (see 11.4 below). Or it could be that an option being considered is found to be suitable in different scenarios. Indeed a criterion of strategy evaluation for Shell is that a chosen strategy needs to be suitable in terms of a range of different crude oil prices.

One of the other advantages of screening through scenarios is that, as managers screen the possible strategies in terms of the different scenarios, they come to see which would be most suitable in different environmental contexts. This can then sensitise managers to the need for changes in strategy, or changes in strategic emphasis, given changes in the environment.

11.2.3 Screening for bases of competitive advantage

One of the key issues in evaluating a strategy is whether it is likely to provide a basis of competitive advantage. Quite possibly the factors relating to this may have been built into the ranking exercises explained above. However, if they have not, then it may be sensible to consider this question specifically. Table 11.4 provides a basis for doing this.

As Chapters 3 and 6 explained, the likely bases of competitive advantage reside in the strategic capabilities of an organisation. Screening for bases of competitive advantage therefore requires the following steps:

- An identification of the key strategic capabilities underpinning a proposed strategy.
- The screening of these strategic capabilities in terms of their suitability to deliver either:
  - (a) Cost leadership or
  - (b) Differentiation benefits as valued by the customer.

  It is these two critical requirements, as explained in Chapter 6, that are the bedrock upon which competitive strategies might be built.

Table 11.4 Assessing bases of competitive advantage

Strategic capabilities underpinning the proposed strategy	Contribution to cost leadership differentiation	Perceived value to customers	Rarity	Inimitability	Non-substitutability

● Screening each of the strategic capabilities against the VRIN criteria explained in Chapter 3 (section 3.3) upon which sustainability of competitive advantage is based:

V value; the potential to achieve competitive advantage in a market, though this has to bear in mind the need to achieve this at a cost that allows an organisation to realise acceptable levels of return (see 11.3.2 below).

R rarity; the extent to which the strategic capability is distinctive or unique to the organisation and, very important, cannot readily be obtained or acquired by a competitor.

I inimitability; how difficult it would be for competitors to imitate the strategic capability.

N non-substitutability in terms of products or services or competences.

Such an analysis may well reveal that very few strategic capabilities are difficult to imitate in isolation. As section 3.4.3 on activity systems made clear, however, it is likely that it is not a generic capability that matters, but rather the linkages between the activities that make up the capability. So care has to be taken in this analysis to ensure that these linkages are identified and taken into consideration. Moreover it is important to remember the important point made in the discussion of inimitability in section 3.3.3. Difficulty of imitation is likely to be because strategic capabilities are complex (not least because of such linkages), causally ambiguous or embedded in an organisation's culture. So, again, care needs to be taken that the bases of strategic capability are well understood through disaggregation rather than expressed in overly abstract terms (see section 3.4.3).

11.2.4 Decision trees

Decision trees can also be used to assess strategic options against a list of key factors. Here options are 'eliminated' and preferred options emerge by progressively introducing requirements which must be met (such as growth, investment or diversity). Illustration 11.2 provides an example.

ILLUSTRATION 11.2

A strategic decision tree for a law firm

Decision trees evaluate future options by progressively eliminating others as additional criteria are introduced to the evaluation.

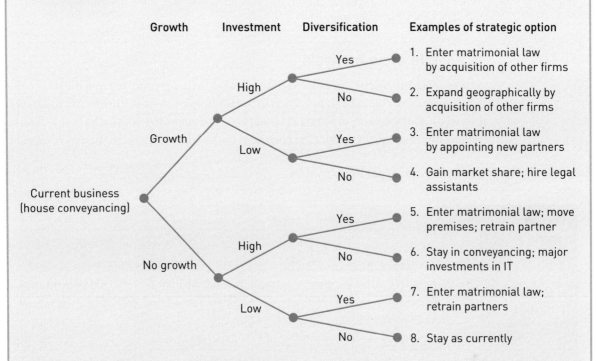

A law firm had most of its work related to house conveyancing (the legal aspects of buying property) where profits had been significantly squeezed. Therefore, it wanted to consider a range of new strategies for the future. Using a strategic decision tree it was able to eliminate certain options by identifying a few key criteria which future developments would incorporate, such as growth, investment (in premises, IT systems or acquisitions), and diversification (for example, into matrimonial law which, in turn, often brings house conveyancing work as families 'reshape').

Analysis of the decision tree reveals that if the partners of the firm wish growth to be an important aspect of future strategies, options 1–4 are ranked more highly than options 5–8. At the second step, the need for low-investment strategies would rank options 3 and 4 above 1 and 2, and so on.

The partners were aware that this technique has limitations in that the choice at each branch of the tree can tend to be simplistic. Answering 'yes' or 'no' to diversification does not allow for the wide variety of alternatives which might exist between these two extremes, for example *adapting the 'style' of the conveyancing service* (this could be an important variant of options 6 or 8). Nevertheless, as a starting point for evaluation, the decision tree provided a useful framework.

Questions

1 Try reversing the sequence of the three parameters (to diversification, investment and growth) and redraw the decision tree. Do the same eight options still emerge?

2 Add a fourth parameter to the decision tree. This new parameter is development by *internal methods* or by *acquisition*. List your 16 options in the right hand column.

The end point of the decision tree is a number of discrete development opportunities. The elimination process is achieved by identifying a few key elements or criteria which possible strategies need to achieve. In Illustration 11.2 these are growth, investment and diversification. As the illustration shows, choosing growth as an important requirement of a future strategy ranks options 1–4 more highly than 5–8. At the second step, the need for low investment strategies would rank options 3 and 4 above 1 and 2; and so on. The danger here is that the choice at each branch on the tree can tend to be simplistic. For example, as the illustration points out, answering 'yes' or 'no' to diversification does not allow for the wide variety of options which might exist within it.

11.2.5 Life cycle analysis

A *life cycle analysis* assesses whether a strategy is likely to be appropriate given the stage of the industry life cycle. Table 11.5 shows a matrix with two dimensions. The market situation is described in four stages, from embryonic to ageing. The competitive position has five categories ranging from weak to dominant. The purpose of the matrix is to establish the appropriateness

Table 11.5 The industry life cycle/portfolio matrix

Competitive position	Stages of industry maturity			
	Embryonic/ Developing	Growth	Mature	Ageing/Decline
Dominant	Fast grow Start up	Fast grow Attain cost leadership Renew Defend position	Defend position Attain cost leadership Renew Fast grow	Defend position Focus Renew Grow with industry
Strong	Start up Differentiate Fast grow	Fast grow Catch up Attain cost leadership Differentiate	Attain cost leadership Renew, focus Differentiate Grow with industry	Find niche Hold niche Hang in Grow with industry Harvest
Favourable	Start up Differentiate Focus Fast grow	Differentiate, focus Catch up Grow with industry	Harvest, hang in Find niche, hold niche Renew, turnaround Differentiate, focus Grow with industry	Retrench Turnaround
Tenable	Start up Grow with industry Focus	Harvest, catch up Hold niche, hang in Find niche Turnaround Focus Grow with industry	Harvest Turnaround Find niche Retrench	Divest Retrench
Weak	Find niche Catch up Grow with industry	Turnaround Retrench	Withdraw Divest	Withdraw

Source: Arthur D. Little.

of particular strategies in relation to these two dimensions. The consultancy firm Arthur D. Little suggests a number of criteria for establishing where an organisation is positioned on the matrix and what types of strategy are most likely to be suitable:

- **Position within the life cycle** can be determined in relation to market growth rate, growth potential, breadth of product lines, numbers of competitors, spread of market share between competitors, customer loyalty, entry barriers and technology. It is the balance of these factors which determines the life-cycle stage. For example, an embryonic industry is characterised by rapid growth, changes in technology, fragmented market shares and pursuit of new customers: an ageing industry by falling demand, declining number of competitors and, often, a narrow product line.

- **Competitive position** within its industry can be determined as follows:

  - A *dominant* position is rare in the private sector unless there is a quasi-monopoly position. In the public sector there is a legalised monopoly status (though this is becoming rarer).

  - *Strong* organisations are those that can follow strategies of their own choice without too much concern for competition.

  - A *favourable* position is where no single competitor stands out, but leaders are better placed (as, for example, in clothing retailing).

  - A *tenable* position is that which can be maintained by specialisation or focus.

  - *Weak* competitors are ones which are too small to survive independently in the long run.

Whilst this matrix is of use in providing guidance and raising questions in the evaluation of possible strategies, the danger is that it is taken over-literally: it does not, of itself, provide directive answers.

(11.3) ACCEPTABILITY

Acceptability is concerned with **whether the expected performance outcomes of a proposed strategy meet the expectations of stakeholders.** These can be of three types, the '3 Rs': *risk, return* and *stakeholder reactions*. It is sensible to use more than one approach in assessing the acceptability of a strategy.

11.3.1 Risk

The first R is the *risk* an organisation faces in pursuing a strategy. **Risk concerns the extent to which the outcomes of a strategy can be predicted**. For example, risk can be high for organisations with major long-term programmes of innovation, where high levels of uncertainty exist about key issues in the environment, or about market behaviour, or where there are high levels of public concern about new developments – such as genetically modified crops.[1] Formal risk assessments are often incorporated into business plans as well as the investment appraisals of major projects. Importantly, risks other than ones with immediate financial impact are included, such as 'risk to corporate or brand image' or 'risk of missing an opportunity'. Developing a good understanding of an organisation's strategic position (Part I of this book) is at the core of good risk assessment. However, the following tools can also be helpful in a risk assessment.

Sensitivity analysis[2]

Sometimes referred to as *what-if* analysis, sensitivity analysis allows each of the important assumptions underlying a particular strategy to be questioned and challenged. In particular, it tests how sensitive the predicted performance or outcome (e.g. profit) is to each of these assumptions. For example, the key assumptions underlying a strategy might be that market demand will grow by 5 per cent a year, or that a new product will achieve a given sales and contribution level, or that certain expensive machines will operate at 90 per cent loading. Sensitivity analysis asks what would be the effect on performance (for example, profitability) of variations on these assumptions. For example, if market demand grew at only 1 per cent, or by as much as 10 per cent, would either of these extremes alter the decision to pursue that strategy? This can help develop a clearer picture of the risks of making particular strategic decisions and the degree of confidence managers might have in a given decision. Illustration 11.3 shows how sensitivity analysis can be used.

ILLUSTRATION 11.3

Sensitivity analysis

Sensitivity analysis is a useful technique for assessing the extent to which the success of a preferred strategy is dependent on the key assumptions which underlie that strategy.

In 2009 the Dunsmore Chemical Company was a single-product company trading in a mature and relatively stable market. It was intended to use this established situation as a 'cash cow' to generate funds for a new venture with a related product. Estimates had shown that the company would need to generate some £4m (~€4.4m; ~$6m) cash (at 2009 values) between 2010 and 2015 for this new venture to be possible.

Although the expected performance of the company was for a cash flow of £9.5m over that period (the *base case*), management were concerned to assess the likely impact of three key factors:

● Possible increases in *production costs* (labour, overheads and materials), which might be as much as 3 per cent p.a. in real terms.
● *Capacity-fill*, which might be reduced by as much as 25 per cent due to ageing plant and uncertain labour relations.
● *Price levels*, which might be affected by the threatened entry of a new major competitor. This could

(a) Sensitivity of cash flow to changes in real production costs

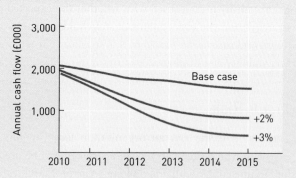

squeeze prices by as much as 3 per cent p.a. in real terms.

It was decided to use sensitivity analysis to assess the possible impact of each of these factors on the company's ability to generate £4m. The results are shown in the graphs.

Financial ratios[3]

The projection of how key financial ratios might change if a strategy were adopted can provide useful insights into risk. At the broadest level, an assessment of how the *capital structure* of the company would change is a good general measure of risk. For example, strategies that would require an increase in long-term debt will increase the gearing (or 'leverage') of the company and, hence, its financial risk. This is not because high long-term debt is the risk in itself, but because of the mandatory interest payments that go with it: if performance dips, these interest payments still have to be paid.

A consideration of the likely impact of a proposed strategy on an organisation's *liquidity* is also important in assessing risk. Indeed many businesses fail, not because they are inherently unprofitable, but because of a lack of cash liquidity and an inability to raise capital. For example, a small retailer eager to grow quickly may be tempted to fund the required shop-fitting costs by delaying payments to suppliers and increasing bank overdraft. Attractive as this may be to

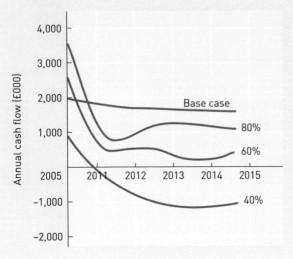

(b) Sensitivity of cash flow to changes in plant utilistion

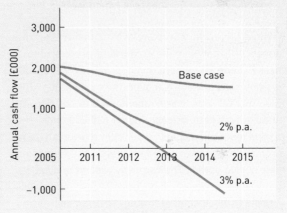

(c) Sensitivity of cash flow to reductions in real price

the extent to which they could protect price levels if such competition emerged. They therefore developed an aggressive marketing strategy to deter potential entrants.

From this analysis, management concluded that their target of £4m would be achieved with *capacity utilisation* as low as 60 per cent, which was certainly going to be achieved. Increased *production costs* of 3 per cent p.a. would still allow the company to achieve the £4m target over the period. In contrast, *price* squeezes of 3 per cent p.a. would result in a shortfall of £2m.

Management concluded from this analysis that the key factor which should affect their thinking on this matter was the likely impact of new competition and

Questions

What should the company do if its marketing campaigns fail to stop real price erosion:

1 Push to achieve more sales volume/ capacity fill?

2 Reduce unit costs of production?

3 Something else?

improve short-term cash flow, it could mean that the survival of the business becomes dependent on the likelihood of either creditors or the bank demanding payments from the company – an issue that clearly requires careful assessment.

Break-even analysis

Break-even analysis[4] is a simple and widely used approach which allows variations in assumptions about key variables in a strategy to be examined. It demonstrates at what point in terms of revenue the business will recover its fixed and variable costs and therefore break even. It can therefore be used to assess the risks associated with different price and cost structures of strategies as shown in Illustration 11.4.

ILLUSTRATION 11.4

Using break-even analysis to examine strategic options

Break-even analysis can be a simple way of quantifying some of the key factors which would determine the success or failure of a strategy.

A manufacturing company was considering the launch of a new consumer durable product into a market segment where most products were sold to wholesalers which supplied the retail trade. The total market was worth about €4.8.m (or $6.6m) (at manufacturers' prices) – about 630,000 units. The market leader had about 30 per cent market share in a competitive market where retailers were increasing their buying power. The company wished to evaluate the relative merits of a high-price/high-quality product sold to wholesalers (strategy A) or an own-brand product sold directly to retailers (strategy B).

The table summarises the market and cost structure for the market leader and these alternative strategies.

The table shows that the company would require about 22 per cent and 13 per cent market share respectively for strategies A and B to break even.

Questions

1 Which option would you choose? Why?

2 What would be the main risks attached to that option and how would you attempt to minimise these risks?

3 Create another option (strategy C) and explain the kind of break-even profile which would be needed to make it more attractive than either strategy A or strategy B.

Market and cost structure	Market leader	Strategy A	Strategy B
Price to retailer	€10.00	€12.00	€8.00
Price to wholesaler	€7.00	€8.40	–
Total variable costs (TVC)	€3.50	€4.00	€3.10
Contribution to profit per unit sold (= Price sold-TVC)	€3.50	€4.40	€4.90
Fixed costs (FC)	€500,000	€500,000	€500,000
Break-even point: no. of units to sell (= FC/Contribution to profit)	142,857	136,363	81,633
Total market size (units)	630,000	630,000	630,000
Break-even point: market share (= Break-even point units/Mkt size)	22.6%	21.6%	13.0%
Actual market share	30.0%	–	–

11.3.2 Return

The second R is returns. These are **the financial benefits which stakeholders are expected to receive from a strategy**. In the private sector typically these are shareholders and lenders; in the public sector the equivalent is funders, typically government departments. Measures of return are a common way of assessing proposed new ventures or major projects within businesses. So an assessment of financial and non-financial returns likely to accrue from specific strategic options could be a key criterion of acceptability of a strategy – at least to some stakeholders. There are different approaches to understanding return. This section looks briefly at three of these. It is important to remember that there are no absolute standards as to what constitutes good or poor return. It will differ between industries and countries and between different stakeholders. So it is important to establish what return is seen as acceptable by which stakeholders. Views also differ as to which measures give the best assessment of return, as will be seen below.

Financial analysis[5]

Traditional financial analyses are used extensively in assessing the acceptability of different strategic options. However, there are three considerations to be borne in mind when carrying out a financial analysis for the purpose of strategy evaluation:

- *The problem of uncertainty.* Be wary of the apparent thoroughness of the various approaches to financial analysis. Most were developed for the purposes of investment appraisal. Therefore, they focus on discrete projects where the additional cash inflows and outflows can be predicted with relative certainty: for example, a retailer opening a new store has a good idea about likely turnover based on previous experience of similar stores in similar areas. Such assumptions are not necessarily valid in many strategic contexts because the outcomes are much less certain. It is as strategy implementation proceeds (with the associated cash-flow consequences) that outcomes become clearer (see the discussion of 'real options' below).

- *The problem of specificity.* Financial appraisals tend to focus on direct *tangible* costs and benefits rather than the strategy more broadly. However, it is often not easy to identify such costs and benefits, or the cash flows specific to a proposed strategy, since it may not be possible to isolate them from other ongoing business activities. Moreover such costs and benefits may have spillover effects. For example, a new product may look unprofitable as a single project. But it may make strategic sense by enhancing the market acceptability of other products in a company's portfolio.

- *Assumptions.* Financial analysis is only as good as the assumptions built into the analysis. If assumptions about sales levels or costs are misguided, for example, then the value of the analysis is reduced, even misleading. This is one reason why sensitivity testing based on variations of assumptions is important.

Three commonly used bases of financial analysis (see Figure 11.1) are:

- Forecasting the *return on capital employed (ROCE)* for a specific time period after a new strategy is in place. For example, a ROCE of 15 per cent by year 3. This, then, is a profit measure of return and is shown in Figure 11.1(a). The ROCE (typically profit before interest and tax – PBIT, divided by capital employed) is a measure of the earning power of the resources used in implementing a particular strategic option. Its weakness is that it does not focus on cash flow or the timing of cash flows (see the explanation of DCF below).

Figure 11.1 Assessing profitability

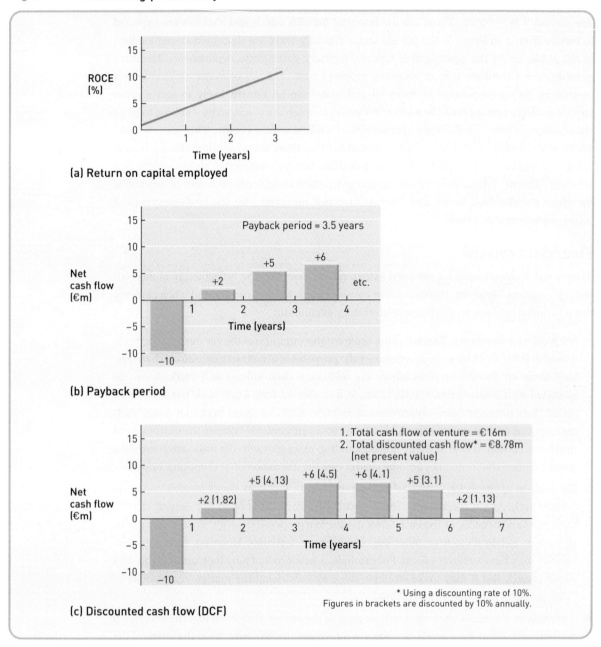

(a) Return on capital employed

(b) Payback period

(c) Discounted cash flow (DCF)

* Using a discounting rate of 10%.
Figures in brackets are discounted by 10% annually.

● Estimating the *payback period* is a cash flow measure. This is the length of time it takes before the cumulative cash flows for a strategic option become positive. In the example in Figure 11.1(b) the payback period is three and a half years. This measure has the virtue of simplicity and is most often used where the difficulty of forecasting is high and therefore risk is high. In such circumstances this measure can be used to select projects or strategies that have the quickest payback. Payback is often used in combination with DCF (see below), for example by setting criteria such as a payback period of, say, three years together with a positive NPV. Of course acceptable payback periods vary from industry to industry. A venture capitalist investing in the turnaround of an existing business may expect a fast return, whereas public infrastructure projects such as road building may be assessed over payback periods exceeding 50 years.

- Calculating *discounted cash flows (DCF)*. This is a widely used investment appraisal technique using common cash-flow forecasting techniques with the purpose of identifying which proposed projects are likely to achieve the best cumulative cash flow. The resulting measure is the net present value (or NPV) of the project, one of the most widely used criteria for assessing the financial viability of a project. Whilst on the face of it the project with the best NPV should be selected, given that a DCF is only as valid as the assumptions built into it, (a) sensitivity testing of assumptions is important and (b) it may be more prudent to regard any project with a positive NPV as worthy of further consideration and evaluation.

Taking the example of DCF in Figure 11.1(c), once the cash inflows and outflows have been assessed for each of the years of a strategic option they are discounted by an appropriate cost of capital hurdle. This reflects the fact that cash generated early is more valuable than cash generated later. The discount rate is also set at a level that reflects the riskiness of the strategy under consideration (i.e. a higher rate the greater the risk). In the example, the cost of capital or discounting rate of 10 per cent (after tax) reflects the rate of return required by those providing finance for the venture – shareholders and/or lenders. The 10 per cent cost of capital shown here *includes* an allowance for inflation of about 3–4 per cent. It is referred to as the 'money cost of capital'. By contrast, the 'real' cost of capital is 6–7 per cent *after* allowing for or *excluding* inflation.

The projected after-tax cash flow of £2m (~€2.2m; ~$3m) at the start of year 2 is equivalent to receiving £1.82m (~€2.00m; ~$2.73m) now – £2m multiplied by 0.91 or 1/1.10. £1.82m is called the *present value* of receiving £2m at the start of year 2 at a cost of capital of 10 per cent. Similarly, the after-tax cash flow of £5m (~€5.5m; ~$7.5m) at the start of year 3 has a present value of £4.13m (~€4.54m; ~$6.20m) – £5m multiplied by 1/1.10 squared. The *net present value (NPV)* of the venture, as a whole, is calculated by adding up all the annual present values over the venture's anticipated life. In the example, this is 7 years. The NPV works out at £8.78m (~€9.66m; ~$13.17m). Allowing for the time value of money, the £8.78m is the extra value that the strategic initiative will generate during its entire lifetime. However, it would be sensible to undertake a sensitivity analysis, for example by assuming different levels of sales volume increases, or different costs of capital in order to establish what resulting NPV measures would be and at what point NPV falls below zero. For example, in Figure 11.1(c) a cost of capital or discounting rate of about 32 per cent would produce a zero NPV. Such sensitivity testing is, then, a way in which DCF can be used to assess risk.

The key debate at the end of the chapter discusses how the use of DCF is regarded differently in different countries.

Shareholder value analysis

Shareholder value analysis[6] (SVA) poses the question: which proposed strategies would increase or decrease shareholder value? From a shareholder's point of view, what matters is the cash-generating capability of the business since this determines (a) the ability to pay dividends in the short term and (b) for a business to reinvest for the future, which, in turn, should enable a future flow of dividend payments. In the public sector the equivalent issue is the need to deliver best-value services within financial limits, though it is often difficult to identify clearly what is meant by 'value' in this context.

Table 11.6 **Measures of shareholder value**

(a) Total shareholder return (TSR)	(b) Economic profit or economic value added (EVA)
Given • Opening share price, £1 • Closing share price, £1.20 • Dividend per share received during financial year, 5p Then • Increase in share price (20p) plus dividend received (5p) = 25p TSR is • 25p divided by opening share price of £1 expressed as a percentage = 25%	Given • Operating profit after tax, £10m • Capital employed, £100m • Cost of capital, 8% Then • The capital or financing charge required to produce the operating profit after tax is the capital employed of £100m × the cost of capital of 8% = (£8m) EVA is • Operating profit (after tax) of £10m less the cost of the capital, £8m = £2m

Managing for shareholder value is, then, concerned with maximising shareholders' return in terms of dividends plus stock appreciation. There are several measures of shareholder value, but two are common. One is external to the company. The other is internal:

● The external measure is referred to as *total shareholder return (TSR)*. In any financial year, it is equal to the increase in the price of a share plus the dividends received per share actually received in that year. This is then divided by the share price at the start of the financial year. A simple example is given as Table 11.6(a).

● The internal measure is called *economic profit* or *economic value added (EVA)*. If the operating profit (after tax) is greater than the cost of the capital required to produce that profit then EVA is positive. An example is given as Table 11.6(b). Quite likely in the early stage of a new venture EVA is negative but the aim is to achieve a growing and positive EVA.

From the point of view of evaluating business strategies, the central question becomes which proposed strategy would maximise shareholders' returns? There are *key value drivers* which have the most influence on the cash generation capability. So, in evaluating proposed strategies, it is important to consider their effects on these value drivers. Some of these are relatively obvious; for example minimising *costs* and maximising *sales growth*, which improves cash flow and may help achieve economies of scale. Others are less obvious:[7]

● *Capital expenditure* can be a major cash outflow that could reduce shareholder value. So, on the face of it, keeping capital expenditure low improves shareholder value. However, doing so can mean that there is a reduced ability to grow a business for the long term. So the emphasis needs to be on how capital expenditure contributes to improving revenues or reducing costs elsewhere. How does the capital expenditure for a proposed strategy *enhance product features* leading to increased sales and/or better prices; or *reduce costs* (for example, through increased labour productivity) or *decrease working capital* (for example, through stock reduction by streamlining production or distribution)?

- *Cost of capital.* It is important that the cash flows generated from a given strategy should exceed the cost of capital. A major limitation of traditional accounting measures such as operating profit (profit before interest and taxation) is that they may ignore the cost of capital and therefore give misleading signals about whether value is created or destroyed. In turn, this can give misleading views about the acceptability of proposed strategies. The cost of capital therefore needs to be taken into account in evaluating a proposed strategy.

- *The management of working capital* such as stock, debtors and creditors will increase or decrease shareholder value. What is the effect of different proposed strategies on levels of working capital?

- *Maintaining and extending competitive advantage over time* can be a significant contributor to shareholder value since margins are particularly sensitive to high levels of competitive rivalry.

Although shareholder value analysis has helped address some of the shortcomings of traditional financial analyses, it has been criticised for over-emphasising short-term returns.[8] Nevertheless, the idea of valuing a strategy may serve to give greater realism and clarity to otherwise vague claims for strategic benefits. Perhaps the major lesson, however, is that firms that most successfully employ SVA do so within an overall approach to managing for value throughout the firm rather than merely as a technique for purposes of analysis.[9]

Cost–benefit[10]

Profit measures may be too narrow an interpretation of return, particularly where intangible benefits are an important consideration. This is usually so for major public infrastructure projects for example, such as the siting of an airport or a sewer construction project (see Illustration 11.5) or in organisations with long-term programmes of innovation (e.g. pharmaceuticals or aerospace). The *cost–benefit* concept suggests, however, that a money value can be put on all the costs and benefits of a strategy, including tangible and intangible returns to people and organisations other than the one 'sponsoring' the project or strategy.

Although in practice monetary valuation is often difficult, it can be done and, despite the difficulties, cost–benefit analysis is useful provided its limitations are understood. Its major benefit is in forcing managers to be explicit about the various factors that influence strategic choice. So, even if people disagree on the value that should be assigned to particular costs or benefits, at least they can argue their case on common ground and compare the merits of the various arguments.

Real options[11]

The previous approaches assume a reasonable degree of clarity about the outcomes of a strategic option. There are, however, situations where precise costs and benefits of strategies only become clear as implementation proceeds. For example, product development in a pharmaceuticals company may take many years. Its early stages in the laboratory are likely to be relatively low-cost. It is only later, if a viable product is developed, that costs become clear and still later, when launched, that demand becomes clear. In these circumstances the traditional DCF approach discussed above will tend to undervalue a 'project' because it does not take into account the value of options that could be opened up by the particular project.[12] For example, the development of a drug may not eventually lead to a viable product and the project may

ILLUSTRATION 11.5

Sewerage construction project

Investment in items of infrastructure – such as sewers – often requires a careful consideration of the wider costs and benefits of the project.

The UK's privatised water companies were monopolies supplying water and disposing of sewage. One of their priorities was investment in new sewerage systems to meet the increasing standards required by law. They frequently used cost–benefit analysis to assess projects. The figures below are from an actual analysis.

Cost/Benefit	£m*	£m*
Multiplier/linkage benefits		0.9
Flood prevention		2.5
Reduced traffic disruption		7.2
Amenity benefits		4.6
Investment benefit		23.6
Encouragement of visitors		4.0
Total benefits		42.8
Costs		
Construction cost	18.2	
Less: Unskilled labour cost	(4.7)	
Opportunity cost of construction	(13.5)	
Present value of net benefits (NPV)	29.3	

* (£1m is about €1.1m or $1.5m)

Note: Figures discounted at a *real* discount rate of 5% over 40 years.

Benefits

Benefits result mainly from reduced use of rivers as overflow sewers. There are also economic benefits resulting from construction. The following benefits are quantified in the table:

- The multiplier benefit to the local economy of increased spending by those employed on the project.
- The linkage benefit to the local economy of purchases from local firms, including the multiplier effect of such spending.
- Reduced risk of flooding from overflows or old sewers collapsing – flood probabilities can be quantified using historical records, and the cost of flood damage by detailed assessment of the property vulnerable to damage.
- Reduced traffic disruption from flooding and road closures for repairs to old sewers – statistics on the costs of delays to users, traffic flows on roads affected and past closure frequency can be used to quantify savings.
- Increased amenity value of rivers (for example, for boating and fishing) can be measured by surveys asking visitors what the value is to them or by looking at the effect on demand of charges imposed elsewhere.
- Increased rental values and take-up of space can be measured by consultation with developers and observed effects elsewhere.
- Increased visitor numbers to riverside facilities resulting from reduced pollution.

Construction cost

This is net of the cost of unskilled labour. Use of unskilled labour is not a burden on the economy, and its cost must be deducted to arrive at opportunity cost.

Net benefits

Once the difficult task of quantifying costs and benefits is complete, standard discounting techniques can be used to calculate net present value and internal rate of return, and analysis can then proceed as for conventional projects.

Source: G. Owen, formerly of Sheffield Business School.

Questions

1 What do you feel about the appropriateness of the listed benefits?

2 How easy or difficult is it to assign money values to these benefits?

have to be closed down. There could, however, be other outcomes of value: the research could create valuable new knowledge or provide a 'platform' from which other products or process improvements spring; or perhaps be a basis for a licensing arrangement or even the sale of know-how to another company. So a strategy should be seen as a *series* of 'real' options (i.e. choices of direction at points in time as the strategy takes shape) which should be evaluated as such. Illustration 11.6 provides an example. A real options approach to evaluation therefore typically increases the expected value of a project because it adds the expected value of possible future options opened up by that project. There are four main benefits of this approach:

- *Bringing strategic and financial evaluation closer together.* Arguably it provides a clearer understanding of both strategic and financial return and risk of a strategy by examining each step (option) separately.

- *Valuing emerging options.* In taking such an approach, it allows a value to be placed on options that might be opened up by an initial strategic decision.

- *Coping with uncertainty.* Advocates of a real options approach argue it overcomes, or provides an alternative to, profitability analyses that require managers to make assumptions about future conditions that may well not be realistic. As such it can be linked into ways of analysing uncertain futures such as scenario analysis (see section 2.2). For example, applying a real options approach might well have two effects. First, to defer decisions as far as possible because (secondly) the passage of time will clarify expected returns – even to the extent that apparently unfavourable strategies might prove viable at a later date.

- *Offsetting conservatism.* One problem with financial analyses such as DCF is that the hurdle rates set to reflect risk and uncertainty mean that ambitious but uncertain projects (and strategies) tend not to receive support. The real options approach, on the other hand, tends to value higher more ambitious strategies. There have, therefore, been calls to employ real options together with more traditional financial evaluation such as DCF. In effect DCF provides the cautionary view and real options the more optimistic view.

It must, however, be stressed that a real options approach is only useful where a strategy is, or can be structured, in the form of options; for example, where there are stages, as in pharmaceutical development, such that each stage gives the possibility of abandoning or deferring going forward. So it would not be suited, for example, to a project where major capital outlay was required at the beginning.

11.3.3 Reaction of stakeholders

The third R is the likely *reaction* of stakeholders to a proposed strategy. Section 4.5.2 and Illustration 4.5 showed how *stakeholder mapping* can be used to understand the political context and consider the political agenda in an organisation. It also showed how stakeholder mapping can be used to consider the likely reactions of stakeholders to new strategies and thus evaluate the acceptability of a strategy. There are many situations where stakeholder reactions could be crucial. For example:

- *Owners'* (e.g. shareholders, family owners, the state) financial expectations have to be taken into account and the extent to which these are met will influence the acceptability of a strategy. A proposed strategy might also call for the financial restructuring of a business, for example an issue of new shares, which could be unacceptable, for example to a powerful group of shareholders, since it dilutes their voting power.

ILLUSTRATION 11.6

Real options evaluation for developing premium beers in India

A real options approach can be used to evaluate proposed projects with multiple options.

A brewer of premium beers had been exporting its products to India for many years. They were considering an investment in brewing capacity in India. Although it was envisaged that, initially, this would take the form of brewing standard products locally and distributing through existing distributors, there were other ideas being discussed, though these were all contingent on the building of the brewery. Management took a real options approach to evaluating the project as set out in the figure below.

The evaluation of the proposal to build the brewery considered three options; to invest now, at a later date, or not invest at all. However, the building of the brewery opened other options. One of these was to cease operating through existing third party distributors and open up their own distribution network. Again, there were alternatives here. Should they invest in this immediately after the brewery was built, at a later date or not invest in it at all and continue through their current distibutors? The investment in the brewery, especially if better distribution systems were to be developed, in turn opened up other options. Currently being discussed, for example, was whether there existed a market opportunity to develop and produce beers tailored more specifically to the Indian market. Again, should there be investment in this soon after the building of the brewery, at a later date, or not at all? It was also recognised that other options might emerge if the project went forward.

The board used a real options approach, not least because they needed to factor in the potential added value of the options opened up by the brewery.

They would employ DCF to evaluate the brewery project. However, they would also evaluate the other options assuming the brewery was built. In each of these evaluation exercises DCF would also be used, adjusting the cost of capital to the perceived risk of the options. This would give them an indication of NPV for each of those options. The possible positive NPVs of the subsequent options could then be taken into account in assessing the attractiveness of the initial brewery project.

They also recognised that, if they invested in the brewery so as to further develop their presence in India, greater clarity on both costs and market opportunities would emerge as the project progressed. So it would make sense to revisit the evaluation of the other options at later stages as such information became available.

Question

What are the advantages of the real options approach to this evaluation over other approaches (a) to building the brewery; and (b) to other ideas being considered?

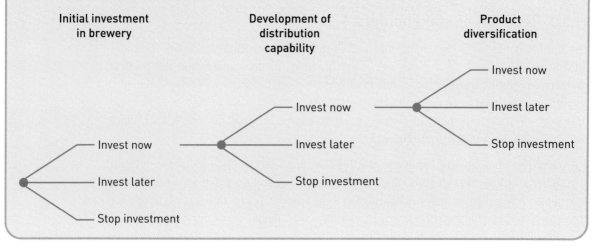

Initial investment in brewery — Invest now / Invest later / Stop investment

Development of distribution capability — Invest now / Invest later / Stop investment

Product diversification — Invest now / Invest later / Stop investment

- *Bankers* and other providers of interest-bearing loans are concerned about the *risk* attached to their loans and the competence with which this is managed. It is likely they will manage this risk through taking securities against it. Nonetheless a good track record in managing that risk could be regarded (in itself) as a reason for bankers to invest further with some companies and not others. The extent to which a proposed strategy could affect the capital structure of the company could also be important. For example, would it increase the gearing ratio (of debt to equity), which determines how sensitive the solvency of the company is to changes in its profit position? Interest cover is a similar measure that relates interest payments to profit. They will also be concerned with the *liquidity* of the company, because a deteriorating liquidity position may require correction through additional loans and an increased risk profile. So the question needs to be asked: how will the proposed strategy affect liquidity?

- *Regulators* are important stakeholders in industries such as telecommunications, financial services, pharmaceuticals and power. They may have what amounts to decision-making powers over aspects of an organisation's strategy, such as price or geographic expansion.

- *Employees and unions* may resist strategic moves such as relocation, outsourcing or *divestment* if they see them as likely to result in job *losses*.

- *The local community* will be concerned about jobs but also with the *social cost* of an organisation's strategies, such as pollution or marketing – an issue of growing concern. Matters of business ethics and social responsibility were discussed in section 4.4.

- *Customers* may also object to a strategy. Their sanction is to cease buying from the company, perhaps switching to a competitor. For example, a new business model, such as marketing online, might run the risk of a backlash from existing retail channels, which could jeopardise the success of the strategy.

Overall, there is a need to be conscious of the impact on the various stakeholders of the strategic options being considered. Managers also need to understand how the capability to meet the varied expectations of stakeholders could enable the success of some strategies whilst limiting the ability of an organisation to succeed with other strategies.

FEASIBILITY

Feasibility is **concerned with whether a strategy could *work in practice*:** therefore whether an organisation has the capabilities to deliver a strategy. An assessment of feasibility is likely to require two key questions to be addressed: (a) do the resources and competences currently exist to implement a strategy effectively? And (b) if not, can they be obtained? These questions can be applied to any resource area that has a bearing on the viability of a proposed strategy. Here the focus is on three areas, however: finance, people (and their skills) and the importance of resource integration.

11.4.1 Financial feasibility

A central issue in considering a proposed strategy is the funding required for it so the *cash flow analysis and forecasting*[13] required for evaluating the acceptability of possible strategies is also relevant here. The need is to identify the cash required for a strategy, the cash generated by following the strategy and the timing of any new funding requirements. This then informs consideration of the likely sources for obtaining funds.

Table 11.7 Financial strategy and the business life cycle

Life cycle phase	Funding requirement	Cost of capital	Business risk	Likely funding source(s)	Dividends
Development/ launch	High	High	High	Equity (venture capital)	Zero
Growth	High	Low/medium	High	Debentures and equity (growth investors)	Nominal
Maturity	Low/medium	Medium	Medium	Debt, equity and retained earnings	High
Decline	Low/negative	Medium/high	Low	Debt	High

Managers need to be familiar with different sources of funds as well as the advantages and drawbacks of these. This is well explained in standard financial texts.[14] This is not only a matter of the feasibility of a strategy, but also its acceptability to different stakeholders, not least those providing the funds. So the discussion in section 11.3 is relevant here too. Decisions on which funding sources to use will also be influenced by the current financial situation of the organisation such as ownership (e.g. whether the business is privately held or publicly quoted) and by the overall corporate goals and strategic priorities of the organisation. For example, there will be different financial needs if a business is seeking rapid growth by acquisition compared with if it is seeking to consolidate its past performance.

A useful way of considering funding is in terms of which financial strategies might be needed for different 'phases' of the development and life cycle of a business – see Table 11.7. In turn this raises the question as to whether such sources of finance are available and, if not, whether the proposed strategy is both feasible and acceptable.

- *Emerging and new-launch businesses*[15] are high-risk businesses. They are at the beginning of their life cycle and are not yet established in their markets; moreover, they are likely to require substantial investment. A stand-alone business in this situation might, for example, seek to finance such growth from specialists in this kind of investment, such as venture capitalists who, themselves, seek to offset risk by having a portfolio of such investments. Schemes for private investors (so-called 'business angels') have also become popular. Such sources of funds are, however, likely to be high-cost since the funders are aware of the high business risk.

- *Growth businesses* may remain in a volatile and highly competitive market position. The degree of business risk may therefore remain high, as will the cost of capital in such circumstances. However, if a business in this phase has begun to establish itself in its markets, perhaps as a market leader in a growing market, then the cost of capital may be lower. In either case, since the main attractions to investors here are the product or business concept and the prospect of future earnings, equity capital is likely to be appropriate, perhaps by public flotation.

- *Mature businesses* are those operating in mature markets and the likelihood is that funding requirements will decline. If such a business has achieved a strong competitive position with a high market share, it should be generating regular and substantial surpluses. Here the business risk is lower and the opportunity for retained earnings is high. In these circumstances, if funding is required, it may make sense to raise this through debt capital as well as equity, since reliable returns can be used to service such debt. Provided increased debt (*gearing* or *leverage*) does not lead to an unacceptable level of risk, this cheaper debt funding will in fact increase the residual profits achieved by a company in these circumstances.

- *Declining businesses* are likely to find it difficult to attract equity finance. However, borrowing may be possible if secured against residual assets in the business. At this stage, it is likely that the emphasis in the business will be on cost cutting, and it could well be that the cash flows from such businesses are quite strong. These businesses may provide relatively low-risk investments.

This life-cycle framework does not, however, always hold. There are exceptions. For example, a company seeking to develop *new and innovative businesses* on a regular basis might, in effect, be acting as its own venture capitalist, accepting high risk at the business level and seeking to offset such risk by 'cash cows' in its portfolio (see section 7.7.1). Or some companies may need to sell off businesses as they mature to raise capital for further investment in new ventures. Public-sector managers know about the need to balance the financial risk of services too. They need a steady core to their service where budgets are certain to be met, hence reducing the financial risk of the more speculative aspects of their service.

11.4.2 People and skills

Chapter 3 showed how organisations that achieve sustainable competitive advantage may do so on the basis of competences that are embedded in the skills, knowledge and experience of people in that organisation. Indeed, ultimately the success of a strategy will likely depend on how it is delivered by people in the organisation. These could be managers but they could also be more junior people in the organisation who are nonetheless critical to a strategy, for example as the front-line contact with customers. Three questions arise: do people in the organisation currently have the competences to deliver a proposed strategy? Are the systems to support those people fit for the strategy? If not, can the competences be obtained or developed?

The first step here is the same as suggested in sections 11.2.1–3 for the screening for competitive advantage. The need is to identify the key strategic capabilities underpinning a proposed strategy, but specifically in terms of the people and skills required. The second step is to determine if these exist in the organisation. It could be, of course, that the proposed strategy is built on the argument that they do. If so, how realistic is this? Or it could be that the assumption is that these can be obtained or developed. Again, is this realistic?

Many of the issues of feasibility in relation to the structures and systems to support such competence development and people are addressed in Chapter 13 on organising and Chapter 14 on managing strategic change. Other critical questions that need to be considered include:[16]

- *Work organisation*. Will changes in work content and priority-setting significantly alter the orientation of people's jobs? Will managers need to think differently about the tasks that need to be done? What are the critical criteria for effectiveness needed? Are these different from current requirements?

- *Rewards.* How will people need to be incentivised? Will people's career aspirations be affected? How will any significant shifts in power, influence and credibility need to be rewarded and recognised?

- *Relationships.* Will interactions between key people need to change? What are the consequences for the levels of trust, task competence and values-congruence? Will conflict and political rivalry be likely?

- *Training and development.* Are current training and mentoring systems appropriate? It may be necessary to take into account the balance between the need to ensure the successful delivery of strategy in the short term and the required future development of people's capabilities.

- *People.* Given these issues, will different people be required than currently and at what levels in the organisation?

11.4.3 Integrating resources

The success of a strategy is likely to depend on the management of many resource areas; not only people and finance, but also physical resources, such as buildings, information, technology and the resources provided by suppliers and partners. It is possible, but not likely, that a proposed strategy builds only on existing resources. It is more likely that additional resources will be required. The feasibility of a strategy therefore needs be considered in terms of the ability to obtain and integrate such resources – both inside the organisation and in the wider value network. Serious problems can result from the failure to think through the need for such integration. This is especially the case where a strategy involves the complex integration of diverse resources. For example, as Illustration 11.7 shows, the highly publicised chaos at the opening of BA's Terminal 5 at Heathrow in 2008 was not the result of a single problem, but of a failure to integrate the many different resources, systems and competences required to ensure its effectiveness.

(11.5) EVALUATION CRITERIA: FOUR QUALIFICATIONS

There are four qualifications that need to be made to this chapter's discussion of evaluation criteria:

- *Conflicting conclusions and management judgement.* Conflicting conclusions can arise from the application of the criteria of suitability, acceptability and feasibility. A proposed strategy might look eminently suitable but not be acceptable to major stakeholders, for example. It is therefore important to remember that the criteria discussed here are useful in helping think through strategic options but are not a replacement for management judgement. Managers faced with a strategy they see as suitable, but which key stakeholders object to, have to rely on their own judgement on the best course of action, but this should be better informed through the analysis and evaluation they have undertaken.

- *Consistency between the different elements of a strategy.* It should be clear from the chapters in Part II that there are several elements of a strategy, so an important question is whether the component parts work together as a 'package'. So *competitive strategy* (such as low cost or differentiation), strategy *direction* (such as product development or diversification) and

ILLUSTRATION 11. 7

Chaos at Heathrow Terminal Five

Thinking through the integration of the elements of a strategy is fundamental to effective strategy implementation.

With an investment of over £4.3 (€4.7; $6.4) billion, the new state of the art Terminal 5 (T5) was a key element of British Airways' strategy to consolidate its international and domestic flights in a showpiece hub at the world's busiest international airport, Heathrow. It opened on 27th March 2008. It was perhaps the worst 'grand opening' of all time. The first day ended with a malfunctioning baggage handling system, resultant travel chaos, passengers stranded, baggage lost and appalling headlines for the airport operator BAA and for BA. It was followed by the resignation of five key executives from these organisations.

This malfunction of the state-of-the-art automated baggage handling system, designed to process 12,000 bags an hour, certainly had a knock-on impact. However, other seemingly more mundane issues also contributed to the problems. Many staff found difficulty locating the staff car parks, reporting unclear road signs and misdirection. Overflow car parks were not open so staff were driving round in circles trying to find a place to park. This led to queues of staff trying to get to 'airside' [restricted access] work stations. One experienced check-in operator commented 'It took an hour for people to get to the right place. The place is so enormous; we don't know where we are going, we've been given no maps, no numbers to ring.'

At 04.00 hrs check-in desks were still closed, so passengers began to queue. When the desks finally opened the rush to the desks created chaos. By 06.00 hrs, passengers on inbound flights were kept waiting to collect their bags and 300 passengers were back-logged waiting to board flights. As the morning continued so did the length of the wait [over $2\frac{1}{2}$ hours] to collect baggage from inbound flights. The cause was a clogged underground baggage conveyer, exacerbated by staff's failure to remove bags quickly enough. By the afternoon, flights were being cancelled but there seemed little understanding of how to process stranded passengers. Finally at 16.30 all check-in was suspended.

Later Willie Walsh [CEO of BA] admitted that many issues contributed to the overall failure.

'There were problems in the car parks, airport areas, computer glitches and the baggage system. In isolation, they would not have had the impact they did, but in combination they led to service disruption. We never took control during the day.'

In fact there had been extensive trials, including twenty fully loaded baggage system tests. However, Jamie Bowden, an aviation analyst and former BA customer services manager, commented:

'Many areas of BA had told managers month after month they were not ready or did not feel confident to move in [to T5] but there was a general feeling of hubris – "Don't worry it'll be alright on the day".'

One eye witness who had attempted to travel on a BA domestic flight from T5 that day reported that many elements and many organisations were part of the unpreparedness.

'The new fancy lifts from the rail link weren't working. Then I was confronted with chaos in departures, BAA staff who were unable to direct me and BA staff who could tell me nothing of the likely departure time, if at all, of my flight. I chose to leave and tried to call home but the payphones weren't connected. I found no one from BAA who could direct me to an exit and eventually a BA person sent me through passport control with no passport. Finally when I tried to leave on a coach, the coach company's computerised ticketing wasn't working. All round chaos: not just BA.'

Sources: C. Buckley, Heathrow's Managing Director Quits after Fiasco at Terminal 5, *The Times*, 14th May 2008; K. Done, Long Haul to restore BA's Reputation, *Financial Times*, 29th March 2008; T. Webb, Walsh Hits Heavy Turbulence, *The Observer*, 20th April 2008; What Did Go Wrong at Terminal 5? BBC News Website, 30th March 2008; What Went Wrong at Heathrow's T5? BBC News website, 7th May 2008.

Questions

1 Identify the key resources and activities that would have contributed to an effective 'grand opening'.

2 Suggest why the chaos occurred.

KEY DEBATE

What is the best approach to strategic investment decisions?

There are differences around the world in the bases and types of analyses used for strategic investment decisions (SIDs). Research has particularly highlighted the difference between the bases of SIDs in the USA and UK where shareholder models of governance prevail and countries where stakeholder models prevail such as Japan and, traditionally, Germany (see section 4.3.2). The differences highlighted are these:

- In the US and UK there is an emphasis on financial bases of appraisal. This goes hand in hand with the widespread use of DCF as a financial basis of evaluation. In a set of studies carried out over a ten year period,[1] 100% of managers in firms questioned in the USA reported using the DCF approach. The comparable figure in the UK was 50% of firms, though this had dropped from 84% in 1986. The widespread use of DCF also went hand in hand with expected internal rates of return for proposed projects. This focus on financial analysis was argued to be associated with the need to meet the expectations of the financial markets and, in particular, the pressures for short term results due to the relatively arm's-length relationships with institutional investors in the US and UK.

- In Japan and Germany there was an emphasis on broader bases of strategic appraisal and the importance of achieving long term viable and secure market positioning. Here, the popularity of DCF was markedly less; in Germany (28%) and Japan (18%). Other methods of analysis such as *Payback* and *Return on Capital Employed* (ROCE) were more widely applied and rates of return expectations were lower, more flexible or, as in Japan, not much emphasised. All this may be because of firms' closer relationships with financial institutions (eg banks) or the higher incidence of family ownership (as in Germany) encouraging a longer term perspective, reducing the threat of acquisition pressure and for short term results. Perhaps because of the emphasis on a broader strategic approach, there was also less of a

concern with more sophisticated methods of financial appraisal.

The evidence of explanations lying in the governance systems seems to be borne out in Germany where changes are occurring. Here family ownership of firms remains common. In these firms, there appears to have been little change in the SID analysis over time. The preference is for measures of payback and ROCE at lower levels of target return and longer time frames: 5/7 years as opposed to 2/3 years in the USA and UK. But in the publicly owned corporations in Germany there has been a shift towards the USA/UK approach.

Others[2] have argued that there really should be no conflict between a financial and a strategic orientation: that good financial analysis complements rather than contradicts good strategy analysis, providing that, built into any financial analysis, are assumptions about markets and bases of sustainable competitive advantage. So the role of financial analysis should be to highlight rather than mask such key issues.

References:
1. C. Carr and C. Tomkins, Context, Culture and the Role of the Finance Function in Strategic Decisions: A comparative Analysis of Britain, Germany, the USA and Japan, *Management Accounting Research*, 9, 213–239, 1998; C. Carr, Are German, Japanese and Anglo-Saxon Strategic Decision Styles Still Divergent in the Context of Globalization? *Journal of Management Studies*, vol. 42, no. 6, pp. 1155–1188, September 2005.
2. P. Barwise, P. Marsh and R. Wensley, Must finance and strategy clash, *Harvard Business Review*, September–October 1989.

Question

1 What are the arguments for the evaluation of strategic options being based on an emphasis: i) on financial bases of evaluation; ii) broader strategic bases of evaluation?

2 What approaches to the evaluation of strategic options would *you* propose, and why?

methods of pursuing strategies (such as organic development, acquisition or alliances) need to be considered as a whole and be consistent. There are dangers if they are not. For example, suppose an organisation wishes to develop a differentiation strategy by building on its capabilities developed over many years to develop new products or services within a market it knows well. There may be dangers in looking to develop those new products through acquiring other businesses which might have very different capabilities that are incompatible with the strengths of the business.

- *The implementation and development of strategies* may throw up issues that might make organisations reconsider whether particular strategic options are, in fact, feasible or uncover factors that change views on the suitability or acceptability of a strategy. This may lead to a reshaping, or even abandoning, of strategic options. It therefore needs to be recognised that, in practice, strategy evaluation may take place through implementation, or at least partial implementation. This is another reason why experimentation, low-cost probes and real options evaluation may make sense.

- *Strategy development in practice.* More generally, it should not be assumed that the careful and systematic evaluation of strategy is necessarily the norm in organisations. Strategies may develop in other ways. This is the subject of Chapter 12 which follows. The final chapter (15) also explains what managers actually do in managing strategic issues.

SUMMARY

- Proposed strategies may be evaluated using the three SAFe criteria:
  - *Suitability* is concerned with assessing which proposed strategies address the *key opportunities and constraints* an organisation faces. It is about the *rationale* of a strategy.
  - The *acceptability* of a strategy relates to three issues: the level of *risk* of a strategy, the expected *return* from a strategy and the likely *reaction of stakeholders*.
  - *Feasibility* is concerned with whether an organisation has or can obtain the capabilities to deliver a strategy.

VIDEO ASSIGNMENT

Visit *MyStrategyLab* and watch the *Inamo* case study.

In setting up Inamo, in terms of the SAFe criteria:

1 On what bases might the founders have judged the project to be 'suitable'?

2 What aspects of 'feasibility' would they need to consider? In particular, consider the need to *integrate* the different aspects of the Inamo business model.

WORK ASSIGNMENTS

✲ *Denotes more advanced work assignments.* * *Denotes case study in the Text and Case edition.*

11.1 Undertake a ranking analysis of the choices available to easySolution, Marks & Spencer (C)*, or an organisation of your choice similar to that shown in Illustration 11.1.

11.2 Using the criteria of suitability, acceptability and feasibility undertake an evaluation of the strategic options that might exist for easySolution, Aids Alliance* or an organisation of your choice.

11.3 Undertake a risk assessment to inform the evaluation of strategic options for an organisation of your choice.

11.4 Write an executive report on how sources of funding need to be related to the nature of an industry and the types of strategies that an organisation is pursuing.

11.5 Suggest how managers could have better considered and managed the integration between the various resources required for a successful opening of Heathrow Terminal 5 (see Illustration 11.7).

11.6✲ Using examples from your answer to previous assignments, make a critical appraisal of the statement that 'Strategic choice is, in the end, a highly subjective matter. It is dangerous to believe that, in reality, analytical techniques will ever change this situation.' Refer to the commentary at the end of Part II of the book.

Integrative assignment

11.7✲ Explain how the SAFe criteria might differ between public- and private-sector organisations. Show how this relates to both the nature of the business environment (Chapter 2) and the expectations of stakeholders (Chapter 4).

RECOMMENDED KEY READINGS

- A companion book which explores techniques of strategy evaluation more fully is V. Ambrosini with G. Johnson and K. Scholes (eds), *Exploring Techniques of Analysis and Evaluation in Strategic Management*, Prentice Hall, 1998.

- Readers may wish to consult one or more standard texts on finance. For example: G. Arnold, *Corporate Financial Management*, 4th edition, Financial Times Prentice Hall,

2009; P. Atrill, *Financial Management for Decision Makers*, 4th edition, Financial Times Prentice Hall, 2006.

- A classic paper that considers the relationship between financial approaches to evaluation and 'strategic' approaches is P. Barwise, P. Marsh and R. Wensley, 'Must finance and strategy clash?', *Harvard Business Review*, September–October 1989.

REFERENCES

1. L. Levidow and S. Carr, 'UK: precautionary commercialisation', *Journal of Risk Research*, vol. 3, no. 3 (2000), pp. 261–70.
2. For those readers interested in the details of sensitivity analysis see: A. Satelli, K. Chan and M. Scott (eds), *Sensitivity Analysis*, Wiley, 2000. For a more detailed exploration of different approaches see A.G. Hadigheh and T. Terlaky. 'Sensitivity analysis in linear optimization: invariant support set intervals', *European Journal of Operational Research*, vol. 169, no. 3 (2006), pp. 1158–76.
3. See C. Walsh, *Master the Management Metrics That Drive and Control Your Business*, Financial Times Prentice Hall, 4th edition, 2005.
4. Break-even analysis is covered in most standard accountancy texts. See, for example, G. Arnold, *Corporate Financial Management*, 4th edition, Financial Times Prentice Hall, 2009.
5. Most standard finance and accounting texts explain in more detail the financial analyses summarised here. For example see G. Arnold (reference 4 above), Chapter 4.

6. The main proponent of shareholder value analysis is A. Rappaport, *Creating Shareholder Value: the New Standard for Business Performance*, 2nd edition, Free Press, 1998. See also R. Mill's chapter, 'Understanding and using shareholder value analysis', Chapter 15 in V. Ambrosini with G. Johnson and K. Scholes (eds), *Exploring Techniques of Analysis and Evaluation in Strategic Management*, Prentice Hall, 1998.

7. S. Williams, 'Delivering strategic business value', *Strategic Finance*, vol. 86, no. 2 (2004), pp. 41–8.

8. A. Kennedy, *The End of Shareholder Value*, Perseus Publishing, 2000.

9. This point is made clear in a research study reported by P. Haspeslagh, T. Noda and F. Boulos, 'It's not just about the numbers', *Harvard Business Review*, July–August, pp. 65–73, 2001.

10. A 'classic' explanation of cost–benefit analysis is J.L. King, 'Cost–benefit analysis for decision-making', *Journal of Systems Management*, vol. 31, no. 5 (1980), pp. 24–39. A detailed example in the water industry can be found in: N. Poew, 'Water companies' service performance and environmental trade-off', *Journal of Environmental Planning and Management*, vol. 45, no. 3 (2002), pp. 363–79.

11. Real options evaluation can get lost in the mathematics, so readers wishing to gain more detail of how real options analysis works can consult one of the following: T. Copeland, 'The real options approach to capital allocation', *Strategic Finance*, vol. 83, no. 4 (2001), pp. 33–7; T. Copeland and V. Antikarov, *Real Options: a Practitioner's Guide*, Texere Publishing, 2001; L. Trigeorgis, *Managerial Flexibility and Strategy in Resource Allocation*, MIT Press, 2002; P. Boer, *The Real Options Solution: Finding Total Value in a High Risk World*, Wiley, 2002. Also see M.M. Kayali, 'Real options as a tool for making strategic investment decisions', *Journal of American Academy of Business*, vol. 8, no. 1 (2006), pp. 282–7; C. Krychowski and B.V. Quelin, 'Real options and strategic investment decisions: Can they be of use to scholars?', *Academy of Management Perspectives*, vol. 24, no. 2 (2010), pp. 65–78.

12. T. Luehrman, 'Strategy as a portfolio of real options', *Harvard Business Review*, vol. 76, no. 5 (1998), pp. 89–99.

13. See G. Arnold on funds flow analysis (ref. 4 above), Chapter 3, p. 108.

14. See: P. Atrill, *Financial Management for Decision Makers*, 4th edition, Financial Times Prentice Hall, 2006, Chapters 6 and 7; G. Arnold (ref. 4 above), Part IV.

15. There has been much research and publication around the funding of this start-up phase. For example: D. Champion, 'A stealthier way to raise money', *Harvard Business Review*, vol. 78, no. 5 (2000), pp. 18–19; Q. Mills, 'Who's to blame for the bubble?', *Harvard Business Review*, vol. 79, no. 5 (2001), pp. 22–3; H. Van Auken, 'Financing small technology-based companies: the relationship between familiarity with capital and ability to price and negotiate investment', *Journal of Small Business Management*, vol. 39, no. 3 (2001), pp. 240–58; M. Van Osnabrugge and R. Robinson, 'The influence of a venture capitalist's source of funds', *Venture Capital*, vol. 3, no. 1 (2001), pp. 25–39.

16. These issues are based on those identified by C. Marsh, P. Sparrow, M. Hird, S. Balain and A. Hesketh (2009) 'Integrated organization design: the new strategic priority for HR directors', in P.R. Sparrow, A. Hesketh, C. Cooper, and M. Hird (eds) *Leading HR*, London: Palgrave Macmillan.

CASE EXAMPLE

EasySolution

The business idea

One thing always annoyed Camilla Oxley as she worked on her biochemistry doctorate at the University of Oxford. Each day she wasted about 20 minutes manually preparing the 'buffer solutions' in which she would carry out her experiments. She calculated that this repetitive and tedious task would consume about 500 hours across her whole time as a doctoral student.

Buffer solutions, though, were absolutely critical to her research work – and that carried out by about 150,000 laboratory research groups in the United Kingdom and United States alone. Buffer solutions involve creating varying mixes of liquid chemicals which must have an exact pH (acid-alkali balance) at a particular temperature. The mixes must be absolutely accurate for the reliability of the experiment. A bad mix could lead to the discarding of chemicals worth up to £100 (~€110; ~$150) or so a litre. Because of the tedium of daily preparation, researchers have been known to create large stocks of buffer solutions which deteriorated over time and so jeopardised the reliability of many weeks of experimental work.

Camilla believed that the tedious process of buffer solution preparation should be automated in a machine. After all, computers were helping to automate other parts of the experimental process. The average number of experiments carried out per day by researchers had trebled in recent years. Manual buffer solution preparation was becoming a bottle-neck.

Camilla mentioned her automation idea to fellow biochemistry doctoral student Jochen Klingelhoefer. Jochen had a background in electrical engineering and technical consulting and was also involved in Oxford University's entrepreneurial community. He knew that the University's business idea competition, Idea Idol, was coming up in March 2009. Camilla and he teamed together to prepare a two-minute 'elevator pitch' for a machine for the automated preparation of buffer solutions, called EasySolution. Against more than one hundred initial competitors, EasySolution emerged as winners of Idea Idol 2009.

Camilla Oxley preparing a buffer solution
Source: Richard Whittington.

After success at Idea Idol, everything began to snowball for EasySolution. The prize was worth £7,500, plus £2,000 worth of free advice from a local law firm. EasySolution's success had also attracted the attention of two Saïd Business School MBA students: Ville Lehtonen, with an MSc in computer sciences and experience in product management, business-to-business sales and private equity; and Andrew Hunt, a graduate in classical languages and with a prize-winning background in marketing. With Ville as Chief Executive Officer, Jochen as Chief Technology Officer, Andrew as Director for Business Development and Camilla as Chief Science Officer, the four formed an equally-owned new company, LabMinds Ltd, in order to take EasySolution to market.

The business plan

The four started work on a business plan for the new company, eventually to be presented to a group of 'business angels' (early-stage investors) in September 2009. A survey of 200 potential users in the University of Oxford, plus discussions with product development companies, helped to refine the original product idea.

Table 1 Product prices and costs

	Sale	Maintenance
Revenue	£9,990	£1,500
Production Cost	−£3,000	−
Delivery	−£750	−
Service	−	−£300
Replacement	−	−£120
VAT (15%)	−£814	−£141
Commission (20%)	−£1,085	−£188
Gross Profit	£4,341	£751
Profit Margin	43.5%	50.1%

EasySolution was now defined as a machine that could make exact mixes of solutions with precise pH values at particular temperatures, according to commands delivered via internet, intranet or touch-screen. Creation of solutions would take one minute, and exact contents, time of creation and name of creator would be recorded in a log entry accessible to the laboratory manager. The proposed price of a machine was £9,990 (about €11,000), just below the level at which complex purchasing procedures are typically triggered in university laboratories. There would also be a maintenance charge of 15% for the machine, in line with rates paid for comparable laboratory devices (see Table 1). The only similar machines were typically much larger: for example, the American scientific products giant Millipore manufactured systems capable of producing solutions of 100 litres upwards, against the 1 litre or so for EasySolution. The only substitute was the purchase of standard buffer solutions from large scientific supplies companies, but these were typically expensive (£20 upwards) and required ordering well in advance.

The business plan proposed development of the core EasySolution machine in five key phases (see Table 2). The first phase would be devoted to a feasibility study funded by the founding team itself, friends and family and hopefully grants from various government schemes supporting new businesses. The feasibility study, development and prototyping would be carried out by specialist companies DC Allen and Design Technology International Ltd. Development work would continue into phase 2, before production and launch of the core EasySolution product in phase 3. Phase 4 represents the continued growth of the company, leading towards eventual exit. Exit was expected to be in the form of either sale to an established large pharmaceutical or scientific equipment company or an initial public offering (IPO) to investors at large. The business plan pointed to the success of earlier start-ups in the specialised scientific products market, such as Harvard Bioscience and PerkinElmer, in achieving exit valuations based on net profit multiples of between 14 and 17.

Table 3 summarises the financial forecasts presented to investors. As above, the first year would be mostly concerned with development and investment. Sales were only expected to take off in year two (phase 3), with 350 units sold. By year three, machine sales were expected to reach £15m, with significant additional revenues from maintenance worth £1.65m. Production and maintenance were to be outsourced to specialised companies. After production, delivery and maintenance costs, LabMinds expected a gross profit of more than £7m in year 3.

Net profits in Table 3 came after significant operating (OPEX) and capital (CAPEX) expenditures. Operating expenditures planned in the first year included modest salaries for the management team, office charges, travel and marketing. In the second year, OPEX was expected to rise significantly, with the hiring of a Finance Director, an office manager, a software team and the building of a professional sales team for the United States as well as the United Kingdom. Capital expenditures were

Table 2 LabMinds' proposed development stages

Phase 1 (Month 1)	Development company DC Allen runs a feasibility study to identify not only the best way to create the whole system (based on the product specification by LabMinds), but also the easiest ways to get around core patents. The 2 core patents (likely described in product description) will be filed in this phase. Financing need: Roughly £30,000
Phase 2 (Months 2–7)	Proof of principles created on a level where the system can be demonstrated to potential customers to support pre-sales efforts. The official goal is to be able to create any solution at any temperature and pH combination, and being able to prove the sterility of the machine. Financing need: Roughly £150,000
Phase 3 (Months 8–19)	Prepare production. All the certifications necessary (nature of the product and the target market requires a rather wide range) will be acquired during this period. In parallel everything is being set up for mass production and the aesthetic aspects of the product are being finished. Financing need: Roughly £500,000
Phase 4 (Unknown)	Day-to-day operations with sales and marketing clearly being in their element now. Financing need: Roughly £1,000,000 mainly to fuel the marketing and sales efforts
Phase 5	Exit

Table 3 LabMinds' Revenue, Profit and Investment Forecasts

(000's)	Year 1	Year 2	Year 3
Unit Sales	0	350	1500
Sales Revenue		£3,496	£14,985
Maint Revenue		£263	£1,650
Gross Profit		£1,653	£7,345
OPEX	−£211	−£1,166	−£2,000
CAPEX	−£432	−£271	−£500
Net Profit	−£643	£216	£4,845
Investment	£650	£1,000	
Government	£270	£126	
Debt Financing	£25	£200	
Founding Capital	£10		

more front-loaded. Plans in the first year included more than £400,000 for payment to the product development companies DC Allen and Design Technology International Ltd, and a further £21,000 to create a family of patents intended to protect LabMinds' intellectual property. The business plan predicted continuing capital expenditures on product development and patents for the second year, though at a lower rate. CAPEX was expected to rise again in Year 3 with the development of further complementary machines.

Funding for the early years was expected to come from various sources. The founders themselves would put in an initial £15,000 and would raise convertible loans for a further £25,000 (a convertible loan gives the lender the option of converting the debt to equity). Various government support schemes were expected to contribute significantly, and a consultant was to be retained to assist in making grant applications. The most important source of funds, however, would be business angels and similar investors, with two rounds of investment in the first year and a third substantial one (£1m) in the second. The investors in the first two rounds were expected to acquire about 40–50 per cent of the equity, and the investor in the third and largest round would receive just under 10 per cent of the equity. By the end of the second year, other employees and advisors were expected to hold a further 10 per cent or so of the equity. The business plan envisaged that at this point the original four founders would still own 25–35 per cent of a company valued at around £10m.

Investors were being offered access to a potentially huge market. The LabMinds team estimated the potential total market for EasySolution machines at about £1.0bn annually in the United Kingdom and the United States alone. Annual maintenance revenues for this market could reach £150m. But laboratories were not the only potential market. The business plan also pointed out that the basic technology could find other applications, for example in coffee-making or the preparation of cocktails for bars. LabMinds had a lot of upside.

Questions

1 Imagine that you are a potential investor hearing a short pitch from the EasySolution team based on the 2009 business plan. Using the SAFe framework, what questions would you raise with the team under:

   (a) Suitability?

   (b) Acceptability?

   (c) Feasibility?

2 If you were interested in investing in EasySolutions, which round of investment would you prefer to participate in? Why?

12

STRATEGY DEVELOPMENT PROCESSES

Learning outcomes

After reading this chapter you should be able to:

● Explain what is meant by *intended* and *emergent* strategy development.

● Identify intended processes of strategy development in organisations including: the role *of strategic leadership, strategic planning systems* and *externally imposed strategy.*

● Identify processes that give rise to emergent strategy development such as: *logical incrementalism, political processes, the influence of prior decisions* and *organisational systems.*

● Explain some of the challenges managers face in strategy development including: managing *multiple strategy processes,* strategy development in *different contexts* and *managing intended* and *emergent strategy.*

PEARSON mystrategylab

MyStrategyLab is designed to help you make the most of your studies. Visit **www.pearsoned.co.uk/mystrategylab** to discover a wide range of resources specific to this chapter, including:

• A personalised **Study plan** that will help you understand core concepts

• **Audio** and **video clips** that put the spotlight on strategy in the real world

• **Online glossaries** and **flashcards** that provide helpful reminders when you're looking for some quick revision.

(12.1) INTRODUCTION

We are familiar with successful strategies: Google's dominance of the internet; Ryanair becoming one of the most profitable airlines in the world; Apple's development of the iPhone; Zara's entrance into the UK fashion market. We know about failed strategies: Lehman Brothers and the Royal Bank of Scotland in banking; Woolworths in UK retailing; high-profile, once successful car manufacturers. Parts I and II of the book addressed how strategists might understand the strategic position of their organisation and what strategic choices are available. Chapter 11 explained different ways in which strategies can be evaluated. However, none of this directly addresses the question that is the theme of this chapter: *how do strategies actually develop?* (Chapter 15 then examines in more detail which people get involved in these processes and what they actually do in developing strategies.)

Figure 12.1 summarises the structure of this chapter. It is organised around two views of strategy development: strategy as intended and strategy as emergent. The *intended strategy* explanation is that strategies come about as the result of the deliberations of top management. This is sometimes known as the *rational/analytic view* of strategy development, or, as in the commentary sections of this book, *a design view* of strategy development. The second view is that of *emergent strategy*: that strategies do not develop on the basis of a grand plan but tend to emerge in organisations over time. The discussion in the commentaries of the experience, Variety and Discourse Lenses relates to this explanation. As the chapter will show, these two views are not mutually exclusive.

● The next section (12.2) of the chapter discusses intended strategy. First, there is an explanation of how strategies may be the outcome of *leadership, 'command'* or *vision* of individuals.

Figure 12.1 Strategy development process

This is followed by a discussion of what formal *planning systems* in organisations might look like and the role they play. The section concludes with a discussion of how strategies might be deliberately *imposed* on organisations from the outside.

● The next section of the chapter (12.3) then switches to explanations of how strategies might emerge in organisations. The common feature of the different explanations here is that they do not see strategy-making as a distinct and separate organisational activity, but rather see strategies developing out of more day-to-day and routine aspects of organisations. The section offers four explanations of how this might occur: *logical incrementalism*, the influence of *political processes* in organisations, the effects of *prior decisions* on future strategy and finally how strategies could be the *outcome of organisational systems*.

● The final section of the chapter (12.4) raises some *implications for managing strategy development* including:

  ● The likelihood that different explanations of strategy development should not be seen as independent or mutually exclusive. Rather that *multiple processes of strategy development* may all be seen within organisations.

  ● How different approaches to strategy development may be more or less well suited to *different contexts*.

  ● The implications for *managing intended strategy and emergent strategy development processes*.

 ## 12.2 INTENDED STRATEGY DEVELOPMENT

KEY CONCEPT

Intended strategy

Intended strategy is deliberately formulated or planned by managers. This may be the result of *strategic leadership, strategic planning* or sometimes the *external imposition* of strategy deliberately formulated elsewhere. Its development may also be associated with the use of the sort of tools, techniques and frameworks for strategic analysis and evaluation explained in this book.

12.2.1 Strategic leadership: the role of vision and command

An organisation's strategy may be influenced by strategic leaders: individuals (or perhaps a small group of individuals) whose personality, position or reputation gives them dominance over the strategy development process. They are therefore personally identified with and central to the strategy of their organisation. Such an individual could be central because he or she is the owner or founder of the organisation. This is often the case in small businesses and family businesses. It may also be that an individual still remains central after a business becomes very large: such is the case with Richard Branson at Virgin or Ratan Tata of the Tata Corporation. Or it could be that an individual chief executive has made major strategic changes and, as such, personifies the success of the organisation's strategy, as was the case with Michael O'Leary at Ryanair. Illustration 12.1 provides examples of strategic leaders' views on how they influence the strategy of their organisations.

In any of these circumstances, strategy may be – or may be seen to be – the deliberate intention of that leader. This may manifest itself in different ways.

● *Strategic leadership as command.* The strategy of an organisation might be dictated by an individual. This is, perhaps, most evident in owner-managed small firms, where that individual

ILLUSTRATION 12.1

CEO influence on strategy development

Different CEOs place different emphases on their influence on strategy in different circumstances.

Take a hard look at what the future might hold.
When Michael Jackson arrived at AutoNation. . . . the auto industry was selling as many as 17 million units a year, but its high fixed costs made him face what would happen if the economic environment changed. At his first management meeting he therefore announced his desire to find a business model that would let AutoNation break even if the auto industry sold only 10 million units. . . . 'Everybody looked at me like I had 6 heads', he recalls.

'Eventually we came to the conclusion that amongst other things it would take a credit crisis to get volumes that low, because in our business nothing moves without credit. So we got out of the finance and leasing business. . . . Without the limitation on risk we put in place, we would be in deep serious trouble at the moment.' (2009 when the credit crisis was at its height)[1]

Put strategy centre stage.
Bill Nuti, Chairman and CEO of NCR:

'The world moves at a pace that requires strategy to be front and centre all of the time. . . . there are too many variables that come into play in a normal cycle, let alone this one (the credit crisis of 2009) that can rapidly change the course of your company, so I bring strategy up at every single meeting.'[1]

The courage to take decisions and back your judgement.
Edward Breen of Tyco International stresses the importance of decisiveness, often with imperfect information:

'A lot of CEOs are slow to react and their problems get away from them. . . . you have to get as much data as quickly as possible. But you will never get all of it – so you need to make decisions quickly.'[1]

Sanjiv Ahuja, Chief Executive, Orange Group:

'You, as a leader, are supposed to make some decisions that are necessarily not going to be very popular. And that is OK; but stand up and be counted for those

decisions. Sometimes those decisions are where you bet your job, but that's OK; stand up and be counted for those.'[2]

Howard Lester, Chairman and CEO, Williams-Sonoma:

'Great leaders have a strength of conviction. You have the responsibility to really think through what you are doing. You ask a lot of opinions; it's not as if you go hide from everybody because you have made up your mind. But I think my point of view has always been that if I have an opinion and people can't argue me out of it, then I must be right. And I have to have the strength of that conviction and the courage to stick to it.'[2]

Communicate and be clear about the mission.
Terry Lundgren, Chairman, President and CEO of Macy's:

'The only way to address uncertainty is to communicate and communicate. When you think you've just about got to everybody, then communicate some more.'[1]

Domenico De Sole, former President and CEO, Gucci Group:

'What I say to everybody is that the mission should be clear and repeated all the time. It is important for a CEO to keep repeating the same basic principle and make sure that everybody at every level of the organisation shares the mission, shares the dream and understands what needs to be done.'[2]

References:
1. D. Carey, M. Patsalos-Fox and M. Useem, 'Leadership lessons for hard times', *McKinsey Quarterley*, July 2009.
2. *Leading by Example*, Harvard Business School Press, 2007.

Questions

1 Do you agree with all the views of the CEOs? If not, why not?

2 What else would you emphasise as an important contribution CEOs make to strategy development?

is in direct control of all aspects of the business. Danny Miller and Isabel Le Breton-Miller suggest there are advantages and disadvantages here. On the plus side it can mean speed of strategy adaptation and 'sharp, innovative, unorthodox strategies that are difficult for other companies to imitate'. The downside can, however, be 'hubris, excessive risk taking, quirky, irrelevant strategies'.[1]

- *Strategic leadership as vision.* It could be that a strategic leader determines or is associated with an overall vision, mission, or strategic intent (see section 4.2) that motivates others, helps create the shared beliefs within which people can work together effectively and shapes more detailed strategy developed by others in an organisation. Some writers see this as *the* role of the strategic leader.[2] For example, CEO of Tesco Sir Terry Leahy is recognised as driving and sustaining the need to regard customers as *the* primary stakeholder in the firm and the associated explicit core purpose: 'to create value for customers to earn their lifetime loyalty'.

- *Strategic leadership as decision-making.* It is likely that, whichever strategy development processes exist, there will be many different views and, perhaps, much but incomplete evidence to support those views. One of the key roles of leaders is to have the ability to weigh such different views, interpret data, have the confidence to take timely decisions and the authority to get others to buy into those decisions.

- *Strategic leadership as symbolic.* A strategic leader might, in effect, embody the strategy of the organisation whether or not he or she directly manages the organisation. Richard Branson no longer runs Virgin on a day-to-day basis; but he is seen as the embodiment of the Virgin strategy (see the Chapter 7 case example) and is frequently the public face of the company.

12.2.2 Strategic planning systems

A second way in which intended strategies develop is through formalised **strategic planning** systems.[3] These **take the form of systematised, step-by-step, procedures to develop an organisation's** strategy. For example, in a study of strategic planning systems of major oil companies, Rob Grant[4] noted the following stages in the cycle for a large corporation:

- *Initial guidelines.* The cycle's starting point is usually a set of guidelines or assumptions about the external environment (e.g. price levels and supply and demand conditions) and the overall priorities, guidelines and expectations of the corporate centre.

- *Business-level planning.* In the light of these guidelines, business units or divisions draw up strategic plans to present to the corporate centre. Corporate centre executives then discuss those plans with the business managers usually in face-to-face meetings. On the basis of these discussions the businesses revise their plans for further discussion.

- *Corporate-level planning.* The corporate plan results from the aggregation of the business plans. This coordination may be undertaken by a corporate planning department that, in effect, has a coordination role. The corporate board then has to approve the corporate plan.

- *Financial and strategic targets* are then likely to be extracted to provide a basis for performance monitoring of businesses and key strategic priorities on the basis of the plan.

Grant found that some of the companies he studied were much more formal and regularised than others (e.g. the French Elf Aquitaine and Italian ENI), with greater reliance on written reports and formal presentations, more fixed planning cycles, less flexibility and more specific objectives and targets relating to the formal plans. Where there was more informality or flexibility (e.g. BP, Texaco and Exxon), companies placed greater emphasis on more general financial targets. Central corporate planning departments also played different roles. In some organisations they acted primarily as coordinators of business plans. In others they were more like internal consultants, helping business unit managers to formulate their plans. Illustration 12.2 is a schematic representation of how strategic planning takes form in a large multinational drinks company.

Formalised strategic planning systems may play a role in how future organisational strategy is determined but this may not always be so. For example, the decisions about competitive

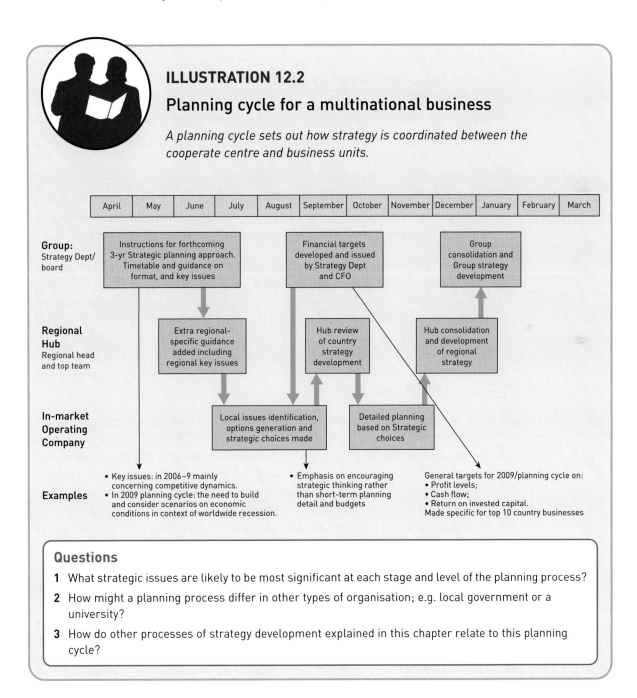

ILLUSTRATION 12.2

Planning cycle for a multinational business

A planning cycle sets out how strategy is coordinated between the cooperate centre and business units.

April	May	June	July	August	September	October	November	December	January	February	March

Group:
Strategy Dept/
board

Instructions for forthcoming 3-yr Strategic planning approach. Timetable and guidance on format, and key issues

Financial targets developed and issued by Strategy Dept and CFO

Group consolidation and Group strategy development

Regional Hub
Regional head and top team

Extra regional-specific guidance added including regional key issues

Hub review of country strategy development

Hub consolidation and development of regional strategy

In-market Operating Company

Local issues identification, options generation and strategic choices made

Detailed planning based on Strategic choices

Examples

- Key issues: in 2006–9 mainly concerning competitive dynamics.
- In 2009 planning cycle: the need to build and consider scenarios on economic conditions in context of worldwide recession.

- Emphasis on encouraging strategic thinking rather than short-term planning detail and budgets

General targets for 2009/planning cycle on:
- Profit levels;
- Cash flow;
- Return on invested capital.
Made specific for top 10 country businesses

Questions

1 What strategic issues are likely to be most significant at each stage and level of the planning process?

2 How might a planning process differ in other types of organisation; e.g. local government or a university?

3 How do other processes of strategy development explained in this chapter relate to this planning cycle?

strategy in a business-level strategic plan will quite likely be taken in management meetings in that business. There the processes associated with strategy development may correspond to any of those explained in this chapter and elsewhere in the book (e.g. see Chapter 15 and the Commentaries). However, such decisions may *then* be built into the formal plan.

A strategic planning system may therefore play several roles within an organisation. Typically four are emphasised:

- *Formulating* strategy by providing means by which managers can understand strategic issues, for example by establishing overall *objectives*, encouraging the use of *analytic tools* such as those explained in this book and by *encouraging a longer-term view* of strategy than might otherwise occur. Planning horizons and associated objectives and bases of analysis vary, of course. In a fast-moving consumer goods company, 3- to 5-year plans may be appropriate. In companies which have to take very long-term views on capital investment, such as those in the oil industry, planning horizons can be as long as 15 years (in Exxon) or 20 years (in Shell).

- *Learning*: Rita McGrath and Ian MacMillan[5] argue that managers can benefit from planning if they see it as a means of learning rather than a means of 'getting the right answers'. They emphasise 'discovery-driven' planning which emphasises the need for *questioning and challenging* received wisdom and the taken-for-granted.

- *Co-ordinating* business-level strategies within an overall corporate strategy.

- *Communicating* intended strategy throughout an organisation and *providing agreed objectives or strategic milestones* against which performance and progress can be reviewed.

However, it should also be recognised that a planning system may also play a *psychological role*. By *involving people* in strategy development it can help to create *ownership* of the strategy. It can also provide a *sense of security* and logic, not least among senior management who believe they *should* be proactively determining the future strategy and exercising control over the destiny of the organisation.

Henry Mintzberg has, however, challenged the extent to which planning provides such benefits.[6] Arguably there are five main dangers in the way in which formal systems of strategic planning have been employed:

- *Confusing strategy with the strategic plan*. Managers may see themselves as managing strategy when what they are doing is going through the processes of planning. Strategy is, of course, not the same as 'the plan': strategy is the long-term direction that the organisation is following, not just a written document. Linked to this may be a confusion between *budgetary processes* and strategic planning processes. The two may come to be seen as the same so that strategic planning gets reduced to the production of financial forecasts rather than thinking through of the sort of issues discussed in this book. Of course it may be important to build the output of strategic planning into the budgetary process; but they are not the same.

- *Detachment from reality*. The managers responsible for the implementation of strategies, usually line managers, may be so busy with the day-to-day operations of the business that they cede responsibility for strategic issues to specialists *or* consultants. However, these rarely have power in the organisation to make things happen. The result can be that strategic planning becomes an intellectual exercise removed from the reality of operations. Specialist strategic planners may also come to believe that centrally planned strategy determines what goes on in an organisation. In fact it is what people do and the experience they draw on to do it that are likely to play a much more significant role (see section 12.3 and the Experience Lens in the Commentary). If formal planning systems are to be useful, those responsible for them need to draw on such experience and involve people throughout the organisation if planning is to avoid being removed from organisational reality.

- *Paralysis by analysis.* Strategic planning can also become over-detailed in its approach, concentrating on extensive analysis that, whilst technically sound, misses the major strategic issues facing the organisation. For example, it is not unusual to find companies with huge amounts of information on their markets, but with little clarity about the strategic importance of that information. The result can be *information overload* with no clear outcome.

- *Lack of ownership.* The strategy resulting from deliberations of a corporate planning department, or a senior management team, may not be owned more widely in the organisation. In one extreme instance, a colleague discussing a company's strategy with its planning director was told that a strategic plan existed, but found it was locked in the drawer of the executive's desk. Only the planner and a few senior executives were permitted to see it! There is also a danger that the process of strategic planning may be so cumbersome that individuals or groups might contribute to only part of it and *not understand the whole*. The result can be that the business-level strategy does not correspond to the intended corporate strategy. This is particularly problematic in very large firms.

- *Dampening of innovation.* Highly formalised and rigid systems of planning, especially if linked to very tight and detailed mechanisms of control, can contribute to an inflexible, hierarchical organisation with a resultant stifling of ideas and dampening of innovative capacity.

Table 12.1 summarises these potential benefits and potential dangers.

The evidence of the extent to which the pursuit of such systemised planning results in organisations performing better than others is equivocal[7] – not least because it is difficult to isolate formal planning as the dominant or determining effect on performance. However, there is some evidence that planning may be beneficial if it is designed to work in conjunction with bottom-up emergent processes of strategy development, approximating to the 'logical incremental' processes explained in section 12.3.1 below.[8] It may also be especially beneficial in dynamic environments, where decentralised authority for strategic decisions is required

Table 12.1 The potential benefits and dangers of strategic planning

Benefits	Dangers
• Helping determine and direct strategy	• Confusing strategy with the strategic plan
• Help understand strategic issues	• Detachment from reality
• Coordinating business-level strategies	• Paralysis by analysis
• A means of implementing an agreed strategy	• Lack of ownership
• Involving people and creating ownership of a strategy	• Dampening of innovation

(see Chapter 13) but where there is a need for co-ordination of strategies arising from such decentralisation.[9]

There has been a decline in the use of formal corporate planning departments[10] and a shift to business unit managers taking responsibility for strategy development and planning (see Chapter 15). Strategic planning is becoming more project-based and flexible.[11] In this respect the emphasised role for strategic planning has become less as a vehicle for top-down development of intended strategy and more of a vehicle for the co-ordination of strategy emerging from below.

12.2.3 Externally imposed strategy

The third way in which intended strategies manifest themselves is in situations where managers face what they see as the imposition of strategy by powerful external stakeholders. Strategies being imposed in such ways may have been determined elsewhere, perhaps through systematic strategic planning; or they may have developed in a more emergent fashion (see section 12.3 below). However, to the managers of the organisation having it imposed on them, it is experienced as an 'intended strategy'.

For example, government may dictate a particular strategic direction as in the public sector, or where it exercises extensive regulatory powers in an industry. Or it may choose to deregulate or privatise a sector or organisation currently in the public sector. In the UK public sector a more direct interventionist approach began to be used in the early 2000s. So-called special measures were employed for schools or hospitals deemed to be under-performing badly, with specialist managers being sent in to turn round the ailing organisations and impose a new strategic direction. Businesses in the private sector may also be subject to such imposed strategic direction, or significant constraints on their choices. A multinational corporation seeking to develop businesses in some parts of the world may be subject to governmental requirements to do this in certain ways, perhaps through joint ventures or local alliances. An operating business within a multidivisional organisation may also regard the overall corporate strategic direction of its parent as akin to imposed strategy. Venture capitalists may impose strategies on the businesses they acquire.[12]

12.3 EMERGENT STRATEGY DEVELOPMENT

Although strategy development is often associated with top-management intentionality, an alternative explanation is that of **emergent strategy**: that **strategies emerge on the basis of a series of decisions, a pattern in which becomes clear over time**. This explains an organisation's strategy, not as a 'grand plan', but as a developing 'pattern in a stream of decisions'.[13] These cumulative decisions may subsequently be more formally described, for example in annual reports and strategic plans, and be seen as the intentional strategy of the organisation. It will not, however, have been the plan that developed the strategy; it will be the emerging strategy that informed the plan.

There are different explanations of emergent strategy[14] and this section summarises these. As Figure 12.2 shows, the different explanations can be thought of in terms of a continuum according to how deliberately managed the processes are. The explanations are: logical incrementalism, strategy as the outcome of political processes, as adaptation from prior decisions and finally as the outcome of organisational systems and routines.

Figure 12.2 A continuum of emergent strategy development processes

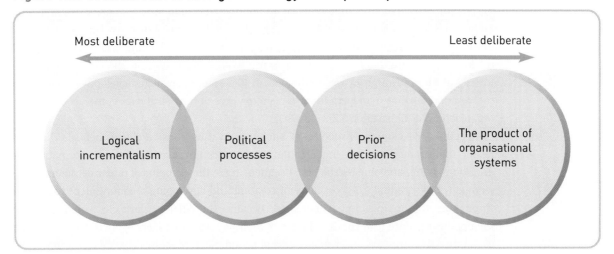

12.3.1 Logical incrementalism

The first explanation of how strategies may emerge is that of *logical incrementalism*. This explanation, in effect, bridges intentionally and emergence in that it explains how management may deliberately cultivate a bottom-up, experimental basis for strategies to emerge. Logical incrementalism **is the development of strategy by experimentation and learning** 'from partial commitments rather than through global formulations of total strategies'.[15] It was a term coined by James Quinn in his study of how strategies developed in multinational businesses.[16] There are four main characteristics of strategy development in this way.

- *Environmental uncertainty*. Managers realise that they cannot do away with the uncertainty of their environment by relying on analyses of historical data or predicting how it will change. Rather, they try to be sensitive to environmental signals by encouraging constant environmental scanning throughout the organisation.

- *General goals*. There may be a reluctance to specify precise objectives too early, as this might stifle ideas and prevent innovation and experimentation. So more general rather than specific goals may be preferred, with managers trying to move towards them incrementally.

- *Experimentation*. Managers seek to develop a strong, secure, but flexible, core business. They then build on the experience gained in that business to inform decisions both about its development and experimentation with 'side-bet' ventures. Commitment to strategic options may therefore be tentative in the early stages of strategy development. Such experiments are not the sole responsibility of top management. They emerge from what Quinn describes as '*subsystems*' in the organisation. By this he means the groups of people involved in, for example, product development, product positioning, diversification, external relations, and so on.

- *Coordinating emergent strategies*. Top managers may then utilise a mix of formal and informal processes to draw together an emerging pattern of strategies from these subsystems. These may then be formed into coherent statements of strategy for stakeholders (e.g. shareholders, financial commentators, the media) who need to understand the organisation's strategy.

Quinn argued that, despite its emergent nature, logical incrementalism can be 'a conscious, purposeful, proactive, executive practice' to improve information available for decisions and build people's psychological identification with the development of strategy. Logical incrementalism therefore suggests that strategy development can be deliberate and intended, whilst relying on organisational subsystems to sense what is happening in the environment and to try out ideas through experimentataion. It is a view of strategy development similar to the descriptions that managers themselves often give of how strategies come about in their organisations as Illustration 12.3 shows.

Arguably, developing strategies in such a way has considerable benefits. Continual testing and gradual strategy implementation provides improved quality of information for decision-making, and enables the better sequencing of the elements of major decisions. Since change will be gradual, the possibility of creating and developing a commitment to change throughout the organisation is increased. Because the different parts, or 'subsystems', of the organisation are in a continual state of interplay, the managers of each can learn from each other about the feasibility of a course of action. Such processes also take account of the political nature of organisational life, since smaller changes are less likely to face the same degree of resistance as major changes. Moreover, the formulation of strategy in this way means that the implications of the strategy are continually being tested out. This continual readjustment makes sense if the environment is considered as a continually changing influence on the organisation.

Given logical incrementalism's emphasis on learning, it is a view of strategy development which corresponds to the **'learning organisation'**[17] – an organisation **that is capable of continual regeneration from the variety of knowledge, experience and skills within a culture that encourages questioning and challenge**. Proponents of the learning organisation argue that formal structures and systems of organisations typically stifle organisational knowledge and creativity. They, too, argue that the aim of top management should be to facilitate rather than direct strategy development by building pluralistic organisations, where conflicting ideas and views are surfaced and become the basis of debate; where knowledge is readily shared and experimentation is the norm such that ideas are tried out in action.

As with logical incrementalism the learning organisation sees organisations as social networks,[18] where the emphasis is not so much on hierarchies as on different interest groups that need to cooperate and learn from each other. It also sees strategy development occurring on the basis of ideas bubbling up from below and being moulded at the top rather than being directed from the top. In these respects there are similarities to the Variety Lens discussed in the Commentaries.

12.3.2 Strategy as the outcome of political processes

The second explanation of how strategies may emerge is that they are the outcome of the bargaining and power politics that go on between executives or between coalitions within the organisation and major stakeholders. Managers may well have different views on issues and how they should be addressed; they are therefore likely to seek to position themselves such that their views prevail. They may also seek to pursue strategies or control resources to enhance their political status. For example, Motorola's inability to move fast enough from analogue to digital technology for mobile phones and its consequent loss of market dominance (see Illustration 5.1 in Chapter 5) was substantially the result of divisional 'warring tribes' across the company seeking to preserve their own interests.[19] The **political view of strategy**

ILLUSTRATION 12.3

An incrementalist view of strategic management

Managers often see their job as managing adaptively: continually changing strategy to keep in line with the environment, whilst maintaining efficiency and keeping stakeholders happy.

● 'You know there is a simple analogy you can make. To move forward when you walk, you create an imbalance, you lean forward and you don't know what is going to happen. Fortunately, you put a foot ahead of you and you recover your balance. Well, that's what we're doing all the time, so it is never comfortable.'[1]

● 'I begin wide-ranging discussions with people inside and outside the corporation. From these a pattern eventually emerges. It's like fitting together a jigsaw puzzle. At first the vague outline of an approach appears like the sail of a ship in a puzzle. Then suddenly the rest of the puzzle becomes quite clear. You wonder why you didn't see it all along.'[2]

● 'We haven't stood still in the past and I can't see with our present set-up that we shall stand still in the future; but what I really mean is that it is a path of evolution rather than revolution. Some companies get a successful formula and stick to that rigidly because that is what they know – for example, [Company X] did not really adapt to change, so they had to take what was a revolution. We hopefully have changed gradually and that's what I think we should do. We are always looking for fresh openings without going off at a tangent.'[3]

● 'In our business you cannot know the future; it's changing so fast. That's why I employ some of the best brains in the industry. Their job is to keep at the forefront of what's happening and, through what they are working on, to help create that future. I don't give them a strategic plan to work to; my job is to discern a strategy from what they tell me and what they are doing. Of course they don't always agree

– why would they, they can't *know* the future either – which means there's a good deal of debate, a good deal of trial and error and a good deal of judgement involved.'[4]

● 'The analogy of a chess game is useful in this context. The objective of chess is clear: to gain victory by capturing your opponent's king. Most players begin with a strategic move, that assumes a countermove by the opponent. If the countermove materialises, then the next move follows automatically, based on a previous winning strategy. However, the beauty of chess is the unpredictability of one's opponent's moves. To attempt to predict the outcome of chess is impossible, and therefore players limit themselves to working on possibilities and probabilities of moves that are not too far ahead.'[5]

References:

1. Quotes from interviews conducted by A. Bailey as part of a research project sponsored by the Economic and Social Research Council (Grant No.: R000235100).
2. Extract from J.B. Quinn, *Strategies for Change*, Irwin, 1980.
3. Extracts from G. Johnson, *Strategic Change and the Management Process*, Blackwell, 1987.
4. CEO of a hi-tech business in an interview with a co-author.
5. From a manager on an MBA course.

Questions

1 With reference to these explanations of strategy development, what are the main advantages of developing strategies incrementally?

2 Is incremental strategy development bound to result in strategic drift (see section 5.2)? How might this be avoided?

development[20] is, then, that **strategies develop as the outcome of bargaining and negotiation among powerful interest groups** (or stakeholders). This is the world of boardroom battles often portrayed in film and TV dramas. Illustration 12.4 shows how the differences of views on strategy between its founder and different company directors at the budget airline easyJet played out over 2008 and 2009.

A political perspective on strategic management suggests that the rational and analytic processes often associated with developing strategy (see section 12.2.2 above and the Design Lens in the Commentary) may not be as objective and dispassionate as they appear. Objectives may reflect the ambitions of powerful people. Information used in strategic debate is not always politically neutral. A manager or coalition may exercise power over another because they control important sources of information. Powerful individuals and groups may also strongly influence which issues get prioritised.[21] In such circumstances it is bargaining and negotiation that give rise to strategy rather than careful analysis and deliberate intent.

None of this should be surprising. In approaching strategic problems, people are likely to be differently influenced by at least:

- *Personal experience* from their roles within the organisation.
- *Competition for resources and influence* between the different subsystems in the organisation and powerful people within them who are likely to be interested in preserving or enhancing their positions.[22]
- *The relative influence of stakeholders* on different parts of the organisation. For example, a finance department may be especially sensitive to the influence of financial institutions whilst a sales or marketing department will be strongly influenced by customers.[23]
- *Different access to information* given their roles and functional affiliations.

In such circumstances there are two reasons to expect strategy development to build gradually on the current strategy. First, if different views prevail and different parties exercise their political muscle, compromise may be inevitable. Second, it is quite possible that it is from the pursuit of the current strategy that power has been gained by those wielding it. Indeed it may be very threatening to their power if significant changes in strategy were to occur. It is likely that a search for a compromise solution accommodating different power bases will end up with a strategy which is an adaptation of what has gone before. So, often organisational politics are seen as constraining strategy development.

There are, however, more positive ways of seeing political processes. The conflict and tensions that manifest themselves in political activity, arising as they do from different expectations or interests, can be the source of new ideas (see the discussion on the Variety Lens in the Commentaries and on 'ambidexterity' in section 12.4.1) or challenges to old ways of doing things.[24] New ideas may be supported or opposed by different 'champions' who will battle over what is the best idea or the best way forward. Arguably, if such conflict and tensions did not exist, neither would innovation. The productive management of such tensions may be a learned competence or dynamic capability (see section 3.2.2) in some organisations that provides them with a basis for competitive advantage. Further, as section 14.4.5 shows, the exercise of power may be important in the management of strategic change.

All of this suggests that political activity has to be taken seriously as an influence on strategy development. Whatever thinking goes into a strategy will need to go hand in hand with activity to address the political processes at work. This is addressed in other parts of this book, in particular sections 4.5.2–3 and 14.4.5 as well as in the Commentaries.

ILLUSTRATION 12.4

Boardroom battles at easyJet

Political processes in organisations can influence the development of strategy.

Sir Stelios Haji-Ioannou founded easyJet in 1995 and was Chairman between 2000 and 2003. He resigned from this position in 2003 saying he wanted to 'concentrate on new ventures' but that he intended to 'remain a significant share holder of this company for a very long time'. His influence took centre stage in autumn 2008 when a private boardroom spat became public, took a subsequent 12 months to resolve, saw a change of 3 senior directors and ended with Sir Stelios getting 50% of his own way.

In 2007, the easyJet share price was flying high at 630p (~€6.9 ~$9.5), but, by autumn 2008 it had nose-dived to 266p per share. Perhaps worried about his investment, perhaps keen to re-extend his influence, Sir Stelios increased his shareholding in the company by taking on the voting rights of the shares held by his sister. He then made his concerns about the growth plans of Andrew Harrison [the CEO at the time] public by writing to Sir Colin Chandler, who was then Chairman, demanding changes to the board of directors as well as the scaling down of growth plans. In particular his objection was to plans to place a £3.4bn (~€3.7bn; ~$5.1bn) order with Airbus.

Press reports at the time claimed that at least two of the non-executive directors of easyJet had threatened to resign if Sir Stelios forced his way back to the helm of the company. In fact, it was the Finance Director who decided to leave for a position elsewhere in the FTSE 100 and in May 2009 Sir Colin Chandler also stepped down earlier than expected amid whispers of his simply being fed-up with the row on the plans for expansion between Stelios and the management team.

During this period, Sir Stelios had attempted to tone down the perception of the disagreement describing it as 'a debate not a dispute' and claiming he was simply exercising his right to protect his investment. Other key figures saw it differently. Sir David Michels, the senior independent non-executive director and widely respected corporate figure, said that the stress of running the company was not helped by a dominant [38%] shareholder: 'it is a company with one large shareholder and that always produces particular pressures. On top of that the shareholder is a very public and on the whole respected figure.'

Sir Stelios had always retained the right, with a shareholding of over 25%, to appoint two non-executive directors and more importantly make himself chairman. The threat of this action and confusion at the rationale for his objection, not only to the plans for growth, but also his suggested alternative [a pay-out to shareholders] left analysts wary of the stock.

As 2009 drew to a close it appeared the matter was reaching a resolution. With a new Chairman [Sir Michael Rake] in place since June 2009 Sir Stelios finally relented and approved a scaled down version of the expansion plans. But the final casualty was CEO Andrew Harrison. At end of the year he announced his plans to step down in the summer of 2010 and seek 'new challenges'. His replacement was Carolyn McCall who joined the board in July 2010. The following week she announced a review of the growth strategy. In the same week Sir Stelios called for an emergency general meeting of shareholders.

Sources: Mark Kleinman, 'easyJet Directors Threaten to Take Off'. *Daily Telegraph*, 15 November 2008; R. Lea, 'O'Leary Faces Lawsuit over Attack on easyJet Founder', *The Times*, 13 February 2010; Lauren Mills, 'Stelios Plays Down his Clash with Directors'. *Daily Mail*, 15 November 2008; Dan Milmo, 'easyJet Entrepreneur Stelios wins Boardroom Battle after Chairman Quits Early'. *Guardian*, 7 April 2009; Dominic O'Connell, 'Stelios Grabs Controls at easyJet', *Sunday Times*, 16 November 2008.

Questions

1 Do you consider the reported events at easyJet exceptional? Can you identify other examples?

2 The influence of Sir Stelios resides in his being the founder of easyJet and a major shareholder. What bases of political influence would executives draw on in disagreements a) with shareholders and b) between themselves?

12.3.3 Strategy informed by prior decisions

The third explanation of how strategies may emerge is as the product of prior decisions which inform or constrain strategy development. In many ways this is to be expected. It would be strange and, arguably, dysfunctional for an organisation to change its strategy fundamentally very often. So one way of explaining emergent strategy is that managers deliberately seek to maintain a continuity of strategy. There are, however, also explanations that suggest that such continuity may be much less deliberate; that it could be the outcome of path dependency or of organisational culture.

Emergent strategy as managed continuity

The strategy of an organisation may develop on the basis of a series of strategic moves each of which makes sense in terms of previous moves. Figure 12.3 illustrates this. A business may start with a new product idea. Its initial success may give rise to product development and product extensions building on this initial success. This may be followed by launches of the product into new markets. An acquisition might follow in the belief that this is synergistic with the current product offering. Over time the company may then become more acquisitive, perhaps seeking to diversify into related products. In this way each strategic move is informed by the rationale of the previous strategic move, such that over time the overall strategic approach of the organisation becomes more and more established. It is common to find management justifying successive strategic moves in this way.

Path-dependent strategy development

There is, however, a less deliberate explanation of such continuity. Path dependency was explained in Chapter 5 (section 5.3). Path dependency is where early events and decisions

Figure 12.3 Strategic direction from prior decisions

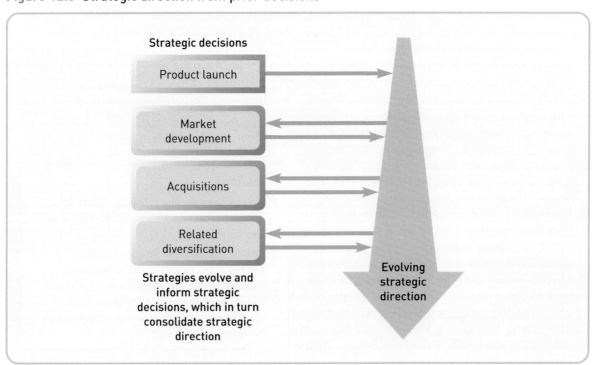

establish 'policy paths' that have lasting effects on subsequent events and decisions.[25] It therefore explains strategic decisions as historically conditioned. It also adds a degree of potential perversity to the pattern of continuity. The same decision sequence shown in the sort of incremental progression explained in Figure 12.3 may hold even if the opening move (in this case a product launch) is not especially successful. For example, a company may develop a product based on technology to which it is wedded and on the basis of which there is some initial success in the market. However, even if the initial success does not continue, further product development and product extensions may take place, perhaps because the company has invested large amounts of capital in the technology. Mixed success with these new products may then encourage the business to acquire another company in a related area in an attempt to strengthen the initial product range. Experience with this acquisition gives the business confidence to make further acquisitions in more diversified product areas. Thus the business ends up as a widely diversified company when it originally sought only to launch a single new product. In effect the company pursues a strategy in which they reinforce suboptimal prior strategic decisions: they 'dig the hole deeper'.

Organisation culture and strategy development

The influence of culture on strategy was also explained in Chapter 5 (section 5.4). Here the emphasis is on strategy development as the outcome of the taken-for-granted assumptions, routines and behaviours in organisations. This taken-for-grantedness works to define, or at least guide, how people view their organisation and its environment. It also tends to constrain what is seen as appropriate behaviour and activity.[26] It is very likely, then, that decisions about future strategy will be within the bounds of the culture and that a pattern of continuity will be the outcome, subsequently post-rationalised by managers. Examples of this are given in Chapter 5 together with the potential problems that can arise. Not least amongst these is that such culturally bounded strategy development can lead to strategic drift (see section 5.2 of Chapter 5).

12.3.4 Strategy as the product of organisational systems

The fourth explanation of how strategies may emerge is on the basis of an organisation's systems. Rather than seeing strategy development as about foresight and anticipation taking form in directive plans from the top of the organisation, strategy development can be seen as the outcome of managers at much lower levels making sense of and dealing with problems and opportunities by applying established ways of doing things. In so doing they are likely to be heavily influenced by the systems and routines with which they are familiar in their particular context. Two useful explanations have developed as to how this occurs: the resource allocation process[27] (RAP) explanation of strategy development and the attention-based view[28] (ABV) of strategy development. Both emphasise that established ways of allocating resources in organisations will tend to play a significant part in what sort of solutions to problems are advocated and those to which resources are allocated.

A classic example of how the resource allocation process can influence strategy is Robert Burgelman's study[29] of how Intel became a microprocessor company in the 1980s. This is explained in Illustration 12.5. There are two main insights that this explanation of strategy development offers, shown graphically in Figure 12.4.

- *Organisational systems as a basis for making sense of issues.* Managers are likely to make sense of issues they face on the basis of the systems and routines with which they are familiar and

Figure 12.4 Strategy development as the product of structures, systems and routines

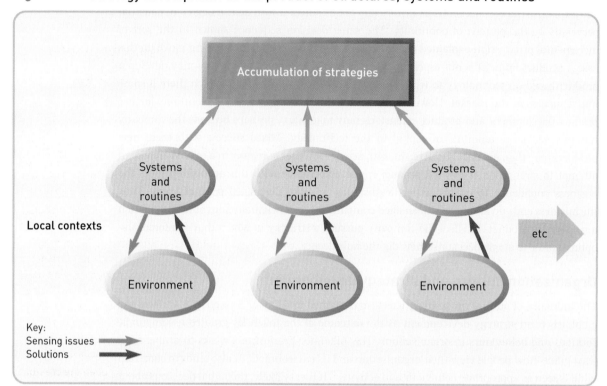

which directly affect them. For example, a finance director will be primarily concerned with the financial systems of the organisation or an operations director with operations. Managers within a business unit will be primarily concerned with the systems relating to that business; managers at the corporate level with systems at that level. Reward systems for company directors based on year-on-year earnings growth can encourage a focus on short-term rather than long-term strategies. Overhead allocation routines can exaggerate the profitability of some products or services and therefore encourage their perceived significance and development at the expense of others. Targets set by government for those managing public services can result in a focus on some issues at the expense of others. Vertical reporting relationships in hierarchies will focus managers' attention on issues within their part of the organisation as distinct from cooperating on wider issues across the wider organisation.

Whereas top-down explanations of strategy development assume that managers' focus of attention will readily cohere around clearly identified overarching 'strategic issues', this explanation emphasises that (a) it may not be analysis of an organisation's overall strategic position so much as local systems that surface issues that get attended to; and (b) such issues are likely to be locally defined.

- *Organisational systems provide bases of solutions to strategic issues.* Systems and routines also provide solutions that managers can draw on when faced with problems. However, responses may differ depending on the context the managers are in and the associated systems and routines. A common example is the way in which different responses emerge as a result of a downturn in company performance. Marketing managers, seeing this as a downturn in the market, may originate solutions which are to do with sales promotion and

ILLUSTRATION 12.5

The development of the microprocessor business at Intel

Resource allocation systems rather than management's intention may drive strategy development.

Between 1968 and 1985 Intel specialised in integrated circuit memory products. By the early 1980s it had two main product areas. DRAM (Dynamic Random Access Memory) had been the basis of the firm's growth and top management remained committed to R&D investment in it. However, given increased competition, DRAMs had lost market share. EPROM (Erasable Programmable Read Only Memory) had become Intel's most profitable product. There was also the emerging business in microprocessors. Microprocessors, however, involved different processes, with an emphasis on chip design rather than manufacturing processes as in the other product areas.

By the end of the 1980s, however, it was the microprocessor business that emerged as the basis of Intel's future growth and identity. This did not happen because of top management's planned direction. They remained committed to the memory business. However, in a company in which there had been an ethos of top-down financial rigour, a resource allocation rule had been created by the first Finance Director designed to maintain Intel as a technological leading-edge company. It stipulated that manufacturing capacity was allocated in proportion to the profit margins achieved in the different product sectors.

The emphasis within the DRAM group was on finding sophisticated technical solutions to DRAM's problems; it was, however, innovation in markets where innovation was no longer commerically viable. DRAM managers nonetheless continued to fight to have manufacturing capacity assigned purely to DRAM, proposing that capacity be allocated on the basis of manufacturing cost. Senior management refused, however, to change the basis of resource allocation.

By the early 1980s DRAMs amounted to only 5 per cent of Intel's revenue, down from 90 per cent. Since DRAM profits were also declining and microprocessor profits were increasing, over time DRAM lost manufacturing capacity within Intel to the microprocessor area. Once this decision was made to keep the resource allocation rule, the strategic freedom left to corporate managers to recover the founding businesses to which they were very attached diminished as market share fell beyond what could be deemed worthwhile recovering. DRAM managers had to compete internally with the technological prowess of the other product areas where morale and excitement were at high levels and innovation was happening in an increasingly dynamic market. And as microprocessors became more and more profitable, the business received increased funding, with manufacturing capacity and investment increasingly allocated away from memory towards them, providing it with the basis for future growth. Eventually corporate managers realised that Intel would never be a player in the 64K DRAM memory game, despite having been the creator of the business. In 1985, top management came to realise they had to withdraw from the DRAM market.

Lingering resistance to the exit continued. Manufacturing personnel ignored implications of exiting from DRAM by trying to show they could compete in the marketplace externally, by explaining failure in terms of the strong dollar against the Japanese yen and battling with poor morale. Eventually Andy Grove, CEO from 1987, took the executive decision to withdraw from EPROM too, leaving no doubt that microprocessors now represented Intel's future strategic direction. The subsequent exit from EPROM was rapidly executed. Staff associated with EPROM left and set up their own start-up.

Source: Based on the case study on Intel by Jill Shepherd (Segal Graduate School of Business, Simon Fraser University, Canada) in 8th edition of *Exploring Corporate Strategy*.

Questions

1 What other examples can you think of where resource allocation processes strongly influence strategy development?

2 What role should top management play in relation to resource allocation processes in organisations?

advertising to generate more sales, research and development managers may see it as a need for product innovation and accountants may see it as a need for tighter controls and cost cutting. Each is drawing on the context in which they find themselves and the associated systems and routines for dealing with such problems.

This explanation highlights two potential problems of strategy development. First, since managers in different contexts have different foci of attention, they may well define issues differently and respond in different ways. Examples were given above in relation to different management functions. Another example is between the business unit and the corporate centre of an organisation. Managers in the business unit, close to a market, may pay attention to routines and systems to do with competitors and customers whereas senior corporate executives may be concerned with balancing resource allocation across businesses, with systems relating to financial markets and with government regulation. There is evidence to suggest that this is one reason why middle-management concerns about changes in markets may go unheeded.[30]

Second, this explanation emphasises that it may not be top-down strategic intent that drives the strategy of an organisation so much as the accumulation of local decisions strongly influenced by local context. These may then be post-rationalised into an apparently coherent strategy. It also helps explain why the strategy development is likely to be a political process (section 12.3.2) since there may be different perceptions of strategic issues and different views on solutions.

12.4 IMPLICATIONS AND CHALLENGES FOR MANAGING STRATEGY DEVELOPMENT

The discussion of different strategy development processes in sections 12.2 and 12.3 has implications for how managers manage the strategy development process.

12.4.1 Multiple strategy development processes

The processes explained above are not discrete or mutually exclusive. It is likely that there will be multiple processes at work in any organisation and the effective management of strategy development needs to take this into account. Indeed, a number of observers of strategy development have suggested that organisations manifest processes that are, in effect, 'planned emergence' with top-down overall intent taking into account and building on bottom-up emergence of strategy.

Even if there is a dominant mode of strategy development in an organisation other processes will, then, be evident too. For example, if a planning system exists in a large organisation, there will also undoubtedly be political activity; indeed the planning system itself may be used for negotiating purposes. It has to be recognised, therefore, that there is *no one right way* in which strategies are developed. The challenge is for managers to recognise the potential benefits of different processes of strategy development so as to build organisations capable of adapting and innovating within a changing environment yet achieving the benefits of more formal processes of planning and analysis to help this where necesssary.[31] There are, however, some useful insights from research that can guide a consideration of appropriate strategy development processes.

Organisational ambidexterity

Multiple strategy processes may need to exist because the strategic needs of organisations require it. For example, an organisation may seek to *exploit* the capabilities that it has built up over time in order to build and sustain competitive advantage. It may seek to do so by top management being fairly directive about the strategy to be followed and coordinating and controlling this through a *planning* system. It will also, very likely, mean that there will be *incremental* development of strategy since strategy will be built on established ways of doing things. The risk, however, is that there may not be enough *exploration* of bases of new capabilities and bases of innovation. If such exploration is to take place there is likely to be a greater need for *organisational learning* (see section 12.3.1) to be more in evidence. The conclusion is that in some organisations there may be a need for both exploitation and exploration – what has become known as '*organisational ambidexterity*'. However, this may be problematic because the different processes associated with exploitation and exploration require different management styles, organisational systems and cultural contexts. In relation to the processes explained in this chapter and elsewhere in the book there are, however, suggestions as to how this might be possible.

- *Structural ambidexterity.* Many organisations have maintained the main core of the business devoted to exploitation with tighter control and careful planning but created separate units or temporary, perhaps project-based, teams for exploration[32] (see section 13.2.5). These separate units devoted to exploration, very likely much smaller in size, may be less tightly controlled[33] with much more emphasis on learning and processes to encourage new ideas.

- *Diversity rather than conformity.* Contradictory behaviours may be beneficial, so there may be benefits from diversity of views in line with the concept of *organisational learning* and with the inevitable consequence of political activity. Such diversity might be on the basis of managers with different experience that gives rise to useful debate. Stanford Univerity's Robert Burgelman argues that somewhere in an organisation, quite likely close to the market and therefore perhaps at junior levels, there will be those who are dissatisfied with the prevailing strategy or think it is inadequate in the face of what they perceive to be changing industry circumstances. He argues[34] that senior executives need to distinguish between dissonant 'noise' in the organisation and such 'strategic signalling', value 'constructive confrontation' and channel it into a 'searing intellectual debate' until a clearer strategic pattern emerges.

- *The role of leadership.* In turn this has implications for leadership roles in organisations. Leaders need to encourage and value different views and potentially contradictory behaviours rather than demanding uniformity.[35] This may well mean running with new ideas and experiments to establish just what makes sense and what does not. However, they also need to have the authority, legitimacy and recognition to stop such experiments when it becomes clear that they are not worthwhile pursuing and make decisions about the direction that is to be followed which, once taken, are followed by everyone in the organisation – including those who have previously dissented.

- *Tight and loose systems.* All this suggests that there needs to be a balance between systems of strategy development that can exploit existing capabilities – perhaps employing the disciplines of strategic planning – and 'looser' systems that encourage new ideas and experimentation. This might, in turn, be linked to the idea that there needs to be some overall common 'glue', perhaps in the form of a clear *strategic intent* in terms of mission and values such that different units in the organisation may be allowed to express how such mission is achieved in their different ways.

Perceptions of strategy development

It is also likely that processes of strategy development will be seen differently by different people. For example, senior executives tend to see strategy development more in terms of intended, rational, analytic planned processes, whereas middle managers see strategy development more as the result of cultural and political processes. Managers in public-sector organisations tend to see strategy as externally imposed more than managers in commercial businesses, largely because their organisations are answerable to government bodies.[36] People who work in family businesses tend to see more evidence of the influence of powerful individuals, who may be the owners of the businesses. The chapter's Key Debate shows very different accounts of the strategy development for a highly successful strategy.

12.4.2 Strategy development and organisational context

Processes of strategy development are likely to differ according to context. Therefore different ways of thinking about strategy development and different processes for managing strategy may make sense in different circumstances. At the risk of over-generalisation there are three major contextual influences. The first two can be considered together.

Organisational characteristics and the nature of the environment

Organisations differ in their characteristics and exist in different environments. The combination of these two contextual dimensions is likely to affect strategy development processes.

First, in terms of the *characteristics of the organisation*, is it *small or large?* In a small organisation individual and fairly detailed direction of strategy may be possible by a chief executive but this may be more difficult in a larger organisation. If the organisation is large, is it also *complex?* Some large organisations, for example, nonetheless operate in a single industry or with a core business model: a major retailer such as Wal-Mart for example. Others are more complex in that they are more diverse, perhaps including many different business units; for example a highly diversified conglomerate such as GE. Or they may comprise diverse and specialised technologies as in universities or a local government with many different services. In such circumstances top management needs to recognise that the possibility of planning detailed strategies from the top is limited, arguably dangerous, since specialists lower down in the organisation know more about the environment in which the organisation operates than they do.

Second, what is the *nature of the environment?*[37]

- *In stable environments* historic tendencies are capable of being understood and are likely to influence the future nature of the environment.
- In relatively *dynamic and uncertain* environments history is less a predictor, so managers need to seek to take a view of the future rather more than the past.
- *Complex* environments are difficult to comprehend; and here complexity is likely to go hand in hand with dynamic change. For example, high-tech industries may be in this category.

Figure 12.5 shows strategy processes are likely to differ according to these organisational characteristics and different environments.[38] For example:

Figure 12.5 **Strategy development contexts**

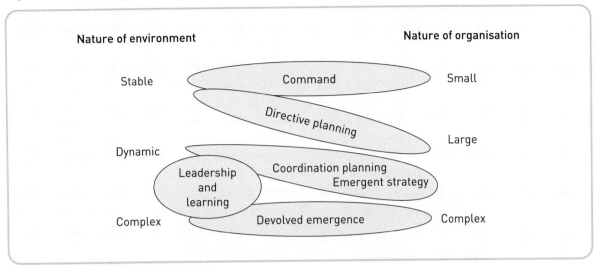

- The *command* mode of strategy is likely to be found most in small organisations in relatively stable environments. A strategic leader – perhaps an owner of a small firm – may be able to draw on extensive experience of how to compete in an industry, use that experience to direct strategy and manage the implementation of that strategy in a fairly hands-on manner given the size of the organisation.

- *Directive planning* in which top management determines and drives strategy is most likely in large stable organisations that are not too complex. Here managers are likely to understand their business units well and, if environmental change does occur, it may be predictable; so it could make sense to analyse the environment extensively on a historical basis as a means of trying to forecast likely future conditions. Examples might include major retailers, raw material suppliers or mass manufacturing. It may also be possible to identify some predictors of environmental influences. For example, in some public services, demographic data such as birth rates might be used as lead indicators to determine the required provision of schooling, health care or social services. There are, however, two problems here. First, competitors in the same sort of environment may all end up following the same strategies; and this could be a recipe for high degrees of competition and low profits (see Chapter 6). Second, environmental conditions may change. Many organisations have found increasingly dynamic and/or complex conditions. When this happens it could be that they find difficulties in adjusting to those changed conditions because their strategy development processes are not suited to them.

- *'Co-ordination planning'*: Where organisations face more turbulent or complex situations there is an important role for planning but it is likely to differ from top-down directive planning.[39] It may play the role of promoting strategic thinking throughout the organisation. For example, a role of strategic planning in many large conglomerates is to provide business units with guideline key assumptions about the future environment together with overall objectives that are to be met. They will then act to integrate the strategies that emerge from those business units.

- *Emergent strategy* processes are also more likely in complex organisations where the environment is also more complex. Professional services such as accountancy and health services are examples. Here specialist units may be dealing with particular markets or needs. In such circumstances it is likely that there will be devolved power of decision-making since top managers at the centre of the organisation cannot expect to understand markets or technologies such that they can take directive decisions at such levels. Strategies will be more likely to emerge from operating units. Top management's role may be more to do with setting overall strategic direction and co-ordinating and shaping emerging strategy from below.

● *Leadership and learning:* The situation of dynamic or complex environments therefore poses an additional challenge. Not only is co-ordination necessary, but it is likely that some stimulus from the top will be needed to galvanise change or to empower and legitimise new ideas from the bottom. So leadership may play an important role here both in establishing clarity of an overall mission or vision and in encouraging organisational learning and development. Further, in terms of the impact new leaders such as CEOs have on organisations, there seems to be evidence that this may vary according to how dynamic the environment is. Whilst the influence of new CEOs in relatively stable environments may be long-lasting, in fast-changing environments their influence may be much more short-lived.[40]

Life cycle effects

The third contextual influence on strategy development processes is how organisations develop over time. For example:

● *Life cycle stages.* In the early stage of an organisation's development, very likely strategy development will be heavily influenced by the founder; as such it is likely to be a 'command' style of management. As organisations develop, especially in new industries there is likely to be a reliance on managers' experience and drawing lessons from what other organisations do, with relatively low use of more rational search mechanisms. As organisations and industries mature, however, they may use more analytic approaches to strategy development.[41]

● *Strategic inflection points.* Burgelman and Grove[42] argue that all organisations face what they call 'strategic inflection points' where there are shifts in fundamental industry dynamics which management needs to recognise and act upon. The problem management faces is how to do this when they are busily working to maximise their competitive advantage and returns in the prevailing industry structure. This is where managers need to take seriously the 'dissonance' that exists in their organisations. So this relates to the challenge of organisational ambidexterity and the strategy development processes required for this (see above).

12.4.3 Managing intended and emergent strategy

This chapter has drawn a distinction between intended and emergent strategy. It has also made the point that the different processes of strategy development are not mutually exclusive; organisations have multiple processes. A problem that managers face, then, is that it is not unusual for organisations to have an intended strategy, perhaps the result of a strategic planning process, but to be following a different strategy in reality. We all experience this as customers of organisations that have stated strategies quite different from what we experience – government agencies that are there purportedly to serve our interests but act as bureaucratic officialdom, companies that claim they offer excellent customer service but operate call centres that frustrate customers and fail to solve problems, universities that claim excellence of teaching but are more concerned with their staff's research, or vice versa. Drawing on the explanations provided in this chapter, Figure 12.6 shows how realised strategy may come to be different from intended strategy.

- *Intended strategy* is the strategy deliberately formulated or planned by senior executives, as explained in section 1.2 and represented by route 1 in Figure 12.6. It may well be expressed in a formal document. It may also be accompanied by mechanisms designed to implement the intentions – project plans or objectives and targets, for example. However, intention and plans are not action; what an organisation actually does can be influenced by other processes.

- *Emergent strategy* is that which emerges on the basis of a series of decisions, a pattern which becomes clear over time. How this happens is explained in section 12.3.3 in terms of the influences of learning, political processes, prior decisions and organisational systems and is represented by route 2 in Figure 12.6.

- *Realised strategy* is what the organisation is actually doing in practice (3 in Figure 12.6). This may have come about as a result of the intended strategy, but it may have come about as the outcome of emergent strategy processes. In truth the likelihood is that it will be a combination of the two: both intended and emergent processes are likely to influence what actually happens.

- *Unrealised strategy* (route 4) is the aspects of the intended strategy that do not come about in practice. There are several reasons for this: the environment changes and managers decide that the strategy, as planned, should not be put into effect; the plans prove to be unworkable or unacceptabel in practice; or the emergent strategy comes to dominate. (Also see the discussion of the drawbacks of planning systems in section 12.2.2 above.)

There are at least four important implications here for strategists:

- *Awareness.* First, and most fundamental, have managers taken steps to check if the intended strategy is actually being realised? It should not be assumed that top management of organisations is always close enough to customers or gets sufficient feedback so as to understand

Figure 12.6 Strategy development routes

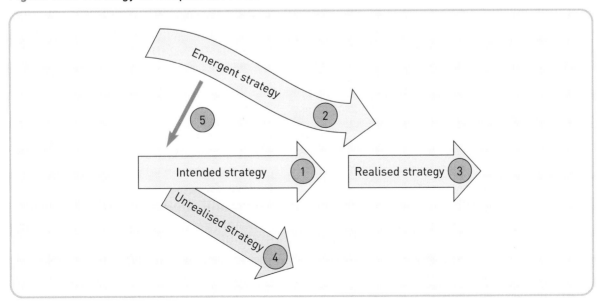

the extent of difference between what is intended as the strategy and what is actually happening.

● *The role of strategic planning.* As has been pointed out, strategic planning might not perform the role of formulating strategies so much as the useful role of co-ordinating the strategies that emerge within the organisation; this is route 5 in Figure 12.6. This may be useful because it may be important that there is a formal explanation of the strategy for the stakeholders of the organisation. However, the danger is that this does little more than pull together 'received wisdom' built up over the years such that the plan merely post-rationalises where the organisation has come from. If strategic planning systems are to be employed managers need to learn two key lessons:

  ● They are not a substitute for other processes of strategy development. These other processes need to be managed too (see below).

KEY DEBATE

Honda and the US motorcycle market in the 1960s

There are different explanations of how successful strategies develop.

In 1984, Richard Pascale published a paper which described the success Honda had experienced with the launch of its motorcycles in the US market in the 1960s. It was a paper that has generated discussion about strategy development processes ever since. First he gave explanations provided by the Boston Consulting Group (BCG):

'The success of the Japanese manufacturers originated with the growth of their domestic market during the 1950s. This resulted in a highly competitive cost position which the Japanese used as a springboard for penetration of world markets with small motorcycles in the early 1960s. . . . The basic philosophy of the Japanese manufacturers is that high volumes per model provide the potential for high productivity as a result of using capital intensive and highly automated techniques. Their market strategies are therefore directed towards developing these high model volumes, hence the careful attention that we have observed them giving to growth and market share.'

Thus the BCG's account is a rational one based upon the deliberate intention of building of a cost advantage based on volume.

Pascale's second version of events was based on interviews with the Japanese executives who launched the motorcycles in the USA:

'In truth, we had no strategy other than the idea of seeing if we could sell something in the United States. It was a new frontier, a new challenge, and it fitted the 'success against all odds' culture that Mr. Honda had cultivated. We did not discuss profits or deadlines for breakeven. . . . We knew our products . . . were good but not far superior. Mr. Honda was especially confident of the 250cc and 305cc machines. The shape of the handlebar on these larger machines looked like the eyebrow of Buddha, which he felt was a strong selling point. . . . We configured our start-up inventory with 25 per cent of each of our four products – the 50cc Supercub and the 125cc, 250cc and 305cc machines. In dollar value terms, of course, the inventory was heavily weighted toward the larger bikes. . . . We were entirely in the dark the first year. Following Mr. Honda's and our own instincts, we had not attempted to move the 50cc Supercubs. . . . They seemed wholly unsuitable for the US market where everything was bigger and more luxurious.

- There needs to be realistic expectations of the role of strategic planning. For example, is its primary role one of co-ordination of emergent strategies; or is the expectation that it will contribute proactively to the development of strategy by, for example, encouraging the challenge of received wisdom and ways of doing things? If it is the latter, then the role of the strategic planner becomes one of internal consultancy as well as analyst and co-ordinator.

- *Managing emergent strategy.* The processes of strategy development that give rise to emergent strategy may be rooted in organisational routines and culture, but they are not unmanageable. Indeed, this is as much about managing strategy as is strategic planning. Resource allocation processes can be changed; political processes can be analysed and managed (see section 4.5 on stakeholder analysis in Chapter 4); challenge to the norms and routines of organisation culture can be encouraged. A clear mission or vision can help

---

... We used the Honda 50s ourselves to ride around Los Angeles on errands. They attracted a lot of attention. But we still hesitated to push the 50cc bikes out of fear they might harm our image in a heavily macho market. But when the larger bikes started breaking, we had no choice. And surprisingly, the retailers who wanted to sell them weren't motorcycle dealers, they were sporting goods stores.'

Two very different accounts, yet they describe the same market success. Since the publication of the paper, many writers on strategy have hotly debated what these accounts actually represent. For example, Henry Mintzberg observed: 'the conception of a novel strategy is a creative process (of synthesis), to which there are no formal techniques (analysis)'. He argued any formal planning was in the implementation of the strategy: 'strategy had to be conceived informally before it could be programmed formally'. He went on to add, 'While we run around being "rational", they use their common sense ... they came to America prepared to *learn*.'

Michael Goold, the author of the original BCG report, defended it on the grounds that

'its purpose was to discern what lay behind and accounted for Honda's success in a way that would help others to think through what strategies would be likely to work. It tries to discern patterns in Honda's strategic decisions and actions and to use these patterns in identifying what works well and badly.'

Richard Rumelt concluded that

'the "design school" is right about the reality of forces like scaled economies, accumulated experience and accumulative development of core competences over time ... but my own experience is that coherent strategy based upon analyses and understandings of these forces is much more often imputed than actually observed.'

And Pascale himself concluded that the serendipitous nature of Honda's strategy showed the importance of learning; that the real lessons in developing strategies were the importance of an organisation's agility and that this resides in its culture, rather than its analyses.

Source: This case example is based on R.T. Pascale, 'Perspectives on strategy: the real story behind Honda's success', *California Management Review*, vol. 26, no. 3 (Spring 1984), pp. 47–72; and H. Mintzberg, R.T. Pascale, M. Goold and R.P. Rumelt, 'The Honda effect revisited', *California Management Review*, vol. 38, no. 4 (1996), pp. 78–116.

Questions

1 Are the different accounts mutually exclusive?

2 Which of the different explanations of strategy development explained in the chapter do you discern in the Honda story?

3 Do you think Honda would have been more or less successful if it had adopted a more formalised strategic planning approach to the launch?

direct the bottom-up strategy development and strategic planning systems can help co-ordinate the outcomes of such processes.

● *The challenge of strategic drift.* A major strategic challenge facing managers was identified in Chapter 5 as the risk of strategic drift (see section 5.2): the tendency for strategies to develop incrementally on the basis of historical and cultural influences, but fail to keep pace with a changing environment. The discussion in section 12.3 of this chapter suggests that such a pattern may be a natural outcome of the influence of organisational culture, individual and collective experience, political processes and prior decisions. This further highlights that strategy development processes in organisations need to encourage people to have the capacity and willingness to challenge and change their core assumptions and ways of doing things.

SUMMARY

This chapter has dealt with different ways in which strategy development occurs in organisations. The main lessons of the chapter are:

- It is important to distinguish between *intended* strategy – the desired strategic direction deliberately planned by managers – and *emergent strategy* which may develop in a less deliberate way from the behaviours and activities inherent within an organisation.

- Most often the process of strategy development is described in terms of intended strategy as a result of *planning systems* carried out objectively and dispassionately. There are benefits and disbenefits of formal strategic planning systems. However, there is evidence to show that such formal systems are not an adequate explanation of strategy development as it occurs in practice.

- Intended strategy may also come about on the basis of central *command, the vision of strategic leaders* or the *imposition of strategies* by external stakeholders.

- Strategies may emerge from within organisations. This may be explained in terms of:

  - How organisations may proactively try to cope through processes of *logical incrementalism and organisational learning.*

  - The outcome of the bargaining associated with *political activity* resulting in a negotiated strategy.

  - Strategy development on the basis of *prior decisions, path dependency* and the taken-for-granted elements of *organisational culture* that favour certain strategies.

  - Strategies developing because *organisational systems* favour some strategy projects over others.

- In *managing strategy development processes*, managers face challenges including:

  - *Multiple processes of strategy development* are likely to be needed if organisations are to achieve both the benefits of the *exploitation* of existing capabilities and the *exploration* for new ideas and capabilities (*organisational ambidexterity*).

  - Recognising that *different processes of strategy development may be needed at different times and in different contexts.*

  - Managing the processes that may give rise to *emergent strategy.*

WORK ASSIGNMENTS

❋ *Denotes more advanced work assignments. * Refers to a case study in the Text and Cases edition.*

12.1   Read the annual report of a company with which you are familiar as a customer (for example, a retailer or transport company). Identify the main characteristics of the intended strategy as explained in the annual report, and the characteristics of the realised strategy as you perceive it as a customer.

12.2   Using the different explanations in sections 12.2 and 12.3, characterise how strategies have developed in different organisations (for example, Google, Cordia* or RACC*).

12.3❋   Planning systems exist in many different organisations. What role should planning play in a public-sector organisation such as local government or the National Health Service and a multinational corporation such as SABMiller*?

12.4❋   Incremental patterns of strategy development are common in organisations, and managers see advantages in this. However, there are also risks of strategic drift. Using the different explanations in sections 12.2 and 12.3, suggest how such drift might be avoided.

12.5   Suggest why different approaches to strategy development might be appropriate in different organisations such as a university, a fashion retailer, a diversified multinational corporation and a high-technology company.

Integrative assignment

12.6❋   Assume you were asked to advise a chief executive of a long-established, historically successful multinational business with highly experienced managers that is experiencing declining profits and falling market share. What might you expect to be the causes of the problems? What processes of strategy development would you propose to address them?

RECOMMENDED KEY READINGS

- A much quoted paper that describes different patterns of strategy development is H. Mintzberg and J.A. Waters, 'Of strategies, deliberate and emergent', *Strategic Management Journal*, vol. 6, no. 3 (1985), pp. 257–72.

- The changing role of strategic planning in the oil industry is explained by Rob Grant; see 'Strategic planning in a turbulent environment: evidence from the oil majors', *Strategic Management Journal*, vol. 24 (2003), pp. 491–517. Also see M. Mankins, 'Stop making plans, start making decisions', *Harvard Business Review*, January 2006, pp. 77–84.

- A fascinating case study of the effects of resource allocation routines on the developing strategy of Intel is provided by Robert Burgelman in 'Fading memories: a process theory of strategic business exit in dynamic environments', *Administrative Science Quarterly*, vol. 39 (1994), pp. 34–56.

- J. Brews and M.R. Hunt, 'Learning to plan and planning to learn: resolving the planning school/learning school debate', *Strategic Management Journal*, vol. 20 (1999), pp. 889–913.

- Insights into the importance of multiple processes of strategy development can be found in S.L. Hart, 'An integrative framework for strategy-making processes', *Academy of Management Review*, vol. 17, no. 2 (1992), pp. 327–51.

REFERENCES

1. The role of a command style in small businesses is discussed in D. Miller and I. Le Breton-Miller, 'Management insights from great and struggling family businesses', *Long Range Planning*, vol. 38 (2005), pp. 517–30. The quotes here are from p. 519.

2. For example see W. Bennis and B. Nanus, *The Strategies for Taking Charge*, Harper and Row, 1985 and J. Collins and J. Porras, *Built to Last: Successful Habits of Visionary Companies*, Harper Business, 2002.

3. In the 1970s and 1980s there were many books written on formal strategic planning approaches to strategy development. They are less common now but, for example, see N. Lake, *The Strategic Planning Workbook*, Kogan Page, 2nd edn (2006); J.M. Bryson, *Strategic Planning For Public and Nonprofit Organizations: a Guide to Strengthening and Sustaining Organizational Achievement*, 3rd edn, Jossey-Bass, 2005; and S. Haines, *The Systems Thinking Approach to Strategic Planning and Management*, St. Lucie Press, 2000.

4. R. Grant, 'Strategic planning in a turbulent environment: evidence from the oil majors', *Strategic Management Journal*, vol. 24 (2003), pp. 491–517.

5. R.G. McGrath and I.C. MacMillan, *Discovery-driven Growth*, Harvard Business School Press, 2009.

6. Many of these dangers are drawn from H. Mintzberg, *The Rise and Fall of Strategic Planning*, Prentice Hall, 1994.

7. Studies on the relationship between formal planning and financial performance are largely inconclusive. Some studies have shown benefits in particular contexts. For example, it is argued there are benefits to entrepreneurs setting up new ventures; see F. Delmar and S. Shane, 'Does business planning facilitate the development of new ventures?', *Strategic Management Journal*, vol. 24 (2003), pp. 1165–85. And other studies actually show the benefits of strategic analysis and strategic thinking, rather than the benefits of formal planning systems; e.g. see C.C. Miller and L.B. Cardinal, 'Strategic planning and firm performance: a synthesis of more than two decades of research', *Academy of Management Journal*, vol. 37, no. 6 (1994), pp. 1649–65.

8. P.J. Brews and M.R. Hunt, 'Learning to plan and planning to learn: resolving the planning school/learning school debate', *Strategic Management Journal*, vol. 20 (1999), pp. 889–913.

9. T.J. Andersen, 'Integrating decentralized strategy making and strategic planning processes in dynamic environments', *Journal of Management Studies*, vol. 41, no. 8 (2004), pp. 1271–99. Also M. Ketokivi and X. Castaner, 'Strategic planning as an integrative device', *Administrative Science Quarterly*, vol. 49 (2004), pp. 337–65.

10. See reference 4 above.

11. See M. Mankins, 'Stop making plans, start making decisions', *Harvard Business Review*, January 2006, pp. 77–84.

12. See B. King, 'Strategizing at leading venture capital firms: of planning, opportunism and deliberate emergence', *Long Range Planning*, vol. 41 (2008), pp. 345–66.

13. H. Mintzberg and J.A. Waters, 'Of strategies, deliberate and emergent', *Strategic Management Journal*, vol. 6, no. 3 (1985), pp. 257–72.

14. See S. Elbanna, 'Strategic decision making: process perspectives', *International Journal of Management Reviews*, vol. 8, no. 1 (2006), pp. 1–20, for a useful explanation of differences between deliberate, intended strategy development and explanations of emergent and incremental strategy development.

15. See J.B. Quinn, *Strategies for Change*, Irwin, 1980. See also J.B. Quinn, 'Strategic change: logical incrementalism' in J.B. Quinn and H. Mintzberg, *The Strategy Process*, 4th edn, 2003, Prentice Hall.

16. See J.B. Quinn, *Strategies for Change*, reference 15, p. 58.

17. The concept of the learning organisation is explained in P. Senge, *The Fifth Discipline: the Art and Practice of the Learning Organization*, Doubleday/Century, 1990. Also M. Crossan, H.W. Lane and R.E. White, 'An organizational learning framework: from intuition to institution', *Academy of Management Review*, vol. 24, no. 3 (1999), pp. 522–37.

18. The concept of the organisation as a set of social networks is discussed by, for example, M.S. Granovetter, 'The strength of weak ties', *American Journal of Sociology*, vol. 78, no. 6 (1973), pp. 1360–80, and G.R. Carroll and A.C. Teo, 'On the social networks of managers', *Academy of Management Journal*, vol. 39, no. 2 (1996), pp. 421–40.

19. See S. Finkelstein, 'Why smart executives fail: four case histories of how people learn the wrong lessons from history', *Business History*, vol. 48, no. 2 (2006), pp. 153–70.

20. For political perspectives on management, see: J.R. DeLuca, *Political Savvy: Systematic Approaches to Leadership behind the Scenes*, Evergreen Business Group, 2nd edn (1999) and G.J. Miller, *Managerial Dilemmas: the Political Economy of Hierarchy*, Cambridge University Press, 2006.

21. For a discussion and an explanatory model of this political perspective, see V.K. Narayanan and L. Fahey, 'The micro politics of strategy formulation', *Academy of Management Review*, vol. 7, no. 1 (1982), pp. 25–34.

22. For an example of how different political coalitions can influence see S. Maitlis and T. Lawrence, 'Orchestral manoeuvres in the dark: understanding failure in organizational strategizing, *Journal of Management Studies*, vol. 40, no. 1 (2003), pp. 109–40.

23. This is sometimes referred to as a 'resource dependency view' of strategy development; for the original argument see J. Pfeffer and G.R. Salancik, *The External Control of Organizations: a Resource Dependence Perspective*, Harper and Row, 1978.

24. This is the argument advanced by J.M. Bartunek, D. Kolb and R. Lewicki, 'Bringing conflict out from behind the scenes: private, informal, and nonrational dimensions of conflict in organizations', in D. Kolb and J. Bartunek (eds), *Hidden Conflict in Organizations: Uncovering Behind the Scenes Disputes*, Sage, 1992.

25. W.B. Arthur, 'Competing technologies, increasing returns and lock in by historical events', *Economic Journal*, vol. 99 (1989), pp. 116–31.

26. Two of the early extensive case studies showing how cultural and political processes give rise to the emergence of strategies are A. Pettigrew, *The Awakening Giant*, Blackwell, 1985; and G. Johnson, *Strategic Change and the Management Process*, Blackwell, 1987.

27. The RAP explanation is sometimes known as the Bower–Burgelman explanation of strategy development after two US professors – Joe Bower and Robert Burgelman. Their original studies are J.L. Bower, *Managing the Resource Allocation Process: a Study of Corporate Planning and Investment*, Irwin, 1972; and R.A. Burgelman, 'A model of the interaction of strategic behavior, corporate context and the concept of strategy', *Academy of Management Review*, vol. 81, no. 1, pp. 61–70; and 'A process model of internal corporate venturing in the diversified major firm', *Administrative Science Quarterly*, vol. 28, pp. 223–44 both in 1983. Also see J.L. Bower and C.G. Gilbert, 'A revised model of the resource allocation process', in *From Resource Allocation to Strategy*, eds J.L. Bower and C.G. Gilbert, pp. 439–55, Oxford University Press, 2005.

28. William Ocasio, 'Towards an attention-based view of the firm', *Strategic Management Journal*, vol. 18 (Summer Special Issue, 1997), pp. 187–206.

29. The Intel case is also written up by Robert Burgelman, see *Strategy as Destiny: How Strategy Making Shapes a Company's Future*, Free Press, 2002. Also see Burgelman, 'Fading memories: a process theory of strategic business exit in dynamic environments', *Administrative Science Quarterly*, vol. 39 (1994), pp. 34–56.

30. J.S. McMullen, D.A. Shepherd and H. Patzelt, 'Managerial (in)attention to competitive threats', *Journal of Management Studies*, vol. 46, no. 2 (2009), pp. 157–80.

31. This idea of a balance between analytic rigour and intuition and imagination is the theme of G. Szulanski and K. Amin, 'Learning to make strategy: balancing discipline and imagination', *Long Range Planning*, vol. 34 (2001), pp. 537–56.

32. M.L. Tushman, and C.A. O'Reilly, 'Ambidextrous organizations: managing evolutionary and revolutionary change', *California Management Review*, vol. 38, no. 4 (1996), pp. 8–30.

33. R. Duncan, 'Characteristics of organisational environments and perceived environmental uncertainty', *Administrative Science Quarterly*, vol. 17, no. 3 (1972), pp. 313–27.

34. Robert Burgelman and Andrew Grove, 'Strategic dissonance', *California Management Review*, vol. 38, no. 2 (1996), pp. 8–28.

35. R.A. Burgelman and A.S. Grove, 'Let chaos reign, then rein in chaos – repeatedly: managing strategic dynamics for corporate longevity'. *Strategic Management Journal*, vol. 28 (2007), pp. 965–79.

36. For a discussion of the differences between strategy development in the public and private sectors, see N. Collier, F. Fishwick and G. Johnson, 'The processes of strategy development in the public sector' in *Exploring Public Sector Strategy*, G. Johnson and K. Scholes (eds), Pearson Education, 2001.

37. See R. Duncan (reference 33).

38. See, for example, S. Hart and C. Banbury, 'How strategy making processes can make a difference', *Strategic Management Journal*, vol. 15, no. 4 (1994), pp. 251–69.

39. See reference 9.

40. A.D. Henderson, D. Miller and D.C. Hambrick, 'How quickly do CEOs become obsolete? Industry dynamism, CEO tenure and company perormance', *Strategic Management Journal*, vol. 27 (2006), pp. 447–60.

41. G. Gavetti and J.W. Rivkin, 'On the origin of strategy: action and cognition over time', *Organization Science*, vol. 18, no. 3 (2007), pp. 420–39.

42. See reference 35.

Google: who drives the strategy?

Phyl Johnson, Strategy Explorers

From an idea to a verb in less than 15 years: 'to Google – to search the Internet'

If you are in need of the answer to a question and close to a computer what do you do: Google it. With the exception of 'Hoover' it is hard to think of another example of an organisation whose product's name has become so synonymous with the activity of the product that it becomes a commonly used verb. Google has achieved this in just a few years, growing at an eye-watering pace to its current internationally dominant position in internet search. It has to be one of the most successful strategies ever; so how did they do it?

Unsurprisingly, Google has attracted the attention of analysts, researchers and other organisations trying to uncover their formula for success. Moreover, their business model has taken over from GE and IBM before it as the model to learn and replicate. At the heart of this hugely successful enterprise is a famously unstructured style of operating and a CEO who claims their strategy is based on trial and error: can this really be the case?

> 'Google is unusual because it's really organized from the bottom up. . . . It often feels at Google people are pretty much doing what they think best and they tolerate having us around. . . . We don't really have a five-year plan. . . . We really focus on what's new, what's exciting and how can you win quickly with your new idea.' Eric Schmidt, Google CEO[1]

About Google

Google started life as the brainchild of Larry Page and Sergey Brin when they were students at the IT power-house Stanford University in the USA. Google was born from coursework the pair undertook in 1998 to improve internet search engine results. After University and when Page and Brin launched their own search engine product, it gained followers and users very quickly, attracted financial backing and enabled them to launch their IPO* in the USA stock market in 2004, so making Google a publicly owned corporation.

* IPO: Initial Public Offering of shares in a company to the public to buy, often referred to as the flotation of a company on a stock market.

Source: Press Association Images/Mark Lennihan/AP.

From the beginning Google has been different. Page and Brin insisted that their IPO follow a very unusual route: instead of using investment banks as dictators of their initial share price, they launched a kind of open IPO. In this auction, buyers decided on the fair price for a share and not the investment banks. A quirky route to market that some saw as arrogant and established a theme for Google: breaking the mould. This continued as Google set up its governance structure with a two-tier board of directors, common in some European countries [e.g. Germany] but extremely rare in the USA. The advantage of the two-tier system for founders Page and Brin was the additional distance it places between them and their shareholders and the increased managerial freedom it offered to them to run their company their way. Page confirmed this by penning an open letter to shareholders claiming that Google was not a conventional company and that they did not intend to become one.

Running the company the Google way involved another curious and unlikely twist in 2001. Page and Brin recruited successful CEO Eric Schmidt from Novell Inc and, between the three of them, they shared power at the top. Schmidt dealt with administration and the company's investors and had the most traditional CEO role. Page was centrally concerned with the social structure of Google whilst Brin took a lead in the area of ethics. There have been very few successful triumvirates in history and many epic failures. Either politics and confusion create rifts in which three become two and two become one; or the three power holders become overly consensual. But against the odds it went well for Google.

With 132 million customers and a network of 1 million computers worldwide, Google is without a doubt the dominant player in internet search with 67.5% market share, way ahead of Yahoo [8.4%].[2] But they are also widely diversified thanks to their highly acquisitive approach to business. Their other areas of operation include Blogging, Radio & TV Advertising, Online Payment Services, Social Networks and Mobile Phone Operating Systems. Their guiding principle in acquisition seems to be: if they can't innovate something in-house, buy it. In this way Google were buying a product, technical expertise and usually a fan base of early adopters. This is in contrast to Apple, for example, who seek to innovate in-house. In the period between 2001 and 2009 they acquired some 50 companies. Many of these were small starts-ups but others were already established with a significant enough band of internet followers to be attractive, the most famous of which was YouTube in 2001 for $1.65 (~€1.15) billion.

In 2010, Google was still expanding at a startling rate,* and following twin tracks in its operation, those of search tools and productivity tools. Their aim to retain their position as the *King of Search* but always follow the same mantra was delivered on multiple YouTube broadcasts by the senior Google executives: *'To organize the world's information'*.

The disorganisation organisation

In many ways, life inside the Googleplex [Google's HQ] is the image of a disorganised organisation where it can be difficult to work out who is responsible for what. An example of this was Google's failure to renew its own domain name in the German market in 2007 as well as an instance when no legal representative for the company appeared at a Belgian law suit.

Google famously launch half-finished products into the market and don't control information flow about their products by advertising: in fact they don't advertise at all. With regard to product development their approach is to launch a part-finished [*beta*] product, let Google fanatics find it, toy with it, essentially error-check and de-bug it. This may be a good use of end users but also a significant release of control.

The legacy of Google's rapid growth is an organisation with less structuring than would be expected for

its size and breadth of operation. Control of workflow, quality and to a large extent the nature of projects that are under way is down to employees and not management. Google is a famously light-managed organisation. They have a 1:20 ratio of employees to managers. This is half the number of managers that would be the case in the average US organisation [1:10] and considerably less than some European countries [France 1:7.5].

Engineers work in small autonomous teams and the work they produce is quality assured using peer review and not classical supervision. So there is the potential for these small work teams, with their freedom for self-initiated project work, to create a situation of project proliferation in which a large percentage of activity may not be contributing to the strategic direction the leadership wish the firm to take. Moreover, engineers at Google are allowed to allocate 20% of their work time to personal projects that interest them as a means to stimulate innovation and create new knowledge as well as potential products. However, some commentators suggest that reports from inside Google estimate many engineers spend more like 30% of their time on labour of their own choice – a lot of opportunity for new ideas but also for chaos.

This form of highly organic organisation [sometimes referred to as an ecosystem] is more familiar in much smaller organisations, under the 300 employee level and in creative industries such as advertising agencies. But for an organisation the size of Google [more than 16,000 employees] the disorganisation and anti-bureaucratic approach is something that they pride themselves on.

> 'Google is run by its culture and not by me. . . . It's much easier to have an employee base in which case everybody is doing exactly what they want every day. They're much easier to manage because they never have any problems. They're always excited, they're always working on whatever they care about. . . . But it's a very different model than the traditional, hierarchical model where there's the CEO statement and this is the strategy and this is what you will do, and it's very very measured. We put up with a certain amount of chaos from that.' Eric Schmidt: CEO[3]

The rigid organisation

Irrespective of the image that Google has as an organisation that sees the benefits in releasing managerial control and rigid hold over strategic direction, there are some significant areas of rigidity built into the system.

One key area is that of recruitment. With an extremely highly rated employment brand, Google can afford to be choosy. Close to 100 talented applicants

---

* An example of their pace in growth being employee numbers, from 1,628 employees in 2003 to 19,604 in 2008.

chase each job at the Googleplex. The pay is competitive but not way ahead of the competition. However, perks, including free meals, a swimming pool and massages, all help attract employees. So too does the 20% of free time engineers can spend on their own interests. In return Google have rigid recruitment criteria and processes and are unashamedly elitist.

Engineers must have either a Masters or Doctorate from a leading University and they must pass through a series of assessment tests and interviews. The criteria for these are derived in a highly scientific manner; after all Google measure *everything*. The end product of this is that Google actually recruit against a psychometric profile* of *googleness* and can therefore hire and retain a fairly predictable employee population: much easier to manage.

Their laissez-faire attitude toward the management of employees can be read as control as well as freedom. Peer review is a famously stringent form of performance management. Amongst professionals, reputation is key and if someone is being reviewed by peers the pattern is toward harder and higher quality work. The way peer reviews are carried out and indeed the way many processes within Google are followed is formulaic and rigid. For example, work teams are kept small and limited to a maximum of six. Projects to be worked on must be limited, deadlines are short [no longer than six weeks] and as ever in Google there is measurement.

> 'Everyone who meets Sergy Brin notices his aptitude as a mathematician. Math is everywhere at Google: in pricing policy, in discussions among engineers, in decisions about whether to develop a new product, in the development of those products in recruiting, and in evaluating employee performance. Google measures and analyzes everything.' Girard (2009 pp. 97–98)

> 'We're very analytical. We measure everything, and we systematized every aspect of what's happening in the company. For example, we introduced a spreadsheet product this week. I've already received hourly updates on the number of people who came in to apply to use the spreadsheet, the number of people using it, the size of the spreadsheet.' Eric Schmidt[4]

* Personality type.

Google's internal technical platform is a major part of its success. They have the capacity to record and analyse vast aspects of data from their user and customer groups. In addition, there is an in-house intranet called 'Moma' that tracks huge amounts of data in real time. Google is all about information, capturing it, tracking it and applying it all in a systematic and organised manner. The technology itself is the strategy and the strategy is the technology.

As Google continues to travel at a high velocity into the future, on some level major decisions have been and remain to be made. Who decided to buy YouTube and make the other acquisitions? Who do the shareholders hold responsible for strategic success and failure? In early 2010, Google back-tracked on a deal they had made with China to allow some content to be censored by the Chinese authorities. However, after a security breach into its gmail system, Google reversed course. Who made these decisions? Moreover, as information capture about users and the personalisation of search engines to those users becomes more advanced, so does the hunger of organisations and perhaps even governments for that information. The triumvirate who run Google find themselves with some big strategic thinking to do around decisions that will have huge ramifications around the Google world.

Primary source: Girard B. (2009) *The Google Way: How one company is revolutionizing management as we know it*. No Starch Press, San Francisco, CA.

References:
1. Interview by Nicholas Carlson with Google CEO Eric Schmidt: 'We Don't Really Have A Five-Year Plan' *Washington Post Leadership series* 20 May 2009.
2. Cited in Web Ultimatum shakes the great firewall of China to its foundations *The Times*, 14 January 2010.
3. As above.
4. Quoted on p. 97 of Girard (2009).

Questions

1 What influences strategy development in Google?

2 What are the strengths and weaknesses of their approach?

3 Is the Google approach transferable to other organisations?

13

ORGANISING FOR SUCCESS

Learning outcomes

After reading this chapter you should be able to:

● Identify *key challenges in organising* for success, including ensuring control, managing knowledge, coping with change and responding to internationalisation.

● Analyse main organisation *structural types* in terms of their strengths and weaknesses.

● Recognise key issues in designing organisational *control systems* (such as planning and performance targeting systems).

● Recognise how the three strands of strategy, structure and systems should reinforce each other in *organisational configurations* and the managerial dilemmas involved.

Key terms

Balanced scorecards p. 447

Configurations p. 453

Cultural systems p. 445

Direct supervision p. 445

Functional structure p. 432

Market systems p. 449

Matrix structure p. 436

McKinsey 7-S framework p. 453

Multidivisional structure p. 434

Performance targets p. 446

Planning systems p. 450

Project-based structure p. 440

Strategy maps p. 447

Structures p. 431

Systems p. 431

Transnational structure p. 439

---

mystrategylab

MyStrategyLab is designed to help you make the most of your studies.

Visit **www.pearsoned.co.uk/mystrategylab** to discover a wide range of resources specific to this chapter, including:

• A personalised **Study plan** that will help you understand core concepts

• **Audio** and **video clips** that put the spotlight on strategy in the real world

• **Online glossaries** and **flashcards** that provide helpful reminders when you're looking for some quick revision.

(13.1) INTRODUCTION

Strategies only happen because people do things. To take one end of the scale: if American multinational retailer Wal-Mart wants to achieve its strategy, it needs to get its 2.1 million employees pointing in the right direction. To take the other end of the scale: even a football team has to ensure that all its members will play the right kind of game. Thus strategies require organisation and this involves both structures and systems. If the organisation does not support the strategy, then even the cleverest strategy will fail because of poor implementation.

This chapter examines organising for successful strategy implementation. It focuses particularly on two key elements of organisational 'design': organisational structures and organisational systems. **Structures give people formally defined roles, responsibilities and lines of reporting with regard to strategy. Systems support and control people as they carry out structurally defined roles and responsibilities**.

KEY CONCEPT

Structures

Figure 13.1 expresses the interdependency between strategy, structure and systems. In the ideal organisational design, all three should support each other in a circular process of mutual reinforcement. This chapter captures the importance of mutual reinforcement between elements with the concept of 'configuration', explained in section 13.4. However, the chapter will also underline how difficult it sometimes can be to configure the organisation in order to support strategy. In particular, the Key Debate at the end of the chapter questions the extent to which formal organisational structures can be simply reshaped to align with strategy. Sometimes the organisational elements of structure and systems can get out of synchrony with the strategy, fatally undermining it or even redefining its direction. In Figure 13.1, it is worth noticing that structure and systems not only flow *from* strategy but also feed *into* it.

This chapter addresses the following topics therefore:

- *Structures*, in other words the formal roles, responsibilities and lines of reporting in organisations. The chapter considers the main types of structures, including functional, multidivisional, matrix, project and transnational structures.

Figure 13.1 Organisational configurations: strategy, structure and systems

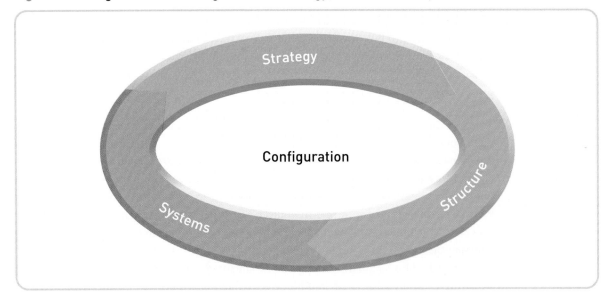

- *Systems*, what supports and controls people within and around an organisation. These systems include formal mechanisms such as performance targeting and planning, and more informal ones such as cultural and market systems.

- *Configurations*, the mutually supporting elements that make up an organisation's design. As well as strategy, structure and systems, these elements can include staff, style, skills and superordinate goals, as encapsulated in the *McKinsey 7-S framework*.

(13.2) STRUCTURAL TYPES

Managers often describe their organisation by drawing an organisation chart, mapping out its formal structure. These structural charts define the 'levels' and roles in an organisation. They are important to managers because they describe who is responsible for what. But formal structures matter in at least two more ways. First, structural reporting lines shape patterns of communication and knowledge exchange: in many organisations people tend not to talk much to people much higher or lower in the hierarchy, or in different parts of the organisation. Second, the kinds of structural positions at the top suggest the kinds of skills required to move up the organisation: a structure with functional specialists such as marketing or production at the top indicates the importance to success of specialised functional disciplines rather than general business experience. In short, formal structures can reveal a great deal about the role of knowledge and skills in an organisation. Structures can therefore be hotly debated (see Illustration 13.1).

This section reviews five basic structural types: functional, multidivisional, matrix, transnational and project.[1] Broadly, the first two of these tend to emphasise one structural dimension over another, either functional specialisms or business units. The three that follow tend to mix structural dimensions more evenly, for instance trying to give product and geographical units equal weight. However, none of these structures is a universal solution to the challenges of organising. Rather, the right structure depends on the particular kinds of challenges each organisation faces. Researchers propose a wide number of important challenges (sometimes called 'contingencies') shaping organisational structure, including organisational size, extent of diversification and type of technology.[2] This implies that the first step in organisation design is deciding what the key challenges facing the organisation actually are. Section 13.2.6 will particularly focus on how the five structural types fit both the traditional challenge of control and the three new challenges of change, knowledge and internationalisation.

13.2.1 The functional structure

Even a small entrepreneurial start-up, once it involves more than one person, needs to divide up responsibilities between different people. The **functional structure divides responsibilities according to the organisation's primary specialist roles such as production, research and sales.** Figure 13.2 represents a typical organisation chart for such a functional organisation. This kind of structure is particularly relevant to small or start-up organisations, or larger organisations that have retained narrow, rather than diverse, product ranges. Functional structures may also be used within a multidivisional structure (see below), where the divisions themselves may split themselves up according to functional departments (as in Figure 13.2).

Figure 13.2 also summarises the potential advantages and disadvantages of a functional structure. There are advantages in that it gives senior managers direct hands-on involvement

ILLUSTRATION 13.1

Volkswagen: a case of disputed centralisation

A new chief executive introduces a more centralised structure over this multi-brand giant.

Figure 1 Volkswagen, November 2006 (simplified)

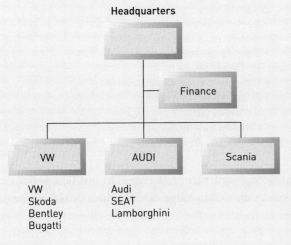

Figure 2 Volkswagen, January 2007 (simplified)

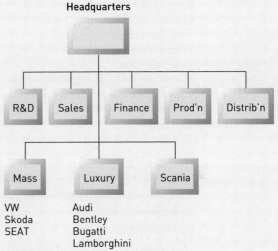

In 2007, following the Porsche car company's building up of a controlling stake and the installation of a new chief executive, German car manufacturer Volkswagen announced a major reorganisation. For the previous few years, Volkswagen had been organised as two groups of brands under the main Volkswagen and Audi labels (see Fig. 1), with technical and marketing expertise clustered around particular brands within these. Now the company was to be reorganised into two main groups, a mass-market group (VW, Skoda, SEAT) and a more luxury market group (Audi, Bentley, Bugatti and Lamborghini). Volkswagen also had a large stake in truck company Scania. The company would be more centralised, with new corporate responsibilities for production, sales, distribution and R&D (see Fig. 2). The new CEO, Martin Winterkorn, would also act as head of R&D and be directly responsible for the VW group of brands.

The stated aim of this more centralised structure was to increase synergies between the various brands. More centralised R&D would help ensure the sharing of engines and components, and centralisa-tion of production would assist the optimisation of factory usage across the company. The departing head of the Volkswagen group took another view. He asserted that, in order to ensure cross-functional integration and motivation, expertise needed to identify closely with particular brands. According to him, the new structure mimicked the centralised Porsche structure, but Porsche was a much smaller company with just one main brand. Porsche's spokespersons responded by recalling that Porsche was the most profitable car company in the world, while Volkswagen was one of the least.

Questions

1 Which type of structure did the old decentralised structure resemble most and which type of structure is Volkswagen moving closer to?

2 What pros and cons can you see in the new Volkswagen structure?

Figure 13.2 A functional structure

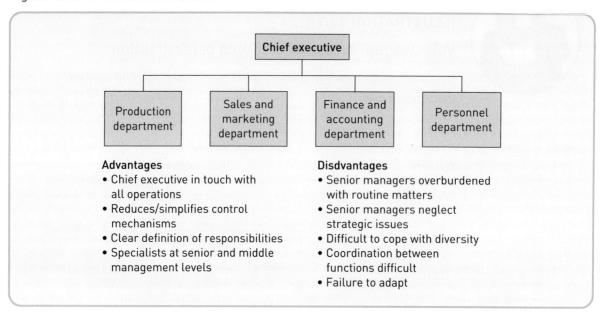

in operations and allows greater operational control from the top. The functional structure provides a clear definition of roles and tasks, increasing accountability. Functional departments also provide concentrations of expertise, thus fostering knowledge development in areas of functional specialism.

However, there are disadvantages, particularly as organisations become larger or more diverse. Perhaps the major concern in a fast-moving world is that senior managers focus too much on their functional responsibilities, becoming overburdened with routine operations and too concerned with narrow functional interests. As a result, they find it hard either to take a strategic view of the organisation as a whole or to coordinate separate functions quickly. Thus functional organisations can be inflexible, poor at adapting to change. Separate functional departments tend also to be inward-looking – so-called 'functional silos' – making it difficult to integrate the knowledge of different functional specialists. Finally, because they are centralised around particular functions, functional structures are not good at coping with product or geographical diversity. For example, a central marketing department may try to impose a uniform approach to advertising regardless of the diverse needs of the organisation's various business units around the world.

13.2.2 The multidivisional structure

A **multidivisional structure is built up of separate divisions on the basis of products, services or geographical areas** (see Figure 13.3). Divisionalisation often comes about as an attempt to overcome the problems that functional structures have in dealing with the diversity mentioned above.[3] Each division can respond to the specific requirements of its product/market strategy, using its own set of functional departments. A similar situation exists in many public services, where the organisation is structured around *service departments* such as recreation, social services and education.

There are several potential advantages to divisional structures. As self-standing business units, it is possible to control divisions from a distance by monitoring business performance

Figure 13.3 **A multidivisional structure**

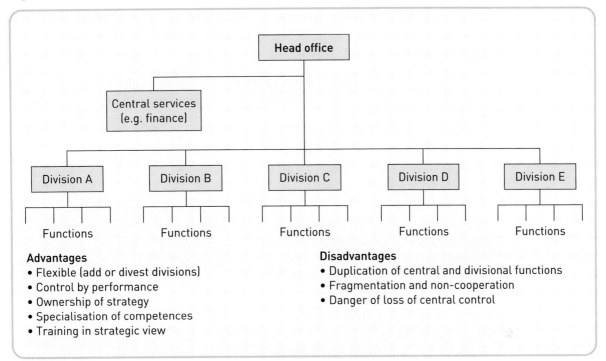

Advantages
- Flexible (add or divest divisions)
- Control by performance
- Ownership of strategy
- Specialisation of competences
- Training in strategic view

Disadvantages
- Duplication of central and divisional functions
- Fragmentation and non-cooperation
- Danger of loss of central control

(see section 13.3.3). Having divisions also provides flexibility because organisations can add, close or merge divisions as circumstances change. Divisional managers have greater personal ownership for their own divisional strategies. Geographical divisions – for example, a European division or a North American division – offer a means of managing internationally (see section 13.2.4). There can be benefits of specialisation within a division, allowing competences to develop with a clearer focus on a particular product group, technology or customer group. Management responsibility for a whole divisional business is good training in taking a strategic view for managers expecting to go on to a main board position.

However, divisional structures can also have disadvantages of three main types. First, divisions can become so self-sufficient that they are *de facto* independent businesses, but duplicating the functions and costs of the corporate centre of the company. In such cases of *de facto* independence, it may make more sense to split the company into independent businesses, and de-mergers of this type are now common. Second, divisionalisation tends to get in the way of cooperation and knowledge-sharing between business units: divisions can quite literally divide. Expertise is fragmented and divisional performance targets provide poor incentives to collaborate with other divisions. Finally, divisions may become too autonomous, especially where joint ventures and partnership dilute ownership. Here, divisions pursue their own strategies almost regardless of the needs of the corporate parent. In these cases, multidivisionals become *holding companies*, where the corporate centre effectively 'holds' the various businesses in a largely financial sense, exercising little control and adding little value. Figure 13.3 summarises these potential advantages and disadvantages of a multidivisional structure.

Large and complex multidivisional companies often have a second tier of *subdivisions* within their main divisions. Treating smaller strategic business units as subdivisions within a large division reduces the number of units that the corporate centre has to deal with directly. Subdivisions can also help complex organisations respond to contradictory pressures. For example, an organisation could have geographical subdivisions within a set of global product divisions (see section 13.2.4).

13.2.3 The matrix structure

A **matrix structure** combines different structural dimensions simultaneously, for example **product divisions and geographical territories or product divisions and functional specialisms.**[4] In matrix structures, middle managers typically report to two or three senior managers each. Figure 13.4 gives examples of such a structure.

Matrix structures have several advantages. They promote *knowledge-sharing* because they allow separate areas of knowledge to be integrated across organisational boundaries. Particularly in professional service organisations, matrix organisation can be helpful in applying particular knowledge specialisms to different market or geographical segments. For example, to serve a particular client, a consulting firm may draw on people from groups with particular knowledge specialisms (e.g. strategy or organisation design) and others grouped according to particular markets (industry sectors or geographical regions). Figure 13.4 shows how a school might combine the separate knowledge of subject specialists to create programmes

Figure 13.4 Two examples of matrix structures

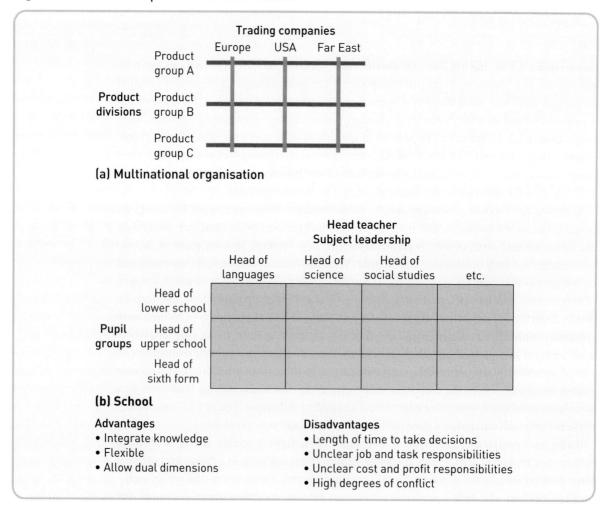

(a) Multinational organisation

(b) School

Advantages	Disadvantages
• Integrate knowledge	• Length of time to take decisions
• Flexible	• Unclear job and task responsibilities
• Allow dual dimensions	• Unclear cost and profit responsibilities
	• High degrees of conflict

of study tailored differently to various age groups. Matrix organisations are *flexible*, because they allow different dimensions of the organisation to be mixed together. They are particularly attractive to organisations operating globally, because of the possible mix between local and global dimensions. For example, a global company may prefer geographically defined divisions as the operating units for local marketing (because of their specialist local knowledge of customers). But at the same time it may still want global product units responsible for the worldwide coordination of product development and manufacturing, taking advantage of economies of scale and specialisation. This combination of dimensions is the approach of American multinational Procter & Gamble, for instance (see Illustration 13.2).

However, because a matrix structure replaces single lines of authority with multiple cross-matrix relationships, this often brings problems. In particular, it will typically take *longer to reach decisions* because of bargaining between the managers of different dimensions. There may also be *conflict* because staff find themselves responsible to managers from two structural dimensions. In short, matrix organisations are hard to control.

As with any structure, but particularly with the matrix structure, the critical issue in practice is the way it actually works (i.e. behaviours and relationships). The key ingredient in a successful matrix structure can be senior managers good at sustaining collaborative relationships (across the matrix) and coping with the messiness and ambiguity which that can bring. It is for this reason that Chris Bartlett and Sumantra Ghoshal describe the matrix as involving a 'state of mind' as much as a formal structure (see also Illustration 13.2).[5]

13.2.4 Multinational/transnational structures

Operating internationally adds an extra dimension to the structural challenge. As in Figure 13.5, there are essentially four structural designs available for multinationals. Three are simple extensions of the principles of the multidivisional structure (section 13.2.2), so are dealt with briefly. The fourth, the transnational structure, is more complex and will be explained at more length.

The three simpler multinational structures are as follows:

- *International divisions*. An international division is a stand-alone division added alongside the structure of the main home-based business. This is often the kind of structure adopted by corporations with large domestic markets (such as in the United States or China), where an initial entry into overseas markets is relatively small-scale and does not require structural change to the original, much bigger, home businesses. For example, a Chinese car, truck and motorbike manufacturer might have separate divisions for each of its product areas in its home market of China, but run its overseas businesses in a separate 'international division' combining all three product areas together. The international division is typically run from headquarters, but not integrated with the domestic business. As in Figure 13.5, the international division structure is centralised but not highly coordinated.

- *Local subsidiaries*. These subsidiaries typically have most of the functions required to operate on their own in their particular local market, for example design, production and marketing. They are thus a form of geographic divisional structure. They have high local responsiveness and are loosely coordinated. A local subsidiary structure is very common in professional services such as law, accounting and advertising, where there are few economies of scale and responsiveness to local regulations, relationships or tastes is very important. This structure fits the multidomestic strategy introduced in Chapter 8.

ILLUSTRATION 13.2

Procter & Gamble's evolving matrix

Having replaced its multidivisional structure in 1987, P&G has constantly revised its matrix, and shown how it is not only a structure but also a 'state of mind'.

In 2010, Procter and Gamble (P&G), the giant American consumer products company, declared of its matrix organisational structure: 'We have made P&G's structure an important part of our capacity to grow. It combines the global scale of a $79 (~€55) billion global company with a local focus to win with consumers and retail customers in each country where P&G products are sold.' The 2010 matrix is summarised alongside. Apparently simple, this structure was the outcome of nearly a quarter of a century of revisions, one of which had cost the Chief Executive his job.

P&G first experimented with a matrix structure in 1987. On top of the existing product divisions in the American market, P&G overlaid a strengthened second axis of central corporate functions. These corporate functions gave functional managers in the divisions access to specialised expertise. For example, divisional sales executives still had a primary ('solid-line') relationship with their divisional top managers, but now had a secondary ('dotted-line') relationship with the central Vice President of Sales overseeing all the American divisions. In the following few years, P&G's central functions extended their responsibilities globally, and central 'category' presidents' took responsibility for innovation in product areas worldwide. By 1995, P&G had created four profit-responsible regions across the world (North America, Latin America, Europe/Middle East/African and Asia). P&G now had a global matrix, with global functions and global categories cross-cutting the four regions.

Declining growth in the late 1990s prompted a major revision of P&G's matrix structure, with the establishment of Global Business Units (with profit responsibility for products worldwide), Market Development Organisations (tasked with sales growth in local markets), plus centralised Global Business Services and Corporate Functions managing internal business processes and providing specialised expertise. This new structure was launched by a new Chief Executive, the aggressive Durk Jager. Management layers were simultaneously reduced from 13 to 7, and 15,000 people were laid off. Jager was a man who said of himself: 'I break kneecaps. I make heads roll'. But performance collapsed in the first year of the new structure, and it was soon Jager that was fired.

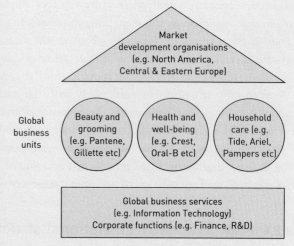

Adapted from: http://www.pg.com/en_US/company/global_structure_operations/corporate_structure.shtml.

In 2000, Alan Lafley took over as Chief Executive. He retained P&G's basic matrix of Global Business Units, Market Development Organizations, Global Business Services and Corporate Functions. But, described as like 'a nerdy college professor', Lafley brought a gentler style. In 2010, Lafley was still at the top of P&G, now as Chairman, with a decade of solid success behind him.

Sources: P&G.com; M. Piskorski and A. Spadini, Procter & Gamble: Organization 2005 (A), Harvard Business School Case no, 707–516; R. Degen (2009), 'Designing Matrix Organizations that Work', International School of Management working paper no. 33, Paris.

Questions

1 Compare the balance of power between categories and regions in the 1995 structure to that between Global Business Units and Market Development Organizations in the post-2000 structure. What implications would this shift have for strategy?

2 How does this case illustrate the claim that a matrix is 'a state of mind', not just a formal structure?

- *Global product divisions.* This kind of structure is often used where economies of scale are very important. Organising the design, production and marketing on the basis of global divisions rather than local subsidiaries typically maximises cost efficiency. To return to the Chinese car, truck and motorbike manufacturer, there would be just three divisions each responsible for their particular product area across the whole world, China included. There would be very little scope for adaptation to local tastes or regulations in particular markets. In global product divisions, local responsiveness would typically be very low. This structure fits the global strategy introduced in Chapter 8.

The international division, local subsidiary and global product division structures all have their particular advantages, whether it is managing relative size, maximising local responsiveness or achieving economies of scale. The fourth structure, however, tries to integrate the advantages of the local subsidiary structure with those of the global product divisional structure.

In terms of Figure 13.5, the **transnational structure combines local responsiveness with high global coordination.**[6] According to Bartlett and Ghoshal, transnational structures are similar to matrices but distinguish themselves by their focus on knowledge-sharing, specialisation and network management, as follows:

- *Knowledge-sharing.* While each national or regional business has a good deal of autonomy, in the transnational they should see themselves as sources of ideas and capabilities for the whole corporation. Thus a good idea that has been developed locally is offered for adoption by other national or regional units around the world.

- *Specialisation.* National (or regional) units specialise in areas of expertise in order to achieve greater scale economies on behalf of the whole corporation. Thus a national unit that has particular competences in manufacturing a particular product, for example, may be given responsibility for manufacturing that product on behalf of other units across the world.

Figure 13.5 **Multinational structures**

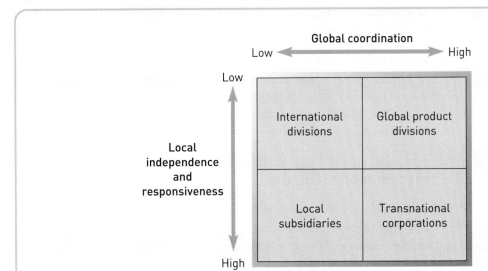

● *Network management.* The corporate centre has the role of managing this global network of specialisms and knowledge. It does so first by establishing the specialist role of each business unit, then sustaining the systems and relationships required to make the network of business units operate in an integrated and effective manner.

The success of a transnational corporation is dependent on the ability *simultaneously* to achieve global competences, local responsiveness and organisation-wide innovation and learning. This requires clarity as to boundaries, relationships and the roles that the various managers need to perform. For example:

● *Global business managers* have the overriding responsibility to further the company's global competitiveness, which will cross both national and functional boundaries. They must be the *product/market strategists*, the *architects* of the business resources and competences, the *drivers of product innovation* and the *coordinators* of transnational transactions.

● *Country or area managers* have potentially a dual responsibility to other parts of the transnational. First, they must act as a *sensor* of local needs and feed these back to those responsible internationally for new products or services. Second, they should seek to *build* unique competences: that is, country managers should seek to become centres of excellence, allowing them to be *contributors* to the company as a whole, in manufacturing or research and development, for instance.

● *Functional managers* such as finance or IT have responsibility for setting standards and ensuring worldwide innovation and learning across the various parts of the organisation. This requires the skill to recognise and spread best practice across the organisation. So they must be able to *scan* the organisation for best practice, *cross-pollinate* this best practice and be the *champions* of innovations.

● *Corporate (head office) managers* integrate these other roles and responsibilities. Not only are they the *leaders*, but they are also the *talent spotters* among business, country and functional managers, facilitating the interplay between them. For example, they must foster the processes of innovation and knowledge creation. They are responsible for the *development* of a strong management centre in the organisation.

Theoretically the transnational combines the best of local decentralisation with the best of global centralisation. However, the transnational can be very demanding of managers in terms of willingness to work not just at their national business units but for the good of the transnational as a whole. Diffuse responsibilities also make for similar complexities and control problems to those of the matrix organisation.[7]

13.2.5 Project-based structures[8]

Many organisations rely heavily on project teams with a finite lifespan. A **project-based structure is one where teams are created, undertake the work (e.g. internal or external contracts) and are then dissolved.**[9] This can be particularly appropriate for organisations that deliver large and expensive goods or services (civil engineering, information systems, films) or those delivering time-limited events (conferences, sporting events or consulting engagements). The organisation structure is a constantly changing collection of project teams created, steered and glued together loosely by a small corporate group. Many organisations use such teams in a more ad hoc way to complement the 'main' structure. For example, *task forces* are set up to make progress on new elements of strategy or to provide momentum where the regular structure of the organisation is not effective.

The project-based structure can be highly flexible, with projects being set up and dissolved as required. Because project teams should have clear tasks to achieve within a defined period, accountability and control are good. As project team members will typically be drawn from different departments within the firm, projects can be effective at knowledge exchange. Projects can also draw on members internationally and, because project lifespans are typically short, project teams may be more willing to work temporarily around the world. There are disadvantages, however. Without strong programme management providing overarching strategic control, organisations are prone to proliferate projects in an ill-coordinated fashion. The constant breaking up of project teams can also hinder the accumulation of knowledge over time or within specialisms.

Overall, project-based structures have been growing in importance because of their inherent flexibility. Such flexibility can be vital in a fast-moving world where individual knowledge and competences need to be redeployed and integrated quickly and in novel ways.

13.2.6 Choosing structures

From the discussion so far, it should be clear that functional, multidivisional, matrix, transnational and project structures each have their own advantages and disadvantages. Organisational designers, therefore, have to choose structures according to the particular strategic challenges (or 'contingencies') they face. Here the various structures are considered in the light of four general challenges that have become particularly important for many contemporary organisations in recent years:

● The need for *control* in a world where organisations are increasingly large, complex and under scrutiny. One extreme of complexity is the American retailer Wal-Mart, which in 2010 had 2.1 million employees. Control is also important because investors, regulators and pressure groups typically watch closely to see that organisations actually deliver on the strategic promises they make.

● The *speed of change* and the increased levels of *uncertainty* in the business environment, as discussed in Chapter 2. As a result, organisations need to have flexible designs and be skilled at reorganising.

● The growing importance of *knowledge creation* and *knowledge-sharing* as a fundamental ingredient of strategic success, as discussed in Chapter 3. Organisational designs should both foster concentrations of expertise and encourage people to share their knowledge.

● The rise of *internationalisation*, as discussed in Chapter 8. Organising for a international context has many challenges: communicating across wider geography, coordinating more diversity and building relationships across diverse cultures are some examples. Wal-Mart operates in Japan, China, India, Latin America and the UK (as ASDA), as well as the United States. Internationalisation also brings greater recognition of different kinds of organising around the world.

Table 13.1 summarises how the five basic structures – functional, multidivisional, matrix, transnational and project – meet these challenges of control, change, knowledge and internationalisation faced by many contemporary organisations. No structure scores high across all four challenges. Organisational designers therefore face trade-offs and choices. If they seek

Table 13.1 Comparison of structures

Challenge	Functional	Multidivisional	Matrix	Transnational	Project
Control	***	**	*	**	**
Change	*	**	***	***	***
Knowledge	**	*	***	***	**
Internationalisation	*	**	***	***	**

* Stars indicate typical capacities to cope with each challenge, with three stars indicating high, two indicating medium and one indicating poor.

control, but are less concerned for flexibility in response to change or global reach, then they might prefer a functional structure. If they want to foster knowledge and flexibility on a global scale, then they might consider a matrix or transnational structure. In other words, structural choice depends on the particular strategic challenges the organisation faces. The difficult trade-offs involved are illustrated by the debate around Volkswagen's structure (Illustration 13.1) and the evolving nature of Procter & Gamble's structure (Illustration 13.2).

In reality, few organisations adopt a structure that is just like one of the pure structural types discussed above. Structures often blend different types into hybrid structures (see section 13.4.1 below), tailor-made to the particular mix of challenges facing the organisation. While Table 13.1 considers general challenges for contemporary organisations, Goold and Campbell provide *nine design tests* against which to check specific tailor-made structural solutions.[10] The first four tests stress fit with the key objectives and constraints of the organisation:

● *The Market-Advantage Test.* This test of fit with market strategy is fundamental, following Alfred Chandler's classic principle that 'structure follows strategy'.[11] For example, if coordination between two steps in a production process is important to market advantage, then they should probably be placed in the same structural unit.

● *The Parenting Advantage Test.* The structural design should fit the 'parenting' role of the corporate centre (see Chapter 7). For example, if the corporate centre aims to add value as a synergy manager, then it should design a structure that places important integrative specialisms, such as marketing or research, at the centre.

● *The People Test.* The structural design must fit the people available. It is dangerous to switch completely from a functional structure to a multidivisional structure if, as is likely, the organisation lacks managers with competence in running decentralised business units.

● *The Feasibility Test.* This is a catch-all category, indicating that the structure must fit legal, stakeholder, trade union or similar constraints. For example, after scandals involving biased research, investment banks are now required by financial regulators to separate their research and analysis departments from their deal-making departments.

Goold and Campbell then propose five more tests based on good general organisational design principles, as follows:

● *The Specialised Cultures Test.* This test reflects the value of bringing together specialists so that they can develop their expertise in close collaboration with each other. A structure scores poorly if it breaks up important specialist cultures.

- *The Difficult Links Test.* This test asks whether a proposed structure will set up links between parts of the organisations that are important but bound to be strained. For example, extreme decentralisation to profit-accountable business units is likely to strain relationships with a central research and development department. Unless compensating mechanisms are put in place, this kind of structure is likely to fail.

- *The Redundant Hierarchy Test.* Any structural design should be checked in case it has too many layers of management, causing undue blockages and expense. Delayering in response to redundant hierarchies has been an important structural trend in recent years.

- *The Accountability Test.* This test stresses the importance of clear lines of accountability, ensuring the control and commitment of managers throughout the structure. Because of their dual lines of reporting, matrix structures are often accused of lacking clear accountability.

- *The Flexibility Test.* While not all organisations will face the same general rise in environmental velocity as referred to with regard to Table 13.1, a final important test is whether the design will be sufficiently flexible to accommodate possible changes in the future. Here Kathleen Eisenhardt argues for structural 'modularity' (i.e. standardisation) in order to allow easy 'patching' (i.e. transfer) of one part of the organisation to another part of the organisation, as market needs change.[12] For example, if strategic business units are similar in structural size and internal management systems throughout a large organisation, it becomes easy to switch them between divisions as new opportunities for collaboration between units become apparent.

Goold and Campbell's nine tests provide a rigorous screen for effective structures. But even if the structural design passes these tests, the structure still needs to be matched to the other key element of an organisation's configuration, its systems. Systems too will have to reinforce strategy and structure.

(13.3) SYSTEMS

Structure is a key ingredient of organising for success. But structures can only work if they are supported by formal and informal organisational systems.[13] Systems give control over the organisation. If structures are like the bones in a body, systems are the muscles that control how things move. Illustration 13.3 on the changing structures and systems of the World Health Organization demonstrates the linkages between structures and systems.

Systems as means of control can be subdivided in two ways. First, systems tend to emphasise either control over inputs or control over outputs. Input control systems concern themselves with the *resources* consumed in the strategy, especially financial resources and human commitment. Output control systems focus on ensuring satisfactory *results*, for example the meeting of targets or achieving market competitiveness. The second subdivision is between direct and indirect controls. Direct controls involve *close supervision* or monitoring. Indirect controls are more *hands-off*, setting up the conditions whereby desired behaviours are achieved semi-automatically. How the five systems we shall consider emphasise input or output controls and direct or indirect control is summarised in Table 13.2.

Organisations normally use a blend of these control systems, but some will dominate over others according to the strategic challenges. As for structures, these challenges include change, knowledge and internationalisation and different systems cope with some of these

ILLUSTRATION 13.3

The World Health Organization's structure comes under pressure

New strategic challenges are shifting the organisation towards centralisation.

2009 was a testing year for the World Health Organization (WHO). The swine flu virus (H1N1), orginating in Mexico in April, swept quickly around the world. In June, the WHO Director-General Dr Margaret Chan declared: 'The world is moving into the early days of its first influenza pandemic of the 21st Century'. It looked like the worst pandemic since the 1968 Hong Kong flu killed an estimated one million people worldwide. Hundreds of millions of people rushed to be vaccinated.

As the coordinator of health policy for the United Nations, the WHO has a staff of 8000 health and other experts. About 1800 work at headquarters in Geneva. The remainder are spread around six regional offices (Africa, Europe, South-East Asia, Americas, East Mediterranean and West Pacific) and 147 country offices. WHO projects range from children's medicine, through leprosy eradication to dealing with HIV/AIDS.

Traditionally the WHO has been decentralised. Regional offices, typically with around 100 professional staff plus support staff, would lead in dealing with the characteristic health problems of their region. They also managed administrative, personnel, medical supply and field security services within their regions. However, criticisms of inefficiency from member states and the apparent rising threat of pandemics (worldwide disease outbreaks) were creating pressures for change. While there had been famous pandemics in history (for example, the Black Death), since the Hong Kong flu of 1968 there had been the emergence of HIV/AIDs in the 1980s, the SARS scare of 2003, the Avian flu scare of 2004–07 and then the H1N1 crisis of 2009.

Dr Margaret Chan had been director of health in Hong Kong since the 1990s, dealing with SARS and early outbreaks of Avian flu. In 2004 she had become an Assistant Director-General of the WHO. One of her first acts on arriving in Geneva was to set up a Strategic Health Operations Centre, a nerve centre for monitoring disease outbreaks across the world. In 2006, Chan became Director-General of the whole of WHO. She launched a further set of managerial reforms.

Principal amongst these reforms was the creation in 2008 of a global service centre, based in Kuala Lumpur. This global service centre provides administrative services and support to all staff in WHO offices worldwide in respect of human resources, payroll, procurement and accounts payable. Most of the previous posts carrying out these functions in Geneva, the regional offices and country offices were suppressed. A second important reform was the creation of a global management system, launched in 2009. This is based on an Enterprise Resource Management system produced by the American company Oracle, and brings together all existing WHO systems in the areas of finance, human resources, travel, programme planning and procurement.

By December, 2009, the H1N1 pandemic had claimed 10,000 lives across 208 countries. This was less than feared, and some accused the WHO of exaggerating the original threat. Margaret Chan told *The Canadian Press* in an interview: 'I can understand all these suspicions and conspiracy thinking, but I must emphasize that there is no basis for that. . . . All the measures that I put in place in Hong Kong in 1997 (an early outbreak of avian flu) became the gold standard. The aggressive approach by WHO . . . to put SARS back in the box is paying dividends. . . . I think we must remain prudent and observe the evolution of the (H1N1) pandemic in the course of the next six to 12 months before crying victory.'

Sources: www.who.int; *The Canadian Press*, 28 December 2009; 'A World Health Organization Primer' (www.medscape.com).

Questions

1 How is the strategy of the WHO changing and with what consequences for its structure and systems?

2 What barriers and threats can be envisaged to the direction of the WHO's structural and system reforms?

Table 13.2 **Types of control systems**

	Input	Output
Direct	Direct supervision; Planning systems	Performance targeting
Indirect	Cultural systems	Internal markets

better than others. As we shall see, input measures tend to require that the controllers have high levels of knowledge of what the controlled are supposed to do. In many knowledge-intensive organisations, especially those generating innovation and change, controllers rarely have a good understanding of what their expert employees are doing, and tend to rely more on output controls. At least they can know when a unit has made its revenue or profitability targets. Direct control relies heavily on the physical presence of management, although now surveillance through information technology can substitute. For this reason, international organisations may make use of indirect controls for their geographically dispersed subsidiaries. On the other hand, direct control systems can be very effective for small organisations on a single site.

13.3.1 Direct supervision

Direct supervision **is the direct control of strategic decisions by one or a few individuals, typically focused on the effort put into the business by employees.** It is a dominant process in small organisations. It can also exist in larger organisations where little change is occurring and if the complexity of the business is not too great for a small number of managers to control the strategy *in detail* from the centre. This is often found in family businesses and in parts of the public sector with a history of 'hands-on' political involvement (often where a single political party has dominated for a long period).

Direct supervision requires that the controllers thoroughly understand what is entailed by the jobs they supervise. They must be able to correct errors, but not cramp innovative experiments. Direct supervision is easiest on a single site, although long-distance monitoring (for instance, of trading strategies in banking) is now possible through electronic means. Direct supervision can also be effective during a *crisis*, when autocratic control through direct supervision may be necessary to achieve quick results. Turnaround managers are often autocratic in style. Quite often, especially in the public sector, there are expectations of direct supervision that go far beyond the controllers' actual competence.

13.3.2 Cultural systems

Organisations typically have distinctive cultures which express basic assumptions and beliefs held by organisation members and define taken-for-granted ways of doing things (see Chapter 5). Despite their taken-for-granted, semi-conscious nature, organisational cultures can seem a tempting means of managerial control. Managers may therefore try to influence organisational culture through various deliberate mechanisms in order to achieve the kinds of employee behaviour required by their strategy.[14] **Such** cultural systems **aim to standardise norms of behaviour within an organisation in line with particular objectives.** Cultural systems exercise an *indirect* form of control, because of not requiring direct supervision: it becomes a matter of willing conformity or *self*-control by employees. Control is exerted on the *input* of employees, as the culture defines the norms of appropriate effort and initiative that employees will put into their jobs.

Three key cultural systems are:

- *Recruitment.* Here cultural conformity may be attempted by the selection of appropriate staff in the first place. Employers look to find people who will 'fit'. Thus some employers may favour recruiting people who have already shown themselves to be 'team-players' through sport or other activities.

- *Socialisation.* Here employee behaviours are shaped by social processes once they are at work. It often starts with the integration of new staff through training, induction and mentoring programmes. It typically continues with further training throughout a career. Symbols can also play a role in socialisation, for example the symbolic example of leaders' behaviours or the influence of office décor, dress codes or language.

- *Reward.* Appropriate behaviour can be encouraged through pay, promotion or symbolic processes (for example, public praise). The desire to achieve the same rewards as successful people in the organisation will typically encourage imitative behaviour.

It is important to recognise that organisations' cultures are not fully under formal management control. Sometimes aspects of organisational culture may persistently contradict managerial intentions, as with peer-group pressure not to respond to organisational strategies. Cynicism and 'going through the motions' are common in some organisations. Sometimes the culture of an organisation may even drive its strategy (see Chapter 5). On the other hand, some cultures can bring about desired results, even without deliberate management intervention. For example, workers often form spontaneous and informal 'communities of practice', in which expert practitioners inside or even outside the organisation share their knowledge to generate innovative solutions to problems on their own initiative.[15] Examples of these informal communities of practice range from the Xerox photocopying engineers who would exchange information about problems and solutions over breakfast gatherings at the start of the day, to the programmer networks which support the development of Linux 'freeware' internationally over the internet.

13.3.3 Performance targeting systems

Performance targets focus on the *outputs* of an organisation (or part of an organisation), such as product quality, revenues or profits. These targets are often known as key performance indicators (KPIs). The performance of an organisation is judged, either internally or externally, on its ability to meet these targets. However, within specified boundaries, the organisation remains free on how targets should be achieved. This approach can be particularly appropriate in certain situations:

- *Within large businesses*, corporate centres may choose performance targets to control their business units without getting involved in the details of how they achieve them. These targets are often cascaded down the organisation as specific targets for sub-units, functions and even individuals.

- In *regulated markets*, such as privatised utilities in the UK and elsewhere, government-appointed regulators increasingly exercise control through agreed *performance indicators* (PIs), such as service or quality levels, as a means of ensuring 'competitive' performance.[16]

- In *the public services*, where control of resource inputs was the dominant approach historically, governments are attempting to move control processes towards outputs (such as quality of service) and, more importantly, towards outcomes (for example, patient mortality rates in health care).

Many managers find it difficult to develop a useful set of targets. There are at least three potential problems with targets:[17]

- *Inappropriate measures* of performance are quite common. For example, managers often prefer indicators that are easily measured or choose measures based on inadequate understanding of real needs on the ground. The result is a focus on the required measures rather than the factors that might be essential to long-term success. In the private sector, focus on short-term profit measures is common, at the expense of investment in the long-run prosperity of the business. To take a public-sector case, inappropriate 'national indicators' appeared to be a problem with child protection services in Illustration 13.4.

- *Inappropriate target levels* are a common problem. Managers are liable to give their superiors pessimistic forecasts so that targets are set at undemanding levels, which can then be easily met. On the other hand, superiors may over-compensate for their managers' pessimism, and end up setting excessively demanding targets. Unrealistically ambitious targets can either demotivate employees who see no hope of achieving them regardless of their effort, or encourage risky or dishonest behaviours in order to achieve the otherwise impossible.

- *Excessive internal competition* can be a result of targets focused on individual or sub-unit performance. Although an organisation by definition should be more than the sum of its parts, if individuals or sub-units are being rewarded on their performance in isolation, they will have little incentive to collaborate with the other parts of the organisation. The struggle to meet individualistic targets will reduce the exchange of information and the sharing of resources.

These acknowledged difficulties with targets have led to the development of two techniques designed to encourage a more balanced approach to target-setting. The most fundamental has been the development of the balanced scorecard approach.[18] **Balanced scorecards** set **performance targets according to a range of perspectives, not only financial**. Thus balanced scorecards typically combine four specific perspectives: the *financial perspective*, which might include profit margins or cash flow; the *customer perspective*, which sets targets important to customers, such as delivery times or service levels; the *internal perspective*, with targets relating to operational effectiveness such as the development of IT systems or reductions in waste levels; and finally the future-oriented *innovation and learning perspective*, which targets activities that will be important to the long-run performance of the organisation, for example investment in training or research. Attending to targets relevant to all four perspectives helps ensure that managers do not focus on one set of targets (e.g. financial) at the expense of others, while also keeping an eye to the future through innovation and learning.

A second more balanced approach to target-setting is strategy mapping, developing the balanced scorecard idea. **Strategy maps** link different performance targets into a mutually **supportive causal chain supporting strategic objectives**. Figure 13.6 shows an extract of a strategy map for a delivery company based on the four perspectives of finance, customers, internal processes, and innovation and learning. In this map, investments in well-trained and motivated drivers under the heading of 'innovation and learning' lead to on-time deliveries under the heading of 'internal processes', and thence to satisfied customers and finally to

KEY CONCEPT

Balanced scorecards

ILLUSTRATION 13.4
Structure, systems and saving children's lives

Changing structures and systems is not a quick fix in protecting children from parental abuse and neglect.

England and Wales have a problem: the homicide of children by their own parents. In the period 1998 to 2008, an average of about 40 children were killed by their parents annually. In 2008, about 200,000 children were living in households with a known high risk of domestic abuse and violence.

The death of nine-year-old Victoria Climbié in 2000 at the hands of her great aunt and boyfriend prompted a major reform of child protection services in England and Wales. Victoria Climbié's death had come after nine months of regular warning signs to the local social, police and medical services. The lack of coordination in picking up signs of abuse between these agencies was seen as a major weakness. One result was the merger of local education and children's social services into *unified children's services department*s. Another was to create *'common assessment frameworks'* (CAFs), a way for all agencies (from police to doctors) to record their dealing with a particular child on a standardised form accessible to all. A system of *national indicators* for measuring child protection was also introduced.

The homicide rate drifted down after the implementation of the reforms between 2003 and 2005, but then started to climb back towards the average, with 43 homicides in 2007–08. The 2007 death by neglect and abuse of 17-month-old 'Baby P' – in the same local authority area as Victoria Climbié and again after months of warning signs to police, medical and social work services – prompted a further review of services. The review found that under 10 per cent of local authorities had adopted the national indicators for child protection: local authorities complained that the targets were focused excessively on proper process and timescales, rather than meaningful outcomes. None the less, the review basically confirmed the new structure and systems, while urging more effective implementation through better training of social workers, revised indicators, more resources, centralised computer support and improved communications between agencies.

On the ground, however, there was considerable dissatisfaction with the post-Climbié reforms. 81 per cent of professionals in one poll claimed that the merger between educational and social services was not working (www.publicservice.co.uk). Most of the merged departments were headed by former directors of education, with little understanding of the social work for which they were responsible. Social workers complained about excessive form filling in order to demonstrate correct procedures. A boy told the review: 'It seems like they have to do all this form filling – their bosses' bosses make them do it – but it makes them forget about us'. An academic commentator estimated that social workers were now spending 80 per cent of their time in front of computers rather than with clients. The common assessment framework (CAF) form is eight pages long. One school head reported to the *Guardian* newspaper: 'You can no longer pick up the phone to the agencies for advice or referral without hearing "Where is the CAF?"'.

Speaking to the *Guardian*, Maggie Atkinson, director for learning and children in the town of Gateshead, urged patience: 'Bringing services together into one department creates a different culture, not immediately, but over a period of time. This change in culture is only really beginning to be embedded in local services and to put it into reverse would be a wasted opportunity. It doesn't matter whether the director comes from education or social services. What you need to do the job is broad shoulders, effective management and a very strong team around you.'

Sources: L. Lightfoot, 'A marriage on the rocks', *Guardian*, 17 March 2009; 'The Protection of Children in England: a Progress Report', *Every Child Matters*, March 2009.

Questions

1 List the advantages and disadvantages of the new structure and systems for children's services.

2 What kinds of actions and initiatives might be appropriate in terms of the cultural systems of children's services?

Figure 13.6 A strategy map

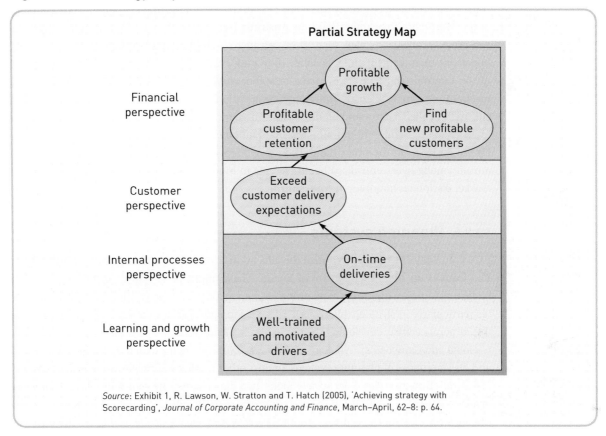

Partial Strategy Map

Source: Exhibit 1, R. Lawson, W. Stratton and T. Hatch (2005), 'Achieving strategy with Scorecarding', *Journal of Corporate Accounting and Finance*, March–April, 62–8: p. 64.

profitable growth. The causal chain between the various targets underlines the need for balance between them: each depends on the others for achievement. Thus strategy maps help in reducing the problem of partial measures referred to above; the problems of inappropriate target levels and internal competition are not so easily resolved.

13.3.4 Market systems

Market disciplines (or *internal markets*) can be brought inside organisations to control activities internally.[19] **Market systems typically involve some formalised system of 'contracting' for resources or inputs from other parts of an organisation and for supplying outputs to other parts of an organisation.** Control focuses on outputs, for example revenues earned in successful competition for internal contracts. The control is indirect: rather than accepting detailed performance targets determined externally, units have simply to earn their keep in competitive internal markets.

Internal markets can be used in a variety of ways. There might be *competitive bidding*, perhaps through the creation of an internal investment bank at the corporate centre to support new initiatives. Also, a customer–supplier relationship may be established between a central service department, such as training or IT, and the operating units. Typically these internal markets are subject to considerable regulation. For example, the corporate centre might set rules for *transfer prices* between internal business units to prevent exploitative contract pricing, or insist on *service-level agreements* to ensure appropriate service by an essential internal supplier, such as IT, for the various units that depend on it.

Internal markets work well where complexity or rapid change makes detailed direct or input controls impractical. Arguably this is the case in the specialised and fast-moving environment of the Macquarie investment bank in Australia (see Illustration 13.5). But market systems can create problems as well. First, they can increase bargaining between units, consuming important management time. Second, they may create a new bureaucracy monitoring all of the internal transfers of resources between units. Third, an overzealous use of market mechanisms can lead to dysfunctional competition and legalistic contracting, destroying cultures of collaboration and relationships. These have all been complaints made against the internal markets and semi-autonomous Foundation Hospitals introduced in the UK's National Health Service. On the other hand, their proponents claim that these market processes free a traditionally over-centralised health service to innovate and respond to local needs, while market disciplines maintain overall control.

13.3.5 Planning systems

Planning systems plan and control the allocation of resources and monitor their utilization. The focus is on the direct control of inputs. These might be simple financial inputs (as in budgeting), human inputs (as in planning for managerial succession) or long-term investments (as particularly in strategic planning). This section concentrates on strategic oversight from the corporate centre, developing the discussion in Chapter 12.

Goold and Campbell's[20] typology of three *strategy styles* helps to determine the advantages and disadvantages of planning systems against other methods of corporate central oversight. The three strategy styles differ widely along two dimensions: the *dominant source of planning influence*, either top-down (from the corporate centre to the business units) or bottom-up (from the business units to the centre); and the *degree of performance accountability* for the business units, either tight or reasonably relaxed. As in Figure 13.7, the three strategy styles align themselves on these two dimensions thus:

Figure 13.7 Strategy styles

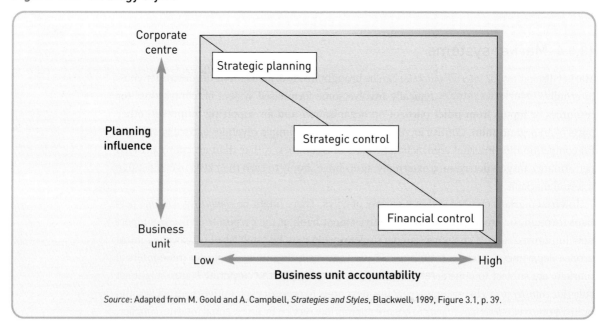

Source: Adapted from M. Goold and A. Campbell, *Strategies and Styles*, Blackwell, 1989, Figure 3.1, p. 39.

ILLUSTRATION 13.5

Controlling investment bankers

Known as the 'Millionaire Factory', Macquarie's entrepreneurial bankers are pursuing deals all over the world. Now there is a new CEO.

Sydney-based Macquarie Bank is Australia's largest investment bank and its most successful division, the Infrastructure Group, is the largest operator of toll roads in the world. Its funds own Copenhagen Airport and the Thames Water company and during 2006 it launched an audacious and ultimately unsuccessful bid for the London Stock Exchange. Despite this set-back, 2006 was another record year for Macquarie. Its total staff has risen from under 5000 in 2003 to just less than 10,000 in 2007; its international staff rose from less than a thousand to 3200 in the same period.

The long-standing chief executive, Allan Moss, joined Macquarie in 1977, when it was still a sub-sidiary of British merchant bank Hill Samuel with about 50 employees. A Harvard MBA (he graduated in the top 5%), Moss became chief executive in 1993 and listed the bank on the Australian Stock Exchange in 1995. According to the *Financial Times*, Moss has an image of a 'bumbling professor', spilling coffee and tripping over telephone cords. He does not travel overseas much, preferring to stay in Sydney, and he works short hours by investment banker standards, 8.30 a.m. to 7.30 p.m.

Moss describes the bank's culture as one of 'freedom within boundaries'. For him, Macquarie is a federation of businesses in which entrepreneurs can thrive: 'we provide the infrastructure, the capital, the brand and a controlled framework – and the staff provide the ideas'. The culture is very competitive internally, with colleagues pitching for 'mandates' (the responsibility for a bit of business) against each other. One former banker observed: 'Walking into Macquarie is like walking into a Turkish bazaar. Everyone has the same rug and they're all competing to sell the same rug.' In fact, though, the internal competition produces highly innovative ideas – for

example, the proposal that the bank should provide financing for patients' operations, including cosmetic surgery such as breast implants. The rule-of-thumb guiding promotion to one of the coveted – and lucrative – 250 executive directorships has been generating an annual profit personally of $5m (Australian; ~€3.5m or ~US$4.5m). The company receives 70,000 un-solicited CVs from would-be Macquarie bankers every year. All hires go through the same distinctive and rigorous psychological testing process.

Of course, some doubt whether Macquarie's successful run can go on for ever. The *Financial Times* quoted one close observer of Macquarie: 'I am starting to detect some hubris at the bank. It has done so well it is inevitable. Allan [Moss] is loyal to those he trusts and only time will tell whether he is trusting his lieutenants a bit too much.' In 2008, Moss retired. His successor as CEO, Nicholas Moore, announced: 'I have been here for 22 years and have grown up with this organisation. I have seen the culture and organisation work year in, year out. I think we have a winning formula.'

The new CEO had to deal with the banking crisis. Macquarie's shares slid from $66 Aus in May 2008 to less than $16 at the bottom of the crisis in March 2009. By early 2010 Macquarie was back at $55, but the gloss had certainly come off the millionaires' factory by then.

Sources: Financial Times, 17 December 2005, 28 May 2008; *Sydney Morning Herald*, 19 August 2006.

Questions

1 In this account, what control systems are particularly important to Macquarie?

2 What threats are there to these systems?

- The *strategic planning* style is the archetypal planning system, hence its name. In the Goold and Campbell sense, the strategic planning style combines both a strong planning influence on strategic direction from the corporate centre with relatively relaxed performance accountability for the business units. The logic is that if the centre sets the strategic direction, business unit managers should not be held strictly accountable for disappointing results that might be due to an inappropriate plan in the first place. In the strategic planning style, the centre focuses on inputs in terms of allocating resources necessary to achieve the strategic plan, while exercising a high degree of direct control over how the plan is executed by the businesses.

- The *financial control* style involves very little central planning. The business units each set their own strategic plans, probably after some negotiation with the corporate centre, and are then held strictly accountable for the results against these plans. This style differs from the strategic planning style in that control is against financial outputs, similar to a performance targeting system. If the businesses devised the plans, then they should take full responsibility for success or failure. Business unit managers in the financial control style have a lot of autonomy and typically receive high bonus payments for success. But failure may easily lead to dismissal. The financial planning style fits with the portfolio manager or restructurer roles of the corporate centre referred to in Chapter 7.

- The *strategic control* style is in the middle, with a more consensual development of the strategic plan between the corporate centre and the business units and moderate levels of business unit accountability. Under the strategic control style, the centre will typically act as coach to its business unit managers, helping them to see and seize opportunities in a supportive manner. This style often relies on strong cultural systems to foster trust and mutual understanding. Thus the strategic control style is often associated with the synergy manager or parental developer roles of the corporate centre discussed in Chapter 7.

Thus the three strategy styles vary with regard to their reliance on, and application of, planning systems. The direct control of inputs characteristic of the strategic planning style is only appropriate in certain circumstances. In particular, it makes sense where there are large, risky and long-range investments to be allocated: for example, an oil company typically has to take the decision to invest in the ten-year development of an oilfield at the corporate centre, rather than risk delegating it to business units whose resources and time-horizons may be limited. On the other hand, the financial control style is suitable where investments are small, relatively frequent and well understood, as typically in a mature, non-capital-intensive business. The strategic control style is suitable where there are opportunities for collaborating across businesses and there is a need to nurture new ones.

The strategic planning style (not the practice of strategic planning in general) has become less common in the private sector in recent years. The style is seen as too rigid to adapt to changing circumstances and too top-down to reflect real business circumstances on the ground. However, it is important to recognise the internal consistency of all three styles, including strategic planning. Each achieves logical combinations of accountability and strategic influence. Problems occur when organisations construct systems of planning and accountability that depart substantially from the diagonal line in Figure 13.7. Too far below the line (the 'south-west' corner) implies an excessively relaxed combination of weak direction from the centre and low accountability for the businesses. Too far above the diagonal line (the 'north-east' corner) implies a harsh combination of strong direction from the centre and strict accountability in the businesses. In the 'north-east' corner, business managers are held accountable even for mistakes that may have their origins in the centre's own plans.

(13.4) CONFIGURATIONS

The introduction of this chapter introduced the concept of configurations. **Configurations are the set of organisational design elements that interlink together in order to support the intended strategy.** Figure 13.1 focused on the mutually supporting elements of strategy, structure and systems. This section begins by extending these three elements with the McKinsey 7-S framework and finishes by considering likely tensions or dilemmas amongst the elements of organisational design and some methods for managing them.

13.4.1 The McKinsey 7-S framework

The McKinsey & Co consulting company has developed a framework for assessing the degree to which the various elements of an organisation's design fit together in a mutually supporting manner. **The McKinsey 7-S framework highlights the importance of fit between strategy, structure, systems, staff, style, skills and superordinate goals.**[21] Together these seven elements can serve as a checklist in any organisational design exercise: see Figure 13.8.

This chapter has already addressed strategy, structure and systems. This section will comment on the remaining four elements of the 7-S framework, as follows:

Figure 13.8 The McKinsey 7 Ss

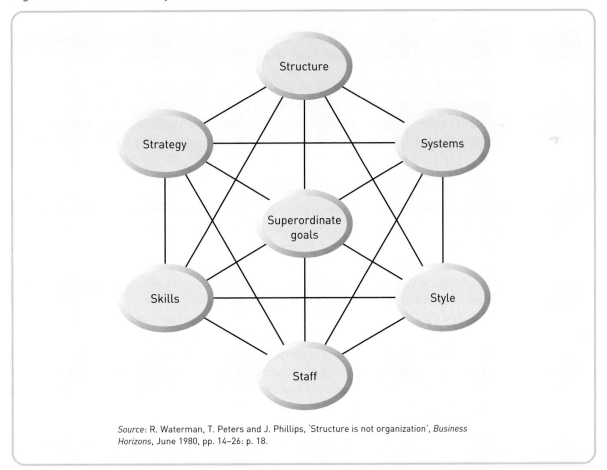

Source: R. Waterman, T. Peters and J. Phillips, 'Structure is not organization', *Business Horizons*, June 1980, pp. 14–26: p. 18.

- *Style* here refers to the leadership style of top managers in an organisation. Leadership styles may be collaborative, participative, directive or coercive, for instance (see Chapter 14). Managers' behavioural style can influence the culture of the whole organisation (see Chapter 5). The style should fit other aspects of the 7-S framework: for example, a highly directive or coercive style is not likely to fit a matrix organisation structure, as in the case of Durk Jager at Procter & Gamble (see Illustration 13.2).

- *Staff* is about the kinds of people in the organisation and how they are developed. This relates to systems of recruitment, socialisation and reward (section 13.3.2). A key criterion for the feasibility of any strategy is: does the organisation have the people to match (see section 11.4.2)? A common constraint on structural change is the availability of the right people to head new departments and divisions (the 'People Test': see 13.2.6).

- *Skills* relates to staff, but in the 7-S framework refers more broadly to capabilities in general (see Chapter 3). The concept of capabilities here raises not only staff skills but also issues to do with how these skills are embedded in and captured by the organisation as a whole. For example, how do the organisation's training schemes, information technology and reward systems transform the talents of individuals into the organisational capabilities required by the strategy?

- *Superordinate goals* refers to the overarching goals or purpose of the organisation as a whole, in other words the mission, vision and objectives that form the organisational purpose (see Chapter 4). Superordinate goals are placed at the centre of the 7-S framework: all other elements should support these.

The McKinsey 7-S framework highlights at least three aspects of organising. First, organising involves a lot more than just getting the organisational structure right; there are many other elements to attend to. Second, the 7-S framework emphasises fit between all these elements: everything from structure to skills needs to be connected together. Third, if managers change one element of the 7-S, the concept of fit suggests they are likely to have to change all the other elements as well in order to keep them all appropriately aligned to each other. Changing one element in isolation is liable to make things worse until overall fit is restored.

13.4.2 Configuration dilemmas

Although the concept of configurations and the 7-S framework emphasise the importance of mutual fit between elements, in practice this is often hard to achieve. Managing typically involves trade-offs and tensions between different desirable states. Seeking perfect solutions on one element of the configuration may very well oblige compromises on another element. Given that many of these tensions are very hard to escape, this section briefly considers various ways in which they can at least be managed.

Figure 13.9 summarises five key dilemmas in organising. First, formal hierarchies are often necessary to ensure control and action, but they can sit uneasily with the informal networks that foster knowledge exchange and innovation. Second, vertical accountability promotes maximum performance by subordinates, but it can easily lead managers to maximise their own self-interest, at the expense of horizontal relationships. Third, empowering employees lower down the organisation gives scope for potentially valuable initiatives and experiments, but over the long term can lead to incoherence. Fourth, while centralisation might be needed for standardisation of products and processes, this can be at the cost of the initiative and flexibility fostered by decentralisation. Finally, adopting best practice on a particular element

Figure 13.9 Some dilemmas in organising for success

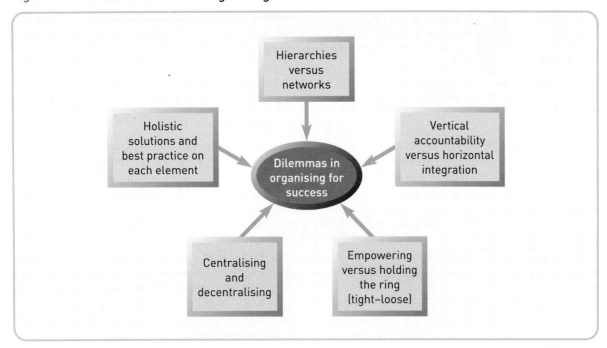

of the organisation, for instance financial controls, may actually be damaging if it does not fit with the needs of the organisation as a whole.

Managers should recognise that any organisational design is likely to face dilemmas of these kinds and that it is hard to optimise on all dimensions. However, they may be able to manage these dilemmas in three ways:

- By *subdividing* the organisation, so that the one part of the organisation is organised optimally according to one side of these dilemmas, while the rest responds to the other. Thus, for example, IBM created its revolutionary personal computer in a specialised new-venture division, kept separate from the traditional mainframe activities which were dominated by principles of hierarchy and vertical accountability highly antagonistic to radical innovation.[22]

- By *combining* different organising principles at the same time. Thus organisation design expert Jay Galbraith argues for the potential of 'hybrid structures': for instance, a 'front–back' structure combines centralised functional specialisms in manufacturing and research at the 'back', while customer-facing units at the front are organised in a more decentralised way around particular market segments, such as industry or geography.[23]

- By *reorganising* frequently so that no one side of the dilemma can become too entrenched. The rate of major reorganisation for large UK companies increased from once every four years to once every three years in the last decade.[24] Given this pace of reorganising, many organisations are like pendulums, constantly swinging between centralisation and devolution, for example, without resting long on one side or the other.[25]

A final dilemma arising from the interconnectedness of configurations is which element drives the others. The extent to which strategic elements drive structural elements is the subject of the Key Debate.

KEY DEBATE

Does structure follow strategy?

A key message of this chapter is that strategy and structure should fit together. But which determines which?

Alfred Chandler, Professor of Business History at Harvard Business School, proposed one of the fundamental rules of strategic management: 'unless structure follows strategy, inefficiency results'.[1] This logical sequence fits the 'design lens' for strategy, but does assume that structure is very much subordinate to strategy: structure can easily be fixed once the big strategic decisions are made. But some authors warn that this dangerously underestimates structure's role. Sometimes strategy follows structure.

Chandler's rule is based on the historical experience of companies like General Motors, Exxon and DuPont. DuPont, for example, was originally an explosives company. During the First World War, however, the company anticipated the peace by deliberately diversifying out of explosives into new civil markets such as plastics and paints. Yet the end of the war plunged DuPont into crisis. All its new businesses were loss-making; only explosives still made money. The problem was not the diversification strategy, but the structure that DuPont used to manage the new civil businesses. DuPont had retained its old functional structure, so that responsibilities for the production and marketing of all the new businesses were still centralised on single functional heads. They could not cope with the increased diversity. The solution was not to abandon the diversification strategy; rather it was to adopt a new structure with decentralised divisions for each of the separate businesses. DuPont thrives today with a variant of this multidivisional structure.

Hall and Saias accept the importance of strategy for structure but warn that the causality can go the other way.[2] An organisation's existing structure very much determines the kinds of strategic opportunities that its management will see and want to grasp. For instance, it is easy for a company with a decentralised multidivisional structure to make acquisitions and divestments: all it has to do is add or subtract divisions, with few ramifications for the rest of the business. On the other hand, it can be very hard for the top managers of a decentralised multidivisional organisation to see opportunities for innovation and knowledge-sharing within the operations of the divisions: they are too far away from the real business. In other words, structures can shape strategies.

Amburgey and Dacin tested the relative impact of strategy and structure on each other by analysing the strategic and structural changes of more than 200 American corporations over nearly thirty years.[3] They found that moves towards decentralised structures were often followed by moves towards increasingly diversified strategies: here, structure was determining strategy. Overall, however, increased diversification was twice as likely to be followed by structural decentralisation as the other way round. In other words, structure does follow strategy, but only most of the time.

Henry Mintzberg concludes that 'structure follows strategy as the left foot follows the right'.[4] In other words, strategy and structure are related reciprocally rather than just one way. Mintzberg warns that a simple 'design' approach to strategy and structure can be misleading. Structure is not always easy to fix after the big strategic decisions have been made. Strategists should check to see that their existing structures are not constraining the kinds of strategies that they consider.

References:
1. A. Chandler, *Strategy and Structure: Chapters in the History of American Enterprise*, MIT Press, 1962, p. 314.
2. D.J. Hall and M.A. Saias, 'Strategy follows structure!', *Strategic Management Journal*, vol. 1, no. 2 (1980), pp. 149–63.
3. T. Amburgey and T. Dacin, 'As the left foot follows the right? The dynamics of strategic and structural change', *Academy of Management Journal*, vol. 37, no. 6 (1994), pp. 1427–52.
4. H. Mintzberg, 'The Design School: reconsidering the basic premises of strategic management', *Strategic Management Journal*, vol. 11 (1990), pp. 171–95.

Question

Hall and Saias suggest that organisational structures can influence the kinds of strategies that management teams will pursue. What kinds of organisations might be particularly susceptible to structural constraints on their strategies?

SUMMARY

- Successful organising means responding to the key challenges facing the organisation. This chapter has stressed control, change, knowledge and internationalisation.

- There are many *structural types* (e.g. functional, divisional, matrix, transnational and project). Each structural type has its own strengths and weaknesses and responds differently to the challenges of control, change, knowledge and internationalisation.

- There is a range of different organisational *systems* to facilitate and control strategy. These systems can focus on either inputs or outputs and be direct or indirect.

- The separate organisational elements, summarised in the *McKinsey 7-S framework*, should come together to form a coherent *reinforcing configuration*. But these reinforcing cycles also raise tough dilemmas that can be managed by *subdividing*, *combining* and *reorganising*.

WORK ASSIGNMENTS

✱ *Denotes more advanced work assignments.* * *Refers to a case study in the Text and Cases edition.*

13.1 Go to the website of a large organisation you are familiar with and find its organisational chart (not all organisations provide these). Why is the organisation structured like this?

13.2 Referring to section 13.2.2 on the multidivisional structure, consider the advantages and disadvantages of creating divisions along different lines – such as product, geography or technology – with respect to a large organisation you are familiar with or a case organisation such as CRH*, SABMiller* or Sony*.

13.3✱ Referring to Figure 13.6, write a short executive brief explaining how strategy maps could be a useful management system to monitor and control the performance of organisational units. Be sure to analyse both advantages and disadvantages of this approach.

13.4 As a middle manager with responsibility for a small business unit, which 'strategy style' (section 13.3.5) would you prefer to work within? In what sort of circumstances or corporate organisation would this style not work so well for you?

Integrative Assignment

13.5 Take a recent merger or acquisition (see Chapter 10), ideally one involving two organisations of roughly equal size, and analyse how the deal has changed the acquiring or merged company's organisational structure. What do you conclude from the extent or lack of structural change for the new company going forward?

RECOMMENDED KEY READINGS

- The best single coverage of this chapter's issues is in R. Daft, *Understanding the Theory and Design of Organizations*, South-Western, 2009.

- For a collection of relevant articles, see the special issue 'Learning to design organizations', R. Dunbar and W. Starbuck (eds), *Organization Science*, vol. 17, no. 2 (2006).

- M. Goold and A. Campbell, *Designing Effective Organizations*, Jossey-Bass, 2002, provides a practical guide to organisational design issues.

REFERENCES

1. A good review of new and old structural types can be found in G. Friesen, 'Organisation design for the 21st century', *Consulting to Management – C2M*, vol. 16, no. 3 (2005), pp. 32–51.

2. The view that organisations should fit their structures to key challenges ('contingencies') is associated with the long tradition of research on contingency theory: see L. Donaldson, *The Contingency Theory of Organizations*, Sage, 2001, or R. Whittington, 'Organizational structure', in *The Oxford Handbook of Strategy*, Volume II, Oxford University Press, 2003, Chapter 28, for summaries.

3. This view of divisionalisation as a response to diversity was originally put forward by A.D. Chandler, *Strategy and Structure*, MIT Press, 1962. See R. Whittington and M. Mayer, *The European Corporation: Strategy, Structure and Social Science*, Oxford University Press, 2000, for a summary of Chandler's argument and the success of divisional organisations in contemporary Europe.

4. For a review of current experience with matrix structures, see S. Thomas and L. D'Annunzio, 'Challenges and strategies of matrix organisations: top-level and mid-level managers' perspectives', *Human Resource Planning*, vol. 28, no. 1 (2005), pp. 39–48, and J. Galbraith, *Designing Matrix Structures that Actually Work*, Jossey-Bass, 2009.

5. See C. Bartlett and S. Ghoshal, 'Matrix management: not a structure, more a frame of mind', *Harvard Business Review*, vol. 68, no. 4 (1990), pp. 138–45.

6. C. Bartlett and S. Ghoshal, *Managing across Borders*, 2nd edition, Harvard Business School Press, 2008.

7. Recent research finds that transnational structures generally perform better than either centralised or decentralised structures: see J.-N. Garbe and N. Richter, 'Causal analysis of the internationalization and performance relationship based on neural networks', *Journal of International Management*, vol. 15, no. 4 (2009), pp. 413–31.

8. The classic article on project-based organisations is by R. DeFillippi and M. Arthur, 'Paradox in project-based enterprise: the case of film-making', *California Management Review*, vol. 40, no. 2 (1998), pp. 125–45. For some difficulties, see M. Bresnen, A. Goussevskaia and J. Swann, 'Organisational routines, situated learning and processes of change in project-based organizations', *Project Management Journal*, vol. 36, no. 3 (2005), pp. 27–42.

9. For a discussion of more permanent team structures, see Thomas Mullern, 'Integrating the team-based structure in the business process: the case of Saab training systems', in A. Pettigrew and E. Fenton (eds), *The Innovating Organization*, Sage, 2000.

10. M. Goold and A. Campbell, *Designing Effective Organizations*, Jossey-Bass, 2002. See also M. Goold and A. Campbell, 'Do you have a well-designed organization?', *Harvard Business Review*, vol. 80, no. 3 (2002), pp. 117–224.

11. A.D. Chandler, *Strategy and Structure: Chapters in the History of American Enterprise*, MIT Press, 1962.

12. This practice of 'patching' parts of the organisation on to each other according to changing market needs is described in K. Eisenhardt and S. Brown, 'Patching: restitching business portfolios in dynamic markets', *Harvard Business Review*, vol. 25, no. 3 (1999), pp. 72–80.

13. The point has been argued by E. Fenton and A. Pettigrew, 'Theoretical perspectives on new forms of organizing', in A. Pettigrew and E. Fenton (eds), *The Innovating Organization*, Sage, 2000, Chapter 1.

14. C. Casey, 'Come, join our family: discipline and integration in corporate organizational culture, *Human Relations*, vol. 52, no. 2 (1999), pp. 155–79; for an account of the socialisation of graduate trainees, see A.D. Brown and C. Coupland, 'Sounds of silence: graduate trainees, hegemony and resistance', *Organization Studies*, vol. 26, no. 7 (2005), pp. 1049–70.

15. E.C. Wenger and W.M. Snyder, 'Communities of practice: the organized frontier', *Harvard Business Review*, vol. 78, no. 1 (2000), pp. 139–46.

16. D. Helm and T. Jenkinson, *Competition in Regulated Industries*, Clarendon Press, 1999, provides a number of in-depth case studies of competitive implications of deregulation.

17. The value of goals and performance targets has been debated vigorously: see L. Ordonez, M. Schweitzer, A Galinksy and M. Bazerman, 'Goals gone wild: the systematic side effects of overprescribing goal setting', *Academy of Management Perspectives*, vol. 23, no. 1 (2009), pp. 6–16 and E. Locke and G. Latham, 'Has goal setting gone wild?', *Academy of Management Perspectives*, vol. 23, no. 1 (2009), pp. 17–23.

18. See R. Kaplan and D. Norton, 'Having trouble with your strategy? Then map it', *Harvard Business Review*, vol. 78, no. 5 (2000), pp. 167–76 and R. Kaplan and D. Norton, *Alignment: How to Apply the Balanced Scorecard to Strategy*, Harvard Business School Press, 2006.

19. Companies like Royal Dutch Shell have been experimenting with internal markets to stimulate innovation. See Gary Hamel, 'Bringing Silicon Valley inside', *Harvard Business Review*, vol. 77, no. 5 (1999), pp. 70–84. For a discussion of internal market challenges, see A. Vining, 'Internal market failure', *Journal of Management Studies*, vol. 40, no. 2 (2003), pp. 431–57.

20. M. Goold and A. Campbell, *Strategies and Styles*, Blackwell, 1987.

21. R. Waterman, T. Peters and J. Phillips, 'Structure is not organization', *Business Horizons*, June 1980, pp. 14–26.

22. R.A. Burgelman, 'Managing the new venture division: implications for strategic management', *Strategic Management Journal*, vol. 6, no. 1 (1985), pp. 39–54.

23. J. Galbraith, 'Organizing to deliver solutions', *Organisational Dynamics*, vol. 31, no. 2 (2002), pp. 194–207.

24. R. Whittington and M. Mayer, *Organising for Success: A Report on Knowledge*, CIPD, 2002.

25. For an analysis of this process at a leading pharmaceutical firm, see S. Karim and W. Mitchell, 'Innovating through acquisition and internal development: a quarter-century of boundary evolution at Johnson & Johnson', *Long Range Planning*, vol. 37, no. 6 (2004), pp. 525–38.

Hurricane Katrina: human-made disaster?

Introduction

Early on Monday morning, 29 August 2005, Hurricane Katrina struck the southern American state of Louisiana, rushing quickly inland to the city of New Orleans. With wind speeds at 125 miles per hour (200 km/h), the levees (dykes) protecting the city collapsed in several places. Over the next few days, the world watched in horror as New Orleans and the surrounding areas struggled with chaos. Hurricane Katrina claimed 1,836 lives and left vivid images of bodies floating in the streets, families stranded on rooftops and 25,000 hungry and thirsty people trapped for days in the notorious Superdome. Six months after the hurricane, more than half of New Orleans' population had still not returned to the city.

Ultimately, of course, the destruction wrought by Hurricane Katrina had natural causes. But there is every sign that the damage and suffering were significantly increased by organisational failures. The disaster of Hurricane Katrina was partly a consequence of organisational design.

A new organisation

The government organisation ultimately responsible for coordinating the response to Katrina was the US Department of Homeland Security. This itself was a recent creation, a reaction to the terrorist attacks of September 11, 2001. One finding from investigations into the circumstances surrounding 9/11 was the difficulty of coordinating all the information regarding terrorist threats. For example, before the attacks, a flight training school had alerted local authorities about a student who only seemed interested in learning how to fly civil airliners, not about how to take off or land. But the information had not been passed on to the Federal Bureau of Investigations (FBI): the student went on to be one of the terrorist hijackers involved in 9/11.

The US government responded to 9/11 by placing terrorism as the highest priority. It believed that one way of improving coordination in response to potential terror threats was by centralising relevant government

Source: Reuters/Robert Galbraith.

departments. Nine days after the 9/11 attack, President Bush appointed Pennsylvania Governor and decorated Vietnam veteran Tom Ridge to create and head a new department. The White House vetoed some of Tom Ridge's more radical proposals, so that both the Justice Department and the FBI remained independent. However, finally 22 departments were swept together in 2002 to create the new Department for Homeland Security (see Figure 1 for an organisational chart).

Involving more than 180,000 employees, this was the biggest reorganisation of the US government since the creation of the Pentagon in 1947. Amongst the major agencies that were gathered together under Tom Ridge's command were Customs, Immigration, Narcotics, the Coast Guard, the Secret Service and, most important here, the Federal Emergency Management Agency (FEMA). All were to unite in the fight against terrorism. As the head of the US Customs Service said: 'Terrorism is our highest priority, bar none. Ninety eight per cent of my attention . . . has been devoted to that one issue.' Tom Ridge anticipated turf battles between the newly amalgamated agencies but declared: 'The only turf we should be worried about protecting is the turf we stand on.'

FEMA, however, resisted the reorganisation. Responsible for responding to natural disasters such as hurricanes or earthquakes, FEMA had since 1993 been represented directly inside the President's Cabinet.

Figure 1 Department of Homeland Security organisation chart

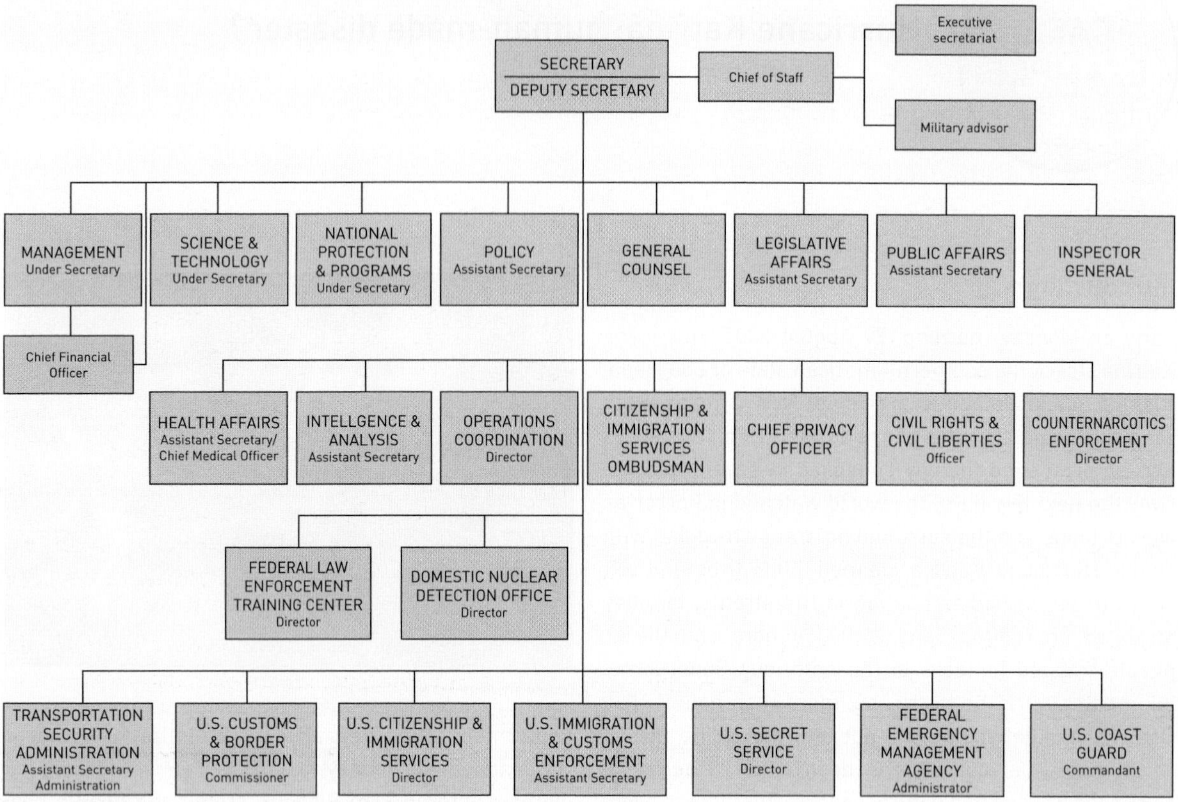

Source: http://www.dhs.gov/xabout/structure/editorial_0644.shtm.

Merger within the new Department of Homeland Security relegated FEMA to a mere internal division, with no direct Cabinet-level representation. FEMA's then head protested to the President's chief of staff: 'I told him it was a big mistake. The fact that FEMA could report to the President, any President – Democrat, Republican or independent – was what made the agency effective.' In the wake of 9/11, of course, this sounded like special pleading.

Within the new organisation, response to natural disasters had a low priority. In 2004, the Department drew up a list of 15 planning scenarios, doomsday events that could cause major fatalities. Twelve of these involved shadowy international terrorist groups, with plots involving mustard gas, sarin, nuclear weapons and anthrax, amongst other imaginative possibilities. One planning scenario did raise the threat of a hurricane flooding a nameless southern city and causing more than a thousand deaths. But terror attacks held the attention and these attracted the budgets.

Resources for protection against natural disasters began to get squeezed. Tom Ridge retired and was replaced by a new Secretary for Homeland Security,

Michael Chertoff, a former judge. Various FEMA functions were stripped off and reallocated to other parts of the reorganisation. FEMA lost $80m (~€56m) from its $550m operating budget. It struggled to get resources for rehearsing a response to a New Orleans hurricane scenario, and when it did do so, funds were denied for a follow-up. Between 2000 and 2005, the budget for the New Orleans Engineering Corps, responsible for the levees protecting the city, was cut by 44 per cent. Meanwhile, the Ohio Fire Service was able to get funds for bulletproof vests to protect their dogs in the event of terrorist attack.

Testing the new organisation

Hurricane Katrina gave several days' notice, forming over the Bahamas on 23 August and sweeping over Florida two days later. Early on Saturday morning, 27 August, a FEMA watch officer posted a warning of a severe hurricane threat to the New Orleans area, capable of causing thousands of fatalities. Michael Chertoff was at home that day, working on immigration issues. On Saturday night, New Orleans Mayor Ray Nagin ordered an evacuation of the city's 400,000 citizens. But, with no certainty that the hurricane would actually hit, and with what force, not everybody wanted to leave their homes for fear of looting. Moreover, many had no means of transport, including tragically many old people who were to be trapped without power in their nursing homes. When the hurricane struck on the Monday morning, 60,000 people were still in New Orleans.

The city was not ready. FEMA's planning for the state of Louisiana as a whole had called for 69 truckloads of water, 69 truckloads of ice and 34 truckloads of food to be in place. It planned for 400 buses and 800 drivers to ferry people to shelters. On the Sunday, FEMA had just 30 truckloads of water, 17 truckloads of ice and 15 truckloads of meals. FEMA had no buses in the state at all.

FEMA had got one officer into the city on the Sunday, but was otherwise not represented locally. When the flooding started, communications broke down. The various services had different communications systems, and the batteries on mobile devices soon ran down, with no power available to recharge. FEMA's high-tech communications wagon only reached New Orleans on the Friday (long after the world's journalists) and in the meantime Mayor Nagin's team had broken into an Office Depot store in order to steal functioning communications equipment. The sole FEMA officer on the ground had to bully his way onto one of the few helicopters available to confirm the broken levees on the first day. The Department of Homeland Security operations centre in Washington, guarding against panic responses, insisted on verification by a second source before passing the message up the chain, but no second source was available. Secretary Chertoff briefed President Bush about immigration issues on Monday morning, and made no mention of the hurricane.

The Department of Homeland Security struggled to cope over the following days. Michael Brown, FEMA's Head, flew to nearby Baton Rouge, but suffered from poor communications and found himself increasingly bypassed by Department Head Michael Chertoff in Washington. The evacuation of the Superdome only began on the Friday, after the instigation of food rationing, and the Washington operations centre overlooked 20,000 refugees at the New Orleans Convention Center for several days, thinking it the same building as the Superdome. Aircraft were delayed because of the lack of air marshals required by anti-terrorist regulations. The Department of Homeland Security insisted that all evacuees would have to be security screened before being allowed on planes, and then took eight hours to fly in security staff. A large consignment of food packs from the United Kingdom was turned away because of fears of Mad Cow Disease.

At a Thursday press conference in Washington, Michael Chertoff praised 'the genius of the people at FEMA' in their response to the disaster. 'I think it is a source of tremendous pride to me to work with the people who've pulled off this really exceptional response.' But television reports direct from New Orleans contradicted this picture every hour. The failure of FEMA, and of local agencies, was becoming very apparent. Facing heavy criticism, FEMA's head, Michael Brown, resigned on 13 September. Michael Chertoff kept his job.

Sources: C. Cooper and R. Block, *Disaster: Hurricane Katrina and the Failure of Homeland Security*, Times Books, 2006; and I. Daaddler and I. Destler, 'Advisors, Czars and Councils', *The National Interest*, 1 July (2002).

Questions

1 What was the 'strategy' of the Department of Homeland Security in the period immediately before Hurricane Katrina?

2 In the light of this strategy, what, if any, changes should be made to the Department's organisational structure after Hurricane Katrina?

3 Who was responsible for the organisational failures surrounding the response to Hurricane Katrina?

14

LEADERSHIP AND STRATEGIC CHANGE

Learning outcomes

After reading this chapter you should be able to:

● Identify *types* of required strategic change.

● Analyse how *organisational context* might affect the design of strategic change programmes.

● Undertake a *forcefield analysis* to identify forces blocking and facilitating change.

● Identify and assess the different styles of leading and managing strategic change.

● Assess the value of different *levers* for strategic change.

● Identify the pitfalls and problems of *managing change programmes*.

Key terms

Coercion p. 475

Collaboration p. 474

Direction p. 475

Education p. 473

Forcefield analysis p. 469

Leadership p. 471

Participation p. 475

Situational leadership p. 473

Symbols p. 481

Turnaround strategy p. 484

(14.1) INTRODUCTION

David Brandon took over as CEO of Domino's Pizza after a period of little change. He introduced himself to his management team as follows: 'If you are the kind of people and type of organisation that loves change, that believes change is good, change is exciting and embracing change is something that you really want to get good at and want to do, then you are going to love me. If you are the kind of person who wants things always to be the way they have been and you want to sit around and talk about the good old days, then I am not your guy, because truthfully I am here to create better days and that is going to require change'.[1] Harvard's John Kotter makes this distinction: 'Management is about coping with complexity . . . without good management complex enterprises tend to become chaotic . . . Leadership, by contrast is about coping with change'.[2] Clearly David Brandon saw himself as a leader of change.

Strategic change is inherent in much of this part of the book. Chapter 11 posed questions about the feasibility of strategies; could they work in practice? Chapter 12 provided different explanations of how strategies develop. Chapter 13 addressed issues to do with organising

Figure 14.1 Key elements in managing strategic change

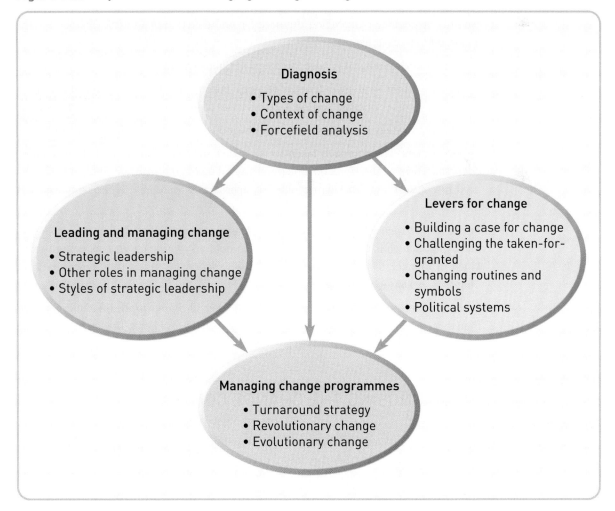

to deliver strategies. These considerations are all important in managing strategic change. However, central to strategic change is ensuring that people make a strategy happen. This chapter is about how managers can lead people to effect strategic change. This leadership role is most often associated with chief executives, but, in fact, it may occur at different levels in organisations: other senior managers and middle managers too may take leadership roles in change.

Figure 14.1 provides a structure for the chapter. Section 14.2 begins by explaining important issues that need to be considered in *diagnosing the context* an organisation faces when embarking on strategic change, in terms of the *types of change* required, the variety of *contextual factors* that need to be taken into account, and the *forces blocking or facilitating change*. Section 14.3 discusses the management of strategic change in terms of the roles played by *leaders of strategic change*. It then goes on to explain how *styles of change leadership* need to align with the context of change. Section 14.4 then reviews *levers for change,* including the need to build a compelling *case for change*, to *challenge the taken for granted*, change organisational *routines, systems and symbols*, the role of *political activity*, and more specific *change tactics*. Section 14.5 draws all this together by considering what overall lessons can be drawn about *managing change programmes*.

In doing this the chapter builds on four key premises:

- *Strategy matters.* What has been written in Parts I and II of the book should be seen as an essential precursor in identifying the need for and direction of strategic change. So it is important to be clear about:

  - Why strategic change is needed (discussed in Chapters 2 to 5).

  - The bases of the strategy in terms of strategic purpose, perhaps encapsulated in a statement of vision or mission (section 4.2) and bases of competitive advantage (Chapter 6).

  - What the strategy is in terms of strategy directions and methods (Chapters 7 to 10).

- *Context matters.* The approach taken to managing strategic change needs to be *context-dependent*. There is, therefore, no 'one right way' of managing strategic change. Managers need to consider how to balance different approaches according to the circumstances they face.

- *Inertia* and *resistance* to change are likely. Managers report that the major problem in managing change is the tendency of people to hold on to existing ways of doing things. Much of Chapter 5 and the discussion of the Experience Lens in the Commentary on Chapter 1 explain why this is so.

- *Leadership matters.* This does not mean that leadership of change is always and exclusively from the top of an organisation – though such leadership does matter. Leadership of change needs to happen at different levels in an organisation.

KEY CONCEPT

Strategic change context

14.2 DIAGNOSING THE CHANGE CONTEXT

How change is managed will depend on the magnitude of the challenge faced in trying to effect strategic change. It is therefore useful to consider the *type* of change required, the wider *context* in which change is to occur, the specific *blockages* to change that exist and forces that exist to *facilitate* the change process.

Figure 14.2 Types of change

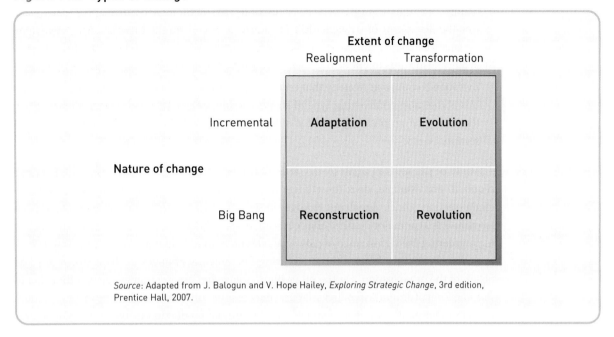

Source: Adapted from J. Balogun and V. Hope Hailey, *Exploring Strategic Change*, 3rd edition, Prentice Hall, 2007.

14.2.1 Types of strategic change

KEY CONCEPT

Types of strategic change

As shown in Chapter 5 (section 5.2.1) and 12 (section 12.3), strategy development is often *incremental* in nature. It builds on rather than fundamentally changes prior strategy. More fundamental change is less common. Balogun and Hope Hailey[3] develop this insight further to identify four types of strategic change (see Figure 14.2), and these have implications for how change might be managed.

The axes in Figure 14.2 are concerned with (a) the extent of change and (b) the nature of change. In terms of the *extent* of change, the question is whether change can occur in line with the current business model and within the current culture as a *realignment* of strategy? Or does it require significant culture change; in effect more *transformational* change? The nature of change is concerned with the speed at which it happens. Arguably, it is beneficial for change in an organisation to be *incremental* since this allows time to build on the skills, routines and beliefs of those in the organisation. However, if an organisation faces crisis or needs to change direction fast a '*big bang*' approach to change might be needed on occasion. Combining these two axes suggests four types of strategic change:

1 *Adaptation* is change that can be accommodated within the current culture and occur incrementally. It is the most common form of change in organisations.

2 *Reconstruction* is change that may be rapid and involve a good deal of upheaval in an organisation, but which does not fundamentally change the culture. It could be a *turnaround* situation where there is need for major structural changes or a major cost-cutting programme to deal with a decline in financial performance or difficult or changing market conditions. How this might be managed is discussed further in section 14.5.1 in this chapter.

3 *Revolution* is change that requires rapid and major strategic as well as culture change. This could be in circumstances where the strategy has been so bounded by the existing

culture that, even when environmental or competitive pressures might require fundamental change, the organisation has failed to respond. This might have occurred over many years (see the discussion of strategic drift in section 5.2) and resulted in circumstances where pressures for change are extreme – for example, a takeover threatens the continued existence of a firm. How this might be managed is discussed further in section 14.5.2.

4 *Evolution* is change in strategy that requires culture change, but over time. In some respects this is the most challenging type of strategic change since, for many in an organisation, there may be no pressing need for change. How this might be managed is discussed in section 14.5.3.

Many of the tools of analysis in Part I of the book can help identify the type of change required. For example, does the change require a substantial reconfiguration of the value chain (section 3.4.2), significant changes in the activities underpinning strategic capabilities (section 3.4.3) or major cultural change (section 5.4.6)? Care does, however, need to be taken in considering the significance of new strategies on required change. For example, a business may launch new products without requiring fundamental changes in the assumptions and beliefs of the organisation. On the other hand, some changes in strategy, even if they do not take the form of dramatic product changes, may require fundamental changes in core assumptions in the organisation. For example, the shift from a production focus for a manufacturer to a customer-led, service ethos may not entail product changes, but will very likely require significant culture change.

14.2.2 The importance of context

Leading change in a small entrepreneurial business, where a motivated team is driving change, would be quite different from trying to do so in a major corporation, or perhaps a long-established public-sector organisation, with set routines, formal structures and perhaps a great deal of resistance to change. So it is dangerous to assume that leading change effectively in one context is the same as in another. Moreover, an assumption that approaches to change are readily transferable between contexts may be risky. For example, many government departments in different parts of the world have sought to import change management practices from consultancies or by recruiting managers from commercial enterprises but have often found this problematic.[4] Illustration 14.1 gives an example of the contextual issues faced in trying to manage change in the UK Ministry of Defence (MOD).[5]

Approaches to leading change therefore need to be differ according to context.[6] Balogun and Hope Hailey's 'Change Kaleidoscope' builds on this point to identify contextual features to take into account in designing change programmes. Figure 14.3 summarises these.

Here are some examples of how the contextual features shown in Figure 14.3 might require different approaches to change:

- The *time* available for change could differ dramatically. A business may face immediate decline in turnover or profits from rapid changes in its markets. This is a quite different context for change compared with a business where the management may see the need for change coming in the future, perhaps years away, and have time to plan it carefully as a staged incremental process.

- The *scope* of change might differ either in terms of the *breadth* of change across an organisation or the *depth* of culture change required. The scope of change in an organisation such as

Figure 14.3 **The Change Kaleidoscope**

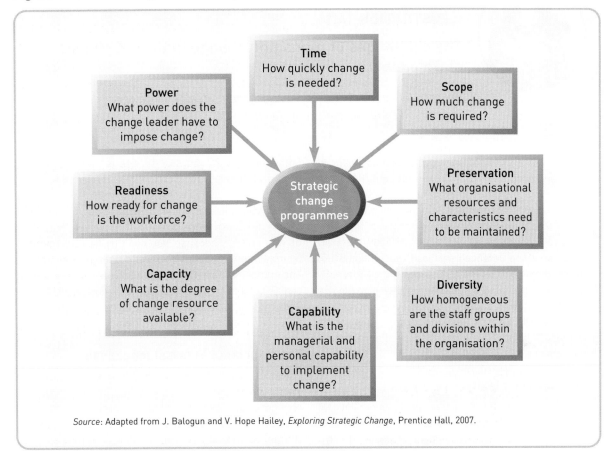

Source: Adapted from J. Balogun and V. Hope Hailey, *Exploring Strategic Change*, Prentice Hall, 2007.

the MOD in Illustration 14.1 is wholly different in terms of both breadth and depth than, for example, adaptive change in a successful small business and would be likely to be a much bigger challenge.

- *Preservation* of some aspects of an organisation may be needed: in particular capabilities on which changes need to be based. Suppose, for example, that a computer software business needs to become more formally organised because of its successful growth. This could well upset technical experts who have been used to a great deal of independence and ready access to senior management when it could be vital to preserve their expertise and motivation.

- A *diversity* of experience, views and opinions within an organisation may help the change process. However, if an organisation has followed a strategy for many decades, such continuity may have led to a very homogeneous way of seeing the world, which could hamper change. So gauging the nature and extent of diversity is important.

- Is there *capability* or experience of managing change in the organisation? There may be managers who have experience of leading change in the past, or a workforce that has been used to and has accepted past changes, whilst people in another organisation may have little experience of change.

- *Capacity* for change in terms of available resources will also be significant: change can be costly, not only in financial terms, but also in terms of management time.

ILLUSTRATION 14.1

The challenges of managing change in the UK Ministry of Defence

Understanding the challenge of managing strategic change requires an understanding of the context of change.

The UK Ministry of Defence (MOD) has found it difficult to make major changes. For example, in 2004, of the seven principles underpinning the recommendations of the Smart Procurement Initiative begun in 1998 only one was properly implemented and, of the other six, some hardly at all. Or, again, in 2000 the MOD established the Defence Logistics Organisation (DLO) to coordinate across the army, navy and air force. By 2005 it was accepted that this had stalled. Drawing on published studies and their own experience working with the MOD, Derrick Neal and Trevor Taylor, of the Defence Academy at Shrivenham, explain some of the reasons that existed in 2005.

Size and complexity

The MOD comprised 300,000 people of whom 200,000 were military personnel. It also relied on a further 300,000 people in its supply chain. Moreover it comprised many parts so: 'Change initiated in one part of the system runs into resistance and difficulty from arrangements elsewhere, or has implications for other parts of the system that were not foreseen by the original change initiators.' It is also difficult to change all the systems simultaneously.

Empowerment

The MOD cannot decide overall defence strategy since that is decided by politicians. However, there is significant autonomy within the MOD. There were 13 top-level budget holders (TLBs), within each of which there was then further delegation of responsibility. The result was some 36 defence agencies and below them 120 'integrated project teams'. When the MOD centre tries to generate change, locally empowered leaders often produce their own version of change programmes. In 2003 it was found that there were 150 uncoordinated change initiatives under way within the DLO.

Personnel systems

The MOD employs both military staff and civilian staff. Military staff expect to move locations frequently.

Someone with 35 years of service is likely to have moved 20 times. Time horizons are therefore short within a 'can do' culture. Those who wished to make a quick impact did so by initiating change but moving on before initiatives were completed. However, follow-up was unlikely because 'you don't make your name by implementing another officer's change initiative'. The number of 'fast-track' civil servants likely to hold a series of jobs in quick succession is much more limited; most are not expected to move regularly. So time horizons are different for them.

The reluctance to invest for change

The MOD viewed change as a 'budget-neutral activity': that it was necessary to make savings in order to fund change, rather than fund change in order to make savings. For example, it was only after the stalled DLO initiative that the MOD recognised the need for investment in that change programme and obtained funding from the Treasury to try and address it.

The lack of urgency

There was no feeling of crisis. Paradoxically, for people who often find themselves at serious risk, they see the institutions that surround them as secure and fixed. The only signal of required change was from the Treasury's financial initiatives, which may be seen as a threat.

Source: Based on D. Neal and T. Taylor, 'Spinning on dimes: the challenges of introducing transformational change into the UK Ministry of Defence', *Strategic Change*, vol. 15 (2006), pp. 15–22.

> ### Questions
>
> 1 Use the checklist of the Change Kaleidoscope in section 14.2.2 to identify the range of contextual issues that need to be taken into account in influencing change in the MOD.
>
> 2 What approach to change should be adopted to improve the MOD's ability to manage change?

- What is the *readiness* for change? Is there a felt need for change across the organisation, widespread resistance, or pockets or levels of resistance in some parts of the organisation and readiness in others?

- Who has the *power* to effect change? Often it is assumed that the chief executive has such power, but in the face of resistance from below, or perhaps resistance from external stakeholders, this may not be the case. It may also be that the chief executive supposes that others in the organisation have the power to effect change when they do not, or do not see themselves having it.

This consideration of context needs to be borne in mind throughout the rest of this chapter. It also raises an important overarching question: *is one-off change possible?* Does the organisation in question have the capacity, capability, readiness and power structures to achieve the scope of change required? For example, in a study of attempts to manage change in hospitals[7] it was found that their governance and organisational structures prevented any clear authority to manage change. This, combined with the resource constraints under which they laboured, meant that major one-off change initiatives were not likely to succeed. In such circumstances, it may be that the context needs to be changed before the strategic change itself can occur. For example, it could be that new managers with experience of leading change need to be introduced to enhance the capability and readiness for change and get the organisation to a point where it is ready to embark on a more significant strategic change programme. Or it may need to be recognised that change has to be managed in stages. The researchers in the hospital study reported above found that change tended to take place by one initiative making limited progress, then stalling, followed by a later one making further advances.

14.2.3 Forcefield analysis

A forcefield analysis **provides an initial view of change problems that need to be tackled by identifying forces for and against change**. It allows some key questions to be asked:

- What aspects of the current situation would block change, and how can these be overcome?
- What aspects of the current situation might aid change in the desired direction, and how might these be reinforced?
- What needs to be introduced or developed to aid change?

A forcefield analysis can be informed by many of the concepts and frameworks already introduced in the book. As explained above, for example, the Change Kaleidoscope can inform a forcefield analysis. But so too, for example, can the following:

- *Mapping activity systems* (section 3.4.3) can provide insights into aspects of the organisation that have provided the basis for an organisation's historical success. These may be a basis upon which future change might be built; or, again, may have taken form in ways of doing things that have ceased to be advantageous but are very difficult to change.

- *Stakeholder mapping* (section 4.5.2) can provide insight into the power of different stakeholders to promote change or to resist change.

- *The culture web* (see section 5.4.6) is a means of diagnosing organisational culture and therefore an understanding of the symbolic, routinised as well as structural and systemic factors that may be taken for granted and can act for or against change. It can also be used to envisage what the culture of an organisation would need to look like to deliver future strategy.[8]

ILLUSTRATION 14.2

A forcefield analysis for the UK Forestry Commission

A forcefield analysis can be used to identify aspects of the organisation that might aid change, blockages to change and what needs to be developed to aid change.

In the late 1990s the Forestry Commission in the UK was wrestling with significant strategic challenges. The collapse in world timber prices meant that alternative sources of income were needed. Additionally, the government's policy was to develop an emphasis on forestry for leisure and social inclusion, not just the production of timber. However, what emerged from a cultural web analysis was that the organisation's current culture raised problems over moving to such a future.

Foresters saw themselves as *the* forestry experts, which translated into an attitude of 'FC knows best', a tendency to see the forests as 'theirs' and the public as a 'nuisance', getting in the way of efficient timber production. There was also an ingrained public sector ethos – a sense of contributing to society rather than working for commercial gain. The command and control style of management had also led to a deference to senior management and there was the bureaucracy of a public sector organisation. It also took at least 50 years to grow trees: linked to this was a deep sense of tradition making the organisation conservative and slow to change.

Forcefield analysis was then used to consider what changes in culture would be needed if the Forestry Commission were to put more emphasis on 'forests for the community'. As well as identifying many barriers to change that needed to be removed, the forcefield analysis identified aspects of the culture that might facilitate change. These included the powerful support for change of the 'Director General', the commitment of employees to the organisation, the ethos of hard work and the potential flexibility, together with a desire from within the organisation to change the command and control culture. It was also possible to identify what might be added to this: for example, widespread participation in the change programme could help achieve ownership of future vision; and increased diversity of personnel together with a more inclusive management style with more listening and less telling could promote more innovation and commitment.

Source: Adapted from The Forestry Commission case study by Anne McCann.

Pushing →

- Hard work ethic that delivers results
- Commitment of employees
- Juggling priorities/potential flexibility
- Forestry know-how
- Encouragement/support of change from the top

Additional

- Encouragement to work in new ways
- Increased diversity of staff
- Clear articulation of a vision for the future
- Participation in the change process
- Skills development

← **Resisting**

- Traditional structure/ways of working
- Bureaucracy
- Departmental silos
- Homogeneous workforce
- Conservative/risk averse/slow to change
- Command and control management style
- Deference to senior staff
- Past experience of change was that nothing really changed

Questions

1 What might be some of the problems in managing changes indicated by the forcefield analysis?

2 Undertake a forcefield analysis for an organisation of your choice.

- *The 7-S framework* (section 13.4.1) can highlight aspects of the infrastructure of an organisation that may act to promote or block change.

As well as helping to identify the current forces acting for and against change, each of these frameworks can also be used to help think through what might be needed as additional forces to promote change. Illustration 14.2 shows how a forcefield analysis was used in the UK's Forestry Commission's strategic change programme.

 LEADING STRATEGIC CHANGE

This section of the chapter is concerned with the role people play in leading strategic change and how they do it. It begins by explaining how *leadership change roles* may exist in different parts and at different levels in an organisation. It then goes on to consider the different *styles of strategic leadership* that might be adopted and how these need to be aligned with different contexts of change.

14.3.1 Strategic leadership roles

Leadership is the process of influencing an organisation (or group within an organisation) in its efforts towards achieving an aim or goal.[9] Without effective leadership of strategic change the risk is that people in an organisation are unclear about its purpose or lack motivation to deliver it. Strategic leadership is therefore central to strategic change. There are three key roles that are especially significant in terms of leading strategic change:

- *Envisioning future strategy.*[10] The effective strategic leader needs to ensure there exists a clear and compelling vision of the future and communicate clearly a strategy to achieve that both internally and to external stakeholders. In the absence of top management doing this, those who attempt to lead change elsewhere in an organisation are likely to construct such a vision themselves. This may be well intentioned but can lead to confusion, highlighting the importance of overall clarity on the purpose of strategic change.

- *Aligning* the organisation to deliver that strategy.[11] This involves ensuring that people in the organisation are committed to the strategy, motivated to make the changes needed and empowered to deliver those changes. There is, then, a need for leaders to build and foster relationships of trust and respect across the organisation.[12] It may, however, also be necessary to change the management of the organisation to ensure such commitment, which is a reason that top teams often change as a precursor to or during strategic change.

- *Embodying change.* A strategic leader will be seen by others, not least those within the organisation, but also other stakeholders and outside observers, as intimately associated with a future strategy and a strategic change programme. A strategic leader is, then, symbolically highly significant in the change process and needs to be a role model for future strategy (see section 14.4.4 below on symbolic levers for change).

Whilst there is often an emphasis on individuals at the top of an organisation, the leadership of change also involves others in and around the organisation.

Middle managers

A top-down approach to managing strategy and strategic change sees middle managers as implementers of top-management strategic plans. Here their role is to ensure that resources are allocated and controlled appropriately and to monitor the performance and behaviour of staff. However, middle managers have multiple roles in relation to the management of strategy.[13] In the context of managing strategic change there are three other roles they play:

- *'Sense making'* of strategy. Top management may set down a strategic direction; but how it is explained and made sense of in specific contexts (e.g. a region of a multinational or a functional department) may, intentionally or not, be left to middle managers. If misinterpretation of that intended strategy is to be avoided, it is therefore vital that middle managers understand and feel an ownership of it. They are therefore a crucial *relevance bridge* between top management and members of the organisation at lower levels, in effect translating a change initiative into a message that is locally relevant. A number of researchers have made the point that, in this role, how they make sense of top-down strategy and how they talk about and explain it to others becomes critically important.[14] In this sense they can play a *local leadership* role.

- *Reinterpretation and adjustment* of strategic responses as events unfold (e.g. in terms of relationships with customers, suppliers, the workforce and so on); this is a vital role for which middle managers are uniquely qualified because they are in day-to-day contact with such aspects of the organisation and its environment.

- *Advisers* to more senior management on what are likely to be blockages and requirements for change.

When it comes to strategic change, middle managers are therefore in a key 'mediating' role between those trying to direct from the top and the operating level. The Key Debate at the end of the chapter takes this into account and considers strategic change in relation to a top-down perspective, but also in relation to some of the roles played by middle managers.

Newcomers and outsiders

Whilst managers in the organisation have important roles to play, 'outsiders' can also play an important role in strategic change. These could include:

- A *new chief executive* from outside the organisation may be introduced into a business to enhance the capability for change or to bring a fresh perspective, not bound by the constraints of the past, or the embedded routines that can prevent strategic change. This is especially so in turnaround situations (see 14.5.1 below).

- *New management* from outside the organisation can also increase the diversity of ideas, help break down cultural barriers to change and increase the experience of and capability for change. However, their successful influence is likely to depend on how much explicit *visible backing* they have from the chief executive. Without such backing they may be seen as lacking authority and influence.

- *Consultants* are often used to help formulate strategy or to plan the change process. They are also increasingly used as facilitators of change processes: for example, in a coordinating capacity, as project planners for change programmes, as facilitators of project teams working on change, or of strategy workshops used to develop strategy and plan means of strategic change. The value of consultants is threefold. First, they do not inherit the cultural baggage of the organisation and can therefore bring a dispassionate view to the process. Second, as a result, they may ask questions and undertake analyses which challenge taken-for-granted ways of seeing or doing things. Third, they signal symbolically the importance of a change process, not least because their fees may be of a very high order.

● *Other stakeholders* may be key influencers of change. For example, government, investors, customers, suppliers and business analysts all have the potential to act as change agents on organisations.

14.3.2 Styles of strategic leadership

There is no one best style of strategic leadership. Moreover there is evidence[15] that **successful strategic leaders are able to adjust their style of leadership to the context they face**. This has become known as '**situational leadership**'. Here this is explained, first by reviewing different generic approaches to managing change, next by considering more specific styles of leading change, then by considering how these may need to differ by context.

Theory E and theory O

On the basis of many years' study of corporate change programmes, Michael Beer and Nitin Nohria observe that, broadly, there are two approaches to managing change which they describe as 'Theory E and Theory O'.[16]

● *Theory E* is change based on the pursuit of economic value and is typically associated with the top-down, programmatic use of the 'hard' levers of change. The emphasis is on changes of structures and systems, financial incentives, often associated with portfolio changes, downsizing and consequent job layoffs.

● *Theory O* is change based on the development of organisational capability. The emphasis here is on culture change, learning and participation in change programmes and experimentation.

However, Beer and Nohria argue that, stark as these alternatives seem to be, a combination of the two approaches may not only be required, but be beneficial. This might involve, for example:

● *Sequencing change* to start with theory E approaches and move on to theory O approaches.

● *Embracing both approaches* simultaneously and being explicit about it to people in the organisation and external stakeholders.

● *Combining direction from the top with participation from below.* By so doing the benefits of both clarity of overall strategic direction and potential upward spontaneity can be achieved.

● *Using incentives to reinforce change* rather than to drive change.

Styles of change leadership

Within these two generic approaches to change there are several styles of change leadership: Table 14.1 summarises these.[17]

● **Education involves persuading others of the need for and means of strategic change**. Four phases of this style of change leadership have been advocated:[18]

  ● Convince employees that change is imperative and why the new direction is the right one. Again this emphasises the necessity for clarity of future vision and strategy.

  ● Since change is likely to be interpreted differently throughout the organisation,[19] frame the changes in ways relevant to the different groups and functions that have to enact the change and gather feedback on how this is understood and communicated within those groups.

Table 14.1 Styles of leading change

Style	Description	Advantages	Disadvantages
Education	Use small group briefings to discuss things with people and explain things to them. The aim is to gain support for change by generating understanding and commitment. This is likely to be accompanied by delegation of responsibility for change.	Spreads support for change. Also ensures a wide base of understanding.	Takes a long time. If radical change is needed, fact-based argument and logic may not be enough to convince others of need for change. Easy to voice support, then walk away and do nothing.
Collaboration	Widespread involvement of the employees on decisions about both what and how to change.	Spreads not only support but ownership of change by increasing levels of involvement.	Time-consuming. Little control over decisions made.
Participation	Strategic leaders retain overall coordination and authority but delegate elements of the change process.	Again, spreads ownership and support of change, but within a more controlled framework. Easier to shape decisions.	Can be perceived as manipulation.
Direction	Change leaders make the majority of decisions about what to change and how. Use of authority to direct change.	Less time-consuming. Provides a clear change direction and focus.	Potentially less support and commitment, and therefore proposed changes may be resisted.
Coercion	Use of power to impose change.	Allows for prompt action.	Unlikely to achieve buy-in without a crisis.

Source: Adapted from J. Balogun and V. Hope Hailey, *Exploring Strategic Change*, 3rd edn, 2008.

- Ensure ongoing communication of the progress of change.
- Reinforce behavioural guidelines in line with the change and reward the achievement of change goals.

However, there are problems here. The assumption that reasoned argument in a top-down fashion will overcome perhaps years of embedded assumptions about what 'really matters' may be optimistic. There may be apparent acceptance of change without its actually being delivered. Such an approach to change can also take a long time and can also be costly, for example in terms of training and management time.

- **Collaboration** in the change process is the involvement of those affected by strategic change in setting the change agenda; for example, in the identification of strategic issues, the strategic decision-making process, the setting of priorities, the planning of strategic change or the drawing up of action plans. Such involvement can foster a more positive attitude to change; people may see the constraints the organisation faces as less significant[20] and feel increased ownership of, and commitment to, a decision or change process. It may therefore be a way of building readiness and capability for change. However, there are potential problems here too. People may come up with change solutions that are not in line with, or do not achieve the expectations of, top management or key stakeholders. For example, there is the risk that solutions will be found from within the existing culture or that the agenda for change will be negotiated and may therefore be a compromise. In either case there is the risk of perpetuating the status quo or merely an adaptation of it. A strategic change leader who takes this approach may, therefore, need to retain the ability to intervene in the process, but this runs the risk of demotivating employees who have been involved in the change process.

- **Participation retains the coordination of and authority over processes of change by a strategic leader who delegates** *elements* **of the change process.** For example, particular stages of change, such as ideas generation, data collection, detailed planning, the development of rationales for change or the identification of critical success factors, may be delegated to project teams or task forces. Such teams may not take full responsibility for the change process, but become involved in it and see their work building towards it. The responsibility for the change is retained by the strategic leader who ensures the monitoring of progress and that change is seen to occur. An advantage is that it involves members of the organisation, not only in originating ideas, but also in the *partial implementation* of solutions, helping build commitment to the change. It may also be that the retention of the agenda and means of change by the strategic leader reduces the possibility of a negotiated compromise and means that more radical change can be achieved. The potential problem is that employees may see this approach as manipulation and become disenchanted and demotivated.

- **Direction involves the use of personal managerial authority to establish a clear strategy and how change will occur.** It is top-down management of strategic change where change 'solutions' and the means of change are 'sold' to others who are tasked with implementing them. The need here is for both clarity of strategic vision and the specifics of a change programme in terms of critical success factors and priorities. The approach may be needed if there is a need for fast change or control over the change agenda (for example to meet the expectations of dominant external stakeholders). The danger is that it can result in explicit resistance to change or people going along with the rhetoric of change whilst passively resisting it. It is also worth noting that even where top management people see themselves adopting participative styles, their subordinates may perceive this as directive and, indeed, may welcome such direction if they see major change as needed.[21]

- **Coercion** is direction in its most extreme form. It **is the imposition of change or the issuing of edicts about change.** This is the explicit use of power and may be necessary if the organisation is facing a crisis, for example.

Illustration 14.3 provides examples of different strategic leadership styles.

Different styles for different contexts

Clearly different styles of change are likely to suit different managers' personality types. However, since strategic leaders with the greatest *capability* to manage change have the ability to adopt different styles in different circumstances, it is useful to consider the appropriateness of different styles to different contexts.

- *Time and scope.* Education or collaboration may be most appropriate for incremental change within organisations, but where transformational change is required, more centralised control or directive approaches may be more appropriate.

- *Capability and readiness for change.* Research on leadership has shown that leadership styles need to differ according to the ability and willingness of employees to change. Translating

ILLUSTRATION 14.3

Leadership styles for managing change

Successful top executives have different leadership styles.

Don't noodle

Terry Lundgren, CEO of Federated Department Stores:

'I have always been a pretty good listener, and I am quick to admit that I do not have all the answers. So I am going to listen. But shortly after I listen, the second piece is to pull the trigger. I have all the input, and here is what we are going to do. People need closure on a decision. If you listen and then noodle on it, people get confused, and that's not effective leadership.'[1]

The promised land

James Strachan, former Chairman of the Audit Commission UK, reporting what a CEO had told him:

'All you have to do is to figure out precisely where you want to go and you need to be able to paint that "promised land" in technicolour. Second you need to ask whether you have got the right people around you, particularly at the top: if not change them tomorrow – literally tomorrow. Third you delegate; but you do so without actually absolving yourself of all responsibility. You still own the ultimate responsibility – the buck stops with you – but you significantly delegate to people to enable them to bring out the best in themselves. Last you praise their success to high heaven.'[2]

He then added:

'The lesson about change for me is that in times of change there is a lot of turbulence, confusion, worry and concern. This is all natural. So people naturally gravitate towards a leadership that tries to take this confusion and describe it in simple terms about why we are doing this, what the "promised land" that we are going to get to is and why all this agony is worthwhile. In terms of change it is simplicity and conviction that rule.'

Coach but don't coddle

Allan G. Laffley, CEO of Procter & Gamble:

'My approach to leadership is to raise aspiration and then achieve great execution . . . communicate priorities clearly, simply and frequently . . . to a large degree our division leaders must define their own future. I play the role of coach; but coaching doesn't mean coddling. I expect our managers to make choices . . . to help managers make these strategic choices leaders must sometimes challenge deeply held assumptions. . . . Being a role model is vital . . . I know that I must be ready for moments of truth that alert the organization to my commitment.'[3]

Be dedicated and collegiate

Sir Terry Leahy of Tesco has overseen one of the biggest retail transformations in the world. Yet he is

'disarmingly ordinary. . . . His speech is serious and straightforward. He's no showman . . . He talks only about Tesco; . . . it's like meeting a religious leader faithfully reciting a creed. . . . His co-workers respect him for his decision-making but he doesn't make his moves on a whim. . . . Everything is analysed, taken apart, discussed and put back together. . . . He's gathered around him senior managers who've been with him and the group for years. He's in charge but he's also collegiate.'[4]

He also likes to talk and listen to people in the stores:

'What makes Leahy different is the extraordinary degree to which he chats with junior staff and absorbs their views and the attention he pays to customers.'

References:
1. Interview by Matthew Boyle, in *Fortune*, 12 December 2005, vol. 152, no. 12, pp. 126–7.
2. *Lessons Learned: Straight Talk from the World's Top Business Leaders: Managing Change*, Harvard Business School Press, 2007.
3. *Leadership Excellence*, November 2006, vol. 23, no. 11, pp. 9–10.
4. Chris Blackhurst, 'Sir Terry Leahy', *Management Today*, February 2004, p. 32. Reproduced from *Management Today* magazine with the permission of the copyright owner, Haymarket Business Publications Limited.

Questions

1 How would you describe each of the styles illustrated here in terms of those explained in section 14.3.2?

2 What might be the benefits and problems of each of the leadership styles? In what circumstances?

3 Only some stakeholders are specifically mentioned in the examples. Does this mean that the style should be the same towards all stakeholders of the organisation? If not, how would they differ?

Figure 14.4 Styles of change leadership according to organisational capability and readiness

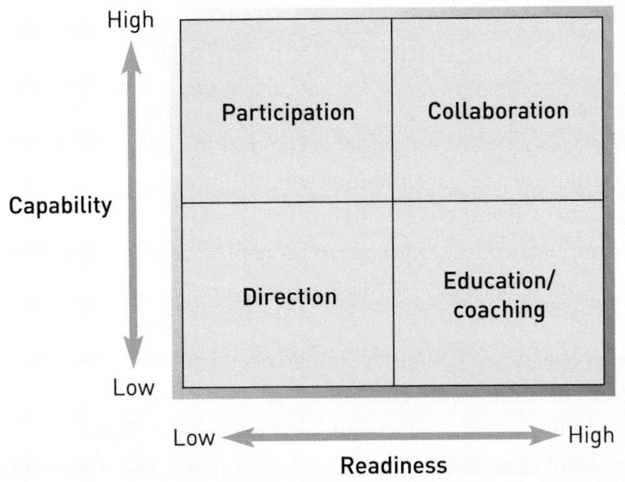

these findings into aspects of the Change Kaleidoscope it is likely that styles of change leadership will need to differ according to the extent of capability and readiness for strategic change in the organisation (see Figure 14.4). Where there is low readiness and capability for change, then direction may be the most appropriate style. Where there is high readiness but low capability then education, training and coaching may be appropriate. Where capability is high but readiness is low, involving people in the change process whilst retaining overall central control (participation) may make sense. Where both readiness and capability are high, then collaboration may be possible and top management may be able to delegate much of the change agenda.

- *Power.* In organisations with *hierarchical power structures* a directive style may be common and it may be difficult to break away from it, not least because people expect it. On the other hand, in 'flatter' power structures, a more networked or learning organisation described elsewhere in this book, e.g. section 12.3.1), it is likely that collaboration and participation will be common, indeed desirable.

- *Styles of managing change are not mutually exclusive.* For example, clear direction on overall vision might aid a more collaborative approach to more detailed strategy development. Education and communication may be appropriate for some stakeholders, such as financial institutions; participation may be appropriate for groups in parts of the organisation where it is necessary to build *capability and readiness*; whereas if there are parts of the organisation where change has to happen fast, *timing* may demand a more directive style.

(14.4) LEVERS FOR MANAGING STRATEGIC CHANGE

Some levers for change have already been discussed elsewhere in the book. The importance of clarity of a strategic vision was discussed in section 5.2 together with the importance of other goals and objectives. The effects of changes in organisational structure and control systems of organisations were addressed in Chapter 13. This section of the chapter examines other possible change levers. In so doing it is worth noting that many of these correspond to the elements of the cultural web (section 5.4.6). The implication is that the forces that act to embed and protect current ways of doing things might also provide bases for change.

14.4.1 A compelling case for change

Whichever style of management is adopted a convincing case for change has to be presented. McKinsey & Co, the consultants,[22] argue that too often the case for change is made in terms of top management's perception of what is important: for example meeting expectations of shareholders or beating competition. When most managers and employees are asked what motivates them, on the other hand, there are many more factors that motivate: the impact on society, on customers, on the local working team, or on employees' personal well-being. A compelling case for change needs to speak to these different bases of motivation, not just to top-management perceptions of change needs. It may, of course, be difficult for top management to understand and relate to these different needs: so it may make sense to involve employees, themselves, in the creation of stories of change that, in effect, 'translate' corporate imperatives of change into local motivating messages. It is also important that the case for change does not just focus on the understanding of why change is needed, but the action required to deliver it.

14.4.2 Challenging the taken-for-granted

A major challenge in achieving strategic change can be the need to change often long-standing mindsets or taken-for-granted assumptions – the paradigm (see section 5.4.6). There are different views on how this might be achieved.

One view is that sufficient evidence, perhaps in the form of careful strategic analysis, will itself serve to challenge and therefore change the paradigm. However, where long-standing assumptions have persisted, they can be very resistant to change. People find ways of questioning, reconfiguring and reinterpreting such analysis to bring it in line with the existing paradigm. It may take much persistence to overcome this. Others argue that encouraging people to question and challenge each other's assumptions and received wisdom by making them explicit is valuable.[23] Scenario planning (see section 2.2.2) is similarly advocated as a way of overcoming individual biases and cultural assumptions by getting people to see possible different futures and the implications for their organisations.[24]

Others argue that senior managers in particular can be too far removed from the realities of their organisations and need to be brought face-to-face with them. They may rarely speak to customers directly or experience themselves the services offered by their own firms. A senior executive of a rail company explained that in the past senior executives in the organisation had always travelled first class or by chauffeur-driven car. Hardly any of them had ever travelled in a crowded railway carriage. He introduced a policy that all senior executives should travel economy class wherever possible.

14.4.3 Changing operational processes and routines

In the end, strategies are delivered through day-to-day processes and routines of the operations of the organisation. These might be formalised and codified or they might be less formal 'ways we do things around here' which tend to persist over time and guide people's behaviour. As has been seen in the discussion in Chapter 3, it may be that such routines can be the basis of its core competences and therefore its competitive advantage. However, they can also be serious blockages to change. The relationship between strategic change and day-to-day processes and routines is therefore important to consider in at least four respects:

- *Planning operational change.* The planning of the implementation of an intended strategy requires the identification of the key changes in the routines required to deliver that strategy. In effect, strategic change needs to be considered in terms of the re-engineering of organisational processes.[25] For example, in Shell Lubricants until 2002 seven people were involved in different aspects of order processing routines. In the search for improved efficiency and customer service, one person was given overall responsibility for an order, with the consequent reduction in order time of 75 per cent, reduction in order processing costs of 45 per cent and vastly improved customer satisfaction.[26]

- *Challenging operational assumptions.* Changing organisational processes and routines may also have the effect of challenging the often taken-for-granted assumptions under-pinning them. In turn this may have the effect of getting people to question and challenge deep-rooted beliefs and assumptions in the organisation. Richard Pascale argues: 'It is easier to act your way into a better way of thinking than to think your way into a better way of acting';[27] in other words, it is easier to change behaviour and by so doing change taken-for-granted assumptions than to try to change taken-for-granted assumptions as a way of changing behaviour. If this is so, the style of change employed (see section 14.3.2 above) needs to take this into account: it suggests that education and communication to persuade people to change may be less powerful than involving people in the activities of changing.

- *Operation-led change.* Operational change may not simply be the outcome of planned strategic change; it could be that opportunities for operational change can stimulate innovation and new strategic thinking. Michael Hammer[28] argues that managers do not consider changes at the operational level sufficiently radically. Typically they benchmark best practice against industry standards rather than looking for best practice wherever it can be found (see section 3.4.1). He gives the example of Taco Bell in the US, which saved costs and improved the quality of its offering by re-examining its operational processes in terms of best practice in manufacturing instead of fast-food operations.

- *Bottom-up changes to routines.* Even when changes in routines are not planned from the top, people do change them and this may result in wider strategic change. Research[29] shows that this can occur proactively through managers deliberately '*bending* the rules of the game'. This could give rise to resistance, but persistent bending may eventually achieve enough support from different stakeholders such that new routines become acceptable. When sufficient questioning of the status quo is achieved, those seeking change may actively *subvert* existing ways of doing things so as to make clear a funda-mental change from the past. This could, for example, be an approach adopted by middle managers in seeking to carry with them both people who work for them and more senior managers, both of whom may be resistant to change. It is an incremental, experimental process that is, however, likely to suffer setbacks and require persistence and political acumen.

The overall lesson is that changes in routines may appear to be mundane, but they can have significant impact. Illustration 14.4 gives some examples of changes in routines linked to strategic change.

ILLUSTRATION 14.4

Changes in routines and symbols

Changes in organisational routines and symbols can be a powerful signal of and stimulus for change.

Changes in routines

- A drug can only be promoted on launch on the basis of claims substantiated by clinical data, so how pharmaceutical firms conduct clinical trials is strategically important. The traditional approach has been to base extensive data collection on a scientific research protocol and then to write a report explaining why all this data had been collected: a highly time-consuming and costly process. Some firms changed their procedures to ensure that scientific tests addressed regulatory and medical need. They created ideal claims statements and drafted the report they would need. Only then did they create research protocols and data collection forms, specifying the data required from the trials to support the claims.

- In a retail business with an espoused strategy of customer care, the chief executive, on visiting stores, tended to ignore staff and customers alike: he seemed to be interested only in the financial information in the store manager's office. He was unaware of this until it was pointed out; his change in behaviour afterwards, insisting on talking to staff and customers on his visits, became a 'story' which spread around the company, substantially supporting the strategic direction of the firms.

Language that challenges and questions

- A chief executive facing a crisis addressed his board: 'I suggest we think of ourselves like bulls facing a choice: the abattoir or the bull ring. I've made up my mind: what about you?'

- When the new management team (Gordon Bethune as Chief Executive and Greg Brennemaan as Chief Operating Officer) took over ailing Continental Airlines they chose their language carefully. The future winning orientation was made clear consistently. The overall strategy was referred to as the 'Go forward plan', the marketing plan was 'Fly to win' and the financial plan 'Fund the future'. It was language reinforced in how Brennemaan explained the determination to succeed: 'Did you know there are no rear view mirrors on an airplane? The runway behind is irrelevant.'[1]

Symbols of change

- In a textile firm the workforce was instructed to take machinery associated with 'old ways of doing things' into the yard at the rear of the factory and smash it up.

- The head nurse of a recovery unit for patients who had been severely ill decided that, if nurses wore everyday clothes rather than nurses' uniforms, it would signal to patients that they were on the road to recovery and a normal life; and to nurses that they were concerned with rehabilitation. However, the decision had other implications for the nurses too. It blurred the status distinction between nurses and other non-professional members of staff. Nurses preferred to wear their uniforms. Whilst they recognised that uniforms signalled a medically fragile role of patients, they reinforced their separate and professional status as acute care workers.[2]

References:
1. J.M. Higgins and C. McCallaster, 'If you want strategic change don't forget your cultural artefacts', *Journal of Change Management*, vol. 4, no. 1 (2004), pp. 63–73.
2. M.G. Pratt and E. Rafaeli, 'Organisational dress as a symbol of multi-layered social idealities', *Academy of Management Journal*, vol. 40, no. 4 (1997), pp. 862–98.

Questions

For an organisation with which you are familiar:

1 Identify at least five important routines, symbols or rituals in the organisation.

2 In what way could they be changed to support a different strategy? Be explicit as to how the symbols might relate to the new strategy.

3 Why are these potential levers for change often ignored by change agents?

14.4.4 Symbolic changes[30]

Change levers are not always of an overt, formal nature: they may also be symbolic in nature. **Symbols are objects, events, acts or people which express more than their intrinsic content**. They may be everyday things which are nevertheless especially meaningful in the context of a particular situation or organisation. (In this sense the organisational processes and routines discussed above are also symbolic in nature.) Changing symbols can help reshape beliefs and expectations because meaning becomes apparent in the day-to-day experiences people have of organisations, such as the symbols that surround them (e.g. office layout and décor), the type of language and technology used and organisational rituals. Consider some examples.

- Many *rituals*[31] of organisations are concerned with effecting or consolidating change. Table 14.2 identifies and gives examples of such rituals and suggests what role they might play in change processes.[32] New rituals can be introduced or old rituals done away with as ways of signalling or reinforcing change.

- Changes in *physical aspects* of the work environment are powerful symbols of change. Typical here is a change of location for the head office, relocation of personnel, changes in dress or uniforms, and alterations to offices or office space.

- The *behaviour of managers*, particularly strategic leaders, is perhaps the most powerful symbol in relation to change. So, having made pronouncements about the need for change, it is vital that the visible behaviour of change agents be in line with such change.

- The *language* used by change agents is also important.[33] Either consciously or unconsciously, language and metaphor may be employed to galvanise change. Of course, there is also the danger that strategic leaders do not realise this and, whilst espousing change, use language that signals adherence to the status quo, or personal reluctance to change.

Illustration 14.4 also gives some examples of such symbolic signalling of change. However, there is an important qualification to the idea that the manipulation of symbols can be a useful lever for managing change. The significance and meaning of symbols are dependent on how they are interpreted. Since their use may not be interpreted as intended (see the nursing

Table 14.2 **Organisational rituals and change**

Types of ritual	Role	Examples in managing change
Rites of passage	Signify a change of status or role	Induction to new roles Training programmes
Rites of enhancement	Recognise effort benefiting organisation Similarly motivate others	Awards ceremonies Promotions
Rites of renewal	Reassure that something is being done Focus attention on issues	Appointment of consultant Project teams and workshops
Rites of integration	Encourage shared commitment Reassert rightness of norms	Celebrations of achievement or new ways of doing things
Rites of conflict reduction	Reduce conflict and aggression	Negotiating committees
Rites of challenge	'Throwing down the gauntlet'	New CEO setting challenging goals

example in Illustration 14.4), whilst they may be a powerful lever for change, their impact is difficult to predict.

14.4.5 Power and political systems[34]

Section 4.5 explained the importance of understanding the political context in and around the organisation. There is also a need to consider strategic change within this political context. This can be important because it may be necessary to build a political context for change. To effect change powerful support may be required from individuals or groups or a reconfiguration of *power structures* may be necessary, especially if transformational change is required. Table 14.3 shows some of the mechanisms associated with managing change from a political perspective.

- *Acquiring resources* or being identified with important resource areas or areas of expertise. In particular the ability to withdraw or allocate such resources can be a valuable tool in overcoming resistance or persuading others to accept change or build readiness for change.

- *Association with powerful stakeholder groups* (elites), or their supporters, can help build a power base or help overcome resistance to change. Or a manager facing resistance to change may seek out and win over someone highly respected from within the very group resistant to change. It may also be necessary to *remove individuals or groups* resistant to change. Who these are can vary – from powerful individuals in senior positions to whole layers of resistance, perhaps executives in a threatened function or service.

Table 14.3 Political mechanisms in organisations

Activity areas	Mechanisms			Problems
	Resources	**Elites**	**Building alliances**	
Building the power base	Control of resources Acquisition of/ identification with expertise Acquisition of additional resources	Sponsorship by an elite Association with an elite	Identification of change supporters Alliance building Team building	Time required for building Perceived duality of ideals Perceived as threat by existing elites
Overcoming resistance	Withdrawal of resources Use of 'counter-intelligence'	Breakdown or division of elites Association with change agent Association with respected outsider	Foster momentum for change Sponsorship/ reward of change agents	Striking from too low a power base Potentially destructive: need for rapid rebuilding
Achieving compliance	Giving resources	Removal of resistant elites Need for visible 'change hero'	Partial implementation and collaboration Implantation of 'disciples' Support for 'young Turks'	Converting the body of the organisation Slipping back

● *Building alliances* and *networks* of contacts and sympathisers may be important in overcoming the resistance of more powerful groups. Attempting to convert the whole organisation to an acceptance of change is difficult. There may, however, be parts of the organisation, or individuals, more sympathetic to change than others with whom support for change can be built. Marginalisation of those resistant to change may also be possible. However, the danger is that powerful groups in the organisation may regard the building of support coalitions, or acts of marginalisation, as a threat to their own power, leading to further resistance to change. An analysis of power and interest using the stakeholder mapping (section 4.5.1) can, therefore, be useful to identify bases of alliance and likely resistance.

However, the political aspects of change management are also potentially hazardous. Table 14.3 also summarises some of the problems. In overcoming resistance, the major problem may simply be the lack of power to undertake such activity. Trying to break down the status quo may become so destructive and take so long that the organisation cannot recover from it. If the process needs to take place, its replacement by some new set of beliefs and the implementation of a new strategy is vital and needs to be speedy. Further, as already identified, in implementing change, gaining the commitment of a few senior executives at the top of an organisation is one thing; it is quite another to convert the body of the organisation to an acceptance of significant change.

14.4.6 Change tactics

There are also more specific tactics of change which might be employed to facilitate the change process.

Timing

The importance of timing is often neglected in thinking about strategic change. But choosing the right time tactically to promote change is vital. For example:

● *Building on actual or perceived crisis* is especially useful the greater the degree of change needed. If there is a higher perceived risk in maintaining the status quo than in changing it, people are more likely to change. Indeed, it is said that some chief executives seek to elevate problems to achieve perceived crisis in order to galvanise change. For example, a threatened takeover may be used as a catalyst for strategic change.

● *Windows of opportunity* in change processes may exist. The arrival of a new chief executive, the introduction of a new, highly successful product, or the arrival of a major competitive threat on the scene may provide opportunities to make more significant changes than might normally be possible. Since change will be regarded nervously, it may also be important to choose the time for promoting such change to avoid unnecessary fear and nervousness. For example, if there is a need for the removal of executives, this may be best done before rather than during the change programme. In such a way, the change programme can be seen as a potential improvement for the future rather than as the cause of such losses.

● *The symbolic signalling of time frames* may be important. In particular, conflicting messages about the timing of change should be avoided. For example, if rapid change is required, the maintenance of procedures or focus on issues that that signal long time horizons may be counter-productive.

Visible short-term wins

A strategic change programme will require many detailed actions and tasks. It is important that some are seen to be successful quickly. Identifying some 'low-hanging fruit' – changes that may not be big but can be made easily and yield a quick payoff – can be useful. This could take the form, for example, of a retail chain introducing a new product range and demonstrating its success in the market or the breaking down of a long-established routine and the demonstration of a better way of doing things. In themselves, these may not be especially significant aspects of a new strategy, but they may be visible indicators of a new approach associated with that strategy. The demonstration of such wins can therefore galvanise commitment to the wider strategy.

One reason given for the inability to change is that resources are not available to do so. This may be overcome if it is possible to identify '*hot spots*' on which to focus resources and effort. For example, William Bratton, famously responsible for the Zero Tolerance policy of the New York Police Department, began by focusing resource and effort on narcotics-related crimes. Though associated with 50–70 per cent of all crimes he found they only had 5 per cent of the resources allocated by NYPD to tackle them. Success in this field led to the roll-out of his policies into other areas and to gaining the resources to do so.[35]

(14.5) MANAGING STRATEGIC CHANGE PROGRAMMES

There are, then, a variety of change levers that change agents may use. Indeed, most successful change initiatives rely on multiple levers for change.[36] So choosing the appropriate levers, rather than following a set formula for managing strategic change, is important. This will depend on the change context and the skills and styles of those managing change. For example, to take the extremes, if the need is to overcome resistance to achieve fast results, then the emphasis may have to be on changing elements of the strategy itself from the top and achieving behavioural compliance to a change programme. On the other hand, if there is a need and the time to 'win hearts and minds' then there will need to be a focus on changing people's values and a much greater emphasis on their involvement in changing the culture. Illustration 14.5 shows these differences.

This section first revisits three types of change identified in section 14.2.1 to consider which levers managers use in which contexts. It concludes by summarising evidence as to why change programmes fail and the lessons that can be learned from that.

14.5.1 Turnaround strategy

There are circumstances where the emphasis has to be on rapid reconstruction, in the absence of which a business could face closure, enter terminal decline or be taken over. This is commonly referred to as a **turnaround strategy**, **where the emphasis is on speed of change and rapid cost reduction and/or revenue generation** and managers need to prioritise the things that give quick and significant improvements. Typically it is a situation where a directive approach to change (see section 14.3.2) is required. Some of the main elements of turnaround strategies are as follows:[37]

- *Crisis stabilisation*. The aim is to regain control over the deteriorating position. This requires a short-term focus on cost reduction and/or revenue increase, typically involving some of

ILLUSTRATION 14.5

Change programmes at IBM and Pace

Change programmes need to be tailored to context.

Values-based change at IBM

Sam Palmisano took over as CEO of IBM in 2002. His predecessor Lou Gerstner had made major changes but, as Palmisano explained: 'Then there was "a burning platform"'. In 2002 there was a need for a continuation of change but 'instead of galvanizing people through fear of failure, you have to galvanize them through hope and aspiration'. Palmisano believed it was impossible to do this in a company as complex as IBM by relying on structures and control systems. It had to be through values.

In July 2003 over a three-day period over 50,000 employees took part in an intranet discussion on company values: the 'ValuesJam'. Much of what was posted was highly critical. IBM talked a lot about trust but spent endless time auditing people; no one questioned the views of senior executives; mistakes were not tolerated or seen as part of learning. It was uncomfortable and some senior executives wanted to pull the plug on the exercise. But Palmisano insisted it continue and joined in, posting his personal views and acknowledging problems.

In many respects the values that emerged extended what IBM already espoused: 'dedication to every client's success', 'innovation that matters – for our company and the world', 'trust and personal responsibility in all relationships'. However they were not being enacted. So the next step was to identify where the values were not being delivered. This was also rolled out to an online jam again (see Illustration 15.2), identifying examples of processes and routines contrary to the values.

Palmisano then instigated changes in control systems to bring them in line with the values. This included changes to the incentive scheme for managing directors of IBM businesses, through to providing funds to line managers to use at their discretion to generate business or develop client relationships. Price setting was also made more client-friendly, especially for products and services crossing IBM businesses, involving significant reworking of the IBM pricing routines.[1]

Turnaround at Pace

Pace manufactures products for the digital TV markets: in particular set-top boxes for customers such as BSkyB and Canal+. When Neil Gaydon took over as Chief Executive in 2006 the company was facing bankruptcy with a loss of £15m (~€16.5m; ~$22.5m) on sales of £175m and a bank facility that had just been withdrawn. By 2010 the company was reporting profits of £69.9m on revenues of over £1 billion.

Gaydon broadened the customer base. At the turn of the century 90% of revenue came from just two customers. By 2010 Pace had more than 100 customers worldwide. In addition he focused on key areas of market development; in particular on high definition television and on pay-TV operations which have a higher price level and offer better margins.

However he also introduced a major reorganisation of the company. He significantly pruned management and organised the company into small teams focused on particular customers. Each team was given a lot of freedom, controlled its own profit and loss account and bonuses were linked to the teams' performance, incentivising everyone to get results. Pace, notorious for late deliveries and over-runs on R&D costs, significantly improved its reliability and cost control.

Reference:
1. Based on Paul Hemp, 'Leading change when business is good', *Harvard Business Review*, vol. 82, no. 12 (2004), pp. 60–70.

Questions

1 Compare the different approaches of Palmisano and Gaydon. Why were they different?

2 How do they compare to that of John Howie and Craig Lockhart at Faslane (see the case example).

3 Which levers for change described in the chapter are evident in each case? Which others might have been used and why?

Table 14.4 Turnaround: revenue generation and cost reduction steps

Increasing revenue	Reducing costs
• Ensuring marketing mix tailored to key market segments	• Reduce labour costs and reduce costs of senior management
• Review pricing strategy to maximise revenue	• Focus on productivity improvement
• Focus organisational activities on needs of target market sector customers	• Reduce marketing costs not focused on target market
• Exploit additional opportunities for revenue creation related to target market	• Tighten financial controls
• Invest funds from reduction of costs in new growth areas	• Tight control on cash expenses
	• Establish competitive bidding for suppliers; defer creditor payments; speed up debtor payments
	• Reduce inventory
	• Eliminate non-profitable products/services

the steps identified in Table 14.4. There is nothing novel about these steps: many of them are good management practice. The differences are the speed at which they are carried out and the focus of managerial attention on them. The most successful turnaround strategies also focus on reducing direct operational costs and on productivity gains. Less effective approaches pay less attention to these and more on the reduction of overheads.[38]

However, too often turnarounds are seen as no more than cost-cutting exercises when a wider alignment between causes of decline and solutions may be important. For example, where the business decline is principally a result of changes in the external environment it may be folly to expect that cost-cutting alone can lead to renewed growth. Other elements of turnaround strategies are therefore important.

● *Management changes.* Changes in management may be required, especially at the top. This usually includes the introduction of a new chairman or chief executive, as well as changes to the board, especially in marketing, sales and finance, for three main reasons. First, because the old management may well be the ones that were in charge when the problems developed and be seen as the cause of them by key stakeholders. Second, because it may be necessary to bring in management with experience of turnaround management. Third, because, if new management come from outside the organisation, they may bring different approaches to the way the organisation has operated in the past.

● *Gaining stakeholder support.* Poor quality of information may have been provided to key stakeholders. In a turnaround situation it is vital that key stakeholders, perhaps the bank or key shareholder groups, and employees are kept clearly informed of the situation and improvements as they are being made.[39] It is also likely that a clear assessment of the power of different stakeholder groups (see section 4.5.1) will become vitally important in managing turnaround.

● *Clarifying the target market(s) and core products.* Central to turnaround success is ensuring clarity on the target market or market segments most likely to generate cash and grow profits. A successful turnaround strategy involves getting closer to customers and improving the flow of marketing information, especially to senior levels of management, so as to focus revenue-generating activities on key market segments. Of course, a reason for the poor performance of the organisation could be that it had this wrong in the first place. Clarifying the target market also provides the opportunity to discontinue or outsource products and services that are not targeted on those markets, eating up management time for little return or not making sufficient financial contribution.

- *Financial restructuring.* The financial structure of the organisation may need to be changed. This typically involves changing the existing capital structure, raising additional finance or renegotiating agreements with creditors, especially banks.

All of this requires the ability of management to prioritise those things that give quick and significant improvements.

14.5.2 Managing revolutionary strategic change

Revolutionary change differs from turnaround (or reconstruction) in two ways that make managing change especially challenging. First, the need is not only for fast change but also cultural change. Second, it may be that the need for change is not as evident to people in the organisation as in a turnaround situation; or that they see reasons to deny the need for change. This situation may have come about as a result of many years of relative decline in a market, with people wedded to products or processes no longer valued by customers – the problem of strategic drift. Or it could be that the problems of the organisation are visible and understood by its members, but that people cannot see a way forward. Managing change in such circumstances is likely to involve:

- *Clear strategic direction.* In these circumstances the need for the articulation of a clear strategic direction and decisive action in line with that direction is critical. So this is the type of change where individual CEOs who are seen to provide such direction are often credited with making a major difference. They may well also become the symbol of such change within an organisation and externally.

- *Combining rational and symbolic levers.* Very likely some of the hard decisions outlined above for turnaround will be taken: for example, portfolio changes, greater market focus, top management changes and perhaps financial restructuring. However, often these are also employed to send major symbolic messages of change. Most common here is the replacement of very senior executives or, perhaps, major changes in board structure signalling both internally and externally the significance of change at the very top. Similarly, the introduction of new managers, often at a senior level, may make sense in gaining the benefits of a fresh perspective, but also signals the significance of change. Consultants may also be used to provide a dispassionate analysis of the need for change but also to signal how meaningful the change process is.

- *Multiple styles of change management.* Whilst a *directive style* of change management is likely to be evident, this may need to be accompanied by other styles. It may be supported by determined efforts to *educate* about the need for change and the use of *participation* to involve people in aspects of change in which they have specific expertise or to overcome their resistance to change.

- *Working with the existing culture.* It may be possible to work with elements of the existing culture rather than attempt wholesale culture change.[40] This involves identifying those aspects of culture that can be built upon and developed and those that have to be changed – in effect a forcefield approach (see section 14.2.3). For example, as Illustration 5.2 showed, when Mary-Adair Macaire became CEO at the struggling Scottish knitwear firm, Pringle, in 2009 she built a change programme that emphasised its past reputation and identity for quality and stylish knitwear and the pride employees took in that.

● *Monitoring change*. Revolutionary change is likely to require the setting and monitoring of unambiguous targets that people have to achieve. Often these will be linked to overall financial targets and in turn to improved returns to shareholders.

14.5.3 Managing evolutionary strategic change

Managing change as evolution involves transformational change, but incrementally. It can be thought of in two ways. The first is in terms of the creation of an organisation capable of continual change, akin to a learning organisation (section 12.3.1) or one that has achieved organisational ambidexterity (section 12.4.1). Insights into how this might be achieved are also explained in the Variety Lens in the Commentaries. Trying to achieve this in practice is a significant challenge for management, not least because it requires:

● *Empowering the organisation*. Rather than top-down management, there is the need here for people throughout the organisation to accept the responsibility for contributing strategic ideas, for innovating, and for accepting change as inevitable and desirable. Clearly, then, there is a need for a high level of involvement in the change agenda.

● *A clear strategic vision*. It is the responsibility of top management to create the context within which new ideas can bubble up from below around a coherent view of long-term goals. This requires them to provide very clear guidelines – vision, mission or 'simple rules' – around which those ideas can cohere. In so doing, they need to find the balance between the clarity of such vision that allows people to see how they can contribute to future strategy whilst avoiding specifying that strategy in such detail as to constrain people's enthusiasm to contribute and innovate.

● *Continual change and a commitment to experimentation* with regard to organisational processes throughout the organisation.

A second way of conceiving of strategic change as evolution is in terms of the movement from one strategy to a changed strategy but over perhaps many years. Here the principles that might guide managers are these:

● *Stages of transition*. Identifying interim stages in the change process is important. For example, in terms of the change context (see section 14.2.2) there may be insufficient readiness or an insufficient capacity to make major changes initially. It will therefore be important to establish these conditions before other major moves are taken.

● *Irreversible changes*. It may be possible to identify changes that can be made that, whilst not necessarily having immediate major impact, will have long-term and irreversible impacts. For example, a law firm or accountancy firm that wishes to manage an evolutionary approach to strategic change might legitimately see this as dependent on the skills and focus of its partners. Changing the criteria for appointment of partners to achieve this might be one way of doing this. The time horizons for the effects of such changes to take effect would be many years but, once made, the effects would be difficult to reverse.

- *Sustained top management commitment* will be required. The danger is that the momentum for change falters because people do not perceive consistent commitment to it from the top.

- *Winning hearts and minds.* Culture change is likely to be required in any transformational change. This may be more problematic than for revolutionary change because people may simply not recognise that there are problems with regard to the status quo. The need is for multiple levers for change to be used consistently: education and participation as styles of managing change to allow people to see the need for change and contribute to what that change should be; the signalling of the meaning of change in ways that people throughout the organisation understand both rationally and emotionally; and levers that signal and achieve improved economic performance.

14.5.4 Why change programmes fail

Research into why change programmes fail can also provide lessons on the pitfalls to avoid. This section summarises seven of the main failings.[41]

- *Death by planning.* The emphasis is put on planning the change programme rather than delivering it. There is a continuous stream of proposals and reports, each one requiring agreement amongst managers affected by the changes. Sub-committees, project teams and working groups may be set up to examine problems and achieve buy-in. The result can be 'analysis paralysis' and a discourse about change rather than the delivery of change. This may also be linked to the politicisation of the change programme where meetings about change become forums for debate and political game-playing.

- *Loss of focus.* Change is often not a one-off process; it might require an ongoing series of initiatives, maybe over years. However, the risk is that these initiatives are seen by employees as 'change rituals' signifying very little. There is also the risk that the original intention of the change programme becomes eroded by other events taking place; for example, a redundancy programme.

- *Reinterpretation.* The attempted change becomes reinterpreted according to the old culture. For example, an engineering company's intended strategy of adding value in ways that customers valued was interpreted by the engineers within the firm as providing high levels of technical specification which they, not customers, determined.

- *Disconnectedness.* People affected by change may not see the change programme connecting to their reality. Senior executives, as proponents of the change, might not be seen to be credible in terms of understanding the realities of change on the ground. Or perhaps new systems and initiatives introduced are seen as out of line with the intentions of the intended change.

- *Behavioural compliance.* There is the danger that people appear to comply with the changes being pursued in the change programme without actually 'buying into' them. Change agents may think they see change occurring, when all they see is superficial compliance.

- *Misreading scrutiny and resistance.* Those promoting change in the organisation are likely to face either resistance to the change programme or critical scrutiny of it. Often the response to this is to see such behaviour as negative and destructive. It can, on the other hand, be seen as ways in which 'change recipients' in the organisation are engaging with the changes likely to affect them. They are likely to question change and evaluate it in terms of its significance for them. Even if resistance occurs, this is a way of keeping the agenda for

KEY DEBATE

The management of change from top to bottom

Strategic change has always been seen as the responsibility of top management: but to what extent can top managers manage change?

John Kotter, one of the world's foremost authorities on leadership and change, argues that problems of strategic change arise because top executives fail to take the necessary steps to manage such changes. These include:

- Establishing a sense of urgency on the basis of market threats or opportunities.
- Forming a powerful coalition of stakeholders for change.
- Creating and communicating a clear vision and strategy to direct the change and ensuring that the behaviour of the guiding coalition is in line with the vision.
- Removing obstacles to change, changing systems that undermine the vision and encouraging non-traditional ideas and activities.
- Creating short-term wins.
- Consolidating improvements but also continuing the process of change.

However, Julia Balogun studied a top management change initiative from the point of view of how middle managers interpreted it. She found that, whilst top managers believed they were being clear about the intended strategy, change actually took place by middle managers making sense of change initiatives in terms of their own *mental models* in relation to their *local responsibilities and conditions*, through discussion with their peers and on the basis of rumour. Top managers were inevitably too far removed from these dynamics and could not be expected to understand them in detail or manage them in specific ways. She argues that 'Senior managers can initiate and influence direction of change but not direct change'. They can:

- Monitor how people respond to change initiatives.
- Engage as much as possible with how people make sense of change and work with their reality, responding to their issues and interpretations.
- Live the changes they want others to adopt, especially avoiding inconsistencies between their actions, words and deeds.
- Focus on creating the understanding of higher-level principles rather than the details.

Hari Tsoukas and Robert Chia go further. They argue that change is an inherent property of organisations. Hierarchy and management control dampen that inherent change.

'Change programmes trigger ongoing change: they provide the discursive resources for making certain things possible, although what exactly will happen remains uncertain when a change programme is initiated. It must first be experienced before the possibilities it opens up are appreciated and taken up (if they are taken up). Change programmes are . . . locally adapted, improvised and elaborated. . . . If this is accepted what is, then, the meaning of "planned change"? . . . Change has been taken to mean that which occurs as a consequence of deliberate managerial action. In the view put forward here such a definition is limited. Although managers certainly aim at achieving established ways of thinking and acting through implementing particular plans, nonetheless, change in organizations occurs without necessarily intentional managerial action as a result of individuals trying to accommodate new experience and realize new possibilities. In the view suggested here, an excessive preoccupation with planned change risks failing to recognize the always already changing texture of organizations' (pp. 578–579).

References:
J. Kotter, 'Leading change: why transformation efforts fail', *Harvard Business Review*, March–April (1995), pp. 59–67.
J. Balogun and G. Johnson, 'Organizational restructuring and middle manager sensemaking', *Academy of Management Journal*, vol. 47, no. 4 (2004), pp. 523–49.
J. Balogun, 'Managing change: steering a course between intended strategies and unanticipated outcomes', *Long Range Planning*, vol. 39 (2006), pp. 29–49.
H. Tsoukas and R. Chia, 'On organizational becoming: rethinking organizational change', *Organization Science*, vol. 13, no. 5 (2002), pp. 567–82.

Questions

1 What are the problems associated with top-down or bottom-up views of change management?

2 If you were a senior executive which approach would you take and in what circumstances?

3 Are the different views irreconcilable? (You will find the perspectives on the management of strategy in the commentaries useful background reading.)

change on the table. Moreover, resistance that is explicit is more capable of being addressed than that which is passive or covert. So those managing the change programme need to see scrutiny and resistance as a basis for engaging others in the change programme.

- *Broken agreements and violation of trust.* The need for a clear message about the need for and direction of change has been emphasised in this chapter. However, if senior management fail to provide honest assessments of the situation or provide undertakings to employees on which they subsequently renege, then they will lose the trust and respect of employees and, very likely, ensure heightened resistance to change.

Many of the problems and challenges of managing strategic change are reflected in the Key Debate for this chapter.

SUMMARY

www.pearsoned.co.uk/mystrategylab
AUDIO SUMMARY

A recurrent theme in this chapter has been that approaches, styles and means of change need to be tailored to the context of that change. Bearing in mind this general point, this chapter has emphasised the following:

- There are different *types of strategic change* which can be thought of in terms of the *extent* of culture change required and its *nature* – whether it can be achieved through incremental change or requires urgent action (the 'big bang' approach). Different approaches and means of managing change are likely to be required for these different types of change.
- It is also important to diagnose wider aspects of organisational context summarised in the Change Kaleidoscope. These include the *resources and skills that need to be preserved*, the degree of *homogeneity or diversity* in the organisation, the *capability, capacity and readiness* for change and the *power to make change happen*.
- *Forcefield analysis* is a useful means of identifying blockages to change and potential levers for change.
- *Situational leadership* suggests that strategic leaders need to adopt different *styles* of managing strategic change according to different contexts and in relation to the involvement and interest of different groups.
- *Levers for managing strategic change* need to be considered in terms of the type of change and context of change. Such levers include building a *compelling case for change*, *challenging the taken-for-granted*, the need to change *operational processes*, *routines* and *symbols*, the importance of *political processes*, and other change *tactics*.

WORK ASSIGNMENTS

*✳ Denotes more advanced work assignments. * Refers to a case study in the Text and Cases edition.*

14.1 Drawing on section 14.2.2 assess the key contextual dimensions of an organisation (such as for the case example on Faslane) and consider how they should influence the design of a programme of strategic change.

14.2 Use a forcefield analysis to identify blockages and facilitators of change for an organisation (such as one for which you have considered the need for a change in strategic direction in a previous assignment). Identify what aspects of the changes suggested by this analysis can be managed as part of a change programme and how.

14.3 Compare and contrast the different styles of managing change of leaders you have read about in the press or in this book (for example, John Howie and Craig Lockhart at Faslane, Fergus Chambers at Cordia* or Stuart Rose at Marks & Spencer*).

14.4✳ In the context of managing strategic change in a large corporation or public-sector organisation, to what extent, and why, do you agree with Richard Pascale's argument that it is easier to act ourselves into a better way of thinking than it is to think ourselves into a better way of acting? (References 30 to 36 will be useful here.)

14.5✳ There are a number of books by renowned senior executives who have led major changes in their organisation. Read one of these and note the levers and mechanisms for change they employed, using the approaches outlined in this chapter as a checklist. How effective do you think these were in the context that the change leader faced, and could other mechanisms have been used?

Integrative assignment

14.6✳ What would be the key issues for the corporate parent of a diversified organisation with a multidomestic international strategy (see Chapter 8) wishing to change to a more related portfolio? Consider this in terms of (a) the strategic capabilities that the parent might require (Chapters 3 and 7), (b) the implications for organising and controlling its subsidiaries (Chapter 13), (c) the likely blockages to such change and (d) how these might be overcome (Chapter 14).

RECOMMENDED KEY READINGS

- J. Balogun and V. Hope Hailey, *Exploring Strategic Change*, Prentice Hall, 3rd edition, 2008, builds on and extends many of the ideas in this chapter. In particular, it emphasises the importance of tailoring change programmes to organisational context and discusses more fully many of the change levers reviewed in this chapter.

- The paper by John Kotter, 'Leading change: why transformation efforts fail', *Harvard Business Review*, March–April 1995, pp. 59–67 (also see the Key Debate) provides a useful view of what a change programme might look like. An alternative but complementary perspective is provided by Julia Balogun, 'Managing change: steering a course between intended strategies and unanticipated outcomes', *Long Range Planning*, vol. 39 (2006), pp. 29–49.

- For an understanding of different approaches to managing change: M. Beer and N. Nohria, 'Cracking the code of change', *Harvard Business Review*, vol. 78, no. 3 (May–June 2000), pp. 133–41.

- The study of change programmes by L.C. Harris and E. Ogbonna, 'The unintended consequences of culture interventions: a study of unexpected outcomes', *British Journal of Management*, vol. 13, no. 1 (2002), pp. 31–49 provides a valuable insight into the problems of managing change in organisations.

REFERENCES

1. *Lessons Learned: Straight Talk from the World's Top Business Leaders: Managing Change*, Harvard Business School Press, 2007, p. 25.

2. J. Kotter, 'What leaders really do', *Harvard Business Review*, December 2001, pp. 85–96.

3. *Exploring Strategic Change* by J. Balogun and V. Hope Hailey, 3rd edition, Prentice Hall, 2008, is a sister text to this book; this part of the chapter draws on their Chapter 3 on the context of strategic change.

4. For a discussion of the problems of importing change programmes from the private sector to the public sector, see F. Ostroff, 'Change management in government', *Harvard Business Review*, vol. 84, no. 5 (May 2006), pp. 141–7.

5. Based on D. Neal and T. Taylor, 'Spinning on dimes: the challenges of introducing transformational change into the UK Ministry of Defence', *Strategic Change*, vol. 15 (2006), pp. 15–22.

6. For an interesting example of how different contexts affect receptivity to change, see J. Newton, J. Graham, K. McLoughlin and A. Moore, 'Receptivity to change in a general medical practice', *British Journal of Management*, vol. 14, no. 2 (2003), pp. 143–53.

7. See J.-L. Denis, L. Lamothe and A. Langley, 'The dynamics of collective change leadership and strategic change in pluralistic organizations', *The Academy of Management Journal*, vol. 44, no. 4 (2001), pp. 809–37.

8. Approaches to how to use the cultural web for the purposes outlined here are dealt with in detail in the chapter, 'Mapping and re-mapping organisational culture', in V. Ambrosini with G. Johnson and K. Scholes (eds), *Exploring Techniques of Analysis and Evaluation in Strategic Management*, Prentice Hall, 1998, and the similar chapter in G. Johnson and K. Scholes (eds), *Exploring Public Sector Strategy*, Prentice Hall, 2000.

9. This definition of leadership is based on that offered by R.M. Stodgill, 'Leadership, membership and organization', *Psychological Bulletin*, vol. 47 (1950), pp. 1–14. For a more recent and more comprehensive discussion of leadership, see G.A. Yukl, *Leadership in Organizations*, 6th edition, Prentice Hall, 2005.

10. See D. Ulrich, N. Smallwood and K. Sweetman, *Leadership Code: the Five Things Great Leaders Do*, Harvard Business School Press, 1999.

11. This is emphasised by John Kotter (reference 2).

12. The importance of relationship building was one of the findings of the research of Paul Hersey and Ken Blanchard (*Management of Organizational Behavior: Utilizing Human Resources*, Prentice Hall, 1988).

13. See S. Floyd and W. Wooldridge, *The Strategic Middle Manager: How to Create and Sustain Competitive Advantage*, Jossey-Bass, 1996.

14. See for example J. Balogun and G. Johnson: 'Organizational restructuring and middle manager sensemaking', *Academy of Management Journal*, August 2004; J. Balogun, 'Managing change: steering a course between intended strategies and unanticipated outcomes', *Long Range Planning*, vol. 39 (2006), pp. 29–49; J. Sillence and F. Mueller, 'Switching strategic perspective: the reframing of accounts of responsibility', *Organization Studies*, vol. 28, no. 2 (2007), pp. 155–76.

15. The discussion on different approaches of strategic leaders and evidence for the effectiveness of the adoption of different approaches can be found in D. Goleman, 'Leadership that gets results', *Harvard Business Review*, vol. 78, no. 2 (March–April 2000), pp. 78–90, and C.M. Farkas and S. Wetlaufer, 'The ways chief executive officers lead', *Harvard Business Review*, vol. 74, no. 3 (May–June 1996), pp. 110–12.

16. See M. Beer and N. Nohria, 'Cracking the code of change', *Harvard Business Review*, vol. 78, no. 3 (May–June 2000), pp. 133–41.

17. Different authors explain change styles in different ways. This section is based on the typologies used by J. Balogun and V. Hope Haley (see 3 above, section 2.4, pp. 31–6) and D. Dunphy and D. Stace, 'The strategic management of corporate change', *Human Relations*, vol. 46, no. 8 (1993), pp. 905–20. For an alternative framework see R. Caldwell, 'Models of change agency: a fourfold classification', *British Journal of Management*, vol. 14, no. 2 (2003), pp. 131–42.

18. For example D.A. Garvin and M.A. Roberto, 'Change through persuasion', *Harvard Business Review*, February 2005, pp. 104–12.

19. See Balogun and Johnson (reference 14).

20. For evidence of the effects of involvement in the strategy development process see: N. Collier, F. Fishwick and S.W. Floyd, 'Managerial involvement and perceptions of strategy process', *Long Range Planning*, vol. 37, no. 1 (2004), pp. 67–83.

21. Evidence for this is provided by D. Dunphy and D. Stace (reference 17 above) and see also Collier, Fishwick and Floyd (reference 20 above).

22. See Carolyn Aiken and Scott Keller, 'The irrational side of change management', *The McKinsey Quarterly*, no. 2, 2009, 101–9.

23. For an example of this approach see J.M. Mezias, P. Grinyer and W.D. Guth, 'Changing collective cognition: a process model for strategic change', *Long Range Planning*, vol. 34, no. 1 (2001), pp. 71–95. Also for a systematic approach to strategy making and change based on such surfacing, see F. Ackermann and C. Eden with I. Brown, *The Practice of Making Strategy*, Sage, 2005.

24. For a discussion of the psychological context, thinking flaws, and the impact that these have for managers as they consider the future, see K. van der Heijden, R. Bradfield, G. Burt, G. Cairns and G. Wright, *The Sixth Sense: Accelerating Organizational Learning with Scenarios*, Wiley, 2002, chapter 2.

25. See M. Hammer and J. Champy, *Reengineering the Corporation: A Manifesto for Business Revolution*, HarperCollins, 2004.

26. This example is given by Michael Hammer in 'Deep change: how operational innovation can transform your

CHAPTER 14 LEADERSHIP AND STRATEGIC CHANGE

company', *Harvard Business Review*, vol. 82, no. 4 (April 2004), pp. 84–93.

27. This quote is on page 135 of R. Pascale, M. Millemann and L. Gioja, 'Changing the way we change', *Harvard Business Review*, vol. 75, no. 6 (November–December 1997), pp. 126–39.

28. See 26 above.

29. See Gerry Johnson, Stuart Smith and Brian Codling, 'Institutional change and strategic agency: an empirical analysis of managers' experimentation with routines in strategic decision-making', in *The Cambridge Handbook of Strategy as Practice*, edited by D. Golsorkhi, L. Rouleau, D. Seidl and E. Vaara, 2010.

30. For a fuller discussion of this theme, see G. Johnson, 'Managing strategic change: the role of symbolic action', *British Journal of Management*, vol. 1, no. 4 (1990), pp. 183–200. Also see J.M. Higgins and C. McCallaster, 'If you want strategic change don't forget your cultural artefacts', *Journal of Change Management*, vol. 4, no. 1 (2004), pp. 63–73.

31. For a discussion of the role of rituals in change, see D. Sims, S. Fineman and Y. Gabriel, *Organizing and Organizations: an Introduction*, Sage, 1993.

32. See H.M. Trice and J.M. Beyer, 'Studying organisational cultures through rites and ceremonials', *Academy of Management Review*, vol. 9, no. 4 (1984), pp. 653–69; H.M. Trice and J.M. Beyer, 'Using six organisational rites to change culture', in R.H. Kilman, M.J. Saxton, R. Serpa and associates (eds), *Gaining Control of the Corporate Culture*, Jossey-Bass, 1985.

33. See C. Hardy, I. Palmer and N. Phillips, 'Discourse as a strategic resource', *Human Relations*, vol. 53, no. 9 (2000), p. 1231.

34. This discussion is based on observations of the role of political activities in organisations by, in particular, H. Mintzberg, *Power in and around Organizations*, Prentice Hall, 1983, and J. Pfeffer, *Power in Organizations*, Pitman, 1981. However, perhaps the most interesting book on political management remains Niccolo Machiavelli's sixteenth-century work, *The Prince* (available in Penguin Books, 2003). It is also the basis of a management book by Gerald Griffin, *Machiavelli on Management: Playing and Winning the Corporate Power Game*, Praeger, 1991.

35. For a fuller discussion of this approach by Bratton and other change agents, see W.C. Kim and R. Mauborgne, 'Tipping point leadership', *Harvard Business Review*, vol. 81, no. 4 (April 2003), pp. 60–9.

36. For a review of research that makes this point see: D. Buchanan, L. Fitzgerald, D. Ketley, R. Gallop, J.L. Jones, S.S. Lamont, A. Neath and E. Whitby, 'No going back: a review of the literature on sustaining organizational change', *International Journal of Management Reviews*, vol. 7, no. 3 (2005), pp. 189–205.

37. Turnaround strategy is more extensively explained in D. Lovett and S. Slatter, *Corporate Turnaround*, Penguin Books, 1999, and P. Grinyer, D. Mayes and P. McKiernan, 'The sharpbenders: achieving a sustained improvement in performance', *Long Range Planning*, vol. 23, no. 1 (1990), pp. 116–25. Also see V.L. Barker and I.M. Duhaime, 'Strategic change in the turnaround process: theory and empirical evidence', *Strategic Management Journal*, vol. 18, no. 1 (1997), pp. 13–38.

38. See the 'Sharpbenders' study (reference 37 above).

39. See K. Pajunen, 'Stakeholder influences in organizational survival', *Journal of Management Studies*, vol. 43, no. 6 (2006), pp. 1261–88.

40. The value of working with aspects of the existing culture is a finding from the research of S. Finkelstein, C. Harvey and T. Lawton, documented in *Breakout Strategy*, McGraw-Hill, 2007.

41. The observations and examples here are largely based on L.C. Harris and E. Ogbonna, 'The unintended consequences of culture interventions: a study of unexpected outcomes', *British Journal of Management*, vol. 13, no. 1 (2002), pp. 31–49; J.D. Ford, L.W. Ford and A.D. Amelio, 'Resistance to change: the rest of the story, *Academy of Management Review*, vol. 23 (2008), pp. 362–77; and D.A. Garvin and M.A. Roberto (18 above).

CASE EXAMPLE

Managing change at Faslane

Thirty miles west of Glasgow is HM Naval Base Clyde (Faslane), the home of the UK's nuclear submarines that carry the Trident weapon system. It is a Ministry of Defence (MOD) installation, but managed by private sector Babcock Marine, part of Babcock International.

The Babcock Marine office overlooks Gareloch on which the naval base is situated and where the ships and the 148-metre-long Trident submarines are maintained. As well as the base's offices there is also accommodation for the sailors, all within a heavily guarded barbed wire perimeter fence. Over the peninsula is Coulport, also part of the base, where nuclear warheads are processed and loaded onto submarines.

John Howie was the Babcock Marine Managing Director from 2002 to 2006.

John, how did Babcock Marine get involved at Faslane?

Faslane had been run entirely by the MOD and the Royal Navy. By 2000 the MOD had decided they needed to significantly reduce the cost and improve operational effectiveness of their naval bases and that in-house MOD management would find that difficult given the restrictions they operated under as part of a wider civil service. So they established partnering arrangements with industrial firms. In 2002 we signed a contract initially for a five-year period to deliver £76 (~€83; ~$114) million of cost savings without affecting the service provided to the Navy. A percentage of that saving would come to us as profit; the bulk would go to the customer as cost reduction. Our profit was entirely a share of the savings, so no cost reduction, no profit; but the contract made sure we couldn't do that by prejudicing service levels.

Over 1,700 civil service posts and nearly 300 Royal Navy personnel and civil servants were seconded to us. In addition there remained 1,000 other civil servants on site, security personnel, police and the MOD Guard Service, Royal Marines, together with the sailors, ships and the submarines. The population of Faslane and Coulport is about 7,500 people.

What was it like when you arrived?

The customer support ethos didn't feel right. Despite being a naval base, the staff saw buildings and infra-

Source: Babcock Faslane.

structure facilities as more important than supporting the Navy. The focus was from the waterfront inward rather than looking outwards to the ships and submarines. I think that was because the people who looked after the site were often civilians who had been here much longer than the Navy people who looked after ships and submarines and generally moved on after 2–3 years. The civilians had built up empires. So the challenge was to become focused on delivering services to the customer, the Navy.

Moreover a public sector manager who's got wide-ranging responsibilities and a fairly large budget has no incentive to reduce costs. They don't share in any benefits and were brought up in a system where, if they hadn't spent their budget, next year it would be cut. So we believed that a big opportunity might come from changing the mindset: to see their job as to deliver with the minimum possible spend.

Another difficulty is that every significant decision of a civil servant could be questioned by an elected politician. That makes people naturally conservative. You also end up with lots of layers in the organisation; lots of people with limited autonomy who focus on doing things within their own control. It's procedural; a 'handle turning' exercise.

With political accountability it's also important to demonstrate an audit path for the decision you made. So speedy decision making is secondary to being able to demonstrate why you made the decision.

What of the management here before Babcock?

The commodore in charge when this process started was willing to change in a way some of his predecessors hadn't been. He'd come to the same conclusion about the need to change from infrastructure focus to naval focus. He saw partnering as the opportunity to better manage the people. The commodore's management team were a mix of people who either believed change was necessary and were willing to give partnering a try or people who were likely to be personally disadvantaged by partnering and were less supportive.

What of the workforce?

There was a perception that because of the base's role supporting the nuclear deterrent, they were ring-fenced from radical changes. Their view was that the base was doing a good job so why would you want to change that? There was no perception of a need to save money. They'd also been through a whole raft of MOD change, not least large-scale outsourcing programmes. There was the feeling of flavour-of-the-month change pro-grammes. So the backdrop was a workforce forcibly transferred to a private company and fearful of what change would mean.

So how did you set about change?

We brought in people from Babcock who had lived through similar changes. What they didn't necessarily understand was how to run a naval base, but the MOD transferred people to us who knew how to do that. Our job was to manage them differently.

The initial aim was to get visibility about how money was being spent whilst focusing on things that matter to the customer. We looked carefully at structures and processes to figure out how they operated and ask how that could be done differently. For example, there was a process that required any change to be documented and passed through a series of review points. After all, in a nuclear naval base you have to be sure that changing something fundamental to safety can be done without unacceptable risk. At each stage of that process people were given 14 days to review it; and of course everyone looked at it on day thirteen. So the overall process took about 56 days. It also became clear that a number of the review points weren't adding value; it was: 'I'm letting you look at this because you might be interested', not because involvement was critical. By taking those stages out you free up people's bureaucratic burden. You also don't give them 14 days to review it; you give them two days. Now that 56-day process is six days; a simple example of process re-engineering.

All that sounds very mechanistic

It's not like that. We are an organisation that doesn't own any physical assets other than the people who walk through the gate every day. So change is very much about people. And with 2,000 people you get access to a whole raft of ideas and change initiatives that we would never have thought of because we had never worked in this environment. So part of it was about removing shackles from people to come up with their own change ideas. But culturally that's a challenge, when for many there's no incentive to come up with a change when it might mean that people next to you get made redundant.

So how do you do it?

We had a management structure that wasn't right to deliver change. We had seven layers in it. It's now (2006) down to a maximum of four layers. We've reappointed all the jobs. We asked other companies which had been through large-scale changes: 'what should we learn from what you did?' The answer was: 'Implement the management structural changes early'. People tried to launch transformational change with the existing team, got two or three years into it, realised it wasn't working, and then changed the structure. We are doing it the other way round. We implemented all the low-level changes upfront because they're easy. That allowed us to deliver £14 million of saving in the first year against a target of £3 million. But once you get into more transformational change – about trying to deliver a strategy of being the best, most profitable organisation supporting the UK submarine fleet – we needed different skill sets. So we've changed the structure. The management team we had was about 250; it's now about half of that.

The problem is that as we get away from the changes which are relatively mechanistic we get into changes that are much more complex in nature.

It also seems a difficult political situation

The first thing is to understand who you need to have as allies, such as the Naval Base Commander. Our success was intertwined. I have a parent company to satisfy, whilst the Commodore has to manage the relationships with the wider MOD and the Navy Board. Beyond that you have to look at the wider stakeholders. If the commanding officers of the ships and submarines were saying 'we're getting a bad service' we'd have struggled. Or if the security people thought we weren't interested in national security. Another key stakeholder was the local community. We did a lot of work upfront with two local councils because the base represents 9.5% of employment in the area and we've reduced by about 400 full-time equivalent posts. Some of those have been naval posts rather than local people. And 98 reductions have been voluntary redundancies. Fairly quickly the meetings with the councils stopped because they became comfortable we were doing things the right way.

So, what has been achieved?

Year 1 the target was £3 million of savings; we delivered £14 million. Year 2 the target was £12 million; we delivered £16 million. By the end of Year 5 we had delivered around £100 million against our £76 million target; that's over 20% reduction in annual running costs. By the end of Year 10 we should have saved £280 million; that's 38.2%. And the Navy's view was that the service they received was better, attitude better, communication better, responsiveness better. So we have delivered both cost reductions and service improvement.

Craig Lockhart, part of the original Babcock management team, succeeded John Howie in 2006. He takes up the story in 2009.

'We are in our second year of having a performance scorecard. We started to measure outputs. Everyone down to team leaders have become acutely aware that business performance is not something to be hidden. It has to be transparent. However, it wasn't just about measurement. Business planning had been top-down. As our journey developed we appreciated that it was a hearts and minds issue: that we had to get the entire workforce aligned around common objectives. We held "the event in the tent" sessions and nearly 3,000 people went through day-long discussions where we allowed them to challenge and express their views about the transformation of Naval Base Clyde.'

'They got to ask real questions and started to see that they got real answers. If there was bad news we would tell them it was bad news. If it was good news we would tell them it's good news but it was always honest news. So, we started to get the trust of the workforce. Now we've got the trade unions talking about "our company". We followed it up with blank business plans. We said, "We've given you the broad headings, the broad objectives from a company point of view, but what's important is where do you think you fit in". They were tasked to generate their own team, their own departmental business plans.'

'By 2009 we were also producing a joint business plan with the customer. It's not a Babcock Marine business plan or an MOD business plan. It's a plan on behalf of Clyde. And by the end of the year the Commodore and his team of directors will co-locate with us. We will be working together.'

In April 2010, Craig was able to announce* that Faslane would become the home base, not just for nuclear submarines but for the entire UK submarines fleet. Together with the associated submarines and nulear training schools, it could mean up to 2000 more jobs at the base by 2014.

* *Source: Helensburgh Advertiser, 29 April 2010.*

> ## Questions
>
> 1 In relation to sections 14.2.1 and 14.5, what is the type of change being pursued at Faslane?
>
> 2 Describe the change styles of John Howie and Craig Lockhart.
>
> 3 What levers of change are being used (see section 14.4)? What others could be used and why?
>
> 4 Assess the effectiveness of the change programme.

15

THE PRACTICE OF STRATEGY

Learning outcomes

After reading this chapter you should be able to:

● Identify *key people involved in strategising*, including top management, strategy consultants, strategic planners and middle managers.

● Assess which people should be included in addressing different strategic issues.

● Evaluate different approaches to strategising activity, including *analysis*, *issue-selling*, *decision-making structures* and *communicating*.

● Recognise key elements in various methodologies commonly used in strategising, including *strategy workshops*, *projects*, *hypothesis testing* and writing *business cases* and *strategic plans*.

Key terms

Business case p. 521

Hypothesis testing p. 521

Strategic issue-selling p. 510

Strategic plan p. 521

Strategic planners p. 502

Strategy projects p. 520

Strategy workshops p. 518

(15.1) INTRODUCTION

If you were to be appointed as a strategic planner, or became a managing director of a business, what would you actually do to develop a strategy? This final chapter examines how managers actually practise strategy, using the theoretical concepts, tools and techniques introduced earlier in the book. Whereas Chapter 12 introduced the overall organisational process of strategy development, this chapter is about what managers do *inside* the process. The aim is to examine the practicalities of strategy-making for top managers, strategic planning specialists, strategy consultants or managers lower down the organisation.

The chapter has three sections as shown in Figure 15.1:

● *The strategists*. The chapter starts by looking at the various people involved in making strategy. It does not assume that strategy is made just by top management. As pointed out in Chapter 12, strategy is often emergent, and involves people from all over the organisation and often from outside. The Key Debate at the end of the chapter addresses the controversial involvement of external strategy consultants. Readers can ask themselves how they fit into this set of strategists, or how they might in the future.

● *Strategising activities*. The chapter continues by considering the kinds of work and activity that strategists carry out in their strategy-making. This includes, not just the strategy analysis that has been central to a large part of this book, but also the managing of strategic issues over time, the realities of strategic decision-making and the critical task of communicating strategic decisions throughout the organisation.

● *Strategising methodologiess*. The final section covers some of the practical methodologies that managers use to carry out their strategising activities. This includes strategy workshops for formulating or communicating strategy; strategy projects and strategy consulting teams; hypothesis testing to guide strategy work; and the writing of strategic plans and business cases.

Figure 15.1 The pyramid of strategy practice

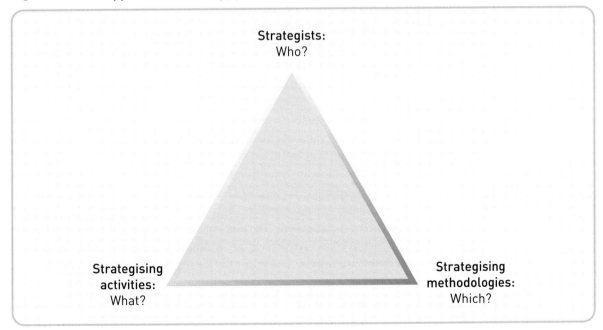

Figure 15.1 integrates these three sections in a *pyramid of practice*.[1] The pyramid highlights three questions that run through this chapter: *who* to include in strategy-making; *what* to do in carrying out strategising activity; and *which* strategising methodologies to use in organising this strategising activity. Placing strategists at the top of the pyramid emphasises the role of managerial discretion and skill in strategy-making. It is the strategists who choose and enact both the strategising activity and the strategy methodologies that are at the base of the pyramid. Strategists' choices and skill with regard to activity and methodologies can make a real difference to final outcomes. The rest of the chapter seeks to guide practising strategists through the key choices they may have to make in action.

(15.2) THE STRATEGISTS

This section introduces the different types of people involved in strategy. It starts at the top-management level, but includes strategic planners, consultants and middle managers. One key issue is how middle managers can increase their influence in strategy-making.

15.2.1 Top managers and directors

The conventional view is that strategy is the business of top management. This view suggests that top management is clearly separated from operational responsibilities, so that it can focus on overall strategy.[2] If top managers are directly involved in operations such as sales or service delivery, they are liable to get distracted from long-term issues by day-to-day responsibilities and to represent the interests of their departments or business units rather than the interests of their organisation as a whole. In the private sector at least, top managers' job titles underline this strategic responsibility: company directors set direction, managers manage.

In reality, the top management role involves much more than setting direction. Also, different roles are played by different members, whether *Chief Executive Officer*, the *Top Management Team* or *Non-Executive Directors*:

- The *Chief Executive Officer* is often seen as the 'chief strategist', ultimately responsible for all strategic decisions. Chief Executives of large companies typically spend about one-third of their time on strategy.[3] Michael Porter stresses the value of a clear strategic leader, somebody capable of setting a disciplined approach to what fits and what does not fit the overall strategy.[4] In this view, the Chief Executive Officer (or Managing Director or equivalent top individual) owns the strategy and is accountable for its success or failure. The clarity of this individual responsibility can no doubt focus attention. However, there are dangers. First, centralising responsibility on the Chief Executive Officer can lead to excessive personalisation. Organisations respond to setbacks simply by changing their Chief Executive Officer, rather than examining deeply the internal sources of failure. Second, successful Chief Executives can become over-confident, seeing themselves as corporate heroes and launching strategic initiatives of ever-increasing ambition.[5] The over-confidence of heroic leaders often leads to spectacular failures. Jim Collins's research on 'great' American companies that outperformed their rivals over the long term found that their Chief Executive Officers were typically modest, steady and long-serving.[6]
- The *top management team*, often an organisation's executive directors, also shares responsibility for strategy. They can bring additional experience and insight to the Chief Executive

Officer. In theory, they should be able to challenge the Chief Executive Officer and increase strategic debate. In practice, the top management team is often constrained in at least three ways. First, except in the largest companies, top managers often carry operational responsibilities that either distract them or bias their strategic thinking: for example, in a business the marketing director will have ongoing concerns about marketing, the production director about production, and so on. In the public sector the top management team will also, very likely, be heads of operating departments. Second, top managers are also frequently appointed by the Chief Executive Officer; consequently, they may lack the independence for real challenge. Finally, top management teams, especially where their members have similar backgrounds and face strong leadership, often suffer from '*groupthink*', the tendency to build strong consensus amongst team members and avoid internal questioning or conflict.[7] Top management teams can minimise groupthink by fostering diversity in membership (for example, differences in age, career tracks and sex), by ensuring openness to outside views, for example those of non-executive directors, and by promoting internal debate and questioning.

- *Non-executive directors* have no executive management responsibility within the organisation, and so in theory should be able to offer an external and objective view on strategy. Although this varies according to national corporate governance systems (see section 4.3.2), in a public company the chairman of the board is typically non-executive. The chairman will normally be consulted closely by the Chief Executive Officer on strategy, as he or she will have a key role in liaising with investors. However, the ability of the chairman and other non-executives to contribute substantially to strategy can be limited. Non-executives are typically part-time appointments. The predominant role for non-executive directors in strategy, therefore, is consultative, reviewing and challenging strategy proposals that come from the top management executive team. A key role for them also is to ensure that the organisation has a rigorous system in place for the making and renewing of strategy. It is therefore important that non-executives are authoritative and experienced individuals, that they have independence from the top management executive team and that they are fully briefed before board meetings.

Top management capability in making strategy should not simply be assumed. Managers are often promoted to strategic roles for their success in dealing with operations or their professional skill in a particular functional specialism. These kinds of experience do not necessarily provide the skills needed for the tasks involved in making strategy. There are at least three important qualities senior managers need if they are to contribute effectively to high-level strategy-making:

- *Mastery of analytical concepts and techniques*, as introduced in this book, cannot be assumed. Sometimes an executive education course can help improve understanding of strategy concepts and techniques.

- *Social and influencing skills* are necessary if analysis is to be understood and accepted by senior colleagues. Again, senior managers are not equally effective in strategic discussions, but there are now many professional coaches who can help.

- *Group acceptance as a player* in strategic discussions. Boards and senior executive teams are social groups like any other, where members have to win respect. Clear and significant success in one's own particular sphere of responsibility is normally a precondition for being respected as a contributor to wider discussions of the organisation's strategy.

15.2.2 Strategic planners

Strategic planners, sometimes known as strategy directors, corporate development managers or similar, **are managers with a formal responsibility for coordinating the strategy process** (see Chapter 12). Although small companies very rarely have full-time strategic planners, they are common in large companies and increasingly widespread in the public and not-for-profit sectors. As in Illustration 15.1, organisations frequently advertise for strategic planning jobs. Here, the personal specifications give a clear picture of the types of role a typical strategic planner might be expected to play. In a large corporation a strategic planner would not only be working on a three-year strategic plan, but investigating acquisition targets, monitoring competitors and helping territory senior managers (country managers) with their own plans. In this the role is not just about analysis in the back office. Strategic planning is also about communications, team work and influencing skills.

Although the job in Illustration 15.1 is being advertised externally, strategic planners are often drawn from inside their own organisations. Internal strategic planners are likely to have an advantage in the important non-analytical parts of the job. As internal recruits, they bring to the planning role an understanding of the business, networks with key people in the organisation and credibility with internal audiences. Moreover, an internal appointment to a strategic planning role can serve as a developmental stage for managers on track for top management roles. Participating in strategy provides promising managers with exposure to senior management and gives them a view of the organisation as a whole.

Strategic planners do not take strategic decisions themselves. However, they typically have at least three important tasks:[8]

- *Information and analysis.* Strategic planners have the time, skills and resources to provide information and analysis for key decision-makers. This might be in response to some 'trigger' event – such as a possible merger – or as part of a regular planning cycle. A background of good information and analysis can leave an organisation much better prepared to respond quickly and confidently even to unexpected events as they occur. Strategic planners can also package this information and analysis in formats that ensure clear communication of strategic decisions.

- *Managers of the strategy process.* Both for the headquarters and for business units, strategic planners can assist and guide other managers through their strategic planning cycles (see Illustration 12.2 in Chapter 12). This will involve acting as a bridge between the corporate centre and the businesses by clarifying corporate expectations and guidelines. It could also involve helping business-level managers develop strategy by providing templates, analytical techniques and strategy training. This bridging role is important in achieving alignment of corporate-level and business-level strategies. Researchers[9] point out that this alignment is often lacking; that 60 per cent of organisations do not link financial budgets to corporate strategic priorities; and that the measures of performance of 70 per cent of middle managers and more than 90 per cent of front-line employees have no link to the success or failure of strategy implementation.

- *Special projects.* Strategic planners can be a useful resource to support top management on special projects, such as acquisitions or organisational change. Here strategy planners will typically work on project teams with middle managers from within the organisation and often with external consultants. Project management skills are likely to be important.

In addition to these tasks, they typically work closely with the CEO, discussing and helping refine his or her strategic thinking. Indeed, many strategic planners are physically located

ILLUSTRATION 15.1

Wanted: Team member for strategy unit

The following advertisement appeared on the UK Cabinet Office website. It gives an insight into the kind of work such strategic planners do and the skills and background required.

Job Description for a Team Member: Band A

About the Strategy Unit

The PMSU (Prime Minister's Strategy Unit) has three main roles:

- to carry out strategy reviews and provide policy advice in accordance with the Prime Minister's policy priorities;
- to support Government Departments in developing effective strategies and policies – including helping them to build their strategic capability; and
- to identify and effectively disseminate thinking on emerging issues and challenges facing the UK e.g. through occasional strategic audits.

Post holders will be members of small teams set up to address issues where innovative approaches and fresh thinking are necessary to ensure the achievement of the Government's objectives. Teams will be drawn from both inside and outside the Civil Service and work intensively on an issue, for periods ranging from 3–4 weeks to 3–4 months or longer depending on the task.

Candidates will need to have first rate policy or strategy experience, strong interpersonal skills, and the ability to write clearly and compellingly. Outstanding analytical and problem solving skills are absolutely essential to the role.

Essential competences for the SU

Strategic Thinking
1. Knowledge and understanding of government priorities
2. Knowledge of the wider policy environment, including political or institutional restraints
3. Ability to derive clear goals and strategies from a complex brief

Analysis and Use of Evidence
1. Knows and deploys a range of analytical tools
2. Uses a variety of tools in collecting and analysing evidence
3. Works in partnership with a wide range of analytical experts to achieve project goals
4. Ability to understand complex statistical data
5. Understands what constitutes good evidence

People Management
1. Able to develop individuals for high performance
2. Champions equality and diversity, and promotes best practice
3. Able to give good feedback that people can act on

Programme and Project Management
1. Can work with a team to develop a project plan
2. Anticipates, manages and monitors programme/project risks
3. Ensures effective communications with stakeholders

Specialist Professional Skills

Essential
1. Good quality qualifications or training in economics, social policy, operational research or similar
2. Excellent quantitative and qualitative analytical skills
3. Sector knowledge – an understanding of social policy is an advantage

Desirable
1. Experience in working in a think-tank or high profile management consultancy role or policy or analytical arm of a government department.

Source: from Extracts from Strategy Unit Job Description for a Team Member: Band A from http://www.cabinetoffice.gov.uk/strategy/jobs/band_a.asp. Crown Copyright material is reproduced with permission under the terms of the Click-Use Licence.

Questions

1 What would be the attractions of this job for you? What would be the disadvantages?

2 What relevant skills and experience do you already have, and what skills and experience would you still need to acquire before you were able to apply for this job?

close to the CEO. In doing all this, they may have relatively few resources – perhaps a small team of support staff – and little formal power, but their closeness to the CEO is likely to mean that managers throughout an organisation are likely to use them to sound out ideas.[10]

15.2.3 Middle managers

As in section 15.2.1, a good deal of conventional management theory excludes middle managers from strategy-making. Middle managers are seen as lacking an appropriately objective and long-term perspective, being too involved in operations.[11] In this view, middle managers' role is limited to strategy implementation. This is, of course, a vital role. However, there is increasing middle management involvement in strategy-making for at least three reasons.[12] First, many organisations are decentralising their organisational structures to increase accountability and responsiveness in fast-moving and competitive environments. As a result, strategic responsibilities are being thrust down the organisational hierarchy. Second, the rise of business education means that middle managers are now better trained and more confident in the strategy domain than they used to be. These higher-calibre middle managers are both more able and more eager to participate in strategy. Third, the shift away from a traditional manufacturing economy to one based more on professional services (such as design, consulting or finance) means that often the key sources of competitive advantage are no longer resources such as capital, which can be handed out from the headquarters, but the knowledge of people actually involved in the operations of the business. Middle managers at operational level can understand and influence these knowledge-based sources of competitive advantage much more effectively than remote top managers.

In this context, there are at least four roles they have in relation to the management of strategy:[13]

- *Information source*. Their knowledge and experience of the realities of the organisation and its market is likely to be greater than that of many top managers. So middle managers are a potential source of information about changes in the strategic position of the organisation.

- '*Sense making*' of strategy. Top management may set down a strategic direction; but how it is explained and made sense of in specific contexts (e.g. a region of a multinational or a functional department) may, intentionally or not, be left to middle managers.[14] They are therefore a crucial *relevance bridge* between top management and members of the organisation at lower levels, in effect translating strategy into a message that is locally relevant. If misinterpretation of that intended strategy is to be avoided, it is therefore vital that middle managers understand and feel an ownership of it. (See also the Key Debate in Chapter 11.)

- *Reinterpretation and adjustment* of strategic responses as events unfold (e.g. in terms of relationships with customers, suppliers, the workforce and so on); this is a vital role for which middle managers are uniquely qualified because of their day-to-day contact with such aspects of the organisation and its environment.

- *Champions of ideas*. Given their closeness to markets and operations middle managers may not only provide information but champion new ideas that can be the foundation of new strategies.

Middle managers may also increase their influence on strategy when they have:

- *Key organisational positions*. Middle managers responsible for larger departments, business units or strategically important parts of the organisation have influence because they are likely to have critical knowledge.[15] Also, managers with outward-facing roles (for example, in marketing) tend to have greater strategic influence than managers with inward-facing roles (such as quality or operations).[16]

- *Access to organisational networks*. Middle managers may not have hierarchical power, but can increase their influence by using their internal organisational networks. Drawing together information from network members can help provide an integrated perspective on what is happening in the organisation as a whole, something that otherwise can be difficult to get when occupying a specialised position in the middle of an organisation. Mobilising networks to raise issues and support proposals can also give more influence than any single middle manager can achieve on their own.[17] Strategically influential middle managers are therefore typically good networkers.

- *Access to the organisation's 'strategic conversation'*. Strategy-making does not just happen in isolated, formal episodes, but is part of an ongoing strategic conversation amongst respected managers.[18] To participate in these strategic conversations middle managers should: maximise opportunities to mix formally and informally with top managers; become at ease with the particular language used to discuss strategy in their organisation; familiarise themselves carefully with the key strategic issues; and develop their own personal contribution to these strategic issues.

In the public sector elected politicians have traditionally been responsible for policy and public officials supposed to do the implementation. However, three trends similar to those in the corporate world are challenging this division of roles. First, the rising importance of *specialised expertise* has shifted influence to public officials who may have made their careers in particular areas, while politicians are typically generalists. Second, public sector reform in many countries has led to increased *externalisation of functions* to quasi-independent 'agencies' or 'QUANGOs' (quasi-autonomous non-governmental organisations) which, within certain constraints, can make decisions on their own. Third, the same reform processes have changed *internal structures* within public organisations, with decentralisation of units and more 'executive' responsibility granted to public officials. All this is supported by the discourse of 'New Public Management', which encourages officials to be more enterprising and accountable. In short, strategy is increasingly part of the work of public officials too.[19]

15.2.4 Strategy consultants

External consultants are often used in the development of strategy. Leading consultancy firms that focus on strategy include Bain, the Boston Consulting Group, Monitor and McKinsey & Co.[20] Most of the large general consultancy firms also have operations that provide services in strategy development and analysis. There are also smaller 'boutique' consultancy firms and individual consultants who specialise in strategy.

Consultants may play different roles in strategy development in organisations:[21]

- *Analysing, prioritising and generating options*. Strategic issues may have been identified by executives, but there may be so many of them, or disagreement about them, that the organisation faces a lack of clarity on how to go forward. Consultants may analyse such issues afresh and bring an external perspective to help prioritise them or generate options for executives to consider. This may, of course, involve challenging executives' preconceptions about their views of strategic issues.

- *Transferring knowledge.* Consultants are the carriers of knowledge and perceived best practice within and between their clients.

- *Promoting strategic decisions.* In doing this, consultants may substantially influence the decisions that organisations eventually take. A number of major consultancies have been criticised in the past for undue influence on the decisions made by their client organisation, leading to major problems. For example, McKinsey & Co. was heavily associated with Enron's controversial 'asset-lite' business model, and was also the proponent of Swissair's failed 'Hunter' strategy of strategic alliances.[22]

- *Implementing strategic change.* Consultants play a significant role in project planning, coaching and training often associated with strategic change. This is an area that has seen considerable growth, not least because consultants were criticised for leaving organisations with consultancy reports recommending strategies, but taking little responsibility for actually making these happen.

The value of strategy consultants is often controversial (see the Key Debate at the end of this chapter). For example, in the UK government departments have increasingly been criticised for spending too much on consultants. The consultancy spend by nineteen UK central government departments was reported to be over £873 million (~€960m; ~$1309m) in 2008–09.[23] But consultants are often blamed for failures when it is the client's poor management of the consulting process that is ultimately at fault. Many organisations select their consultants unsystematically, give poor initial project briefs and fail to act on and learn from projects at the end. There are three key measures that client organisations can undertake to improve outcomes in strategy consulting:[24]

- *Professionalise purchasing of consulting services.* Instead of hiring consulting firms on the basis of personal relationships with key executives, as is often the case, professionalised purchasing can help ensure clear project briefs, a wide search for consulting suppliers, appropriate pricing, complementarity between different consulting projects and proper review at project-end. The German engineering company Siemens has professionalised its consultancy purchasing, for example, establishing a shortlist of just ten preferred management consulting suppliers.

- *Develop supervisory skills* in order to manage portfolios of consulting projects. The German railway company Deutsche Bahn and automobile giant DaimlerChrysler both have central project offices that control and coordinate all consulting projects throughout their companies. As well as being involved in the initial purchasing decision, these offices can impose systematic governance structures on projects, with clear responsibilities and reporting processes, as well as review and formal assessment at project-end.

- *Partner effectively* with consultants to improve both effectiveness in carrying out the project and knowledge transfer at the end of it. Where possible, project teams should include a mix of consultants and managers from the client organisation, who can provide inside information, guide on internal politics and, sometimes, enhance credibility and receptiveness. As partners in the project, client managers retain knowledge and experience when the consultants have gone and can help in the implementation of recommendations.

15.2.5 Who to include in strategy development?

There is a potentially wide range of people to involve in any strategic issue: as well as the Chief Executive and the top management team, non-executive directors, strategic planners,

Figure 15.2 The access/execution paradox

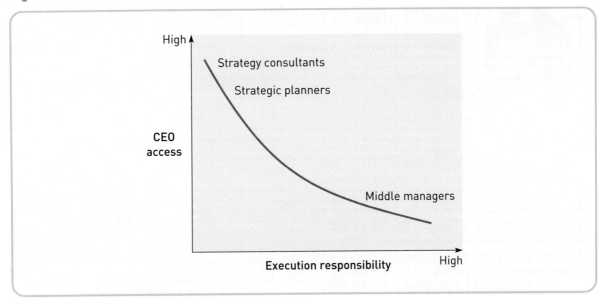

strategic consultants and middle managers. This raises questions about who should be included in addressing particular strategic issues. The paradox of strategy inclusion is that those with the most access to the CEO on strategy are often strategic planners and strategy consultants who have little responsibility for strategy implementation and little knowledge of business on the ground (see Figure 15.2). The middle managers who have both the knowledge and the implementation responsibility can have least access to the CEO in strategy discussions, either because they are too busy with operational realities or because they are seen as biased. Strategy is not necessarily being made by the most appropriate people.

There is no general rule about inclusion or exclusion in strategy-making, but there are criteria that can guide managers about whom to include according to the nature of the strategic issues in hand. Research by McKinsey & Co. indicates that the people involved should vary according to the nature of the issue (see Figure 15.3[25]). For example, issues that are urgent and could involve major changes to strategy (such as a merger or acquisition opportunity) are best approached by small special project teams, consisting of senior managers and perhaps planners and consultants. Issues which may be important but are not urgent (such as deciding on key competitors) can benefit from more prolonged and open strategic conversations, both formal and informal. Urgent issues that do not involve major change (such as responding to competitor threats) require only limited participation. Issues that may involve major changes but require idea generation over time (such as the search for global opportunities) might benefit from more open participation, though this might be organised more formally through a series of planned events, such as conferences bringing together large groups of managers in particular geographical regions.

Illustration 15.2 shows two approaches to achieving productive inclusion in strategy-making at IBM, with its 'strategy jam' and the International Trade Centre's value chain mapping in Uganda. The public sector also often uses the internet for public consultations and discussion forums with regard to controversial policy issues: see for example www.communities.gov.uk/.

ILLUSTRATION 15.2

Jamming and mapping

Participation in strategy making can be important in global businesses and developing enterprises alike.

Jamming at IBM[1]

IBM has developed a $3m (~€2.1m) information technology platform that allows its 300,000 employees to participate in global debates about strategic issues (see Illustration 14.5). These debates are called 'jams' after the structured improvisation ('jamming') used in jazz music. Jams typically combine off-site face-to-face brain-storming sessions with 'threaded' discussions, theme-based forums and electronic idea-ratings organised through the corporate intranet site. All IBM employees have equal access to the jam sessions. IBM manager Mike Malloney explained: 'It's like jazz collaboration, with people building on other people's ideas in a structured format. Jams are a blend of technology and a kind of grassroots discussion of ideas.'

IBM has used jams to address managerial roles, post-merger integration, organisational barriers to innovation and revenue growth (informally dubbed the 'logjam') and the development of a new values statement (the 'ValuesJam'). The ValuesJam took place over three days, generating 2.3 million page views and over a million words of input. Tens of thousands of employee ideas were refined into 65 key ideas, using online voting and IBM's proprietary natural language analytical software ('jamalyzer'). A small team then set to work on refining these further into three overarching values based on innovation, the customer and trust. Chief Executive Sam Palmisano commented on the ValuesJam:

> 'Yes, the electronic argument was hot and contentious and messy.... We had done three or four big online jams before ... Even so, none of those could have prepared us for the emotions unleashed by this topic.'

Mapping in Uganda[2]

The International Trade Centre (ITC) in Geneva (www.intracen.org) is responsible for helping enterprises improve exports. In many developing countries where it operates there is little reliable published information available, development activities can be fragmented and people tend to be reticent unknown individuals. The Ugandan fish processing and exporting

sector provides one example of how these difficulties can be overcome.

ITC worked alongside the Uganda Export Promotion Board to facilitate meetings of stakeholders from all stages of the fish value network on a strategy for export growth. Stakeholders included enterprise owners, community leaders, government and development agencies, services providers such as transport, inspections, customs, banks, freight forwarders and packagers. Meeting in Kampala, they collaborated on a series of exercises to identify market opportunities, diagnose sector performance issues and organise development activity implementation.

They mapped the core stages of their value chains on large wall sheets from target markets back to sources of supply. Sector-wide issues and market requirements were broken down into value chain stage components and illustrated on these maps. The process surfaced tacit information and 'market realities' and stimulated new ideas for value addition, cost cutting and diversification (see Illustration 3.4). It also helped participants see 'the big picture opportunities', understand their mutual dependency and participate in the design of solutions, agree on the priorities to raise sector performance and who should implement which parts of the strategy and how.

Source: (1) S.J. Palmisano, 'Leading change when business is good', *Harvard Business Review*, December (2004), pp. 60–70; PR Newswire, 30 November (2005); (2) Ian Sayers, Senior Advisor for the Private Sector, Division of Trade Support Services, the International Trade Centre, Geneva.

Questions

1 Why was it important at IBM and in the Ugandan fishing industry to obtain wide input on strategic issues? What strategic issues would not require the same kind of input?

2 If you were a smaller company, without the information technology resources of IBM or the help of government agencies as in Uganda, how might you be able to get employee input into strategy development?

Figure 15.3 Who to include in strategy making?

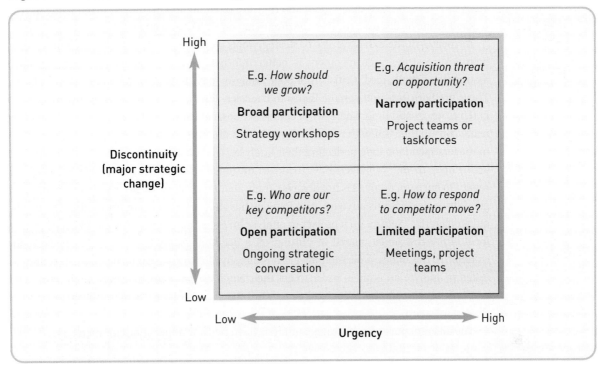

15.3 STRATEGISING

The previous section introduced the key strategists; this section concentrates on what people do in strategising. The section starts with strategy analysis, then issue-selling, decision-making and communications about the chosen strategy. In practice, of course, these activities rarely follow this logical sequence; or they may not happen at all. As Chapter 12 made clear, strategies do not always come about in such ways and strategic decisions are often made without formal analysis and evaluation. So the section ends with a reminder about the often 'messy' nature of strategy development.

15.3.1 Strategy analysis

A good deal of this book is concerned with strategy analysis, and indeed analysis can be an important input into strategy-making. However, as suggested in Chapter 12, strategy is often not the outcome of rational analysis. Analysis is frequently done in an ad hoc and incomplete fashion and not always followed through. Or the analysis activity itself may serve other functions than a simple input into subsequent decisions. Research shows that managers typically use a 'strategy toolkit' of between one and nine tools, with just four being the most common number of tools cited.[26] SWOT (strengths, weaknesses, opportunities and threats) analysis is the most widely used tool in strategy, but even this simple tool is typically used in a way far from the technical ideal. One study found frequent deviations from textbook recommendations, by both managers and consultants.[27] For example, in practice SWOT analyses tend to produce unmanageably long lists of factors (strengths, weaknesses, opportunities and threats), often well over 50 or so. The result is these factors are rarely probed or refined, little substantive analysis is done to investigate them and they are often not followed up systematically in subsequent strategic discussions. (See the discussion on SWOT in section 3.4.4.)

Advocates of the extensive use of strategy tools would argue that their greater use would help ensure strategy development is better informed and managerial bias and ingrained assumptions challenged. Criticism of poor analysis may, however, sometimes be misplaced. There are both *cost* and *purpose* issues to consider. First of all, analysis is costly in terms of both resources and time. There are of course the costs of gathering information, particularly if using consultants. But with regard to time there is also the risk of '*paralysis by analysis*', where managers spend too long perfecting their analyses and not enough time taking decisions and acting upon them.[28] Managers have to judge how much analysis they really need. Second, with regard to purpose, analysis is not always simply about providing the necessary information for good strategic decisions anyway. Ann Langley has shown that the purposes of analysis can be quite different.[29] Setting up a project to analyse an issue thoroughly may even be a deliberate form of *procrastination*, aimed at putting off a decision. Analysis can also be *symbolic*, for example to rationalise a decision after it has already effectively been made. Managers may be asked to analyse an issue in order to get their *buy-in* to decisions that they might otherwise resist. Analyses can also be *political*, to forward the agenda of a particular manager or part of the organisation.

The different purposes of strategy analysis have two key implications for managers:

- *Design the analysis according to the real purpose*. The range and quality of people involved, the time and budget allowed, and the subsequent communication of analysis results should all depend on underlying purpose, whether informational, political or symbolic. For example, prestigious strategy consulting firms are often useful for political and symbolic analyses. Involving a wide group of middle managers in the analysis may help with subsequent buy-in.

- *Invest appropriately in technical quality*. For many projects, improving the quality of the technical analysis will make a valuable addition to subsequent strategic decisions. On other occasions, insisting on technical perfection can be counter-productive. For example, a SWOT analysis that raises lots of issues may be a useful means of allowing managers to vent their own personal frustrations, before getting on with the real strategy work. It may sometimes be better to leave these issues on the table, rather than probing, challenging or even deleting them in a way that could unnecessarily alienate these managers for the following stages.

15.3.2 Strategic issue-selling

Organisations typically face many strategic issues at any point in time. But in complex organisations these issues may not be appreciated to the same extent, or may not even be recognised at all, by those involved in developing strategy. Some issues will be filtered out in the organisational hierarchy; others will be sidelined by more urgent pressures. Moreover, senior managers will rarely have sufficient time and resources to deal with all the issues that do actually reach them. So strategic issues compete for attention. What get top management attention are not necessarily the most important issues.[30]

Strategic issue-selling is the process of gaining the attention and support of top management and other important stakeholders for strategic issues. Managers need to consider at least four aspects in seeking attention and support for their issues:

Figure 15.4 Formal channels for issue-selling

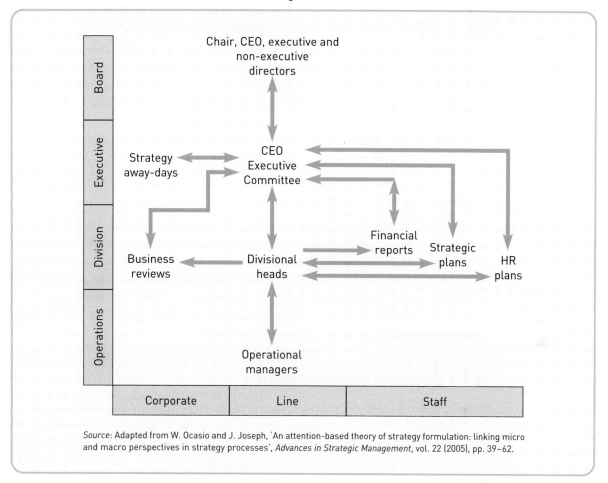

Source: Adapted from W. Ocasio and J. Joseph, 'An attention-based theory of strategy formulation: linking micro and macro perspectives in strategy processes', *Advances in Strategic Management*, vol. 22 (2005), pp. 39–62.

- *Issue packaging.* Care should be taken with how issues are packaged or framed. Clearly the strategic importance of the issue needs to be underlined, particularly by linking it to *critical strategic goals* or *performance metrics* for the organisation. Generally clarity and succinctness win over complexity and length. It also usually helps if the issue is packaged with *potential solutions*. An issue can easily be put aside as too difficult to address if no ways forward are offered at the same time.

- *Formal and informal channels.* Managers need to balance formal and informal channels of influence. Figure 15.4 indicates some *formal channels* for selling issues in a multidivisional organisation (based on General Electric). Here formal channels are split between corporate, line and staff. On the corporate side, they include the annual business reviews that the CEO carries out with each divisional head, plus the annual strategy retreats (or workshops) of the top executive team. The line channel involves the regular line interaction of operational managers, divisional heads and the CEO and other executive directors. Finally, there are the various reporting systems to staff functions, including finance, human resources and strategic planning. Formal channels are of course not just for upwards influence, but typically two-way: for example, strategic plans often iterate between divisions and corporate headquarters until a mutually satisfactory position is reached. Moreover, formal channels are rarely enough to sell strategic issues. *Informal channels* can, however, be very important and often decisive in some organisations. Informal channels might include ad hoc conversations with influential managers in corridors, on journeys or over meals or drinks. For example, Illustration 15.3 shows how informal channels can be important for consultants.[31]

● *Sell alone or in coalitions.* Managers should consider whether to press their issue on their own or to assemble a *coalition of supporters*, preferably influential ones. A coalition adds credibility and weight to the issue. The ability to gather a coalition of supporters can be a good test of the issue's validity: if other managers are unpersuaded, then the CEO is unlikely to be persuaded either. But notice that enlisting supporters may involve compromises or reciprocal support of other issues, so blurring the clarity of the case being put forward.

● *Timing.* Managers should also time their issue-selling carefully. For example a short-term performance crisis, or the period before the handover to a new top management team, is not a good time to press long-term strategic issues.

Selling an issue is only the start, of course. Even after an issue has been successfully sold, and actions and resources agreed, managers should make sure that attention is *sustained*.[32] Initial commitments in terms of top management attention and other resources need to be protected. As the strategic issue evolves over time, it may require more attention and resources than originally promised. Establishing at the outset a regular series of reviews and a set of relevant performance metrics will help keep top management attention focused on the issue and hopefully prepared to release more resources as required.

15.3.3 Strategic decision-making

Strategic issues are ultimately decided upon in many ways. Strategic decision-making is not always rational and is liable to several biases.[33] The notion of strategic issue-selling points to the so-called *champion's bias*: the likelihood that people will exaggerate their case in favour of their particular proposal. Similarly, there is the *sunflower syndrome*, the tendency (like sunflowers following the sun) to follow the lead of the most senior person in the decision-making process, or to try to anticipate their view even before they have expressed it. Decision-makers often hold exaggerated opinions of their competence, leading to over-optimistic decisions, especially where there are few data available. At the same time, they can be risk-averse, being unduly deterred by substantial downsides, even when the chances of such downsides are very slight.

Just putting decisions in the hands of a team of managers, therefore, does not on its own guarantee rigorous and effective decision-making. Katherine Eisenhardt's research on strategic decision-making in fast-moving environments suggests four helpful guidelines for managers:[34]

● *Build multiple, simultaneous alternatives.* Having several alternatives on the table at the same time helps to encourage critical debate. This can help counter phenomena such as the champion's bias and the sunflower syndrome. It is also faster than taking proposals sequentially, where alternatives are only sought out after a previous proposal has been examined and rejected. Examining multiple, simultaneous alternatives is a practice adopted by Barclays Bank, for example, where the rule is that proposals should never be presented in isolation, but always alongside at least two other alternatives.[35]

● *Track real-time information.* Eisenhardt's research found that fast decision-makers do not cut back on the amount of information; they use a different type of information – real-time

ILLUSTRATION 15.3

Dinner with the consultants

Consultants operate through both formal and informal channels to influence strategic thinking.

Locco* was a major European automotive component manufacturer. In the mid 1990s, it began to experience declining profits. The CEO therefore invited consultants to undertake a strategic review of the firm. This consultancy team included a partner, a senior consultant and a junior consultant. Their recommendations led to changes in Locco's product and market strategy.

Like all other consultancy assignments the consultants undertook extensive analysis of industry data and company data. However in addition to this more formal work, there was more informal engagement between the consultants and the management, including three dinners held during the period of the project.

At home with the CEO

At the beginning of the assignment the CEO invited the partner and senior consultant to meet senior managers at his home for dinner 'to get together in a more informal way . . . to get to know each other better . . . and . . . learn more about the history of our company', but also to establish trust between the managers and the consultants.

Others saw it differently. For example the marketing and sales manager viewed it as an attempt by the CEO to influence the outcome of the project: '(he) likes to do this. While dining in his home you can hardly oppose his views'. The consulting partner was somewhat wary, fearing a hidden agenda but nonetheless seeing it as an opportunity to 'break the ice' as well as gaining political insight and understanding of the management dynamics.

Over dinner discussion was largely between the CEO and the consultants with the CEO setting out some concerns about the project, not least the danger of cost cutting leading to a loss of jobs. As they mingled over after dinner drinks other sensitive issues were raised by other managers.

At the castle

In the third week of the project the consultant invited the CEO to a restaurant in a converted castle. He saw this as an opportunity to get to know the CEO better, to gain his agreement to the consultants' approach to the project, but also to gain a clearer understanding of the politics amongst the senior management and establish more insight into the CEO's perceived problems of Locco.

Over the meal the consultant established that there were two management 'camps' with different views of strategy. The consultant also took the opportunity to influence and gain the CEO's approval for the agenda for the next management meeting.

At the pizzeria

Some weeks later the senior consultant invited middle managers who he saw as 'good implementers' for pizza and beer at an Italian restaurant to 'exchange information and get opinions on some of our analyses, see how some of the middle managers react . . .'. Some of those who attended were sceptical about the meeting but went along. Senior managers were not invited.

At the dinner the consultant discussed his initial analysis, particularly on strategic competences. He also raised some issues to do with the political dynamics within the senior management team. The consultant regarded the dinner as a success both in terms of establishing a rapport but also in establishing that 'some (of the managers) know exactly why the company has a problem . . . they already have some ideas for solutions . . . but their voices are not heard'. The managers who attended were, on the whole, also positive about the dinner, many regarding it as 'good fun' though others who were not there felt threatened by their absence.

* A pseudonym used by the researchers.

Adapted from A. Sturdy, M. Schwarz and A. Spicer, 'Guess who's coming to dinner? Structures and uses of liminality in strategic management consultancy', *Human Relations*, vol. 59, no. 7, pp. 929–60 (2006).

Questions

1 Why are informal settings such as dinners useful?

2 Could the consultants have influenced the agenda in more formal ways ? How?

3 If you had been one of the managers at the Italian restaurant, what would your views of the meeting been?

information. These managers prefer immediate information from current operations, rather than statistical trends and forecasts. They tend to spend a lot of time in face-to-face meetings, 'managing by wandering around' and reviewing the most up-to-date indicators, such as weekly and even daily measures of sales, cash, stocks or work-in-progress. In fast-moving environments especially, a quick decision may be better than a delayed decision, and trend data are liable to be rapidly outdated anyway.

● *Seek the views of trusted advisers.* Experienced managers can provide fast feedback on what is likely to work or not based on extensive knowledge from their past. They can also ask tough questions given what they have seen before. The instincts of experienced managers are faster, and often both more reliable and more credible, than lengthy analysis undertaken by junior managers or consultants. Older middle managers whose careers have plateaued can also be good people to listen to, especially to identify risks and problems: not only do they have the experience, but they usually have less self-interest at stake.

● *Aim for consensus, but not at any cost.* Fast decision-makers seek consensus amongst the decision-making team, but do not insist on it. Consensus can be too slow and often leads to mediocre choices based on the lowest common denominator. Fast decision-makers recognise that debates cannot always be resolved to everybody's satisfaction. Eisenhardt's advice is that the Chief Executive or some other senior person should have the courage at a certain point simply to decide. Having had the chance to voice their position, the responsibility of other managers is to accept that decision and to get on with implementation.

However, it is easy to exaggerate both the importance and the effectiveness of decision-making. Many decisions are not followed through with actions. Many strategies are emergent rather than consciously decided (see Chapter 12).

Two widely held views about decision-making have been implicitly challenged so far. First, *intuition* is not always a bad thing.[36] Immersion in real-time information or the long experience of older middle managers can provide a strong 'gut feel' for what should be done. This gut feel can provide the basis for inspired hunches where there are few reliable data to be analysed anyway, for instance in the creation of radically new markets or products. Such intuition can also be beneficial, especially in the idea generation stage of problem solving and in circumstances where fast decisions are needed. Higher levels of intuition are also found more amongst entrepreneurs than the population of managers generally and seem to be related to an orientation towards intentions of organisational growth.[37] Table 15.1 provides suggested guidelines as to how managers might harness and develop their intuitive capabilities.

Second, constructive *conflict* in decision-making teams can be positively useful.[38] Conflict can expose champion's biases. It can challenge optimistic self-assessments of managerial competence. Conflict is fostered by having diverse managerial teams, with members prepared to be devil's advocates, challenging assumptions or easy consensus. But productive conflict needs careful management. Table 15.2 uses the idea of games with rules to summarise ways in which this might be done (also see the discussion on 'organisational ambidexterity' in section 12.4.1).

15.3.4 Communicating the strategy

Deciding strategy is only one step: strategic decisions need to be communicated. Managers have to consider which stakeholders to inform (see Chapter 4) and how they should tailor their messages to each. Shareholders, key customers and employees are likely to be particularly

Table 15.1 Guidelines for developing intuitive capabilities

1. Open up the closet	To what extent do you: experience intuition; trust your feelings; count on intuitive judgements; suppress hunches; covertly rely upon gut feel?
2. Don't mix up your I's!	Instinct, insight and intuition are not synonymous; practise distinguishing between your instincts, your insights, and your intuitions.
3. Elicit good feedback	Seek feedback on your intuitive judgements; build confidence in your gut feel; create a learning environment in which you can develop better intuitive awareness.
4. Get a feel for your batting average	Benchmark your intuitions; get a sense for how reliable your hunches are; ask yourself how your intuitive judgement might be improved.
5. Use imagery	Use imagery rather than words; literally visualise potential future scenarios that take your gut feelings into account.
6. Play devil's advocate	Test out intuitive judgements; raise objections to them; generate counter-arguments; probe how robust gut feel is when challenged.
7. Capture and validate your intuitions	Create the inner state to give your intuitive mind the freedom to roam; capture your creative intuitions; log them before they are censored by rational analysis.

Source: E. Sadler-Smith and E. Shefy, 'The intuitive executive: understanding and applying "gut feel" in decision making', *Academy of Management Executive*, vol. 18, no. 4, pp. 76–91 (2004).

Table 15.2 Managing conflict

Rulebook	• Establish clear behavioural boundaries. • Encourage dissenting voices. • Keep debate professional, not emotional.
Referees	• Ensure the leader is (a) open to differing views, (b) enforces the rules.
Playing field	• Ensure each side of the debate has a chance to win. • Be clear on the basis of resolution (e.g. decision from the top or consensus).
Gaps to exploit	• Does each group have a specific objective to champion?
Relationships	• Ensure individuals (a) deliver on their commitments, (b) behave with integrity. • Ensure leaders throughout the organisation further test perspectives up and down the hierarchy.
Energy levels	• Ensure sufficient tension to promote useful debate, but monitor this. • Do leaders understand what people really care about?
Outcomes	• Ensure leader gives bad news without damaging relationships. • Ensure dignity in losing and risk-taking rewarded.

Source: Reprinted by permission of *Harvard Business Review*. Exhibit from 'How to pick a good fight' by S.A. Joni and D. Beyer, December 2009, pp. 48–57. Copyright © 2009 by the Harvard Business School Publishing Corporation. All rights reserved.

central, all with different needs. For every new strategy, there should be a communications strategy to match. It is also important to remember that communication is a two-way process. Harvard's Michael Beer and Russell A. Eisenstat[39] argue that effective communication needs to involve *both* advocacy of a strategy by senior management and inquiry about the concerns of influential internal and external stakeholders. In the absence of the former, there is lack of clarity, confusion and frustration. In the absence of the latter, concerns will surface in any case, but in ways that actively or passively undermine the new strategy.

As a minimum, effective employee communications are needed to ensure that the strategy is understood. In the absence of this there are two likely consequences:

- *Strategic intent will be reinterpreted.* As the Key Debate in Chapter 12 showed, it is inevitable that people in the organisation will interpret intended strategy in terms of their local context and operational responsibilities.[40] The more such reinterpretation occurs, the more unlikely it is the intended strategy will be implemented.

- *Established routines will continue.* Old habits die hard; so top management may underestimate the need to make very clear what behaviours are expected to deliver a strategy. Of course, effective communication is only one way in which change can be managed; the wider lessons of managing strategic change in this regard need to be taken into account (see Chapter 14).

One example of an organisation seeking high understanding of strategy by all employees is the Volvo Group, where the target is that 90 per cent of employees will be aware of the company's strategic goals, tested by an annual attitude survey.[41]

In shaping a communications strategy for employees, four elements need to be considered in particular:[42]

- *Focus.* Communications should be focused on the key issues that the strategy addresses and the key components of the strategy. If top management cannot show they are clear on these, then it cannot be expected that others will be. If possible it also helps to avoid unnecessary detail or complex language. CEO Jack Welch's famous statement that General Electric should be 'either Number One or Number Two' in all its markets is remembered because of this clear focus on the importance of being a dominant player wherever the company competed.

- *Media.* Choosing appropriate media to convey the new strategy is important.[43] Mass media such as e-mails, voicemails, company newsletters, videos, intranets and senior manager blogs can ensure that all staff receive the same message promptly, helping to avoid damaging uncertainty and rumour-mongering. However, face-to-face communications are important too in order to demonstrate the personal commitment of managers and allow for interaction with concerned staff. So, for example, senior managers may undertake *roadshows*, carrying their message directly to various groups of employees with conferences or workshops at different sites. They may also institute *cascades*, whereby each level of managers is tasked to convey the strategy message directly to the staff reporting to them, who in turn are required to convey the message to their staff, and so on through the organisation. Of course, if this is to be effective, it is essential that the key issues and components of the strategy are clear. Such roadshows and cascades may, of course, also raise new issues and should therefore be part of a two-way communication process.

- *Employee engagement.* If a two-way process of communication is to be achieved, it needs to involve multiple levels of management. Indeed, it is often helpful to engage employees more widely in the communication strategy, so that they can see what it means for them personally and how their role will change. Interchanges through roadshows and cascades can help, but some organisations use imaginative means to create more active engagement. For example, one British public-sector organisation invited all its staff to a day's conference introducing its new strategy, at which employees were invited to pin a photograph of themselves on a 'pledge wall', together with a hand-written promise to change at least one aspect of their work to fit the new strategy.[44] However, employee engagement also means listening to employees. For example, in 2010 Toyota had to recall 5.6 million vehicles in the US alone due to safety defects, so damaging its reputation for reliability. Toyota's top management had apparently ignored warnings of potential problems by its own long-serving factory workers. In 2006 they had sent a two-page memo to the company's president warning that the focus on lowering cost and increasing speed of production was threatening safety standards.[45]

- *Impact.* Communications should be impactful, with powerful and memorable words and visuals. A strong 'story-line' can help by encapsulating the journey ahead and imagined new futures for the organisation and its customers. One struggling medical centre in New Mexico communicated its new strategy, and inspired its staff, with a story-line representing the organisation as 'The Raiders of the Lost Art', conveying a simultaneous sense of courage in adversity and recovery of old values.[46]

15.3.5 The messiness of everyday strategising

There is a danger of seeing strategising as part of a neat, linear process driven by management rationality. Chapter 12 made it clear that this is not always so; that there are multiple processes at work that contribute to the development of strategy. There may be careful analysis and design of strategy communications, but these go hand in hand with more everyday practices. Senior executives do meet over lunch or coffee and discuss strategic issues. Managers spend most of their time in face-to-face, telephone and increasingly e-mail discussion with other managers. A large proportion of face-to-face contact is in meetings. Some of these may be formally designated as strategy meetings; but in others that are not, issues with strategic implications will arise and be discussed. As sections 12.3.2 and 12.3.4 explained, in such settings, strategic issues and solutions may arise on the basis of organisational politics and as the product of organisational systems. In such circumstances, centrally important to managers is their political acumen within their network of contacts, their ability to use persuasive language[47] and also their ability to build coherent narratives of strategy from the often fragmented discussions that take place and views that get aired.[48]

(15.4) STRATEGY METHODOLOGIES

Strategists may use a range of methodologies to organise and guide their strategising activity. The methodologies introduced here are not analytical concepts or techniques such as in most of the rest of the book, but approaches to managing the strategising process. These could include strategy workshops (or 'away-days') and strategy projects. Projects may be driven by hypothesis-testing techniques. Finally, strategising output typically has to fit the format of a business case or strategic plan. This section introduces key issues in each of these methodologies.

15.4.1 Strategy workshops

Strategy workshops (sometimes called strategy away-days or off-sites) are a common methodology for making strategy.[49] These workshops usually **involve groups of executives working intensively for one or two days, often away from the office, on organisational strategy**. Such executives are typically senior managers in the organisation, although workshops can also be a valuable mechanism for involving a wider group of managers. Workshops are used typically to formulate or reconsider strategy, but also to review the progress of current strategy, address strategy implementation issues and to communicate strategic decisions to a larger audience. Workshops can be either ad hoc or part of the regular strategic planning process, and they may be stand-alone or designed as a series of events. As well as facilitating strategy-making, workshops can have additional roles in team-building and the personal development of individual participant. Illustration 15.4 shows how they can contribute to strategy development as well as how they can go wrong.

Strategy workshops can be a valuable part of an organisation's strategy-making activity. Research suggests, however, that their form can influence the nature of participants' debate of strategy and its likely success;[50] so their design matters. First, whatever the purpose of the workshop is, clarity of that purpose is strongly correlated with perceived success.[51] Given this, if the purpose is to *question existing strategy or develop new strategy* successful workshops are likely to involve:

- *Strategy concepts and tools* likely to promote questioning of the current strategy.

- *A specialist facilitator to* guide participants in the use of such tools and concepts, free managers to concentrate on the discussion, help keep the discussion focused on the strategic issues and ensure participants contribute equally to discussion.

- *The visible support of the workshop sponsor* (perhaps the CEO) for the questioning and the facilitator. In the absence of this the workshop is unlikely to succeed.[52]

- *The diminishing of everyday functional and hierarchical roles.* This may be aided by a distinctive off-site location to signal how different from everyday routine the workshop is, help detach participants from day-to-day operational issues and symbolically affirm the occasion is not subject to the usual norms of executive team discussion. Ice-breaking and other apparently playful exercises – sometimes called 'serious play'– at the beginning of a workshop can help generate creativity and a willingness to challenge orthodoxies.[53]

On the other hand, workshops with the purpose of *reviewing the progress of current strategy* are likely to be successful if they have a more operational agenda and if participants maintain functional and hierarchical roles.

Workshops are, however, prone to at least two problems. First, if the purpose is to encourage questioning, there is the danger that the structure of the workshop, or the absence of support of the workshop sponsor, fails to do this, such that participants simply draw on their existing preconceptions. Especially when reduced to a routine part of the strategic planning cycle, and involving the usual group of senior managers, workshops may not be able to produce new ideas that significantly challenge the status quo.[54] Second, workshops can become detached from subsequent action. Precisely because they are separated from the ordinary routines of the organisation, it can be difficult to translate workshop ideas and enthusiasm back into the workplace.

ILLUSTRATION 15.4

A tale of two workshops

How strategy workshops are designed is a significant influence on their success.

Given the growth of the business the directors of Hotelco* decided to hold two two-day workshops to re-think the organisational structure needed for the company's future strategic direction. Both workshops were facilitated by an external consultant.

Workshop 1

The first workshop was held in a luxury rural hotel in the South of England far away from Hotelco's modest offices. This was not just to 'get away from the office', but also because: 'It freed up the mind . . . It was a great experience'.

Together with one of the directors, the facilitator had organised the agenda. The 'command style' of the CEO was replaced by a participative approach orchestrated by the facilitator: 'He made it a more level playing field'. He had interviewed staff about the core values of the business and provided a report to the directors as a basis for the discussion: 'Does everyone know what Hotelco stands for?'

The directors became genuinely engaged with the discussion: 'It focused our minds. It made us all understand the things we were good at and . . . the things we were weak at and what we needed to do.' They regarded the workshop as a success, concluding that a change was needed from an authoritarian, command management style to a more structured and devolved approach to management, with responsibility being passed to middle levels, so freeing up the top team to focus more on strategy.

This outcome was not, however, carried forward. On their return to the office, the directors came to the conclusion that what was agreed during the workshop was unrealistic, that they were 'carried away with the process'. The result was significant back-tracking but without a clear consensus on a revised structure for the business.

Workshop 2

The second two-day workshop, two months later, was for the top team and their seven direct reports

and used the same facilitator. It took place in one of the group's own hotels. Again the workshop began with a discussion of the interviews on Hotelco's values. One of the directors then made a presentation raising the idea of an operational board. However, in discussion it emerged that the directors were not uniformly committed to this – especially the CEO. Eventually, as the facilitator explained:

> 'I had to sit the four directors in another room and say: look, until you sort this out; you're just going to create problems. . . . The four directors got into a heated argument and forgot about the other seven.'

This was not, however, how the directors saw it. Their view was that the facilitator was seeking to impose a solution rather than facilitate discussion.

With the directors in one room and the direct reports in another, the comments of each group were transmitted between rooms by the facilitator. It was a situation that satisfied no one. In the afternoon the CEO intervened, replacing the idea of a seven person 'operational board' with an intermediary level of three 'divisional directors'.

No one was content with the workshop. One of the seven who was not to be a divisional director commented: 'I didn't know where I sat any more. I felt my job had been devalued.' A director also recognised: 'We left these people feeling really deflated.'

* Hotelco is a pseudonym for a small UK hotel group.

Questions

1 Evaluate the design of the two workshops in terms of the guidelines in section 15.4.1.

2 If you were a facilitator, how would you have organised the workshops differently?

3 What benefits (or disadvantages) might such workshops have in comparison with other approaches to strategy development for such an organisation?

In designing workshops that will be closely connected to subsequent action, managers should consider:

- *Identifying agreed actions* to be taken. Time should be set aside at the end of the workshop for a review of workshop outputs and agreement on necessary actions to follow up. However this, of itself, may well not make a sufficiently powerful bridge to operational realities.
- *Establishing project groups.* Workshops can build on the cohesion built around particular issues by commissioning groups of managers to work together on specific tasks arising from the workshop and report on progress to senior management.
- *Nesting of workshops.* Especially if a workshop has expected participants to question current strategy and develop radical new ideas, it may be useful to have a series of workshops, each of which gradually becomes more and more grounded in operational realities.
- *Making visible commitment by the top management.* The chief executive or other senior manager needs to signal commitment to the outcomes of the workshop not only by their statements but by their actual behaviours.

15.4.2 Strategy projects

Both strategy-making and strategy implementation are often organised in the form of projects or task forces.[55] **Strategy projects involve teams of people assigned to work on particular strategic issues over a defined period of time.** Projects can be instituted in order to explore problems or opportunities as part of the strategy development process. Or they might be instituted to implement agreed elements of a strategy, for example an organisational restructuring or the negotiation of a joint venture. Translating a strategic plan or workshop outcomes into a set of projects is a good means of ensuring that intentions are translated into action. They can also include a wider group of managers in strategy activity.

Strategy projects should be managed like any other project. In particular they need:[56]

- *A clear brief or mandate.* The project's objectives should be agreed and carefully managed. These objectives are the measure of the project's success. 'Scope creep', by which additional objectives are added as the project goes on, is a common danger.
- *Top management commitment.* The continuing commitment of top management, especially the top management 'client' or 'sponsor', needs to be maintained. Top management agendas are frequently shifting, so communications should be regular.
- *Milestones and reviews.* The project should have from the outset clear milestones with an agreed schedule of intermediate achievements. These allow project review and adjustment where necessary, as well as a measure of ongoing success.
- *Appropriate resources.* The key resource is usually people. The right mix of skills needs to be in place, including project management skills, and effort should be invested in 'team-building' at the outset. Strategy projects are often part-time commitments for managers, who have to continue with their 'day jobs'. Attention needs to be paid to managing the balance between managers' ordinary responsibilities and project duties: the first can easily derail the second.

Projects can easily proliferate and compete. Programme managers should manage overlaps and redundancies, merging or ending projects that no longer have a distinct purpose because of changing circumstances. Senior management should have careful oversight of the whole portfolio, and again be ready to merge and end projects or even programmes, in order to prevent the 'initiative fatigue' that is often the result of project proliferation.

15.4.3 Hypothesis testing

Strategy project teams are typically under pressure to deliver solutions to complex problems under tight time constraints. **Hypothesis testing is a methodology used particularly in strategy projects for setting priorities in investigating issues and options** and is widely used by strategy consulting firms and members of strategy project teams.

Hypothesis testing in strategy is adapted from the hypothesis testing procedures of science.[57] It starts with a proposition about how things are (*the descriptive hypothesis*), and then seeks to test it with real-world data. For example, a descriptive hypothesis in strategy could be that being large-scale in a particular industry is essential to profitability. To test it, a strategy project team would begin by gathering data on the size of organisations in the industry and correlate these with the organisations' profitability. Confirmation of this initial descriptive hypothesis (i.e. small organisations are relatively unprofitable) would then lead to several *prescriptive hypotheses* about what a particular organisation should do. For a small-scale organisation in the industry, prescriptive hypotheses would centre on how to increase scale: one prescriptive hypothesis in this case would be that acquisitions were a good means to achieve the necessary scale; another would be that alliances were the right way. These prescriptive hypotheses might then become the subjects of further data testing.

This kind of hypothesis testing is ultimately about setting practical priorities in strategy work. Hypothesis testing in business therefore differs from strict scientific procedure (see Illustration 15.5). The aim finally is to concentrate attention on a very limited set of promising hypotheses, not on the full set of all possibilities. Data are gathered in order to support favoured hypotheses, whereas in science the objective is formally to try to refute hypotheses. Business hypothesis testing aims to find a robust and satisfactory solution within time and resource constraints, not to find some ultimate scientific truth. Selecting the right hypotheses can be helped by applying *Quick and Dirty Testing* (QDT). Quick and Dirty Testing relies on the project team's existing experience and easily accessed data in order to speedily reject unpromising hypotheses, before too much time is wasted on them.

15.4.4 Business cases and strategic plans

Strategising activities, such as workshops or projects, are typically oriented towards creating an output in the form of a *business case* or *strategic plan*. Keeping this end goal in mind provides a structure for the strategising work: what needs to be produced shapes the strategising activities. A **business case** usually **provides the data and argument in support of a particular strategy proposal, e.g. investment in new equipment**. A **strategic plan provides the data and argument in support of a strategy for the whole organisation**. It is therefore likely to be more comprehensive, taking an overall view of the organisation's direction over a substantial period of time. Many organisations have a standard template for making business cases or proposing a strategic plan, and where these exist, it is wise to work with that format. Where there is no standard template, it is worth investigating recent successful business cases or plans within the organisation, and borrowing features from them.

A project team intending to make a business case should aim to meet the following criteria:[58]

ILLUSTRATION 15.5

Hypothesis testing at a bank

This outline of a consulting engagement for a large, diversified bank shows how the hypothesis testing process can shape a strategy project.

1 Defining the problem/question

The consultants' first step is to define the problem. As usual, the strategic problem has to do with the existence of a gap between what the client wants (here a certain level of profitability for a particular product) and what it has (declining profitability). In short, the consultants' problem is that the bank's profitability for this product is below target levels.

2 Develop a set of competing descriptive hypotheses about problem causes

The consultants gather some preliminary data and draw on their own experience to generate some possible descriptive hypotheses about the causes of the problem. Thus they know that some large national competitors are already exiting from this type of product; that profitability varies dramatically across competitors involved in this product; and that some specialised new entrants have taken significant market share. Three possible hypotheses emerge: that the industry structure is basically unattractive; that the bank lacks the right strategic capabilities; that the bank is targeting the wrong customer segments. The consultants use quick and dirty testing to reject the first two hypotheses: after all, some competitors are making profits and the bank has strong capabilities from long presence in this product area. Accordingly, the starting descriptive hypothesis is that the bank is targeting unprofitable customer segments.

3 Testing the starting descriptive hypothesis

The consultants next design a study to collect the data needed to support the descriptive hypothesis. They carry out a market segmentation analysis by customer group by doing interviews with customers across different geographies and income levels. They analyse the kinds of service different segments require and the fees they might pay. The consultants find that their data supports their starting hypothesis: the bank's branches are concentrated in locations which prosperous customers willing to pay higher fees for this product do not use. (Had they not been able to confirm their hypothesis, the consultants would have returned to the other two competing hypotheses, step 2.)

4 Develop prescriptive hypotheses

The consultants then develop prescriptive hypotheses about actions necessary to attract more profitable customer segments. One prescriptive hypothesis is that a better portfolio of branch locations will enhance profitability. The consultants carry out data gathering and analysis to support this hypothesis, for example comparing the profitability of branches in different kinds of locations. They find that the few branches that happen to be in the right locations do have higher profitability with this product.

5 Make recommendations to the client

The consultants prepare a set of preliminary recommendations based on the descriptive hypothesis and validated prescriptive hypotheses: one of these is that the branch locations need changing. These recommendations are checked for acceptability and feasability with key managers within the bank and adjusted according to feedback. Then the consultants make their formal presentation of final recommendations.

Source: Jeanne Liedtka, Darden School of Management, University of Virginia.

Questions

1 Select an important strategic issue facing an organisation that you are familiar with (or an organisation that is publicly in trouble or a case study organisation). Try generating a few descriptive hypotheses that address this issue. Use quick and dirty testing to select an initial descriptive hypothesis.

2 What data should you gather to confirm this descriptive hypothesis and how would you collect it? Should the descriptive hypothesis be confirmed, what possible prescriptive hypotheses follow?

- *Focus on strategic needs.* The team should identify the organisation's overall strategy and relate its case closely to that, not just to any particular departmental needs. A business case should not look as if it is just an HR department or IT department project, for example. The focus should be on a few key issues, with clear priority normally given to those that are both strategically important and relatively easy to address.

- *Supported by key data.* The team will need to assemble appropriate data, with financial data demonstrating appropriate returns on any investment typically essential. However, qualitative data should not be neglected – for example, striking quotations from interviews with employees or key customers, or recent mini-cases of successes or failures in the organisation or at competitors. Some strategic benefits simply cannot be quantified, but are not the less important for that: information on competitor moves can be persuasive here. The team should provide background information on the rigour and extent of the research behind the data.

- *Provide a clear rationale.* Analysis and data are not enough; make it clear *why* the proposals are being made. The reasons for the choice of recommendations therefore need to be explicit. Many specific evaluation techniques that can be useful in a business cases are explained in Chapter 11.

- *Demonstrate solutions and actions.* As suggested earlier, issues attached to solutions tend to get the most attention. The team should show how what is proposed will be acted on, and who will be responsible. Possible barriers should be clearly identified. Also recognise alternative scenarios, especially downside risk. Implementation feasibility is critical.

- *Provide clear progress measures.* When seeking significant investments over time, it is reassuring to offer clear measures to allow regular progress monitoring. Proposing review mechanisms also adds credibility to the business case.

Strategic plans have similar characteristics in terms of focus, data, actions and progress measures. Strategic plans are, however, more comprehensive, and they may be used for entrepreneurial start-ups, business units within a large organisation, or for an organisation as a whole. Again formats vary. However, a typical strategic plan has the following elements, which together should set a strategy team's working agenda:[59]

- *Mission, goals and objectives statement.* This is the point of the whole strategy, and the critical starting place. While it is the starting place, in practice a strategy team might iterate back to this in the light of other elements of the strategic plan. It is worth checking back with earlier statements that the organisation may have made to ensure consistency. Section 4.2 provides more guidance on mission, goals and objectives.

- *Environmental analysis.* This should cover the key issues identified in terms of the whole of the environment, both macro trends and more focused issues to do with customers, suppliers and competitors. The team should not stop at the analysis, but draw clear strategic implications. (See Chapter 2.)

- *Capability analysis.* This should include a clear identification of the key strengths and weaknesses of the organisation and its products relative to its competitors and include a clear statement of competitive advantage. (See Chapter 3.)

- *Proposed strategy.* This should be clearly related to the environmental and organisational analyses and support the mission, goals and objectives. It should also make clear options that have been considered and why the proposed strategy is preferred. Particularly useful here are Chapters 6 to 11.

KEY DEBATE

What good are strategy consultants?

Strategy consultants are frequent participants in strategy making, and typically bring good analytical and project management skills. Why are they so controversial then?

There is no shortage of books criticising strategy consultants. Titles such as *Con Tricks*, *Dangerous Company* and *Rip Off!* provide the flavour. And there have been some spectacular failures. As in section 15.2.4, McKinsey & Co. took a good deal of blame for the strategic mistakes of Enron and Swissair.

The accusations made against strategy consultants are at least three-fold. First, they rely too much on inexperienced young staff fresh out of business school, who typically have the slimmest understanding of how client organisations and their markets really work. Second, they are accused of handing over strategy recommendations, and then walking away from implementation. Third, they are perceived as expensive, overpaid individually and always trying to sell on unnecessary extra projects. Clients end up paying for more advice than they really need, much of it unrealistic and unimplementable.

These accusations may be unfair. Most large strategy consulting firms are now organised on industry lines, so building up expertise in particular areas, and they increasingly recruit experienced managers from these industries. Most consultants also prefer to work in joint client–advisor teams, so that clients are involved in generating the recommendations that they will have to implement. Some consultancies, such as Bain, make a point of getting closely involved in implementation too. Finally, consultants are in a competitive market and their clients are typically sophisticated buyers, not easily fooled into buying advice they do not need: the fact that strategy consulting business increased in Europe from €3bn (~$4.2bn) in 1996 to €8bn in 2004 suggests there is plenty of real demand.

There are some successes too. Bain claims that, since 1980, its clients' stock prices have on average outperformed the Standard & Poor's 500 large American companies index by four to one (www.bain.com). Some great corporate managers have originated in strategy consulting: Lou Gerstner, who turned around IBM, and Meg Whitman, leader of eBay, both started as McKinsey & Co. strategy consultants. And one of the world's most influential management books ever, *The Concept of the Corporation*, came from Peter Drucker's consulting assignment with General Motors during World War II.

There are clues to managing strategy consultants in the criticisms, however: for example, make sure to hire consultants with relevant experience; connect analysis to implementation; and keep a close eye on expenditure. James O'Shea and Charles Madigan close their book with a provocative quotation from Machiavelli's *The Prince*: 'Here is an infallible rule: a prince who is not himself wise cannot be wisely advised. . . . Good advice depends on the shrewdness of the prince who seeks it, and not the shrewdness of the prince on good advice.'

Sources: The European Federation of Management Consultancy Associations (www.feaco.org); J. O'Shea and C. Madigan, *Dangerous Company: Consulting Powerhouses and the Businesss they Save and Ruin*, Penguin, 1998; C.D. McKenna, *The World's Newest Profession: Management Consulting in the Twentieth Century*, Cambridge University Press, 2006.

Questions

1 What measures can a strategy consultant take to reassure a potential client of his or her effectiveness?

2 Are there any reasons to suspect that some people might want to exaggerate criticisms of strategy consultants' conduct?

- *Resources.* The team will need to provide a detailed analysis of the resources required, with options for acquiring them. Critical resources are financial, so the plan should include income statements, cash flows and balance sheets over the period of the plan. Other important resources might be human, particularly managers or people with particular skills. A clear and realistic timetable for implementation is also needed.

- *Key changes.* What does the plan envisage are the key changes required in structures, systems and culture and how are these to be managed? Chapters 13 and 14 are most relevant here.

SUMMARY

- The practice of strategy involves critical choices about *who to involve* in strategy, *what to do* in strategising activity, and *which strategising methodologies* to use in order to guide this activity.

- Chief executive officers, senior managers, non-executive directors, strategic planners, strategy consultants and middle managers are all involved in strategising. Their degree of appropriate involvement should depend on the nature of the strategic issues.

- Strategising activity can involves *analysing, issue-selling, decision-making* and *communicating.* Managers should not expect these activities to be fully rational or logical and can valuably appeal to the non-rational characteristics of the people they work with.

- Practical methodologies to guide strategising activity include *strategy workshops, strategy projects, hypothesis testing,* and creating *business cases* and *strategic plans.*

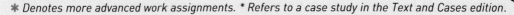

WORK ASSIGNMENTS

✱ *Denotes more advanced work assignments.* * *Refers to a case study in the Text and Cases edition.*

15.1 Go to the careers or recruitment web page of one of the big strategy consultants (such as www.bain.com, www.bcg.com, www.mckinsey.com). What does this tell you about the nature of strategy consulting work? Would you like this work?

15.2 Go to the website of a large organisation (private or public-sector) and assess the way it communicates its strategy to its audiences. With reference to section 15.3.4, how focused is the communication; how impactful is it; and how likely is it to engage employees?

15.3 If you had to design a strategy workshop, suggest who the participants in the workshop should be and what roles they should play in (a) the case where an organisation has to re-examine its fundamental strategy in the face of increased competitive threat; (b) the case where an organisation needs to gain commitment to a long-term, comprehensive programme of strategic change.

15.4✱ For any case study in the book, imagine yourself in the position of a strategy consultant and propose an initial descriptive hypothesis (section 15.4.3) and define the kinds of data that you would need to test it. What kinds of people would you want in your strategy project team (see sections 15.2.5 and 15.4.2)?

15.5✱ Go to a business plan archive (such as the University of Maryland's www.businessplanarchive.org or use a Google search). Select a business plan of interest to you and, in the light of section 15.4.4, assess its good points and its bad points.

Integrative assignment

15.6✱ For an organisation with which you are familiar, or one of the case organisations, write a strategic plan (for simplicity, you might choose to focus on an undiversified business or a business unit within a larger corporation). Where data are missing, make reasonable assumptions or propose ways of filling the gaps. Comment on whether and how you would provide different versions of this strategic plan for (a) investors; (b) employees.

RECOMMENDED KEY READINGS

- For an overview of top management involvement in strategy, see P. Stiles and B. Taylor, *Boards at Work: How Directors View their Roles and Responsibilities*, Oxford University Press, 2001. For an overview of the middle management role, see S. Floyd and B. Wooldridge, *Building Strategy from the Middle*, Sage, 2000.

- For an explanation of the role of strategic planners, see D. Angwin, S. Paroutis and S. Mitson, 'Connecting up strategy; are senior strategy directors a missing link?', *California Management Review*, vol. 51, no. 3 (2009), pp. 74–94.

- *Strategy as Practice*, by Gerry Johnson, Ann Langley, Leif Melin and Richard Whittington (Cambridge University Press, 2007) provides examples of academic studies of strategy practice, as do three journal special issues: the 'Micro strategy and strategizing', *Journal of Management Studies*, vol. 40, no. 1 (2003); 'Strategizing: the challenges of a practice perspective', *Human Relations*, vol. 60, no. 1 (2007); and R. Whittington and L. Cailluet, 'The crafts of strategy', *Long Range Planning* (Special Issue, June 2008).

- A practical guide to strategising methodologies is provided by E. Rasiel and P.N. Friga (2001), *The McKinsey Mind*, which has much more general relevance than that particular consulting firm.

REFERENCES

1. A theoretical basis for this pyramid can be found in R. Whittington, 'Completing the practice turn in strategy research', *Organization Studies*, vol. 27, no. 5 (2006), pp. 613–34 and P. Jarzabkowski, J. Balogun and D. Seidl, 'Strategizing: the challenges of a practice perspective', *Human Relations*, vol. 60, no. 1 (2007), pp. 5–27.

2. The classic statement is A. Chandler, *Strategy and Structure: Chapters in the History of American Enterprise*, MIT Press, 1962.

3. S. Kaplan and E. Beinhocker, 'The real value of strategic planning', *MIT Sloan Management Review*, Winter 2003, pp. 71–6.

4. M.E. Porter, 'What is strategy?', *Harvard Business Review*, November–December 1996, pp. 61–78.

5. M. Haywood and D. Hambrick, 'Explaining the premium paid for large acquisitions: evidence of CEO hubris', *Administrative Science Quarterly*, vol. 42, no. 1 (1977), pp. 103–28.

6. J. Collins, *Good to Great*, Random House, 2001.

7. I. Janis, *Victims of Groupthink: a Psychological Study of Foreign-Policy Decisions and Fiascoes*, Houghton Mifflin, 1972; R.S. Baron, 'So right it's wrong: groupthink and the ubiquitous nature of polarized group decision making', in Mark P. Zanna (ed.), *Advances in Experimental Social Psychology*, vol. 37, pp. 219–53, Elsevier Academic Press, 2005.

8. E. Beinhocker and S. Kaplan, 'Tired of strategic planning?', *McKinsey Quarterly*, special edition on Risk and Resilience (2002), pp. 49–57; S. Kaplan and E. Beinhocker, 'The real value of strategic planning', *MIT Sloan Management Review*, Winter 2003, pp. 71–6.

9. R.S. Kaplan and D.P. Norton, 'The office of strategy management', *Harvard Business Review*, October 2005, pp. 72–80.

10. D. Angwin, S. Paroutis and S. Mitson, 'Connecting up strategy; are senior strategy directors a missing link?', *California Management Review*, vol. 51, no. 3 (2009), pp. 74–94.

11. See A. Chandler (reference 2).

12. G. Johnson, L. Melin and R. Whittington, 'Micro-strategy and strategising: towards an activity-based view', *Journal of Management Studies*, vol. 40, no. 1 (2003), pp. 3–22.

13. S. Floyd and W. Wooldridge, *The Strategic Middle Manager: How to Create and Sustain Competitive Advantage*, Jossey-Bass, 1996 and S. Mantere, 'Role expectations and middle manager strategic agency', *Journal of Management Studies*, vol. 45, no. 2 (2008), pp. 294–316.

14. See for example J. Balogun and G. Johnson: 'Organizational restructuring and middle manager sensemaking', *Academy of Management Journal*, August 2004; J. Balogun, 'Managing change: steering a course between intended strategies and unanticipated outcomes', *Long Range Planning*, vol. 39 (2006), pp. 29–49.

15. A. Watson and B. Wooldridge, 'Business unit manager influence on corporate-level strategy formulation', *Journal of Managerial Issues*, vol. 18, no. 2 (2005), pp. 147–61.

16. S. Floyd and B. Wooldridge, 'Middle management's strategic influence and organizational performance', *Journal of Management Studies*, vol. 34, no. 3 (1997), pp. 465–85.

17. S. Mantere 'Strategic practices as enablers and disablers of championing activity', *Strategic Organization*, vol. 3, no. 2 (2005), pp. 157–84.

18. F. Westley, 'Middle managers and strategy: microdynamics of inclusion', *Strategic Management Journal*, vol. 11 (1990), pp. 337–51.

19. See D. Moyniham, 'Ambiguity in policy lessons: the agentification experience', *Public Administration*, vol. 84, no. 4 (2006), pp. 1029–50 and L.S. Oakes, B. Townley and D.J. Cooper, 'Business planning as pedagogy: language and control in a changing institutional field', *Administrative Science Quarterly*, vol. 43, no. 2 (1997), pp. 257–92.

20. The websites of the leading strategy consultants are useful sources of information on strategy consulting and strategy in general, as well as strategy consulting careers: see www.mckinsey.com; www.bcg.com; www.bain.com; www.monitor.com.

21. For theoretical discussion of advisers in strategy, see L. Arendt, R. Priem and H. Ndofor, 'A CEO-adviser model of strategic decision-making', *Journal of Management*, vol. 31, no. 5 (2005), pp. 680–99.

22. C.D. McKenna, *The World's Newest Profession*, Cambridge University Press, 2006; R. Whittington, P. Jarzabkowski, M. Mayer, E. Mounoud, J. Nahapiet and L. Rouleau, 'Taking strategy seriously: responsibility and reform for an important social practice', *Journal of Management Inquiry*, vol. 12, no. 4 (2003), pp. 396–409.

23. 'Whitehall spending on consultants rises', *Daily Telegraph*, 22 February 2010.

24. S. Appelbaum, 'Critical success factors in the client-consulting relationship', *Journal of the American Academy of Business* (March 2004), pp. 184–91; M. Mohe, 'Generic strategies for managing consultants: insights from client companies in Germany', *Journal of Change Management*, vol. 5, no. 3 (2005), pp. 357–65.

25. E. Beinhocker and S. Kaplan (reference 8) Figure 2, p. 56.

26. P. Jarzabkowski, M. Giulietti and B. Oliveira, 'Building a strategy toolkit: lessons from business', AIM Executive briefing, 2009. Also see G. Hodgkinson, R. Whittington, G. Johnson and M. Schwarz, 'The role of strategy workshops in strategy development processes: formality, communication, coordination and inclusion', *Long Range Planning*, vol. 30 (2006), pp. 479–96.

27. T. Hill and R. Westbrook, 'SWOT analysis: it's time for a product recall', *Long Range Planning*, vol. 30, no. 1 (1997), pp. 46–52.

28. A. Langley, 'Between paralysis by analysis and extinction by instinct', *Sloan Management Review*, vol. 36, no. 3 (1995), pp. 63–76.

29. A. Langley, 'In search of rationality: the purposes behind the use of formal analysis in organisations', *Administrative Science Quarterly*, vol. 34 (1989), pp. 598–631.

30. This draws on the attention-based view of the firm: see W. Ocasio and J. Joseph, 'An attention-based theory of strategy formulation: linking micro and macro perspectives in strategy processes', *Advances in Strategic Management*, vol. 22 (2005), pp. 39–62.

31. For an insightful analysis of the role of mealtimes and other informal moments to influence strategy, see A. Sturdy, M. Schwarz and A. Spicer, 'Guess who's coming to dinner? Structures and the use of liminality in strategic management consultancy', *Human Relations*, vol. 10, no. 7 (2006), pp. 929–60.

32. B. Yakis and R. Whittington, 'Sustaining strategic issues: five longitudinal cases in human resource management', paper to the *Academy of Management*, Philadelphia, 2007.

33. D. Lovallo and O. Siboney, 'Distortions and deceptions in strategic decisions', *McKinsey Quarterly*, no. 1 (2006). A good review of decision-making biases is in G. Hodgkinson and P. Sparrow, *The Competent Organization*, Open University Press, 2002.

34. K.M. Eisenhardt, 'Speed and strategic choice: how managers accelerate decision making', *California Management Review*, Spring 1990, pp. 39–54.

35. M. Mankins, 'Stop wasting valuable time', *Harvard Business Review*, September 2004, pp. 58–65.

36. C. Miller and R.D. Ireland, 'Intuition in strategic decision-making: friend or foe in the fast-paced 21 century?', *Academy of Management Executive*, vol. 21, no. 1 (2005), pp. 19–30.

37. G.P. Hodgkinson, E. Sadler-Smith, L.A. Burke, G. Claxton and P.R. Sparrow, 'Intuition in organizations: implications for strategic management', *Long Range Planning*, vol. 42, no. 3 (2009), pp. 277–97.

38. K.M. Eisenhardt, J. Kahwajy and L.J. Bourgeois, 'Conflict and strategic choice: how top teams disagree', *California Management Review*, vol. 39, no. 2 (1997), pp. 42–62. Also R.A. Burgelman and A.S. Grove, 'Let chaos reign, then rein in chaos – repeatedly: managing strategic dynamics for corporate longevity', *Strategic Management Journal*, vol. 28 (2007), pp. 965–79.

39. M. Beer and R.A. Eisenstat, 'How to have an honest conversation', *Harvard Business Review*, vol. 82, no. 2 (2004), pp. 82–9.

40. See J. Balogun and G. Johnson (reference 14).

41. C. Nordblom, 'Involving middle managers in strategy at Volvo Group', *Strategic Communication Management*, vol. 10, no. 2 (2006), pp. 24–8.

42. This builds on M. Thatcher, 'Breathing life into business strategy', *Strategic Communication Management*, vol. 10, no. 2 (2006), pp. 14–18. Also Beer and Eisenstat (see reference 39 above).

43. R.H. Lengel and R.L. Daft, 'The selection of communication media as an executive skill', *Academy of Management Executive*, vol. 2, no. 3 (1988), pp. 225–32.

44. R. Whittington, E. Molloy, M. Mayer and A. Smith, 'Practices of strategizing/organizing: broadening strategy work and skills', *Long Range Planning*, vol. 39 (2006), pp. 615–29.

45. 'The Toyota way is famous. In reality it is to ignore warnings from within the firm', *The Times*, 12 March 2010, p. 55.

46. G. Adamson, J. Pine, T. van Steenhoven and J. Kroupa, 'How story-telling can drive strategic change', *Strategy and Leadership*, vol. 34, no. 1 (2006), pp. 36–41.

47. See D. Samra-Fredericks, 'Strategizing as lived experience and strategists' everyday efforts to shape strategic direction', *Journal of Management Studies*, vol 42, no. 1 (2003), pp. 1413–42.

48. J.D. Ford, 'Organizational change as shifting conversations', *Journal of Strategic Change*, vol, 12, no. 6 (1999), pp. 480–500.

49. For a survey of strategy workshops in practice, see G. Hodgkinson, R. Whittington, G. Johnson and M. Schwarz, 'The role of strategy workshops in strategy development processes: formality, communication, coordination and inclusion', *Long Range Planning*, vol. 30 (2006) pp. 479–96.

50. This is based on research by G. Johnson, S. Prashantham, S. Floyd and N. Bourque, 'The ritualization of strategy workshops', *Organization Studies*, forthcoming.

51. G. Hodgkinson et al. (see reference 49).

52. For a discussion of a failed strategy workshop from different points of view, see G. Hodgkinson and G. Wright, 'Confronting strategic inertia in a top management team: learning from failure', *Organization Studies*, vol. 23, no. 6 (2002), pp. 949–78 and R. Whittington, 'Completing the practice turn in strategy research', *Organization Studies*, vol. 27, no. 5 (2006), pp. 613–34.

53. L. Heracleous and C. Jacobs, 'The serious business of play', *MIT Quarterly*, Fall 2005, pp. 19–20.

54. C. Bowman, 'Strategy workshops and top-team commitment to strategic change', *Journal of Managerial Psychology*, vol. 10, no. 8 (1995), pp. 4–12; B. Frisch and L. Chandler, 'Off-sites that work', *Harvard Business Review*, vol. 84, no. 6 (2006), pp. 117–26.

55. P. Morris and A. Jamieson, 'Moving from corporate strategy to project strategy', *Project Management Journal*, vol. 36, no. 4 (2005), pp. 5–18. A comparative study of strategy project development teams is in F. Blackler, N. Crump and S. McDonald, 'Organizing processes in complex activity networks', *Organization*, vol. 72, no. 2 (2000), pp. 277–300.

56. H. Sirkin, P. Keenan and A. Jackson, 'The hard side of change management', *Harvard Business Review*, October 2005, pp. 109–18; J. Kenny, 'Effective project management for strategic innovation and change in an organizational context', *Project Management Journal*, vol. 34, no. 1 (2003), pp. 43–53.

57. This section draws on E. Rasiel and P.N. Friga, *The McKinsey Mind*, McGraw-Hill, 2001, H. Courtney, *20/20 Foresight: Crafting Strategy in an Uncertain World*, 2001, and unpublished material from J. Liedtka, University of Virginia.

58. J. Walker, 'Is your business case compelling?', *Human Resource Planning*, vol. 25, no. 1 (2002), pp. 12–15; M. Pratt, 'Seven steps to a business case', *Computer World*, 10 October 2005, pp. 35–6.

59. Useful books on writing a business plan include: C. Barrow, P. Barrow and R. Brown, *The Business Plan Workbook*, Kogan Page, 2008 and A.R. DeThomas and S.A. Derammelaan, *Writing a Convincing Business Plan*, Barron's Business Library, 2008.

Ray Ozzie, software strategist

During 2005 and 2006, Ray Ozzie took an increasingly important strategic role at the computer software giant Microsoft, finally emerging as the company's Chief Software Architect. At the centre of Ozzie's new strategy was the endeavour to 'webify' Microsoft, widely perceived to have fallen behind Internet upstarts such as Google and Yahoo!. Developing this new strategy involved more than formulating a bold and challenging new vision for Microsoft. Ozzie faced difficult decisions even in the sheer practicalities of strategy making. Thus Ozzie had to design a top management strategy retreat; he had to find a way of maintaining the momentum after that retreat; and finally, he had to decide how best to communicate the key themes of the emerging new strategy.

Ozzie was regarded by many experts as a software genius. In 1984 he had founded Iris Associates, which five years later launched, under contract for the Lotus Development Corporation, the first commercial e-mail and collaboration software for major corporations, Lotus Notes. Lotus Development Corporation bought Iris for $84m (~€59m) in 1994, and the next year computer giant IBM in turn bought Lotus. Three years later, Ozzie left IBM to found Groove Networks, another collaboration software company. In March 2005, Microsoft bought Groove Networks in order to integrate its collaboration features into the next generation of its Office products. Ozzie joined Microsoft as a new employee.

What Microsoft paid for Groove Networks was undisclosed, but it certainly made Ozzie an even wealthier man. In other respects, however, Ozzie's position was not so comfortable. Ozzie's starting position was as only one of three chief technology officers at Microsoft, a company with 70,000 employees. Initially he would be commuting weekly from his home in Boston on the East Coast to the Microsoft headquarters in Redmond on the West Coast. Besides, Groove Networks had been Ozzie's own show, and much smaller, with just 200 employees. As Ozzie said in an interview with MSNBC: 'The great thing about a small company is that you can put a lot of effort into one thing – but you can have limited impact. In a larger

Bill Gates (left) and Ray Ozzie (right)
Source: Press Associated Images/Jeff Chiu/AP.

role, I'll probably have less focused impact, across a broader range of things.'

The company that Ozzie was joining did indeed operate across a broad range of products. It was responsible for the near universal Microsoft Windows operating system; for the equally pervasive Microsoft Office range of products; for the Xbox games business; for the MSN Internet portal; and for MSNBC cable television. Total turnover was $40bn and the company had $35bn cash reserves. The company was still dominated by Bill Gates, who had founded it in 1975 and boasted in 2005 that he had worked every single day in the intervening 30 years. In 2005, Gates was still the company's Chief Software Architect.

But by 2005 the company was apparently stagnating. Turnover and profits were still climbing, but the stock price had been stuck for several years. From a peak of nearly $60 a share, Microsoft had been fluctuating around $25 (see the figure). Microsoft's core business model relied on selling proprietary software direct either to users or to computer manufacturers for pre-installation on machines. This model was being challenged by free open-source software (such as Linux) and web-based companies whose software was free off the Internet and supported by advertising (such as Google or Yahoo!). Microsoft was widely perceived as yesterday's company.

Microsoft corporation
Price history – MSFT (9/11/1996–9/8/2206)

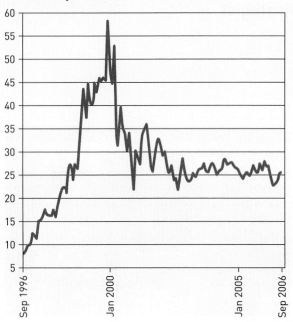

Source: www.msnbc.com.

The first strategy retreat

Ozzie was not going into Microsoft blind. As a *Fortune* article describes, even before being hired, Ozzie had attended the March retreat of the company's top 110 or so executives, including Bill Gates. The two-day retreat was organised by Microsoft's CEO, Steve Ballmer, and took place at the luxurious Semiahmoo Resort, over-looking the Pacific and with a spa and two golf courses. According to *Fortune*, the retreat kicked off with a team-building exercise in which the executives broke into groups of six or seven. Each group was given a bag of parts for a battery-powered Mars rover. The goal: build the rover quickly, but with the fewest parts. Bill Gates's team won. On the second day, groups were assigned to breakout sessions in order to brainstorm various strategic issues. Gates, Ozzie and several other top technologists were put in a group tasked with defin-ing Microsoft's 'core' – the set of things Microsoft does uniquely well that could be used across all Microsoft's product lines. Ozzie recalled the breakout session: 'It was the first time I had a chance as an insider to see how people within the company relate to Bill.' When the group went into its appointed conference room, he told *Fortune*, 'they tended to just naturally fall with Bill at one end and other people around the sides. In some ways they were being deferential, and in some ways he was just one of the gang in a really lively peer discussion.'

The nature of Microsoft's core emerged as the key strategic issue from Semiahmoo. Ballmer, however, seemed unable to push the issue forward. The group of executives he had asked to arrange a larger event to develop the issue refused to organise it. They argued it was premature and likely to cause undue alarm to involve more people at that stage. The momentum from Semiahmoo seemed to have evaporated, until Ballmer turned to Ozzie to ask him to take forward the concept of the strategic core. Soon after, Ballmer asked Ozzie to take the lead with another top management retreat, to take place in June. As Ozzie commented to *Fortune*: 'I had more than a bit of anxiety, given I had never worked with these folks before'.

The second strategy retreat

Ozzie worked closely with Gates, Ballmer and some other senior executives to design this second retreat. It would take place over one day at Robinswood House, a small hotel based on a nineteenth-century pioneer lodge close to Microsoft's headquarters. Just 15 senior executives were to attend; Gates was not invited. The Robinswood facilities were cramped and somewhat basic, with everybody sitting elbow to elbow in a small room. The room was cold and the food attracted complaints. Everybody had been circulated before the meeting with a 51-page memo from Ozzie with his diagnosis of the strategic challenge facing Microsoft.

Ozzie kicked off the retreat by restating the strategic challenge to Microsoft. *Fortune* reports that Ozzie main-tained his usual genial and non-confrontational style, but no punches were pulled about Microsoft's past mis-takes. Ozzie recalled how the group of senior managers then went through a 'cathartic exercise of venting about every negative thing' in the company's technical and organisational strategy of recent years. 'It was story after story after story.' For 14 hours, the senior Microsoft executives worked continuously debating the future of the company. The group's conclusion was that Microsoft needed major change. At the end of the debate, Ballmer demanded of his colleagues: 'If there are any concerns, you've got to say them now.' There was no dissent.

The follow-up

This time Ballmer and Ozzie worked hard to ensure follow-through. A series of weekly half-day meetings were scheduled for the executives who had been at the retreat, with strong pressure for attendance. Ozzie set the agenda for the meetings and for eight weeks the executives debated specific aspects of the new strategy in a conference room right next door to Ballmer's office. There was a good deal of controversy still, but progress was made. In mid-September, Ballmer announced a set of major organisational changes and promotions. Most significant was the merger of Windows and MSN to create a new Platform Products and Services group within Microsoft, firmly based on the web. Significant too was Ozzie's promotion to chief technology officer for Microsoft as a whole, and the movement of his office and staff to the high-security top-floor suite where Gates and Ballmer had their offices too.

The web strategy moved forward. In late October Bill Gates and Ray Ozzie each released important internal memos (soon leaked to the Internet). The Gates memo was dated Sunday 30 October, subject Internet Services Software and e-mailed to all Microsoft Executive Staff and Direct Reports and the Distinguished Engineers group. Gates recalled his memo of 10 years earlier, entitled the 'Internet Tidal Wave', which had launched a revolution within Microsoft to catch up with the first-generation Internet challenge. He then introduced the new issue of Internet software (or web-based) services. He attached Ozzie's own memo on which he commented: 'I feel sure we will look back on [this] as being as critical as the Internet Tidal Wave. Ray outlines the great things we and our partners can do using the Internet Services approach. The next sea change is upon us.'

Ozzie's own attached memo dated from the Friday before and was addressed to Executive Staff and Direct Reports. It was 5,000 words long, with the subject line 'The Internet Services Disruption'. The memo started positively, by asserting that Microsoft was in the midst of its most important new product phase in its history, referring to the launch of the Xbox 360 and many other products. But it continued quickly to remind readers that the company was innovating at a time of great turbulence and change. This was not unprecedented, however. The memo continued by recalling that the company had needed to review its core strategy and direction roughly every five years throughout its history.

Ozzie recalled three previous changes, including the Internet Tidal Wave, on a five-year cycle going back to 1990. He then proposed the existence of a new business model, Internet-based software supported by advertising. He insisted that everybody should reflect on the environmental change, on the company's strengths and weaknesses and on its leadership responsibilities. He warned that if his fellow employees did not reflect and respond quickly and decisively, the company as it stood was seriously at risk. He repeatedly used the word 'we' to underline the common challenge.

The final parts of Ozzie's memo were particularly significant. Invoking 'Bill' Gates and 'Steve' Ballmer by their first names, he insisted that the senior leadership was absolutely committed to the vision outlined in the memo. As evidence, he cited the recent reorganisation of the company into three divisions, including the creation of the new Platform Products and Services group. Ozzie also carefully outlined what he called 'Next Steps'. Here he specified a timetable by which division presidents would be assigning individual managers as 'scenario owners' to take forward various initiatives, to work together with Ozzie, to consult within Microsoft and finally to develop concrete new plans. Ozzie provided the address for an internal blog that he would keep, which would provide relevant documents and his own thoughts as they continued to develop. He also promised to experiment with various other ways to allow Microsoft employees to engage with him directly in the strategic conversation.

On 1 November, Bill Gates and Ray Ozzie jointly unveiled the new strategy to a press conference in San Francisco. In June 2006, Gates announced that he would be retiring from a full-time role in Microsoft, easing out over two years. Ozzie took over Gates's role as the company's Chief Software Architect. He had meanwhile bought himself an apartment near the Microsoft headquarters, overlooking Seattle harbour. His wife started commuting to him.

Main sources: D. Kirkpatrick and J.L. Yang, 'Microsoft's new brain', *Fortune*, 15 May (2006), pp. 52–63; 'Bill Gates: Internet Software Services', at http://blogs.zdnet.com/web2explorer/?page_id=53; 'Ray Ozzie: the Internet Services Disruption', at http://www.scripting.com/disruption/ozzie/TheInternetServicesDisruptio.htm; 'Microsoft to buy Groove Networks', MSNBC, 10 March (2005).

Questions

1 Why was the Semiahmoo retreat not successful in creating sustained momentum around the issue of Microsoft's 'core'?

2 Why was Ozzie more successful in creating follow-on action after the Robinswood retreat?

3 Comment on Ozzie's communications strategy with regard to the Internet Services Disruption.

COMMENTARY ON PART III

This Part of the book was concerned with strategy in action. A central question is what role managers can play to ensure that a strategy is pursued effectively. In Chapter 1 the overall model for this book was introduced in section 1.2. The point was made that managing strategy should not necessarily be seen as a linear process: that the activities and challenges raised in different parts of this book interact and inform each other. However, by necessity, the book is presented in a linear fashion and strategic management is often discussed in terms of strategy formulation followed by strategy implementation.

Design lens

Building on the notion that thinking precedes organisational action, managing strategy is, indeed, seen as a linear process. So managers should:

- Systematically evaluate the relative merits of strategic options so as to select the optimum strategy in terms of the economic benefit to the organisation.
- Persuade managerial colleagues, other people throughout the organisation and external stakeholders to accept the logic of the strategy by employing the evidence of high-quality objective analysis.
- Implement that strategy through project planning to ensure appropriate resourcing, timing and sequencing.
- And establishing an appropriate organisational structure and set of control systems to monitor the progress of strategy implementation.

Experience lens

The idea of implementation of strategy following strategy formulation is misleading. Rather:

- Strategies typically develop from what the organisation is doing and the issues that people perceive on the basis of their experience and culture; current strategy therefore informs and moulds future strategy. In effect 'strategy follows structure'.
- Moreover, political processes of bargaining and negotiation play an important role in what strategies are chosen and pursued. So the strategy followed is likely to be political compromise.

The implication is that significant strategic change is likely to be resisted because of cultural inertia or if it threatens the political status quo.

Managers therefore face a choice:

- Accept the likelihood of a strategy based on incremental change from the status quo and have low expectations of change.
- If they believe a more radical change of strategy is required, challenge and change to the underlying assumptions and political structures that preserve the status quo are needed. Whilst analytic persuasion might play a role in this, it is likely that it will be necessary to employ means of cultural change and overcome political blockages to change.

STRATEGY IN ACTION

In this commentary the strategy lenses are used to explore this key issue further. Does it make sense to manage strategy as a process of formulation followed by implementation of strategy? Note that:

- There is no suggestion here that one of these lenses is better than another, but they do provide different insights into the problems faced and the ways managers cope with the challenge.
- If you have *not* read the Commentary following Chapter 1, which explains the four lenses, you should now do so.

Variety lens

Strategies emerge as patterns of order from the ideas that bubble up from within and around an organisation. Managers are one, but not the only, mechanism by which strategies get selected. This also occurs by new ideas attracting 'positive feedback' from inside and outside the organisation (e.g. customers in the market); and by their becoming embedded in organisational routines. So, again, the neat division between strategy formulation and strategy implementation is misleading.

If a strategy is to be pursued effectively, but also allow new ideas to continue to arise, managers have three roles to play:

- It is top managers' role to identify the potential of new ideas and mould these into a coherent strategy that people inside and outside the organisation can understand.
- They need to translate this strategy into a few key guiding principles or 'simple rules' that ensure the coherence of strategy but within which there is sufficient latitude to permit people to experiment and try out new ideas. Extensive and cumbersome controls and overly tight structural boundaries should be avoided.
- Given the variety of different experience and ideas that exist in organisations, managers should assume that there will be potential but variable readiness for change. The bases for this may well differ across the organisation, as will ideas about how a change of strategy should be enacted. So managers need to be prepared to work with such variation rather than assume or insist on uniformity.

Discourse lens

Strategy and its management are essentially about discourse – written and spoken. Its use, deliberately or not, is central to which strategies are followed and how they take effect. This raises the question of the role of such discourse. It needs to be recognised that:

- Discourse that is appropriate to the needs of stakeholders can have a powerful effect on getting strategies accepted and put into effect. Managers seeking to persuade others of the 'rightness' of a strategy need to tailor strategic messages with stakeholders' expectations and identities in mind.
- Given that power of language, especially in framing and motivating change, managers should pay particular attention to the language they use to present and justify change and motivate people to follow a strategy.
- In the selection of a strategy managers may also employ the language of strategy to justify its benefits and to signal its inevitable success. Those interested in establishing if there is substance to such claims need to be prepared to question and challenge below the surface of such language.

GLOSSARY

Acceptability expected performance outcomes of a proposed strategy to meet the expectation of the stakeholders (p. 371)

Acquisition when one firm takes over the ownership ('equity') of another; hence the alternative term 'takeover' (p. 329)

Backward integration develop activities that involve the inputs into a company's current business (p. 240)

Balanced scorecards performance targets set according to a range of perspectives, not only financial (p. 447)

Barriers to entry factors that need to be overcome by new entrants if they are to compete in an industry (p. 55)

Blue Oceans new market spaces where competition is minimised (p. 73)

Boston Consulting Group (BCG) matrix uses market share and market growth criteria to determine the attractiveness and balance of a business portfolio (p. 249)

Business case provides the data and argument in support of a particular strategy proposal, e.g. investment in new equipment (p. 521)

Business-level strategy the plan of how an individual business should compete in its particular market(s) (p. 7)

Business model describes how an organisation manages incomes and costs through the structural arrangement of its activities (p. 301)

Buyers the organisation's immediate customers, not necessarily the ultimate consumers (p. 58)

CAGE framework emphasises the importance of cultural, administrative, geographical and economic distance (p. 278)

Cash cow a business unit within a portfolio that has a high market share in a mature market (p. 250)

Coercion the imposition of change or the issuing of edicts about change (p. 475)

Collaboration all those affected by strategic changes are active in setting the change agenda (p. 474)

Collaborative advantage the benefits received when a company achieves more by collaborating with other organisations than it would when operating alone (p. 338)

Collective strategy how the whole network of an alliance, of which an organisation is a member, competes against rival networks of alliances (p. 338)

Complementor (i) customers value your product more when they have another organisation's product than if they have your product alone; (ii) it's more attractive to suppliers to provide resources to you when they are also supplying another organisation than if they are supplying you alone (p. 62)

Competences the ways in which an organisation may deploy its assets effectively (p. 84)

Competitive advantage how a strategic business unit creates value for its users which is both greater than the costs of supplying them and superior to that of rival SBUs (p. 199)

Competitve strategy how a strategic business unit achieves competitive advantage in its domain of activity (p. 199)

Configurations the set of organisational design elements that interlink together in order to support the intended strategy (p. 453)

Conglomerate (unrelated) diversification diversifying into products or services that are not related to the existing business (p. 233)

Control systems the formal and informal ways of monitoring and supporting people within and around an organisation (p. 178)

Core competences the linked set of skillls, activities and resources that, together, deliver customer value, differentiate a business from its competitors and, potentially, can be extended and developed (p. 89)

Corporate entrepreneurship refers to radical change in an organisation's business, driven principally by the organisation's own capabilities (p. 328)

Corporate governance concerned with the structures and systems of control by which managers are held accountable to those who have a legitimate stake in an organisation (p. 123)

Corporate-level strategy concerned with the overall scope of an organisation and how value is added to the constituent businesses of the organisation as a whole (p. 7)

Corporate social responsibility (CSR) the commitment by organisations to behave ethically and contribute to economic development while improving the quality of life of the workforce and their families as well as the local community and society at large (p. 134)

Cost-leadership strategy this involves becoming the lowest-cost organisation in a domain of activity (p. 200)

Critical success factors (CSF) those factors that are either particularly valued by customers or which provide a significant advantage in terms of costs. [Sometimes called key success factors (KSF)] (p. 73)

Cultural systems these aim to standardise norms of behaviour within an organisation in line with particular objectives (p. 445)

Cultural web shows the behavioural, physical and symbolic manifestations of a culture (p. 176)

Differentiation involves uniqueness in some dimension that is sufficiently valued by customers to allow a price premium (p. 203)

Diffusion the process by which innovations spread amongst users (p. 303)

Direction the use of personal managerial authority to establish a clear strategy and how change will occur (p. 475)

Direct supervision direct control of strategic decisions by one or a few individuals, typically focused on the effort put into the business by the employees (p. 445)

Disruptive innovation this creates substantial growth by offering a new performance trajectory that, even if initially inferior to the performance of existing technologies, has the potential to become markedly superior (p. 309)

Diversification increasing the range of products or markets served by an organisation (p. 232)

Dogs business units within a portfolio that have a low share in static or declining markets (p. 250)

Dominant logic the set of corporate-level managerial competences applied across the portfolio of businesses (p. 238)

Dynamic capabilities an organisation's ability to renew and re-create its strategic capabilities to meet the needs of changing environments (p. 85)

Economies of scope efficiency gains made through applying the organisation's existing resources or competences to new markets or services (p. 237)

Education involves persuading others of the need for, and means of, strategic change (p. 473)

Emergent strategy a strategy that develops as a result of a series of decisions, in a pattern that becomes clear over time, rather than as a deliberate result of a 'grand plan' (p. 404)

Entrepreneurial life cycle this progresses through start-up, growth, maturity and exit (p. 311)

Exploring Strategy Model this includes understanding *the strategic position* of an organisation (context); assessing *strategic choices* for the future (content); and managing *strategy in action* (process) (p. 14)

Feasibility whether a strategy can work in practice (p. 383)

First-mover advantage where an organisation is better off than its competitors as a result of being first to market with a new product, process or service (p. 307)

Five forces framework *see* Porter's five forces framework

Focus strategy this targets a narrow segment of domain of activity and tailors its products or services to the needs of that specific segment to the exclusion of others (p. 205)

Forcefield analysis this provides an initial view of change problems that need to be tackled by identifying forces for and against change (p. 469)

Forward integration developing activities concerned with the output of a company's current business (p. 240)

Functional structure this divides responsibilities according to the organisation's primary specialist roles such as production, research and sales (p. 432)

Game theory this encourages an organisation to consider competitors' likely moves and the implications of these moves for its own strategy (p. 217)

Global–local dilemma the extent to which products and services may be standardised across national boundaries or need to be adapted to meet the requirements of specific national markets (p. 274)

Global sourcing purchasing services and components from the most appropriate suppliers around the world, regardless of their location (p. 272)

Global strategy this involves high coordination of extensive activities dispersed geographically in many countries around the world (p. 266)

Governance chain this shows the roles and relationships of different groups involved in the governance of an organisation (p. 124)

Hypercompetition this occurs where frequency, boldness and aggression of competitor interactions accelerate to create a condition of constant disequilibrium and change (p. 6)

Hypothesis testing a methodology used particularly in strategy projects for setting priorities in investigating issues and options; widely used by strategy consulting firms and members of strategy project teams (p. 521)

Industry a group of firms producing products and services that are essentially the same (p. 54)

Inimitable capabilities those capabilities that competitors find difficult to imitate or obtain (p. 91)

Innovation the conversion of new knowledge into a new product, process or service *and* the putting of this new product, process or service into actual use (p. 296)

Intended strategy a strategy that is deliberately formulated or planned by managers (p. 398)

International strategy a range of options for operating outside an organisation's country of origin (p. 266)

Key drivers for change the environmental factors likely to have a high impact on the success or failure of strategy (p. 50)

Leadership the process of influencing an organisation (or group within an organisation) in its efforts towards achieving an aim or goal (p. 471)

Learning organisation an organisation that is capable of continual regeneration due to a variety of knowledge, experience and skills within a culture that encourages questioning and challenge (p. 406)

Legitimacy this is concerned with meeting the expectations within an organisational field in terms of assumptions, behaviours and strategies (p. 171)

Logical incrementalism the development of strategy by experimentation and learning (p. 405)

Managing strategy in action this is about how strategies are formed and how they are implemented (p. 18)

Market a group of customers for specific products or services that are essentially the same (for example, a particular geographical market) (p. 54)

Market development this offers existing products to new markets (p. 253)

Market penetration this implies increasing share of the current markets with the current product range (p. 234)

Market segment a group of customers who have similar needs that are different from customer needs in other parts of the market (p. 71)

Market systems these typically involve some formalised system of 'contracting' for resources or inputs from other parts of an organisation and for supplying outputs to other parts of an organisation (p. 449)

Matrix structure this combines different structural dimensions simultaneously, for example product divisions and geographical territories or product divisions and functional specialisms (p. 436)

McKinsey 7-S framework this highlights the importance of fit between strategy, structure, systems, staff, style, skills and superordinate goals (p. 453)

Merger the combination of two previously separate organisations, typically as more or less equal partners (p. 329)

Mission statement this aims to provide the employees and stakeholders with clarity about the overriding purpose of the organisation (p. 120)

Monopoly formally an industry with just one firm and therefore no competitive rivalry (p. 60)

Multidivisional structure this is built up of separate divisions on the basis of products, services or geographical areas (p. 434)

Objectives statements of specific outcomes that are to be achieved (often expressed in financial terms) (p. 121)

Oligopoly a few firms dominate an industry, with the potential for limited rivalry and great power over buyers and suppliers (p. 60)

Open innovation this involves the deliberate import and export of knowledge by an organisation in order to accelerate and enhance its innovation (p. 300)

Operational strategies these are concerned with how the components of an organisation effectively deliver the corporate- and business-level strategies in terms of resources, processes and people (p. 7)

Organic development this is where a strategy is pursued by building on and developing an organisation's own capabilities (p. 328)

Organisational culture the taken-for-granted assumptions and behaviours that make sense of people's organisational context (p. 168)

Organisational field a community of organisations that interact more frequently with one another than with those outside the field and that have developed a shared meaning system (p. 169)

Organisational justice this refers to the perceived fairness of managerial actions, in terms of distribution, procedure and information (p. 337)

Organisational knowledge the collective intelligence, specific to an organisation, accumulated through both formal systems and the shared experience of people in that organisation (p. 94)

Organisational structures the roles, responsibilities and reporting relationships in organisations (p. 178)

Outsourcing activities that were previously carried out internally are subcontracted to external suppliers (p. 241)

Paradigm the set of assumptions held in common and taken for granted in an organisation (p. 174)

Parental developer an organisation that seeks to use its own central capabilities to add value to its businesses (p. 248)

Participation elements of the change process are delegated by a strategic leader, who still retains authority over, and coordinates, the processes of change (p. 475)

Path dependency where early events and decisions establish 'policy paths' that have lasting effects on subsequent events and decisions (p. 163)

Perfect competition this exists where barriers to entry are low, there are many equal rivals each with very similar products, and information about competitors is freely available (p. 60)

Performance targets these focus on the *outputs* of an organisation (or part of an organisation), such as product quality, revenues or profits (p. 446)

PESTEL framework this categorises environmental influences into six main types: political, economic, social, technological, environmental and legal (p. 50)

Planning systems these plan and control the allocation of resources and monitor their utilisation (p. 450)

Platform leadership this refers to how large firms consciously nurture independent companies through successive waves of innovation around their basic technological 'platform' (p. 300)

Political view of strategy development stategies develop as the outcome of bargaining and negotiation among powerful interest groups (or stakeholders) (p. 406)

Porter's Diamond this suggests that locational advantages may stem from local factor conditions; local demand conditions; local related and supporting industries; and from local firm strategy structure and rivalry (p. 271)

Porter's five forces framework this helps identify the attractiveness of an industry in terms of five competitive forces: the threat of entry; the threat of substitutes; the power of buyers; the power of suppliers; and the extent of rivalry between competitors (p. 54)

Portfolio manager he or she operates as an active investor in a way that shareholders in the stock market are either too dispersed or too inexpert to be able to do so (p. 247)

Power the ability of individuals or groups to persuade, induce or coerce others into following certain courses of action (p. 145, p. 177)

Project-based structure teams are created, undertake their work (e.g. internal or external contracts) and are then dissolved (p. 440)

Problem child *see* **Question mark**.

Product development organisations deliver modified or new products, or services, to existing markets (p. 234)

Profit pools the different levels of profit available at different parts of the value network (p. 102)

Question mark a business unit within a portfolio that is in a growing market but does not yet have high market share (also called 'problem child') (p. 250)

Rare capabilities those capabilities that are possessed uniquely by one organisation or by a few (p. 90)

Recipe a set of assumptions, norms and routines held in common within an organisational field about the appropriate purposes and strategies of organisational field members (p. 169)

Related diversification diversifying into products or services that are related to the existing business (p. 232)

Resource-based view (RBV) of strategy this states that the competitive advantage and superior performance of an organisation is explained by the distinctiveness of its capabilities (p. 83)

Resources assets possessed by an organisation, or that it can call upon (e.g. from partners or suppliers) (p. 84)

Returns the financial benefits that stakeholders are expected to receive from a strategy (p. 375)

Risk the extent to which the outcomes of a strategy can be predicted (p. 371)

Rituals particular activities or special events that emphasise, highlight or reinforce what is important in the culture (p. 177)

Rivals organisations with similar products and services aimed at the same customer group (NB not the same as substitutes) (p. 59)

Routines 'the way we do things around here' on a day-to-day basis (p. 177)

Scope indicates how far an organisation should be diversified in terms of products and markets (p. 231)

S-curve the shape of the curve reflects a process of initial slow adoption of an innovation, followed by a rapid acceleration in diffusion, leading to a plateau representing the limit to demand (p. 304)

Situational leadership successful leaders are able to adjust their style of leadership to the context they face (p. 473)

Social entrepreneurs individuals and groups who create independent organisations to mobilise ideas and resources to address social problems, typically earning revenues but on a not-for-profit basis (p. 315)

Staged international expansion model this proposes a sequential process whereby companies gradually increase their commitment to newly entered markets as they build market knowledge and capabilities (p. 282)

Stakeholder mapping this identifies stakeholder expectations and power, and helps in the understanding of political priorities (p. 141)

Stakeholders those individuals or groups that depend on an organisation to fulfil their own goals and on whom, in turn, the organisation depends (p. 119)

Star a business unit within a portfolio that has a high market share in a growing market (p. 250)

Statements of corporate values these communicate the underlying and enduring core 'principles' that guide an organisation's strategy and define the way that the organisation should operate (p. 121)

Strategic alliance where two or more organisations share resources and activities to pursue a strategy (p. 338)

Strategic business unit (SBU) this supplies goods or services for a distinct domain of activity (p. 198)

Strategic capabilities the capabilities of an organisation that contribute to its long-term survival or competitive advantage (p. 84)

Strategic choices these involve the options for strategy in terms of both the *directions* in which strategy might move and the *methods* by which strategy might be pursued (p. 17)

Strategic customer the person to whom the strategy is primarily addressed because they have the most

influence over which goods or services are purchased (p. 72)

Strategic drift the tendency for strategies to develop incrementally on the basis of historical and cultural influences, but fail to keep pace with a changing environment (p. 158)

Strategic groups organisations within an industry or sector with similar strategic characteristics, following similar strategies or competing on similar bases (p. 69)

Strategic issue-selling the process of gaining attention and support of top management and other important stakeholders for strategic issues (p. 510)

Strategic lock-in this is where users become dependent on a supplier and are unable to use another supplier without substantial switching costs (p. 210)

Strategic plan this provides the data and argument in support of a strategy for the whole organisation (p. 521)

Strategic planners (also known as strategy directors or corporate managers): managers with a formal responsibility for coordinating the strategy process (p. 502)

Strategic planning systemised, step-by-step procedures to develop an organisation's strategy (p. 400)

Strategic position this is concerned with the impact on strategy of the external environment, the organisation's strategic capability (resources and competences), the organisation's goals and the organisation's culture (p. 16)

Strategy the long-term direction of an organisation (p. 3)

Strategy as design this views strategy development as a logical process of analysis and evaluation (p. 27)

Strategy as discourse the view that the language is important as a means by which managers communicate and explain and change strategy, but by which they also gain influence and power and establish their legitimacy and identity (p. 27)

Strategy as experience this views strategy development as the outcome of people's (not least managers) taken-for-granted assumptions and ways of doing things (p. 27)

Strategy as variety this is the view that strategy bubbles up from new ideas arising from the variety of people in and around organisations (p. 27)

Strategy canvas this compares competitors according to their performance on key success factors in order to develop strategies based on creating new market spaces (p. 73)

Strategy lenses ways of looking at strategy issues differently in order to generate many insights (p. 20)

Strategy maps these link different performance targets into a mutually supportive causal chain supporting strategic objectives (p. 447)

Strategy projects these involve teams of people assigned to work on particular strategic issues over a defined period of time (p. 520)

Strategy statements these should have three main themes: the fundamental *goals* that the organisation seeks, which typically draw on the organisation's stated mission, vision and objectives; the *scope* or domain of the organisation's activities; and the particular *advantages* or capabilities it has to deliver all of these (p. 8)

Strategy workshops (also called strategy away-days or off-sites): these involve groups of executives working intensively for one or two days, often away from the office, on organisational strategy (p. 518)

Structures these give people formally defined roles, responsibilities and lines of reporting with regard to strategy (p. 431)

Substitutes products or services that offer a similar benefit to an industry's products or services but by a different process (p. 57)

Suitability assessing which proposed strategies address the *key opportunities and restraints* an organisation faces (p. 364)

Suppliers those who supply the organisation with what it needs to produce the product or service (p. 58)

SWOT the strengths, weaknesses, opportunities and threats likely to impact on strategy development (p. 106)

Symbols objects, events, acts or people that convey, maintain or create meaning over and above their functional purpose (p. 177, p. 481)

Synergy the benefits gained where activities or assets complement each other so that their combined effect is greater that the sum of parts (p. 238)

Synergy manager a corporate parent seeking to enhance value for business units by managing synergies across business units (p. 248)

Systems these support and control people as they carry out structurally defined roles and responsibilities (p. 431)

Three horizons framework this suggests that every organization should think of itself as comprising three types of business or activity, defined by their 'horizons' in terms of years (p. 4)

Threshold capabilities those capabilities that are needed for an organisation to meet the necessary requirements to compete in a given market and achieve parity with competitors in that market (p. 87)

Tipping point this is here demand for a product or service suddenly takes off, with explosive growth (p. 304)

Transnational structure combines local responsiveness with high global coordination (p. 439)

Turnaround strategy here the emphasis is on speed of change and rapid cost reduction and/or revenue generation (p. 484)

Value strategic capabilities are of value when they provide potential competitive advantage in a market at a cost that allows an organisation to realise acceptable levels of return (p. 90)

Value chain the categories of activities within an organisation which, together, create a product or a service (p. 97)

Value curves a graphic depiction of how customers perceive competitors' relative performance across the critical success factors (p. 74)

Value innovation the creation of new market space by excelling on established critical success factors on which competitors are performing badly and/or by creating new critical success factors representing previously unrecognised customer wants (p. 74)

Value net a map of organisations in a business environment demonstrating opportunities for value-creating cooperation as well as competition (p. 62)

Value network inter-organisational links and relationships that are necessary to create a product or service (p. 97)

Vertical integration entering into activities where the organisation is its own supplier or customer (p. 240)

Vision statement concerned with the desired future state of the organisation (p. 121)

Yip's globalisation framework this sees international strategy potential as determined by market drivers, cost drivers, government drivers and competitive drivers (p. 268)

INDEX OF NAMES

GENERAL INDEX

ACKNOWLEDGEMENTS

We are grateful to the following for permission to reproduce copyright material:

Figures

Figures 2.2 and 6.9 adapted from Michael E. Porter (1998) *Competitive Strategy: Techniques for Analyzing Industries and Competitors*, adapted with the permission of The Free Press, a Division of Simon & Schuster, Inc., copyright © 1980, 1998 by The Free Press, all rights reserved; Figure 2.3 adapted from and reprinted by permission of *Harvard Business Review*, A. Brandenburger and B. Nalebuff (1996) 'The right game', July–August, pp. 57–64, copyright © 1996 by the Harvard Business School Publishing Corporation, Boston, MA, all rights reserved; Figure 2.6 adapted from Richard A. D'Aveni with Robert Gunther (1995) *Hypercompetitive Rivalries: Competing in Highly Dynamic Environments*, adapted with the permission of The Free Press, a Division of Simon & Schuster, Inc., copyright © 1994, 1995 by Richard A. D'Aveni, all rights reserved; Figures 3.4, 3.5 and 6.2 adapted from Michael E. Porter (1998) *Competitive Advantage: Creating and Sustaining Superior Performance*, adapted with the permissions of The Free Press, a Division of Simon & Schuster, Inc., copyright © 1985, 1998 by Michael E. Porter, all rights reserved; Figure 4.2 adapted from David Pitt-Watson, Hermes Fund Management; Figure 5.6 adapted from P. Grinyer and J.C. Spender (1979) *Turnaround: Managerial Recipes for Strategic Success*, Associated Business Press, p. 203, reprinted with permission of Peter H. Grinyer and J.C. Spender; Figure in Illustration 6.5 from Avinash K. Dixit and Barry J. Nalebuff (1991) *Thinking Strategically: The Competitive Edge in Business, Politics, and Everyday Life*, copyright © 1991 Avinash K. Dixit and Barry J. Nalebuff, used by permission of W.W. Norton & Company, Inc.; Figure 6.5 adapted from D. Gursoy, M. Chen and H. Kim (2005) 'The US Airlines Relative Positioning', *Tourism Management*, 26(5), pp. 57–67, simplified from Figure 1 on p. 62, with permission from Elsevier; Figure 6.7 adapted from Richard D'Aveni with Robert Gunther (1994) *Hypercompetition: Managing the Dynamics of Strategic Manoeuvring*, with the permission of The Free Press, a Division of Simon & Schuster, Inc., copyright © 1994 by Richard D'Aveni, all rights reserved; Figure 6.6 adapted from D. Faulkner and C. Bowman (1995) *The Essence of Competitive Strategy*, Prentice Hall, reproduced with permission; Figure 6.8 reprinted by permission of *Harvard Business Review* from N. Kumar (2006) 'A framework for responding to low-cost rivals', December, Exhibit, reprinted by permission of the Harvard Business School Publishing Corporation, copyright © 2006 by the Harvard Business School Publishing; Figure 7.2 adapted from H.I. Ansoff (1988) *Corporate Strategy*, Chapter 6, Penguin, with permission of the Ansoff Family Trust; Figures 7.5 and 7.9 adapted from M. Goold, A. Campbell and M. Alexander (1994) *Corporate Level Strategy: Creating value in the multibusiness company*, Wiley, copyright © 1994 John Wiley & Sons, Inc., reproduced with permission of John Wiley & Sons, Inc.; Chapter 7 References, p. 259, figure from H. Ansoff (1988) *The New Corporate Strategy*, John Wiley & Sons, Inc., copyright © 1988 (and owner), reproduced with permission of John Wiley & Sons, Inc., and the Ansoff Family Trust; Figure 8.1 from www.bigcharts.com, Marketwatch.Online by www.bigcharts.com, copyright 2006 by Dow Jones & Company, Inc., reproduced with permission of Dow Jones & Company, Inc. in the format Textbook via Copyright Clearance Center; Figure 8.3 adapted from Michael E. Porter (1990), *The Competitive Advantage of Nations*, Palgrave, reproduced with permission of Palgrave Macmillan in World territory excluding USA, Canada and Dependencies and with the permission of The Free Press, a Division of Simon & Schuster, Inc., copyright © 1990, 1998 by Michael E. Porter, all rights reserved in USA, Canada and Dependencies; Figure 8.4 adapted from M. Porter (1987) 'Changing patterns of international competition', pp. 9–39, Figure 5, copyright © 1987 by The Regents of the University of California, reprinted from the *California Management Review*, vol. 28, no. 2, by permission of The Regents; Figure 8.5 from M. Javidan, P. Dorman, M. de Luque and R. House (2006) *Academy of Management Perspectives*, copyright 2006 by Academy of Management (NY), reproduced with permission of Academy of Management (NY) in the format Textbook via Copyright Clearance Center; Figure 8.6 by permission of *Harvard Business Review*, Exhibit adapted from I. Macmillan, S. van Putten and R. McGrath (2003) 'Global gamesmanship', May, copyright © 2003 by the Harvard Business School Publishing Corporation, Boston, MA, all rights reserved; Figure 8.8 reprinted by permission of Harvard Business School Press, from C.A. Bartlett and S. Ghoshal (1989) *Managing Across Borders: The Transnational Solution*, pp. 105–11, copyright © 1989 by the Harvard Business School Publishing Corporation, Boston, MA, all rights reserved; Figure in Chapter 8, Case Example, from http://finance.yahoo.com/echarts?s= LHL.F#chart7:symbol=lhl.f;range=20011224,20070102; compare=^ixic;indicator=ke_sd+volume;charttype=line;crosshair =on;ohlcvalues=0;logscale=off, reproduced with permission of Yahoo! Inc. © 2010 Yahoo! Inc., YAHOO! and the YAHOO! logo are registered trademarks of Yahoo! Inc., data in the figure is reproduced with permission from the NASDAQ OMX Group, Inc.; Figure 9.2 adapted from W.J. Abernathy and J.M. Utterback (1975) 'A dynamic model of process and product innovation', *Omega*, 3(6), pp. 639–56, copyright © 1975, with permission from Elsevier; Figure 9.4 adapted and reprinted by permission of Harvard Business School Press, from C. Christensen and M.E. Raynor (2003) *The Innovator's Solution*, copyright © 2003 by the Harvard Business School Publishing Corporation, Boston, MA, all rights reserved; Figure 9.5 reprinted by permission of Harvard Business School Press from I. MacMillan and R.G. McGrath (2000) *The Entrepreneurial Mindset*, p. 176, copyright © 2000 by the Harvard Business School Publishing Corporation, Boston, MA, all rights reserved; unnumbered figure, Chapter 9, Case Example, from Phil Wolff (2010), *Skype Journal*, 8 March, reproduced with permission; Figure 10.2 from P. Haspeslagh and D. Jemison (1991) *Managing Acquisitions*, The Free Press, reproduced with permission from the authors; Figure 10.4 adapted from E. Murray and J. Mahon (1993) 'Strategic alliances: Gateway to the new Europe, *Long Range Planning*, 26, p. 109, copyright 1993, with permission from Elsevier; unnumbered figure in Illustration 13.2 from Proctor & Gamble, http://www.pg.com/en_US/company/global_structure_operations/corporate_structure.shtml, reproduced with permission; Figure 13.5 adapted and reprinted by permission of Harvard Business School Press from C.A. Bartlett and S. Ghoshal (1998) *Managing Across Borders: The Transnational Corporation*, 2nd Edition, copyright © 1998 by the Harvard Business School Publishing Corporation, Boston, MA, all rights reserved; Figure 13.6 from R. Lawson, W. Stratton and T. Hatch (2005) 'Achieving strategy with scorecarding', *Journal of Corporate Accounting and Finance*, March–April, p. 64 John Wiley & Sons Ltd, reproduced with permission; Figure 13.7 adapted from M. Goold and A. Campbell (1989) *Strategies and Styles*, Figure 3.1, p. 39, Wiley-Blackwell, reproduced with permission; Figure 13.8 from R. Waterman, T.J. Peters and J.R. Phillips (1980) 'Structure is not organization', *Business Horizons*, vol. 23, pp. 14–26, McKinsey & Company, reproduced with permission; Figures 14.2 and 14.3 adapted from J. Balogun and V. Hope Hailey (1999) *Exploring Strategic Change*, Prentice Hall, reproduced with permission; Figure 15.4 was published in G. Szulanski, J. Porac and Y. Doz (eds) (2005) 'An attention-based theory of strategy formulation: linking micro and macro perspectives in strategy processes', *Advances in Strategic Management, 22: Strategy Process*, December, pp. 39–62, copyright Elsevier (2005); unnumbered figure in Chapter 15, Case Example, from www.msnbc.msn.com, MSNBC.COM (Online) (only staff-produced materials may be used) by MSNBC, copyright 2006 by MSNBC INTERACTIVE NEWS, LLC, reproduced with permission of MSNBC INTERACTIVE NEWS, LLC in the format Textbook via Copyright Clearance Center.

Tables

Table 1.4 adapted and reprinted by permission of Harvard Business School Press from K.M. Eisenhardt and D.N. Sull (2001) 'Strategy as simple rules', *Harvard Business Review*, January, Exhibit, copyright © 2001 by Harvard Business School Publishing Corporation, all rights reserved; Table 2.3 from *Strategies for Growth in an Increasingly Consolidated Global Beer Market*, Euromonitor International (2010) reproduced with permission; Table 14.1 adapted from J. Balogun *et al.* (2008) *Exploring strategic change*, 3rd Edition, FT/Prentice Hall, reproduced with permission; Table 15.1 from E. Sadler-Smith and E. Shefy (2004) 'The intuitive executive: understanding and applying "gut feel" in decision making', *Academy of Management Executive*, 18(4), pp. 76–91, copyright 2004 by the Academy of Management (NY), reproduced with permission of the Academy of Management (NY) in the format Textbook via Copyright Clearance Center; Table 15.2 adapted and reprinted by permission of *Harvard Business Review*, from S.A. Joni and D. Beyer (2009) 'How to pick a good fight', December, pp. 48–57, copyright © 2009 by the Harvard Business School Publishing Corporation, all rights reserved.

Text

Illustration 1.2 extract from www.ucc.ie, reproduced with permission; Illustration 1.2, extract from www.nokia.com, reproduced with permission; Illustration 3.1, extract from Tony Hall, Chief Executive of Royal Opera House, in *Royal Opera House Annual Review 2005/6*, p. 11, reprinted by permission of Royal Opera House; Illustration 3.3 adapted from www.smt.sandvik.com/sandvik, © AB Sandvik Materials Technology, reproduced with permission; Chapter 4, Case Example, extract from P. Vallely (2007) 'The Big Question: does the RED campaign help big eastern brands more than Africa?', *Independent*, 9 March, copyright *Independent*, 9 March 2007; Chapter 4, Case Example, extract p. 153 from Gerard Baker (2006) 'Mind the Gap: With this attack on globalization', *The Times*, 24 October, © The Times/The Sun/nisyndication.com; Illustration 4.2 from *The Times*, 16 September 2008, p. 2, © The Times/The Sun/nisyndication.com; Illustration 5.4 adapted from Mark Jenkins and Veronique Ambrosini (2002), *Strategic Management*, Palgrave, reproduced with permission of Palgrave Macmillan; Illustration 7.4 extracts adapted from 2009 Berkshire Hathaway, Inc.'s Annual Report, the material is copyrighted and used with permission of the author; Illustration 10.4 adapted from the document Oxfam's Partnership Policy at www.oxfam.org/uk/resources/accounts, reproduced with the permission of Oxfam GB, Oxfam House, John Smith Drive, Cowley, Oxford OX4 2JY, UK, www.oxfam.org.uk, Oxfam GB does not necessarily endorse any text or activities that accompany the materials; extract Chapter 14 p. 489 reprinted by permission from H. Tsoukas and R. Chia (2002) 'On organizational becoming: Rethinking organizational change', *Organization Science*, 13(5), pp. 578–9, copyright 2002, the Institute for Operations Research and the Management Sciences (INFORMS), 7240 Parkway Drive, Suite 310, Hanover, MD 21076, USA; quote in Illustration 14.3 (p. 475) from Sir Terry Leahy, in Chris Blackhurst (2004) *Management Today*, February, p. 32, reproduced with the permission of the copyright owner, Haymarket Business Publications Limited; Illustration 15.1 from 'Extracts from Strategy Unit job description for a team member: Band A', http://www.cabinetofficegov.uk/strategy/jobs/band_a.asp, Crown Copyright material is reproduced with permission under the terms of the Click-Use License.

The Financial Times

Illustration 6.2 from J. Leahy (2009) 'Volvo takes a lead in India', © *Financial Times*, 31 August.

Photographs

Alamy Images: p. 79 Picturesbyrab; **Babcock Faslane:** p. 495; **Getty Images:** pp. 24, 115; **iStockphotos:** p. 353; **Press Association Images:** p. 291 Kin/Cheung/AP; p. 426 Mark Lennihan/AP; p. 529 Jeff Chiu/AP; **Reuters:** p. 459 Robert Galbraith; **Rex Features:** p. 226 Lehtikuva OY; p. 260 Steve Bell; p. 322 Steve Forrest; **Shutterstock:** p. 187.

All other images © Pearson Education.

In some instances we have been unable to trace the owners of copyright material, and we would appreciate any information that would enable us to do so.